Ancient Community
and Economy
at Chinchawas
(Ancash, Peru)

YALE UNIVERSITY PUBLICATIONS IN ANTHROPOLOGY

EDITORIAL COMMITTEE

Richard L. Burger
*Curatorial Editor-in-Chief*
*Charles J. MacCurdy Professor of Anthropology*
*Chair, Council on Archaeological Studies*

Andrew Hill
*J. Clayton Stephenson Professor of Anthropology*

Roderick J. McIntosh
*Professor of Anthropology*

The Yale University Publications in Anthropology series, published by the Yale University Department of Anthropology and the Peabody Museum of Natural History at Yale University, is supported by the Theodore and Ruth Wilmanns Lidz Endowment Fund for Excellence in Scholarly Publications, dedicated to the dissemination of scholarly research and study of the world and its cultures.

The Yale University Publications in Anthropology series embodies the results of researches in the general field of anthropology directly conducted or sponsored by the Yale University Department of Anthropology and the Yale Peabody Museum of Natural History Division of Anthropology. Occasionally other manuscripts of outstanding quality that deal with subjects of special interest to the faculty of the Department of Anthropology may also be included.

For a complete list of available titles in this series visit www.yalebooks.com.

# Ancient Community and Economy at Chinchawas (Ancash, Peru)

## George F. Lau
*Sainsbury Research Unit for the Arts
 of Africa, Oceania & the Americas*
*School of World Art Studies and Museology
University of East Anglia*

Number 90

Published by
the Yale University Department of Anthropology
and the Yale Peabody Museum of Natural History

Distributed by
Yale University Press
NEW HAVEN AND LONDON

# Yale

YALE UNIVERSITY PUBLICATIONS IN ANTHROPOLOGY
Number 90

Rosemary Volpe, *Publications Manager*

Index by Aardvark Indexing

Distributed by Yale University Press
New Haven and London | www.yalebooks.com

*Cover:* View of Peru's Cordillera Blanca from Punta Kayán, the pass connecting the Chinchawas site (A.D. 300–900) to the Recuay heartland in the Callejón de Huaylas. Photograph by George F. Lau.

*Title page:* A two-faced painted design from the interior surface of a Chinchawasi 2 phase Ware A bowl (see Figure 51).

Copyright © 2010 Yale University. All rights reserved.
This book may not be reproduced, in whole or in part, including illustrations, in any form (beyond that copying permitted by Sections 107 and 108 of the U.S. Copyright Law and except by reviewers for the public press), without the written permission of the publishers.

For submission guidelines send inquiries to:
Publications Office, Peabody Museum of Natural History, Yale University,
P. O. Box 208118, New Haven CT 06520-8118 USA; peabody.publications@yale.edu

ISSN 1535-7082
ISBN 978-0-913516-26-3
Printed in the United States of America.

Library of Congress Cataloging-in-Publication Data

Lau, George F., 1969-
  Ancient community and economy at Chinchawas (Ancash, Peru) / George F. Lau.
    p. cm. -- (Yale university publications in anthropology ; v. 90)
  Includes bibliographical references and index.
  ISBN 978-0-913516-26-3 (trade pbk. : alk. paper)
  1. Chinchawas Site (Peru) 2. Recuay culture--Peru--Ancash. 3. Indian pottery--Peru--Ancash. 4. Excavations (Archaeology)--Peru--Ancash. 5. Ancash (Peru)--Antiquities. I. Title.
F3429.1.A45L38 2010
985'.21--dc22
                                                                                    2010031126

∞ This paper meets the requirements of ANSI/NISO Z39.48-1992 (Permanence of Paper).

10  9  8  7  6  5  4  3  2  1

# Contents

vii  Figures
xi  Tables
xii  Acknowledgements

1  ONE • Introduction
    1  Objectives
    5  Comparative Considerations
    10  Organization of Chapters

11  TWO • The North Highlands of Peru, the Recuay Culture and Wari Expansion into Highland Ancash
    11  Environment and Geological Processes
    21  Prehistory in the Callejón de Huaylas and Recuay Culture

37  THREE • Fieldwork Methodology and Sector 1 Excavations
    37  Chinchawas Ceramic Sequence
    39  Archaeological Fieldwork
    41  Enclosures
    45  Room Complexes
    61  The Torreón
    65  Conclusions

69  FOUR • Excavations of Terrace Areas, Sector 1
    69  Terrace 1
    85  Terrace 2
    87  Terrace 3
    94  Terrace 4
    106  Terrace 5
    109  Terrace 6
    111  Terrace 7
    111  Terrace 8
    112  Terrace 9
    113  Conclusions

115  FIVE • Investigations of Sector 2 Mortuary Constructions
    115  Background and Reconnaissance
    118  Sector 2 Investigations
    133  Discussion
    137  Conclusions

139 SIX • CERAMICS OF THE KAYÁN AND CHINCHAWASI PHASES
    140  Methodology
    141  Kayán Phase Ceramics
    151  Chinchawasi 1 Phase Ceramics
    177  Chinchawasi 2 Phase Ceramics

207 SEVEN • CERAMICS OF THE WARMI AND CHAKWAS PHASES
    207  Warmi Phase Ceramics
    235  Chakwas Phase Ceramics
    246  Post-Chakwas Occupation
    246  Overview of the Ceramic Chronology of Chinchawas
    247  Conclusions

249 EIGHT • FANCY AND IMPORTED CERAMICS
    249  Fancy Pottery in Subterranean Tombs, Sector 2
    253  Fancy Pottery in Chullpa Tombs, Sector 2
    255  Fancy and Imported Pottery in Sector 1
    282  Distributions of Fancy and Imported Ceramics at Chinchawas
    289  Cultural Interaction at Chinchawas
    292  Discussion

295 NINE • LOCAL ECONOMY AND TRADE:
           EVIDENCE FROM OTHER ARTIFACTS
    295  Methodology
    297  Chipped Stone Artifacts
    312  Groundstone Artifacts
    321  Miscellaneous Stone Artifacts
    327  Spindle Whorls and Discs
    333  Bone Artifacts
    344  Shell Artifacts
    346  Metal Artifacts
    351  Conclusions

353 TEN • REVIEW AND CONCLUSIONS
    353  Results of the Chinchawas Research
    365  Concluding Comments

367 APPENDIX: Provenience Information

373 REFERENCES

393 INDEX

# Figures

| | | |
|---|---|---|
| 2 | Figure 1. | The Central Andes and sites mentioned in the text. |
| 4 | Figure 2. | Cultural chronology of northern Peru. |
| 12 | Figure 3. | North Central Peru and sites mentioned in text. |
| 14 | Figure 4. | Chinchawas, Sector 1. |
| 16 | Figure 5. | The Chinchawas site and the surrounding region. |
| 18 | Figure 6. | Monthly precipitation levels at different elevations in the Callejón de Huaylas, Peru. |
| 20 | Figure 7. | Schematic reconstruction of ecological floors and land use zones around Chinchawas. |
| 22 | Figure 8. | General schedule for sowing and harvesting crops in the Callejón de Huaylas. |
| 24 | Figure 9. | Oxygen isotope ratios from Huascarán Core 2. |
| 38 | Figure 10. | Chinchawas site, showing the location of Sector 1 and Sector 2. |
| 40 | Figure 11. | Sector 1: architectural zones, excavation operations and stone sculptures. |
| 42 | Figure 12. | Reconstruction of Chinchawas site. |
| 44 | Figure 13. | Enclosure 2, Sector 1. |
| 46 | Figure 14. | West profile of Operation 32 within Enclosure 2, with drainage canal and low-lying platform. |
| 50 | Figure 15. | Plan of northern structures and excavation operations in Room Complex 3. |
| 52 | Figure 16. | North façade of Room Complex 3. |
| 54 | Figure 17. | Section of Room Complex 3 stairwell. |
| 56 | Figure 18. | Plan of southeast structure (Operation 51), Room Complex 3. |
| 58 | Figure 19. | Excavated structure (Operation 49) in Room Complex 4. |
| 60 | Figure 20. | Plan of excavated structure (Operation 45) in Room Complex 5. |
| 62 | Figure 21. | Profile of tall structure (Operation 52), Room Complex 6. |
| 64 | Figure 22. | Plan of Torreón structure excavation (Operation 54) |
| 76 | Figure 23. | East stratigraphic profile of Terrace 1 excavations (Operations 9, 12 and 18). |
| 80 | Figure 24. | Plan of Operation 46, Level H, showing Warmi and Chakwas phase re-use. |
| 88 | Figure 25. | Plan of walls in Terrace 3 (Operation 47), Sector 1. |
| 94 | Figure 26. | Three 1 by 2 m test excavations in Terrace 4. |
| 98 | Figure 27. | Plan of Terrace 4 excavations, Sector 1. |
| 100 | Figure 28. | North profile of Terrace 4, Sector 1. |
| 116 | Figure 29. | Sector 2: subterranean and chullpa tombs, stone sculptures and project operations. |

122 Figure 30. Plan of subterranean tombs, ST-1 (A) and ST-3 (B), from Sector 2.
124 Figure 31. Plan and east profile of Subterranean Tomb 2 (Operation 63), Sector 2.
126 Figure 32. Plans of chullpa tombs, Sector 2.
130 Figure 33. Plan and west profile of Chullpa Tomb 2, Sector 2.
132 Figure 34. The northern façade of Chullpa Tomb 2.
134 Figure 35. East profile of Chullpa Tomb 8, investigated as Operation 60, Sector 2.
136 Figure 36. Plan of Chullpa Tomb 7, Sector 2.
148 Figure 37. Kayán phase Ware A pottery: bowls.
150 Figure 38. Kayán phase pottery: jars.
152 Figure 39. Chinchawasi 1 phase Ware A pottery: bowls.
154 Figure 40. Chinchawasi 1 phase Ware A pottery: bowls.
156 Figure 41. Chinchawasi 1 phase Ware A pottery: bowls and cups.
158 Figure 42. Chinchawasi 1 phase Ware A pottery: jars.
160 Figure 43. Chinchawasi 1 phase Ware B pottery: bowls.
162 Figure 44. Chinchawasi 1 phase Ware C pottery: jars and bowls.
164 Figure 45. Chinchawasi 1 phase Ware D pottery: jar.
166 Figure 46. Chinchawasi 1 phase Ware D pottery: jars.
168 Figure 47. Chinchawasi 1 phase Ware D pottery: jars and olla.
170 Figure 48. Chinchawasi 1 phase Ware D pottery: bowls.
172 Figure 49. Chinchawasi 1 phase Ware D pottery: cups, bottles and spoons.
174 Figure 50. Chinchawasi 1 phase Ware D pottery: colanders and plastic decoration.
175 Figure 51. Chinchawasi 2 phase Ware A pottery: bowl.
176 Figure 52. Chinchawasi 2 phase Ware A pottery: bowl.
178 Figure 53. Chinchawasi 2 phase Ware A pottery: bowls and cup.
180 Figure 54. Chinchawasi 2 phase Ware A pottery: jars and spoon.
182 Figure 55. Chinchawasi 1 and Chinchawasi 2 phase bowls with interior decoration.
185 Figure 56. Chinchawasi 2 phase Ware B pottery: bowl, jars, cup, spoons and bottle.
188 Figure 57. Chinchawasi 2 phase Ware C pottery: bowls.
190 Figure 58. Chinchawasi 2 phase Ware C pottery: bowls, cup, ring-bases.
192 Figure 59. Chinchawasi 2 phase Ware C pottery: colanders, ollas, bottles, spoons.
193 Figure 60. Chinchawasi 2 phase Ware C pottery: jars.
194 Figure 61. Chinchawasi 2 phase Ware C pottery: jars.
195 Figure 62. Chinchawasi 2 phase Ware C pottery: jar.
196 Figure 63. Chinchawasi 2 phase Ware C pottery: jars.
197 Figure 64. Chinchawasi 2 phase Ware C pottery: jars.
198 Figure 65. Chinchawasi 2 phase Ware C pottery: jars.

## Figures

199 FIGURE 66. Chinchawasi 2 phase Ware C pottery: jars.
200 FIGURE 67. Chinchawasi 2 phase Ware C pottery: jars and plastic decoration.
202 FIGURE 68. Reconstruction of shapes represented in Kayán and Chinchawasi 1 phases.
204 FIGURE 69. Reconstruction of shapes represented in Chinchawasi 2 phase.
208 FIGURE 70. Warmi phase Ware A pottery: bowls.
210 FIGURE 71. Warmi phase Ware A pottery: bowls.
212 FIGURE 72. Warmi phase Ware A pottery: bowls and jar.
214 FIGURE 73. Top and profile views of Warmi phase bowls with interior decoration.
216 FIGURE 74. Warmi phase Ware B pottery: jar.
218 FIGURE 75. Warmi phase Ware B pottery: jar.
220 FIGURE 76. Warmi phase Ware B pottery: jar.
222 FIGURE 77. Warmi phase Ware B pottery: jars.
224 FIGURE 78. Warmi phase Ware B pottery: jars.
226 FIGURE 79. Warmi phase Ware B pottery: jars.
228 FIGURE 80. Warmi phase Ware B pottery: jars, bottle and olla.
230 FIGURE 81. Warmi phase Ware B pottery: bowls.
232 FIGURE 82. Warmi phase Ware B pottery: colanders, spoons and plastic decoration.
234 FIGURE 83. Warmi phase Ware B pottery from Sector 2 chullpas: jars and bowls.
236 FIGURE 84. Warmi phase Ware B pottery from Sector 2 chullpas: bowls.
238 FIGURE 85. Reconstruction of shapes represented in Warmi and Chakwas phases.
240 FIGURE 86. Chakwas phase pottery: bowls.
242 FIGURE 87. Chakwas phase pottery: jars.
244 FIGURE 88. Chakwas phase pottery: jar, bottle and plastic decoration.
250 FIGURE 89. Fancy pottery from subterranean tombs, Sector 2.
252 FIGURE 90. Fancy pottery from chullpa tombs, Sector 2.
256 FIGURE 91. Fancy kaolinite pottery, Cajamarca and Cajamarca-related.
260 FIGURE 92. Wilkawaín resist-painted bowl, Nievería effigy bottle and fine pinkware spoons.
262 FIGURE 93. Press-molded tumblers.
264 FIGURE 94. Press-molded tumblers and bowls.
269 FIGURE 95. Polished blackware pottery: tumblers, bowls, spout and exterior plastic decoration.
271 FIGURE 96. Wari-related pottery: polychrome bowls.
273 FIGURE 97. Wari-related pottery: polychrome jars, bottle and tumblers.
274 FIGURE 98. Modeled figurines and adornos.
277 FIGURE 99. Face-neck jars.

278 Figure 100. Other fancy wares.
280 Figure 101. Miniature vessels.
281 Figure 102. Fired pottery whorls and ground ceramic objects.
286 Figure 103. Strap handle marks.
287 Figure 104. Comparison of fancy and imported frequencies by phase.
288 Figure 105. Distribution of fancy and imported styles by context.
302 Figure 106. Kayán phase lithics.
303 Figure 107. Chinchawasi 1 phase lithics.
304 Figure 108. Chinchawasi 1 phase lithics.
305 Figure 109. Chinchawasi 2 phase lithics.
306 Figure 110. Chinchawasi 2 phase lithics.
307 Figure 111. Chinchawasi 2 phase lithics.
308 Figure 112. Chinchawasi 2 phase lithics.
309 Figure 113. Chinchawasi 2 phase lithics.
310 Figure 114. Warmi phase lithics.
311 Figure 115. Warmi phase lithics.
312 Figure 116. Distributions of chipped stone artifacts at Chinchawas, by context and phase.
313 Figure 117. Materials used at Chinchawas in chipped stone assemblage.
316 Figure 118. Hand grinding stones, Sector 1.
317 Figure 119. Mortars and large grinding stones, Sector 1.
320 Figure 120. Hammerstones and stone polishers, Sector 1.
321 Figure 121. Pebble and slingstone objects.
322 Figure 122. Carved stone figurines, Sector 1.
324 Figure 123. Small stone carvings, Sector 1.
325 Figure 124. Large hafted stone implements.
326 Figure 125. Stone beads and pendants, spindle whorls and small stone discs.
328 Figure 126. Ceramic spindle whorls and blanks.
329 Figure 127. Bone implements: spindle whorls and blanks, ornament, rib tools and scapula scrapers.
334 Figure 128. Bone implements: small spatulas and scraping tools.
336 Figure 129. Bone implements: needles, awls and perforators.
339 Figure 130. Bone implements: cranial spoons.
341 Figure 131. Bone implements: pelvic trowels and miscellaneous modified bone objects.
344 Figure 132. Antler objects: awl and reaming tools, worked base and shaft straightener.
345 Figure 133. Shell ornaments.
347 Figure 134. Metal artifacts: Chinchawasi 1 phase, Chinchawasi 2 phase.
348 Figure 135. Metal artifacts: Chinchawasi 2 phase.
350 Figure 136. Metal artifacts: Warmi phase.

# Tables

| Page | Table | Description |
|---|---|---|
| 48 | Table 1. | Radiocarbon assays from Chinchawas. |
| 102 | Table 2. | Relative abundance of Chinchawas vertebrate taxa from Sector 1. |
| 104 | Table 3. | Faunal remains from Operation 38, Sector 1, Chinchawas. |
| 120 | Table 4. | Comparison of funerary construction sizes, Sector 2, Chinchawas. |
| 128 | Table 5. | Human skeletal remains from Sector 2 funerary structures. |
| 140 | Table 6. | Analyzed pottery wares and proportions of open and closed forms by phase. |
| 142 | Table 7. | Plainware forms and percentages by phase. |
| 144 | Table 8. | Miscellaneous plainware forms and percentages by phase. |
| 146 | Table 9. | Decorated pottery and forms by phase. |
| 205 | Table 10. | Maker's marks by phase. |
| 258 | Table 11. | Fancy and imported pottery by architectural contexts, all phases. |
| 296 | Table 12. | Lithic artifacts. |
| 298 | Table 13. | Lithic artifacts by architectural contexts, all phases. |
| 314 | Table 14. | Grinding stones by phase. |
| 318 | Table 15. | Statistics of hammerstones. |
| 318 | Table 16. | Hammerstones by phase. |
| 319 | Table 17. | Pebble and slingstone objects by phase. |
| 319 | Table 18. | Statistics of pebble and slingstone objects. |
| 330 | Table 19. | Statistics and chart of mean dimensions of perforated ceramic spindle whorls. |
| 331 | Table 20. | Statistics and chart of mean dimensions of ceramic spindle whorl blanks. |
| 335 | Table 21. | Bone spatula artifacts by phase and architectural context. |
| 337 | Table 22. | Bone needle artifacts by phase and architectural context. |
| 338 | Table 23. | Bone awl and perforator objects by phase and architectural context. |
| 338 | Table 24. | Cranial spoon artifacts by phase and architectural context. |
| 340 | Table 25. | Pelvic trowel artifacts by phase and architectural context. |
| 340 | Table 26. | Rib tools by phase and architectural context. |
| 340 | Table 27. | Scapula scrapers by phase and architectural context. |
| 342 | Table 28. | Bone ornament objects by phase and architectural context. |
| 342 | Table 29. | Bone tool production debris by phase and architectural context. |
| 342 | Table 30. | Antler artifacts by phase and architectural context. |
| 342 | Table 31. | Antler artifacts by type and phase. |
| 346 | Table 32. | Copper-metal objects by phase and architectural context. |
| 346 | Table 33. | Copper-metal objects by type and phase. |

# Acknowledgements

This book could not have been completed without the generous support of many individuals and institutions. I thank the National Science Foundation and Wenner-Gren Foundation for Anthropological Research for enabling the field research, under grants SBR-9612574 and No. 6066, respectively. Yale University's Josef Albers Fund facilitated initial reconnaissance. Different laboratory studies were supported by grants from Yale's John F. Enders Fellowship (ceramic and faunal analysis) and Sigma Xi GIAR (metals characterization). Support from the Sainsbury Research Unit and a Sterling Memorial Dissertation Writing Fellowship (Yale Graduate School of Arts and Sciences) facilitated different phases of the writing. I am also indebted to Dumbarton Oaks for a fellowship in Pre-Columbian Studies, which facilitated the development of ideas and script.

The Instituto Nacional de Cultura, Peru, under Resolución Directoral Nacional 419-96/INC, provided generous permission for the archaeological investigations. I owe many thanks to the Lima office, especially members of the Comisión Técnica, for favorable consideration of my research project and for the exportation of artifact samples. I am also indebted to César Serna Lamas, Mirtha Antúnez, César Aguirre and Benjamín Morales of the INC–Huaraz office, who furnished research facilities and important supervision at different stages of the project.

The field investigations could not have been completed without the support and dedicated participation of the modern community of Chinchawasi and members of the field crew, especially Martín Justiniano, Jorge Luis Alvarez, César Valverde, Scott R. Hutson, John Geer and James Schumacher. Victor Rodriguez and Habrán Alberto, the community leaders during our time at Chinchawasi, provided invaluable help, humor, and perspective.

The fieldwork and materials research would have been far less enjoyable without the many friendships and scholarly collaborations forged abroad. In addition to generous logistical support, Steve Wegner shared his expert knowledge of Recuay archaeology and the Callejón de Huaylas. Victor Ponte, Javier Barrio, Alex Herrera, Joan Gero, Kevin Lane, Gabriel Ramón and Carolina Orsini shared freely of their data and knowledge. I thank Ysabel Meza, Julio and Gudi Olaza, Christopher Benway and Ankur Tohan for their support and conversation in Huaraz; and the South American Explorers Club (Lima office), Willy García and Alison Sálazar for their assistance and hospitality in Lima.

This manuscript has benefited from the advice and comments of various people, including Richard Burger, Katharina Schreiber, Jeffrey Quilter, Michael Coe, Frank Hole, Karen Stothert, Mickey Dietler, Elsa Redmond, George R. Miller, Takeshi Inomata and Tom Tartaron; any errors, of course, are mine alone. John Verano, Christine Pink, Richard Burger and Heather Lechtman generously coordinated technical studies of materials from the Chinchawas investigations. Yale's Anthropology Department staff, especially Karen Phillips and Donna Del Buco, furnished timely administrative assistance in the initial stages of the fieldwork. Bridget Gazzo, of the Dumbarton Oaks Library, was always generous and supportive. In Norwich, preparation of this volume has received gracious support from Steve Hooper, Pat Hewitt, Francine Hunt and the Sainsbury Research Unit in general.

I extend special thanks to Richard Burger, Lucy Sálazar and Steve Wegner, all veterans of fieldwork in the Callejón de Huaylas, for their encouragement and friendship throughout the project.

# CHAPTER ONE

# Introduction

The investigation of Andean prehistory focuses, traditionally, on large regional centers or specialized ceremonial sites. Especially for societies of the Early Intermediate Period (A.D. 1 to 700) and the Middle Horizon (A.D. 700 to 1000), research often takes a "top-down" approach, shaping the impression of one or more powerful hegemonic states based in a central place and competing for the geopolitical control of others. Thus, provincial settlements and groups in a given region are construed as simple ancillary components within a larger sociopolitical apparatus. The repeated emphasis on regional centers and their political systems eclipses, through sampling, the character and importance of rural communities. In so doing, the ongoing bias in current research obscures the very diversity in prehistory that archaeologists propose to understand.

The present study is an examination of the prehistoric occupation of Chinchawas, a small agropastoral community in the North Central Highlands of Ancash Department, Peru (Figure 1). The discussion presents a site-level reconstruction of highland community patterns and organization in the Recuay cultural tradition of the first millennium A.D. (Lau 2004a). The Chinchawas investigations enable a fuller picture of Recuay sociopolitical complexity by advancing the current knowledge of pre-state Andean societies from a rural highland perspective. Specifically, describing the local socioeconomic transformations at Chinchawas helps to elucidate the character and role of North Highland societies during the Early Intermediate Period and the Middle Horizon.

## Objectives

*Chronology*
Archaeological data will be presented to achieve five basic objectives. The most fundamental goal is to improve the cultural chronology of the Callejón de Huaylas region, especially during the period following the height of Chavín influence, known as the Early Horizon (Rowe 1962). The fieldwork used a single-site methodology that included local mapping, surface collection and excavation sampling. Most studies focusing on regional settlement systems, by their very nature, produce data sets that are better suited to address certain questions than others. Because of powerful natural and anthropogenic forces that disturb, cover and completely displace

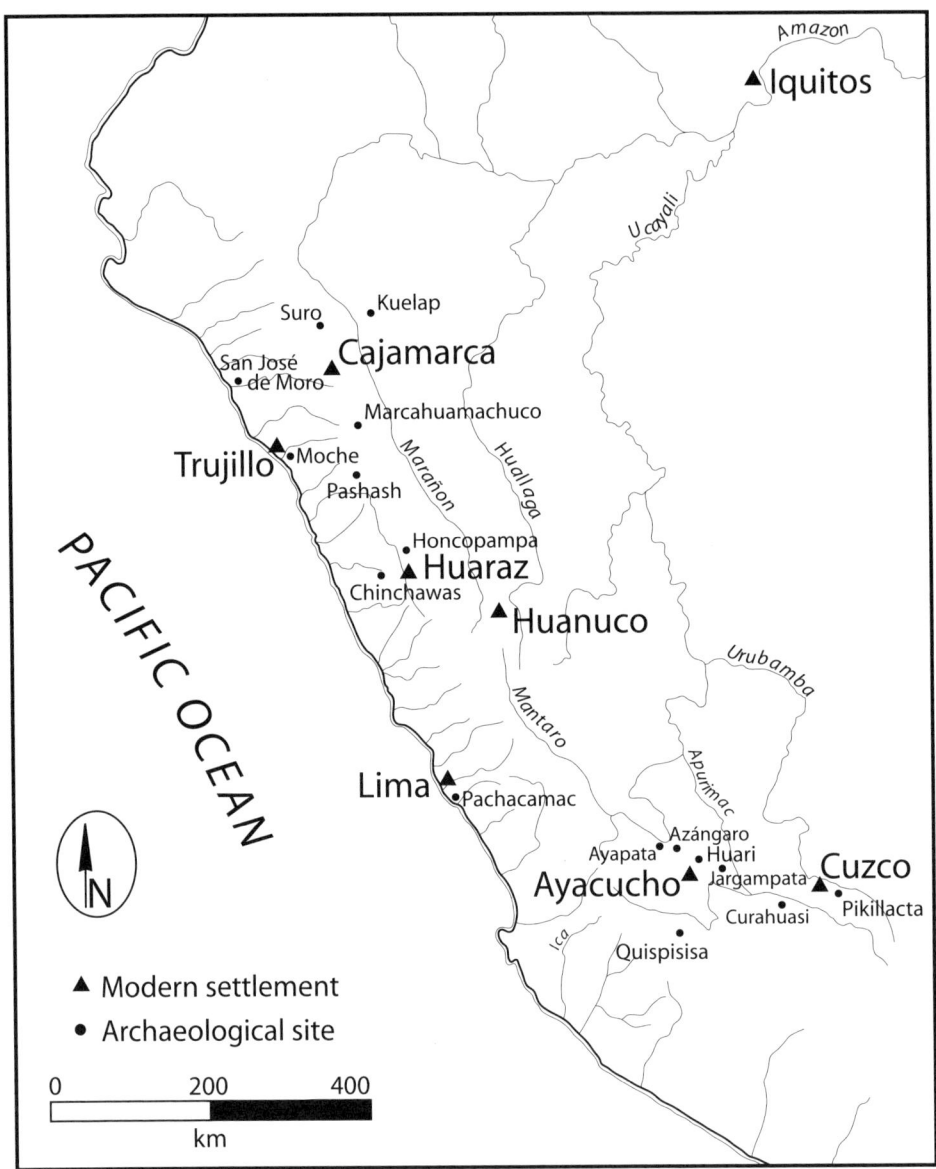

Figure 1. The Central Andes and sites mentioned in the text.

ancient deposits, regional settlement survey is notoriously difficult in highland Ancash and the Central Andes, in general. Moreover, the classification of pottery types based solely on surface materials has often proven inconclusive or too coarse-grained to discern sociocultural transformations at the local or intrasite level.

A five-phase sequence based on ceramic analysis and classification is presented here to understand the local culture history (Figure 2). The primary focus of this study concerns the first four occupations of the site, approximate cal A.D.

300 to 900 (all date ranges hereafter are based on calibrated ages), a period that overlaps with the latter portion of the Early Intermediate Period and Middle Horizon in Central Andean chronology (Rowe and Menzel 1967). Ten radiocarbon determinations provide absolute age ranges to frame and test the accuracy of the relative chronology. Together, the new chronological data are used to build a new cultural sequence for the region that will be useful for future archaeological studies in highland Ancash.

*Settlement Organization*
Site mapping and stratigraphic excavations were conducted to understand the settlement layout of Chinchawas and its change through time. Based on the architecture and corresponding artifact assemblages, the research identifies a series of activity contexts: domestic (midden areas, open terrace areas and room structures), defensive, public–ceremonial and mortuary constructions. Like the overall settlement organization, the different zones illustrate patterns of continuity and change in architecture as well as in artifact distributions.

*Economy*
Changing patterns in local economy will be a major theme of this book. The longstanding emphasis on the art and iconography of Recuay culture has left major gaps in the understanding of North Highland societies after Chavín (ca. 900 to 200 B.C.). The conventional economy of agriculture and camelid herding is often assumed implicitly in considerations of highland groups, especially of Recuay culture. Data from Chinchawas, including faunal and tool assemblages, will be used to detail the character of local economic practices.

As part of the focus on economic patterns, evidence will be marshaled to examine domestic activities at the site, including descriptions of pottery, chipped stone, groundstone and bone tool assemblages. The research identifies a wide range of small-scale craft activities at the site, including preparation of raw textile fiber and production of bone tools, lithics, spindle whorls and other implements. Although there is strong continuity in the types of domestic activities, significant transformations occur in their scale and contexts.

Finally, patterns of exchange will be charted to examine Chinchawas's interregional relationships through time. Stylistic analysis of local decorated ceramics and stone sculpture will be combined with data on imported products (exotic pottery, obsidian, metal artifacts and other sumptuary goods) to interpret the socioeconomic role of Chinchawas in broader, regional contexts. Evidence for trade is limited during the early occupation of the site. Exchange intensified greatly during the period of Wari expansion from about A.D. 700 to 900.

*Ceremonial Practices*
Despite its small size, the Chinchawas site is unusual for its exceptional preservation of standing stone architecture and monolithic stone sculptures. The archi-

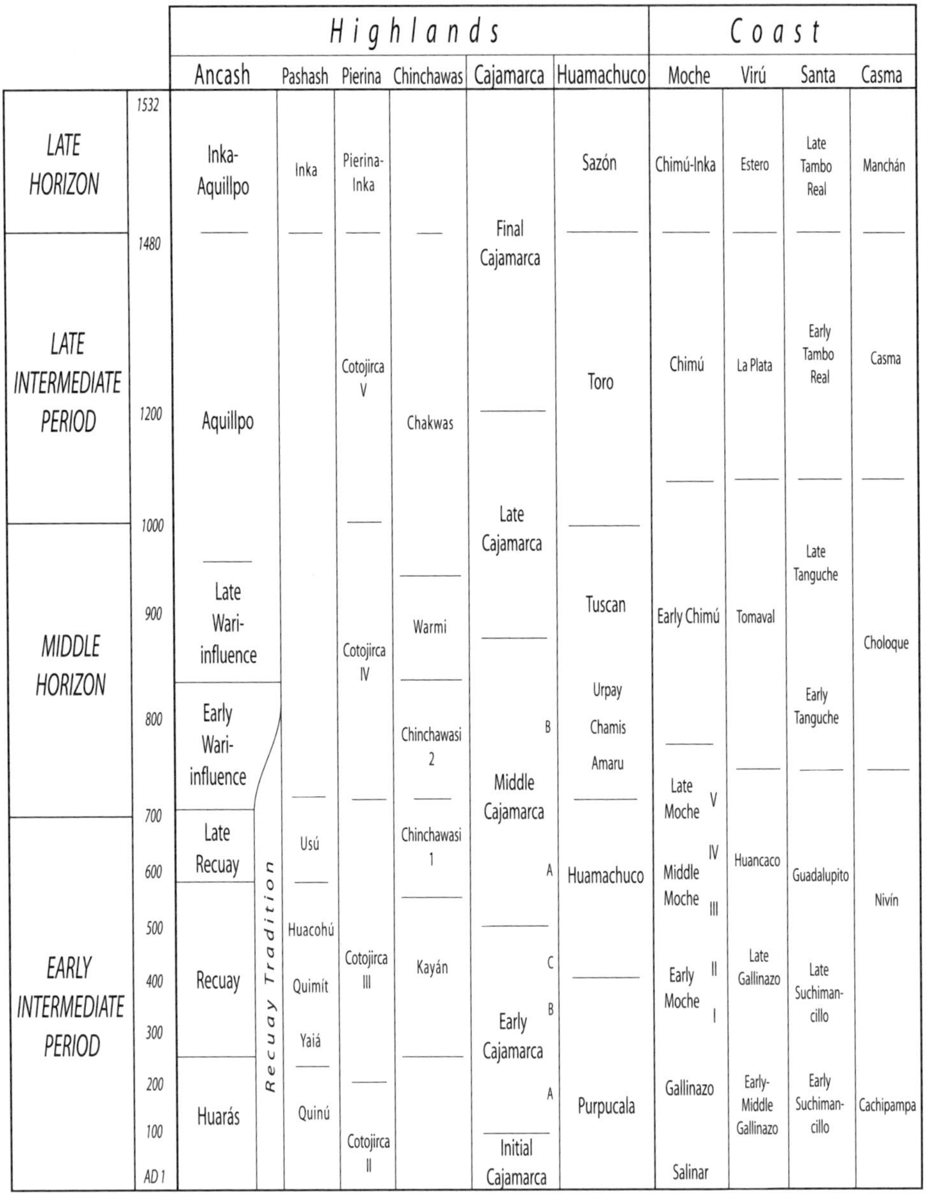

| Date | Period | Highlands | | | | | | Coast | | | |
|---|---|---|---|---|---|---|---|---|---|---|---|
| | | Ancash | Pashash | Pierina | Chinchawas | Cajamarca | Huamachuco | Moche | Virú | Santa | Casma |
| 1532 | LATE HORIZON | Inka-Aquillpo | Inka | Pierina-Inka | | | Sazón | Chimú-Inka | Estero | Late Tambo Real | Manchán |
| 1480 | | | | | | Final Cajamarca | | | | | |
| 1200 | LATE INTERMEDIATE PERIOD | Aquillpo | | Cotojirca V | Chakwas | | Toro | Chimú | La Plata | Early Tambo Real | Casma |
| 1000 | | | | | | Late Cajamarca | | | | Late Tanguche | |
| 900 | MIDDLE HORIZON | Late Wari-influence | | Cotojirca IV | Warmi | | Tuscan | Early Chimú | Tomaval | | Choloque |
| 800 | | Early Wari-influence | | | Chinchawasi 2 | Middle Cajamarca B | Urpay / Chamis / Amaru | Late Moche V | | Early Tanguche | |
| 700 | | | | | | | | | | | |
| 600 | EARLY INTERMEDIATE PERIOD | Late Recuay | Usú | | Chinchawasi 1 | A | Huamachuco | Middle Moche IV | Huancaco | Guadalupito | Nivin |
| 500 | | | Huacohú | | | | | | | | |
| 400 | | Recuay | Quimit | Cotojirca III | Kayán | C | | Early Moche II | Late Gallinazo | Late Suchimancillo | |
| 300 | | | Yaiá | | | Early Cajamarca B | | I | | | |
| 200 | | | | | | A | Purpucala | Gallinazo | Early-Middle Gallinazo | Early Suchimancillo | Cachipampa |
| 100 | | Huarás | Quinú | Cotojirca II | | Initial Cajamarca | | | | | |
| AD 1 | | | | | | | | Salinar | | | |

(Recuay Tradition spans the Pashash column from ~AD 1 to ~600)

FIGURE 2. Cultural chronology of northern Peru, with the position of the occupations at Chinchawas and other regions. The ancient site, termed "Chinchawas" by Mejía (1941), should be distinguished from "Chinchawasi," a phase or style designation after the modern community.

tecture includes funerary structures as well as open enclosures made of elaborate stone work. The research identifies these elements, in addition to fancy pottery and other luxury goods, as part of community patterns of ceremonial practice centered on ancestor veneration and public display. Data from analyses of ritual spaces and their contents are presented to provide additional detail for previous general interpretations (Lau 2000, 2002, 2006b).

*Local Sociopolitical Complexity*
Together, inferences about patterns in architecture and artifact collections will be made to consider Chinchawas's sociopolitical arrangement by phase. Specifically, architectural differences, distribution of sumptuary or exotic items, and organization of economic directions (including domestic activities, exchange and craft production) are examined. Despite remarkable patterns of variability, the ancient community of Chinchawas was largely composed of small-scale groups, apparently with little permanent social hierarchy. The Chinchawas evidence will be compared to other areas and developments in the Recuay heartland.

## Comparative Considerations

*Scale of Research*
This study uses a research methodology that focuses on archaeological patterns at the community level. *The American College Dictionary* (1947) defines community as "a social group of any size whose members reside in a specific locality, share government and have a cultural and historical heritage." On purely definitional grounds, therefore, the term "community" is useful because it carries both physical and abstract dimensions that can be examined archaeologically.

In the archaeological literature, "community" often describes the physical dimension. Archaeologists may speak of village or urban communities. Each usage carries a separate meaning, but often holds specific expectations in demographics or complexity. The usefulness of the term is that it can be multi-scalar and refer to a range of settlements and settlement sizes.

By its very nature, a community should be composed of different parts. In cultural anthropology, community studies often focus on the diversity and histories of constituents within the entire social group, often in terms of families, lineages, work–status groups and enclaves. In archaeology, related forms of diversity can be distinguished on the basis of function and activities, as reflected in architectural spaces and artifact assemblages. As the physical setting in and through which people conduct activities, a community may be considered the amalgam of diverse sets of cultural activities and practices; these may especially include zones for residence, in addition to zones for administration, ceremony, defense and economic production.

The term "community" also integrates a more abstract dimension of shared connectedness, through things and ideas held in common, among its constituents. In the definition above, communities share a "cultural and historical heritage." What often distinguishes a particular community are the ways of doing things (cuisine, language, fashion, material culture and common pasts, among others). For ancient cases, this dimension might be promisingly considered as local compared with external cultural traditions—often examined through material remains of stylistic change or continuity, in iconography and special behavioral patterns (such as funerary practices). Trade items should also provide indicators of the degree to which a local community is connected or separated from larger sociopolitical arrangements.

Reference to community also presupposes that its constituent parts, whether people or physical spaces, are flexible and prone to change. The term, by itself, resists some of the evolutionary and normative expectations attached to site categories, such as hamlet, village, city, central places, secondary centers and others. The fluidity of the composition and socially constituted forms of communities has been a traditional emphasis in cultural anthropology, but has only recently become formalized in archaeology (Canuto and Yaeger 2000).

The present contribution proceeds under the basic premise that communities are dynamic units of archaeological study. The simple term "community" holds utility in evaluating the variability of cultural remains from ancient sites, because it acknowledges intrinsic internal diversity and common traditions, as well as the potential for change at different levels. I will describe by phase the character and articulation of different human activities within the confines of the Chinchawas site. In this way we can track the growth and decline of the community and discern patterns of socioeconomic change that may be interpreted alongside broader transformations in Andean prehistory.

*Interregional Interaction*
Cultural transformations examined through comparisons at the local and interregional level have long been the hallmarks of Andean culture history (Uhle 1903; Tello 1940, 1942; Kroeber 1944; Willey 1945; Bennett 1948). Rowe (1962) instituted an enduring framework to understand relative chronology in the Central Andes, dividing Andean prehistory into a series of temporal units. "Horizons," or those brief units of time characterized by cultural integration across a wide geographic area, intercalated with "periods," those intermediate units of time falling between horizons, often characterized by more regional developments. Although Rowe's sequence aimed largely to do away with chronological systems based on "stages," it has served also as the primary framework to locate and periodize interregional interaction in Andean prehistory.

My study focuses on the Early Intermediate Period and Middle Horizon. After the collapse of Chavín civilization, important new patterns distinguished the Early Intermediate Period, including the rise of urbanism and expansionist polities, the florescence of regional art styles, and major technological innovations in pottery, metalwork and water management. In contrast to the widespread benefits enabled by Chavín interaction (Burger 1992), the Early Intermediate Period has often been characterized as a time of insularity, describing both the balkanization of art styles and group territories (Lanning 1967; Lumbreras 1974a).

The subsequent Middle Horizon witnessed the dispersion of more uniform cultural patterns, specifically of pottery, architecture and other materials affiliated with Wari culture (Menzel 1964; Schaedel 1966, 1993; Isbell and McEwan 1991).

The traditional standpoint interprets Wari cultural expansion as the material correlate of geopolitical statecraft of a militaristic empire centered at the Huari site, in the Central Highlands of Ayacucho (Menzel 1964; Lumbreras 1974a, 1974b; Isbell 1977; Isbell and Schreiber 1978; Schreiber 1992). (I follow Isbell's proposal [2000] to use "Huari" to refer to the Ayacucho site and "Wari" for the culture and art style outside of Huari. For style designations, I follow the original spelling, such as "Huari" in "Huari Norteño" [Larco 1948]). Some scholars question this perspective, proposing, in lieu, that Wari expansion resulted from intensive relationships between regional polities (e.g., Mackey 1982; Shady 1982, 1988, 1989; J. Topic 1991; T. Topic 1991). Under a scenario of peer polity interaction, Wari may have risen to a status of *primus inter pares*. Some scholars deny the utility of the Middle Horizon concept by identifying problems of contemporaneity and strong cultural variability even within core areas of Wari influence (Schaedel 1993).

Before the 1970s, the examination of interregional relationships relied on stylistic analyses of pottery (e.g., Menzel 1964; Willey 1945). While these are consistently powerful tools, scholars have begun to use other independent lines of evidence to verify and improve interpretations of interaction based on ceramics. Certainly, more common use of radiocarbon determinations has enabled finer-grain cultural associations for Early Intermediate Period and Middle Horizon interaction (Ziółkowski et al. 1994). Stylistic analyses of administrative architecture (Hyslop 1990; Isbell and McEwan 1991) show utility in identifying extensive architectural programs of archaic states.

Sourcing studies may provide the most direct evidence for long-distance interaction. Spondylus shell (*Spondylus* sp.), found along the coast of Ecuador, has been a traditional indicator of trade (Paulsen 1974). Clay sourcing studies, currently in its infancy in Andean studies, may prove to be useful in distinguishing pottery production areas, especially in the North Highlands (e.g., Czwarno 1983; Druc 1998). Perhaps the major boon to prehistoric Andean exchange studies has been characterization analyses of obsidian artifacts (Burger and Asaro 1977; Burger and Glascock 2000; Burger et al. 2000, 2006). The scarcity of obsidian sources and its common use in toolmaking often resulted in obsidian exchange over long distances. By determining the chemical composition of each artifact back to its parent source archaeologists can study diachronic patterns in the frequency and distribution of obsidian exchange.

In addition to temporal issues, cultural interaction inheres an important geographical dimension. The Central Andes region consists of three major life zones: the coast, highlands and tropical forest (*selva*) regions. Discussions of trade or cultural interaction have tended to focus within each life zone. There have been fewer systematic treatments of cultural interaction crossing geographical frontiers, either as theoretical models (e.g., Topic and Topic 1983; Burger 1984b; Shimada 1987) or investigations of boundary interaction at the site level (e.g., Church 1996).

Intermontane and coast–highland interactions are evident at Chinchawas. At different times of its occupation, peoples at the Chinchawas site maintained a suite of cultural and economic connections with outside areas. One of the primary aims of this study is to elucidate the scale, source and significance of these external relationships. In addition to stylistic analyses of local decorated pottery, data on fancy pottery, obsidian, marine shell and other nonlocal items will be used to reconstruct site-level patterns of interregional interaction.

*Rural Complexity*
The present study contributes to a growing literature about rural communities in early complex societies (MacEachern et al. 1989; Schwartz and Falconer 1994; Canuto and Yaeger 2000). In lieu of a "top-down" approach to sociopolitical complexity, the research adopts the perspective of a rural agropastoral community. The present case study aims to provide some counterbalance to interpretations of Andean prehistory based on studies of regional centers or central places alone.

As components of larger sociopolitical systems, rural communities have been viewed typically as simple, undifferentiated settlements subordinate to more complex centers. Drawing from the influential concept of "closed corporate communities" in anthropology, archaeologists often characterize peasant villages as insular and homogeneous, with flexible social arrangements and enduring domestic traditions. Social and cultural changes are usually ascribed to external causes, especially as policy administered by more powerful governments (Schwartz and Falconer 1994:2–3).

Site-level studies from rural perspectives remain unorthodox in Andean studies, but there are several germane examples. At Jargampata, Isbell (1977:56) identifies a rural settlement "occupied by peasant agriculturalists under the supervision of state officials" and established to manage agricultural surplus for the urban capital of Wari. On the basis of extensive household archaeology at Lukurmata, Bolivia, Bermann (1994) concludes that the site was largely an autonomous community until the advent of the Tiwanaku state (A.D. 700). Major changes in architecture and material culture indicate that the site evolved into a secondary center subordinate to the Tiwanaku capital. In both cases, agrarian settlements are absorbed to sustain regional political systems. Further, external sources promote local transformations. Similar insights are reached through important projects focused on valley-wide settlement systems (e.g., Willey 1953; Wilson 1988; D'Altroy 1992; Stanish 1992; Aldenderfer 1993).

Under top-down models, therefore, archaeologists expect that local communities were largely administered during periods of political integration. We know from ethnographic and ethnohistorical records, however, that Andean peoples often find ways to accommodate new sociopolitical conditions (e.g., Rowe 1946; Stern 1987; Allen 1988; Rasnake 1988). One can ask whether we see analogues of this in the archaeological record. To what degree were ancient communities autonomous during periods of integration? Do aspects of domination and resistance play out in material culture?

By examining a small Recuay community before, during and after Wari expansion, this study offers data to understand local transformations as the results of local traditions and priorities in relation to broader external pressures. Chinchawas's architecture, ceramics, stone sculpture and other cultural remains express distinct local patterns, each with affinities to more familiar regional styles. By reconstructing the site's changing character of occupation, the research tracks shifting cultural ties that relate the community uniquely to different regions and sociopolitical processes of the Central Andes through time.

Taken together, the evidence indicates considerable local economic and political autonomy throughout the Chinchawas sequence. Exchange relations and cultural influences from external sources are particularly strong during the Middle Horizon, but they are not illustrative of foreign takeover or pressure. The resilience and sometimes intensification of local traditions in material culture, especially during the Chinchawasi 2 phase, are interpreted as internal, community-level responses to conditions created by Wari expansion. Different lines of data, particularly in local decorated pottery and burial practices, suggest that appropriation of intrusive influences was strongest long after the first cultural contacts with Wari. Thus, local practices at Chinchawas mapped onto, but were independent of, core patterns. As shifting configurations of local cultural dispositions, they were neither complete emulations nor forced adoptions of core practices (Lau 2005).

The research will also show that even a modest highland community, such as Chinchawas, manifests considerable diversity in material culture, economic specialization and differentiation in socioeconomic arrangements. The investigations confirm that the ancient inhabitants of Chinchawas subsisted with high altitude agriculture and animal husbandry. Perhaps more significant is that local peoples also pursued a broad range of ancillary activities that complemented the economy.

One of these took the form of trade. The quantity of exotic items, especially finely made pottery, exceeded the wherewithal and interest in "elite" things expected for the inhabitants. Fiber production was also particularly prominent at the site. Abundant faunal remains and spindle whorls indicate the central role of camelids in the local economy and imply the importance of textiles and raw spun fiber as trade goods.

Finally, the research elucidates how local peoples constituted and reinvented their ceremonial practices under changing sociopolitical conditions. Religion at Chinchawas focused on ancestor cults, as expressed in burial structures, stone sculptures and enclosures used for public festivities (Lau 2002, 2006b). Earlier ceremonial practices are rooted in Recuay traditions: subterranean tombs, grave offerings and imagery. These are later replaced by practices centered around the building and use of above-ground tombs. Archaeological remains indicate that feasts and stonecarving were integral activities of local ancestor cults; such ceremonies facilitated the social cohesion of descent groups as well as provided avenues to establish and legitimate political authority.

The overall objective of this book is to present the various lines of evidence that show that communities, even those without permanent hierarchy, such as

Chinchawas, could have remarkably vigorous developments. Rural communities are not merely the building blocks of complex agrarian societies. They also provide valuable empirical information on local-level cultural practices and organization, which occur alongside, accommodating and often disregarding the interventions of larger political systems. The findings from Chinchawas reiterate the importance of a community-level perspective for understanding ancient social complexity.

## Organization of Chapters

Having laid out the principal objectives, the rest of the study details the background, fieldwork, artifact analyses and results of the overall research. Chapter 2 describes the local environment of highland Ancash and considers paleoenvironmental evidence and its implications for contemporary and prehistoric land use. It follows with a brief account of Recuay culture, its history of research, character and transformations. Wari expansion into the highland Ancash is considered, with a focus on the role of the Wari state in local trade and interaction, especially in the Callejón de Huaylas. I then review the archaeological excavations and the stratigraphic contexts of the Chinchawas settlement. Chapters 3 and 4 describe the results of test pits and trenches within the main residential sector of the Chinchawas site. And Chapter 5 summarizes the investigations of the mortuary constructions in the site's principal cemetery area.

Chapters 6 through 8 describe the ceramic sequence of Chinchawas and furnish the basic chronological apparatus to consider diachronic transformations of the community. Chapter 6 treats the Kayán, Chinchawasi 1 and Chinchawasi 2 phases, followed by the Warmi and Chakwas phase descriptions in Chapter 7. Chapter 8 summarizes the corpus of fancy imported ceramics found in the Chinchawas site and discusses the character of long-distance cultural contacts by phase.

As indicators for economic production and cultural relationships, Chapter 9 describes additional artifact classes at Chinchawas, including flaked lithic, groundstone, metal, bone and shell artifacts. In light of the archaeological investigations at Chinchawas, Chapter 10 reviews the research results and examines sociocultural patterns and transformations in the North Highlands during the Early Intermediate Period and Middle Horizon.

CHAPTER TWO

# The North Highlands of Peru, the Recuay Culture and Wari Expansion into Highland Ancash

The ancient community of Chinchawas developed in Peru's spectacular North Central Highlands, in the Department of Ancash. The environmental setting of this region played a vital role for its inhabitants throughout the site's history. After an introduction to regional-level geological processes and local ecological zonation, this chapter examines paleoclimatic conditions as seen in proxy ice core records. It is suggested that, during the period A.D. 500 to 900, new patterns of land use attributed to changing paleoclimatic conditions may have been adopted.

Assessment of the natural setting and paleoclimate is followed by a brief review of previous work in the region. The review focuses on the later prehistory of highland Ancash and, more specifically, the Callejón de Huaylas, one of the most important intermontane valleys of Peru (Figure 3). Although great strides have been made in understanding Recuay culture and subsequent developments, much additional research is needed, especially for basic chronology, socioeconomic patterns and human–environment interaction.

## Environment and Geological Processes

### Geography

The archaeological site of Chinchawas lies at the headwaters of the Río Casma, within the jurisdiction of the District of Pira, Province of Huaraz, Department of Ancash, Peru. The site has coordinates of 206395E latitude and 8942015S longitude (Zone 18L). The site designation PAn 5-26 refers to Peruvian valley of Ancash number 5, site number 26 (there may be some overlap with other site numbering systems for the region). The system, made popular by John Rowe and his students at Berkeley, was used by Duccio Bonavía (1966) for the Callejón de Huaylas; the initial list included 25 sites. Since then investigators have claimed numbers but have not made them known in governmental records or in publications. I use "no. 26" to follow the original record, in which site PAn 5-25 was the last entry recorded.

The principal archaeological zone of Chinchawas straddles a mountain ridge on the western slopes, or Pacific-facing flanks, of the Cordillera Negra (Figure 4). With the main sector of the site reaching an elevation of 3853 meters above sea level (masl), Chinchawas is one of the highest sites in highland Ancash ever to have been investigated systematically. "Chinchawas" refers to the ancient settlement, as first

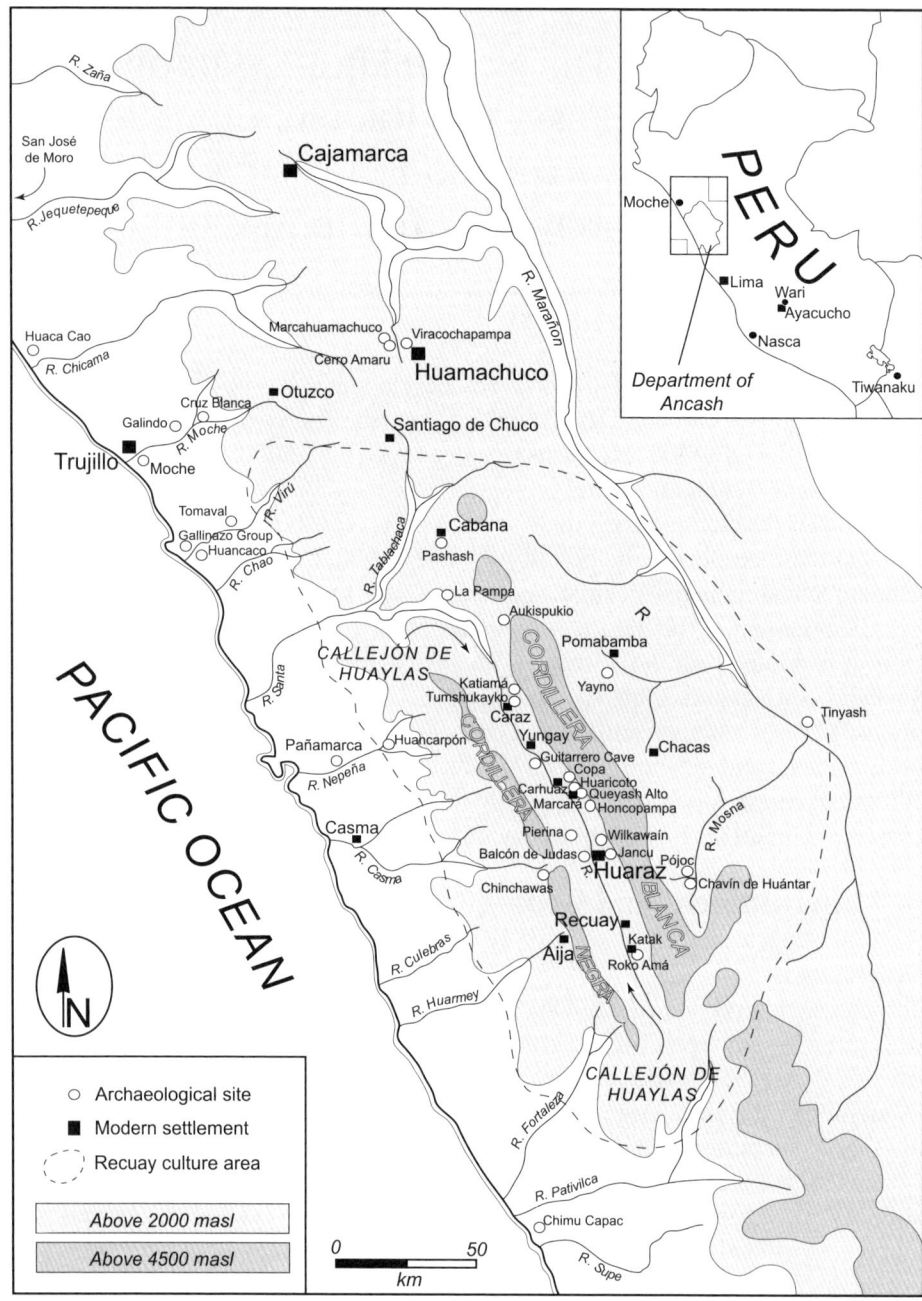

FIGURE 3. North Central Peru and sites mentioned in text. Dashed line shows the general area of Recuay development.

described by Mejía Xesspe (1941), while Chinchawasi (or Chinchayhuasi) refers to the modern community.

During the Pliocene and Pleistocene, the Andes were formed in massive orogenic events of mountain uplift. Local differences in the scale of the vertical movement resulted in the two cordillera systems, known as the Cordillera Blanca and Cordillera Negra. Subsequent volcanism during the Late Cretaceous and Early Tertiary, between 33 and 10 Ma, known as the Calipuy Formation, formed much of today's uppermost belt of peaks and plateaus of the Cordillera Negra (Cossio 1964; Hollister and Sirvas B. 1978; Cobbing et al. 1981). While Calipuy outcroppings of extrusive rock in the Cordillera Negra are dominated by andesites, the formation also consists of volcanic flows, breccias and tuffs of mainly dacitic and rhyolitic composition (Bodenlos and Straczek 1957; Wilson et al. 1967; Hollister and Sirvas B. 1978).

Mineral deposits are abundant in the Cordillera Negra. Base metals such as lead, zinc and copper occur as small stocks throughout the Calipuy Formation (Bodenlos and Straczek 1957; Wilson et al. 1967). Currently, several small mines operate near the town of Pira to the southwest and still more on the Callejón de Huaylas side of the cordillera. As few as 30 years ago, Chinchawasi was also mined for copper and lead (Victor Rodriguez, pers. comm. 1997). Two nearby mineshafts and one wide debris talus to the east of the Chinchawas ridgetop are remnants of this activity.

The Pliocene–Pleistocene uplift of the Andes also initiated the process of downward incision by the region's current structure of river systems. The Río Pira flows into the Río Chacchan and forms one of the principal headwater tributaries of the Río Casma (Figure 5). The Chinchawas site overlooks the confluence of the Pira with smaller feeder streams that wind in from the north through the Quebrada Yupanca and Quebrada Potrero Ruri, and from the south through the Quebrada Pishan. In the local Ancash Quechua language, these confluences are known as *tinku*, and are advantageous locales for small villages, roads and bridges. Because of the steep gradient, the streams are fast-flowing and especially active during the rainy season from October to April (Figure 6).

Chinchawasi, it should be noted, can be reached by a small dirt path that veers away from the village of Tinco, located at a junction of two small valleys farther east. The Río Pira and its stream, the Quebrada Tinco, represent the effective northern boundary for settlements to the south. During the dry season, the Pira can be crossed with little problem almost everywhere down to the village of Yupash. Today, local farmers construct makeshift bridges of wood planks, logs and river cobble foundations. Ancient peoples in the region probably negotiated the river in like manner. My brief inspections of this area did not identify evidence for more permanent bridges.

The Cordillera Blanca, or "white mountains," is famous for its snow-capped peaks (*nevados*), many of which rise over 6000 masl. The tallest, Nevado Huascarán, is the highest mountain in the tropics at 6768 masl. In contrast, the Cordil-

Figure 4. View of Chinchawas, Sector 1 (looking northwest). The modern town of Cantu, on the northern side of the Río Pira, is in the background. Most farming takes place in agricultural plots located below 3800 masl.

lera Negra, the "black mountains," today sustains no permanent glaciation. Compared to the Cordillera Blanca, the Cordillera Negra gives the general appearance of being less rugged and more "rolling," even though its topography boasts many summits surpassing 5000 masl. In addition, the Cordillera Negra has undergone considerable geological metamorphism (Offler et al. 1980). For this reason, silica-rich crystalline raw materials for stone tools are very common throughout the Cordillera, such as fine quartzites and cherts (Lynch 1980).

*Environmental Diversity and Zonation*

The focus of this study concerns the Andean highland regions roughly above 2800 to 3000 masl in elevation and consisting of the *quechua, suni, puna* and *jalca* zones (Figure 7). Chinchawas, at 3,850 masl, lies at the upper limit of the suni life zone (Pulgar Vidal 1972). It is a nonforested region of transitory grass steppe, with scattered shrubbery highly dependent on the seasonal rains. At present, thorny vegetation, broken by small patches of tough grass and periodic rain-green plants, characterizes the land around the site. Cacti and other plants colonize areas of crumbling stone walls, rubble heaps or small isolated boulders.

Directly above the suni altitudinal band lies the puna—essentially mountain grassland characterized by ichu bunch grasses, cushion and rosette-shaped vegetation, and some dwarf shrubs (Pulgar Vidal 1972). The puna provides natural and abundant pasturage for herd animals such as camelids or, more commonly today, sheep and goats. Directly below the suni is the quechua life zone, typified by well-watered valley slopes and rockier tracts of cultivable land, but otherwise abundant in xerophytic shrubs and cactus. In addition, along watercourses or steep quebrada valleys are ribbon-like bands of more diverse and lush vegetation, including the zone's only consistent native tree, the quenual (*Polylepis* sp.), a tree of the rose family.

Today various species of eucalyptus thrive at the expense of indigenous trees, favoring well-watered areas, such as the stream-cut quebradas. Local villagers, "Chinchawasinos," understand the tendency for eucalyptus trees to preferentially strip soils of nutrients and inhibit colonization of local species, referring to zones with eucalyptus as *suelos quemados* (literally, "burnt soils"). But because locals rely almost exclusively on the fast-growing eucalyptus stands for firewood and for construction, they rarely make an effort to plant local saplings that would be more ecologically sound. It is unclear whether the zone once supported large stands of native trees, such as the quenual. *Polylepis* forests today thrive only in parts of the high Andes too inaccessible for pasturing animals or the systematic collection of firewood.

## Current Land Use

As in the past, the modern community of Chinchawasi, or Chinchayhuasi, relies on a combination of high-altitude agriculture and the raising of livestock for its economic well being. For this reason, the livelihood of Chinchawasi is very much dependent on the unique and sometimes extreme environmental conditions that are typical of the high Andes.

A Central Andean highland climate characterizes the higher elevations of the Cordillera Negra, with distinct seasonal differences in temperature and precipitation. There is marked seasonality in the availability of precipitation and the growth of plant life. The wet season begins in the highlands around October, peaking from January to March and ending about April. The wet season is the principal factor in scheduling agricultural activity for local communities in the Chinchawasi area. Rains are frequent during the wet season and are especially strong in the late afternoons, with steady precipitation until mid-evening. Huaraz, at 3100 masl, receives nearly 800 mm of rainfall over the course of one year (ONERN 1973:3). Higher up in the Callejón de Huaylas, another meteorological station at 3750 masl, which approximates the elevation of Chinchawasi, averaged roughly 860 mm of annual rainfall (see Figure 6). Almost all the rainfall occurs during the very pronounced local wet season.

The Callejón de Huaylas is the intermontane drainage of the Río Santa between the Cordillera Negra and Cordillera Blanca. Located in the tropics, the valley does not see much seasonal variation in temperature (ONERN 1973:5, 133). However, there is considerable diurnal temperature change, based on time of day and altitude. Although it is often hot during the early afternoon, temperatures can drop below freezing at

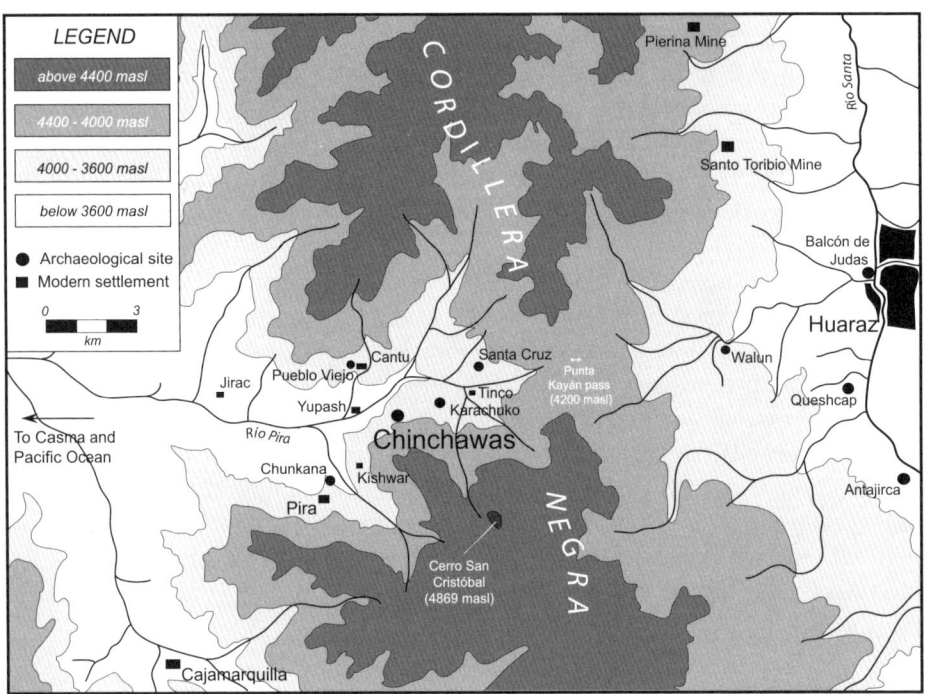
FIGURE 5. The Chinchawas site and the surrounding region.

night, causing frosts, particularly at higher altitudes. Even today, frosts and occasional flurries of freezing rain reiterate the marginal quality of the local environment.

A limited amount of arable land also debilitates local agricultural production. The steep gradients mean that soil horizons are shallow and often depleted in nutrients. Frequent bedrock outcrops and erosion further hinder farming. Except for rare and flat low-lying areas close to stream bottoms, most of the upper Quebrada Tinco basin is analogous to poor Class 6 soil areas described for the Callejón de Huaylas (ONERN 1973). One study showed that, even in the verdant Callejón de Huaylas, only a small percentage (8.1%) of the evaluated drainage area could be considered conducive for intensive agricultural production (ONERN 1973:94–95).

*Local Economy and Settlement*
The modern settlement of Chinchawasi consists of around 30 to 35 residences dispersed within a belt of land 3600 to 3700 masl, spanning about 2 km$^2$. Officially, Chinchawasi is known as a *caserío*, referring to the community, political representation, and the land nestled between the ancient site of Chinchawas in the far west and the hilltop of Karachuko to the east (see Figure 5). In this pocket, most of the arable land owned and cultivated by the modern community lies to the south upslope (about 3700 to 3900 masl). Members of the neighboring villages of Tinco and Kishwar farm up to the Karachuko and

Chinchawas hilltops, respectively. Chinchawasinos also help farm lower altitude fields to the west and north, frequently for wages or as reciprocal labor exchanges. People living in Huaraz own many key plots in the Chinchawas area.

Ascending from the north, the land around Chinchawasi slopes steeply. By about 4,000 masl, however, lands to the east and southeast level off into more rolling plateau areas. In these zones, high altitude puna grasslands proliferate and would have been ideal for camelid herds in antiquity. Today the current herding economy focuses on sheep. Flocks are led, usually by women and children, every morning up the southern slopes to higher grassland zones and returned to protective corrals near the residences in the late afternoon. Production occurs nearly exclusively at the family or household level. Larger flocks are commonly aggregations of sheep from different families. Local peoples also raise goat, pig, chicken and cattle. Cattle are particularly valuable. In the region today, only residents of Santa Cruz, on the other side of valley (to the north), herd camelids.

Local agriculture is also conducted basically at a small-scale, subsistence level. Wheat, barley, tubers and habas beans are the major crops. The most popular native cultivars in the greater Chinchawasi area include beans (*Phaseolus* sp.), potato (*Solanum andigenum*), oca (*Oxalis tuberosa*), ulluco (*Ollucus tuberosus*) and quinua (*Chenopodium quinoa*). Imported cereals, especially barley and wheat, are today the dominant components of the local diet. Wheat, as a storable food source, is the year-round staple. It is often consumed as a side dish when boiled (eaten like plain rice), used in soups, and is ground into flour for simple breads. Maize and maize products are purchased or bartered from inhabitants from lower elevations.

Potatoes are important in local diet, though the region is less productive than in recent history. There is tuber cultivation up to roughly 3900 to 3950 masl, but relict agricultural plots higher up suggest more intensive practices in the past. Older members of the community reminisced proudly that the area once was so productive in its potato agriculture that it had supplied parts of the Callejón de Huaylas.

The steep topography, irregular plots and lack of roads preclude, effectively, machined-based agriculture. In addition, most families cannot afford the expense of insecticides and nutrient-replacing chemicals common in more systematic cultivation methods. Instead, local peoples grow a diversity of crops and rotate them annually (ONERN 1973:17). They told me that that they generally preferred cultigen(s) that promised to be the most productive or the least risky. The unpredictability of rainfall makes agriculture, even with such risk-minimizing strategies, especially problematic.

Agricultural plots are managed largely through individual nuclear families or extended households and rely less on communally administered systems (e.g., Mayer 2002). The community, however, plays a major role in organizing work groups and scheduling of irrigation activities. During the critical periods of sowing

| | Elevation of station | Jan | Feb | Mar | Apr | May | Jun | Jul | Aug | Sep | Oct | Nov | Dec | Year total |
|---|---|---|---|---|---|---|---|---|---|---|---|---|---|---|
| Yungay (1953-69) | 2585 | 33.6 | 54.2 | 97.5 | 42.2 | 5.4 | 0.2 | 0.4 | 0.7 | 5.3 | 17.4 | 16.1 | 22.8 | 295.8 |
| Huaraz (1965-70) | 3207 | 116.2 | 98.4 | 133 | 75.1 | 33.4 | 2.1 | 2.7 | 7.4 | 41.2 | 123.4 | 68.4 | 93.1 | 794.4 |
| Recuay (1966-70) | 3420 | 89.3 | 104.9 | 96.2 | 63.6 | 30.1 | 1.6 | 3.2 | 11.7 | 35.6 | 113.6 | 82.2 | 68.1 | 700.1 |
| Ticapampa (1953-69) | 3550 | 105.2 | 116.6 | 141.4 | 83.5 | 27.7 | 2.4 | 2.3 | 7.9 | 36.9 | 71.2 | 69.2 | 76 | 740.3 |
| San Lorenzo (1965-70) | 3750 | 126.1 | 113.9 | 135.4 | 80.3 | 38.2 | 3.9 | 6.8 | 15.6 | 46.4 | 102.3 | 76.5 | 112.9 | 858.3 |

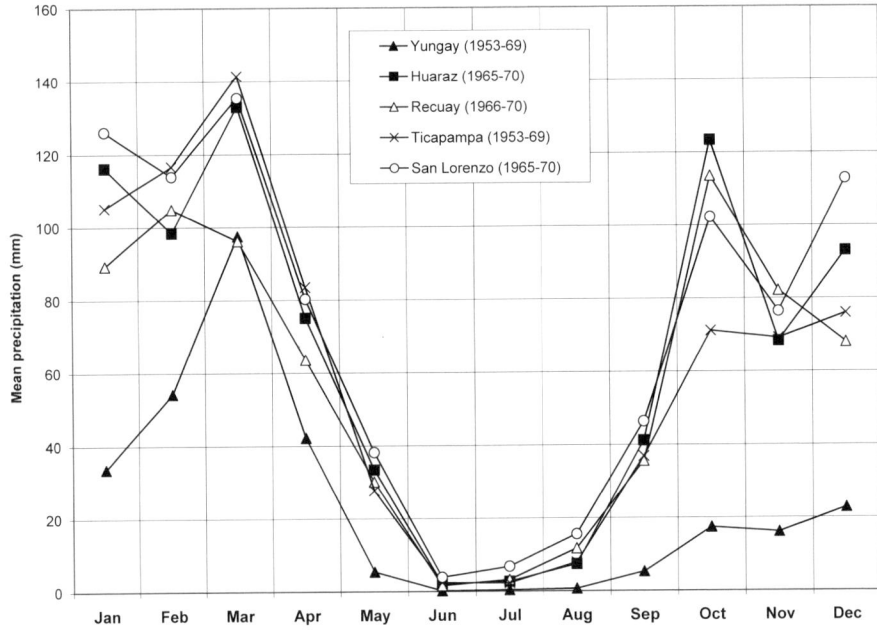

FIGURE 6. Monthly precipitation levels (in millimeters) at different elevations (in meters) in the Callejón de Huaylas, Peru. Note the sharp decline in rainfall during the dry season months between May and September.

and harvest (Figure 8), when timing is essential, individual families often recruit other Chinchawasinos or nearby villagers to help, with the promise of compensation or reciprocal labor. In general, these are male relatives or friends who are in favorable standing with the plot's owner.

When harvests are substantial, any surplus injects some modest cash flow into the household budget. A family member may truck the goods directly to the largest market in the region, Huaraz (about two hours by vehicle, due east) in the Callejón de Huaylas, or to large agricultural villages in the lower cis-*yunga* zones towards the coast, such as Yaután or Pariacoto. Because of the large highland populations in these small towns, high altitude products such as potatoes, oca, and quinoa are very much in demand. Another common strategy is to sell to, or contract, an intermediary to make the necessary transactions.

Today Chinchawas overlooks a major road from Casma on the coast to Huaraz in the highlands. Although this road is unpaved, it is a major trade route for the interchange of regional products. Highland tubers, grains, and sheep are unloaded for coast-grown fruits, maize, and marine foods. For highland communities, the exchange diversifies local diets. Various conversations with Chinchawasinos reiterated the value of coastal products in local highland culture, especially as occasional prized treats that add, literally, flavor to their daily routine.

The Casma–Huaraz road also connects people from the sierra to the coast and to the much larger fishing port city of Chimbote. During the last two or three decades, older Chinchawasinos reported to me that there has been substantial outmigration. Younger members of the community have moved to lower parts of the Pira drainage towards the coast or over the Punta Kayán pass (4100 masl) to the Callejón de Huaylas, especially its hub in Huaraz. The promise of steady wages, in particular, and the related benefits of consistent employment, seems to be the prime mover. Hence, through exchange and interaction, there is substantial communication between the Chinchawasi community and people elsewhere. As I will show later, ancient Chinchawas also maintained close cultural and economic ties with both the coast and neighboring highlands throughout its occupation in pre-Columbian times.

## Sources of Water

Three very small streams flowing roughly north–south provide water to the modern community. As mentioned previously, annual rainfall is critical for local cultivation practices. In addition, water for year-round cultivation is also available from irrigation systems tapping into high water sources to the southeast, flowing in from the Quebrada Chiliac (within the area of caserío San Juan de Maquir) and Quebrada Chihua Paccha (within the area of Chinchawasi). Currently, local arrangements for water distribution are coordinated between communities.

The most likely water source for the archaeological site is a small streamlet 120 m due south of the main ridgetop. The stream flows year-round, but slows to a trickle during the dry season. It is reached by a footpath that, at some stretches, cuts into exposed bedrock. The path leads to a small, low fieldstone wall that encloses a small pond where the water gathers. Although it cannot be determined whether this wall is an ancient construction, redware fragments of large water jars suggest that water collection occurred here at least before the introduction and widespread use of plastic or aluminum containers.

Two older community members asserted that there was once a spring on the main mound of Chinchawas, just southwest of the Torreón structure. The archaeological investigations could neither confirm nor refute this information.

It is unclear the degree to which tectonic uplift may have played a role in shaping past hydrological patterns of the Casma headwaters region. Long-term geological patterns affecting water distribution, water management systems, and the archaeological record are better documented for the coastal region. Specifically, studies of the North Coast detail that natural tectonic movements affect local water table conditions and precipitate the displacement of ancient irrigation systems. Thus, continual long-term geological processes encourage agrarian collapse through abandonment of irrigated land (Moseley 1983). In the Chinchawas region,

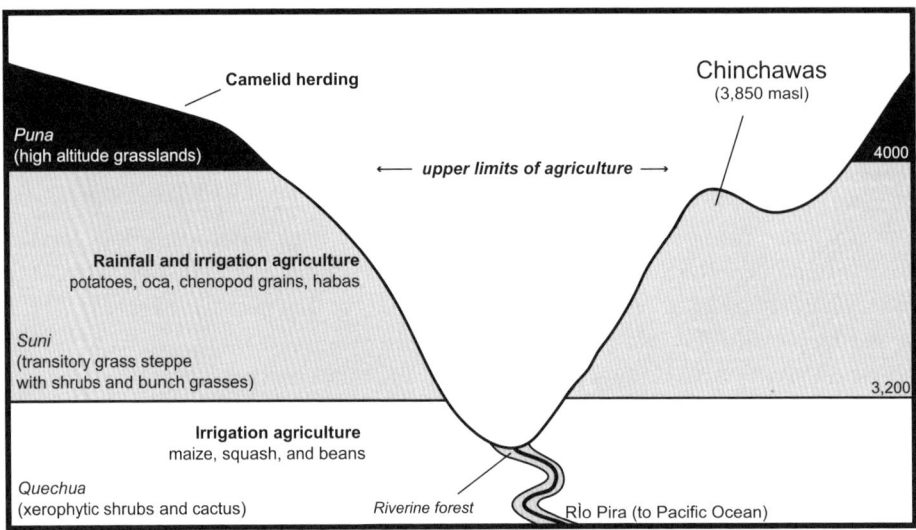

FIGURE 7. Schematic reconstruction of ecological floors and land use zones around Chinchawas. At 3850 masl, the site is at the upper limits of intensive agriculture in the region, well within reach of the rich pasture areas of the Cordillera Negra.

it is surmised that gradual uplift would likely accelerate the pace of erosion along watercourses. But given the current data, its effect on ancient sources of water such as springs and canal systems cannot yet be fully reconstructed.

## *Ice Core Records and Changing Paleoclimatic Conditions*

Ancient climatic conditions almost certainly affected natural resources and economic production for the Chinchawas community. Located at the upper limits of agriculture, its ancient inhabitants developed new strategies to accommodate long-term patterns of change in paleoclimate and the productive capacities of the local environment.

Ice cores from high altitude Andean glaciers furnish key records of climate change during the Holocene (Thompson and Mosley-Thompson 1989; Thompson et al. 1992; Thompson 2001). Annual growth layers of ice provide detailed evidence for local rainfall, temperature and vegetation cover, as evidenced through their dimensions and contents (e.g., pollen, dust and chemical elements). The thickness of each growth layer, for example, is a proxy index of yearly precipitation. Drier conditions correspond to periods of low ice accumulation, while wetter conditions correlate with thicker ice layers. Comparisons between historical and ice core records demonstrate a correlation between isotopically lighter precipitation (more negative $\partial^{18}O$ values) and colder temperatures in the Central Andes (Thompson, et al. 1986, 1992; Thompson and Mosley-Thompson 1989).

Ice core records are especially useful, because annual variations as well as long-term trends can be discerned for paleotemperatures (Thompson et al. 2003). In addition, $\partial^{18}O$ values correlate positively with rainfall patterns, where less negative values indicate generally wetter conditions; in contrast, more negative values indicate generally drier conditions (Thompson and Mosley-Thompson 1989:18–19).

Scholars have used ice core evidence, specifically of the Quelccaya ice cap in the south-central Andes, to model the rise and collapse of ancient Andean polities (e.g., Shimada et al. 1991; Shimada 1994; Kolata 1996). The need for high resolution paleoclimatic data has overshadowed reservations about the temporal precision of the cores. The lowermost levels of the Quelccaya cores, which extend back some 1500 years, are so compressed that the differentiation between annual layers and their contents becomes problematic. Thus, the correlation of absolute years from the lowermost sequence of the ice core should be subject to a ± 20-year standard deviation (Thompson et al. 1986:363; for additional discussion of general concerns with ice core data, see also Alley 2000). Notably, a preliminary review of the cores from Huascarán shows close correlation with overall temperature and precipitation trends outlined by the Quelccaya records (Thompson et al. 1995). It also remains to be verified whether ice core records, taken from one region, reflect ancient conditions in other parts of the Central Andes.

Recent ice cores from Nevado Huascarán, approximately 50 km from Chinchawas, indicate that mean temperatures in highland Ancash fell greatly during the last half of the first millennium A.D. (Figure 9). Colder conditions prevailed, especially during the sixth and eighth centuries A.D. The century-long averages for this time are comparable to those of the "Little Ice Age" (around A.D. 1400 to1800) (Thompson et al. 1986, 1992; Thompson 2001;). Colder weather, as indicated by the Huascarán cores, would have encouraged the advance of puna-like grasslands over the greater Chinchawas area during the site's primary occupations (A.D. 500 to 900). In the Andean highlands, there is a strong dependence between altitude and temperature (Tosi 1960; Pulgar Vidal 1972). Decreases of 1 to 2 °C could lower the upper limits of cultivation 200 to 400 m (Cardich 1985).

It is argued that such conditions favored new strategies for local land use and economic production. First, local peoples probably exploited lower altitude lands for tuber cultivation. Second, there would have been an downward expansion of puna vegetation. Such conditions would have promoted more intensive occupation of the Chinchawas zone for camelid stockraising.

## Prehistory in the Callejón de Huaylas and Recuay Culture

### Highland Ancash before Recuay

In addition to its wealth in natural resources and scenery, soon after the Spanish Conquest highland Ancash became increasingly known for its cultural riches (Espinoza Soriano 1978; Varón Gabai 1980; Cook 1981). There are brief descriptions of local cultures and socioeconomic arrangements by Spanish chroniclers and administrators of the region, including, among others, Cieza de León, Vasquez de Espinoza and Es-

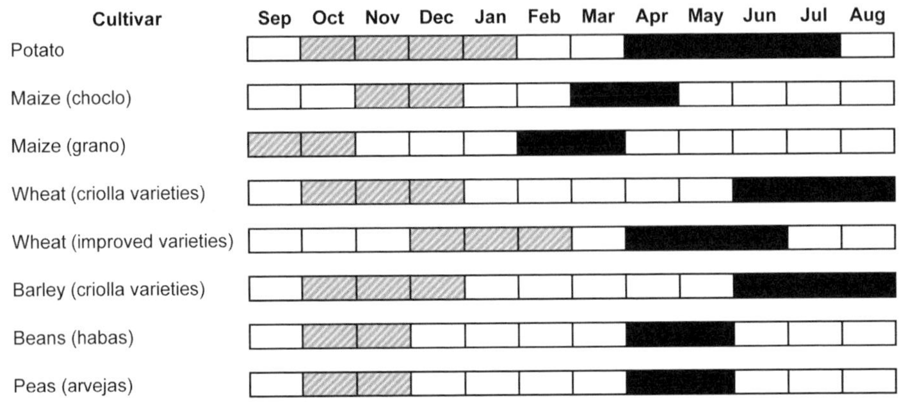

FIGURE 8. General schedule for sowing and harvesting crops in the Callejón de Huaylas. (Modified from ONERN 1973, cuadro 3.) Gray fill denotes sowing season, while black fill indicates months for harvesting.

tete. Not surprisingly, the Spanish were quick to identify the herd and mineral wealth of the highland Ancash groups. Priests also documented local religious practices based around ancestor cults while missionizing and destroying idolatry (Hernández Príncipe 1923; Millones 1979). Later, important travel writings and natural history explorations, on occasion, reported pre-Inka tombs, ceramics and stone sculptures (Raimondi 1873; Wiener 1880; Middendorf 1893–1895; Sievers 1914). It was Julio C. Tello's early expeditions (1923, 1929), however, that established highland Ancash as one of Peru's great archaeological regions.

Prehistoric research in highland Ancash has focused largely on preceramic and early ceramic cultures, emphasizing the emergence of agriculture and civilization in the Andes. Human occupation of highland Ancash dates back to the Preceramic (ca. 8000 to 1800 B.C.). Intensive foraging and hunting activities have been documented in various cave and open-air sites (Lanning 1965; Lynch 1970, 1971, 1980; Malpass 1983, 1985). A broad spectrum of foods, including wild plants and animals, was acquired from intermontane valley and puna settings. Lithic assemblages are associated with broader regional Andean traditions and, together with the food evidence, indicate highly mobile societies characterized by hunting and foraging subsistence practices.

Lynch (1971) argued that small mobile groups cycled through different ecological floors at strategic times of the year. The pattern of transhumance mapped onto zonal resources that were available seasonally. Notably, very early evidence for New World agriculture, at approximately 8000 to 7000 B.C., appears at Guitarrero Cave in the heart of the Callejón de Huaylas. The first cultigens—gourds, squashes and chili peppers—seem to have been easily grown supplements to the overall diet, rather than replacements for the regimen of wild foods (Lynch 1980).

Although temporary shelters continued to function (Lynch 1980; Ponte Rosalino 1999a), sedentism became widespread in highland Ancash by the Late

Preceramic (2500 to 1800 B.C.) and Initial Period (1800 to 800 B.C.). Small villages proliferated because of intensive food production, especially in areas suitable for farming, and irrigation agriculture was established (Bonnier et al. 1983; Bueno Mendoza 1989; Burger and Salazar-Burger 1980; Grieder et al. 1988).

Ceremonial sites centered on cultural practices associated with the Kotosh Religious Tradition (Burger and Salazar-Burger 1980, 1986). With a distribution mainly in the north-central highlands, sites of the tradition, such as La Galgada, Piruru and Huaricoto, are characterized by chambers with central fireplaces and subfloor flues. The structures served as venues for episodic ceremonies based on the burning of offerings. After a period of use, the structures would be cleaned, filled, sealed and then constructed anew, in a pattern termed "temple entombment" (Burger 1992:45–46).

Important transformations in economic and religious practices characterize the subsequent Early Horizon, the period known for the emergence and expansion of the Chavín cult (Tello 1960; Rowe 1967; Patterson 1971; Lumbreras 1989; Burger 1992). Named for the pilgrimage site of Chavín de Huántar, east of the Cordillera Blanca, the cult circulated an ideology and art style based on mythic supernatural beings and shamanistic beliefs and practices.

Although grave goods and monumental architecture suggest some social differentiation in earlier periods, the Early Horizon witnessed sustained evidence for stratification, differential access and privileged theocratic authority. In Ancash, Chavín influence was highly variable. It was prominent, for example, in sites with large public architecture (Chavín de Huántar, Pomakayán), while less prominent in small residential settlements (Huaricoto). Interregional trade, fine craft activities and economic innovations such as camelid herding and transport were integral to the success of Chavín civilization (Burger 1992). These patterns were to characterize highland Ancash until the Spanish Conquest in the 16th century.

*Recuay Culture and the Early Intermediate Period*
By the end of the 1st millennium B.C., Chavín de Huántar fell into ruins and its influence ebbed throughout Peru. In the following centuries groups associated with the Recuay tradition emerged in highland Ancash (Lau 2004a). Recuay became established during a time of unprecedented sociocultural dynamism known as the Early Intermediate Period, around A.D. 1 to 700 (Rowe and Menzel 1967). Terms such as "Mastercraftsmen" and "Florescent" describe this period's achievements and cultural diversity, which included the first expansionistic polities, urbanism, a radical pluralization of art styles and technologies, and widely different sociopolitical systems (e.g., Patterson 1966; Donnan 1978; Terada and Onuki 1982; Topic 1982; Makowski 1994; Shimada 1994; Uceda and Mujica 1994; Bawden 1996; Pillsbury 2001; Silverman and Proulx 2002; Stanish 2003).

Tello (1923, 1929, 1930, 1940) first recognized the importance of Recuay culture. On the basis of fine ceramics and stone monoliths, he emphasized the style because he felt that the first critical developments towards civilization occurred

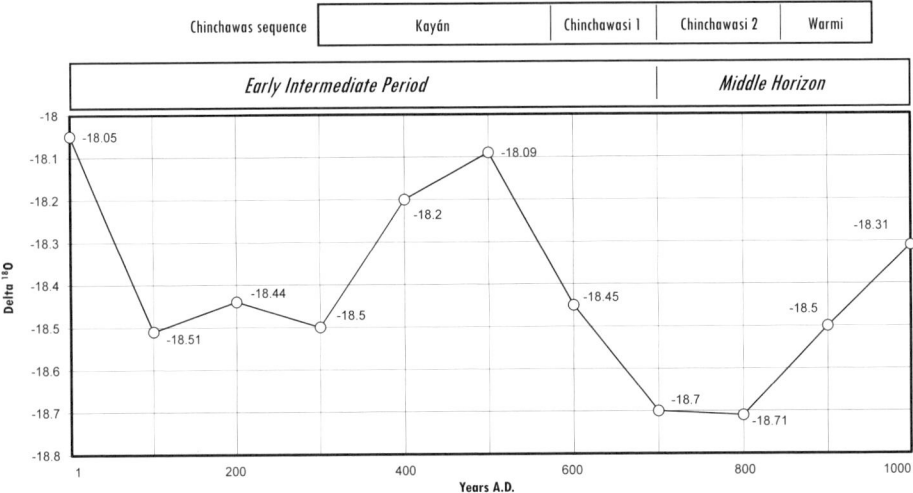

Figure 9. Oxygen isotope ratios from Huascarán Core 2.

not on the coast, as many believed, but rather in the highlands. Born and raised in the montane region above Lima, Tello believed that the highlands had until recently formed the traditional demographic, economic and cultural backbone of the Andes. The "Archaic" culture of Recuay (Tello's "Huaylas" or "Copa") was an integral component of a long tradition of highland civilization that nurtured cultural growth elsewhere. The adaptation of high altitude farming and herding enabled Andean civilization to emerge and spread to other geographical regions. Furthermore, Peruvian art and cosmology, as exemplified through Chavín and Recuay, centered on feline symbolism and fertility cults (Tello 1923).

Tello's rival, Rafael Larco Hoyle (1960, 1962), also acknowledged Recuay's significance, but under the term "Santa." Larco Hoyle, born into a wealthy hacienda family of Peru's North Coast, favored a coastal origin for the style, because he recovered Recuay pottery from the mid-valley portions of the Santa drainage. Although most scholars now consider highland Ancash—the Callejón de Huaylas, parts of the Conchucos (the region to the east of the Cordillera Blanca) and the western slopes of the Cordillera Negra—to be the heartland of Recuay development, Larco Hoyle's recognition of strong Recuay presence in middle and upper parts of coastal valleys remains valid.

Prompted by Tello's pioneering work, Wendell C. Bennett mounted an expedition in 1938 to the Callejón de Huaylas to elucidate the region's prehistory, especially the position of Chavín and subsequent local cultures in the Andean sequence. Like Tello, Bennett (1944) conducted highland investigations to complement studies on better-known coastal cultures, at the time spearheaded by the Virú Valley Project and the Institute of Andean Research. On the basis of stratigraphic testing at Chavín and excavations of mortuary contexts in the Huaraz region, Bennett (1944) formulated the basic periodization still in use today: Chavín to White-on-red to

Recuay to "Tiahuanacoid"–Recuay. Conducted nearly 70 years ago, his research remains the only published assemblage with contextual information that spans the entire Recuay sequence. Bennett's work also managed to salvage valuable Recuay materials that would have been destroyed by the growth of towns in the Callejón de Huaylas, especially Huaraz. I follow the general convention of differentiating the White-on-red archaeological culture, "Huarás," from the modern city of "Huaraz" (Lumbreras 1970, 1974a; Amat Olazábal 1976a, 1976b, 2003).

Subsequent Recuay research has focused mainly on its art and material culture. In addition to Recuay iconography on ceramics and stone sculpture, there has been important research on techniques of pottery manufacture and decoration, such as use of kaolinite clays, resist, and polychrome painting and figure modeling (Clothier 1943; Eisleb 1960, 1987; Mejía Xesspe 1965–1966; Bankmann 1973, 1979, 1988; Bruhns 1976; Reichert 1977a, 1977b, 1982a, 1982b; Grieder 1978, 1992; Smith 1978; Makowski and Rucabado Yong 2000; Wegner 2000, 2003; Laurencich and Wegner 2001; Orsini 2007). Monolithic stonecarving is also one of the hallmarks of Recuay tradition groups (Bennett 1944; Schaedel 1948a, 1948b, 1952; Disselhoff 1956; Kauffmann Doig 1966, 1980; Grieder 1978; Lau 2000, 2006b). Many sculptures, featuring representations of anthropomorphic and animal supernatural beings, adorned the walls of tombs and other high status ceremonial buildings.

Although fancy ceramics and monolithic stone carving are its best known artistic expressions, Recuay textiles (Porter 1992; Manrique P. 1999; Oakland and Fernandez 2000) and metalwork (Grieder 1978; Schindler 2000) were among the most technologically sophisticated and innovative during the Early Intermediate Period.

Settlement survey data with Recuay-related occupations exist primarily for coastal valleys, especially Casma (Wilson 1995), Nepeña (Proulx 1968, 1973, 1982, 1985; Daggett 1987), Santa (Wilson 1988), Virú (Bennett 1939; Ford and Willey 1949; Strong and Evans 1952) and Moche (Topic and Topic 1978, 1987; Billman 1996). Settlement patterns in the highlands are less well-known (Amat Olazábal 1976a, 1976b), but newer studies are underway (Herrera 1999, 2005; Ponte Rosalino 1999a, 1999b, 2000; Capra et al. 2002; Ibarra 2003a, 2003b; Orsini 2003; Herrera et al. 2006).

The current data from both the coastal valleys and highlands suggest a strong preference for hilltop settlements that served as nodes for multiple purposes, including defense, residence, trading relations and ceremonial activities. There is currently very little evidence, however, to reconstruct diachronic patterns in Recuay settlement. Very few Recuay sites on the western slopes have been investigated by systematic excavation (e.g., Montoya Vera 1989).

The best known excavations of Recuay tradition occupations are from highland settlements (Bennett 1944; Tello 1960; Lumbreras 1974c; Grieder 1978; Gero 1990; Ponte 1999a; Wegner 2003; Orsini 2007). Many of these studies, however, exposed Recuay levels only to reach earlier remains. Grieder's study (1978) of Pashash tombs has been the only site report since Bennett's (1944) monograph.

Recuay tradition architecture is quite distinctive, particularly in form and construction techniques (Lau 2000). The Recuay erected residential as well as special ceremonial buildings, including shrines, tombs and plazas. Some of the most impressive buildings are tall compounds enclosing a central open space, with multistory apartments along the outer wall (Lau and Ramón 2007). Almost all Recuay buildings are of stone. The finest constructions featured boulder and spall masonry, known as "wanka-pachilla." Frequently, the stones are arranged in visually impressive patterns that highlight their height, monumentality and volume (e.g., Tello 1929, 1940; Antúnez de Mayolo 1935; Kauffmann Doig 1956). Many Recuay sites feature defensive architecture, including perimeter walls, restricted access, protected enclosures and sometimes dry moats. Some domestic architecture has been described, ranging from the dwellings of small modest villages to elite residences (e.g., Lumbreras 1970, 1974c; Ponte Rosalino 1999a; Lau 2001).

Most descriptions are of mortuary constructions, including different subterranean and aboveground forms (e.g., Soriano Infante 1940, 1941; Mejía Xesspe 1941, 1948; Bennett 1944; Espejo Nuñez 1957, 1959; Grieder 1978; Wegner 1988; Isbell 1997; Lau 2000; Paredes et al. 2000; Ibarra 2003b). Most Recuay tombs seem to have been used for group interments and many show signs of reuse and renovation. The mortuary constructions indicate that funerary cults, focused on ancestor veneration, formed a critical dimension of Recuay culture and religion.

Recuay subsistence practices are virtually unknown. Preliminary analyses from several sites near the modern city of Huaraz—Balcón de Judas (Wegner 2003), Huaricoto (Burger 1985b; Sawyer 1985), Queyash Alto (Gero 1992), and Pierina mine area settlements (Grimaldo G. 1999)—suggest that Recuay peoples derived most of their meat protein from domestic camelids. Imagery on pottery has long suggested that Recuay peoples valued camelids in subsistence and ceremonial practices (Lumbreras 1974a; Smith 1978; Bonavia 1991). Recent analyses of the faunal remains from Chinchawas confirm the reliance on camelid meat, as well as the importance of fiber production, in small Recuay tradition communities (Lau 2007). The plant component of Recuay diet has never been investigated systematically.

*Recuay Chronology*
Tello (1929), Kroeber (1926, 1930) and Bennett (1944) provided the earliest cultural sequences of Recuay pottery. They drew stylistic and formal distinctions, however, that do not seem to relate to temporal subdivisions. Grieder (1978) proposed a three-phase Recuay sequence from Pashash, with radiocarbon dates spanning A.D. 400 to 700 (Lau 2004a). There are also references to sequences from the Marcará area (Buse 1965; Lanning 1965) and from sites along the Mosna (Amat Olazábal 1976a, 1976b, 2003; Lynch 1977; Gambini Escudero 1984). Wegner (2003) identified nonkaolin, utilitarian wares to broaden the range of Recuay diagnostic pottery. A general overview (Lau 2004a) of Recuay absolute and relative chronology argued that various cultural expressions, frequently using disparate terms, could be consid-

ered within periods of a Recuay tradition, namely the Huarás, Recuay, Late Recuay and Wari-influenced (Wilkawaín) periods.

It is commonly held that Recuay emerged out of an earlier pottery culture known as White-on-red, or Huarás style. This order is present stratigraphically from several highland sites (Tello 1960; Lumbreras 1974c; Burger 1985a; Isbell 1989; Gero 1991, 1992). The social and cultural implications of stylistic changes from Huarás to Recuay are unclear. At Huaricoto, a village settlement during both phases, there is considerable cultural continuity in pottery, architecture and domestic refuse (Burger 1985a). At the ceremonial center of Queyash Alto, Gero (1992) argues that the Recuay occupation showed greater evidence of social segmentation, feasting activity and access to luxury goods. Notably, the radiocarbon evidence for contexts with Huarás pottery differs widely in absolute age (Lau 2004a:180–181).

Recuay culture, as defined by the well-known fancy ceramics and stone sculpture, belongs primarily to the latter part of the Early Intermediate Period. Notably, Recuay pottery bears technological and iconographic affinities to its contemporaries. The distribution of Recuay pottery in nonlocal contexts, imported wares (Bennett 1944; Amat Olazábal 1976a, 1976b; Grieder 1978; Terada 1979), and imagery (Bruhns 1976; Reichert 1977a, 1982a; Bankmann 1979; Lau 2004b) all indicate intense cultural contact with Moche groups. Huamachuco and Cajamarca traditions are also linked to Recuay. There are stylistic similarities in ceramics (McCown 1945; King 1948; Thatcher 1979; Terada and Onuki 1982, 1985; Topic 1985; Matsumoto 1988, 1994; Lau 2006a), stone sculpture (Schaedel 1948a, 1952; Kroeber 1950) and architectural conventions (Tello 1929; Soriano Infante 1940; Bennett 1944; Mejía Xesspe 1957; Shady and Rosas 1976; Terada 1979). Matsumoto (1988) contended that Recuay's close ties with Cajamarca might be, in part, due to economic relations, such as the importation of camelids from the Callejón de Huaylas. Recuay also features coastal affinities in imagery and decorative techniques to Lima and Gallinazo cultures (Reichert 1977a; Smith 1978; Makowski and Rucabado 2000).

*Social Complexity among the Recuay*
Differences in Recuay social ranking are expressed through high status objects (fancy wares, sumptuaries and monolithic sculptures), especially from elite burials (e.g., Grieder 1978). In addition, there are iconographic depictions of important individuals which are often taken as evidence for institutionalized leadership roles (Lumbreras 1974a; Grieder 1992; Gero 1999, 2001); some Recuay vessels show warriors or leaders surrounded by attendants (smaller and less elaborated), often in multistory, palace-like buildings.

The variability in Recuay architecture, with considerable differences in size, quality and elaboration, also indicates different levels of control over corporate labor. For example, there is a range of subterranean tombs: from single-interment cist tombs, often associated with very modest grave offerings, to elaborate, multichambered mausolea, often associated with higher status interments (e.g., Bennett

1944). Special buildings were often adorned with elaborate stonemasonry.

Most scholars conceive of Recuay as composed of small, independent polities sharing strong ties in iconography, technology and burial practices. On the basis of early Spanish writings, scholars have used the terms *curacazgos* or *cacicazgos* to describe this type of social arrangement in highland Ancash, referring to politically autonomous and self-sufficient systems in which institutionalized responsibilities seem to have been vested in individuals who wielded political and economic influence over several interdependent communities (Espinoza Soriano 1978; Millones 1979; Varón Gabai 1980). Wegner (1988) identified this arrangement in several agriculturally productive subregions of the North Highlands.

Other scholars ascribe more centralization to Recuay groups (Smith 1978; Pozorski and Pozorski 1987a; Shimada 1987, 1994). Recuay culture is presented as constituting a large political entity that competed for territorial and economic resources with other geopolitical regions. Shimada (1994:258) contended that the "Recuay polity," perhaps driven westward by highland droughts, had the military capacity to be a persistent threat to Moche settlements in valley zones valuable both for food resources and controlling the uppermost intakes of coastal irrigation systems. Smith (1978) divided the Recuay region into two distinct political zones: (1) a southern Recuay zone based in Huaraz and the Callejón de Huaylas and (2) a northern zone that coalesced around the civic–ceremonial center of Pashash. Smith (1978) postulated that the southern Recuay flourished through mobile agropastoralism. The northern Recuay focused on intensive agriculture and eventually displaced their southern counterparts, in political terms, during the later portion of the Early Intermediate Period.

Gero (1990, 1991) argued that certain segments of Recuay communities were able to organize production through festive labor and generous displays of wealth and redistribution. Leaders and their respective kin groups acquired socioeconomic status as they exploited traditional Andean idioms of reciprocity, offering food and drink in ritualized, communal contexts to individuals in return for their labor in corporate projects. Emerging elites began to invent positions of prestige and obligation that allowed them to obtain goods and labor differently than before (Moseley 1975; Godelier 1977; Morris and Thompson 1985; Isbell 1988b; Hastorf 1993; Kolata 1993). Lau (2000, 2002) added that ancestor cults were vital dimensions of public ceremony and political authority among Recuay tradition groups.

The Recuay pattern of increasingly asymmetrical social relations seems to coincide with a shift towards secular administration in coeval cultures (e.g., Moche) and increased competition for key resources. Coastal interaction is shown through settlement pattern studies. In Nepeña, Moche peoples occupied the lower valley, while Recuay groups controlled the upper zones, but the chronology and nature of the territoriality are unresolved (Proulx 1982; Daggett 1985, 1987). There is evidence for Recuay trading caravans on key routes into the mountains, including corrals, kaolinite ceramics and ground drawings of llamas (Wilson 1988). Coast–highland cultural frontiers, separated by differences in ethnicity and adaptation, also developed in other regions of northern Peru about the same time (Ravines 1982a; J. Topic and T. Topic 1983; Dillehay 2001) and continued into subsequent epochs (Julien 1988).

Warfare plays a major role in the interpretation of Recuay culture (Lumbreras 1974a; Bonavia 1991; Makowski and Rucabado Yong 2000; Lau 2004b). Recuay ceramics and sculpture often depict warriors, weapons, and trophy heads and hands, probably to aggrandize the authority and achievements of important leaders (e.g., Tello 1929; Schaedel 1948a; Disselhoff 1956; Eisleb 1987; Wegner 1988). Fine line depictions from several Middle Moche vessels may show battling Mochica and Recuay warriors (Smith 1978; Lau 2004b; cf. Reichert 1989; Schuler-Schömig 1979). Settlement fortifications and the common location of Recuay sites on ridgetops also point to the importance of defense (Tello 1930; Proulx 1982; Daggett 1987; Wilson 1988). Recuay political development and its consequences for the Chinchawas community during the Early Intermediate Period were therefore likely linked to intensive, frequently competitive, interaction with contemporary cultures.

## The Middle Horizon and Transformations in the North Highlands

By about A.D. 700 new cultural patterns emerged throughout the Central Andes. The Middle Horizon (ca. A.D. 700 to 1000) featured the widespread proliferation of cultural styles, especially in pottery and architecture, associated with Wari expansion. In pioneering analyses, Menzel (1964, 1968, 1977) isolated stylistic transformations in Wari culture and identified two main surges of Wari expansion: during Middle Horizon 1B and Middle Horizon 2B. The rapid spread and distribution of Wari culture have been interpreted as the expansion of the Wari state into regions outside its heartland in the Ayacucho highlands (Lumbreras 1960, 1974b; Menzel 1964, 1977; Isbell and McEwan 1991; Schreiber 1992, 2001). The principal expressions of Wari cultural and political expansion occurred from about A.D. 750 to 1000 (Schreiber 2001).

The debate on the sociopolitical meaning of the wide distribution of Wari material culture remains lively. There are some who believe it reflects a powerful empire able to exploit territories through military coercion, diplomacy and tribute arrangements, much the same way as did the Inka state (Menzel 1964; Schaedel 1966; Lumbreras 1974b; Isbell 1977; Schreiber 2001). Others also highlight the importance of Wari religion and ceremonial practices in the spread of Wari-style material culture (Menzel 1964; Cook 1994, 2001; Schreiber 2004; McEwan 2005).

Other investigators are less sanguine about the political might or integration of the Wari state, especially for areas away from the Wari heartland. They emphasize the relative autonomy of local regional powers from the Wari state, often in areas lacking the material correlates of Wari administrative control (Mackey 1982; Shady 1988; Castillo 2001; Jennings 2006a, 2006b). Others focus on patterns of economic interaction between Wari and local provincial groups. In such cases, Wari influence, while still very palpable in trade goods and stylistic exchange, seems to have been part of a larger broader pattern of economic interaction in which Wari was certainly a major player, but, according to some, not the only one (Shady 1988; Topic and Topic 2000).

Finally, single functional interpretations do not readily take into account the range of socioeconomic relationships possible in the Wari state at any given time. Schreiber (1992:269) identifies this plurality in her consideration of Wari imperialism, calling it a "mosaic of control." Rather than ascribing totalizing functions, research centers increasingly on how Wari appears in local assemblages in, but especially outside, the Wari heartland. Hence even within the same time frame, such as Middle Horizon 2, different areas within the Wari interaction sphere may be characterized by territorial takeover or colonization (e.g., Williams 2001), abandonment of building programs (e.g., Topic and Topic 2000), or trade and stylistic interaction (e.g., Castillo 2000).

Another important dimension for considering the implications of Wari material culture is change through time. In accordance with Menzel's contention of different "waves" of Wari expansion (i.e., Middle Horizon 1b and 2b), recent research has documented that Wari "provincial" influence changed in character, especially along its frontiers (Schreiber 2001; Glowacki 2002). For example, Castillo has shown (2000, 2001) that Wari polychrome traditions become more fully integrated into the local fineware repertoire during the Late Moche and "Transitional" periods at San José de Moro. As will be described later, Wari intervention at Chinchawas is manifested mainly by trade interaction early in the Middle Horizon, followed by a period of greater stylistic borrowing, or emulation, in local decorated pottery.

The North Highlands region has often been understood to be a key province during Wari expansion. The presence of Wari-style architecture and Wari pottery in the Callejón de Huaylas and farther north in Huamachuco indicates a vital highland corridor under Wari control. Thus, archaeologists interpreted the northern sierra up to Cajamarca as an important provincial region for Wari (McCown 1945; Menzel 1964; Buse 1965; Lanning 1965; Thatcher 1972, 1975, 1977; Lumbreras 1974a; Williams and Piñeda 1985; Isbell 1989, 1991a; Schreiber 1992; Jennings and Craig 2001).

Work in Huamachuco problematizes Wari's presence in the North Highlands. Specifically, excavations at key sites reveal that state influence took the form mainly of sumptuary goods and that the Wari-style administrative center of Viracochapampa was abandoned before it was ever completed or occupied. Not only is evidence for military conquest negligible, it seems that local cultural forms and styles in ceramics and architecture flourished in spite of Wari intrusion. Local lords were able to maintain power and their political center, Marcahuamachuco, continued to thrive during Middle Horizon times (J. Topic 1991; T. Topic 1991; J. Topic and T. Topic 1992, 2000).

Although some adhere to a very strong Wari presence in highland Ancash

(Paredes et al. 2000), most scholars are more skeptical of direct Wari control (Ponte Rosalino 2000; Lau 2002, 2005; Tschauner 2003; Herrera 2005). If Wari presence was based on the extraction of local staple or labor resources for the state heartland in Ayacucho, we would expect positive evidence for Wari infrastructure in the Callejón de Huaylas, especially in those areas central for control of the region. But there is little evidence for Wari-maintained roads, storage systems or military control and vigilance, such as forts.

Bennett (1944) was the first to systematically document evidence of the Wari in highland Ancash. He recovered Wari pottery in the Wilkawaín area, just northwest of Huaraz. Wilkawaín actually refers to a series of sites, including the large *chullpa* (above-ground burial structure) of Wilkawaín and an enclosed complex of chullpas, rooms and galleries, together called Ichik Wilkawaín, roughly 2 km to the southeast (Bennett 1944). Both locations were used principally during the Middle Horizon, but at Ichik Wilkawaín excavations also recovered a clear superposition of Middle Horizon and Wari materials over Recuay remains. Later work at Wilkawaín has confirmed an intensive Middle Horizon occupation focused on chullpa-based funerary practices and ceremonial offerings, sometimes with Wari-style artifacts (Paredes 2005). Other studies substantiate the association between chullpa funerary practices and Wari-influenced, Wilkawaín period materials (Wegner 1988; Paredes et al. 2000; Ponte Rosalino 2000; Lau 2001; Ibarra 2003a).

Honcopampa is generally understood to be Wari's provincial administrative center of the region (Isbell 1989, 1991a). Some have argued, principally on the basis of its distinctive architecture, that the site served as a major administrative center or a type of frontier settlement for a Wari conquest state (Vescelius, in Lanning 1965; Buse 1965). Honcopampa has architectural forms consistent with the general canons of Wari administrative architecture found at provincial settlements, as well as at the Huari type site (rectangular patio groups, D-shaped structures, galleries). Investigations in the main sector reported several sherds of Wari imports, one Viñaque, and another perhaps Chakipampa (Isbell 1989:109). Chullpas also occur at Honcopampa. One prominent cluster lies just south of the main sector of the site. In the largest chullpa of the group, excavations by Gary Vescelius and Hernán Amat reported finding Wari pottery, including Middle Horizon 2 Viñaque style, dating the use of the structure to later Wari expansion (Buse 1965; Amat Olazábal 1976b).

Closer scrutiny indicates that Honcopampa was not a typical Wari center. For one thing, the site shows little of the integrated spatial organization, construction techniques or pottery diagnostic for Wari satellite settlements (Tschauner 2003), such as Pikillacta, Viracochapampa, Jincamocco or Azángaro. Far above the valley floor of the Callejón de Huaylas and away from easy transport routes, especially north–south routes, Honcopampa is not particularly central to the Callejón de Huaylas, either for broadcasting imperial power or for administering goods and labor. Most inhabitants of the Callejón de Huaylas would have needed to go far out of their way to get there, much less bring products. Located right at the mouth of the Quebrada Honda, it may have been a route through the Cordillera Blanca to the Conchucos region. But it is poorly suited to control goods or labor from populations from the Cordillera Negra or from the rich valley floors of the Callejón de Huaylas (e.g., Pikillacta or Viracochapampa). It is well protected on its northern flanks, but is wide open from the southern approach.

The innovation of Honcopampa's architecture may actually result from prior vagaries in region's archaeological record. Recent investigations at Yayno, near Pomabamba, Ancash, show rectangular compounds formally akin to those at Honcopampa, and radiocarbon dated to at least A.D. 400 (Lau and Ramón 2007). Several of the Yayno examples are larger, taller and more elaborate than the Honcopampa cases. The other major Wari form at Honcopampa, the D-shaped structure, may also have local predecessors, sometimes known as "circular patio groups" in the Conchucos, that were dedicated to residential and ceremonial activities (Herrera 2005:224ff). Much of Honcopampa's patio-group architecture, it should be noted, uses large flattened monolithic slabs, especially as lintels, jambs and supporting members. This was a local convention and is not common outside the North Highlands (Tschauner 2003). None of the above precludes Wari use of Honcopampa, but any Wari affiliation or occupation becomes problematic without additional positive evidence, such as ceramics.

Regardless of their origins, the D-shaped structures, sometimes called "temples," do not seem to have been secular administrative structures: the buildings are relatively small (not intended for large groups) and were likely dedicated to more intimate religious activities, perhaps along the lines of veneration of the local deceased or sacrificial rituals (Cook 2001; Meddens and Cook 2001). At present, the D-shaped structures remain the most identifiably Wari of the buildings at the site, and would link it formally and temporarily to border settlements such as Cerro Baúl (Schreiber 2001:90–91; Williams 2001; not enough is known about Pariamarca, also called Palacio del Inca, and Tocroc to affiliate them with Wari [Williams and Piñeda 1985]. I have visited Pariamarca and could not find any surface material to indicate cultural affiliation. The long halls are reminiscent of Inka *kallankas*).

In sum, the villages and towns of the Middle Horizon in the Callejón de Huaylas show continuity in patterns of architecture, in spite of contact with Wari. This is not to argue that there was no Wari presence in the Callejón de Huaylas. Quite the contrary, Wari expansion seems to have had a profound effect on local groups, but evidence is scant for the annexation of the Callejón de Huaylas into the Wari empire. In other words, the available settlement data do not accord with a territorial control model of highland Ancash, wherein Wari administrators, based at a purpose-built site, actively extracted labor or goods from the local populace.

Elsewhere I have suggested that Wari expansion in the Callejón de Huaylas was probably mediated through a major center in the Huaraz basin, probably based in present-day Huaraz (Lau 2005:83). It is worth elaborating on the logic for this argument here. First, the Wilkawaín area, today a suburb of Huaraz, accounts for some of the largest and most numerous chullpas in the region, some associated with very rich grave lots (Bennett 1944; Paredes 2005). Additional chullpa sites on the outskirts of Huaraz, such as Waullac and Antajirca, suggest the coexistence of multiple, dense and stratified population centers in the same basin. Second, the Huaraz basin forms an especially rich agricultural area: it coincides with the portion of the Callejón de Huaylas that widens greatly into flat arable lands, where maize cultivation becomes possible at a large scale. It is also located at the convergence of two significant road systems. One runs north–south along the Callejón de Huaylas and the other connects Huaraz to Casma on the coast. Finally, given the rich archaeological remains scattered through the modern city, the Huaraz basin was also the seat of an important late Recuay period polity, whose leaders would have been the first points of contact with Wari administrators. This would help to explain the rich Wari period materials in the Wilkawaín area sites, but not at Honcopampa. Unfortunately, any remains lie buried underneath the Spanish colonial city, which in turn lies under the rubble of the 1970 earthquake and the extensive urbanization today. While a Huaraz-based intermediary between Callejón de Huaylas and Wari groups remains largely hypothetical, it is an equally suitable starting point for considering Wari geopolitics in the region.

Most of the incontrovertible evidence for Wari interaction in the Callejón de Huaylas comes from grave lots, especially from chullpas, which show a range of high to low quality Wari-related offerings, including polychrome and modeled ceramics, and pottery figurines. Quispisisa obsidian from the Ayacucho highlands also appears in Middle Horizon sites in the Callejón de Huaylas, especially in those with other Wari-related materials (Burger et al. 2006). There are unpublished cases of a Wari-style greenstone figurine (Carhuaz) and a Wari ceramic offering cache of unbroken vessels found during construction in the plaza of modern Yungay, after Yungay (Viejo) was buried in the 1970 mudslide (some works are on exhibit in the town museum, Ranrahirca).

Wari-related pottery is most common in the Callejón de Huaylas and in parts of the Cordillera Negra. Imported ceramics include Chakipampa and Viñaque, North Highland wares (slipcast spoons, blackware keros), and coastal Middle Horizon styles, such as Nievería and Huari Norteño. Slightly later trade goods included press-molded and painted styles typical of the central and north–central coasts. Derived styles also occur, suggesting local emulation of Wari polychromes, Wamanga and blackware polished (e.g., Bennett 1944; Menzel 1964; Lau 2005). Interestingly, some ceramic figurines depict males with four-cornered hats often identified as Wari dress (Paredes et al. 2000:259); one has his hands tied behind his back, like a captive (Ponte Rosalino 2000:242), while another holds a shield and drinking tumbler (Herrera 2005, fig. 7.19).

It is unlikely that the graves were of Wari people, given their ubiquity across highland Ancash (chullpas) and the fact that other prestige regions are also referenced in the grave lots (Cajamarca, North Coast and North Central Coast). Conservatively, what this shows is that local groups, especially higher status and wealthier groups, found Wari culture desirable and actively took measures to appropriate it for display and funerary purposes. Such measures included acquiring pottery imports and spurring local production to emulate Wari forms and imagery.

Wari culture is clearly intrusive in the Callejón de Huaylas, but the precise character and contexts of Wari interaction have remained elusive. Besides Honcopampa, other Wari-related settlements have been reported in different parts of the Callejón de Huaylas, although few have been studied systematically (Williams and Piñeda 1985; Ponte Rosalino 1999a; Paredes et al. 2000; Herrera 2005). In contrast to the Callejón de Huaylas, the region to the east of the Cordillera Blanca, known as the Conchucos or Callejón de Conchucos, has produced relatively little Wari material, whether ceramics, Wari-related architectural forms or construction style (Ibarra 2003a; Herrera 2005).

In comparative terms, the Wari presence in the Callejón de Huaylas resembles some of the archaeological patterns at Huamachuco. Both areas show evidence of early relationships with Wari by Middle Horizon 1B (Menzel 1964). Wari-style administrative architecture is present in both regions, but it is uncertain whether the structures were ever used by Wari or Wari-governed groups. In those locations, furthermore, the architecture draws strongly from local construction canons (Isbell 1991a; J. Topic 1991; Tschauner 2003). Finally, investigations within the administrative complexes recover diagnostic Wari pottery in conspicuously rare amounts. Fancy Wari pottery, on the other hand, occurs more commonly as luxury goods in mortuary contexts (Topic and Topic 1992).

The patterns emerging for Wari in the North Highlands reflect sociocultural transformations that are more complex than previously thought. Rather than direct military control, Wari penetration of the Huamachuco region may have emphasized commercial and ideological interests, probably to maintain access to key trade routes for the movement of obsidian, fineware ceramics (Wari styles and Cajamarca), lapis lazuli, *Spondylus* shell and other sumptuary goods (Shady 1988; J. Topic 1991:161–163; T. Topic 1991:242–244). Given the intermediate geographical location of Callejón de Huaylas between Huamachuco and the Central Highlands, as well as the lack of strong evidence for territorial control, it stands to reason that Wari interest in the region could have also focused on exchange relations. As both Huamachuco and the Callejón de Huaylas show Wari influence by Middle Horizon 1B, exchange interests might have fueled initial Wari expansion, at least into the North Highlands.

The material evidence suggests interaction with Wari, both through stylistic and physical exchanges. The ceramic evidence indicates very complex local interchanges with Wari that cannot at present be readily subsumed under terms such as "control," "domination" or "resistance." Wari forms and ideology became, apparently, compatible with local practices and were appropriated for ceremonial practices, especially in chullpa funerary ritual. The relations may have also included conflict, diplomatic strategies and exchange. Just as important, interaction between Wari and groups of highland Ancash occurred over at least three centuries, changing forms and character during that time.

The ancient community of Chinchawas therefore emerged under unique environmental and sociocultural conditions that shaped the lifeways and material culture of its residents. The overview of local environmental history, current land use and paleoclimatic changes contextualizes our consideration of the community's economy in antiquity. Like today, the ancient groups of Chinchawas followed a broad highland subsistence pattern, based on agropastoralism. Exploitation of the diversity of resources in the Andean landscape encouraged and benefited from networks of exchange. The inhabitants of Chinchawas emerged out of the Recuay cultural tradition, following general dispositions in settlement, subsistence practices, material culture and funerary practices. As will become clear in the following chapters, however, important cultural changes occurred, especially during the period of Wari state expansion.

CHAPTER THREE

# Fieldwork Methodology and Sector 1 Excavations

The Chinchawas field investigations used a methodology of site mapping, clearing, surface collections and excavation sampling. The data recovered with these methods provide the basis for the reconstruction of the local cultural chronology and changing patterns of occupation. Following brief summaries of the rationale and methodology for the field research, this section details the archaeological excavations in Sector 1.

Four principal types of architectural spaces were investigated through sampling: enclosures, room structures and complexes, terraces and special-purpose buildings (the Torreón structure and mortuary buildings). This chapter details the excavations within enclosures, room complexes and the Torreón structure, while later chapters describe the operations in terrace areas and mortuary constructions.

Pilot surveys of the site, conducted in July 1995 and March 1996, concluded that Chinchawas contained a diversity of surface material. Variability in pottery, architecture and stone sculpture indicated from the beginning that the site had a multicomponent and multipurpose occupation. One of the major objectives of the work was to develop a reliable cultural sequence of occupation at the site. Chinchawas's excellent preservation and manageable size, at under 4 hectares, were considered favorable for sampling (Figure 10). The different forms of the standing architecture suggested that the site's spatial organization could be related to its cultural sequence (see Figure 2).

The research at Chinchawas also aimed to provide comparative data on North Highland ridgetop settlements. By far the most frequent Recuay site type is the fortified hilltop settlement. Most of these sites are fairly small, marginal in terms of cultivable land, and populated by a small groups of dispersed households. Thus, Chinchawas was studied as a highland settlement type typical for many parts of the Callejón de Huaylas and the western flanks of the Cordillera Negra during the Early Intermediate Period.

## Chinchawas Ceramic Sequence

The pottery and associated radiocarbon ages of the Chinchawas ceramic sequence are detailed in subsequent chapters. Here a brief review of the general phases is provided to help contextualize the excavation descriptions. As based on local decorated

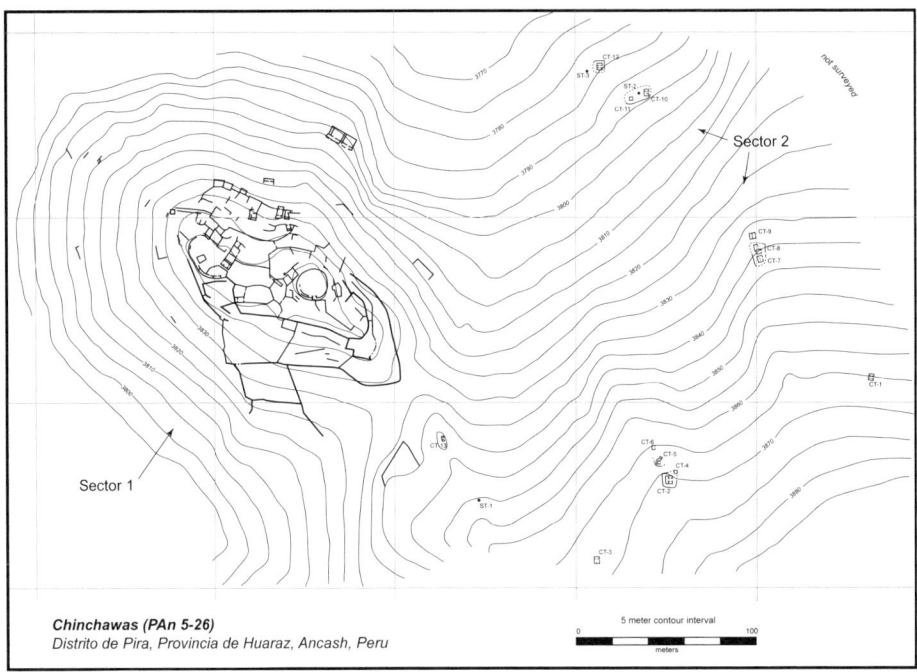

FIGURE 10. The Chinchawas site, showing the location of Sector 1 and Sector 2.

and utilitarian ware groups, Chinchawas's main occupation consists of five ceramic phases (Figure 2), which correspond to the Early Intermediate Period (A.D. 1 to 700) and the Middle Horizon (A.D. 700 to 1000) in Andean chronology (Rowe and Menzel 1967).

In general, the plainware ceramics are strongly consistent in form, paste and surface treatment across the different phases. Local decorated wares, however, show the most innovation and stylistic borrowing. The earliest occupation is represented by the Kayán phase, a local variant of classic Recuay kaolinite pottery of the middle Early Intermediate Period. The subsequent Chinchawasi 1 represents a late Recuay style (Lau 2004a). Chinchawasi 1 derived stylistic features from the Huaraz area and dates to the end of the Early Intermediate Period.

New patterns in form and painted decoration help distinguish Chinchawasi 2 ceramics. They indicate the decline of earlier Recuay elements and the uptake of foreign traits. Radiocarbon data and trade wares, including early Wari contemporary styles, indicate an early to middle Middle Horizon age.

The subsequent Warmi style constitutes the last phase of intensive occupation of Chinchawas and pertains to the middle to late Middle Horizon. It was largely a replacement of local pottery traditions by derived Wari styles. The following Chakwas phase, characterised by plain earthenwares adorned with basic plastic decoration, began around the turn of the millennium. Within a few centuries, however, intensive use of the Chinchawas hilltop for residential purposes came to end.

# Archaeological Fieldwork

*Site Mapping and General Layout*
Datum points were established to create a site grid and map. The benchmark was situated near the center of the site and the grid was laid out following the long dimension of the main plaza on the Chinchawas ridgetop (Figure 11). Topographer César Valverde mapped the site using a theodolite and correlated the various datum points with absolute elevations. A GPS unit measured the highest part of the Sector 1 to 3,853 masl.

All test excavations were located through basic surveying techniques, using metal measuring tapes, plumb-bobs and triangulation along the north–south axis. Some operations followed the limits of surface architecture. All elevations in the excavations can be referenced to the northwest point of the excavation unit, which are in turn based on the primary datum point's elevation of 3,842 masl.

The layout of Chinchawas consists of two main sectors, Sector 1 and Sector 2. Sector 1 refers to the main ridgetop settlement (Figure 11). Ringed by a series of well-built and imposing perimeter walls, Sector 1 has a variety of standing stone architecture, including enclosures, terraces, room complexes and a circular tower, named the "Torreón" structure (Figure 12). Sector 2 consists exclusively of subterranean and aboveground mortuary structures. The mapping identified 16 such constructions to the east and southeast of Sector 1. Most of these buildings are in clusters ranging between 3,825 and 3,885 masl in elevation.

*Excavations*
The investigations sampled different architectural spaces of the Chinchawas site through stratigraphic excavations (Figure 11). A strategy of systematic clearing, test pits and areal excavations was considered the best compromise for the objectives of the fieldwork. The following descriptions summarize the subsurface architectural and other cultural features in relation to their stratigraphic contexts and artifact associations.

All intrusive excavations and discrete exposures were referred to as "operations," which covered a range of fieldwork procedures, including test pits, larger areal exposures and excavations defined by architectural units, as well as nonexcavation exposure strategies such as clearing fallen walls or vegetation. Each procedure, from test pits to horizontal exposures to buildings, was given an operation number, beginning with Operation 1 (OP1) and ending at Operation 66 (OP66). Stratigraphic excavations exposed over 304 m$^2$ during the course of investigation. Another 40 to 50 m$^2$ were exposed through systematic surficial clearing. All the excavations in 1996, Operations 1 to 37, consisted of 1 by 2 m test pits. Operations 38 to 66 were completed in 1997 and consisted of larger exposures, trenches or clearings.

*Excavation Methodology*
In all cases, the excavations were carried out systematically to enable vertical and

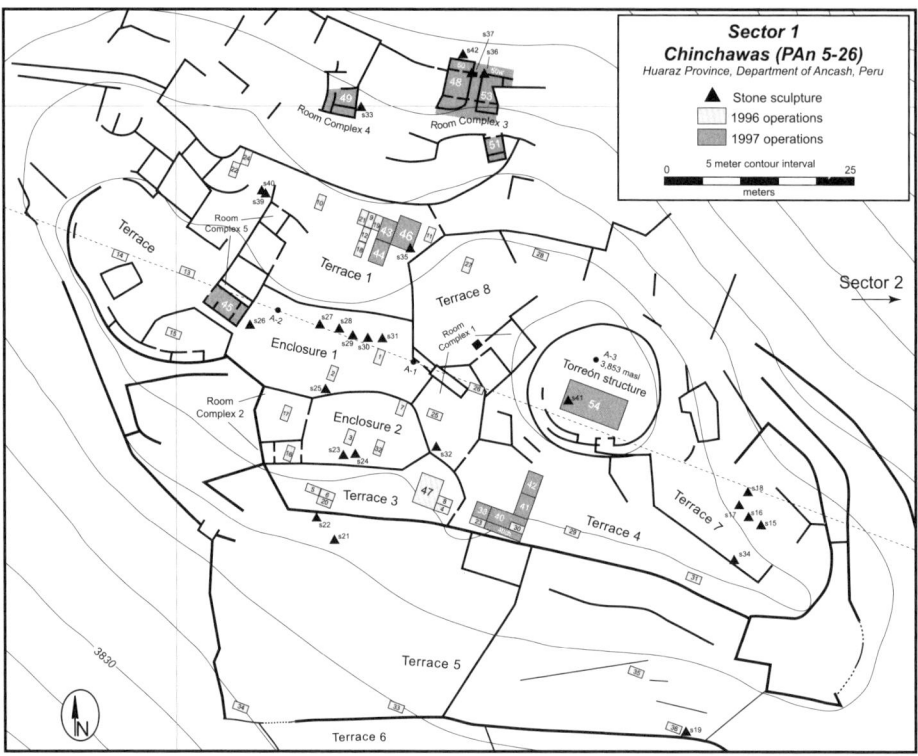

FIGURE 11. Sector 1, Chinchawas, showing the architectural zones, excavation operations and stone sculptures at the site.

horizontal control and metrical documentation of strata, cultural features and artifacts. All soil was sieved through 0.5 cm mesh screens to maximize artifact recovery. During excavations of floor levels and features such as cooking areas, or when otherwise appropriate, 2 mm mesh screens were used on selected occasions.

All excavations proceeded according to natural levels and, when possible, cultural layers or floors as distinguished by color, texture or contents. Thick homogeneous layers were sometimes subdivided so that vertical and horizontal control of artifacts could be more precise. This was executed especially when excavation was through a homogeneous stratum that exceeded 15 to 20 cm in thickness. All excavations were taken down to bedrock, which, given its geological setting, occurs throughout the site. The depths of deposit ranged from 0.4 to 3 m. All pits were backfilled with the rocks and soil from the excavations. To alert future researchers, plastic sheets and cuttings (blue and yellow) were placed on the exposed bedrock surface before backfilling.

As would be expected for a small hilltop village, the depositional history of Chinchawas was very complex and included a range of primary and reworked deposits. Many of the excavations encountered easily identifiable reworked materials, especially in levels with fallen walls and upper surficial levels. Modern agricultural activity and other use have affected different parts of the site, especially the upper levels (sometimes referred to below as "plowzones"). Intentional construction fill or midden deposits were less affected. Levels or features with mixed ceramics were often the measure of identifying secondary deposits and, where notable, are mentioned noted in the following unit descriptions. All of the excavations within the Sector 2 mortuary constructions also encountered reworked material from previous looting activities. In the forthcoming descriptions, primary deposits associated with intact floors, middens and construction fill levels are emphasized. By the second field season, the ceramic sequence, which was largely defined after the first season of test pits, helped to identify optimal areas for further investigation and also to discern reliable deposition.

## Enclosures

Enclosures were defined as large, generally freestanding constructions surrounded entirely or in large part by one contiguous wall or series of walls (Figure 11). At Chinchawas these are quadrangular without strongly defined corners and probably unroofed. Rooms were sometimes added to them. Sector 1 contains two enclosure structures along its central portion, named Enclosure 1 and Enclosure 2. Notably, the constructions use well-built walls that enclose relatively large interior spaces; they also feature adjoining rooms with or without doorways. Stratigraphic test excavations investigated the two enclosures.

### *Enclosure 1*

OPERATION 1
OP1 was a 1 by 2 m test unit in the topmost enclosure structure, Enclosure 1. There were seven stone sculptures on the surface of the enclosure; the excavations, in large part, aimed to recover data about their architectural and phase association. The test pit confirmed expectations that the depth and quality of deposit in this zone were negligible. Not including the surface layer, two levels were excavated. The associations were mixed. OP1B, the lowest, sat directly above bedrock. Levels A and B showed very little internal differentiation, with Level B slightly less compact and browner. There were very few diagnostic artifacts from this pit. Most sherds were small and frequently rounded, suggesting that the material had been reworked, probably by agricultural activity.

OPERATION 2
OP2, a 1 by 2 m test unit, was just east of OP1. Although the stratigraphy was essentially the same as OP1, we encountered a slightly deeper depth of deposit, reaching 40 cm at the northwestern corner of the pit. This small depression was rimmed by the footings of a possible wall set directly into the bedrock. All of the 15 phase diagnostic sherds in the lowest levels (OP1A and OP1B) were Chinchawasi 2 wares,

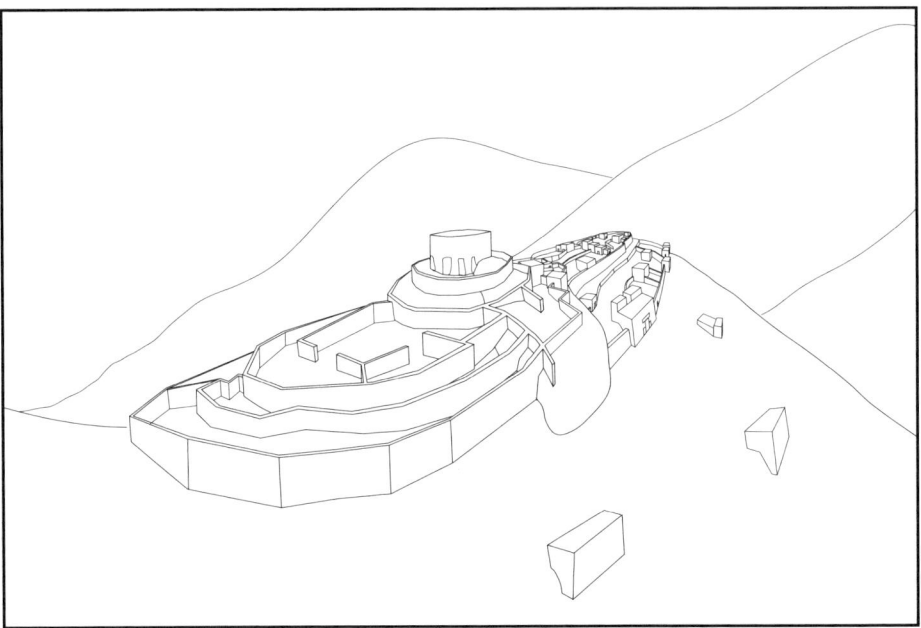

Figure 12. Reconstruction of Chinchawas site, looking towards the northwest. The settlement had residential structures in its western half and was fortified with a series of perimeter walls built atop bedrock. The topmost portion of the community featured a circular building, which contained evidence of ceremonial activities.

suggesting that the wall might date to this phase. Like OP1, the material in OP2 was probably reworked through modern farming activity.

*Enclosure 2*

Enclosure 2 is directly south of Enclosure 1 and is fully enclosed by walls (Figure 13). The interior space descends very slightly toward the southern slope of the ridgetop. A series of carved monoliths are associated with the enclosure (see Chapter 10), which features curved walls built to an irregular quadrangular plan. The well-preserved walls are of the distinctive *wanka–pachilla* style: large upright boulders (*wankas*) separated by rows of fitted small, flat chinking stones (*pachillas*). Test operations aimed to determine the character and context of this surficial architecture.

OPERATION 3

OP3, a 1 by 2 m test pit, had deeper deposits than OP1 or OP2, reaching a maximum depth of 82 cm in the center of the unit. This unit also provided much clearer stratigraphy. At the deepest cultural layer of the pit, Level C, we encountered a find level with a concentration of phase diagnostics, which included 13 Kayán and five Chinchawasi 1 sherds, most of finer quality. These materials were deposited mostly in the southern half of the pit, and were located roughly 10 cm above the sterile bedrock layer. In the same level, we found a stone pendant (Figure 125J).

The remains place the enclosure's use and construction in the late Early Intermediate Period. Together with OP32, the elaborate architecture and the surficial presence of stone sculptures, it is surmised that this patio was of special status, perhaps akin to complexes for the festive public events described for other ceremonial constructions in the Callejón de Huaylas (Gero 1990, 1991; Lau 2002).

Level OP3C was directly overlain by Level B (OP3B), which was composed mostly of wall debris containing no phase diagnostic materials. This is interpreted as a destruction episode that effectively separated the Chinchawasi and Kayán phases from subsequent occupations. Surficial and Level A strata contained very little diagnostic material. This area was used as a small farming plot in recent times, which explains the paucity and poor condition of remains in the uppermost layers.

## Operation 7

OP7 was opened to test for cultural associations in Enclosure 2 and to look at the construction process for the enclosure wall. The unit, 1 by 2 m in size, confirmed that the walls were built directly on bedrock. Elsewhere in the enclosure complex walls with comparable masonry were associated with Chinchawasi pottery dating to the Early Intermediate Period. The depth of deposit in OP7 was very shallow, ranging from 10 to 30 cm. In the primary level, Level B, there were mixed materials, the earliest dating to the Kayán occupation. At the southern end of the pit we encountered the footings of a small, low wall of unknown function and association. The intact portion of the wall faces north.

## Operation 32

OP32 was a 1 by 2 m test pit, in the southeast corner of Enclosure 2. OP32sf was the modern surface level, a loose and dusty stratum with frequent small rocks and mixed, eroded cultural materials. OP32A was a slightly harder level than OP32sf, composed of dark brown soil with frequent small rocks. The accumulation of fallen wall rocks and large fragments of broken domestic pottery distinguished OP32B. The soil was the same dark brown color, but it was usually composed of small granules. The level resembled the destruction levels of rock rubble found in Room Complex 1 (see below). OP32C was a darker layer of moister, harder, sticky soil. Contents included various plainware sherds from jars and open serving vessels. Mixed pottery associations suggest a considerable amount of post-depositional disturbance. Below OP32C was a stratum of sterile dark yellowish brown soil, OP32D, with gritty and sandy mottles. This soil is typical of the sterile fill layers in many parts of the site, such as the sandy fills in Terrace 1 operations of Middle Horizon association (described later).

About 70 cm below the modern surface the enclosure's builders exploited a natural step-like rise in the bedrock to distinguish a higher platform floor level in the northern end of the pit (Figure 14). The contemporary floor in the southern end was identified 10 to 15 cm beneath this rise (OP32E). A stone-lined drainage canal located at the border of the platform divided the two levels. Measuring 15 to

FIGURE 13. View of Enclosure 2, Sector 1 (looking west). Note the uprights on the far end of the enclosure, typical of the wanka–pachilla stonework at Chinchawas. Excavators are working on the western portion of Terrace 3.

20 cm wide and 20 to 25 cm high, the canal used aligned flat stones for sidewalls, bedrock for the base, and carefully positioned capstones for the roof. The canal and split floors extended to other parts of the enclosure's interior space, most likely to drain rainwater. Underneath the northern end, a very dark brown clayey stratum was probably laid down to even out the floor above (OP32F). This stratum was directly above bedrock and contained very little material. OP32 reached a maximum excavated depth of 1.05 m.

The lack of artifacts in the bottom levels suggests that the floor surface was assiduously maintained and that there was no discard of refuse during the drain's construction. Given the superposition of the Warmi destruction level and the contents of the other operations in Enclosure 2, the canal and platform were probably built during Kayán or Chinchawasi 1 times, before the advent of Warmi type pottery.

SUMMARY OF ENCLOSURE 2 OPERATIONS
The available data from OP32, combined with those from OP3 and OP7, indicate that the earliest use of Enclosure 2 dated to the Kayán or Chinchawasi 1 occupation of the site. This enclosure area is an irregular quadrangle and represents an open patio area. The area was surrounded by a series of finely constructed walls of wanka–pachilla masonry. The central area featured a slightly higher platform, ringed by a stone-lined drainage canal. During this time frame this area was characterized by careful maintenance of floors and, when present, pottery of the fancy

decorated types, suggesting a construction of special importance. Stratigraphy and cultural associations indicate that these constructions dated to a late Early Intermediate Period occupation. The area's special importance is reinforced by the presence of three stone sculptures in the Recuay tradition (Lau 2006b).

When Warmi pottery became popular, the area was co-opted into the larger Warmi settlement. Leveled off with deposits of fill, the zone became a place for dumping domestic refuse, perhaps from Room Complex 1. Also, large accumulations of wall debris levels occurred throughout the open enclosure areas. At the end of the Warmi occupation, the enclosure walls were either destroyed or fell into disrepair through general abandonment.

## Room Complexes

Most rooms at Chinchawas are agglutinated. They are rarely freestanding or isolated from other architectural elements. In all cases, the chambers are part of larger architectural units, which I refer to as "room complexes" (Figure 11). Simply, room complexes are arrangements of agglutinated rooms (at least two). All six room complexes were located in Sector 1 and each is very different. The rooms often connect to unroofed, walled areas. Because of the great amount of wall debris, the full dimensions and number of rooms of each complex cannot be identified unequivocally. Nevertheless, it seems likely that each served as the domestic living and work space of an extended family or kin group lineage. Stratigraphic excavations sampled several of the complexes.

### Room Complex 1

#### OPERATION 25

OP25, a 1 by 2 m test unit, was in an area characterized by several adjoining rooms that form Room Complex 1, located just west of the Torreón mound. Our objective with OP25 and OP26 was to determine the character and functional context of these constructions, especially in comparison to other sectors of the site. Given the proximity of the rooms to the Torreón mound, we expected that excavations would uncover evidence of differential status. One other reason for exploring this area more thoroughly was because several older community members informed me that there was once a natural spring near OP25.

OP25 was in an open area in the southernmost room of Room Complex 1, between several walls. OP25sf was the typical surface level. OP25A was a grayish black layer with common inclusions of small rocks and mixed plain and decorated ceramics. OP25sf and OP25A were interpreted as surface and plowzone levels, respectively.

OP25B constituted a destruction layer of a very dark brown soil matrix with charcoal flecks. The level was characterized by plentiful small- and medium-sized rocks, which I surmise as debris from the surrounding walls. OP25C was an arbi-

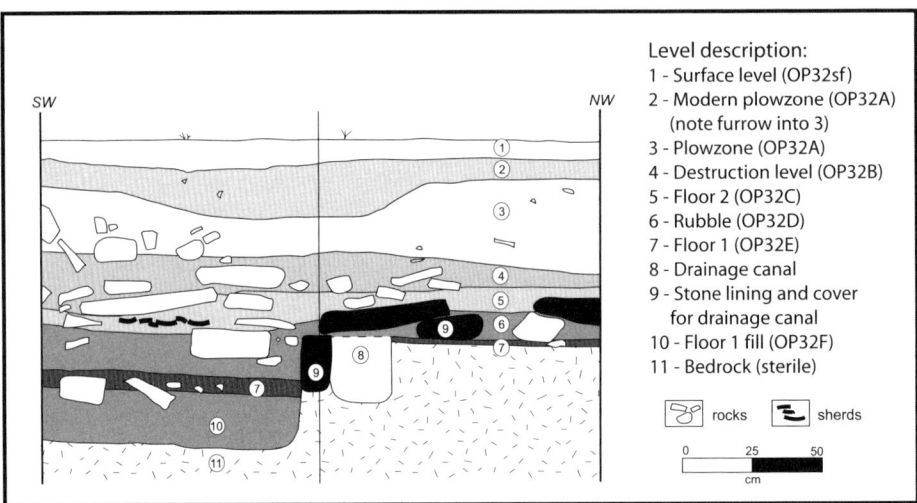

FIGURE 14. West profile of Operation 32 within Enclosure 2, showing drainage canal and low-lying platform.

trary level change for stratigraphic control and was essentially a deeper part of the same destruction level. OP25B and OP25C ceramics contained a range of diagnostics, including Chinchawasi (12%), Warmi (44%), Chakwas (24%) and Middle Horizon exotics (16%) such as press-molded redwares and Wilkawaín negative. The Chakwas pottery suggests that the level's deposition—the collapse or general disrepair of nearby walls—probably occurred in the late part of the Middle Horizon or during the Late Intermediate Period.

OP25D was a hard-beaten dirt floor of brown soil. Broken grinding stones and abundant plainware ceramics littered the surface, suggesting everyday domestic activities. Decorated ceramics were less frequent, but included Chinchawasi phase 2. OP25E was a level of very dark brown to black soil, compact in consistency, with frequent inclusions of small to medium stones. This level is interpreted as another wall debris level. Plainware ceramics suggest a Chinchawasi 1 association.

OP25F was the basal level of the pit, a hard-beaten dirt floor, with frequent flecks of charcoal. Abundant evidence of domestic functions included plainware ceramics, burnt animal bone and grinding stones, including a large gray-green quartzite grinding slab referred to as a *batán*. The batán had use polish on the top surface and a slight depression near the slab's center, indicating grinding activities. Throughout the floor were interbedded lenses of ashy soil that contained many small fragments of burnt animal bone. It is very likely that the floor was a living and cooking surface for the room's occupants. One Kayán kaolinite sherd constitutes the only phase diagnostic from the level. At the northwest corner of the operation we encountered the foundations of a partition wall (OP25-w1) measuring roughly 35 cm in width. The wall ran north–south and extended into the north profile, so its length could not be determined. Built directly on bedrock, the wall was leveled during the formation of the floor surface in OP25D. The operation reached 82 cm in maximum depth.

## Operation 26

OP26 was located several meters to the northeast of OP25 and was excavated within a room of Room Complex 1. Although there was no surficial architecture when the 1 by 2 m pit was opened, we found a large wall (OP26-w1) immediately beneath the initial level OP26sf, running approximately east–west across the northern half of the operation. OP26sf featured a moist and soft brown soil and corresponds to the modern surface level throughout the site.

OP26A was very hard, bearing a dense quantity of small to large rocks corresponding to the destruction level encountered nearby in OP25B. OP26B constituted a deeper continuation of the wall debris stratum (corresponding to OP25C). The soil was slightly softer and grayer, and contained frequent plainware ceramics as well as charcoal flecks. No diagnostics were recovered from either OP26sf or OP26A, and only four in OP26C, including two Chakwas phase sherds. The Chakwas sherds provide a *terminus ante quem* for the date of the destruction and are consistent with associated materials from the wall debris found in OP25B.

OP26D designates the soil underneath several flat rocks at the base of OP26C at the western end of the operation. The level contained a loose dark brown matrix with very little artifactual material. The soil resembled the soil from the wall debris stratum above. The level contained one Warmi phase sherd. OP26E was a stratum found exclusively on the eastern portion of the pit. It was partially beneath OP26D, with a very dark brown soil and harder in consistency. The area was richer also in animal bone, with common flecks of charcoal, suggesting refuse from a hearth-cleaning episode. One Warmi phase sherd was found from this level. OP26F was a stratum on the western portion of the operation, partly overlain by OP26E, and was lighter and softer. It was a continuation of the stratum in OP26D and contained small to large rocks throughout. OP26F held three Warmi phase diagnostics.

OP26G began a thick level of midden refuse. It consisted of a soft matrix of dark reddish brown soil mixed with fewer large rocks, but with similar amounts of small rocks. Faunal and chipped stone debris was common, as was broken plain and decorated pottery. Eighteen diagnostic sherds were identified to the Chinchawasi 2 phase.

A radiocarbon measurement using accelerator mass spectrometry (AMS) was taken from a wood charcoal point sample retrieved from the topmost portion of OP26G ($x$: –0.60N, $y$: –9.28W, $z$: –0.50 m). The sample yielded a radiocarbon age of 1180 ± 45 B.P. (A.D. 770 ± 45 uncalibrated or A.D. 883 ± 45 calibrated), with a 2-sigma range of A.D. 726 to 733 and A.D. 771 to 979 (Table 1). The sample pertains to the late portion of the Chinchawasi 2 phase, when the refuse materials were deposited.

OP26H was a continuation of the OP26G stratum with no discernible change in stratigraphy. The soft and reddish brown soil continued, but with fewer flecks

TABLE 1. Radiocarbon assays from Chinchawas. All dates were calibrated using Radiocarbon Calibration Program Rev. 4.3 (Stuiver and Reimer 1993).

| Lab ID | Unit, level | Phase | $^{14}$C age (B.P.) | Age (uncal a.d.) | Age (cal A.D.) | 1–sigma range (A.D.) | 2–sigma range (A.D.) |
|---|---|---|---|---|---|---|---|
| AA32365 | OP9J | Kayán | 1710 ± 50 | 240 | 347, 360, 374 | 256–412 | 233–434 |
| AA32369 | OP19L | Chinchawasi 1 | 1395 ± 45 | 555 | 655 | 634–669 | 600–689 |
| AA32371 | OP49D | Chinchawasi 1 | 1375 ± 45 | 575 | 661 | 646–677 | 610–763 |
| AA32368 | OP31H | Chinchawasi 1 | 1305 ± 45 | 645 | 687 | 667–776 | 654–855 |
| AA32367 | OP4G | Chinchawasi 2 | 1290 ± 45 | 660 | 711, 746, 755 | 673–781 | 659–875 |
| AA32366 | OP21I | Chinchawasi 2 | 1255 ± 45 | 695 | 777 | 688–861 | 668–888 |
| AA32372 | OP26G | Chinchawasi 2 | 1180 ± 45 | 770 | 883 | 787–953 | 726–979 |
| AA32373 | OP36G | Warmi | 1170 ± 55 | 780 | 886 | 787–965 | 718–998 |
| AA32374 | OP43I | Warmi | 1160 ± 45 | 790 | 888 | 827–965 | 778–991 |
| AA32370 | OP20F | Warmi | 1150 ± 50 | 800 | 891 | 870–973 | 778–1006 |

of charcoal. The 63 diagnostics identified from this level were all Chinchawasi 2. OP26I was a beaten dirt floor stratum distinguished by a dark brown color and significantly harder texture. OP26I lay directly above sterile bedrock and was associated with the foundations of the east–west wall (OP26-w1). This stratum contained two Chinchawasi 2 diagnostics. OP26 reached a depth of 1.38 m.

## Room Complex 2

At the west end of Enclosure 2, two irregularly shaped rooms constitute Room Complex 2. Their walls, constructed in the wanka–pachilla masonry style, are plainly visible on the surface. The east wall of both buildings forms the west wall of Enclosure 2 and is in an excellent state of preservation. Our aim with the following two test excavations was to elucidate their cultural associations and to gauge the intrasite variability in cultural remains and stratigraphy.

### Operation 16

OP16, a 1 by 2 m unit, was located in the southern room of Room Complex 2. The southern room was remarkable because it opened out into Enclosure 2 through a narrow doorway to the east. On the west end of the room there was a small architectural addition, with a small centrally located opening above the floor measuring roughly 40 cm on a side. The structure could have been a tomb. We did not excavate here because it was clear from inspection that bedrock was very close to the surface.

OP16sf was the plowed upper surface level, as found in many parts of the site. The soil was soft and dry, dark grayish brown, and contained roots and small stones in addition to small eroded sherds. OP16A corresponded to a deeper component of the same plowzone level as OP16sf, with no noticeable change in soil color. Diagnostic pottery was predominantly of the Warmi style (80%), with the exception being a single Kayán kaolinite sherd.

OP16B was a darker soil layer, which corresponded to a floor level. The layer was very hard and the remains of a single vessel and scattered large sherd fragments suggest the layer was a floor surface. Only Warmi phase artifacts were found in this layer. OP16C was a stone pavement at bedrock level that served as the base for the beaten dirt floor described above. The pavement fitted large flat stones to grade depressions in uneven portions of the bedrock. OP16C referred to the soil (mixed black and very dark grayish brown) between the stones. There was no identifiable diagnostic pottery in this level. This pavement was probably a continuation of the Chinchawasi 2 paved floor in OP5. The maximum depth of 46 cm from the surface was at the center of the pit.

OPERATION 17

OP17 was a 1 by 2 m test unit located in the northern room of Room Complex 2. OP17sf was the plowzone layer, consisting of a loose dark grayish brown soil with small tubers and roots. OP17A was a harder dry soil, slightly darker, with occasional flecks of carbon. At the base of Level A, we encountered an even more compacted surface, designated OP17B. It was a floor level, with some grading pavement stones on top of bedrock. The floor was more gray in profile, rich with pottery and flecks of carbon. We encountered a broken but largely complete jar at this floor level. OP17C was a softer subfloor level that extended to bedrock. Diagnostic pottery was largely of the Chinchawasi 1 style, especially in OP17C, suggesting that the floor dated to this occupation.

*Room Complex 3*

Room Complex 3 is a large complex of agglutinated rooms and related constructions located roughly northeast of Terrace 1. The complex occupies a steep slope in the northern quadrant of Chinchawas, which today is covered mostly by wall collapse and debris, especially the back section directly north of Terrace 1. The best preserved portion of Room Complex 3 consists of a series of five rooms, which were cleared and partially excavated (Figures 15 and 16). The complex is composed of two agglutinated rooms on the east side and three agglutinated rooms on the west side.

A central staircase divides the two sides. The stairwell consists of large stone blocks built directly atop stone fill and, in many parts, above bedrock (Figure 17). There are 10 steps in the primary portion of the staircase. Two large flat stones placed at the base of the staircase extend the descent, and two additional stairs at the southern end follow after a small landing area. A drain runs underneath the large steps from the top of the room complex to an outtake opening in the north façade. The channel is stone-lined and uses both aligned stones and bedrock for the sides and the bottom surface. The stairwell descends downhill towards the north.

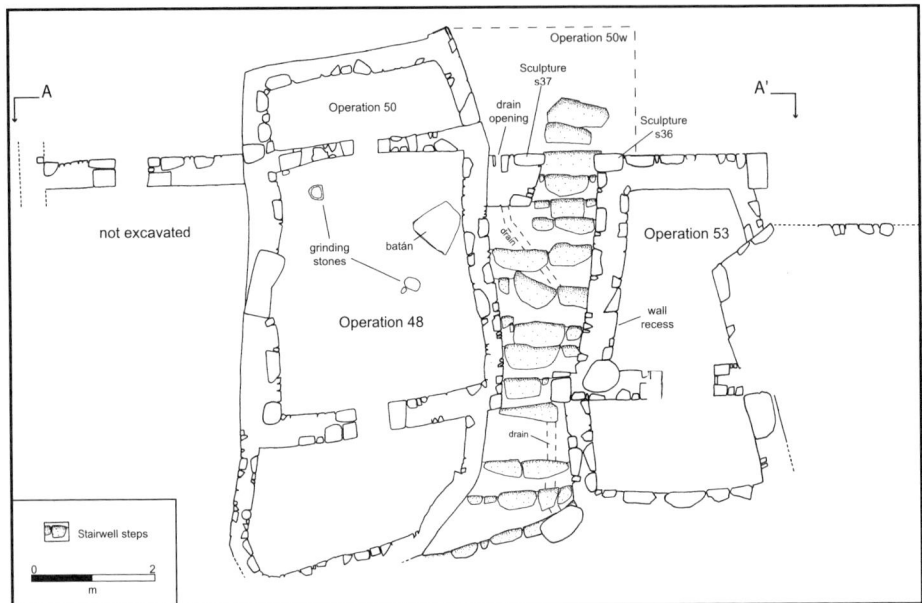

FIGURE 15. Plan of northern structures and excavation operations in Room Complex 3. The earliest occupation was residential and domestic, followed by multiple episodes of reuse and dense refuse accumulation. An elaborate stone-lined canal originating in the southeast portion of the complex runs underneath the stairwell and empties out of an opening on the northern façade.

The tall walls of the façade provide a measure of protection from strong winds and restrict unwanted access from below.

The masonry of the rooms is of the high quality wanka–pachilla type, cemented by sandy mud mortar. Along the east side of the complex the façade stands more than 4 m in height. At the base of the stairwell, flanking each side, are two in situ stone sculptures that bear frontal representations of anthropomorphs (Lau 2006b:209–211). These two sculptures represent several of the only examples of Recuay tradition stone sculpture ever found in situ. As the only accessway into Room Complex 3 from the north, entry to the interior had to pass the impressive façade, stairwell arrangement and jamb sculptures (Figure 16).

Intensive clearing of the area removed wall rocks that had largely covered over the room complex. In all likelihood, the infilling of the rooms from debris was responsible for the remarkable preservation of the buildings and sculpture.

## Operation 48

The structure on the west side consists of three rooms (Figure 15). The largest is the middle chamber, which is entered through the room to the south that connects to a small platform from the stairwell. The middle chamber also provides access into the north chamber. OP48 was the clearing and excavation of the large, middle room (3.05 by 3.16 m).

Because of the steep slope, the west structures of Room Complex 3 occupy at least two levels. The rooms along the north are on a lower part of the slope, while the southern entry room floor rises roughly 1.5 to 2 m above the height of the middle room's floor. Further, the doorway between the southern and middle rooms measures about a meter above the floor of the middle room. The bottom-most floor levels use several small stone steps installed directly into bedrock to help enter the threshold.

The middle chamber was almost completely filled in from rock debris and soil from above. We excavated this deposit in natural and arbitrary levels until the original floor level was reached. After clearing the wall collapse debris, we removed an initial layer of loose and dry dark brown soil as OP48sf. This level had common inclusions of small to large rocks and turned up mixed ceramic remains, including Middle Horizon and later styles. OP48A constituted a level of similarly loose dirt, but was very dark grayish brown and ashy in texture. Interbedded lenses of ash and burnt materials were concentrated in the southwest corner of the chamber, suggesting this could have been a hearth area, but the dark soil, the ashy scatters, and pieces of charcoal were dispersed throughout the stratum. Grinding stones and burned animal bones indicate that this area was probably used at the time as a discard area, almost certainly dumped from above. Given the types of artifacts, including a heavy copper-metal axe (Figure 135J) and fancy ceramics, the discard seems to have been from a group of some prestige. Considerable amounts of mixed diagnostic ceramics characterized this stratum, including Chinchawasi 2 (61%), Middle Horizon imported (13.6%), Warmi (11.9%) and Chakwas (3.4%) style pottery. Imported sherds included three blackware-polished, two fine pinkware spoon and three fine orangeware fragments.

OP48B was a dark brown layer directly underneath the black ashy layer. Despite the change in soil color and consistency, there was considerable continuity in the types of cultural remains recovered: including small grinding stones, faunal remains and broken pottery. Notable artifacts included several hammered copper-metal lamina ornaments, two copper-metal shawl pins and a broken obsidian point. The pottery was mostly Chinchawasi 2 phase types (74.5%), followed by Middle Horizon imported (10.4%), Warmi (8.5%), one Chakwas (0.9%) sherd and one Kayán (0.9%) kaolin sherd. The Middle Horizon imported materials included five blackware polished pieces, two Cajamarca, two Cajamarca-related pieces and two fine pinkware spoon fragments.

OP48C consisted of large rock debris containing dense quantities of camelid bone. The soil matrix was similar in color to OP48B, but is somewhat looser. The deposit can be interpreted as the initial destruction of an early occupation of the house structure, first by the tumbling down of large rocks (OP48C), probably from the original construction of the middle chamber itself, and then the immediate dumping of cultural materials over this (OP48B). In this rocky level we encountered bone implements, grinding stones and several copper-metal artifacts, including two complete shawl pins and a copper-metal lamina ornament. The pottery consisted of a large assemblage of broken plainware and 206 sherds of decorated pottery, most

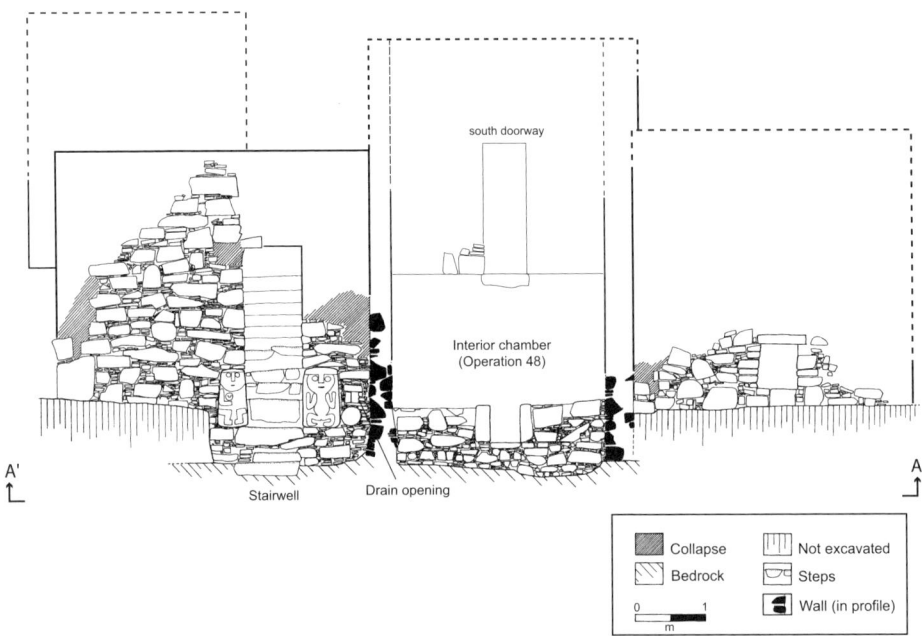

FIGURE 16. North façade of Room Complex 3 (facing south). Given the hilltop location, rooms at Chinchawas were added to existing buildings at different elevations, in modular and organic fashion. Two- and three-chamber buildings, rectangular in plan, were the basic construction units.

notably Chinchawasi 2 (84%) and Middle Horizon imports (7.8%). The Middle Horizon imported pieces included six fine orangeware fragments, six Wari polychrome, two blackware-polished and two fink pinkware spoon fragments.

The topmost portion of OP48D was likely a continuation of the previous level above, in that it consisted of large rocks, uncompacted soils and frequent animal bones and pottery under rocks. When the rocks diminished, however, we encountered a dense midden accumulation of very dark brown soil, mixed with large quantities of animal bone, broken pottery and other cultural remains, including bone implements. OP48D's pottery was represented primarily by Chinchawasi 2 style (94.3%) and Middle Horizon imports (1.4%). The imports consisted of one fine orangeware and two blackware-polished sherds.

OP48E represented the original beaten dirt floor surface of the middle chamber. The level consisted of a compact, near black deposit with small chips of rocks and spalled bedrock. This level lay over bedrock throughout OP48. The unit reached 2.04 m below the modern surface at its northwest interior corner. The floor had several in situ features, including several mortars and pestles and a large batán in the northeast corner that sat on a shallow rise in the bedrock. Other cultural remains included two points, a hafted stone implement (perhaps a clod breaker; Figure 124C) and a stone spindle whorl (Figure 125M). In addition, there was a low masonry wall in the southwest corner built directly above bedrock. This feature was probably the support for a low platform and work surface for domestic activities within the chamber. In the southeast corner, against an outcrop of bedrock, was evidence of a small hearth. Of the 37 diagnostic sherds found in OP48E, 33 were Chinchawasi 2 phase and four were fine orangeware sherds. The primary construction and use of OP48 likely correspond to the early Chinchawasi 2 occupation.

In sum, levels OP48sf, OP48A and OP48B consisted mainly of Chinchawasi 2 debris mixed with some intrusive Warmi and Chakwas materials. These levels can be considered a single massive deposit of reworked refuse and wall debris from above; the topmost part showed signs of burning, suggesting deliberate destruction. Stratigraphically, OP48C had more integrity and represented the deposition of Chinchawasi 2 trash, especially camelid bone; the level post-dated the original use of the chamber, but predated the destruction stratum above. Underneath, intact deposits and the original floor (OP48D and OP48E, respectively) were excavated, indicating that the initial building and use of the middle chamber occurred during Chinchawasi 2. The general associations found in OP48 can be extended for the rest of the complex, including the stairway, entrance and the structures east of the stairwell.

### Operation 50

OP50 was a clearing and excavation operation (measuring 2 by 3 m) in the northern portion of Room Complex 3. The work sought to elucidate the relationships between the staircase, stone sculptures and floor outside the structure. Two levels were defined. The first was OP50sf, which was the modern surface level. Here we encountered the combination of wall debris and soil present also in the upper strata of OP48. The second level, OP50A, continued the wall debris and soil level, and reaches bedrock. Warmi phase remains indicate that domestic refuse was discarded over the buildings after the room complex fell into disrepair.

Operation 50 west (OP50w) was an excavation just outside the façade of Room Complex 3. Located at the foot of the central staircase, the operation (1.5 by 1 m) confirmed that the upper refuse deposits reflected post-Chinchawasi 2 phase destruction and discard activity. Below, Chinchawasi materials accumulated at the very lowest (floor) level, 55 cm below the modern surface, and were associated with two flat staircase stones.

### Operation 51

In OP51 in the southeast portion of Room Complex 3 we investigated the remains of a small room and platform (Figure 18). The operation followed the dimensions of the building, measuring 3.7 m long and 2.9 wide at the front (north) and 2.3 m wide at the back (south). Because the entire structure was underneath wall collapse from above, our initial work here consisted of rock clearing and then defining the structure through excavations. Underneath the pile of rocks was a very shallow surficial layer of soil and cultural debris.

The excavation consisted of only two fairly homogeneous levels, OP51sf and

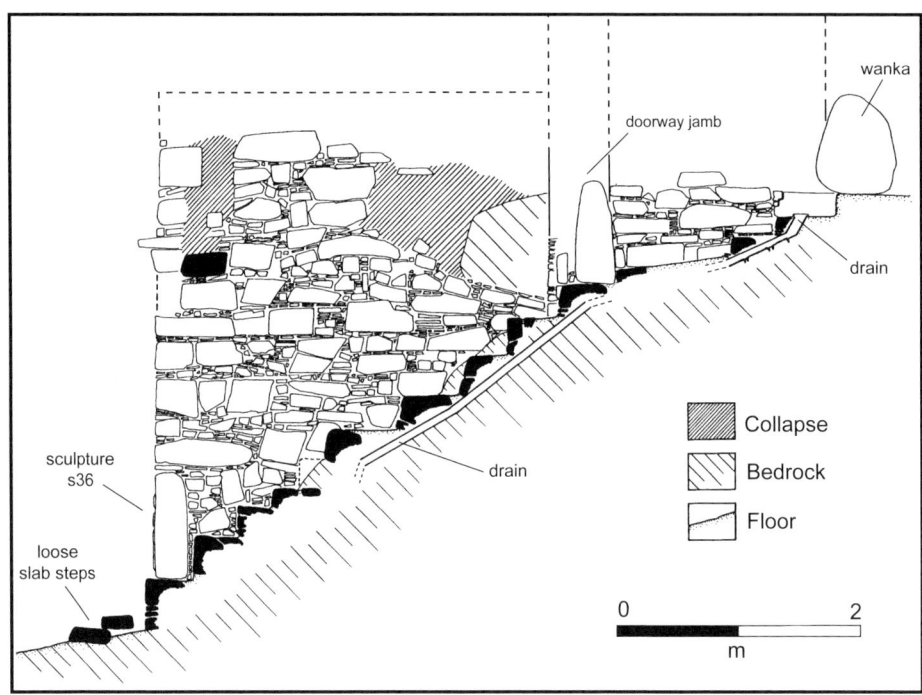

FIGURE 17. Section of Room Complex 3 stairwell, facing east. Loose slab steps were added to the staircase. The buildings no longer have their roof structures, but most probably stood roughly 4 to 6 m tall.

OP50A. We encountered no diagnostic artifacts in OP51sf, but found eight phase diagnostics from later phases in OP51A. The ceramics suggest primary use during the late Middle Horizon occupation of Chinchawas, probably after Middle Horizon 2. It is likely that the post-Chinchawasi 2 midden and rubble levels of OP50 and OP48 resulted from general domestic activities associated with OP51. The deepest excavated part of OP51 was at the back of the structure, 70 cm below the modern surface.

OPERATION 53

OP53 was the excavation of the east building in Room Complex 3. The operation followed the irregular interior dimensions of the chamber (ca. 2.9 by 2 m). The east wing is composed of two chambers: a primary room to the north and a smaller southern room. Like the west wing, the floors of each room are on separate levels and thus accord a duplex-like quality to the building. Access into OP53 is through the south chamber. There is a well-made doorway and, as in OP48, a steep drop onto the floor of the primary chamber. There is also a series of stone steps installed into bedrock connecting the lower floor with the doorway to the south room.

The deposition within the primary chamber was very similar to that found in

OP48. It consisted of a thick initial layer of recent wall rubble (OP53sf) underlain by a black ashy deposit of midden refuse and wall debris (OP53A), then a dark reddish brown level (OP53B), which was the original floor level. The basal level, OP53C, was an arbitrary level change within the same stratum, but was essentially sterile. The unit went down to a maximum depth of 1.8 m below the modern surface in the northwest corner.

Despite the stratigraphic and general architectural similarities, there were several features that distinguish the eastern portion (OP53) from the western (OP48). First, there were far fewer artifacts found in OP53. Second, in the northwest corner of the floor there was a stone-lined construction, quadrangular in plan and measuring approximately 30 by 40 cm. The bottom of the pit extended to bedrock, 40 cm below the floor level, which was even with the top of the stone lining. There were very few artifacts within this pit, except several Chinchawasi sherds and the neck of a crude face-neck vessel. There were, however, thin interbedded lenses of ash within, suggesting small and not very intensive episodes of burning. Finally, on the southwest corner around a natural overhang of the bedrock, a masonry wall formed a pocket-like, walled-in recess. The recess contained only a soft, whitish ashy soil, with some broken potsherds in the Chinchawasi style and snail shells. There were also several camelid bones, suggesting the burning of offerings.

Level OP53B was the primary occupation stratum of the building and corresponds to OP48D and OP48E. Almost all the phase diagnostics (n=33) were Chinchawasi 2 style (93.5%) and three were imports (press-molded, Cajamarca-related and fine orangeware). Notable artifacts included a large trapezoidal copper-metal plate (Figure 134N) that was folded and perforated, and was probably an adornment or cutting tool.

The differential patterning between the east and west buildings indicates spaces with different functions. The two unique architectural features of OP53 distinguish the primary room. The small size of the principal chamber and the lack of household implements such as grinding stones and bone tools indicate that the east wing was not a typical domestic dwelling. Rather, our data suggest that the small, walled-in recess was used for a dedicatory offerings or small-scale storage, perhaps of venerated objects. And the stone-lined feature probably functioned as a pit for intermittent burning episodes, perhaps of small ritual offerings organized at the household level.

### Room Complex 4

Fifteen meters to the west of Room Complex 3, the clearing of wall collapse revealed the remains of another construction complex. Designated Room Complex 4, these structures form part of the larger building program north of Terrace 1. Compared to Room Complex 3, Room Complex 4 lies much closer to the fallen rubble of Terrace 1. Much of the southern end is unreachable, buried underneath a massive slope of collapsed material. Farther north, clearing activities encountered an enclosed patio space, perhaps to pen animals or for open-air domestic activities.

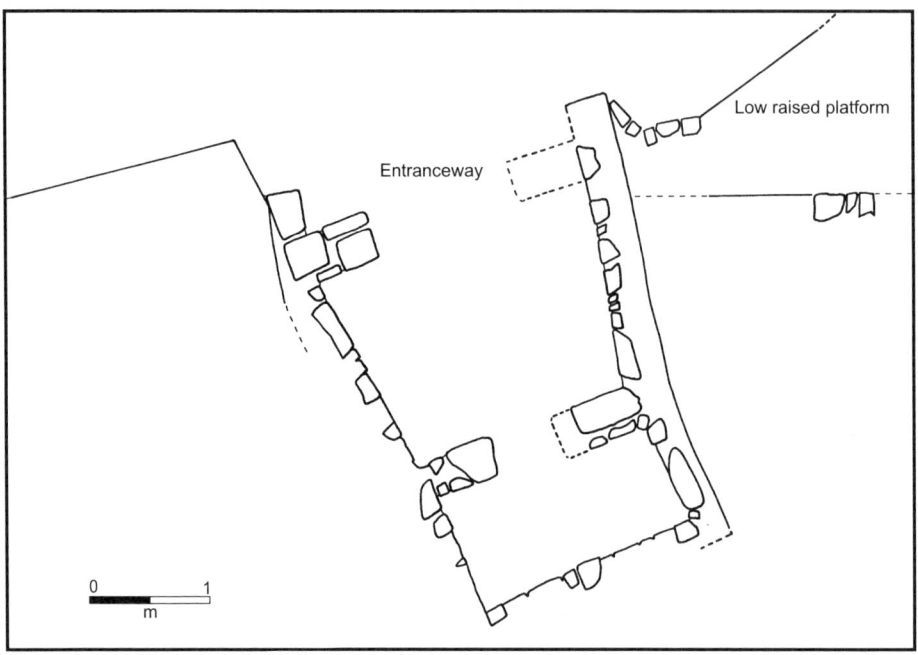

Figure 18. Plan of southeast structure (Operation 51), Room Complex 3. A wide threshold allows access into an open patio area.

Operation 49

OP49 was an excavation of two agglutinated rooms within the larger complex (Figure 19). It is possible that additional rooms were part of the original structure in the south. To the north, OP49 is delimited by a wall that was exposed, for safety reasons, only on the interior face. The operation followed the general dimensions of the two-room building, which was about 4.2 m long and 4.3 m wide (eastern end).

Except for some distinct features, the ground plan of OP49 has an architectural layout consistent with the domestic architecture from the rest of the site, that of a two-chambered house structure. The main chamber is entered through a southern passageway, which affords protection from upvalley winds and unwanted access from below. A stair provides the transition from the doorway to a large meter-wide platform that was also the cooking area for the structure. On the top platform, excavations recovered evidence for food preparation activities, including a large batán, several grinding stones and several bone implements. The platform was built directly above bedrock and the masonry carefully follows its irregularities. At the east end, there is a small niche in the north façade of the platform that could have been used to hold small items and tools. We did not encounter cultural materials within the feature.

The main chamber itself is roughly square in plan, and measures 3.2 m in maximum length and 2.7 m in maximum width. In the west end, a small door, for which only the sill and southern jamb remain, furnishes entry to a small west chamber. Our excavations were conducted in both rooms. The large principal room was designated Room 1 (Ambiente 1) and the smaller west chamber Room 2 (Ambiente 2).

Six levels were excavated in Room 1. The first three were somewhat arbitrary divisions of a deep overburden of ancient domestic debris and rubble from above. The final three levels featured an ashy debris and wall debris level (OP49C) covering the original floor surface (OP49D) and an underlying floor fill (OP49E), which evened the bedrock surface for habitation.

The thick debris level of OP49sf, OP49A and OP49B contained mainly Chinchawasi 2 ceramics, with some intrusive Warmi, Chakwas and imported Middle Horizon style fragments. These levels also had notable discarded items: one stone camelid miniature (Figure 122B); two ceramic figurines representing an anthropomorph and a llama; a bone spindle whorl; and one hammered copper-metal lamina.

OP49C began an ashy debris deposit and was very rich in animal bones and pottery. Diagnostics included Chinchawasi 2 ceramics (63.6%) and substantial amounts of imported Middle Horizon materials (30.3%), suggesting that this grayish black soil stratum formed during this period. Two obsidian points were also found in this level.

OP49D was a hard beaten dirt deposit with substantial amounts of Chinchawasi 1 phase domestic debris and pottery (91.9%). This represented the original floor surface of the building, which extended throughout the house. From the principal room, including its platform, we recovered items of everyday domestic use such as bone implements and various grinding stones, including a large flat milling stone batán on the platform's west side. In the main room's floor we also encountered a copper-metal lamina. OP49E was a subfloor fill composed of dense soil matrix with frequent small, unworked rocks, most of which were bedrock spalls. This stratum contained very little material, but included Chinchawasi 1 pottery, a bead and several broken bone tool fragments. Bedrock was reached in the northern portion of the excavation, 2.52 m below modern surface.

An AMS radiocarbon measurement (see Table 1) was taken for a wood charcoal sample from OP49D, found directly beneath the batán on the kitchen platform. The sample yielded a radiocarbon age of 1375 ± 45 B.P. (A.D. 575 ± 45 uncalibrated, or A.D. 661 ± 45 calibrated, with a 2-sigma range of A.D. 610 to 763). The age fits well within the time range expected for the Chinchawasi 1 phase and accords with the rest of the cultural stratigraphy in OP49.

In Room 2, the deposit was not nearly as dense and deep, and only two levels were defined: OP49sf(a2) and OP49A(a2). The diagnostics consisted mainly of Chinchawasi ceramics, with three fragments of Kayán kaolinite.

In summary, the OP49 structure of Room Complex 4 was a Chinchawasi 1 residence occupied by the latter part of the Early Intermediate Period. In general, the layout resembles other residential structures at Chinchawas: a multiroom

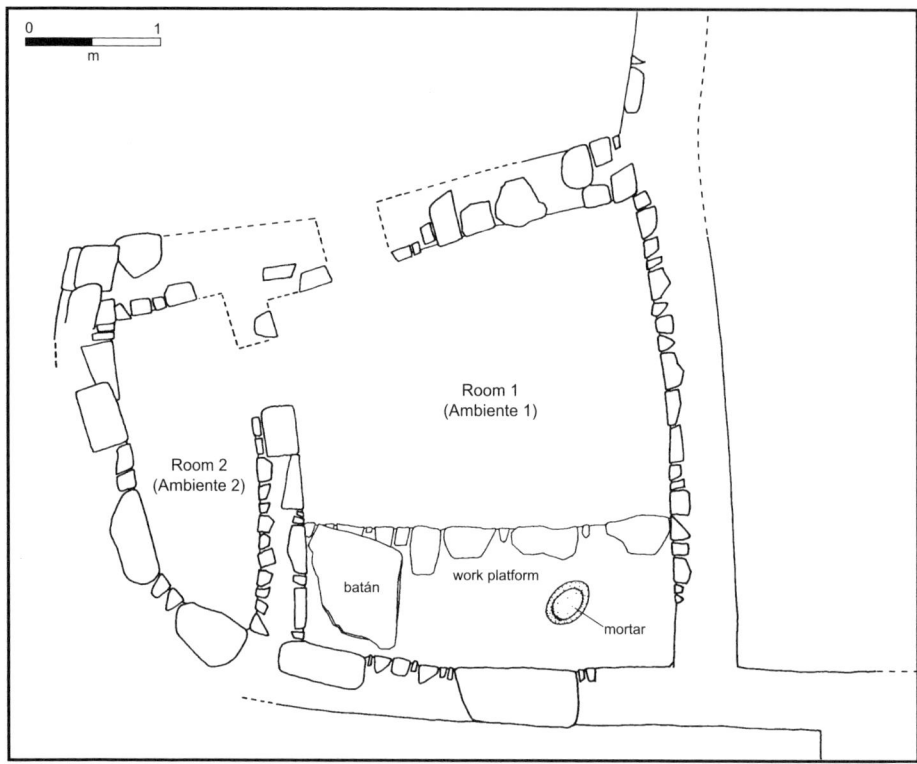

Figure 19. Excavated structure (Operation 49) in Room Complex 4. Large grinding stones, other tools, and domestic debris were uncovered atop a low raised platform on the southern end of the operation.

structure (two- or three-chamber) with one primary chamber dedicated to food preparation and eating. The structure adjoins a small open enclosure that would have functioned for open-air household activities.

## Room Complex 5

Room Complex 5 is located in the western central portion of Sector 1 (Figure 11). One building, OP45, was investigated because of its good preservation and central location. The structure was part of a larger complex, as the western and eastern end walls of OP45 continue uninterrupted to the north to form the lateral walls of four other structures. The rest of this complex is less well defined, as it was not excavated. It looks to be open without interior partition walls, perhaps used for the temporary corralling of animals or for household activities. No passageway connects OP45 directly with the rest of Room Complex 5.

### Operation 45

OP45 (Figure 20), a shallow excavation of the interior of a house structure, was located centrally between Enclosure 1 and Terrace 2. The structure has a rectangular layout and measures 3.8 m by 6.4 m. Today most of its foundations are visible on the surface and survive to a maximum height of 60 cm above the level of the modern surface. During the course of clearing wall rubble, the eastern face of a low platform was uncovered; this elevated OP45 above the floor of Enclosure 1.

OP45's walls are made of the wanka–pachilla style masonry and show very good preservation compared with other structures in the same area. The structure has three chambers: an entry "porch," a larger middle chamber and an end chamber. OP45 was entered from the west. Only the basal stones of the entrance foundation wall survive today. The entry chamber (Ambiente 2) is an irregularly shaped room, with a southern wall that sags inward.

The middle chamber (Ambiente 1) is entered through an opening to the north. While there is a southern partition wall, there is no definite counterpart in the north, although there are several aligned flagstones. The middle chamber, measuring roughly 2.5 by 2 m, is the largest of the three rooms and is divided into two spaces: the lower northern end and a slightly higher southern end. An alignment of low-lying flat stones extends a natural rise in the bedrock, creating a low platform about 10 cm above the floor in the southern area.

The easternmost end chamber (Ambiente 3) is the smallest room of the three, with maximum dimensions of 0.80 by 2.90 m. A small 20 cm opening between two partition walls furnishes entry. There is also a small, narrow channel built into the southern end of the chamber wall. The channel measures 10 cm in height, 14 cm in width, and spans the thickness of the wall; it therefore connects this chamber with the exterior and perhaps functioned to draw air into the chamber. It could have also been used to secure a perishable door across the passage.

Our excavations focused on the interior spaces of OP45. The depth of deposit throughout the room was fairly shallow, measuring 40 to 65 cm. OP45sf was the modern surface level, a dark brown loose soil with granular texture and ashy deposits. There were common inclusions of roots and small to large stones, presumably the result of wall collapse and surficial erosion processes. Cultural materials were small and eroded, but included eight diagnostic sherds: seven Kayán kaolinite sherds and one piece of porcelain. OP45A was essentially a continuation of the previous surface level with fewer roots and large rocks. Although plainware pottery was common, only three diagnostics (all Recuay kaolin) were identified in this artificial level. OP45B constituted a more compact layer of hard, very dark grayish brown soil of a thin, beaten dirt floor above bedrock. Charcoal flecks were especially common in the middle chamber. We encountered a large angular batán in the northwestern part of the middle chamber and its companion implement, a large hand grinding stone nearby. There were 10 diagnostic sherds in OP45B: seven were Kayán phase kaolinite, one was a local Warmi fragment and two were press-molded pieces.

The small diagnostic ceramic sample and general architectural style indicate Recuay cultural associations for the construction and initial use of the house structure. The late Middle Horizon fragments could be intrusive or part of a reoccupation. The location of the batán suggests that the northern end of the middle cham-

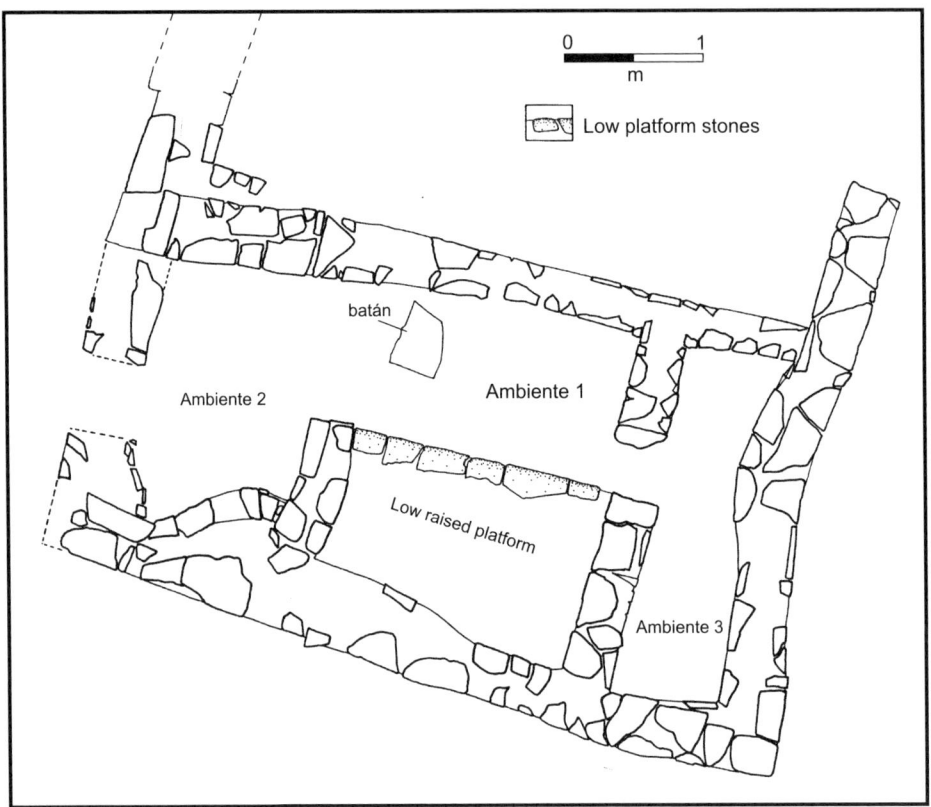

Figure 20. Plan of excavated structure (Operation 45) in Room Complex 5.

ber was used as a food preparation area. The ashy consistency of the OP45B floor surface also indicates preparation activities. The southern platform was probably a small multi-use area for eating, food preparation and sleeping. Except for pottery, no other cultural remains were encountered in the end chamber, suggesting that it was used for storage or sleeping.

## Room Complex 6

### Operation 52

Room Complex 6 is located north of Room Complex 4: clearing and excavations were conducted as OP52 (Figure 21). The large well-preserved walls of the construction are visible on the surface, but the full plan of the building was not revealed until there was a systematic clearing of the area.

The building's ground plan is roughly rectangular, defined by four large perimeter walls. The north façade, 5 m in length, is solid masonry built atop bedrock and currently stands 2.9 m in height. The side walls run between 4.5 and 5 m from the back wall. The entrance on the east side was largely destroyed. The southern wall is formed by masonry facing over a natural rising fracture in the bedrock. Some parts of the back (south) wall rise to 1.2 m above bedrock.

An east–west partition wall defines a long interior chamber located in the north. The chamber measures 4 m long, 1 m wide at the base, and 1.9 m at its maximum height. It is entered through a low doorway opening in the partition wall. Just south of this opening is a small compartment formed by short parallel north–south walls and masonry on the south face. The deepest part of the compartment, built on bedrock, measured 1.18 m below the modern surface.

We excavated within the chamber and in the open patio area. The unit within the patio (OP52s) was essentially a 1 m wide trench south of the partition wall. It extended for 4.7 m (east–west) and had a maximum depth of 1.08 m at the northeast corner of the trench. The excavation defined four levels underneath the rocks of a destruction rubble level. The first two levels were essentially mixed arbitrary divisions and included Warmi and Chakwas style sherds. The underlying two levels, OP52B and OP52C, contained a preponderance of Chinchawasi 2 phase pottery.

The excavations also defined two levels for the chamber interior (up to 4.2 m long and 0.93 m wide). Underneath a Warmi-associated stratum were Chinchawasi 2 phase deposits (OP52c.A). Notable remains included a stone spindle whorl (Figure 125Q) and a bone needle. Along the north wall we encountered a secondary human burial of a juvenile with the skull placed over ribs and some of the long bones. The burial lay above the original surface of the chamber and therefore likely post-dated the original use of the building. There were deposits associated with the original surface of the floor, especially in the eastern end of the chamber where it was considerably deeper (40 cm below the modern surface to bedrock).

The exact function of the area sampled by OP52 remains unclear. The excavations yielded far fewer remains than expected. Considering the amount of domestic pottery within the chamber and open patio, however, the construction likely had a domestic character. The building layout is different than the layout of other residential buildings at Chinchawas in several ways. First, the long chamber uses corbel vaulting. The north façade wall and the interior partition wall both have a series of short flat rocks jutting inwards to form a conical dome-like interior space. It is unclear how high the original building stood or whether there was a small second story. Regardless, the chamber is the tallest roofed space at Chinchawasi and has masonry of a consistent fine quality. The two short parallel walls forming the small compartment are also puzzling, as we did not encounter artifacts there. Perhaps the walls were buttresses for the load-bearing partitions. It is also possible that the compartment furnished a small space for storage, offerings or even burials.

## The Torreón

The Torreón structure occupies a natural circular rise in the eastern part of the Chinchawas ridgetop. The apex, at 3,853 masl, constitutes the highest part of Sec-

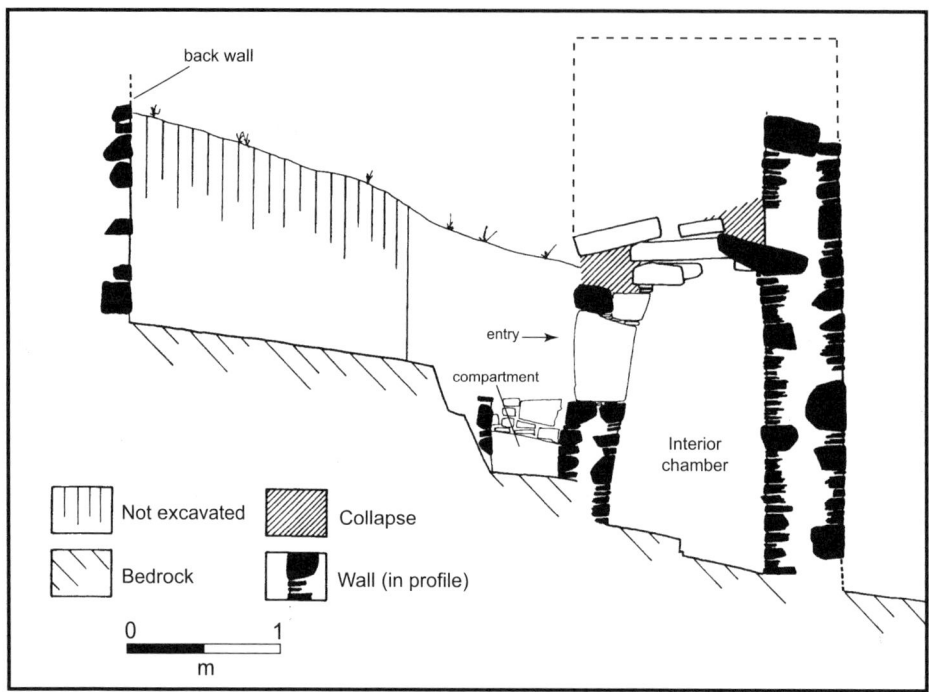

Figure 21. Profile of tall structure (Operation 52), Room Complex 6, facing west. On the right is a tall narrow building, with one long chamber, entered from the back. Underneath the small entryway is a small quadrangular compartment; it was found largely devoid of artifacts, but probably was an offering or burial space. To the rear of the building is small walled and unroofed area.

tor 1. The bedrock provides a natural platform for construction. The area, in addition to its location and vantage, may have held importance for its large natural outcroppings of grayish white bedrock. The outcrops were incorporated as integral segments of the structure, including a prominence in the center. Surficial evidence and pottery indicated that there were important remains underneath the modern surface, despite our expectation that the depth of deposit would be quite shallow.

*The Torreón Structure*

Operation 54

Our excavation took the form of a 4 by 8 m unit (Figure 22). Although there was no surficial evidence of architecture, circular wall foundations began to emerge several centimeters into the excavation. The concentric walls extend as arcs along the entire length of the operation. The deposits were very shallow throughout, from 20 to 60 cm below the modern surface. The initial level (OP54sf) was the modern surface level, a soft light grayish brown with roots and eroded ceramics of the Chinchawasi, Warmi and Chakwas styles. The next level (OP54A) was a continuation of OP54sf, but was somewhat harder and darker grayish brown. Both plainware and decorated ceramics (50 sherds) were more plentiful in this level, which had mixed ceramics from the Kayán to Chakwas phases. A camelid or deer cranial spoon was found in this level, as well as a portion of a copper-metal shawl pin.

OP54B began a series of intact superimposed levels that contained evidence of considerable burning activity in the eastern side of the pit, giving the soil a very light gray brown color and ashy texture. This deposit developed both within and outside the circular building foundations and therefore is likely associated with its use. Of the 27 diagnostic sherds, nearly all were Chinchawasi 2 style and early Middle Horizon contemporary.

The ashy deposit in the eastern side was especially concentrated outside the inner wall of the structure and was documented as a different locus: OP54B(cen). Today only the interior facing of the wall has survived; most of the outer facing was destroyed. Level OP54B(cen) was outside the circular wall, where the ash was especially dense and cultural remains were very rich. Of the 53 diagnostics, most were Chinchawasi style (83%). In association with these were three copper-metal artifacts, including a complete needle and a complete awl-like implement. There was also one cranial spoon and several broken obsidian tool fragments.

The next level (OP54C) was the basal level directly underneath OP54B(cen) outside of the circular Torreón structure. In texture it was basically a continuation of the ashy deposit found above, but was darker and moister. The high status items continued in this level, including a fine nail-top copper-metal pin (Figure 134A), a stone spindle whorl (Figure 125O) and two perforated shell ornaments (Figure 133E and F). Several domestic items included bone spatulas and a stone axe (Figure 124B). Fancy ceramics were also common: of the 28 diagnostics, 25 were Chinchawasi 1 phase and three were Kayán kaolinite.

Within the Torreón structure, three additional stratigraphic levels were defined. The first level underneath OP54B was OP54C(t) and contained 11 phase diagnostics, 10 of which were Chinchawasi 2 and one a Wari polychrome piece. OP54D(t) represented the floor level, which was part flagstone and part bedrock. The soil was dark brown and contained bedrock spalls. Of the 37 diagnostic sherds encountered in OP54D(t), all were Chinchawasi 1 style. A copper-metal sheet artifact was found within the building at this level. The final level defined for the interior of the Torreón structure was OP54E(t), represented by soil within the interstices of the flagstones and any soil in the unit underneath the previous level. The soil was essentially the same, with the same bedrock spalls and occasional fragments of charcoal flecks. Of the 25 diagnostics, all but two were Chinchawasi 1.

Faunal remains were quite common in the operation, especially in Levels A, B and B(cen). The total assemblage contained at least six camelids (the minimum number of individuals, or MNI = 6), in addition to a range of other animals, including one deer, several birds, three cuys and three smaller rodents.

The evidence from OP54 indicates that the Torreón structure was built by the Chinchawasi 1 phase and was used until Chinchawasi 2 times. The circular building is unique at Chinchawas. It has an interior low-step platform ringing the circular

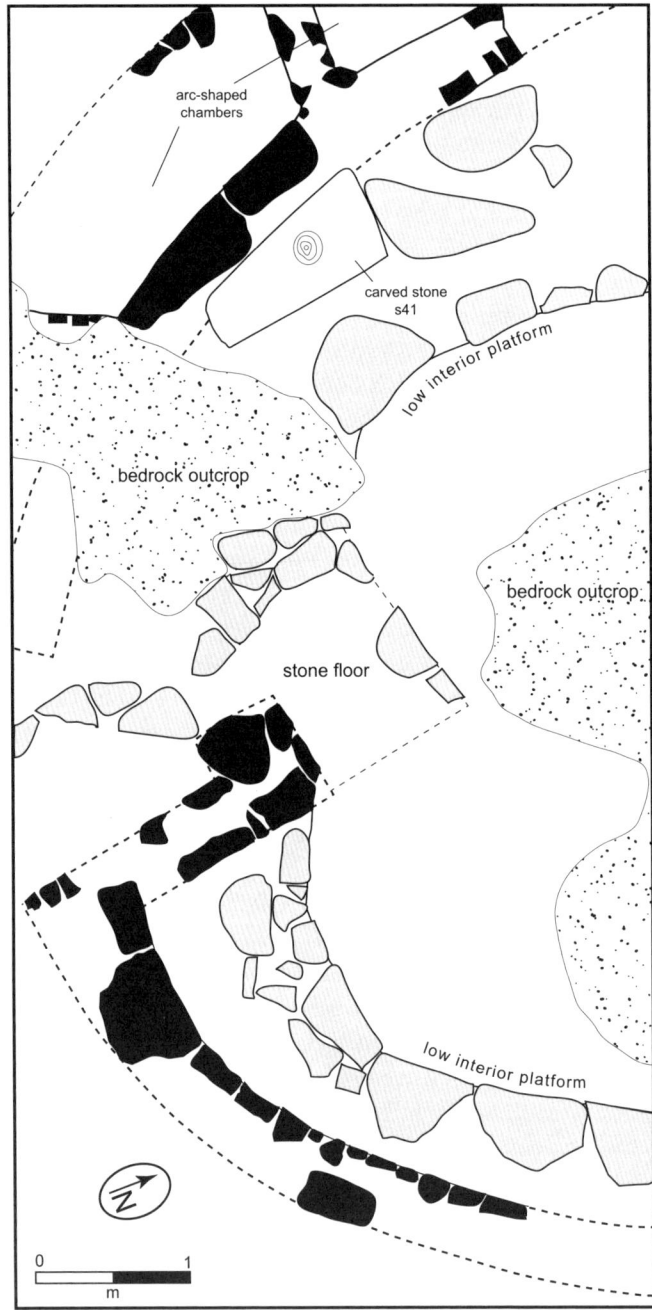

FIGURE 22. Plan of the Torreón structure excavation (Operation 54). Located in the topmost part of Sector 1, the structure has a circular plan incorporating and surrounding a prominent bedrock outcrop. It features a low platform, possibly a bench, on the outer wall of the inner chamber. Arc-shaped chambers were created by adding radial projections. Excavations uncovered fancy pottery, large amounts of animal bone, metal artifacts and other rare objects, suggesting repeated episodes of camelid consumption and display or offering activities, or both.

wall, perhaps used for sitting and viewing special activities that took place inside. These activities could have been partly related to the outcrops of rock on which the building was located. At least one entry was from the south; it was oriented towards the southeast and roughly aligned with another entrance on an outer wall.

The building had at least three concentric walls, with radiating partitions forming segmented "arc chambers" around the structure. Such circular structures elsewhere in the Recuay heartland, such as at La Pampa and Yayno, are also in prominent locales of important sites (Tello 1929; Terada 1979; Lau 2000). Curiously, one of the fallen wankas that formed part of the interior wall has a carved design of concentric circles (Figure 22). The interior floor of this building was part flagstone and part beaten dirt. Although it remains unclear what specific activities occurred in the interior, directly outside in the eastern end we found considerable evidence for burning activities against the exterior construction wall or perhaps within one of the peripheral arc chambers. Overall, the plentiful faunal remains (found inside and outside the structure) suggest that episodic, but intensive, consumption or offering of meat, or both, were among the prominent activities at the Torreón.

The ashy deposit was also very rich in high status items, suggesting that burning was associated with their discard or use as votives in episodic offering rituals. Within the inner structure, high status items are far fewer, but fancy pottery is very common and in a better state of preservation, including several whole or near complete vessels. We may therefore conjecture that whatever took place within the structure also involved the use of these vessels. The lack of domestic implements and general refuse also indicates special activities in the building. We do not have a clear end date for the use of the Torreón structure, but it probably stopped serving its original purpose during the end of the Chinchawasi 2 phase, mainly because later pottery styles do not occur in primary contexts. By Warmi times, the building fell into disuse.

## Conclusions

The excavations in Sector 1 offered key evidence to help reconstruct the spatial and functional organization of the ancient occupations at Chinchawas. Three main forms have been described in this chapter: room complexes, enclosures and a circular walled building known as the Torreón structure. The results from the study indicate that these constructions were among the most important architectural contexts for the residential and ceremonial activities of the inhabitants of Chinchawas.

*Room Complexes*
Residential life in ancient Chinchawas centered in the room complexes of Sector 1. The investigations documented six such complexes, and at least several more probably lie underneath the rubble covering parts of the site. These constructions featured agglutinated buildings (those that share walls) and were often connected

to open patio areas. Each complex contained at least two rectangular buildings or chambers (probably houses), and as many as five. Some complexes could have had additional buildings, which today are buried; only intensive excavation and clearing will reveal their full layout. All evidence suggests that these complexes were the domestic residences and work loci of extended families or small corporate groups, probably numbering from around 12 to 20 people.

The stratigraphic evidence indicates that room complexes were especially prominent during the Chinchawasi phases. The house forms and their contents were very consistent, both across the site synchronically and across phases. Most dwellings had fairly similar dimensions (about 4 to 5 m long and 2 to 3 m wide) and consisted of two or three chambers with a single entranceway. The main large room often contained a large batán grinding stone and other remains of food preparation and discard. A smaller back room connected to the main chamber and, in most cases, was found to be very clean; the back rooms were likely used mainly for sleeping or storage of perishables and food.

The room complexes are characterized by flexibility of arrangement. No two complexes are exactly alike. Buildings seem to have been added and renovated as necessary, without following rigid plans (e.g., axial, symmetric or orthogonal layouts). The only dispositions adhered to were an interest in contiguity, containment within the overall complex and the sharing of patios. This would suggest that the groups who used the complexes were also flexible, adding members or reducing their size as needed.

There is also some variability in the construction quality and architectural features of the room complexes. For example, the best preserved case, Room Complex 3, boasted two-story buildings, a central staircase, fine stonemasonry featuring in situ stone sculpture (as wall elements) and drainage works, while others (e.g., Room Complex 4) lack such elaboration. Therefore, some room complexes seem to manifest differences in the capacity to organize architectural projects.

The earliest residences at Chinchawas were in the uppermost parts of Sector 1. There seems to have been a gradual expansion of buildings outwards and downhill. Residences (e.g., Room Complex 4) in the northwest part of Sector 1 were buried by wall collapse and by erosion. In other complexes, after their initial use, some rooms (such as in OP48 of Room Complex 3) were used as special midden areas, sometimes for episodic, massive deposition of camelid bone and broken fine and plainware ceramics. This type of discard is very similar to that found in other parts of the site associated with feasting activities and subsequent discard patterning during the Chinchawasi occupation of the site (Lau 2002). Although the discard of material was certainly purposeful, it is unclear whether the discard sought to highlight specific buildings or areas previously thought of as important or sacred.

### Enclosures and the Torreón Structure

Two enclosures were identified in Sector 1 and both were sampled with test pits. In general, the enclosures are fairly small, measuring around 15 to 20 m long and about 10 m wide. These constructions were especially interesting because of their fine wanka–pachilla stonemasonry and association with stone sculptures found today on the surface (Lau 2006b). Although most of the sculptures are not in situ, they may have been architectural elements of the enclosures or nearby buildings (Lau 2001, 2006b).

In general, the deposits within the enclosure interiors were shallow and fairly clean of material, probably a result of episodic cleaning. Materials were especially scant in Enclosure 1, but some fine ceramics, fancy objects and a drainage canal were found in Enclosure 2, which dated to the early occupation of Chinchawas. Adjacent to these enclosures, however, were areas that were used for intensive food preparation and the episodic dumping of large quantities of refuse; see descriptions of Terrace 4 (below) and OP48 (above). Elsewhere, the patterns of consumption, discard and display have been interpreted as the results of corporate feasting activities and ancestor ceremonies in Sector 1 in the enclosures (Lau 2002). Such activities ceased during the Warmi phase, when parts of the enclosures fell into disrepair, were appropriated for other more utilitarian buildings, or both.

The Torreón structure was also a focus of ceremonial activities in Sector 1 during the Kayán and Chinchawasi occupations of Chinchawas. The structure is notable because it was located at the highest part of Sector 1, encompasses low bedrock outcrops, and is the only monumental building on the site with multiple concentric walls. The Torreón's concentric walls are of fine boulder and spall stonework. A fallen boulder upright has a petroglyph of concentric circles (Lau 2006b:211). The walls were built around a small outcrop of light-colored andesite, which rises in the central part of the interior space towards the north. Along the wall of the innermost room is a low, circular bench or platform, probably for observing rituals in a small private setting. Small arc chambers formed by radial partitions were probably dedicated to storing or displaying ritual objects and offerings. Excavations in the Torreón structure documented evidence of burning and offerings of camelid meat, along with fancy bowls and special objects made of rare stone, metal and shell.

In sum, the Sector 1 investigations of Chinchawas documented a range of domestic and ceremonial activities. General domestic activities centered on room complexes, while special ceremonial activities focused on open enclosures and the Torreón structure. In general, the dimensions of the site grew over time, at its largest during the Chinchawasi 2 and Warmi occupations. The form and arrangement of residential complexes at Chinchawas shows strong continuity. Ceremonial practices in Sector 1 changed dramatically by the beginning of the Warmi phase. The enclosures and the Torreón structure had fallen into disuse by this time, and ceremonial activities came to emphasize the Sector 2 cemetery area (see Chapter 5).

# CHAPTER FOUR

# Excavations of Terrace Areas, Sector 1

The Chinchawas investigations included archaeological excavations of "terrace areas" in Sector 1 (Figure 11). These are long unroofed spaces, typified with a long wall on the lower, or outer, edge. Many of the terrace areas only resemble modern terraces because of infilling and intermittent use as small agricultural plots today. Our excavations show that, in antiquity, most of the outer walls of these "terraces" were largely freestanding. They served as defensive walls and partitioned open interior spaces on the ridgetop.

Although the term "terrace" is useful for identification purposes, in no way should these areas be associated a priori with agricultural terraces, nor should their walls be assumed to be for retention purposes. Terrace areas were open activity spaces and served diverse functions for the community, including craft activities and refuse discard. Nine terrace areas were defined, and eight of these were examined through excavation sampling. The terrace areas were integral work and activity spaces for the Chinchawas community.

## Terrace 1

Terrace 1 lies directly north of Enclosure 1 and had been used until recently as a small agricultural plot for local farmers. It rises above the northern edge of the main ridgetop, and provides a vantage point over the valley to the north as well as the Casma–Huaraz road directly below. Walls in all directions border Terrace 1. The most prominent is the northern retaining wall. Although of common quality, this wall protects the prehistoric cultural remains from eroding down the steep northern slope.

We opened up a series of test operations after determining that this zone offered the deepest accumulation of prehistoric deposits in the Chinchawas site. The excavations consisted of isolated units (OP10, OP11, OP22 and OP24), as well as a series of adjoining units that can be considered together as a trench (OP9, OP12, OP18, OP19 and OP21). Larger exposures were conducted in the zone during the second field season.

*Terrace 1 East*

OPERATION 11

OP11 (1 by 2 m) was opened to test for stratigraphy and cultural materials in the eastern fringe of the terrace. As in the other pits in the zone, we encountered abundant cultural remains as well as architecture not visible on the surface. A sterile layer was reached at 1.65 m below datum.

OP11sf corresponded to the initial surface layer. OP11A was distinguished from the preceding level by its harder consistency and for the frequent presence of tiny dirt clumps and unworked rocks of variable size, especially at the base of the level. OP11B represented a continuation of the OP11A level with no change in soil color or texture. The rocks found at the basal portion of Level A continued into Level B, frequently with air pockets between them, suggesting rapid local deposition of collapsed construction elements.

OP11C was a darker and more compact soil with the frequent occurrence of large unworked rocks. The stratum contained local Warmi phase pottery as well as fragments of imported wares. Evidence of burning occurred with this fill and wall debris layer. OP11C represents late Middle Horizon reuse of the structure, perhaps to prop water storage containers. In OP11D, a Chinchawasi 2 phase level, we encountered the remains of a large in situ olla in the northern half of the operation. OP11E was a harder, very dark brown soil.

OP11F consisted of a darker brown soil; in the southern half of the pit, OP11F lay directly on bedrock. OP11F represented the floor level for the walls and contained Chinchawasi 1 pottery. The domestic character of the refuse—plainware, lithics and burnt bone—from OP11F indicates that the area defined by the walls was the northeast corner of a domestic residence. OP11G consisted of a hard, sterile level underneath OP11E in the northern half of the operation and contained frequent spalls of bedrock and small stones. The deposit seems to have been associated with the foundation for the structure's entranceway, perhaps to stabilize the basal stones in the trench.

*Terrace 1 West*

OPERATION 10

OP10 (1 by 2 m) was opened to test the northern terrace for stratigraphy and cultural remains. We chose an area that did not have any surficial architecture and that was situated away from the current agricultural plot to the east. Despite some internal variability, OP10sf to OP10D can be considered modern plowzone levels characterized by dark brown soil matrix and dark gray ashy deposits from burning, mixed in with large plowing dirt clods. Artifacts were rare in the plowzone levels.

OP10E and OP10F were similar levels, consisting of more even soil throughout: a dark brown silty loam with fewer dirt clods, but with large rocks interspersed with some air pockets. OP10E and OP10F were deposits over destroyed architecture or rubble. It is unclear whether the deposit was the result of natural or cultural activity. The presence of intrusive modern materials and the mixed phase diagnostics, however, indicate that infilling occurred in the recent past. OP10G was the final level of the operation and was composed of a compact and silty dark brown soil that contained very few artifacts. The pit's excavation reached a depth of 1.98 m.

On the east, north and south sides of the unit we encountered walls built atop bedrock almost completed aligned with the unit's profiles. It seems that OP10G was the only stratum intact from prehistoric times. The walls, however, are original and ancient. At some point in the recent past large stones and a distinctive soil matrix completely covered the original surface. The partial collapse of the east and south walls contributed to the filling in of the area. The surfaces may have been evened to grade the area for farming activities. The filling in seems to have been a relatively rapid and recent process, because there were frequent pockets of air between soil and the large wall debris rocks.

## Operation 22

OP22 was 9 m west of OP10. We excavated the 1 by 2 m test unit to test for stratigraphy and cultural remains in the westernmost part of the northern terrace. OP22sf and OP22A constituted the typical surface layer. OP22A was moister and contained a mix of rolled ceramics, roots, small rocks and significant amounts of lithic debris. OP22B was a hard layer with a rocky soil matrix and substantial mottling. In the southern half of the pit, OP22B was the basal layer above bedrock. To the north we found a harder compact floor. This floor had several ashy deposits within a broken hearth arrangement of burnt stones surrounded by plainware fragments and a grinding stone (*mano*). Only Warmi phase artifacts were found in OP22B and OP22A.

Beneath the beaten dirt floor was another layer of compact dense soil (OP22C), on which was a broken stone pavement. The compact layer and the paving stones represented an earlier floor level. Some of the floor stones formed the capping stones for a drainage canal of elaborate craftsmanship. The canal was stone-lined on three sides, with the base gouged into bedrock. It was almost certainly a continuation of the canal found in OP18 (discussed below) to the east. The canal drained from east to west, leading away from the Terrace 1 area.

There was a small box-like compartment directly above the canal near the western profile of the unit. The feature was made of flat rocks; the opening faced east and was 10 cm long and 6 cm high. The opening proceeded inward about 10 cm and then dropped off into the canal. It is unclear what this feature was used for, except to connect the canal with a feature on the surface. Artifacts were few and associated with the Chinchawasi 2 phase. This is consistent with the associations for the portion of the canal in OP18.

OP22D was a dark brown layer in the north part of the unit, underneath the paving level of the canal stones. There were very few diagnostic artifacts in this level. As the basal level, OP22E was composed of the dark brown matrix of OP22D and mixed with eroding bedrock (gritty light yellow) mottles. OP22E was completely sterile.

Operation 24

Because we did not encounter either nearby surface architecture or subterranean architecture that associated with the canal in OP22, we opened OP24 (1 by 2 m) directly northeast of OP22 to elucidate the context of this unique drainage feature. OP24sf corresponded to the surface layer. OP24A was a harder level in some places, but maintained the color of OP24sf. Near the base of the level we encountered the remains of two intersecting walls that created two distinct areas: the northwest corner and the southern portion of OP24.

The south part of OP24B was much harder and had no distinctive features. Level OP24F, a more compact dark brown layer with frequent inclusions of flat but unworked stones, lay beneath OP24B. The only phase diagnostic for OP24F suggests early Middle Horizon associations. OP24G, between OP24F and bedrock, was a very rocky brownish yellow soil. OP24G contained very little material, but included some plainware sherds of Chinchawasi 2 association.

The northwest corner deposit of OP24B began as a soft and moist soil mixed with dusty ash, and may have been a hearth area. OP24C was excavated in the northwest corner of the unit, bounded by walls OP24-w1 on the west and OP24-w2 on the south. The soil varied from soft to hard with the frequent presence of fist-sized unworked rocks. OP24D represented deposition within the northwest corner of hard brown soil intermingled with a substantial amount of large rocks, interpreted as wall debris. We encountered a mixture of Warmi, Chinchawasi and later phase materials in Levels C and D. OP24C and OP24D probably formed over the course of the area's gradual disuse after the Middle Horizon.

OP24E, beneath OP24D in the northwest corner, was composed of dark brown soil with common inclusion of fist-sized stones. At the base of OP24E we encountered a beaten dirt floor rich with domestic refuse and a small hand grinding stone. The OP24E floor seems to have been laid over a demolished wall (OP24-w3) that parallels OP24-w1; together with the south wall, OP24-w2, they date to the original construction and created a small narrow compartment, perhaps used for storage.

OP24E, including the floor, contained only one phase diagnostic of the Warmi style. The underlying level contained Chinchawasi 2 style ceramics as well as one Wari polychrome sherd. OP24I lay below OP24H in the northwest corner of the unit and contained a softer soil with fewer rocks. OP24I contained only Chinchawasi 1 style ceramics and was associated with the original construction of the building. Although we did not reach bedrock in this corner, we excavated to the footings of the wall as part of OP24I. The soil at these footings was basically sterile at a depth of 1.6 m.

The evidence indicates that the building was built and first used during the Chinchawasi 1 occupation. The narrow gallery or compartment enclosed by parallel walls suggests storage and access from the north. After the Chinchawasi use, the inner wall (OP24-w3) was leveled and a dirt floor put over it, thus expanding the area of usable room in this corner (southeast corner). The artifacts above the floor indicate cooking and domestic activities at this corner during a period of re-use during Warmi times. Because the modern terrace wall occurs immediately to the north and west, the building was either very small or, more likely, destroyed for the most part, having collapsed down the northern ridgetop slope.

*Terrace 1 Center*
We opened five 1 by 2 m test operations in the central zone of Terrace 1 (Figure 11). The zone merited extra attention because of: (1) its intact stratigraphy, with a maximum depth of three meters; (2) the quality and preservation of subsurface architecture; and (3) the presence of an intact Recuay occupation deposit underneath more recent occupations.

OPERATIONS 9, 19 AND 21
OP9 was the initial test unit of the zone and was opened in an area with no surficial architecture. We excavated OP9 until bedrock was reached at a depth of 2.70 m. OP9 provided a rich, intact deposit of Recuay materials (Kayán phase) underneath more recent Chinchawasi and Warmi phase strata. For this reason, it was expanded to the east (OP19) and to the west (OP21). For simplicity, this section will discuss the three operations together.

OP9sf was the typical dry and dusty plowzone level, yielding a variety of mixed ceramics, most very small and eroded. OP9sf corresponded to OP19sf and OP21sf. OP9A was a slightly more compact layer and reddish-brown in color. The level was distinguished mainly on the basis of the frequent presence of hard dirt clods, which were probably the result of recent agricultural plowing. Cultural remains were scarce and mixed in this level. OP9A corresponded to OP19A and OP21A. In OP21 there was a large wall, running east–west, in Level A. Level B in the three pits (OP9B, OP19B and OP21B) was a level of wall rubble and dirt clods. The rocks were sometimes quite large; air pockets indicated a fairly recent and quick destruction process. Cultural materials were rare in this level, but included small pieces of animal bone.

The major feature of Level B in all three pits was the northern wall first appearing in OP21A. The wall, OP9-w1, stretched further east into OP9 and OP19 and, like in OP21, represented the northern limits of those operations. It is likely that the wall ran the length of Terrace 1. It reached nearly 2.5 m deep in some pits; this is even more impressive when one considers that no part of the wall stands to its original height today. Thus the northern wall was probably considerably higher and more imposing in the past. The wall probably served as a northern wall for the entire area, given its size and position.

We found an addition to the northern wall of OP9-w1 in OP21B. It is a north–south wall, OP21-w1, which ran the length of the rest of the unit (1.5 m).

However, it was less well built in masonry and size, and terminated before OP9-w1. Therefore, OP21-w1 was probably an addition dating to after the construction of OP9-w1. OP19C was a continuation of the clod and wall debris layer that began in OP19B; the rocks were probably used in constructions in the past. There was a range of sizes, including larger stones (more than 35 cm) and most frequently the pachilla type flat chinking stones.

The next level, directly beneath the layer of wall rubble, dirt clods and air pockets, was present in all three operations as OP9C, OP19D, OP19E and OP21C. It was generally a layer of a dark brown soil, which contrasted with the clumpy and loose stratum above. But there were also softer, sometimes large, lenses of soil of similar texture and color within this level, although they graded together seamlessly with very little differentiation, except to the trowel.

The level also marked the appearance of concentrated deposits of animal bones and more frequent and better-preserved pottery remains. In addition, several grinding stones in the level suggest that Terrace 1 was used for some domestic activities during the Warmi and Chakwas occupations. It is also possible that the grinding stones were part of the reworked refuse that characterized this level. Late pottery indicated reuse of the wall OP21-w1, probably between the late Middle Horizon and Late Intermediate Period.

OP9D, OP19F, OP21D and OP21E constituted the level corresponding to the initial construction and use of OP21-w1. Compared with the previous level, it was drier, more compact, and hard throughout. At the bottom of this level we encountered a poorly preserved beaten dirt floor, which corresponded to the base of the north–south wall (OP21-w1). Carbon flecks occurred throughout the floor; the remains of a small hearth were at the bottom of OP19F.

OP19 contained another north-south wall addition, OP19-w1. This addition first appeared at this level, and abuts the wall, rather than being integrated into it. Therefore it should predate the construction and initial use of OP21-w1. The pottery from this level belonged predominantly to the Warmi occupation (24 sherds out of 29 identified to phase). Because of its stratigraphic position, the floor was probably laid down late in the Warmi phase.

Underneath the floor level was a layer of yellowish brown soil with a sandy consistency and frequent inclusions of small rocks. This deposit was for the most part sterile, with very few artifacts. This yellow sandy level was represented by OP9E, OP19G, OP19J and OP21F and can be considered an intentional fill that helped grade the surface for the floor detailed above. Frequent large stones at the bottom of this layer underlie the fill. Most of these stones were flat and ordered to provide a uniform floor surface, especially in OP21.

The paving was more intact in the western end of the three pits combined. The stones occurred throughout OP21 and OP9, but seemed only intact as a possible floor in OP21. In OP19, the paving was not encountered, only small stones. Surprisingly, we encountered were very few artifacts on top of or within the soils between the paving stones. The base of the OP19-w1 north–south wall addition was associated with the bottom of OP19J and the use of this floor. Only two diagnostic sherds were encountered in this level, one press-molded and one fine pinkware, both of late Middle Horizon stylistic association.

Underneath the large stones and the yellow sandy layer began a series of alternating rich refuse deposits and floor surfaces containing frequent inclusions of ceramics, animal bone and other artifacts. The first consisted of OP9F, OP19K and OP21H—a dark layer directly below the pavement floor. The soil was largely moist and silty, but there was some yellow-brown mottling with the gritty consistency of the sandy fill layer.

Of the 42 identified decorated diagnostics from this level, 27 were from the Chinchawasi 2 phase (or 62.7%), 10 from the Warmi (23.2%) and five were of an imported polished blackware. The ceramics suggest principal use by Chinchawasi 2 groups. Warmi presence was stronger in OP9F. This refuse layer can be associated with the building and initial use of the east–west wall in Operation 12 (i.e., OP12-w1).

The next layer was distinguished by the gradual disappearance of the yellow sandy mottles and was represented by OP9G and OP21I. The soil was darker, moist and silty, with common inclusions of Chinchawasi 2 pottery. An AMS radiocarbon measurement for a wood charcoal sample from OP21I (see Table 1) yielded a radiocarbon age of 1255 ± 45 B.P. (A.D. 695 ± 45 uncalibrated or A.D. 777 ± 45 calibrated), with a 2-sigma range of A.D. 668 to 888. This age determination fits within the late end of the Chinchawasi phase.

The bottom-most part of the midden layer consisted of OP9H, OP19L and the lower portion of OP21I. A darker black color and deeper stratigraphic position distinguished the new level. We also noted that the soil was moister, but looser than previously, prompting a change in level. An AMS radiocarbon measurement of a sample (wood charcoal or carbonized bone) from OP19L yielded a radiocarbon age of 1395 ± 45 B.P. (A.D. 555 ± 45 uncalibrated or A.D. 655 ± 45 calibrated), with a 2-sigma range of A.D. 600 to 689. This date falls within the expected range of the Chinchawasi 1 phase and pertains to the late Early Intermediate Period.

This midden layer is attributed to the initial use of the large east–west wall, the primary northern boundary of all of Terrace 1. The wall exhibited some of the finest wanka–pachilla stonemasonry at Chinchawas. Its stratigraphic position, cultural affiliation and radiocarbon measurements indicate a building date of around A.D. 600 to 650.

The final level in the three operations consisted of a Kayán phase stratum, represented by OP9I, OP19M and OP21J. The layer was distinguished by a more reddish color, an ashy texture and frequent inclusions of small stones. In the northern part of the operation, the soil was burnt and included concentrations of animal bone and charcoal flecks, suggesting cooking or at least burning activities. Fourteen Kayán kaolinite sherds made up the predominant style represented in the layer. At the base of this reddish Recuay stratum were the remains of a poorly preserved compacted dirt floor. It was best seen in the western portion of the excavation (i.e.,

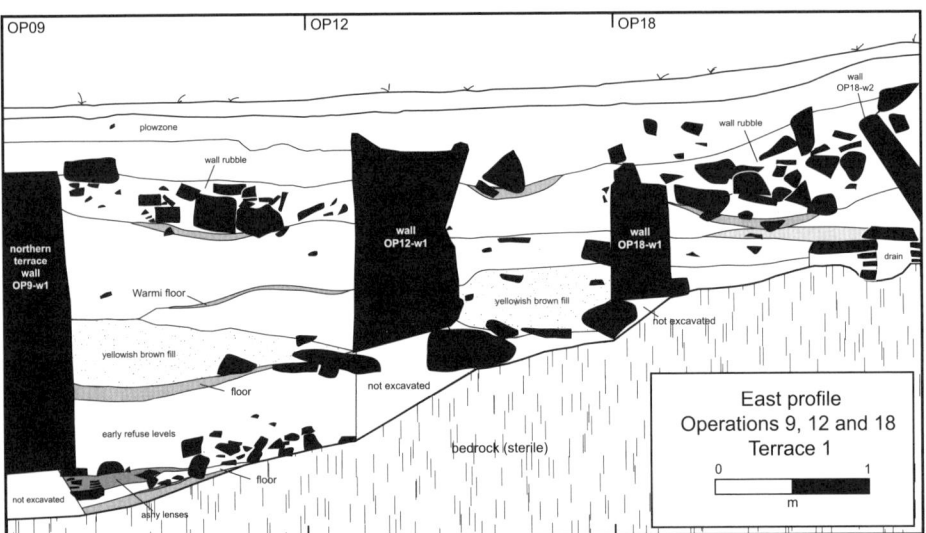

FIGURE 23. East stratigraphic profile of Terrace 1 excavations (Operations 9, 12 and 18). Terrace 1 was intensively re-used throughout the course of Chinchawas's principal occupation. Later groups added walls, fill deposits, drains and floors (some paved) over the course of four or five centuries.

OP21J and portions of OP9I) and was indicated by a much more dense, compact composition. The overlying Recuay deposits, then, seem to have accumulated over this surface.

OP9J was a burned area in the northern third of the pit, composed of a combination of the previously mentioned reddish brown soil and a blackish charcoal-rich soil. It lay directly beneath OP9I, but could have been part of the same use episode(s) that created the burnt area. Diagnostics consisted entirely of Kayán sherds.

An AMS radiocarbon measurement for a wood charcoal sample from OP9J yielded an age of 1710 ± 50 B.P. (A.D. 240 ± 50 uncalibrated or A.D. 360 ± 50 calibrated), with a 2-sigma range of A.D. 233 to 434 (see Table 1). The measurement furnished the earliest age determination for Chinchawas and falls within the range expected for Kayán pottery. The evidence suggests that this zone of Chinchawas, if not the entire site, was not occupied substantially before A.D. 300.

The basal layer in the entire three-pit operation was a silty gray soil bearing a gritty texture (probably from spalling bedrock). The stratum was largely sterile and contained no diagnostic pottery. This basal layer lay directly on bedrock, represented by OP9K and OP21K, and only traces in OP19.

## Operation 12

OP12 (1 by 2 m), directly south of OP9, was excavated to a depth of 2.23 m at its northern end (Figure 23). OP12sf was the typical dry and dusty plowzone level. This surficial layer yielded very small and eroded varieties of pottery. OP12A constituted a slightly more compact layer, was reddish brown and resembled OP9A. The level was distinguished by the presence of hard dirt clods. At the bottom of

OP12A we encountered the remains of an east–west wall, OP12-w1, in the northern half of the operation. We decided at this point to excavate the two different sides as OP12n (north) and OP12s (south).

The stratigraphy of OP12north correlated directly with the stratigraphy of the three-unit operation (OP9, OP19 and OP21). Level B of OP12south (or OP12s.B) consisted of rock rubble and dirt clods, and corresponded to the general level first identified in OP9B. The rocks were sometimes quite large and air pockets indicated that the event was probably fairly recent and quick. Cultural remains included small worn pieces of animal bone and pottery with mixed associations. OP12s.C was a deeper portion of the wall rubble level above. The soil was dark grayish brown, compact, and in some parts troweled out like small balls or pellets. Only a fine pinkware spoon fragment was encountered in this level, although plainware ceramics were abundant.

OP12s.D was the layer of yellowish brown soil defined in OP9E, OP19G, OP19J, OP21F and OP21G. The soil had a sandy consistency with frequent inclusions of small rocks. This deposit was mostly sterile, with a few artifacts of Warmi affiliation. We encountered many large rocks in the yellow sandy soil, suggesting that the level was probably deposited as an intentional fill that graded the surface during Warmi times. OP12s.E is a deeper portion of OP12s.D. The soil was slightly lighter and contained very few artifacts. There were northern (OP12-w1) and southern (OP18-w1) walls in OP12, both built during the Warmi phase to partition spaces along the terrace.

OP12s.F corresponded to the refuse level identified in OP21I, with a darker brown soil with common charcoal flecks. However, the stratum went down only about 10 to 15 cm farther, until the pit reached bedrock. Chinchawasi 1 pottery predominated and is consistent with OP21I.

## Operation 18

OP18 (1 by 2 m) was directly south of OP12. Together, OP9, OP12 and OP18 functioned as a 1 by 6 m trench (Figure 23). OP18sf, with its loose and dry soil, was the typical plowzone surface. OP18A corresponded to the layer of dirt clods and rock fill, and contained mixed pottery associations. OP18B was composed of a dense concentration of large and small rocks within the soil and dirt clod matrix of OP18A. We uncovered two walls at the base of Level B. The constructions defined the operation in its northern (wall OP18-w1) and southern ends (OP18-w2). The rocks were an accumulation of rubble and likely resulted from the intentional destruction of OP18-w2.

Wall 2, OP18-w2, slumps in the profile. Many of the rocks in the deposit (OP18B) came from the collapse of this wall's upper portions. Because of its stratigraphic position, the destruction of the wall probably occurred at the end of Chinchawasi 2 occupation. OP18C was a very hard dark brown soil layer underneath the overlying wall debris. The floor layer was compacted with common inclusions of charcoal flecks and Chinchawasi 2 domestic refuse.

Under the floor was OP18D, the level of yellowish brown soil with a sandy consistency and frequent inclusions of small rocks. This deposit was for the most part sterile, with few artifacts. OP18D represented a fairly thin level and feathered out in the northern end of the pit. In the southern third of OP18D, we uncovered several aligned flat stones that formed the roof of a stone-lined drainage canal built at the base of the east–west wall OP18-w2. The canal was elaborately constructed, and great care had been taken to align the small flat pachillas on either side of the canal. Surprisingly, the dimensions of the canal were fairly large, measuring roughly 22 cm in width and a maximum height of 26 cm, suggesting that the canal was intended to redirect large amounts of water. Because of the resemblance in construction and orientation, the OP18 canal almost certainly connected with the canal segment found in OP22. The canal was constructed directly atop bedrock and is associated with levels containing only Chinchawasi 1 phase materials.

OP18E was a dark grayish brown level characterized by a more compact consistency. The OP18E level was located exclusively north of the canal. OP18G was a thin beaten dirt floor surface directly above bedrock. Flat stones were integrated into this feature, with the flat facing of the stones flush with the floor surface. Only Chinchawasi 1 sherds were found in this stratigraphic level.

On the basis of the stratigraphy, then, the drainage canal in OP18 seems to have been built during the Chinchawasi 1 phase as part of an intensive construction program in Terrace 1. This program witnessed the creation of the large terrace wall (OP9-w1), which defined the northern limit of Terrace 1, and the wall (OP18-w2) that flanked the southern face of the canal.

*Terrace 1 Larger Exposures*
Because of the deep stratigraphy revealed by test pits in the center of Terrace 1, larger exposures of this area were conducted during the 1997 field season. The excavations aimed to retrieve additional materials useful for the local chronology and to determine the cultural contexts for the deposits. The findings indicate that this area was used as special domestic living quarters during the Warmi phase. During the Chinchawasi phases, Terrace 1 functioned as a partitioned terrace space with zones for midden accumulation. Very little Kayán material occurred east of OP19. A diachronic consideration of the use of Terrace 1 follows the excavation summaries.

Operations 43 and 44
OP43 and OP44 were both 2 by 3 m excavations. Because the pits were contiguous and excavated almost simultaneously, I will describe the excavations of OP43 and OP44 as a single 2 by 6 m operation. OP44 turned out to be a much shallower pit, broken by a late prehistoric flagstone floor.

The operation initiated with a level of modern topsoil surface (OP43sf and OP44sf), a loose, dusty and dry soil matrix, mixed with frequent roots of grass, small stones and eroded surface sherds of mixed modern and prehistoric affiliation. The underlying stratum (OP43A and OP44A) consisted of a harder continuation of the same plowzone. The stratum contained dry granular soil with frequent inclusions of dirt clods. OP43B, OP43C and OP44B comprised a deeper plowzone level with the same soil matrix, but with more frequent inclusions of large hard dirt clods. The plowzone levels revealed very few artifacts.

Underneath was a much darker stratum of dark grayish brown soil (OP43D and OP44C), with denser cultural remains. Wall rubble became more common, especially in OP44. The stratum represents the buildup of trash on top of a floor paved with many large flagstone slabs. The floor showed much better preservation in OP44, but portions of the floor survived also in OP43. Near the southern extent of OP43 a small open channel (running east–west) was formed by the intentional alignment of floor stones on top of a hard beaten dirt surface. Unlike water drainage canals found in other parts of the site, we did not encounter any capping stones, and the channel terminated at the foundations of a low-lying north–south partition wall (OP44-w1), so the exact interpretation of the channel remains uncertain. The level represented by OP43D and OP44C contained mixed diagnostic pottery. Given its stratigraphic position, the debris likely accumulated during or after the Chakwas phase.

OP43E represents the soil associated with the floor stones in OP43. Because of the better preservation of the floor in OP44, we decided to forego excavating this portion of the pavement. The soil was dark grayish brown, very compact, but still dry. We encountered a hoe or foot-plow blade fragment made of greenish gray schist and a cranial spoon (Figure 130J). Common Warmi pottery indicates that the floor was built during or after the Warmi phase.

Underneath the paved floor level, we encountered a rock fill stratum (OP43F) deposited to level the area for the floor above. The soil was fairly compact and contained frequent small to large unworked rocks. The level, especially in the upper portion, was very rich in domestic and decorated Warmi pottery (75.9%). It was also associated with scattered refuse, including a batán and lozenge-shaped grinding stone. There were several burnt areas with small lenses of ash and flecks of charcoal and burnt bone, suggesting repeated cooking episodes, especially with OP43 by the northern terrace wall.

OP43G was a level of dark yellowish brown soil with frequent occurrence of rock rubble. The soil was moist, grainy and sandy. The sandy soil was typically loose, while the concentrations of dark brown soil were more compact. Both the contents and the character of this yellowish brown stratum resembled similar layers found in other parts of Terrace 1, representing a distinct level of sterile fill or destruction throughout the site. Only two diagnostics were recovered from this level and both were Warmi phase. OP43H continued this level of dark yellowish brown sandy matrix, but with dense concentrations of rock rubble, especially in the middle of the operation. Only one fragment of late Middle Horizon imported pottery was encountered.

OP43I constituted a dark grayish brown-black beaten dirt floor surface, with

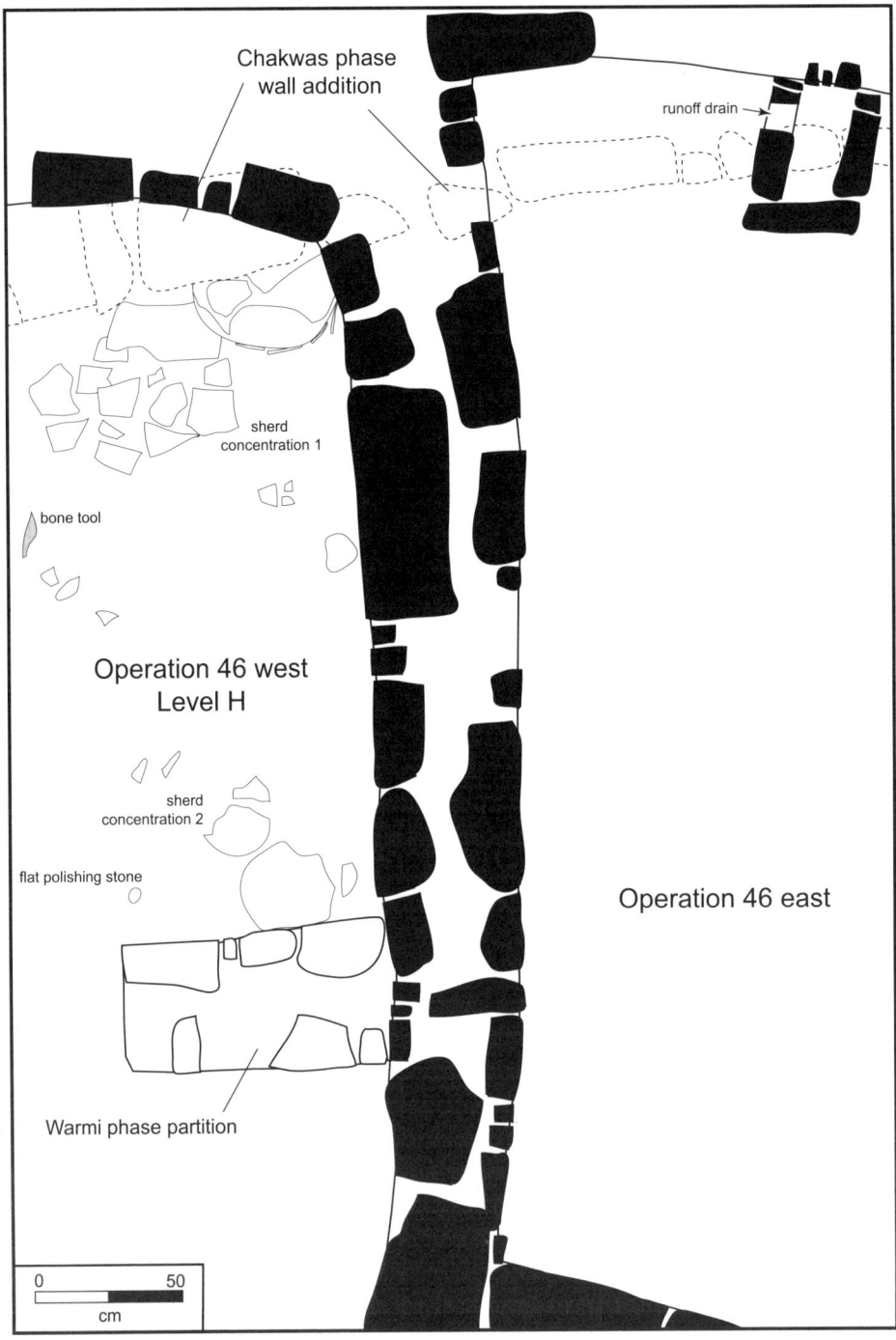

FIGURE 24. Plan of Operation 46, Level H, showing Warmi and Chakwas phase re-use of Chinchawasi 1 terrace and enclosure wall (Terrace 1, Sector 1). The western portion seems to have been a roofed space with residential functions, while the eastern side featured dense bone and broken refuse typical for open patio areas.

a very dark brown soil matrix containing dense quantities of domestic refuse, including animal bones, hearth discard, and plainware and decorated ceramics. There were many areas of dark accumulations of hearth refuse, in which chunks of carbon were common. The soil was moist and clayey, with contained lenses of the dark yellowish brown sandy soil. The ceramic assemblage was composed mainly of local Warmi phase decorated ceramics, and also had 28 fragments of exotic Middle Horizon sherds, including 17 blackware polished pieces, four press-molded, two Cajamarca and five fine pinkware sherds.

An AMS radiocarbon measurement was taken for a wood charcoal sample from OP43I ($x$: 9.8W, $y$: 15.6N, $z$: −1.71m). The sample yielded a radiocarbon age of 1160 ± 45 B.P. (A.D. 790 ± 45 uncalibrated or A.D. 888 ± 45 calibrated), with a 2-sigma range of A.D. 778 to 991 (see Table 1). This determination corroborates the late Middle Horizon association represented by the Warmi style and exotic Middle Horizon styles.

The position of the topmost part of OP43I was associated with the initial building and use of the north–south wall addition (OP19-w1). At the beginning of the level OP43I, on the northwest corner, we encountered a window opening built as part of the large northern terrace wall during the Chinchawas 1 phase. At its base to the south, a series of shoddily placed stones emerged to form the sides of a low box-like addition (roughly 65 by 50 cm) abutting the opening. The feature, as part of the Warmi phase reuse of the terrace wall and opening, likely was as a buffer against the wind or a makeshift wall to keep guinea pigs within the domestic area. This feature is comparable to the window–entryway in OP30.

Directly underneath the Warmi floor surface and floor fill of OP43I was a very dark brown soil level: OP43J. It was moist and with common flecks of charcoal, but without the yellowish brown sandy lenses and with fewer small rocks. The pottery assemblage also changed distinctively as well, and was mostly of the Chinchawasi 2 style (86.7%).

OP43K continued the previous very dark brown soil level, but we encountered more frequent small rocks and spalls of bedrock mixed within the moist and sticky soil matrix. The cultural remains pertained exclusively to the Chinchawasi 1 (16 diagnostics, 84.2%) and Kayán (three sherds, 15.8%) phase. Concentrations of bone from young camelids were encountered along the northern terrace wall and interpreted as offerings. These were found in association with a large oval-shaped mortar, a cranial spoon and other household implements.

OP43L was essentially a sterile level of dark grayish brown soil with small- to medium-sized unworked stones and some spalling bedrock fragments. No diagnostic pottery was identified from the level. OP43M constituted a dark yellowish brown stratum, very rocky, lying just above bedrock. The level was for the most part sterile, but scattered domestic pottery was recovered. In addition, one Kayán kaolinite sherd emerged from this layer.

OPERATION 46

OP46 was a 3 by 4 m pit (Figure 24) located just east of OP43. OP46sf was the modern plowzone surface. OP46A was a harder continuation of the loose dry material found above. OP46B was the level of plowzone with large dirt clods, mixed with the granular and dry soil matrix found above. OP46C was a very dark brown stratum of loose dry granular soil, but without the large dirt clods. In lieu of these, there were many rocks of various sizes, some of the large wanka size. At the basal level of OP46C we began to see the outlines of five different walls. The dense scatter of rocks found throughout OP46C likely was from the destruction of these walls. Cultural remains in the uppermost levels were scarce and show mixed associations.

One wall (OP46-w1) emerged down the center of the operation, effectively separating the pit into two sections. The west side was excavated as the following levels: OP46w.D, OP46w.H, OP46w.I and OP46w.J. The east side was excavated as OP46e.E, OP46e.F, OP46e.G and OP46e.H. To the central wall (OP46-w1) abutted four distinct walls, all running east–west, which partitioned the zone into separate room chambers and activity areas. Because of their joins, stratigraphic position and associated artifacts, these additions post-date the central wall's construction.

Two walls date to the late Warmi occupation: OP46-w5 and OP46-w4. In both, only the shallow basal footings of aligned stones were preserved. Wall thickness, join and condition indicate a construction of poorer quality typical for late Warmi or Chakwas architectural practice and are consistent with their association to late pottery styles. These walls probably functioned simultaneously with the floor pavement to the west.

To the south of OP46-w4 was partition wall OP46-w3, the best preserved of the additions in the east side. This wall went deeper than OP46-w4 and OP46-w5, and its basal layer was associated with Warmi and Chinchawasi 2 pottery, which is consistent with the masonry style and quality.

On the east side, under OP46C, was a deposit of wall collapse and domestic debris and fill recorded as OP46e.E. The soil contrasted with the previous layer in being hard and very dark brown. In the southeast corner of the operation, we uncovered a floor surface with rich cultural remains characteristic of a kitchen refuse area. The beaten dirt floor surface covered the northwest corner of the chamber. Potsherd concentrations of large reconstructible vessels, a complete open bowl and hand grinding stones suggest a relatively quick abandonment. This area was the source of most of the Chinchawasi 2 pottery from OP46e.E. The kitchen area and the OP46-w3 partition seem to have been part of a very late use in the Chinchawasi 2 occupation.

The three eastern partitions were then removed to excavate further into the eastern portion of OP46. OP46e.F was distinguished by being slightly darker in general and moister than OP46e.E, but the transition was smooth with no clear breaks. The dense deposit of domestic refuse continued, made up almost completely of Chinchawasi 2 phase ceramics and the sherds of a near-complete resist painted plate (Figure 92A); the plate is very similar to specimens found in stone-lined tombs near Huaraz (Bennett 1944, fig. 8).

In the northeast corner of OP46, there was a small masonry feature attached to the northern terrace wall. In plan, it takes the form of a rough rectangle and could have been used perhaps as a small trough-like container, probably for water. This is made more plausible because the stones were held together by a very hard and packed clay, and because at the west side of the trough a small opening for a stone-lined canal ran east–west along the northern terrace wall. We were unable to expose this canal completely, because it sat within the deposit just below a large slumping wall addition, but our excavations into the trough indicate that the sides and the bottom of the channel were stone-lined. Within the small portion excavated we found a dense cache of bone, almost fully articulated, suggesting an offering. The feature is associated with level OP46e.F, the Chinchawasi 2 domestic occupation of the zone. Artifacts became scarcer at the end of OP46e.F.

OP46e.G was a nearly black stratum, very moist and clayey; the soil stuck to artifacts. Cultural remains were very abundant in this level and included bone tools, stone spindle whorls, cranial spoons and many polished river stones (from 2 to 5 cm in diameter), probably used as polishers or slingstones.

Pottery, especially decorated ceramics, was also quite dense in OP46eG. Many (248 of 1,845) were painted (13.4%), a large proportion compared with the percentage for all levels throughout the site (3.25%). Of these sherds, nearly all (96.7%) were Chinchawasi 1, one was Kayán and seven fragments were indeterminate. Up against the central section of north–south wall was a burnt soil area, about 70 cm (maximum dimension), which held a large deposit of well-articulated animal bones, especially of camelids. The scatter and density of the remains indicate intensive discard of refuse in this area.

The basal layer on the east side of OP46 was level H, or OP46e.H. The soil remained dark (black), but became rockier as fragments of spalling bedrock became more frequent. There were also far fewer artifacts associated with an early component of the Chinchawasi occupation. Only 11 Chinchawasi 1 and three kaolinite Kayán sherds were found, in addition to one incised piece and two ground sherd fragments (Figure 102K). The large north–south wall of OP46-w1 was built atop bedrock.

On the west side of OP46, OP46w.D was, in soil consistency and color, a continuation of OP46C above, with small lenses of yellow sandy brown soil. At the base of OP46w.D, in the southwest corner of the operation, we encountered the continuation of the flat stone pavement found in OP43 and OP44. OP46w.D was relatively clean of artifacts, following OP46C's pattern. No diagnostics were encountered in the level, although there were scattered plainware sherds. By association, the paved stone flooring seems to have been terminal Warmi or post-Warmi.

OP46w.H, a stratum of the dark yellowish brown sandy soil, lay beneath OP46D. The level contained Warmi phase remains, increasing in density towards the bottom of the level, a Warmi living surface. The base of the partition wall, OP46-w2, ended with the beginning of this level, suggesting that it was not constructed before the Warmi occupation. The sandy fill level (OP46w.H), on the basis of its stylistic associations and its stratigraphic position elsewhere in the site, seems to date directly to the Warmi phase occupation. This yellow sandy level did not occur in the eastern side of OP46.

OP46w.I represented a dark find horizon underneath the yellow sandy layer. It was composed of very dark brown soil and contained dense cultural remains, including in situ vessels of different sizes, bone tools, grinding stones, a copper-metal lamina disc and obsidian fragments. The early Middle Horizon pottery consisted of Chinchawasi 1 and 2 phase material (73.5%), as well as four pieces of Wari polychrome and one bowl fragment from a Cajamarca style spoon (Figure 91E).

The basal layer in the western portion of OP46 was OP46w.J. The soil was very dark grayish brown and had a more ashy and moist texture than the previous level. The level lay directly above bedrock and, like basal strata elsewhere, contained broken pieces of bedrock spalls. Artifacts also became scarcer. Only 10 diagnostics were encountered in this level and all were Chinchawasi 1. The western side of OP46 was excavated to a depth of 2.53 m (northwest corner). Moving eastward, the bedrock ascended upward so that the maximum depth excavated on the eastern side was 1.95 m from surface level (northeast corner). The bedrock also sloped from south to north, so that the deep end of the eastern side measured 1.27 m below the surface.

*Summary of Terrace 1 Operations*

Terrace 1 was a focus of activity throughout the ancient occupation of Chinchawas. Initial use of the terrace was by Kayán peoples. The scarce Kayán artifacts, associated with the deep burnt area and ashy lenses of OP9, suggest only sporadic and ephemeral use of this area, perhaps the result of one or possibly several cooking episodes.

Terrace 1 witnessed major changes with the onset of Chinchawasi 1, when Terrace 1 first saw intensive use. Two major walls were built: the northern terrace wall and the north–south wall in OP46. Even in its initial construction and use phase, the enclosed area was considerable, and probably was unroofed. In OP18, we encountered the back wall to this structure, 5 m from the northern terrace wall. And in OP43, there was a small window opening that would have opened out into a steep slope. Window features occur in other parts of the site as elements of perimeter walls and large structures; they probably provided vantage points to areas below, as well as restricted access to interior spaces.

During Chinchawasi times the zone probably served general residential purposes. Two basic activity patterns can be identified. The interior space (west of the north–south wall in OP46) was kept fairly clean, while the eastern side contained dense deposits of domestic refuse, including faunal remains, grinding stones, domestic pottery and fancy Chinchawasi 1 phase ceramics. The midden accumulation on the east side can be interpreted as the discard from household activities associated with the east enclosure; wall segments of residential structures may be identified either in OP11 or OP10, or in both.

Drastic changes occurred by the onset of the Warmi phase. In the western section of the complex, the enclosure area was leveled and graded with a yellowish brown sandy fill. Local Warmi groups built small rooms by adding partitions to the northern terrace wall and north–south wall in OP46. Walls reaching at least 2 m in height during their initial use in the Chinchawasi 1 phase served only as knee-high foundations for mud-brick superstructures. We can reconstruct a room (roughly 2 by 3 m) in the northern part of the former patio area. There may have been additional rooms in the southeast corner of OP46 and in the space between the walls of OP12 and OP19. These chambers were domestic in function given the character of the cultural remains inside: circular burned hearth areas, spindle whorls, domestic pottery, bone tools and typical kitchen debris.

At the end of the Warmi phase well-made flagstone pavement floors are found in some areas. This new architectural practice broke from the more customary beaten dirt floors of earlier phases.

## Terrace 2

Terrace 2 is directly west and northwest of Enclosure 1; it is the westernmost part of the ridgetop's principal architecture, a flat outcropping of andesitic bedrock that serves as a natural platform. The area features a variety of stone constructions, including rectangular residential buildings and tall perimeter walls. On the northern end are a series of aligned stone uprights, probably the remnants of a wanka–pachilla wall of an important building, now largely destroyed. Leading up to this structure (and Terrace 2) on the north side are the remains of five or six long (about 4 m), but low, step-like platforms, each about 10 cm tall. The steps have stone facing and may have been part of a wide staircase (layer-cake profile). Terrace 2 also features long narrow constructions, or "gallery structures," on the southern portion of the terrace (near OP15). These constructions, also unique at Chinchawas, use the outer terrace walls as their back walls; two small entrances provide access through the inner wall. The three test excavations aimed to elucidate the cultural associations for the surficial architecture.

### Terrace 2 Operations

#### OPERATION 13
OP13, a 1 by 2 m pit located in an open area within the central portion of Terrace 2, tested for cultural remains and stratigraphy. OP13sf was the surface level, with a dry and loose dark grayish brown soil. OP13A was the deepest layer in this operation. Composed of a dark yellowish brown matrix, it sat directly above bedrock throughout the unit. We concluded the excavations at a maximum depth of 32 cm. Diagnostic pottery was of mixed associations. No intact architecture was encountered.

#### OPERATION 14
OP14 was a 1 by 2 m test pit near the western edge of the Terrace 2 platform. OP14sf was the surface level, a dusty dry soil matrix held together by roots and

bunch grasses. OP14A began as a slightly lighter soil with fewer roots. It was harder in some areas than the previous level, while softer in others. Together these formed the Terrace 2 surface layer, with considerable mixing of diagnostic sherds.

OP14B was the beginning of the intact stratigraphy and was composed of a very dark gray soil containing mainly Chinchawasi phase materials. A small, perforated tabular pendant of mica was found in this layer. Below OP14B was the final level, OP14C, a very dark grayish brown matrix that, when it neared the sterile layer, became very rocky with spalling bedrock. In this shallow operation, which reached a depth of only 62 cm, most of the ceramics were of the Chinchawasi 2 phase, with the exception of a Kayán sherd. OP14 contained no architecture.

OPERATION 15

OP15, a 1 by 2 test unit, was located just outside a row of gallery structures with window openings. Our objective aimed to find cultural associations for these constructions, because the interiors had long been emptied of its original contents. OP15sf was the surface layer with a dark brown loose soil, with common occurrence of roots, wall rocks and small, mixed ceramics. OP15A was a somewhat more compact level, with small rocks and sherds of plainware pottery. Cultural associations were mixed.

At the base of OP15A was a dark beaten floor level with large scatters of ash and carbon, referred to as OP15B. On the floor were two grinding stones: a mortar turned over backward, which covered a round mano. Burnt camelid bone and plainware pottery were frequent inclusions in this floor level. The floor level of OP15B also contained two phase diagnostics, both from the Warmi phase.

Under OP15B was another dark grayish brown soil level, found between the floor level and the bedrock throughout the unit. This level was designated OP15B2. In the southwest corner of the pit a shallow depression in the bedrock served as a hearth or burning area. In this depression, there were frequent remains of burnt camelid bone, broken pottery and silex flakes in a dark gray ashy matrix. Near the hearth we recovered a perforated copper-metal pin (Figure 136E) with a flat head embossed with two small indentations that resemble eyes. The materials were Warmi in association.

*Summary of Terrace 2 Operations*

Our three test excavations suggest that Terrace 2 was used especially intensively during the Warmi phase. The gallery structures and the defensive walls were probably built during the Warmi phase occupation. Fragments of Warmi pottery and Middle Horizon imported types are predominant. Further, the masonry style of the gallery structures and perimeter walls, typically made up only of smaller rocks and chinking stones, is consistent with this interpretation. The gallery structures, possibly storage chambers or tombs, were not excavated because inspections identified exposed bedrock throughout the interiors.

# Terrace 3

Terrace 3 is the walled zone immediately south of Enclosure 2. Today, it is used occasionally as an agricultural plot. The eastern and western areas of Terrace 3 were sampled with 1 by 2 m test units. Operation 47 was a larger operation (3 by 4 m) in the eastern portion.

## Terrace 3 East

OPERATION 4

Despite its proximity to pits within Enclosure 2, OP4 showed a completely different depositional character. It furnished the initial evidence to isolate the Chinchawasi cultural components from the later Warmi phase. OP4, a 1 by 2 m test unit, was to the southeast of OP3 in the east corner of Terrace 3. The stratigraphy in OP4 represented the accumulation of refuse and fill near a complex of walled structures located within this corner. The depth of deposit here reached a maximum of just over 1 m, for which eight levels were defined.

The topmost layers (OP4sf, OP4A and OP4B) consisted of mixed materials, probably due to agricultural activity. The underlying levels of OP4C through G showed superposition of a Warmi phase level over Chinchawasi phase materials. The cultural transition occurred between Level D and E, as distinguished by different wares. All 48 phase diagnostic sherds from the Level C and D were exclusively from the Warmi phase or late Middle Horizon styles, including two sherd concentrations of reconstructible drinking cups (or *keros*), one in Central Coast press-molded style (Figure 93A) and another polychrome example, which featured Viñaque style elements (Figure 97H).

A sharp cultural break occurred by Levels E and F. Diagnostic ceramics belonged almost entirely to the Chinchawasi 2 phase. By Level F, we had also recovered some kaolinite materials. Level G contained both Chinchawasi 1 and 2 phase materials. An AMS radiocarbon measurement for a wood charcoal sample from OP4G yielded a radiocarbon age of 1290 ± 45 B.P. (A.D. 660 ± 45 uncalibrated or A.D. 711, 746 or 755 ± 45 calibrated), with a 2-sigma range of A.D. 659 to 875 (see Table 1).

There are two notable features in this operation. First, the remains of a small, low wall built directly atop bedrock ran almost perfectly aligned with the southern profile. We exposed only this face of the wall. In some parts it reached about 18 to 20 cm in height. This wall crossed the second notable feature: a small rut or canal in the surface of the bedrock. The canal ran north–south and seems to have been intentionally gouged out of the bedrock. It measured roughly 16 to 20 cm in width and between 5 and 10 cm deep, and was better preserved in its southern stretch. On the basis of ceramic and stratigraphic associations, the wall and the canal were constructed during the Chinchawasi 1 occupation of the site.

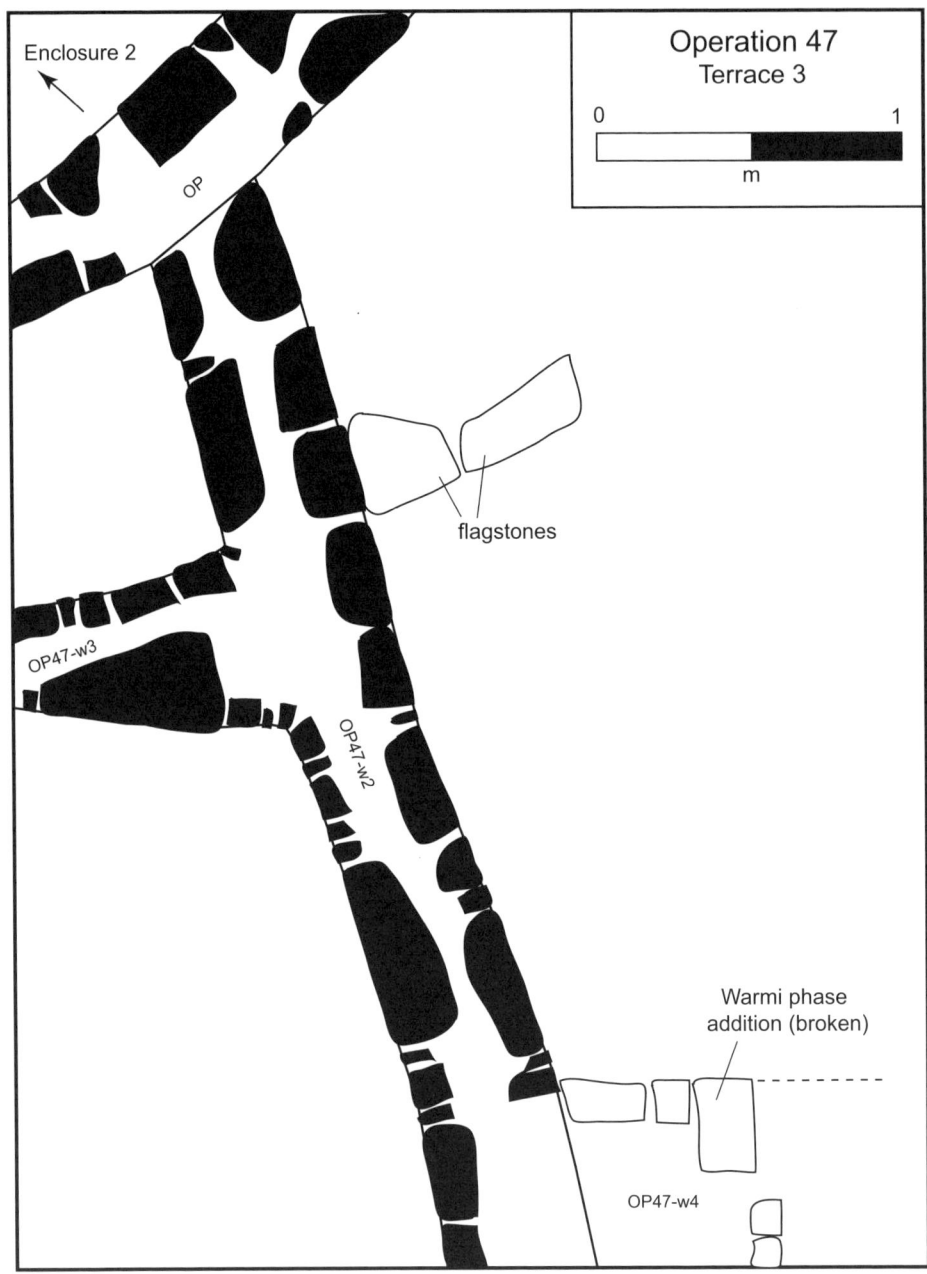

FIGURE 25. Plan of walls in Terrace 3 (Operation 47), Sector 1. The western building was probably roofed.

## OPERATION 8

OP8 was a 1 by 2 m test excavation. OP8sf and OP8A were several layers that have been reworked by modern activity. Level OP8B, the first intact stratum in the pit, featured a very dark grayish brown soil mixed with frequent inclusions of wall rubble, especially in the uppermost half of the stratum. The level most likely reflects a period of disuse during the late part of the Middle Horizon and the gradual destruction of nearby walls and buildings after the Warmi occupation.

Level C (OP8C) was of a lighter brown matrix, but with considerably fewer rocks. Like OP8B, it contained only Warmi phase pottery. Near the base of OP8C, we uncovered three dense sherd concentrations of domestic vessels, especially of large necked jars. Level D (OP8D) was a layer of grayish soil with very few large or medium-sized rocks. Like OP8C, however, it contained several dense sherd concentrations, almost exclusively of plainware vessels. OP8D graded into soil types of different colors and textures, which were given their own level designations: OP8E, OP8F and OP8G. OP8E was a layer of fine dark gray and yellow clayey soil found only on the southern half of the pit. There were very few remains in this layer. Level F was a hard, rocky, reddish brown soil immediately beneath OP8E. Like OP8E, Level F was restricted to the southern half of the operation. Levels D, E and F were characterized by Warmi phase pottery.

Level G (OP8G) lay directly beneath OP8D on the northern and western ends. The level was composed of a layer of hard, dark yellowish brown soil with frequent inclusions of fist-sized, rough stones. Cultural remains included the occasional Chinchawasi 2 sherd and a fine-stemmed obsidian point (Figure 110A).

Level H (OP8H) had a dark brown matrix with patches of black soil, and spanned the entire excavation unit. The soil was much more compact in this layer than in the previous one and yielded Chinchawasi 2 phase material. In the east half of the unit we encountered a sherd concentration of large plainware vessels with associated animal bone, some burnt. Level H in the north and west lay basically on top of bedrock. A deeper level, OP8I, consisting principally of the dark brown soil, was found to the south and east. Like Level H, Level I contained only Chinchawasi phase pottery.

## OPERATION 47

Because of the productivity of test pits OP4 and OP8, we decided to expose a larger portion of the eastern end of Terrace 3, with the dual objective of identifying the cultural associations for nearby architecture and to elucidate the spatial contexts for the cultural remains. OP47 was a 3 by 4 m operation (Figure 25). Immediately below the plowzone (OP47sf), we encountered a large wall debris destruction level, designated OP47A. The soil matrix was dark grayish brown, more compacted and finer than the modern surface soil; it surrounded collapsed rocks of different sizes. Pottery from these two levels included mixed diagnostics and was consistent with the initial layers throughout the site.

OP47B consisted of a continuation of the wall debris level found above. The soil matrix was a fine loamy silt with common medium-sized to small rocks, but fewer large rocks. Cultural materials were much more common, including domestic refuse such as pottery, animal bones and burnt clay clumps. The diagnostic ceramics indicate mixing; Level B is interpreted as a late prehistoric surface layer covered over by recent wall collapse and agricultural activity.

Beginning in OP47B and reaching into bedrock were three interconnected walls: OP47-w1, OP47-w2 and OP47-w3. These walls are in different states of preservation now, but were made in the wanka–pachilla masonry style. The northernmost wall (OP47-w1) represented the section of Enclosure 2's southeastern wall. It was connected, with fitted stones, to a north–south wall, or OP47-w2. OP47-w3 connected to the western side of OP47-w2 and seems to have been a partition. Because of the north–south wall and the emerging differences in stratigraphy, the east and west sides were excavated as distinct units.

*East Side.* OP47C was a darker soil stratum, very dark brown and was excavated on either side of the north–south wall (OP47-w2). However, the east side contained a compacted and slightly darker soil, especially in the southern portion of the operation. The bulk of the cultural remains was recovered from this darker area, and included mainly Warmi pottery; there was also one Wari polychrome sherd. Artifacts included several grinding stones and a copper-metal shawl pin. The east side seems to be a poorly preserved floor deposit. The cultural materials and stratigraphic position indicate a Warmi phase association. OP47e.D was a deposit of a dark yellowish brown sandy layer and stratigraphically seems to correlate with the Warmi phase building episodes throughout the site. The level did not yield a phase diagnostic.

Underneath the yellow sandy layer was OP47e.E, which began a series of three Chinchawasi phase deposits. The soil was clayey loamy silt, yellowish brown and very moist. In the northwest corner, there was a hearth area with burned soil and small flecks of charcoal. We encountered a folded and perforated copper-metal ornament in the southeast corner. Twelve Chinchawasi 2 diagnostics were recovered from this level. In the southernmost portion of the eastern side, there was a masonry addition (OP47-w4) to the north–south wall (OP47-w2). Only a portion of the addition survived, apparently destroyed or fallen into disuse in antiquity. The addition is associated with the bottom of level OP47e.E.

OP47e.F occurred only in the southeastern quadrant of OP47. This level was a darker continuation of the clayey loamy silt of OP47e.E, with some mixing of yellowish brown sandy soil. The basal stratum in OP47 was OP47e.G, a near black level with a silty loam matrix. This level was extremely rich in cultural remains, all corresponding to an early to middle Chinchawasi occupation. Sixty-one out of 64 decorated sherds were Chinchawasi 1, and three could not be identified to a known style. Other artifacts included several bone implements and a polished bone spindle whorl (Figure 127H). OP47e.G was also characterized by the intentional placement of at least three flat flagstones in the level to pave the irregular bedrock. The eastern side excavation was taken down to a maximum depth of 1.7 m under the modern surface. We reached bedrock in the northern section of the operation just 0.88 m under the modern surface.

*West Side.* OP47w.C was a thin level of sterile soil. OP47w.D in the western side of the operation began as a dark, nearly sterile stratum, with no evidence of the yellowish brown sandy level. We found predominantly Warmi materials in the deeper portion of OP47w.D.

OP47w.E was similar to the previous Level D, but represented the basal stratum on the western side. OP47w.E lay directly above bedrock and extended to a depth of 1.59 m below the modern surface. The level contained four Chinchawasi 1 sherds. Bone tools and carbonized wood tools were found directly atop bedrock in the southwest corner of the operation and are associated with the rich materials found in OP47e.G.

*Terrace 3 West*

### Operations 5, 6 and 20

OP5, a 1 by 2 m test unit, was situated in the western portion of Terrace 3. Unlike OP4, the deposit for most of OP5 was much shallower because we encountered a wall (OP5-w1) crossing the long axis of the pit and a stone floor 30 to 40 cm below the surface.

The floor (OP5-f1), which covered the western half of the pit, was paved with rough, flat stones. They were carefully fitted together, with soil packed in the interstices. The floor would have continued to the west, south and north of OP5. Because of the steep slopes to the west and south, and rock debris to the north, we did not excavate in these directions. OP6 and OP20 sampled to the east of the floor.

The masonry of the floor and wall were identical and interlocked, suggesting that the features were likely contemporary. The deeper remains in the far east end of OP5 were excavated as a component of OP6.

Differentiation between the three levels in OP5 was determined on the basis of compactness of soil and the frequent presence of fist-size rocks above the level of the floor. There was very little internal differentiation in terms of artifacts. Six out of the seven phase diagnostics found directly above the floor in OP5 were of the Kayán kaolin type. The floor and wall may have been used during the late part of the Early Intermediate Period as part of the Enclosure 2 patio complex.

OP6, a 1 by 2 m test unit, was directly east of OP5 along the same grid axis. OP6 had a much deeper depth of deposit, reaching 1.66 m at the east end of the unit, and contained rich materials from the Chinchawasi and Warmi phases. An east–west wall (OP6-w1), bisecting the pit, ran the length of the unit and very likely extended further east. It abutted the aforementioned wall (OP5-w1), but was built up against it and does not interconnect. Further, unlike OP5-w1, the wall was erected atop a soft yellow ashy layer rather than on footings directly above bedrock. And given the preponderance of Warmi pottery in the layer, it is likely that the wall was a late Middle Horizon addition. The wall's masonry was typical, with small flat chinks filling the interstices between large uprights.

Rich midden layers, typically dark blackish brown with yellow and grayish black ashy lenses, accumulated after the construction of the Middle Horizon wall, including deposits with large broken jars, burnt animal bone and rocks. The type and buildup of material suggest multiple discard and burning events of domestic trash after the wall's construction. Because of the wall's position in the unit, we only excavated in deposits to the south of the wall. It is unclear whether there were similar deposits to the north of OP6-w1.

Deeper strata also showed ample evidence for earlier discard and burning, indicating a continuity of such activities in this zone (OP5, OP6 and OP20). A yellow sandy matrix with patches of dark brown silty soil characterized Level E. A dark brown-black soil with common yellow sandy lenses characterized the basal level of the operation, or Level F. There were only Chinchawasi 2 phase sherds in this level.

OP20, a 1 by 2 m test unit, was directly south of OP6. Once begun, it became immediately apparent that it would be very difficult to excavate the pit fully. Everywhere south of OP6, there was a terrace retaining wall (OP20-w1) that delimits the area today. This terrace wall was an addition, built cursorily of piled fieldstones over the foundations of the original southern wall (OP20-w2). OP20 overlapped with this piling. We therefore excavated only the unit's northern half.

The stratigraphy of OP20 was nearly identical to OP6, with the same superposition of Warmi over Chinchawasi phase materials. Levels B to E were represented almost exclusively by Warmi diagnostics. Burnt rocks and broken cooking pottery suggested a possible cooking hearth roughly 50 cm from the surface of the pit in the southwestern corner. The hearth ran up against the piled rocks of the late terrace wall, suggesting that the wall was either Warmi or later in date.

Farther below we encountered a series of broken ollas in a homogenous matrix of very dark grayish brown soil and large rocks. These remains were consistent with the pattern of domestic trash discard activity for OP6. It is possible that the rocks were also the remains from the destruction of the original terrace wall (OP20-w2).

An AMS radiocarbon measurement was taken for a wood charcoal sample from OP20F, located within a Warmi pit dug into an earlier deposit and used for burning. The sample yielded a radiocarbon age of 1150 ± 50 B.P. (A.D. 800 ± 50 uncalibrated or A.D. 891 ± 50 calibrated), with a 2-sigma range of A.D. 778 to 1006 (see Table 1). The range falls nicely within the range associated with the late Middle Horizon Warmi style.

In Level G, we exposed the foundations of an east–west stone wall (OP20-

w2), which probably served as the outer terrace wall for the zone. It abutted the north–south wall in OP5, OP5-w1. Although the masonry was not fitted, it was similar and both walls were built on top of bedrock.

On the basis of its stratigraphic and architectural relationships, OP20-w1 can be considered an addition to OP5-w1, but it was not built considerably later. The southern face of the wall, which overlooks the gradual southwestern slope of the hilltop, was not identified in the excavation. This face was partly destroyed, probably by natural causes given its steep position. Stratigraphic evidence shows that the disrepair of the original terrace wall (OP20-w2) occurred some time during the Chinchawasi 2 occupation. All ceramics from OP20G pertained to the Chinchawasi 2 phase.

In OP6 we also encountered the wall facing for a slightly elevated platform or step. The facing (OP6-w2) was built directly on bedrock and connected with the original southern wall (OP20-w2). The step served as an architectural transition between the lower floor and the platform level, similar to the feature found in the residence structure of OP45.

## Summary of Terrace 3 West Operations

OP5, OP6 and OP20 exposed the southwest corner of Enclosure 2. The excavations uncovered a series of superimposed walls that formed part of a large room attached to Enclosure 2. The considerable evidence for repeated episodes of burning and discard activity within the area indicates that the room, at least in the areas excavated, was used for cooking and disposal activities, most likely for the intensive ceremonial activities of Enclosure 2. Initial use began during the late Early Intermediate Period occupation of the site.

Two walls (OP5-w1 and OP20-w2) were built atop bedrock and formed a corner, which was a common area for refuse discard and fill accumulation. Very small fragments of carbonized animal bone, ash and large plainware jars were common in the deposits. Interspersed within these deposits were painted Chinchawasi phase ceramics, typically exterior decorated jars and interior decorated open bowls. Two separate hearths indicate food preparation was performed in the area. In OP5 there was careful stone paving, perhaps the floor to an adjoining elevated chamber or a small stretch of parapet.

During the Chinchawasi 2 occupation, the original southern wall (OP20-w2) was dismantled or destroyed naturally, leaving only its northern foundations intact. Chinchawasi peoples did not rebuild this wall, but did reuse the now open area for cooking and continued trash disposal. During the Warmi phase, another southern wall was built. This new wall, OP6-w1, was built directly on top of the Chinchawasi phase midden strata and connected with the older wall in OP5, OP5-w1. Probably to ward against the possibility of falling down the terrace drop-off, this new wall was erected roughly 20 to 30 cm north of the old wall.

The deposits to the south of the OP6-w1 were a combination of Warmi trash

FIGURE 26. View of three 1 by 2 m test excavations in Terrace 4 (looking southwest). Operations shown, from left to right, include OP29, OP30 and OP23. Paths in the background lead to the town of Pira.

and fill layers. There were burnt bone concentrations as well as evidence for deep burned pits, indicating that burning and food preparation continued in this area. During the end of the Warmi occupation, when intensive use of the enclosure complex ceased, a rough wall of fieldstones (OP6-w1) was built to re-enclose this zone, probably as a makeshift corral to keep in animals. This fieldstone wall was approximately 40 to 50 cm above the foundations of the OP6-w2.

## Terrace 4

Terrace 4 is a zone of the site just south of the Torreón structure (Figures 11 and 26). A large wall, roughly 50 m, is the southern boundary for Terraces 3 and 4. For the most part the wall is well preserved, built with ancient wanka–pachilla masonry. Some segments, though, are in considerable disrepair, having fallen from slumping or been deliberately knocked over. Many segments seem to have been repaired or patched by stacking stones without mortar, perhaps by modern herders to make a corral. Local members of the community told me that Terrace 4 had never been used for agricultural purposes. The objective was to probe the area for prehistoric patterns of cultural activity and function, and their change through time. We excavated four 1 by 2 m test units in Terrace 4 (OP23, OP29, OP30 and OP31), all located along the edge of the terrace wall to maximize retrieval of stratigraphic deposits. Because of artifact density and stratigraphy, larger, more horizontal exposures (OP38, OP40, OP41 and OP42) were opened during the second field season (Figure 27).

## Terrace 4 Operations

### Operation 23

OP23 was a 1 by 2 m test unit located on the western end of Terrace 4. OP23sf was the surface level previously described for other parts of the site. OP23A was a layer composed of a more compact, dark brown soil, with contents similar to OP23sf. OP23B was a continuation of the plowzone level, with little change in soil texture and contents. The top of a north–south wanka–pachilla wall emerged at the base of OP23B. OP23C was a more compact surface, possibly a living surface, composed of a light brown soil matrix with frequent flecks of carbon. There were common occurrences of dirt clods, some of which were burned. This could be evidence of food preparation, because dirt clods are often used to build mounded earth ovens for cooking foods, especially tubers. In these modern plowzone levels, cultural associations were mixed.

OP23D was a level of compact soil beneath OP23C. The soil texture and content resembled a reworked fill and refuse layer. Diagnostics included Warmi pottery as well as one piece of fancy Wari polychrome. OP23E represented another possible beaten dirt floor level. The soil matrix of this level was dark brown and was consistent throughout the operation.

OP23F was made up of a dense refuse layer of animal bone (mainly camelid), ceramics and the shells of land snails. Most of this discarded refuse occurred west of the north–south wall. OP23F itself was a level of soil and refuse, with common air pockets.

The level became less compact in OP23G and contained burnt dirt clods. The refuse accumulation had abundant camelid remains and broken plain and decorated ceramics, especially in the northwest corner of the operation. The topmost portion of an east–west wall, OP23-w2, was first seen at the bottom of level OP23G. OP23H, the basal portion of this refuse heap, was composed of an ashy soil, dark grayish brown with black charcoal flecks. The animal bones throughout this midden deposit were in excellent condition; some cut marks and intentional fracturing indicate human consumption.

There were diverse ceramics in levels OP23F, OP23G and OP23H. Chinchawasi 2 phase pottery was the most common, but Warmi pottery was also represented. The assemblage also included diverse imported Middle Horizon styles, including Nievería (Figure 92B), Cajamarca-related, blackware-polished, Wari polychrome and press-molded specimens.

OP23I was the basal level throughout OP23 and was composed of an ashy very dark brown soil matrix that lay directly above bedrock. This level reached a maximum depth of 1.28 m. The artifacts became less common and more fragmentary in this level. The two walls were constructed above bedrock; there were no wall foundation trenches. OP23I corresponded to the original construction level and floor surface during Chinchawasi 1.

## Operation 29

OP29, a 1 by 2 m test unit, was located to the east of OP23 in the Terrace 4 sector and provided additional evidence for the superposition of Warmi over Chinchawasi phase materials. The depositional patterns found in OP29 were different than those found in OP23. OP29sf was the current surface layer and was characterized by a soft and loose soil with reworked inclusions. OP29A was a harder, more compact layer further differentiated by many more small rocks and some dirt granules and small clods (greater than or equal to 1 cm). OP29B was essentially a stratigraphic continuation of OP29A, distinguished only by the presence of much larger rocks and a lighter soil matrix color. OP29C was a similar level, composed of very large rocks. This stratum is interpreted as the result of the accumulation of wall debris coming in from the Torreón structure located to the operation's north. Warmi phase diagnostics were encountered in Levels A, B and C.

OP29D was made up of a much harder level, composed of a very dark brown soil and containing fewer large rocks. OP29E was a continuation of the level, characterized by a compact soil with a very dark grayish brown matrix, frequent small stones and yellowish brown mottling. Chinchawasi 2 ceramics characterized OP29D and OP29E. OP29F represented the basal level of the operation and consisted of a dense, very dark brown soil (almost blackish). Nearly all diagnostics show a Chinchawasi 1 affiliation, with one Kayán phase kaolinite and a ceramic miniature fragment. The excavation reached 1.6 m in maximum depth in the south–central part of the operation. No architectural features were encountered.

## Operation 30

OP30, a 1 by 2 m test excavation, was just a few meters east of OP23 in Terrace 4. OP30sf was the surface layer. OP30A was a subsurface level characterized by a loose, dry brown soil matrix with small rocks and frequent occurrence of small granular dirt clods. OP30B resembled OP30sf and OP30A in soil color and texture. The topmost portion of an east–west wall, OP30-w1, was revealed midway into the level's removal and was located in the southern third of the operation. Pottery associations were mixed in these upper levels.

OP30C was the basal level of the plowzone levels previously described. OP30C was composed of a very dark brown soil with frequent charcoal flecks. Refuse was abundant, with animal bones and common plain and decorated ceramics. These included both Chinchawasi 2 sherds as well as two local Wari polychrome fragments.

OP30D began a series of intact strata. The level was distinguished by the frequent occurrence of small to large wall debris rocks. The ceramics were also clearly phase-affiliated (Chinchawasi 2), with one Warmi sherd. The destruction of the Torreón complex above to the north likely contributed to the wall debris deposit in

OP30D. OP30E was of a compact, hard dark reddish brown soil without the rock rubble of OP30D. This floor level contained small grinding stones and frequent plainware pottery. Three phase diagnostics, all Chinchawasi 2 style, suggest this floor was in use principally during the early Middle Horizon.

OP30F lay directly below the OP30E floor level and was a thick, soft ashy layer of thin strata of interbedded red, black and gray ash lenses. Forty-nine diagnostic sherds were recovered from Level OP30F; 48 were of Chinchawasi 2 phase, the other an unidentified sherd with pre-fire incision.

Underneath, OP30G was a hard, compact layer, composed of a very dark brown soil matrix. The layer was the dirt floor for the structure associated with the wall to the south (OP30-w1). The level was represented by eight diagnostics, all Chinchawasi 2 phase. The basal level, OP30H, was a hard black layer with frequent inclusions of small, unworked rocks. OP30H lay directly atop bedrock throughout the operation and was completely sterile. OP30 reached a maximum depth of 1.23 m below the surface (southwest corner).

## Operation 31

OP31 was at the far southwest end of Terrace 4 and proved to be a very productive 1 by 2 m test pit for stratigraphy and cultural remains. OP31sf was the typical surface level, with a loose and dry very dark brown soil. The next level, OP31A, consisted of a similar soil matrix, but mixed with small dirt granules. OP31B constituted a layer with more frequent inclusions of the granules. At the bottom of this level, especially in the northeast corner, we encountered a much harder soil (but of the same color). OP31sf, OP31A and OP31B, collectively, were considered plowzone components. OP31C was a level of darker softer soil preceded by a thin interbedded layer of small to medium-sized rocks. One Chinchawasi phase sherd was encountered.

OP31D began a series of levels showing intense discard activity. OP31D had a very dark brown soil matrix, somewhat hard and moist to the trowel, with interbedded black lenses and yellow, orange and black mottles. The refuse included dense quantities of painted and plainware ceramics, animal bone, charcoal and feathers out in the southwestern corner of the pit. OP31E was a continuation of the midden deposit encountered in OP31D. The soil matrix was essentially the same—very dark brown to black, with yellow mottles, and moist—but a little softer in texture. OP31D and OP31E contained typical Chinchawasi 2 style pottery.

In OP31F, the mottling found above disappeared and there was a greater abundance of small to medium-sized rocks. At this level we encountered the remains of a north–south wall, OP31-w1, that lay underneath a large wanka stone. In addition to plentiful animal bone, Chinchawasi 1 phase refuse was common. OP31G was the floor level on which the refuse deposit accumulated. The soil matrix was very dark brown to black, moist and compact, though soft in many parts. In the north–central part of the operation, a hearth (defined by burned soil and its contents) was uncovered near a grinding stone. The hearth took an ovoid form in plan, measuring 45 cm in its long dimension. For stratigraphic control, OP31G

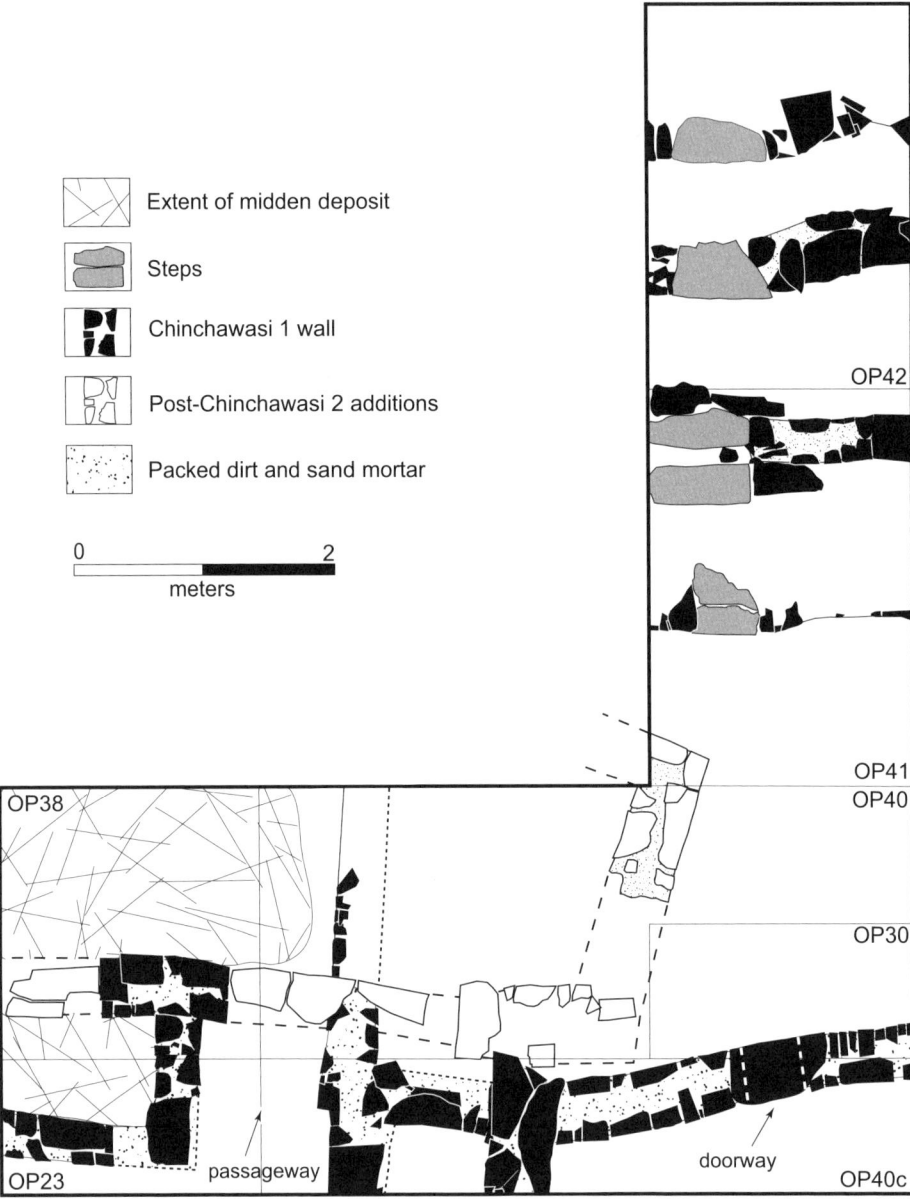

FIGURE 27. Plan of Terrace 4 excavations, Sector 1. A dense midden deposit was found in the western end of the excavation, especially in OP38. A staircase with large stone steps was built on low narrow terraces and provided access into the Torreón structure.

was limited to 10 cm, because it was considered a floor. OP31H was a continuation of the floor deposit; evidence of burning, including charcoal and ashy lenses, was prevalent. Two diagnostics were both of the Chinchawasi 1 style.

An AMS radiocarbon measurement was taken for a wood charcoal sample from OP31H. The sample was found lodged into the Chinchawasi 1 floor. The assay yielded a radiocarbon age of 1305 ± 45 B.P. (A.D. 645 ± 45 uncalibrated or A.D. 687 ± 45 calibrated), with a 2-sigma range of A.D. 654 to 855 (see Table 1). The age is consistent with the stylistic association to the terminal Early Intermediate Period.

OP31I was a dark, wet and clayey soil. The level sat directly above bedrock in all portions of the pit and has frequent inclusions of small angular rocks. No diagnostic artifacts were found in this level. Bedrock was reached 1.83 m below the modern surface in the southwest corner of the pit.

*Terrace 4 Larger Exposures*

OPERATIONS 38, 40, 41 AND 42

Larger exposures (OP38, OP40, OP41 and OP42) aimed to furnish better architectural and spatial contexts for the rich cultural remains and stratigraphy of Terrace 4. The four operations are described as one unit, because they form a single contiguous excavation and because depositional processes, in general, crosscut the operation boundaries (Figures 27 and 28). Exceptions to the general stratigraphy will then be described individually. I will refer to individual operation numbers to identify or locate features and to reference artifact proveniences.

OP38 was a 2 by 2 m unit. OP40 was a 3 by 6 m unit (including OP30). And OP41 and OP42 were 2 by 3 m units. The four operations, incorporating test pits OP23 and OP30, covered 33 m². The initial level was the modern surface level with a dry, dusty and loose soil matrix, with small, eroded sherds, animal bones and mixed ceramic associations (OP38sf, OP40sf, OP41sf and OP42sf).

The underlying level was a stratum of a loose granular soil matrix with common inclusions of small rocks and some medium-sized to large rocks. Cultural materials were scarce and had the character of being reworked, typical of plowzone levels (OP38A, OP40A, OP41A and OP41B).

A darker rocky level (OP38B, OP40B and OP41C) underneath this plowzone featured wall debris and domestic refuse. This level did not occur evenly throughout the operation. Just west of wall OP40-w1 the stratum was even. In the north profile, the rocky debris level was thicker and more concentrated in the west. Moreover, it feathered out to the east, suggesting that the deposit could have been formed by the destruction of the wall dividing Terrace 3 and Terrace 4 (of which the foundations still remain). Because the pottery diagnostics within the destruction layer included Warmi and Chinchawasi 2 styles, we can infer a middle to late Middle Horizon association.

The next level, an ancient compacted floor, extended throughout the west side away from OP40-w1 and was represented by OP38C, OP40C and OP41D. The stratum contained fewer wall debris rocks and more frequent cultural remains. In OP38C, directly underneath the wall debris deposit of OP38B, a compact, dark grayish brown soil matrix was comparatively free of the wall collapse rocks. Farther east toward the wall OP40-w1 the stratum was even harder and more consolidated,

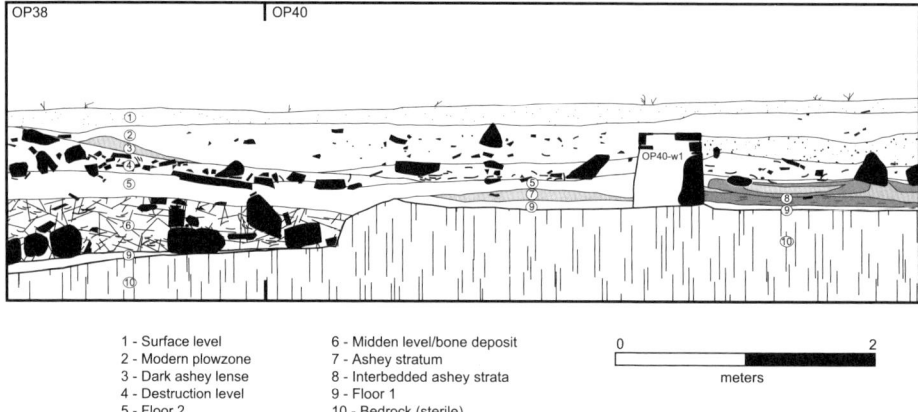

FIGURE 28. North profile of Terrace 4, Sector 1. The lower levels of OP38 featured dense deposits of animal bone, while the eastern portion showed discrete ashy layers, probably from repeated burning activities.

suggesting that, at least on this end, this area had been trodden down considerably and represented an ancient surface on which the darker refuse layer (OP40B) was deposited. In OP38C, OP40C and OP41D, beside common cultural remains such as animal bones, plainware and decorated pottery, we also recovered two copper-metal laminas, broken tools and other exotic raw materials, an antler tine tool, beads of stone and bone, a bone needle and a broken painted animal figurine. Diagnostics included mainly Warmi and imported fancy pottery with late Middle Horizon associations.

East of wall OP40-w1 and underneath the beaten dirt floor surface of OP40C and OP41D was an ashy layer with very fine interbedded gray and black lenses of ash (designated OP40D and OP41E). The ash could be the remnants of nearby cooking events responsible for the midden accumulation to the west. Note that, however, no hearth area was defined in the excavated zone.

Cultural remains were rich in this level and included several bone implements (spatula and scraper), fine lithics such as a point and flakes of obsidian, several pieces of hammered copper-metal laminas and a copper-metal shawl pin fragment. The diagnostic ceramic assemblage for the ashy level (OP40D) contained Chinchawasi 2 pottery almost exclusively.

Underlying the ashy level is OP40E, a very compact, hard and dark blackish brown soil level. The level corresponded to the original floor surface associated with the wall OP40-w1. Unusual artifacts included a fragment of a cranial spoon, a copper-metal shawl pin, a stone bead, a clay spoon, a miniature olla and a bone spindle whorl. This surface corresponded to OP38F and OP41F and was represented by early Chinchawasi phase diagnostics. There were also four fragments of Kayán kaolinite.

On the west side of OP40-w1, OP38D was a thick deposit of dense midden refuse containing mainly animal bone, pottery and rock rubble in a very loose and unconsolidated soil matrix (see also below). There were also abundant amounts of terrestrial snail shells. The diagnostics (n=169) in the dense midden deposit (OP38D) are mainly Chinchawasi 2 and exotics of early Middle Horizon association. The midden deposit was unique to the Chinchawas site both because of its density of artifacts and organic remains and the many imported fancy Middle Horizon period fragments. Except for several small open bowls, a nearly intact fine pinkware spoon and a miniature, no vessel was found complete.

Underlying OP38D was the Chinchawasi 2 occupation floor surface beneath the midden deposit, referred to as OP38E. The soil was far more compact, dark yellowish brown and contained far fewer organic remains. Small bedrock spalls, however, were commonly interspersed within the soil matrix. The refuse in this level included a small nodule of obsidian with flaking scars typical of a core and three spindle whorls of bone, stone and ceramic. Below and directly above bedrock is OP38F, which is characterized by darker color, frequent inclusion of eroding rock and pottery of the Chinchawasi 1 phase. A Kayán fragment was also encountered. Bedrock was reached in different parts of the OP38 and OP40 between 1.28 and 0.8 m below the modern surface.

The Terrace 4 midden was especially remarkable because of its faunal assemblage. The unit, constituted mainly by OP38, recovered over 102.6 kg of faunal materials in a stratum measuring 0.13 to 0.47 m in thickness. The dense bone midden continued to the north and west of the pit boundaries. Although animal remains were prevalent in other parts of Sector 1 (Table 2), the midden deposit in OP38 was distinguished by its density and excellent preservation. The faunal assemblage did not show the intensive fracturing, gnawing or burning one would expect from everyday consumption and disposal patterns (Miller 1979). Further, most of the stratum was still uncompacted and loose to the trowel, with many small pockets containing little soil matrix between bones and debris, suggesting that its deposition was not a gradual process or that very little time elapsed during accumulation episodes.

The faunal assemblage derived mainly from camelids (MNI=64, based on left distal humerus), but small quantities of deer (MNI=2, based on right distal tibia), small mammals (*Canis* sp. and *Lagidium* sp.), guinea pigs (*Cavia* sp.) and other small rodents were also represented (using antler elements would give a deer an MNI of five, but it is unlikely that all antler elements should be attributed to consumption activities; based on antler identification, species represented include the taruca [*Hippocamelus antisensis*] and white-tailed [*Odocoileus virginianus*] varieties). The camelid MNI consists of three categories: small camelid fused (n=35), large camelid fused (n=4) and unfused (n=25). Using an index of usable meat weight (Miller 1979:137–138), the camelid sample totals to 1867.5 kg of usable meat weight, representing 96.9% of all species (Table 3).

Since the small size category likely pertains to alpacas, rather than larger llamas, and the unfused category pertains to younger animals, the sample bears

TABLE 2. Relative abundance of Chinchawas vertebrate taxa from Sector 1, reporting all analyzed materials. MNI, minimum number of individuals; NISP, number of individual specimens. Usable meat weight (in kilograms) estimates follow carcass weight values in Miller (1979).

| Phase | Camelid | Cervid | Indeter. artiodactyl | Cavia sp. | Indeter. rodent | Canis f. | Lagidium p. | Bird | Indeter. small mammal | Totals |
|---|---|---|---|---|---|---|---|---|---|---|
| *Kayán* | | | | | | | | | | |
| NISP | 118 | 9 | 12 | 3 | 0 | 1 | 0 | 0 | 2 | 145 |
| Percentage | 81.4 | 6.2 | 8.3 | 2.1 | — | 0.7 | — | — | 1.4 | 100 |
| MNI | 5 | 1 | — | 1 | — | 1 | — | — | — | 8 |
| Percentage | 62.5 | 12.5 | — | 12.5 | — | 12.5 | — | — | — | 100 |
| Usable weight (kg) | 175 | 36.5 | — | 0.7 | — | 22 | — | — | — | 234.2 |
| Percentage | 74.7 | 15.6 | — | 0.3 | — | 9.4 | — | — | — | 100 |
| *Chinchawasi 1* | | | | | | | | | | |
| NISP | 2025 | 102 | 346 | 37 | 131 | 1 | 12 | 6 | 55 | 2715 |
| Percentage | 74.6 | 3.8 | 12.7 | 1.4 | 4.8 | 0.04 | 0.4 | 0.2 | 2.0 | 100 |
| MNI | 26 | 2 | — | 8 | 4 | 1 | 2 | 2 | — | 45 |
| Percentage | 57.8 | 4.4 | — | 17.8 | 8.9 | 2.2 | 4.4 | 4.4 | — | 100 |
| Usable weight (kg) | 845 | 73 | — | 5.6 | 0.2 | 22 | 2.2 | 1 | — | 949 |
| Percentage | 89.0 | 7.7 | — | 0.6 | 0.02 | 2.3 | 0.2 | 0.1 | — | 100 |
| *Chinchawasi 2* | | | | | | | | | | |
| NISP | 6577 | 115 | 1244 | 48 | 196 | 4 | 7 | 7 | 65 | 8263 |
| Percentage | 79.6 | 1.4 | 15.1 | 0.6 | 2.4 | 0.05 | 0.1 | 0.1 | 0.8 | 100 |
| MNI | 96 | 3 | — | 9 | 19 | 2 | 3 | 1 | — | 133 |
| Percentage | 72.2 | 2.3 | — | 6.8 | 14.3 | 1.5 | 2.3 | 0.8 | — | 100 |
| Usable weight (kg) | 3320 | 109.5 | — | 6.3 | 0.95 | 44 | 3.3 | 0.5 | — | 3484.55 |
| Percentage | 95.3 | 3.1 | — | 0.2 | 0.03 | 1.3 | 0.1 | 0.01 | — | 100 |
| *Warmi* | | | | | | | | | | |
| NISP | 745 | 18 | 75 | 63 | 172 | 1 | 4 | 12 | 26 | 1116 |
| Percentage | 66.8 | 1.6 | 6.7 | 5.6 | 15.4 | 0.1 | 0.4 | 1.1 | 2.3 | 100 |
| MNI | 14 | 1 | — | 2 | 11 | 1 | 1 | 2 | — | 32 |
| Percentage | 43.8 | 3.1 | — | 6.3 | 34.4 | 3.1 | 3.1 | 6.3 | — | 100 |
| Usable weight (kg) | 480 | 36.5 | — | 1.4 | 0.55 | 22 | 1.1 | 1 | — | 542.55 |
| Percentage | 88.5 | 6.7 | — | 0.3 | 0.1 | 4.1 | 0.2 | 0.2 | — | 100 |
| *Chakwas* | | | | | | | | | | |
| NISP | 20 | 0 | 0 | 0 | 0 | 0 | 0 | 0 | 2 | 22 |
| Percentage | 90.9 | — | — | — | — | — | — | — | 9.1 | 100 |
| MNI | 2 | — | — | — | — | — | — | — | — | 2 |
| Percentage | 100.0 | — | — | — | — | — | — | — | — | 100 |
| Usable weight (kg) | 90 | — | — | — | — | — | — | — | — | 90 |
| Percentage | 100.0 | — | — | — | — | — | — | — | — | 100 |

a strong bias (93.8% of MNI, or 87.7% of usable meat) towards camelids with more palatable meat. The low representation of noncamelid species indicates that the disposal activities responsible for the midden focused nearly exclusively on camelids.

Bone artifacts (n=35) were also well represented in Terrace 4. Like the pottery, many have serving functions and show clear use-polish on handles or wear on work edges, including a ladle made from a camelid cranium (Gero 1991, 1992), three bone spatulas, a pelvic "trowel" (Miller 2003:55–57) and eight rib tools. Several of the latter have ground edges or blunt points and could have been used as scraping tools or skewers for meat. The assemblage included two taruca deer crania (*Hippocamelus antisensis*) as well as 12 antler fragments consisting of antler tines, burrs or beam fragments (six taruca [*Hippocamelus antisensis*], two white-tailed deer [*Odocoileus virginianus*] and four unidentified species). The antler was most likely brought from kill sites or curated from outside the Chinchawas area, probably from the puna or the valley bottom; it was used to manufacture tine implements and perhaps also symbolic objects. There were also two thin bone artifacts: a fragment of a round disk with four perforations and an effigy ornament in the shape of a fish (Figure 127I).

Sumptuary items included seven copper-metal artifacts: four hammered lamina ornaments and three shawl pins. The lamina ornaments are circular, with two perforated for hanging. One is particularly large (with a diameter of 6.5 cm) and uses repoussé dots and concentric circles; two holes attach the ornament to a garment or headdress (Figure 134L). The shawl pins have narrow tapering shafts and flat discoidal heads. Other rare objects included several figurines, a miniature vessel and beads of stone or shell. Viewed together, the quantity and character of the Terrace 4 remains indicate that the deposit resulted from corporate activities involving large-scale consumption, particularly of camelids, accompanied by the use or display of special high status accessories.

*Summary of Terrace 4 Operations*
Terrace 4 was used throughout the occupation of the Chinchawas site. Excavations revealed important architectural features and artifact assemblages. The stratigraphy and the superposition of walls suggests that there were at least two main building phases within the area excavated. The space connected to several key areas of the Chinchawas site: the enclosures and terraces to the west and to the Torreón (by way of a staircase to the north).

The first building phase dates to the Chinchawasi 1 occupation. An integral part of the spatial configuration of the sector was a large open space defined in the south by an enclosure wall (Figure 27). Excavations revealed a portion of this wall, measuring 4.5 m in length. Only fallen masonry and debris were encountered south of the wall, indicating that it was the original southern boundary separating Terrace 4 and Terrace 5. Parts of this wall measure 1.2 m in height today and probably stood at least 1.5 m taller. Moreover, it was built atop a natural rise in the bedrock, which provided a platform further elevating it and making the perimeter wall more imposing.

Like other segments of perimeter walls at Chinchawas (e.g., OP43), we identified a small threshold at the foot of the wall. Although the sill of the opening is flush with the interior floor to the north, the threshold would have still been at least 3 m above the height of the terrace surface immediately below (south of the wall).

TABLE 3. Faunal remains from Operation 38, Sector 1, Chinchawas. MNI, minimum number of individuals; NISP, number of individual specimens. Usable meat weight (in kilograms) estimates follow carcass weight values in Miller (1979).

| Remains | Camelid (small) | Camelid (large) | Camelid (unfused) | Camelid (indeter.) | Total camelid | Cervid | Small mammal | Cuy | Other rodents |
|---|---|---|---|---|---|---|---|---|---|
| **Cranial** | | | | | | | | | |
| Maxilla | — | — | — | 120 | 120 | — | — | 1 | 3 |
| Mandible | — | — | — | 53 | 53 | — | — | 2 | 5 |
| Condyle arch | — | — | — | 58 | 58 | — | — | — | — |
| Antler | — | — | — | — | — | 14 | — | — | — |
| **Forelimb** | | | | | | | | | |
| Scapula (glenoid) | 40 | 21 | — | 34 | 95 | 1 | — | 2 | — |
| Scapula (miscellaneous.) | 8 | 1 | — | — | 9 | 1 | — | — | — |
| Humerus (proximal and distal) | 1 | — | 3 | — | 4 | — | — | — | 4 |
| Proximal humerus | 18 | 11 | 56 | — | 85 | 1 | — | — | — |
| Distal humerus | 66 | 16 | 54 | — | 136 | 2 | 1 | 1 | 1 |
| Radio-ulna (proximal and distal) | 2 | — | 2 | — | 4 | — | — | 1 | — |
| Proximal radio-ulna | 52 | 12 | 79 | — | 143 | — | — | 1 | — |
| Distal radio-ulna | 31 | 18 | 81 | — | 130 | 1 | 1 | — | — |
| Radius | — | — | — | — | — | — | 1 | — | — |
| **Hind limb** | | | | | | | | | |
| Tibia (proximal and distal) | — | — | 8 | — | 8 | — | 1 | 2 | 3 |
| Proximal tibia | 40 | 21 | 116 | — | 177 | — | — | — | — |
| Distal tibia | 30 | 18 | 81 | — | 129 | 2 | — | — | — |
| Patella | 28 | 10 | — | 2 | 40 | — | — | — | — |
| Femur (proximal and distal) | 1 | — | 3 | — | 4 | — | 2 | — | 8 |
| Proximal femur | 21 | 17 | 86 | — | 124 | 2 | — | — | — |
| Distal femur | 37 | 19 | 106 | — | 162 | 1 | — | 1 | — |
| Pelvis (acetabulum) | 75 | 36 | — | 137 | 248 | — | 2 | 2 | 5 |
| **Podial** | | | | | | | | | |
| Carpal | 198 | 50 | — | 2 | 250 | 3 | — | — | — |
| Metacarpal (proximal and distal) | 4 | 3 | 12 | — | 19 | 2 | — | — | — |
| Proximal metacarpal | 48 | 12 | 28 | — | 88 | 2 | — | — | — |
| Distal metapodial | 66 | 34 | 199 | — | 299 | 12 | — | — | — |
| Metatarsal (proximal and distal) | 10 | 1 | 4 | — | 15 | — | — | — | — |
| Proximal metatarsal | 61 | 16 | 19 | — | 96 | 2 | — | — | — |
| Tarsal | 163 | 34 | — | 1 | 198 | 4 | — | — | — |
| Astralagus | 85 | 17 | — | — | 102 | — | — | — | — |
| Calcaneum | 39 | 9 | 55 | — | 103 | — | — | — | — |
| Phalanx 1 | 122 | 31 | 147 | — | 300 | 6 | — | — | — |
| Phalanx 2 | 69 | 35 | 38 | — | 142 | 7 | — | — | — |
| Phalanx 3 | 38 | 11 | 1 | — | 50 | 5 | — | — | — |
| **Axial** | | | | | | | | | |
| Atlas | 25 | 12 | 19 | — | 56 | — | — | 1 | — |
| Axis | 19 | 8 | 15 | — | 42 | — | — | — | — |
| Sternum | 12 | 5 | — | — | 17 | — | — | — | — |
| Sacrum | 13 | 13 | 35 | — | 61 | 2 | — | — | — |
| Caudal | — | — | — | — | — | — | 2 | — | — |
| **Total NISP** | 1,422 | 491 | 1,247 | 407 | 3567 | 70 | 10 | 14 | 29 |
| MNI | 35 | 4 | 25 | | 64 | 2 | 2 | 1 | 4 |
| Usable meat (kg) | 1,137.5 | 230 | 500 | | 1,867.5 | 55 | 4.8 | 0.7 | 0.2 |

Total usable meat = 1928.2 kg

The wall ends abruptly near the western end of OP40 and intersecting wall segments proceed northward and southward. To the north, only the lowermost exterior register of this wall remains, built on a very low rise of bedrock. How far this wall extended is unclear, but the southern segment probably did not go beyond the limit of the bedrock platform.

Roughly 1 m to the west of the enclosure's southwest corner we encountered an L-shaped segment of a Chinchawasi 1 wall, similarly built on bedrock. The open space between the two perimeter wall segments could have been an access into the Terrace 4 zone. However, we did not find evidence of steps, either of stone or as depressions cut into the bedrock, that would verify this. There was a dense concentration of heavy rocks and mixed refuse between the two walls.

North of the wall threshold we uncovered a series of four parallel walls that functioned as low terrace platforms leading up to the Torreón structure (OP41 and OP42; see Figure 27). In alignment between the wall opening and the crest of the Torreón structure, the walls of the low terraces use large flat stones as steps upwards. We found six steps, possibly seven.

In addition to the unique architecture, this area during the Chinchawasi 1 phase is distinguished by considerable amounts of finely crafted objects. Hammered copper-metal ornaments, beads, figurines and fancy spindle whorls indicate the presence of individuals with greater access to prestige goods. Most of these artifacts were found in a diagnostic layer of fine gray, light brown and black ash. Deposition or discard of these artifacts probably occurred intermittently under the context of repeated burning episodes throughout the operation.

The Chinchawasi 2 use of Terrace 4 manifests a different character. The stone steps fell into disuse at this time and earlier walls were destroyed, built over or reused. The window was sealed off from the inside with a flat slab and rock fill was inserted into the small passageway. A structure of unknown size was built in the western end of the operation. It is enclosed by a series of new walls, in parts mixing new "patchwork" masonry with co-opted segments of the old wanka–pachilla architecture. The building seems to have been at least partially trapezoidal, and not at right angles. The structure measured more than 5 m long and about 1.5 m wide at its east end.

By far the most prominent activity discernible in the western portion of Terrace 4 was massive dumping of animal bones, pottery and other refuse. This pattern is prominent as early as Chinchawasi 1 and seems to have been the result of activities in adjacent architectural spaces (e.g., Enclosure 2 and the Torreón). Evidence for displays of status and ostentation included sumptuary items, such as fancy exotic (serving) ceramics, copper-metal artifacts, antler and lapidary work. Elsewhere I have interpreted these materials as the remains of intensive feasting episodes, sponsored by local leaders and groups to acquire political authority and labor debts (Lau 2002). By the Warmi phase, the accumulation of refuse from such activities ceased, almost certainly because both Enclosure 2 and the Torreón fell into disuse.

# Terrace 5

Terrace 5 is directly south of Terrace 4 and is lower in elevation. Large ancient walls delimit the northern and southern boundaries of the sector. The sector, in turn, is partitioned into smaller areas by modern fieldstone walls; these areas today are corrals or small agricultural plots. Test pits in Terrace 5 sought to determine the chronology of the large ancient retaining walls and evaluate what types of activities were taking place in the outer areas, as reflected in depositional patterns.

## Terrace 5 Operations

### OPERATION 33

OP33 was a 1 by 2 m unit close to the southern terrace wall. OP33sf was the plowzone surface level. OP33A was a harder soil layer, typical of the level of plowzone just underneath the soft loose soil of the modern surface. There was no change in soil color. Cultural materials in both levels were mixed. OP33B, a level of rock rubble and fill, was of a dark brown granular soil type with frequent inclusions of large and small rocks. Near the top of this level we found the aligned stones of two masonry walls. One, referred to as OP33-w1, running east–west, crossed with OP33-w2, a wall that ran north–south. Cultural materials included three Chinchawasi sherds. Given the obstacle of the wall, excavation was terminated. OP33 reached a maximum excavated depth of 0.62 m.

### OPERATION 34

OP34, a 1 by 2 m unit, was located at the far western end of Terrace 5, just north of the southern retaining wall. The southern retaining wall at this location was massive and uses wanka–pachilla architecture. Today the area is built up because of erosion from the hilltop, and from agricultural and pastoral activities. Local people use broken portions of the southern retaining wall to cross between Terrace 5 and Terrace 6.

OP34sf was the modern surface level of loose and dry plowzone soil. It was dark brown with no diagnostic artifacts. OP34A was the typical harder plowzone soil stratum just below the modern surface. It had the same color soil and included mixed pottery associations.

OP34B formed a massive destruction layer characterized by frequent large rocks of different sizes. The soil was a slightly darker brown and had a granular texture, but remained dry and soft. OP34C was a continuation of the wall debris destruction level, but in a sandy, dark yellowish brown soil matrix. Like OP34B, Level C had abundant wall debris rocks, including very big rocks (larger than 30 cm). We found no diagnostic potsherds in OP34B or OP34C. OP34D consisted of a darker brown soil. The rock rubble diminished, although there were still frequent small rocks. The soil was relatively loose and there were considerably more artifacts, although the associations were mixed. OP34E was a very hard dark brown stratum with flecks of charcoal. A deeper portion of the same effective layer was referred to as OP34F, which represented the basal stratum lying directly above bedrock. The soil matrix was moist and very compact. Diagnostic pottery pertained to the Warmi occupation. OP34 reached a depth of 1.02 m below the modern surface.

## Operation 35

OP35, a 1 by 2 m test unit, was in the east–central portion of Terrace 5. No architecture was visible on the surface. OP35sf was the modern surface, but was exceptionally dry and hard, in contrast to the loose and soft agricultural plowzone surfaces elsewhere. The matrix was dark grayish brown. Slightly farther down the soil became softer and darker (OP35A). Small clods of earth were also present. In Level A the foundations of several walls emerged. A wall (OP35-w1) in the eastern half of the pit ran southwest to northwest. This was the foundation of a late wall of unknown date, perhaps fairly recent, although diagnostics included Chinchawasi and Warmi specimens. The wall was of large rocks and good craftsmanship, but represented the basal foundations of the wall and does not continue farther down.

After the wall's (OP35-w1) removal, excavations proceeded in an area bounded in the southwest corner by a second wall (OP35-w2). The first stratum was OP35B, a very dark soil without the clods of earth found in the previous level. The artifacts indicate that there was considerable disturbance even before the construction of the first wall (OP35-w1). In the southwest corner, a small hearth emerged containing a dense concentration of ashy soil, with frequent flecks and some chunks of charcoal. OP35C, a stratum excavated only within the southwest corner, was a brown layer of burnt earth below the ashy layer.

OP35D was a harder, more compact stratum underneath OP35C, that is, in the southwest corner bounded by OP35-w2. It was dark yellowish brown and had a gritty, sandy consistency. OP35E represented the same stratum on the other side of the wall (OP35-w2). Although no diagnostics were encountered in Level D, Level E (OP35E) revealed common Chinchawasi 2 remains. There was also a small, carved figurine in the Recuay style (Figure 122D). OP35F bore the same consistency (compact with frequent small to medium-sized rocks), but was darker, a very dark brown to black. Of the 20 diagnostics found in this stratum, all were associated with the Chinchawasi 2 style, including a fine pinkware spoon fragment.

OP35G contained no rocks at all and was dark (very dark brown) with a moist and sticky consistency. OP35H represented an arbitrary level change, because of no discernible natural level change after some 25 cm in each corner. The soil continued to be moist and very dark brown, with very few rocks. In the northwest corner a hearth feature was identified with burnt earth, flecks of carbon and abundant amounts of domestic refuse, including burnt animal bone and ceramics. OP35I was a more compact soil matrix, but of the same soil color. It is further distinguished by having substantially fewer artifacts. OP35J was a dark black soil, which was very moist, with some small rock inclusions. The artifacts became increasingly scarce; no decorated pottery was recovered. Levels G to J of OP35 were deposited during the Chinchawasi 1 phase.

OP35K was a sharp break, with the soil a dark brown with occasional pieces of fragmented bedrock mixed in. This represented the basal layer directly above bedrock. The level was essentially sterile, with only a few potsherds, none of which could be identified to phase. OP35 reached a maximum excavated depth of 2.14 m below the unit datum.

## Operation 36

OP36, a 1 by 2 m test unit, was located to the southeast of OP35, near the southern retaining wall of Terrace 5. OP36sf was a very loose and dusty soil (dark grayish brown). OP36A represented the harder plowzone level underlying the modern surface level. OP36B pertained to a stratum defined by a very dark soil. The remains of three circular or ovoid concentrations of very dark ashy soil indicate the presence of three burned areas. OP36C constituted a new stratum of loose dark brown matrix, interspersed with very dark grayish brown soil granules. The investigations recovered very few artifacts from the uppermost levels. OP36D was a wall debris destruction level consisting of a loose brown and granular soil matrix mixed with frequent small to medium-sized rocks. No diagnostic artifacts were recovered from this stratum.

OP36E consisted of very dark brown to black soil, hard and compact, with common inclusions of small rocks and occasional medium-sized rocks. Warmi pottery was common in Level E. OP36F was a stratum of a dark yellowish brown soil mixed with lenses of the soil from OP36E. Frequent wall debris types of rocks characterized this level and seem to correspond to the filling in or collapse of areas throughout the site. The level was relatively sterile; no diagnostics were encountered. Given its intermediate stratigraphic position, Level F was likely laid down during Warmi times.

OP36G was a distinct very dark grayish brown to black soil level, very compact and moist. The level was a beaten dirt floor surface found throughout the operation. It is below the destruction level described in OP36F. The cultural refuse was diverse and included only late Middle Horizon types: 48 local Warmi sherds (60%), 28 press-molded pieces (35%) and three sherds with appliqué or plastic decoration (3.75%). In association with this deposit of material were complete plainware vessels. The pottery was surprisingly intact given their provenience in an outer terrace area.

An AMS radiocarbon measurement was taken from a wood charcoal point sample retrieved from the OP36G floor deposit ($x$: –34.43N, $y$: –48.60W, $z$: –1.65 m). The sample yielded a radiocarbon age of 1170 ± 55 B.P. (A.D. 780 ± 55 uncalibrated, or A.D. 886 ± 55 calibrated), with a 2-sigma range of A.D. 718 to 998 (see Table 1). The age agrees with the late Middle Horizon stylistic association of the ceramics and other Warmi dates.

OP36H was the basal layer of the pit and was distinguished by a lighter brown color mixed with lenses of yellow clayey soil. The upper portion of OP36H, a beaten dirt floor, also featured three depressions (from 5 to 10 cm in depth) to hold large jars. These depressions were associated with a hearth feature in the northeast corner. Chinchawasi 1 ceramics characterized the deposit. Underneath the floor the matrix was similarly compacted, while in others it was looser and mixed with small stones. This stratum was thicker on the western end than on the eastern end. OP36 reached a maximum depth of 2.16 m below the northwest datum.

*[sh1]Summary of Terrace 5 Excavations*
Although the size of the sample precludes a precise understanding of activities, the excavations were very useful in defining the chronology of the occupation and use of Terrace 5. In brief, Chinchawasi 1 groups seem to have favored the eastern portion. By the Warmi phase, the inhabitants of Chinchawas expanded into the western portion (a steeper area) and used the eastern portion of the terrace, probably for some habitation and refuse disposal.

# Terrace 6

Terrace 6 lies just south of Terrace 5 and is delimited by ancient terrace walls to the north and south. Modern rock pilings have partitioned Terrace 6's eastern and western ends. The southern retaining wall, covered by overburden and modern vegetation, probably continues to the east and west. Terrace 6 is much steeper than Terrace 5 and its southern retaining wall spans about a third of the length of the southern terrace wall of Terrace 5. Today parts of the terrace are used to pasture sheep and in the far eastern end there are small agricultural plots for potatoes.

*Terrace 6 Operations*

OPERATION 37
Test excavation OP37 was located at the bottom of the terrace slope, just north of the southern retaining wall, and the modern partition separated the terrace from an agricultural plot. OP37 aimed to examine the area's cultural associations and use.

OP37sf, OP37A and OP37B consisted of modern surface and plowzone layers. OP37C began a thick stratum of wall and destruction debris, with abundant small to large rocks. Larger rocks were especially dense in the western half of the operation. The dark yellowish brown soil was gritty and dry. No diagnostics were recovered from this layer. In OP37C, the top of a large north–south wall emerged, referred to as OP37-w1, and effectively cut the operation in half. The wall was well made in the wanka–pachilla masonry style. The eastern side of the operation continued as OP37e-D, while the western side continued as OP37w-D.

OP37e-D was a continuation of the wall and destruction debris level above in OP37C. The soil matrix became a little darker brown than its counterpart in OP37C, but remained a dark yellowish brown sandy soil mixed with unworked rocks of various sizes. There was also the frequent occurrence of small cream-white hard granules or pebbles, interpreted as small calcium carbonate accretions. In some areas the soil got darker, probably from the mixing of ash and burned midden materials during the wall debris accumulation. Cultural associations were mixed. In OP37e-E the soil became a darker brown, more moist and less gritty. In addition, the rock rubble petered out. As expected, cultural associations were mixed in these upper fill levels.

OP37e-F was a stratum of very dark brown moist soil, but showed occasional interbedding of the yellowish sandy soil lenses from above. This level was rich in pottery refuse, including eight Chinchawasi 2 diagnostics and a fine pinkware spoon fragment. At the base of OP37e-F we encountered the remains of a floor level paved by two large flagstones and many smaller flat stones.

This level was designated OP37e-G. OP37e-G's pavement was located only on the east side of the wall, suggesting that this floor functioned as the principal interior surface of the building, probably the wall or floor section of a domestic cooking area. Around and just underneath the paving stones in the south was a dense oval concentration of animal bone associated with burnt soil and frequent flecks of carbon. The remains included cuy (guinea pig) and camelid bone, as well as deer antler fragments. This deposit is interpreted as the remains of a hearth containing domestic refuse. OP37e-G held six diagnostic sherds, all Chinchawasi 2 style.

Beneath the flagstones was the basal stratum of the operation. OP37e-H was a dark black, very moist and compact soil level directly above bedrock. The few artifacts in this stratum belonged to the Chinchawasi 2 occupation. The primary use of the wall, OP37-w1, was associated with this final layer and the flagstone floor of OP37e-G.

In the western half of the pit, OP37w-D lay under OP37C and was represented by a dark brown stratum of wall debris rock with small creamy white calcium carbonate accretions. The cultural associations were mixed. OP37w-D was identical to OP37e-D in soil color, texture and content.

Subsequent levels were Chinchawasi 2 in association. OP37w-E began a very dark brown layer, with a moist and sticky, and somewhat sandy, consistency. The white granules diminished and refuse discard became more common. This level corresponds to OP37e-E and OP37e-F. OP37w-F was a dark reddish brown stratum directly above bedrock. It was a thin layer and had a gritty and rocky consistency, probably resulting from spalling bedrock. This level corresponds to OP37e-H.

OP37 provided useful insights into the prehistoric settlement layout of Chinchawas. First, it established that domestic occupation of the site by Chinchawasi 2 and Warmi peoples occurred as far south as Terrace 6. Second, we encountered a Chinchawasi 2 domestic floor level. An orderly pavement out of flat rocks, some of which are large flagstones, distinguishes the interior. The exterior meanwhile has no such pavement, but does seem to have been used for dumping activity.

## Operation 39

OP39 was an extension of test pit OP37; together both pits formed a 2 by 3 m unit. The operation was extended because the pit showed productive stratigraphy and the presence of fancy pottery. In addition, we were surprised to encounter these in association with wanka–pachilla walls so far from the central part of the site and aimed to investigate the spatial context for the deposits.

The stratigraphy of OP39 resembled that of OP37. After a series of mixed plowzone and wall debris levels, we encountered a level that contained Chinchawasi 2 ceramics and an imported Wari polychrome fragment. The north–south wall found initially as OP37-w1 continued into the larger operation and similarly divided it into an east and west side. The bottom of level OP39C was a compact beaten dirt floor surface with almost none of the rocks typical of the wall debris levels above. On the west side, this floor surface revealed a broken human cranium, a bead and a grinding stone.

Below an almost sterile yellowish brown fill layer (OP39e.D) we encountered several strata containing Chinchawasi 2 pottery. The yellow sand seems to have been for grading the east side of the wall for some type of construction. Pottery from the underlying levels (OP39e.E and OP39e.F) belonged exclusively to the Chinchawasi 2 style.

In the west side we did not encounter substantial amounts of the yellow sandy level, but instead a large deposit of rocks and fill. Underneath there was a Warmi phase level (OP39w.F); in addition to pottery and animal bones, the level contained a copper-metal lamina, a point and a small stone disc. There was a small hearth area in the southwest corner.

## Terrace 7

Terrace 7 is located mainly in the southeast of Chinchawas Sector 1 and is composed mainly of low to medium height retaining walls, or foundations of both modern and ancient buildings. The entire zone is highly eroded with very little depth of cultural deposit anywhere; there are outcrops of bedrock throughout this zone. For these reasons, Terrace 7 was not sampled through archaeological excavation.

## Terrace 8

Terrace 8 is to the east of Terrace 1 and is defined by a series of walls to the north and Room Complex 1 and the Torreón complex to the southeast (Figure 11). "Terrace" may again be a misnomer, because in antiquity the sector seems to have been composed of several agglutinated room structures now buried. Today only the northern wall is visible on the surface. Two test operations elucidate the use and cultural sequence of Terrace 8.

### *Terrace 8 Operations*

#### Operation 27

OP27 was a 1 by 2 m test unit located in the central portion of Terrace 8. OP27sf and OP27A were plowzone levels with mixed cultural associations. OP27B began a new level distinguished especially by many large plainware pottery sherds, mainly from large jars and cooking ollas. The pottery was mixed in with large wall rocks and debris. This new stratum was called OP27B, although the soil matrix resembled OP27A. The deposit contained several Warmi phase sherds and two exotic Middle Horizon sherds, a fragment with raised dots and another press-molded, suggesting a late Middle Horizon component. In the northwest corner of the operation the end of partition wall, OP27-w1, ran more or less diagonal to the operation.

Levels C to E in OP27 contained Chinchawasi 2 pottery. OP27C consisted of dark yellowish brown soil with fewer artifacts, mainly plainware ceramics. OP27D was a deeper continuation of OP27C, but the soil was harder and there were much fewer artifacts. A ground slate point was recovered from this level. OP27E was a beaten dirt floor surface with very dark brown layer, almost black, with common charcoal flecks and fragments, right above bedrock throughout the operation. OP27 reached a maximum excavated depth of 1.39 m.

OPERATION 28

OP28 was a 1 by 2 m test unit in the eastern portion of Terrace 8. OP28sf constituted the modern surface layer and was composed of a dry and loose dark brown soil matrix. OP28A was a harder and rockier stratum, with concentrations of domestic pottery in the south–central portion. A large east–west wall was at the base of the stratum, OP28-w1. Cultural remains indicate Warmi associations.

OP28B was the final level encountered in the operation, and graded into bedrock. The soil was more compact, but the color and texture resembled the previous level. Six Chinchawasi 1 phase sherds were recovered, as well as one Kayán kaolinite fragment and several fragments from a polished modeled face. These may have been from face-neck vessels. OP28 reached a maximum depth of 0.60 m (northwest corner).

## Terrace 9

Terrace 9 is located directly opposite Sector 1, approximately 100 m south of the Torreón structure. The terrace wall faces the Chinchawas ridgetop. At the base of a mountain slope, its interior space rises to the south away from Sector 1. Today sections of this large angular enclosure are used as a corral and there are foundations of abandoned modern buildings above (to the south). The wall is built of wanka–pachilla masonry, at least in the basal registers. The wall is topped almost everywhere by rough stone pilings without mortar. Some segments of the wanka–pachilla wall have undergone patchwork renovation in less finely crafted stonework.

*Terrace 9 Operations*

OPERATION 62

OP62 was a 1 by 2 m unit opened to test for stratigraphy and cultural remains on the far north end of Terrace 9. It was located at the northernmost part of the area enclosed, near the large terrace wall, at the foot of a gentle slope. Although the test operation reached bedrock at a maximum depth of 1.78 m below pit datum, very few diagnostic artifacts were recovered from the unit. The most common type was domestic plainware pottery. Diagnostic associations were few and inconclusive, although Chinchawasi and Warmi styles were represented most frequently in the assemblage. The most common artifacts accompanied a thick deposit of rock rubble eroding in from the south. Most notable among these were several broken copper-metal adornment fragments.

Based on this scant evidence, one can argue nevertheless that this southern area saw at least limited use both initially during the Chinchawasi phase and again during the Warmi phase. In addition to the pottery, the wanka–pachilla masonry style places the construction of the terrace wall during the Chinchawasi phases. The pottery was occasional and there is very little evidence that the area was used intensively, and most likely not for residential purposes. It is possible that the area, like today, was used to pen animals.

## Conclusions

The terrace area excavations of Sector 1 show that, throughout the occupation of the main ridgetop, local Chinchawas peoples used and transformed the terrace areas for vital activities (Figure 11). The Kayán and Chinchawasi 1 occupations were mainly limited to the central portion of uppermost ridgetop. By Chinchawasi 1 times many of the major perimeter walls still extant today had been erected. Later occupations, associated with the Middle Horizon florescence of the site, expanded the overall settlement by moving away from the ridgetop and creating new walled areas.

The terrace areas were open spaces that served and facilitated different functions, including refuse discard, domestic and craft activities, and interior construction. Refuse discard was prominent during the Chinchawasi phases in Terrace 1 and in Terrace 3, but was especially intensive along the western portion of Terrace 4. This seems to have been related to episodic public ceremonies located in the central portion of the village. The contents of the middens suggest that the activities involved large-scale consumption of camelid meat, the use and discard of fancy local and imported wares (probably for serving), and display of prestige objects.

In areas of primary deposition, domestic and other economic activities were documented throughout the terrace areas, including spinning fiber, food preparation and the production of implements out of chipped stone, antler and bone. These activities were most intensive in Terrace 1 (eastern portion) and the western portion of Terrace 3 during the Chinchawasi phases. The western portion of Terrace 3 and Terrace 2 became more important as activity areas during the subsequent Warmi phase. Terrace 5 and Terrace 9, meanwhile, were almost certainly used for penning animals.

We found small canals in different terrace areas, including Terrace 1 and Terrace 3. These were small channels, usually just above bedrock and covered by flat stones, used to divert rainwater away from areas vulnerable to pooling water. The great elaboration of the canals, especially in higher status areas, indicate that drainage was a perennial concern of Chinchawas's inhabitants and their village planning.

At different times during the occupation of Chinchawas, local peoples moved the perimeter walls outward, probably to reclaim larger portions of the upper ridgetop. The widening of the perimeter walls also probably shielded a larger population from raids and group-level hostilities. By the height of its occupation during Chinchawasi 2 and Warmi times, Chinchawas extended to include the walled areas of Terrace 6 and Terrace 9. Today many of these outer terraces are used as small agricultural plots or makeshift corrals.

Finally, the program of excavation sampling at Chinchawas also shows that subsurface architecture is very common in terrace areas. In many of the terrace locations, processes of erosion have buried prehistoric architecture and activity areas. At any given highland site under such conditions, therefore, site mapping alone may not capture the full diversity of architecture and occupation.

CHAPTER FIVE

# INVESTIGATIONS OF SECTOR 2 MORTUARY CONSTRUCTIONS

The archaeological investigations at Chinchawas included the clearing and excavation of three subterranean tomb structures and seven aboveground chullpa structures in the Sector 2 portion of the site (see Figures 10 and 29). Despite prior looting activities in all of these structures, our excavations were able to salvage useful archaeological data. Specifically, the data provide insights on the cultural and temporal associations for two distinct funerary traditions and on changing patterns of mortuary architecture at the site. The study also furnishes a basic bioarchaeological profile of the interments, although these should be considered preliminary until systematic analyses, currently in progress, become available. As part of the larger study on sociocultural transformations of the ancient Chinchawas community, the data on the mortuary structures and their contents are central to understanding changing local ceremonial patterns.

## Background and Reconnaissance

One of my primary reasons for working at Chinchawas was to study its diversity of standing stone architecture. My initial visits to the site in 1995 and 1996 identified strong formal variability in funerary architecture, with multiple examples of different types exposed on the surface. One form was the subterranean chamber tomb. Others were of the chullpa tomb type, an aboveground mortuary structure, or more rarely, a long row or gallery structure along perimeter walls. Such architectural forms are not uncommon in the Callejón de Huaylas and have analogues in other parts of the Central Andes.

Unfortunately, all of the examples had been looted. As is often the case with looted tombs in the Andes, the human remains frequently survive. While looking for intact collectibles and whole vessels, looters generally leave the bone material and broken artifacts within the tomb chamber, albeit tossed around and disarticulated.

Although recovery of precise information on burial position and provenience of grave goods would be difficult, other potentially important data could be salvaged through systematic research of these tombs. In particular, we aimed to recover information on the number and types of individuals in a given tomb and cultural associations with other parts of the site. Perhaps most fundamental,

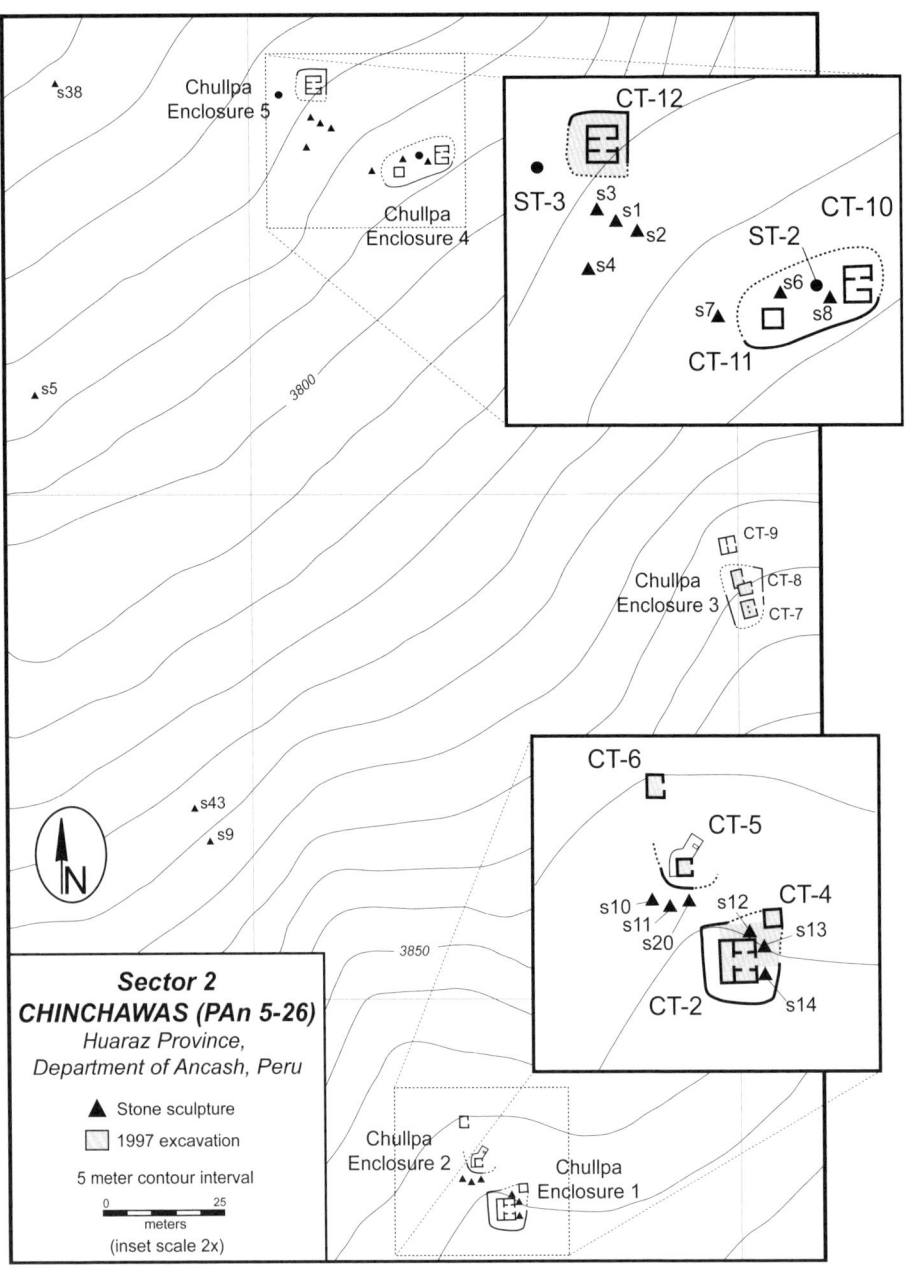

FIGURE 29. Sector 2, Chinchawas, showing the location of subterranean and chullpa tombs, stone sculptures and project operations.

we were interested in the chronological placement and basic use of these tombs, persistent sources of confusion in the literature. Are these chullpas, in fact, tombs or were they, as some have claimed, houses or temples?

Wendell Bennett (1944) pioneered a relative chronology for the Callejón de Huaylas region: the Chavín, Huarás, Recuay, Tiahuanacoid and Inca periods. Through association, he was able to place the middle three periods with architecture, which, on the basis of his study and more recent research, can be interpreted as clearly mortuary in character. The Huarás (or "Huaraz") period interments were modest graves underlying large rocks or boulders. On the basis of stratigraphy, Bennett surmised that Recuay culture antedated the Middle Period or "Tiahuanacoid" Wari-influenced culture in the Callejón de Huaylas.

Bennett was able to associate, in general, subterranean galleries with Recuay culture and aboveground chullpas with Middle Period materials. The principal function, however, remained ambiguous. For example, Bennett (1944:104) described the Wilkawaín examples as "burial galleries," but said similar galleries at Shankaiyan were used for habitation purposes. Similarly, Bennett (1944:106) maintained that some, if not most, of the chullpas were domestic structures, or "houses." Indeed, human skeletal remains found inside the structures were "intrusive." Bennett (1944:104) did not believe chullpas had a mortuary purpose. Rather, burials took other forms, such as deep stone-lined and stone-covered tombs, and small stone-lined boxlike graves under boulders. For Bennett, even some of the subterranean chamber tombs ("subterranean houses") had a domestic character.

Later, in the 1960s, as part of the multidisciplinary Cornell–Vicos Project, Gary Vescelius and Hernan Amat did extensive work in the Callejón de Huaylas using survey, test quadrats and areal excavations in the zone above Carhuaz. In several secondhand, much abridged summaries, they were said to have refined the regional cultural sequence, as well as have come up with a typology of mortuary forms to fit into the cultural sequence (cited in Buse 1965; Lanning 1965). In addition, Vescelius and Amat were said to have found Viñaque style (Middle Horizon) pottery in their excavations of a large Honcopampa chullpa (Buse 1965; Amat 1976b; Isbell 1989, 1991a). However, the results were never published in full.

Subsequent work has done little to improve Bennett's original framework of mortuary practices. Scholars have provided useful lists of mortuary settlements (Soriano Infante 1940; Tello 1956; Mejía Xesspe 1957). Several studies have focused on high-status Recuay tombs, such as the excavations at Pashash (Grieder 1978) and the accidental discovery of the Jancu tomb (Wegner 1988), which reiterate the primary pattern of subterranean graves in the Recuay heartland. Other research has broadened the range of prehistoric burial practices in the Callejón de Huaylas. At Huaricoto, Burger and Salazar-Burger (Burger 1985a) discovered the secondary burial of 12 individuals within a stone-cyst construction associated with the Huarás period. In the summer of 1997, in preparation for a predicted heavy El Niño season, officials at the site of Chavín de Huántar discovered a mass burial of primary and secondary interments in a drainage canal underneath the sunken rectangular plaza (east side); pottery was reported to be in the Recuay style.

Chullpas are relatively well known through excavations and other investigations (Zaki 1978a, 1987; Ponte Rosalino 1999a, 1999b, 2000; Paredes et al. 2000; Lau 2001, 2002; Ibarra 2003b; Herrera 2005). However, there has been little research on the relationship of mortuary architecture to residential communities, on patterns of cultural change and on how there emerged a rapid shift to aboveground chullpa type mausolea (Isbell 1997).

## Sector 2 Investigations

The Sector 2 zone lies due east of the main part of the Chinchawas site. It featured small mortuary constructions on low-lying ridges of exposed bedrock (Figure 29). We identified 16 discrete mortuary constructions of two general types (Table 4): the chullpa and the subterranean chamber tomb. Of these, we excavated seven chullpas and three subterranean tombs. This section summarizes the distinctive features of each construction and provides a brief description of each construction's inventory. Their contents indicate distinct cultural and temporal associations for the two mortuary traditions.

### Subterranean Chamber Tombs

We encountered three subterranean chamber tombs in Sector 2 (Figures 30 and 31). Two of the three are short gallery tombs. These are rectangular in plan and are entered from the top. Each features a small chamber immediately on entry, providing a small vestibule that leads to the larger main chamber, which is shaped in more or less the form of a shoebox. The other example's main chamber is roughly oval in plan, but has a similar entry chamber.

The tombs share several attributes. In addition to their placement below the surface and the entry vestibule, the tombs use bedrock as sides or walls. In addition, they have wanka–pachilla type masonry and, for roofs, use large tabular slabs or boulders. All had been disturbed by looting and reopening, probably in prehispanic times.

OPERATION 56 (ST-1)
OP56 (ST-1) was a subterranean chamber tomb, with its primary chamber shaped in plan like an irregular oval (Figure 30A). The main chamber had a maximum length of 1.94 m and a height of 1.2 m. Two small rooms were attached, on the west and east sides. The east attachment served as an antechamber or vestibule. The doorway is narrow at only 40 cm wide and low at 80 cm high. The top of this antechamber was probably capped by a flat stone or boulder, which no longer survives. The west addition was a back-recess chamber. The stonework is of the wanka–pachilla type and used bedrock for both walls and its floor surface. At least two large flat boulders concealed the tomb and served as the roof.

In addition to human skeletal remains, 22 decorated sherds were encountered during excavation of the tomb. Of these, two were Chinchawasi phase, seven were of a small single-spouted bottle in late Moche style, and 13 small fragments were of a polished and molded blackware style. The pottery suggests a late Early Intermediate Period tomb association.

Located directly above the tomb is a large round wanka, roughly a meter tall, of reddish-brown stone. The upright is flat on two sides and is lodged atop a low masonry platform (about 5 cm tall) that evens the sloping bedrock. The wanka apparently marks the location of the OP56 tomb (also at Jancu).

## Operation 63 (ST-2)

Subterranean Tomb 2 was investigated as OP63 (Figure 31). The principal rectangular chamber is entered from the top and through a small entry portal in the northern end. The long dimension of the tomb runs 3.54 m, including the vestibule, and the principal chamber has a maximum width of just less than a meter. Large flat horizontal slabs covered the entire tomb. The floor of the tomb consists of part bedrock and beaten dirt. The interior passageway, in antiquity, was blocked by a large flat rock resting on the grave floor, sealing off the vestibule from the principal chamber.

The principal chamber of the tomb was almost completely devoid of cultural remains, except for a few scattered sherds and highly eroded fragments of human bone. One of the smaller roof slabs above the main chamber is missing. The chamber was probably entered by looters through this opening and then emptied of its contents. Only six phase diagnostics were recovered, four of which were Chinchawasi phase.

In the vestibule, nine small decorated vessels were uncovered together in a ritual offering cache. Apparently, when the looters entered the primary chamber the slab that sealed off the chamber either blocked or concealed access into the antechamber. Included in this cache were two small semi-globular incurving bowls (Figure 49E, F), a small nubbin-rim jar (Figure 42L), a recurved jar rim with appliqué decorations (Figure 47O), a small face effigy jar (Figure 42K), a single burnished plainware bottle (Figure 49K), a dual chambered double spout and bridge vessel (Figure 49J), a small cup (Figure 49G) and an exterior-decorated, incurving bowl (Figure 41H).

Except for the bottles and the appliqué-decorated rim, which are unique to the entire pottery assemblage from Chinchawas, the forms and exterior decoration on the other vessels are consistent with the Chinchawasi 1 style. The red-on-cream exterior painting in up-pointing arrows and bands with dots, especially, are typical Chinchawasi 1 treatments. On stylistic grounds, the offering was made by during the late Early Intermediate Period and most likely dates to the original sealing of the primary chamber.

## Operation 65 (ST-3)

Subterranean Tomb 3, investigated as OP65, resembles OP63 (ST-2) in shape and form (Figure 30B). The length of the tomb, including the vestibule, measures 2.93

TABLE 4. Comparison of funerary construction sizes, Sector 2, Chinchawas. Unless noted otherwise, all measurements are in meters; all interior measurements are maximum values.

| Tomb ID no. | Operation | Interior shape or plan | Interior length | Interior width | Interior height [a] | Volume [b] (m³) | Length | Width | (m²) |
|---|---|---|---|---|---|---|---|---|---|
| ST-1 | OP56 | Irregular/oval | 1.9 | 1.1 | 1.2 | 2.7 | — | — | — |
| ST-2 | OP63 | Gallery/rectangular | 3.5 | 1.0 | 1.2 | 3.4 | — | — | — |
| ST-3 | OP65 | Gallery/rectangular | 2.9 | 1.2 | 0.9 | 2.5 | — | — | — |
| CT-1 | — | Quadrangular | 4.0 | 2.2 | — | 12.2 | 4.9 | 3.2 | 15.7 |
| CT-2 | OP57 | Quadrangular | 3.4 | 2.9 | 1.5 | 14.4 | 4.6 | 4.0 | 18.4 |
| CT-3 | — | Quadrangular | 3.2 | 2.4 | — | 10.6 | 4.2 | 3.4 | 14.3 |
| CT-4 | — | Quadrangular | — | — | — | — | — | — | — |
| CT-5 | OP59 | Quadrangular | 1.3 | 1.3 | 0.7 | 2.4 | 2.1 | 1.8 | 3.7 |
| CT-6 | OP58 | Quadrangular | 1.9 | 1.3 | 0.8 | 3.4 | 2.9 | 2.5 | 7.4 |
| CT-7 | OP61 | Quadrangular | 2.8 | 2.2 | 1.4 | 8.3 | 3.6 | 3.2 | 11.5 |
| CT-8 | OP60 | Quadrangular | 2.1 | 1.3 | 1.5 | 3.9 | 3.2 | 2.3 | 7.5 |
| CT-8 sub | OP60 | Quadrangular | 3.2 | 1.6 | 1.2 | 4.7 | 4.1 | 2.1 | 8.6 |
| CT-9 | — | Quadrangular | 2.7 | 2.3 | — | 8.8 | 3.6 | 3.4 | 12.1 |
| CT-10 | — | Quadrangular | 3.1 | 1.7 | — | 7.2 | 4.1 | 2.2 | 9.3 |
| CT-11 | — | Quadrangular | 1.1 | 1.3 | — | 2.0 | 2.3 | 2.1 | 4.7 |
| CT-12 | OP64 | Quadrangular | 3.5 | 2.4 | 1.5 | 12.4 | 4.6 | 3.7 | 16.8 |
| CT-13 | OP55 | Irregular | 3.6 | 1.9 | — | 9.3 | 4.2 | 2.4 | 10.1 |

[a] Estimated average height is 1.4 m (n=5).
[b] Estimated; does not account for interior partitions or possible second stories.

m and has a maximum width of 1.20 m. Large, flat horizontal slabs cover the entire structure. The tomb also has a bedrock floor and uses outcrops for parts of the sides and back wall. Like the other subterranean tombs, OP65 had been looted. Because all the roof stones were in situ, I surmise the looters entered through a narrow gap (of removed or collapsed masonry) in the west side between the side wall and the middle roof stone. The opening drew our initial attention to the construction during reconnaissance.

Like OP63, we encountered very few remains in the tomb, except for scattered human skeletal fragments such as small pieces of bone and several complete teeth. Artifacts of note included a small turquoise bead (Figure 125I) and a perforated copper-metal shawl pin with an eroded nail head (Figure 134B). There were only three fragments of pottery, all pertaining to the late Early Intermediate Period occupation: two fragments of a small open bowl, with an exterior painted (red-on-cream) nested diamond design (Figure 41G), and a low, squat jar with a spout emerging from the shoulder (Figure 38E). Its slip is eroded, but some parts indicate it was cream or white. Although this form is relatively rare to the Chinchawas pottery assemblage and could be an import, the form and the spout are typical Recuay style attributes. This accords well with other Chinchawasi 1 pottery and the nail-head shawl pin. In addition to the relative chronology, we conducted an AMS radiocarbon assay on a human premolar found within with the shallow deposit of artifacts and soil above the bedrock (AA32376; CW-012). The tooth was found in the third of three arbitrary levels, Level OP65C. The sampled yielded a radiocarbon age of 675 years B.P. ± 50, which calibrates to A.D. 1299 ± 50 with a 2-sigma range of A.D. 1272 to 1402. The age probably dates Late Intermediate Period re-use of the tomb.

## Summary of Subterranean Tomb Operations

Three subterranean tombs were investigated in Sector 2. These constructions are characterized by a primary burial chamber (located underground) and a roof made out of large stone slabs. One tomb features a circular groundplan, while the other two are of rectangular plan. In each tomb the principal chamber is entered through a vestibule. In one such vestibule, we found an intact grave offering of vessels. All three tombs had been looted, but the excavated remains include disarticulated human skeletal material, ceramics, and some associated metal and lapidary objects. A consideration of subterranean tomb architecture and contents, cultural affiliation and their social implications will follow presentation of the chullpa tombs.

## Chullpa Tombs

Of the 16 mortuary constructions in Sector 2 of Chinchawas, 13 were chullpas. Seven were investigated by clearing surface debris, systematic excavation and archaeological documentation. The chullpa form at Chinchawas is an aboveground tomb, almost always quadrangular. Typically, each building has a rectangular groundplan, with the façade on one of the longer sides. Their sizes range from smallest (from about 1.75 m lengthwise) to largest (just under 5 m).

The most basic chullpas have just one chamber, while more elaborate examples, through use of interior walls or columns, are partitioned into multiple spaces. Most of the chullpas were one story, but at least one may have had a second, upper floor, like larger well-known examples from elsewhere in the Callejón de Huaylas. The chullpas are often in clusters, usually two or three to a group. The remains of a low-lying perimeter wall sometimes enclose these clusters (Figure 29).

All the Chinchawas chullpas are situated on high ground, usually on slight rises of bedrock promontories. At Chinchawas there are at least two cases where the constructions are on top of a raised terrace platform, such as the better-known examples at Wilkawaín and Katiamá, among others. There are also isolated chullpa structures. In all the examples from Chinchawas, there was only one single doorway, generally facing towards the east or northeast. Often, on entering the threshold, one needs to take a step or two down, as if to distinguish inner and outer spaces through height differentials.

The chullpas show considerable variability in form and quality of craftsmanship (Figure 32). Many of the buildings are composed of only one chamber, while there are others with additional partitioned spaces. OP57 (CT-2) and OP64 (CT-12) probably had second stories, now collapsed. Moreover, the quality of stone masonry differs from one chullpa to another. In CT-2, we encounter the best preserved

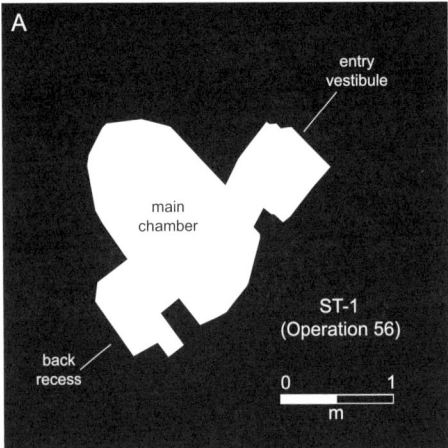 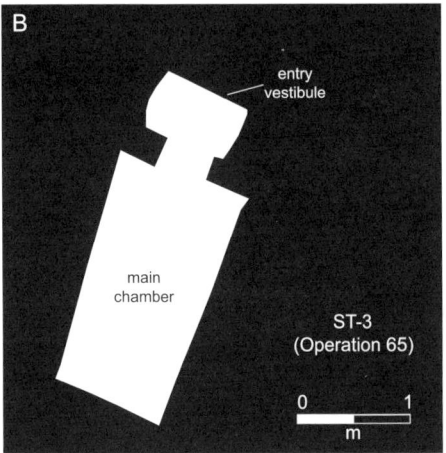

Figure 30. Plan of subterranean tombs, ST-1 (A) and ST-3 (B), from Sector 2. Entry vestibules provided access into the main chambers of the tombs, which featured elaborate stonemasonry and often incorporated bedrock features on the inner walls.

stonework anywhere on the Chinchawas site, while CT-5, for example, is small, poorly made, and single story.

Operation 55 (CT-13)

Chullpa Tomb 13, investigated as OP55, was located in a deep bedrock recess within a small, low ridgetop just southeast of Sector 1 (Figure 32J). Its position provides a good vantage point on the southern portion of the main mound. The construction is unique in its choice of location as well as in its construction technique.

OP55 is partly aboveground, having at least its east wall exposed on the surface. Large tabular flat stones, approximately 1 m above the floor, roofed the structure. The east wall survives only to its footings, but two roof stones are still supported by several well-preserved interior partitions. OP55 has an interior space that is roughly rectangular. The north, south and west walls follow the curves of exposed bedrock and in some parts serve only as a retaining facing for fill. Therefore only the east wall, where the doorway is located, is completely freestanding.

The walls are made of stonework, in a general wanka–pachilla style, but with less attention to detail than others. In some segments of the walls, parts curve and have chinking stones falling out. Large stones are preferred for jambs and supporting members.

Three small walls partition the interior into four spaces, where large amounts of mixed human skeletal material and other cultural remains were concentrated (Table 5). These were divided into five "groups" on the basis of distinct clusters of disarticulated human bone. However, note that these "groups" more than likely do not represent the original positions of individuals, and may not represent individual persons, because many bones were found dispersed throughout the clusters. Based on mandibles, a minimum number of nine individuals were found in OP55.

Special artifacts were also found in the mortuary construction. Two marine shells (*Conus* sp.; Figure 133A, B), with sawn cuts near the narrow top, may have been roped through to hang as adornments or as clicking musical instruments. A copper-metal lamina, a dual-chambered pottery miniature (Figure 101F) and a very small flat redware plate (Figure 101J) were also part of the assemblage.

The broken pottery was almost exclusively of small serving vessels. Besides shallow plates and open bowls, there are two small jars with punctated decoration on the neck that is typical of the Chakwas style. Both of these specimens were blackened, perhaps as part of an offering ritual. The miniature and the small open bowls and plates, especially in paste and finish, are characteristic of the Warmi style. However, remains of the later style suggest that either funerary activities continued into the Chakwas phase or that there was re-use of the structure into the Late Intermediate Period.

## Operation 57 (CT-2)

Chullpa Tomb 2, investigated as OP57, is the largest and the best preserved of all the funerary constructions at Chinchawas (Figure 33). The building stands at 3,870 masl and is the second highest of all the chullpas. Indeed, its fine masonry and general construction, high location, placement on a low platform and nearby associated stone sculpture make CT-2 perhaps the most visually impressive single building extant at Chinchawas (Figure 34).

CT-2 is the principal structure in a larger complex of the two chullpas comprising Chullpa Enclosure 1 (Figure 29). Low foundations of a roughly circular perimeter wall ring the entire enclosure and connect CT-2 and CT-4 spatially. Constructed of large rocks and stone pilings, the wall is best preserved in the western and southern ends, but is in poorer condition in the north and east. A doorway in the east end provided access. Within the perimeter wall, CT-2 was built on top of a low masonry platform (15 cm tall on the northern end) that leveled the sloping bedrock for the building.

The chullpa measures 4.6 by 4.0 m. It stands 3.5 m above its bedrock floor and may have once supported a second story of two low, narrow galleries east and west of a middle interior wall. It is likely that with the typical tomb roof stones and reconstructed walls, CT-2 probably stood over 4.5 to 5 m in height and was the most prominent building in Sector 2.

The builders elaborated the chullpa with the finest and best-preserved example of wanka–pachilla style stonemasonry at the site, except for perhaps the northern terrace wall of Terrace 1. Walls are largely uniform and true. The corners are sharp and the faces of the walls remain vertical. Large stones were preferred for the jambs and supporting members. A hard and gritty mud clay mortar cemented the stones together. Four partition walls divide the interior into four usable spaces: a central chamber or vestibule, two narrow side chambers and a long back room. The entire first floor was capped by two rows of large tabular roof stones running

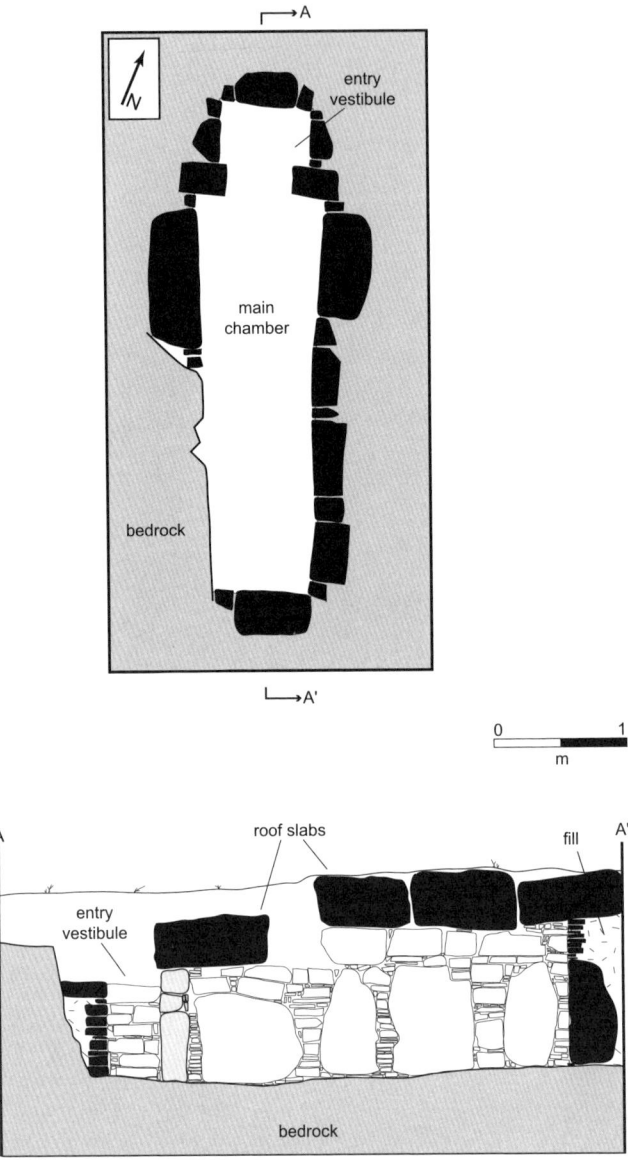

FIGURE 31. Plan (top) and east profile (bottom) of Subterranean Tomb 2 (Operation 63), Sector 2.

east–west, over which survive the middle interior wall and several exposures of a flat stone-lined floor of the second story. The structure was entered through a low east doorway that measured only 60 cm in width, which from afar gives the illusion of a larger, more imposing building. Excavations within the chullpa (Table 5) recovered large quantities of human osteological remains representing at least four individuals. The minimum number of individuals is preliminary, and based on an analysis only of the mandibles. Considerable quantities of human bones were recovered from OP57 and I expect that additional skeletal analysis will increase the MNI for the operation.

OP57 was also remarkable because scattered around its periphery are six stone sculptures. At least one of these came from the interior of the tomb, where there is a jamb cavity that matches the dimensions of a sculpture found outside (Lau 2002). All evidence indicates that many of the stone sculptures are at least partially, if not completely, contemporary with the building and use of the chullpa structures.

Diagnostic pottery was recovered from the excavations within the chullpa. One was Chinchawasi in style. Three were of polished blackware vessels, one with exterior modeled bands and dots (Figure 90A). There was also a spout and bridge fragment from an imported Wari period bottle from the central coast, Nievería in style (Figure 90K), as well as a llama figurine leg in the interior assemblage. The other pottery is represented mostly by small serving vessels (especially open bowls, shallow plates and incurving bowls) in forms characteristic of the Warmi phase. In addition to the relative chronology, we conducted an AMS radiocarbon measurement on a human ulna fragment found within the shallow deposit of artifacts and soil above the bedrock (AA32377; Chinchawasi-013). The bone was found in the second of three arbitrary levels, Level OP57A. The radiocarbon age for the sample was 655 years B.P. ± 50, which calibrates to A.D. 1304 ± 50 with a 2-sigma range of A.D. 1279 to 1407. This age seems too recent given the architectural context and the internal consistency of the Warmi phase cultural remains. The sample probably dates re-use of the chullpa in Chakwas phase times.

In addition to the pottery, we encountered special artifacts in the tomb, including two copper-metal nail-head shawl pins (Figure 136A, B), a copper-metal spearthrower hook (Figure 136H) and a stone spindle whorl (Figure 125L). The pins resemble Chinchawasi phase specimens and could be curated items.

During the course of OP57 we also conducted excavations outside of the tomb structure. A shallow 2 by 4 m trench abutted the northern exterior face of Chullpa Tomb 2 (CT-2) and aimed to examine the enclosure's interior stratigraphy as well as the height of the platform on which CT-2 was built. Excavations went down between 30 and 40 cm, and revealed that the platform stood only 15 cm above bedrock.

The excavation, OP57x, recovered a series of broken fancy Warmi phase bowls lying directly above bedrock (some with ring-bases and tripods), an eroded white paste carinated vessel (Figure 90E) and rim fragments of Huari Norteño flasks (Figure 90H). The plainwares consisted mainly of open serving vessels, but necked ollas and jars were also represented. In addition, two miniature vessels (Figure 101B, I) were found abutting the northern wall of CT-2 and are interpreted as small dedicatory offerings. Like the pottery within the chullpas, the ceramics from the trench date the use of Chullpa Enclosure 1 to Warmi times. The excavations recovered no identifiable faunal material. These remains can be understood best as the residue from small-scale rites involving drinking and offering activities within Chullpa Enclosure 1.

FIGURE 32. Plans of chullpa tombs, Sector 2.

OPERATION 58 (CT-6)
Chullpa Tomb 6, investigated as OP58, was just northwest of CT-2 and is part of the chullpa cluster in this zone. Compared to CT-2, this chullpa is far more modest, both in architecture and in archaeological remains. CT-6 is single-chambered, with a doorway to the east (Figure 32B). Only the foundations of this structure remain. The stonework is of the wanka–pachilla style, but is irregular and the angles are not true. The architecture elicits the general impression of being poorly made.

The structure measures 2.90 by 2.40 m, with an interior space of 1.86 by 1.30 m. The roof structure probably only stood 1.5 m above the ground. A small projecting corbelling stone in the southwest corner is the only remnant of the roof structure. It is unlikely that there were two stories. At least two individuals were interred in Chullpa Tomb 6, as represented by human mandibles.

In addition to a single bent fragment of a hammered copper-metal lamina, five diagnostic sherds recovered from the excavation of the interior were found in association with the human bones. All were from a squat jar with Chakwas style punctated dots and an incised line just above the shoulder (Figure 87J). The vessel had at least one strap handle and was blackened, indicating it had been put over a fire before it was placed in the tomb.

Several fragments of open bowls and very small jars were also found in the CT-6 structure. The offering and serving emphasis of all the pottery is consistent with the chullpa ritual patterns at Chinchawas. The Chakwas phase association suggests that it may have continued after the Warmi phase. By extension, the ideology behind chullpa mortuary customs seems to have been resilient and was maintained after the Middle Horizon.

## Operation 59 (CT-5)

Chullpa Tomb 5, investigated as OP59, is the smallest chullpa excavated (Figure 32A). The structure measures only 2.08 by 1.80 m. The interior space measures 1.33 by 1.31 m. Like CT-6, Chullpa Tomb 5 contains a single chamber, a doorway in the east side, and is characterized by the same common craftsmanship.

CT-5, however, was far richer in archaeological remains. At least four individuals were interred in the tomb. Three complete skulls and associated jaws were found, representing three older adults. The dentition of one mandible (Individual 2) showed many carious lesions.

The tomb contents are internally consistent and bear a late Middle Horizon signature. Of the 25 diagnostic pottery sherds recovered, all were Middle Horizon and most were from imported vessels, including one fragment of a press-molded drinking cup and 20 fragments from a Huari Norteño bottle or flask (Figure 90F, G). There were also two steep-sided shallow bowl miniatures (Figure 101G, H) and several recurved necked jar sherds with ribbed appliqué fillets. Other plainware diagnostics included the typical open bowls and small jars. A complete disc-headed copper-metal shawl pin (Figure 136F) was recovered, as was a dark gray stone bead (Figure 125F).

## Operation 60 (CT-8)

Chullpa Tomb 8 was investigated as OP60. CT-8 is the middle construction in an aligned cluster of three chullpas, all positioned on a low ridge of exposed bedrock (Figure 29). CT-8 is composed of an upper and lower story (Figure 35). The upper portion is a single-chambered construction of medium quality wanka–pachilla stonework. It measures 2.33 by 3.2 m. The roof on the upper story survives to a

TABLE 5. Summary of human skeletal remains from Sector 2 funerary structures. MNI, minimum number of individuals; weight is given in grams.

| Operation | Context | Weight (g) | Total percentage | MNI | Total percentage |
|---|---|---|---|---|---|
| *Chullpa tombs* | | | | | |
| OP55 | CT–13 | 8280 | 14.9 | 9 | 16.4 |
| OP57 | CT–2 | 3430 | 6.2 | 4 | 3.0 |
| OP58 | CT–6 | 3309 | 6.0 | 2 | 3.6 |
| OP59 | CT–5 | 3929 | 7.1 | 4 | 7.3 |
| OP60 | CT–8 | 1358 | 2.4 | 1 | 1.8 |
| OP61 | CT–7 | 9671 | 17.4 | 8 | 14.5 |
| OP64 | CT–12 | 24769 | 44.6 | 24 | 43.6 |
| Total | | 54746 | 98.6 | 52 | 94.5 |
| *Subterranean tombs* | | | | | |
| OP56 | ST–1 | 784 | 1.4 | 1 | 1.8 |
| OP63 | ST–2 | 28 | 0 | 1 | 1.8 |
| OP65 | ST–3 | 10 | 0 | 1 | 1.8 |
| Total | | 822 | 1.4 | 3 | 5.5 |
| Total (all tombs) | | 55568 | 100 | 55 | 100 |

height of 2.34 m above the building's floor. The upper story's interior space is entered from the east and measures 1.26 by 2.1 m, with a maximum height of 1.47 m above the floor. The well-preserved roof of CT-8 shows the typical roofing technique of using large, flat slabs over short, projecting cantilevers.

The lower story is in far poorer condition, with many portions of its walls surviving only to the foundations. It contains two chambers: (1) a large quadrangular primary chamber, with an east building entrance and (2) a small oval-shaped chamber to the south. The small chamber makes use of bedrock sides, with some portions chinked to furnish even sides and surfaces. Several projecting cantilevered stones at the base of the upper story's north wall suggest that the interior space rose to a height of 1.10 m from floor to ceiling, and that the structure had an exterior height of about 1.7 m. In addition to the shared walls and supporting members between the two stories, the flat slab roof of the grotto chamber represents the floor surface of the upper story, indicating that the buildings were designed as a single unit.

Very few archaeological remains were encountered in either portion of CT-8. Based on one fragment of a poorly preserved mandible, at least one adult individual was interred in the upper story of the building. There was one fragment of eroded marine shell in the upper chullpa. Only four decorated sherds were recovered and all were Huari Norteño in style: black on light brown, exterior painted, and polished body sherds. In addition, several local Warmi rim sherds of open and incurving bowls support a late Middle Horizon use of the mortuary structure.

Operation 61 (CT-7)
Chullpa Tomb 7, investigated as OP61, located just 1 m south of CT-8, is part of the same chullpa cluster (Figure 36). The chullpa measures 3.6 by 3.2 m and is relatively well preserved. It features only a single chamber, but its interior space is unusually large. Two solid masonry piers supporting massive horizontal roof slabs allow for a wider span and enclose an area measuring 2.75 by 2.2 by 1.38 m. Most of the roof still stands and all evidence indicates that the structure was only one story. A small eastern doorway facilitates entry. The floor lies beneath the level of the entryway sill. The structure was built directly on bedrock. At least eight individuals were interred in the chullpa. There was one perforated bone fragment.

Excavations in OP61 also recovered 36 diagnostic decorated pottery sherds, all with Warmi-contemporary associations. Represented in this assemblage were several local Warmi style open bowls with interior painted band and meander designs (Figure 90C, D). Twelve sherds came from a closed redware vessel, probably a bottle, with a pinkish red slip, polished surface and press-molded relief designs (Figure 90M–P). Eleven sherds were from a Huari Norteño style carinated bottle with dot–sausage and step fret designs (Figure 90I, J). There were also two sherds of an open bowl with raised dots on the exterior sides and base (Figure 90B).

Operation 64 (CT-12)
Chullpa Tomb 12 represents the northernmost chullpa identified in Sector 2. Like the others, CT-12 is situated on a small rise in the local topography, where there are exposures of bedrock outcrops and little vegetation (Figure 29). CT-12 is the second largest chullpa at Chinchawas, measuring 4.6 by 3.65 m. The walls are in a medium-grade wanka–pachilla style and remain fairly well preserved. There are several horizontal slabs topping the side and interior walls, but it is unclear whether these formed a roof or the ceiling or support for another story, as in CT-2.

The interior chambers are entered through an eastern doorway, which measures roughly 60 cm in width and has two steps leading down into the chullpa. CT-12 had three chambers (Figure 32I). Four short east–west partition walls define the central, north and south chambers, all narrow quadrangular rooms. Beneath the floor of the chullpa we encountered three large flat stones; on turning them over we found three pits built atop or excavated directly into bedrock.

At least 24 individuals were interred in the chullpa, based on distinct mandibles (Table 5). Diagnostic pottery was also relatively common in the interior of the chullpa. The assemblage included one Warmi open bowl rim sherd with a star design, 11 polished blackware sherds (four from a closed carinated bottle with a blackware bird adorno; Figure 90L), one polished press-molded redware sherd and a handle for a polished pinkware bottle or jar. In addition to these decorated sherds,

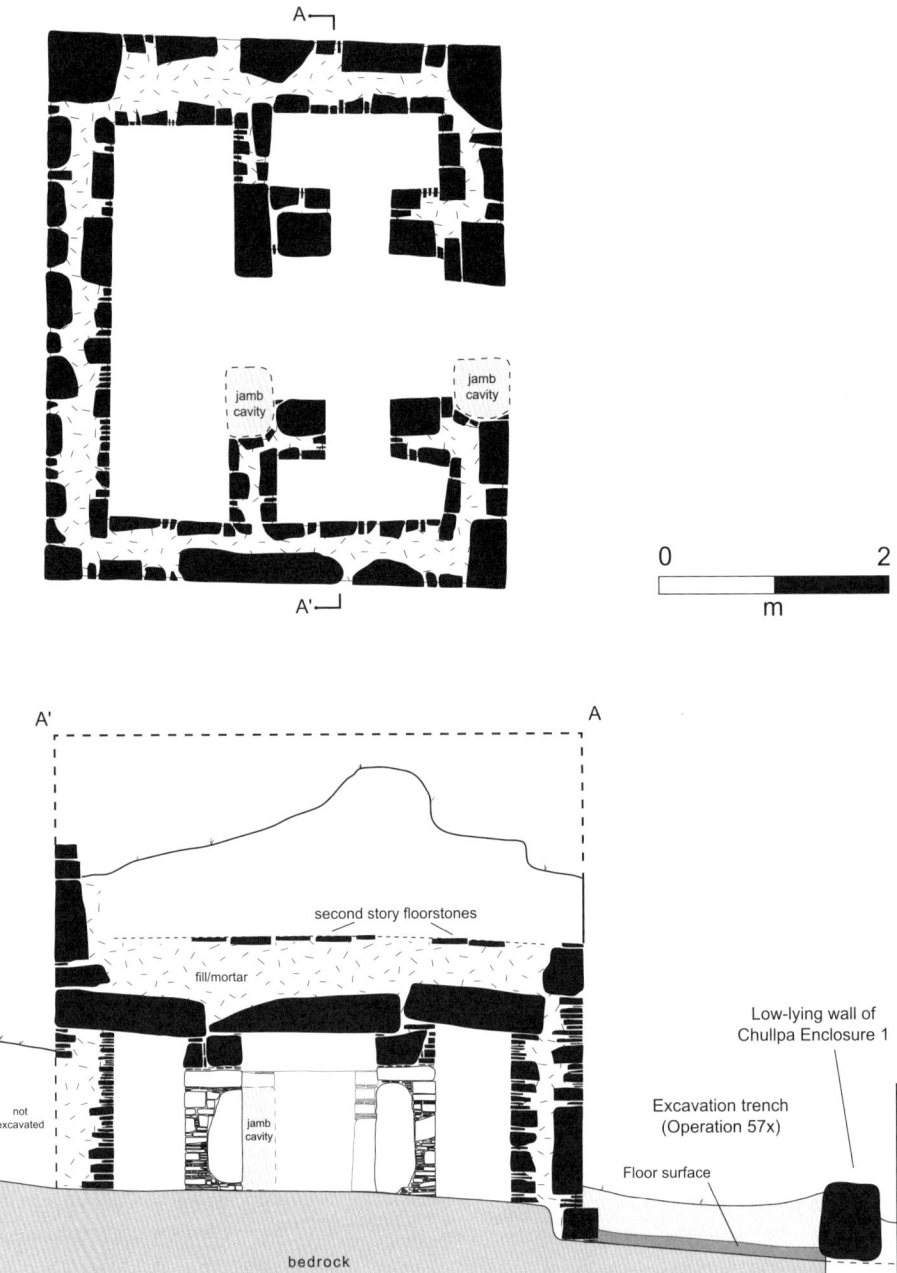

FIGURE 33. Plan and west profile of Chullpa Tomb 2 (CT-2), Sector 2. The chullpa is distinguished by its construction quality, four discrete chambers and association with stone sculptures. It also likely had a second story of two narrow north–south chambers. The chullpa contained mixed human remains as well as broken exotic pottery and metal artifacts. Excavations outside encountered evidence of burning and offering activities, especially of miniature pottery vessels.

typical Warmi phase forms (especially plainware open and thin-sided bowls, small jars and pitchers) were common. Although the pottery assemblage pertains mainly to the Warmi phase, there are pottery elements that seem to indicate re-use of the chullpa during post-Warmi times.

Burial Pits under CT-64

Turning over the three flat stones beneath the floor surface of the chullpa revealed three burial pits built atop or excavated directly into bedrock. The sides of Burial Pit 1 in the north chamber are stone-lined. Burial Pits 2 and 3 were in the central chamber and were not stone-lined. We also detected another pit, Burial Pit 4, covered by a flat stone partly underlying the southeast partition wall, which was not excavated because we did not want to destroy the wall.

All the burial pits contained poorly preserved skeletal remains of human interments. Probably due to the subsurface humidity, the osteological material had decomposed into very small fragments and mostly a powdery tan dust, so that very few intact bones were recovered. Teeth were better preserved, however, and indicate that the osteological materials, indeed, derived from human burials. Moreover, on the basis of the dentition and the size of the pits, there seems to have been only one interment per grave.

The pits did not contain very many objects. In Burial Pit 2 we recovered a leg of a small llama figurine. In Burial Pit 3 there were two corroded copper-metal rings (Figure 136I, J), perhaps ear ornaments (e.g., Lechtman 2003, fig. 17.15 and 17.16). In Burial Pit 1 we recovered many fragments of a brown fiber textile, presumably deposited in antiquity. Some fragments, better preserved than others, retain their woven fabric and measure roughly 3 to 4 cm on a side. Other fragments, less well preserved, were in decomposing clumps or shreds.

The burial pits, on the basis of their architectural position and contents, most likely predate the construction the chullpa. Pit 3 was partially underneath the doorway stair and Pit 4 lay underneath a partition wall. Pit 1, however, could have been an intrusive feature or was re-used in recent times. One sample of the textile in Pit 1 was submitted for a radiocarbon determination. The AMS assay (AA32375) returned a modern age date. Until additional evidence can be acquired, the best interpretation for Burial Pit 1 is that it is an ancient feature re-used in recent times. The other burial pits must antedate the chullpa, because of their location beneath its foundation stones.

*Summary of Chullpa Tomb Operations*

The Sector 2 area of Chinchawas consists of several funerary constructions located within or atop rock outcrops. The most prominent are a series of 12 to 13 aboveground chullpa tombs. These buildings are largely rectangular and in various states of preservation. Seven of the 12 in Chinchawas Sector 2 were investigated through systematic excavation and archaeological documentation. In all cases building in-

FIGURE 34. View of the northern façade of Chullpa Tomb 2 (CT-2). The tomb is ringed by a low-lying wall (stones on the right). The chullpa features elaborate wanka–pachilla stonework, consisting of large uprights and fitted chinking stones. A small stonecarving is at the bottom left.

teriors were the focus of investigation and excavations followed the entire interior dimensions.

The excavations indicate that each of the seven chullpas was used for interment. Investigations along the exterior of some of the chullpas suggest that there were ritual activities in these areas, which included offerings of ceramic vessels and miniatures as well as burning events. In contrast to Sector 1 ceremonial events, camelid meat does not seem to have played a major role in the activities around chullpas.

Considerable variability characterized the architecture of the chullpas and their respective assemblages. While they all share features, such as the rectangular layout and small eastern-facing doorway, no two are identical in any way. Each differs in form, size and construction quality. Several have only one small chamber, while others contain as many as five. The larger chullpas have interior wall partitions, pilasters and a second story. Unequal investment of labor was especially apparent in the size and quality of craftsmanship, as seen in the stone masonry, the thickness and trueness of the walls, size of roofing stones, and overall finish.

The range in the forms and construction quality of the chullpa tombs shows different potential for labor mobilization. The tombs were not built together according to a rigid plan in a single program. Rather, each was an individual project, with different solutions and building specifications, for a similar end.

## Discussion

*Cultural Associations and Function*
In the subterranean tombs, we found artifacts that are identical to materials we encountered in late Early Intermediate Period strata of Sector 1. The ceramics share important features with the Chinchawasi 1 style, including red-on-cream surface treatment, exterior painted design elements (dots within bands, upward facing triangles and nested triangles on low drinking cups) and forms (squat jar with cylindrical tube spout, cup, small effigy jars and globular open bowls). These features are associated with the local terminal Recuay tradition during the late Early Intermediate Period.

In all likelihood, the subterranean tombs held interments of Chinchawasi 1 people who resided or interacted intensively with people on the main mound. Given the relative rarity and construction quality of the subterranean gallery tombs, one can argue that the interments were of relatively high status. The grave goods found in the three examples of subterranean tombs are consistent with this interpretation.

The artifacts from the chullpas also form a coherent assemblage of material, with consistent earliest association to late Middle Horizon styles—from Chinchawas Sector 1 and elsewhere in the Central Andes. Especially diagnostic elements include press-molded wares, local Warmi style pottery, diagnostic forms (e.g., lenticular flasks, tapering spouts, the double spout and bridge vessel, and interior-painted cumbrous bowls) and imported Middle Horizon pottery (Huari Norteño, Nievería and blackware-polished). The imported pottery found in the chullpas can be readily associated with Warmi phase counterparts from Sector 1. Thus, by Warmi times, the cultural remains show that local groups were building and using chullpas at Chinchawas. Later re-use of chullpas seems to have been quite common, with intermittent activities, funerary and otherwise, occurring during Chakwas phase, colonial and contemporary times (see also Salomon 1995).

The ceramic evidence, together with other long-range trade goods such as shell and obsidian, indicates that local peoples were intensifying and extending their range of contacts by the late Middle Horizon. In contrast, the sample from the late Early Intermediate Period graves in Sector 2 had very few imported artifacts, suggesting a more insular population. Apparently referencing exotic contacts and style associations through imported finely crafted items was a critical new component to the local burial custom during the late Middle Horizon.

The Warmi situated their chullpas purposefully in the same area of earlier burials, sometimes on top of previous mortuary constructions. Some argue that this physical intervention or displacement was done purposefully to co-opt ancestral associations of the zone and their supernatural efficacy (DeLeonardis and Lau 2004). This may have been the intention with the construction of Chullpa Tomb CT-12 (OP64) over Burial Pits 2, 3 and 4. It could also have been the case for Chullpa Tomb CT-8's subfloor chamber.

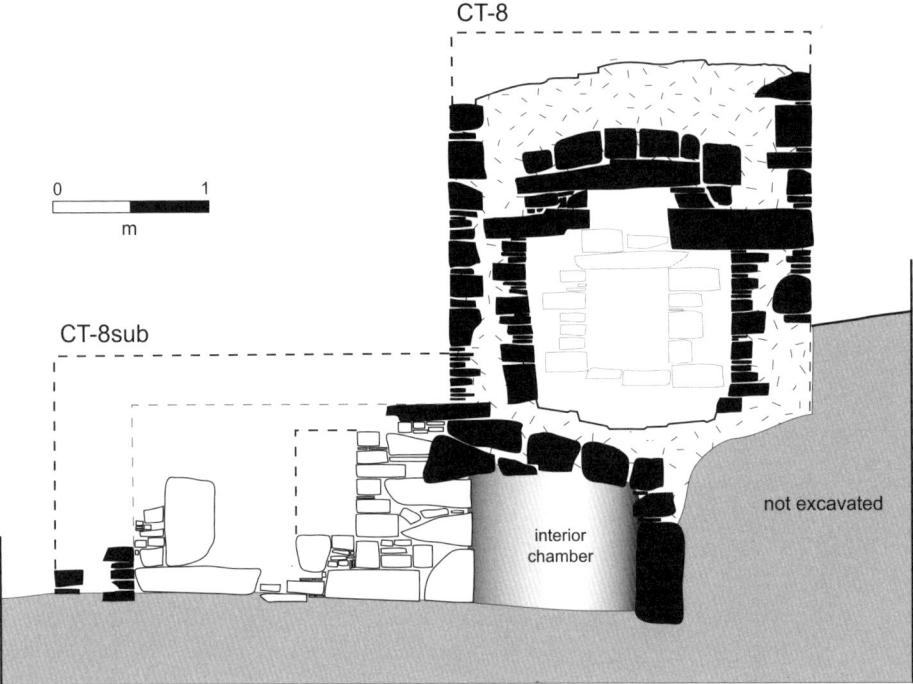

Figure 35. East profile of Chullpa Tomb 8 (CT-8 and CT-8sub) investigated together as Operation 60, Sector 2. CT-8 was built directly above a natural hollow, roughly ovoid in plan. With contiguous constructions directly above and to the north, this chamber probably once housed the remains of a key ancestor whose descendants claimed physical association.

Note that the funerary structures at Chinchawas show considerable variability in cultural patterning, because they have long and complex life histories. Several chullpas, for example, cannot not be confined to single phase occupations in which their construction, use and abandonment are neatly delineated. On the contrary, although ranges can be assigned for their construction and principal use, it is more difficult to generalize about their final use. This is partly because chullpas were constructed to be re-used in regular ceremonies. But it is also clear that tombs were disturbed, looted (e.g., OP63) and added onto (e.g., OP60) in antiquity. In many cases at Chinchawas, chullpas were reused for various purposes, including later interments (e.g., OP64); even residential structures were co-opted for later burials (e.g., OP52). Moreover, they are used today as field landmarks, as well as for penning animals and as repositories for hay.

## Human Skeletal Evidence

In addition to the differences in artifacts and architecture, the human remains from the tombs provide another index of change in mortuary practice. We recovered over 55 kg of human osteological material from the 10 tombs (see Table 5). The chullpas held most of the human remains. My preliminary observations are presented here, but final reporting awaits the results of more specialized metric and characterization analyses that are underway (J. Verano, pers. comm. 2007).

The chullpas are characterized by multiple interments, ranging from one individual in one chullpa (MNI=1) to the high count of 24 individuals in another. In contrast, the counts from the subterranean tombs indicate that they were probably used only for one, or at most, for only several individuals. There is quite a bit of variability in the morphology, size, robustness and dentition within the mandibular and cranial sample from the chullpas, indicating that both women and men, youths and older individuals, were interred. For instance, examples indicative of older individuals show teeth that are heavily worn or missing, with the root holes sutured. A wide range of age categories is therefore represented in our sample. In other words, there does not seem to be an outward preference to select from a specific age or sex group as a prerequisite for chullpa interment.

With these observations in mind, the current evidence supports the argument that the chullpas at Chinchawas served as multi-interment mausolea for specific social groups during the Middle Horizon. Whether these groups were arranged along kin-based lines, as I suspect they were, or other criteria cannot be resolved fully at the moment. However, the modest size of the chullpas and the number and variability of individuals found in them suggest that we may be dealing with burial monuments that held the dead members of a small lineage or extended family group.

*Ancestor Veneration and the Chinchawas Evidence*
The Chinchawas data are consistent with models of chullpa monuments as corporate constructions for local ancestor cults. In particular, they were repositories for ancestor mummies (*malqui*) and the foci for their veneration (Tello 1929; Isbell 1997; Kaulicke 1997). Ancestor cults were significant for historical Andean groups, because they linked landscapes with local pasts and provided the logic through which corporate groups mapped mythic deeds and social boundaries (e.g., Zuidema 1973, 1978, 1988; Salomon 1991, 1995). For the Recuay, ancestor veneration and related funerary practices also fueled the production of an elaborate material culture that included very fancy pottery and stone sculpture (Grieder 1978; Lau 2000, 2002).

Different lines of reasoning suggest that the human remains from the Chinchawas chullpas were flexed interments or bundles. First, there is very little soil or space in the chullpas, or the subterranean tombs for that matter, that would facilitate primary burials. The floors of all the mortuary constructions at Chinchawas survive as thin beaten dirt surfaces that lie directly above bedrock. Further, the size of the tombs and the many individuals found in certain chullpas, such as in CT-12, preclude the likelihood of inhumation-style interments. It is more plausible that some of the individuals were packaged in compact flexed burials, perhaps bundles, and then positioned within the chullpa. No evidence of textiles or wrapping was found, but the concentrations of articulated bone ("bone groups") without much

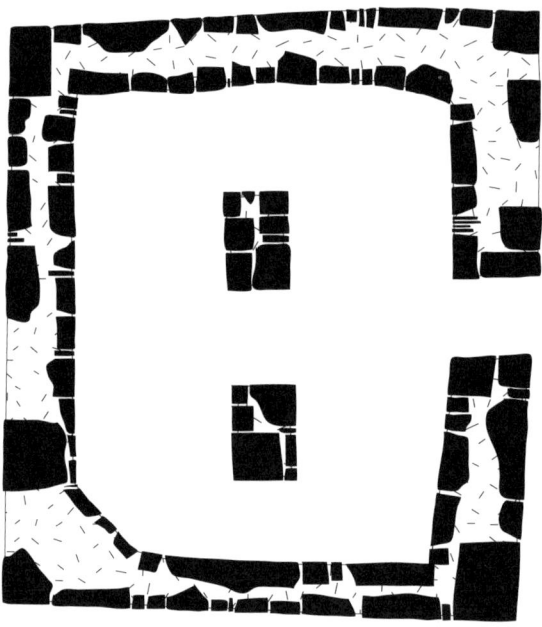

Figure 36. Plan view of Chullpa Tomb 7, Sector 2. Freestanding supports (piers) were not common at Chinchawas, but were used in CT-7 to support the heavy roof structure. They still stand today.

overburden do indicate open air exposure and decomposition typical of chullpa mummy burials in the Central Andes (e.g., Isbell 1997).

Considerable formal and artifact variability characterize the chullpa mortuary structures at Chinchawas. There are probably at least several reasons for the variability. First, the chullpas may not have been built at any one single time, so there could be temporal differences in stylistic popularity. Given the number of chullpas as well as the general contemporaneity of many of the assemblages, many likely operated simultaneously. In addition, the chullpas reflect different scales of investment. That is, groups who chose to devote more resources to their execution made the larger and more elaborate constructions (and vice versa). Lastly, the groups responsible for each construction differed in size, orientation and their ability to obtain goods and labor. A likely interpretation of the tomb variability is that Chinchawas groups built and used tombs to distinguish themselves from other coresident groups.

The stone sculpture of Chinchawas was an additional and distinctive dimension of local ancestor cult practices (Lau 2002, 2006b). Around these tombs, just described, are 17 examples of stone sculptures on the surface that once probably formed integral members of the chullpa structures. Most show a single frontal anthropomorphic figure in splayed or squatting position, as if representing deceased individuals. The figures often show a headdress with serpent-like appendages, incised crosses on the torso and other supernatural elements. Despite these common elements, they display considerable individuality and variability in execution and degree of elaboration, suggesting that they could be representations of different individuals. Overall, the attributes and poses seem to portray the special deceased in altered physical forms and states of transformation (Lau 2006b). As objects of veneration, the stone effigies enabled crucial physical interactions between people and divinities in the chullpas.

## Conclusions

Important changes in mortuary practice occurred during the Middle Horizon, between the Chinchawasi 2 and Warmi phases. Local peoples switched from building subterranean tombs to erecting aboveground chullpa mausolea. Whereas the earlier practices favored single interments, the chullpas contained multiple burials, probably mummy bundles. A greater quantity and new styles of grave goods mirrored these new dispositions.

The transformations in local mortuary practices reflect major changes in how local groups in the Chinchawas community opted to identify and manage their relationships with their dead. Instead of interring one special individual underground, they began to collect their deceased in stone buildings, very much like mini-houses, often with multiple rooms. Perhaps at times during the annual round these individuals were reclaimed from the chambers and celebrated and honored, like the ancestor mummies documented ethnohistorically for the Inka and other groups, to create and reinforce social relationships. Unlike earlier Recuay tradition subterranean tombs, chullpas could regularly be seen and experienced. Not only are Chinchawas's chullpas, located along a low ridge, easily visible from Sector 1, the chullpas marked the western boundary of the pocket of arable land between the Chinchawas and Karachuko hilltops (Figure 5 and 10). In this way, the chullpas were instrumentalized as part of daily community life and mapped ancestry and territory in the local landscape.

The local transformations occurred during the period of late Wari presence in the Callejón de Huaylas. It does not seem coincidental that Wari political presence in the region coincides with changing patterns of material culture and iconography. Yet the character of the mortuary remains, which show certain technological and stylistic continuities, such as in masonry or stone sculpture, does not speak of a complete replacement of people (say, of colonizers) or of a forced acceptance of new funerary rules. Rather, we seem to be witnessing local peoples at Chinchawas synchretizing religious preferences and making adjustments in lifestyle that integrated older traditions into newer, more current priorities. Chullpa practices at Chinchawas grew increasingly significant, and were local measures that materialized ties between land and corporate groups during a period of sociopolitical instability.

CHAPTER SIX

# CERAMICS OF THE KAYÁN AND CHINCHAWASI PHASES

The next three chapters detail the relative cultural chronology of the Chinchawas site, as reconstructed from ceramic evidence. Chapters 6 and 7 will describe the local decorated and plainware styles and establish stylistic and temporal associations. Chapter 8 will detail the fancy and exotic pottery.

Because the general aims of the project are diachronic in nature, I emphasized building the site's culture history on the basis of, in large part, the pottery collected from excavation. Our field investigations recovered 180,776 pottery sherds. Because it was impossible to give equal attention to all sherds, the study focuses on a sample deemed diagnostic for temporal and functional information. The diagnostic assemblage numbered over 17,752 sherds, or 9.8% of the total recovered from the field investigations, and form the corpus of data that the following chapters describe.

For the purposes of the study, it was more expedient to give priority to formal, design and decorative attributes over aspects of manufacture. Through field observation of stratigraphic associations and a subsequent ceramic analysis based on similarity and frequency seriation of chosen attributes (Rowe 1961), I have developed a five-phase sequence for the occupation of the site.

The Chinchawas pottery is classified according to "ware" categories. I follow Rice's definition (1987:484) of "ware" as "a class of pottery whose members share similar technology, fabric and surface treatment." Hence, a suite of manufacturing and decorative attributes defines a ware. The analysis opts for this terminology in part because it fits the data we have from Chinchawas nicely. In addition, I use "wares" to move away from the biases given to manufacturing attributes and the sometimes difficult vocabulary inherent in a type-variety system (Rice 1987, ch. 9).

The presentation of the site's pottery sequence is organized into two chapters. This first chapter contains a brief summary of the analysis' methodology, followed by descriptions of the Kayán, Chinchawasi 1 and Chinchawasi 2 phases. Each ware is treated as a separate component of the phase (Table 6); a comparative discussion follows the characterization of each ware's manufacture, decoration and vessel shapes (Tables 7, 8 and 9). The next chapter reviews the final two phases, the Warmi and Chakwas, and concludes with a phase-by-phase comparison of the Chinchawas sequence with other relative and absolute chronologies of the Central Andes.

TABLE 6. Summary of analyzed pottery wares and proportions of open and closed forms by phase.

| Ware | Count | Percentage of open forms | Percentage of closed forms |
|---|---|---|---|
| *Kayán* | | | |
| A | 194 | 90.9 | — |
| B | 134 | 43.3 | 40.3 |
| *Chinchawasi 1* | | | |
| A | 648 | 83 | 17 |
| B | 26 | 98 | — |
| C | 131 | 80.1 | 19.9 |
| D | 975 | 30.6 | 60.4 |
| *Chinchawasi 2* | | | |
| A | 1,398 | 78.8 | 22.2 |
| B | 221 | 73.3 | 13.8 |
| C | 3,526 | 36.6 | 56.9 |
| *Warmi* | | | |
| A | 948 | 91.8 | 1.5 |
| B | 2,033 | 46.4 | 47.4 |
| *Chakwas* | | | |
| — | 125 | 43.2 | 34.4 |

## Methodology

All ceramic and nonceramic artifacts from excavations at Chinchawas were transported to Huaraz, where our laboratory was based, and there washed and prepared for general study. Common pottery body sherds were tallied on the basis of gross ware types primarily by visual inspection of paste and surface treatment and returned to numbered bags. These await further study in the Museo Arqueológico de Ancash of the Instituto Nacional de Cultura, Huaraz.

Diagnostic materials useful for describing form, function, ware or style were separated and labeled to operation and level and, if applicable, to specific locus. This pottery was separated into two main classes: decorated ceramics and plainwares. The decorated pottery included sherds with painted decoration, slip painting, plastic decoration, modeling or special surface treatment. Plainwares consisted mainly of rim sherds diagnostic of form and shape, or other distinctive fragments, such as tripod supports, handles or colander sherds. Specific attributes were individually counted and entered as spreadsheet data organized according to operation and level. These were later transferred to a database to simplify the pottery calculations for each element, pottery type or phase. We emphasized illustrating the pottery, resulting in over 1,400 drawings of separate sherds or complete vessels. This visual record helped to reference the remaining formal diagnostics with comparable attributes.

## Kayán Phase Ceramics

The Kayán phase is the earliest documented pottery style identified at Chinchawas. We were able to isolate Kayán phase pottery in separate areas of the site: Terrace 1 (OP9, OP12, OP19, OP21, OP43), Enclosure 2 (test pit OP3) and OP45, a house structure in Sector 1. The Kayán assemblage consists of 391 diagnostic sherds and can be divided into two ware categories (Figures 37 and 38).

*Kayán Ware A*

Kayán Ware A Paste
Kayán Ware A consists of 194 diagnostic sherds characterized by a white, pinkish white or light gray color kaolin or kaolinite paste. The paste is very fine and hard. Inclusions of small angular grit are small and well sorted. Surface treatment is fine and smooth, although surfaces are either left with a nongloss matte finish of the paste color, or with red-orange or a faded black or gray slip, especially in the interior. Typically, monochrome or polychrome paint covers the exterior surfaces, especially around the rim, in repeated linear, curvilinear and geometric motifs.

Kayán Ware A Vessel Shapes
The predominant form for Kayán Ware A vessels are small open bowls or cups, accounting for 90.9% of the form diagnostics. At least some of the examples stood with the help of ring bases. No Kayán bowls could be reconstructed in full, but the sample indicates that there were two main shapes. Bowls in either group may have had ring-bases (Figure 38B, C).

*Bowl 1.* Vertical or very slightly slanting walls characterize Bowl 1 bowls (Figure 37A–G). Often the vessel walls, between 0.4 and 0.7 cm wide, are slightly convex and incurving, and taper gently towards the rim. The lip is sometimes left tapered, but more commonly is beveled. Bowl 1 examples are small bowls, with rim diameters of 10 to 20 cm, and averaging around 14 cm. Kaolinite ring bases found at Chinchawas probably derived from Bowl 1 forms.

The white to light gray kaolinite paste in Bowl 1 examples is always very fine, with few inclusions of white to black grit, typically well sorted. Painted decoration, in monochrome and polychrome, occurs exclusively on the exterior. The interior of Bowl 1 examples frequently shows a red or reddish orange slip and, less commonly, a gray or faded black slip.

TABLE 7. Summary of plainware forms and percentages by phase.

| Forms | Kayán Count | Kayán Percentage | Chinchawasi 1 Count | Chinchawasi 1 Percentage | Chinchawasi 2 Count | Chinchawasi 2 Percentage | Warmi Count | Warmi Percentage | Chakwas Count | Chakwas Percentage |
|---|---|---|---|---|---|---|---|---|---|---|
| *Jar (small)* | — | — | — | — | — | — | 2 | 0.1 | — | — |
| Straight rim | — | — | 13 | 1.8 | 10 | 0.3 | 5 | 0.2 | — | — |
| Everted rim | 7 | 5.2 | 31 | 4.4 | 135 | 3.8 | 99 | 4.9 | 19 | 15.2 |
| Short, straight | — | — | 4 | 0.6 | — | — | 5 | 0.2 | — | — |
| *Jar (regular)* | 25 | 18.7 | 62 | 8.8 | 160 | 4.5 | 96 | 4.7 | 8 | 6.4 |
| Straight rim | 3 | 2.2 | 12 | 1.7 | 71 | 2.0 | 26 | 1.3 | — | — |
| Everted rim | 6 | 4.5 | 163 | 23.1 | 1026 | 29.1 | 430 | 21.2 | 10 | 8.0 |
| Short, straight | — | — | 10 | 1.4 | 31 | 0.9 | 23 | 1.1 | — | — |
| Small spout | — | — | — | — | 1 | 0.0 | 1 | 0.0 | — | — |
| Short, everted | 9 | 6.7 | 82 | 11.6 | 362 | 10.3 | 125 | 6.1 | — | — |
| *Jar (large)* | 3 | 2.2 | 12 | 1.7 | 83 | 2.4 | 66 | 3.2 | 4 | 3.2 |
| Straight rim | — | — | — | — | 6 | 0.2 | 4 | 0.2 | — | — |
| Everted rim | — | — | 18 | 2.5 | 59 | 1.7 | 46 | 2.3 | — | — |
| *Jar (other)* | | | | | | | | | | |
| Bulge rim | 1 | 0.7 | 6 | 0.8 | 7 | 0.2 | 7 | 0.3 | — | — |
| Everted or bulge rim | — | — | 3 | 0.4 | 14 | 0.4 | 17 | 0.8 | — | — |
| Short neck | — | — | — | — | 2 | 0.1 | — | — | — | — |
| Flange rim | — | — | 2 | 0.3 | 7 | 0.2 | — | — | — | — |
| *Pitcher* | — | — | — | — | 3 | 0.1 | 4 | 0.2 | 1 | 0.8 |
| Decorated strap handle | — | — | — | — | 3 | 0.1 | — | — | — | — |
| *Bottle* | | | | | | | | | | |
| (base) | — | — | 1 | 0.1 | 4 | 0.1 | 4 | 0.2 | 1 | 0.8 |
| (body) | — | — | 2 | 0.3 | 4 | 0.1 | 2 | 0.1 | — | — |
| (spout) | — | — | 1 | 0.1 | 8 | 0.2 | 1 | 0.0 | — | — |
| *Neckless olla* | — | — | 5 | 0.7 | 12 | 0.3 | — | — | — | — |
| *Bowl or dish* | | | | | | | | | | |
| Open (rim) | 55 | 41.0 | 189 | 26.7 | 1174 | 33.3 | 863 | 42.4 | 34 | 27.2 |
| Open (base) | — | — | — | — | 13 | 0.4 | 14 | 0.7 | — | — |
| Pedestal | — | — | 1 | 0.1 | 15 | 0.4 | 8 | 0.4 | 1 | 0.8 |
| Tripod | — | — | 1 | 0.1 | 9 | 0.3 | 4 | 0.2 | — | — |
| Incurving | 2 | 1.5 | 2 | 0.3 | 38 | 1.1 | 42 | 2.1 | 1 | 0.8 |
| Straight-sided | — | — | 4 | 0.6 | 6 | 0.2 | — | — | — | — |
| With ledge handle | 1 | 0.7 | 1 | 0.1 | 3 | 0.1 | — | — | — | — |
| Small shallow dish | — | — | 10 | 1.4 | 25 | 0.7 | 12 | 0.6 | 18 | 14.4 |
| Bulge | — | — | — | — | 2 | 0.1 | — | — | — | — |
| *Cup* | — | — | — | — | — | — | 1 | 0.0 | — | — |
| Small incurving | — | — | 8 | 1.1 | 3 | 0.1 | — | — | — | — |

TABLE 7 CONTINUED.

| Forms | Kayán | | Chinchawasi 1 | | Chinchawasi 2 | | Warmi | | Chakwas | |
|---|---|---|---|---|---|---|---|---|---|---|
| | Count | Percentage | Count | Percentage | Count | Percentage | Count | Percentage | Count | Percentage |
| *Colander* | | | | | | | | | | |
| Small | — | — | 3 | 0.4 | 10 | 0.3 | 2 | 0.1 | — | — |
| Medium | — | — | — | — | 1 | 0.0 | — | — | — | — |
| Large | — | — | 36 | 5.1 | 114 | 3.2 | 36 | 1.8 | — | — |
| *Spoon* | | | | | | | | | | |
| Small | 1 | 0.7 | 3 | 0.4 | 3 | 0.1 | 5 | 0.2 | — | — |
| Large | — | — | 2 | 0.3 | 2 | 0.1 | 2 | 0.1 | — | — |
| *Kanchero or dipper* | — | — | — | — | 3 | 0.1 | 1 | 0.0 | — | — |
| *Miniature* | — | — | — | — | — | — | 6 | 0.3 | — | — |
| *Panpipe* | — | — | — | — | 1 | 0.0 | — | — | — | — |
| *Funnel* | — | — | — | — | 1 | 0.0 | 3 | 0.1 | — | — |
| *Waster* | — | — | — | — | — | — | 1 | 0.0 | — | — |
| *Flat or corner* | — | — | — | — | 1 | 0.0 | 1 | 0.0 | — | — |
| *Indeterminate rim* | 21 | 15.7 | 20 | 2.8 | 94 | 2.7 | 69 | 3.4 | 28 | 22.4 |
| Total | 134 | 100.0% | 707 | 100.0% | 3,526 | 100.0% | 2,033 | 100.0% | 125 | 100.0% |

*Bowl 2.* Bowl 2 specimens (Figure 37H–W) have a slightly more slanted profile and, in general, a more sturdy appearance than Bowl 1 examples. Walls measure between 0.5 and 0.8 cm, and are straight or slightly convex. The lips are generally left tapered, without much flattening, as in Bowl 1 examples. The white to light gray kaolinite paste in Bowl 2 examples grades from very fine to fine, with occasional inclusions of white to black grit, typically well sorted. Painted decoration, in monochrome and polychrome, occurs exclusively on the exterior. Bowl 2 interiors often have a red or reddish orange slip and, less frequently, a gray or faded black slip.

## Kayán Ware A Surface Treatment

Ware A vessels show very fine burnishing, with very few striations from the shaping process. The white surfaces of the paste have a smooth matte finish, while slipped or painted surfaces have a dull luster.

## Kayán Ware A Painted Decoration

In addition to the kaolinite paste, painted decoration is one of the main diagnostic characteristics of Kayán phase Ware A pottery, occurring in 42.8% (n=83) of the Ware A diagnostics.

TABLE 8. Summary of miscellaneous plainware forms and percentages by phase.

| Forms | Kayán Count | Kayán Percentage | Chinchawasi 1 Count | Chinchawasi 1 Percentage | Chinchawasi 2 Count | Chinchawasi 2 Percentage | Warmi Count | Warmi Percentage | Chakwas Count | Chakwas Percentage |
|---|---|---|---|---|---|---|---|---|---|---|
| *Strap handle* | | | | | | | | | | |
| (indeterminate) | 4 | 8.5 | 18 | 11.0 | 75 | 8.8 | 63 | 14.0 | 6 | 28.6 |
| (small) | 6 | 12.8 | 20 | 12.3 | 79 | 9.3 | 47 | 10.4 | 5 | 23.8 |
| (regular) | 25 | 53.2 | 100 | 61.3 | 569 | 66.6 | 238 | 52.9 | 6 | 28.6 |
| (large) | 12 | 25.5 | 12 | 7.4 | 76 | 8.9 | 52 | 11.6 | 1 | 4.8 |
| Maker's mark | — | — | 1 | 0.6 | 4 | 0.5 | 11 | 2.4 | — | — |
| Plastic decoration | | | | | | | | | | |
| (ticks) | — | — | 1 | 0.6 | 2 | 0.2 | 8 | 1.8 | — | — |
| (dimple) | — | — | — | — | 13 | 1.5 | 1 | 0.2 | — | — |
| (other) | — | — | 1 | 0.6 | 5 | 0.6 | 4 | 0.9 | — | — |
| Painted | — | — | — | — | — | — | — | — | 1 | 4.8 |
| *Ledge handle* | — | — | 8 | 4.9 | 17 | 2.0 | 23 | 5.1 | — | — |
| Maker's mark | — | — | — | — | 1 | 0.1 | 2 | 0.4 | 1 | 4.8 |
| Decorated | — | — | 1 | 0.6 | 1 | 0.1 | 1 | 0.2 | — | — |
| *Loop handle* | — | — | 1 | 0.6 | 10 | 1.2 | — | — | — | — |
| *Kanchero handle* | — | — | — | — | 2 | 0.2 | — | — | 1 | 4.8 |
| Total | 47 | 100.0% | 163 | 100.0% | 854 | 100.0% | 450 | 100.0% | 21 | 100.0% |
| *Tripod leg or support* | — | — | 3 | 33.3 | 7 | 7.7 | 7 | 9.5 | — | — |
| U-shaped | — | — | 1 | 11.1 | 18 | 19.8 | 9 | 12.2 | — | — |
| Conical | — | — | 5 | 55.6 | 57 | 62.6 | 41 | 55.4 | 2 | 100.0 |
| Indeterminate base | — | — | — | — | 9 | 9.9 | 17 | 23.0 | — | — |
| Total | — | — | 9 | 100.0% | 91 | 100.0% | 74 | 100.0% | 2 | 100.0% |
| *Drilled ceramic* | 1 | 100.0 | 3 | 100.0 | 10 | 100.0 | 2 | 100.0 | 1 | 100.0 |
| Colander | | | | | | | | | | |
| (small) | 2 | 13.3 | 14 | 15.1 | 62 | 18.2 | 27 | 18.2 | 2 | 40.0 |
| (medium) | — | — | 7 | 7.5 | 7 | 2.1 | 3 | 2.0 | 1 | 20.0 |
| (large) | 13 | 86.7 | 66 | 71.0 | 267 | 78.5 | 117 | 79.1 | 2 | 40.0 |
| Painted | — | — | — | — | — | — | — | — | — | — |
| Square holes | — | — | — | — | 2 | 0.6 | — | — | — | — |
| Rim handle | — | — | 6 | 6.5 | 2 | 0.6 | 1 | 0.7 | — | — |
| Total | 15 | 100.0% | 93 | 100.0% | 340 | 100.0% | 148 | 100.0% | 5 | 100.0% |
| Total all forms | 63 | | 268 | | 1295 | | 674 | | 29 | |

The principal mode of color addition consists of a red slip over the light-colored clay and is found in 55.4% of the Kayán Ware A sample. An interior-only red slip is the most common (39.8%), followed by exterior-only slip (8.4%) and interior–exterior slip (7.2%). The red slip varies from a reddish brown to reddish orange.

Exterior line painting is another popular technique in Ware A bowls, occurring in 44.6% of the painted sample. This treatment occurs almost exclusively along the register just below the lip. The painting is typically monochrome (black, red and dark brown) and is executed in fine lines or slightly wider bands. Polychrome painting is rarer and is found exclusively on bowl exteriors.

Common motifs include parallel lines running across the exterior register just below the lip. Sometimes these are combined with a series of vertical lines and dashes to create rectangle fields, mazes and linear faces. Such faces resemble the grinning face motif of the following Chinchawasi phases and similar images in Recuay and Cajamarca style pottery. Curvilinear designs include multiple meandering bands, a repeating band of circles and a circle within a teardrop.

### Kayán Ware A Plastic Decoration

In general, the Kayán Ware A sample includes very little plastic decoration, although the few examples are noteworthy. A ring base from a kaolinite vessel shows an incised S-shape, which may be a maker's mark (Figure 38C). The sample also includes a modeled kaolin sherd in the shape of a camelid head (Figure 38A). The sherd is cylindrical, with an exterior red slip. The eyes are made of two small dollops of clay, with two incisions defining the eye; the nose has broken off. Such modeled pieces are common in Recuay pottery and come from effigy vessels depicting camelids (Eisleb 1987, Abb. 209, 240, 241).

## Kayán Ware B

Ware B, represented by 134 formal diagnostic sherds, is the other ware type for the Kayán phase and differs markedly from Ware A.

### Kayán Ware B Paste

Ware B is a less fine redware, characterized by very little painting. Ware B ceramics use nonkaolinite redware pastes. This paste is much coarser than Ware A kaolinite. Inclusions, typically grit and sand, are coarser and more frequent. The paste sometimes contains casts of plants, suggesting the presence of organic fiber inclusions.

### Kayán Ware B Vessel Shapes

There are a greater variety of forms in Kayán Ware B than in Ware A. Given the diversity of Ware B shapes and the more resilient nature of the paste, Ware B could be a more utilitarian line of pottery. Bowls, including open, incurving and shallow forms, represent 43.3% of the Kayán Ware B sample.

TABLE 9. Summary of decorated pottery and forms by phase.

| Forms | Count | Percentage |
|---|---|---|
| *Kayán* | | |
| Bottle | 1 | 1.8 |
| Open or cumbrous bowl | 50 | 90.9 |
| Pedestal or ring-base bowl | 4 | 7.3 |
| Total | 55 | 100.0% |
| *Chinchawasi 1 and Chinchawasi 2* | | |
| Small jar | 4 | 0.3 |
| Regular jar | 255 | 20.5 |
| Bottle | — | — |
| Open or cumbrous bowl | 969 | 77.8 |
| Incurving bowl | 7 | 0.6 |
| Pedestal or ring-base bowl | 1 | 0.1 |
| Shallow bowl or dish | 1 | 0.1 |
| Straight-sided cup or tumbler | 9 | 0.7 |
| Total | 1246 | 100.0% |
| *Warmi* | | |
| Regular jar | 21 | 4.0 |
| Bottle | 2 | 0.4 |
| Open or cumbrous bowl | 481 | 91.8 |
| Tripod bowl | 11 | 2.1 |
| Pedestal or ring-base bowl | 4 | 0.8 |
| Shallow bowl or dish | 1 | 0.2 |
| Kero or tumbler | 4 | 0.8 |
| Total | 425 | 100.0% |
| *Chakwas* | | |
| Small jar | 2 | 6.3 |
| Regular jar | 13 | 40.6 |
| Open or cumbrous bowl | 16 | 50.0 |
| Incurving bowl | 1 | 3.1 |
| Total | 32 | 100.0% |
| *Indeterminate or unphased decorated* | | |
| Small jar | 1 | 0.3 |
| Regular jar | 41 | 13.6 |
| Bottle | 23 | 7.6 |
| Open-cumbrous bowl | 226 | 75.1 |
| Shallow dish or bowl | 3 | 1.0 |
| Straight sided cup | 5 | 1.7 |
| Kero or tumbler | 2 | 0.7 |
| Total | 301 | 100.0% |

*Bowl 1.* Most of the sample consists of shallow bowl shapes (Bowl 1) with slightly convex sides, no basal angle and coarse interior or exterior painting, or both, in dark red. The rims show very little treatment besides a pinching and slight flattening of the exterior lip.

Jars and related closed forms of differing sizes account for 40.3% of the Kayán Ware B sample. Of this total, regular-sized jars (with rim diameters of 15 to 30 cm) represent 32.1%; everted and short, everted rims are the most common neck treatments. Small jars with everted rims represent 4.7% of the Ware B sample and large everted neck jars total 2%.

*Jar 1.* Jar 1 is the most common closed vessel and has a short, everted rim whose diameter measures between 14 and 18 cm. Occasionally, notched ledge nubbins are attached to the neck wall (Figure 38D).

*Jar 2.* Jar 2 is a small squat jar, with a short cylindrical pouring spout and a flat base (Figure 38E).

### Kayán Ware B Surface Treatment
In general, compared to Ware A, surface treatment in Kayán Ware B pottery is less fine, but is considerably more varied. Smoothing is common, as is burnishing to a matte finish and, less commonly, to a dull luster. No examples had very fine burnishing or polishing.

### Kayán Ware B Painted Decoration
Monochrome painting is present in several examples of Ware B bowls, rendered predominately in broad red strokes over paste color. Painting occurs typically as linear and curvilinear designs on the interior or exterior, or both. No clear designs could be identified from the sample.

### Kayán Ware B Plastic Decoration
One jar rim (Figure 38D) has a small ledge handle or nubbin, with three small notches or incisions.

### Discussion: Kayán Phase
The Kayán phase is named for the pass referred to as Punta Kayán (Punta Kallán), which separates the upper Pira drainage from the Callejón de Huaylas. This pass, as described earlier, is one of the major routes in the Huaraz area today and likely was exploited frequently in prehistory to traverse the Cordillera Negra. The region just west of Huaraz and east of Chinchawas seems to have been a locus for the type of Recuay ceramics referred to as the Kayán style.

The Kayán phase assemblage, especially the Ware A sample, resembles the Recuay period pottery of the Huaraz area just east of the pass. Bennett (1944:59–

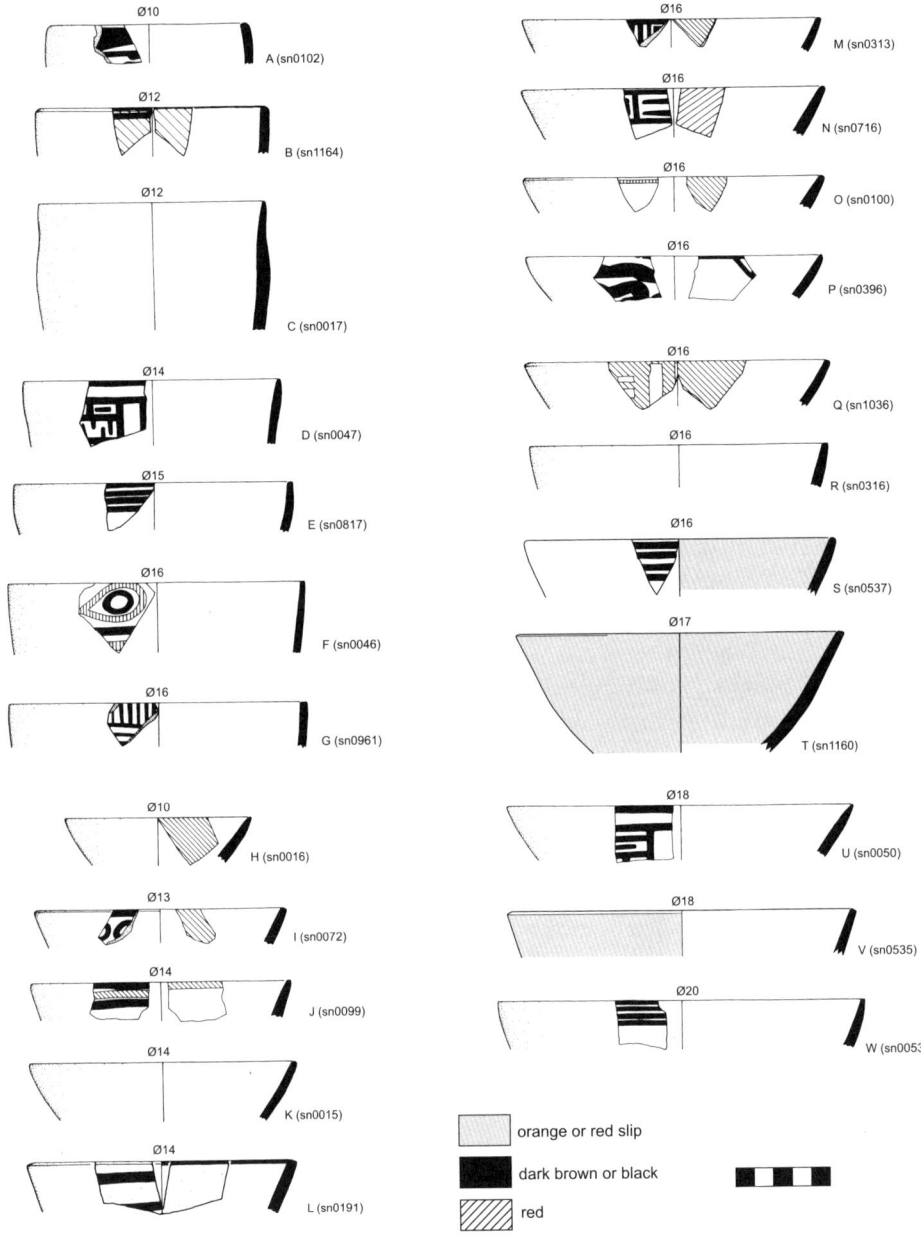

FIGURE 37. Kayán phase Ware A pottery: A–G, Bowl 1; H–W, Bowl 2.

60) found similar ceramics through surface reconnaissance at Balcón de Judas; he referred to the site as San Gerónimo and described the remains as "Incaic" in affiliation, despite having excavated sites bearing very similar Recuay ceramics. Subsequent research by Wegner at Balcón de Judas, however, has shown that the

kaolinite pottery can be attributed to the Recuay culture approximately a thousand years before the Inka (Wegner 1982, 1988, 2003).

Kayán phase materials from Chinchawas and the Recuay period pottery from Balcón de Judas are directly comparable and show formal and decorative similarities. First, the emphasis on bowl forms, especially the vertical and near vertical shape of Bowl 1, is shared. Second, both assemblages have exterior painting of linear and curvilinear designs on the uppermost rim register. Finally, the frequent use of a red interior slip is also a common shared mode.

More broadly, Kayán phase ceramics can be categorized with Recuay pottery found in other parts of the North Highlands. Lynch (1980, fig. 9.23f–k) recovered positive and negative painted kaolinite fragments in Guitarrero Cave, near Mancos on the Cordillera Negra side of the Callejón de Huaylas. Assemblages from sites such as Katak (Eisleb 1987), Pashash (Grieder 1978) and Chavín de Huántar (Tello 1960; Lumbreras 1970, 1977) feature impressive kaolinite ceramics in the Recuay tradition. Exterior-painted kaolinite bowls from these sites provide the best comparisons, as does the use of ring bases (Grieder 1978:212–218; Eisleb 1987, Abb. 2–32;). The short cylindrical spouts and squat jar forms of Ware B are also characteristic Recuay features. Modeled llama figurines are a hallmark of the Recuay style and are representative especially of the Callejón de Huaylas (Reichert 1977a:170–175; Smith 1978:64–66). The Kayán specimen (Figure 38A) may be comparable to examples from Queyash Alto (Gero 1990:53) and Katak (Eisleb 1987, Abb. 207–211). Maker's marks (Figure 38C) have also been documented on Recuay pottery from Pashash (Grieder 1978:79). The affinities therefore indicate that Kayán Ware A ceramics are directly related to the Recuay tradition of the North Highlands.

Ware A vessels represent the fancy class of Kayán phase ceramics, designated for either serving or other special purposes. As the dual wares of the Kayán phase indicate, Recuay peoples of the North Highlands used multiple types of pottery simultaneously. While kaolinite pottery was probably reserved for special purposes at Chinchawas, more quotidian activities probably used coarser wares, such as Kayán Ware B.

Kayán Ware A pottery was likely a prestige ware for local peoples. Systematic investigations have only recovered substantial Recuay kaolinite materials from high-status Recuay contexts. Moreover, these contexts are almost exclusively mortuary in nature (Bennett 1944; Grieder 1978; Eisleb 1987). Kaolinite ceramics seem to have played a crucial role in funerary ceremonies.

In addition, the recovery of Ware A pottery in patio enclosures suggests that use of kaolinite pottery also extended to local episodes of ostentation, likely under the context of feasting and community gatherings. Kaolinite sherds from OP45 also indicate that Recuay style pottery somehow functioned in residential practice, probably as occasional special-use serving vessels. The relative proportions of fancy Kayán pottery indicate that its residential function was secondary to its use in the patio enclosures.

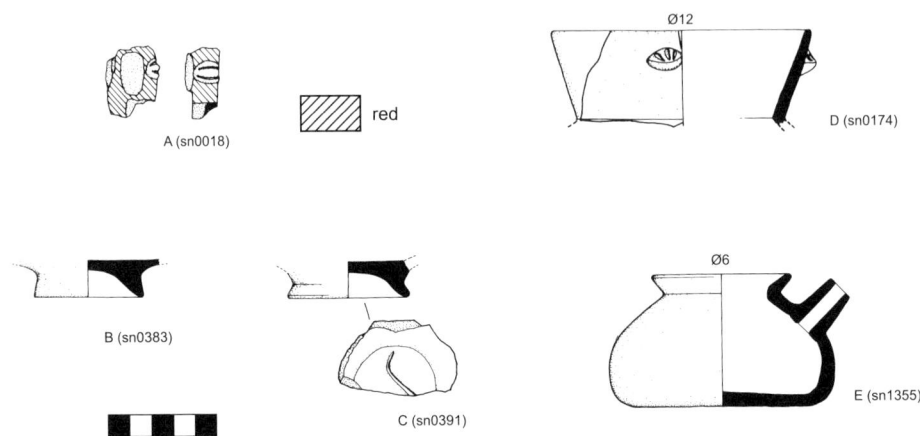

FIGURE 38. Kayán phase pottery: A–C, Ware A; D, Ware B Jar 1; E, Ware B Jar 2.

Ware B, on the other hand, seems to have been used for normal quotidian purposes, namely cooking and storage. The coarser pastes and utilitarian add-ons, such as strap handles and nubbins, suggest that the durability of daily-use pots was a priority. By extension, Kayán phase Ware B seems indicative of more local production, that is, near the Chinchawas site. The persistence of Ware B paste use in later phases, such as the Chinchawasi and Warmi, supports such an interpretation. In contrast, the infrequency of Ware A and its limited function suggest that this may have been an imported ware, probably from the Callejón de Huaylas near the kaolin sources bordering the Río Santa (Czwarno 1983).

Although the results from the Chinchawas research widens the functional contexts of Recuay fancy pottery, more research needs to be done to clarify the diversity and variability of Recuay material culture, especially over time.

## Kayán Phase Absolute Dating

The few radiocarbon measurements for Recuay investigations indicate a middle to late Early Intermediate Period placement for the culture (Lau 2004a). The best dated Recuay materials come from the site of Pashash, near Cabana in the provincial region of Pallasca (Grieder 1978). Related dates for younger or older ceramic associations from Chavín de Huántar, Queyash Alto, La Pampa, Honcopampa, Huaricoto and sites in the Pierina Survey bracket Recuay culture within a 400 to 500 year period that terminates with the end of Early Intermediate Period.

Our single radiocarbon assay from a trench excavation with Kayán artifacts comes from OP9, Level J, and has an age of 1710 ± 50 B.P. (A.D. 240 ± 50 uncalibrated, or A.D. 360 ± 50 calibrated), with a 2-sigma range of A.D. 233 to 434. This Kayán phase assay accords well with the general placement of Recuay culture in the late half of the Early Intermediate Period.

# Chinchawasi 1 Phase Ceramics

The appearance of a new, distinct ceramic style marks the onset of the next occupation. The phase is named after the local modern community of Chinchawasi (or Chinchayhuasi).

Certain Kayán phase features hold over, but the new pottery constitutes a reformulation of the local tradition and undergoes at least one major transformation: Chinchawasi 1 into Chinchawasi 2. Our investigations located Chinchawasi pottery in all of the horizontal excavations and in nearly all of the test excavations performed in Sector 1. In these, Chinchawasi levels lay directly above Kayán deposits, or constituted the initial find level, indicating both a larger and more intense occupation than the preceding, lighter Kayán occupation. The Chinchawasi 1 phase diagnostic sample consists of 1,810 sherds: 835 decorated sherds and 975 plainware form diagnostics. Four major pottery wares were distinguished for the Chinchawasi 1 phase.

*Chinchawasi 1 Ware A*
The most recognizable Chinchawasi 1 pottery is Ware A, distinguished by red-on-cream treatment (Figures 39, 40, 41 and 42). The sample consists of 648 sherds.

CHINCHAWASI 1 WARE A PASTE
A distinctive cream, tan or yellowish tan paste characterizes Ware A. The paste typically contains common medium-sized to coarse (well-sorted) inclusions.

CHINCHAWASI 1 WARE A VESSEL SHAPES
Bowls are the most common vessel shape in Ware A pottery, accounting for 82.4% (n=330) of the formal diagnostics.

*Bowl 1.* The general Bowl 1 shape is Ware A's predominant shape, accounting for 81.2% of all recognized shapes. The defining attributes for this open bowl form are exterior painting and the general vessel shape. All examples with complete profiles indicate that the bowls were roughly globular, without any pronounced basal angle. There are two Bowl 1 variants; because the decoration and surface treatment are essentially the same, differentiation between the variants is based on mainly bowl shape and profile.

The Bowl 1a variant is a steep-sided bowl, with a slight to pronounced convex profile (Figure 39A–E). These bowls have mouth diameters between 18 and 22 cm, with the average at 19 to 20 cm. Lip treatment is typically a simple rounding and, less commonly, flattening. There are occasionally rim nubbins, typically in the form of a rounded rectangle (Figure 39A) or semicircle. The nubbin is typically ribbed or notched (Figure 39D) or is left unribbed.

The Bowl 1b variant is a shallow bowl form, with a slight convex profile (Figures 39F–S and 40A–N). Bowl 1b examples have mouth diameters between 14 and 32 cm, with the average at 18 cm. Lip treatment includes simple rounding and, less

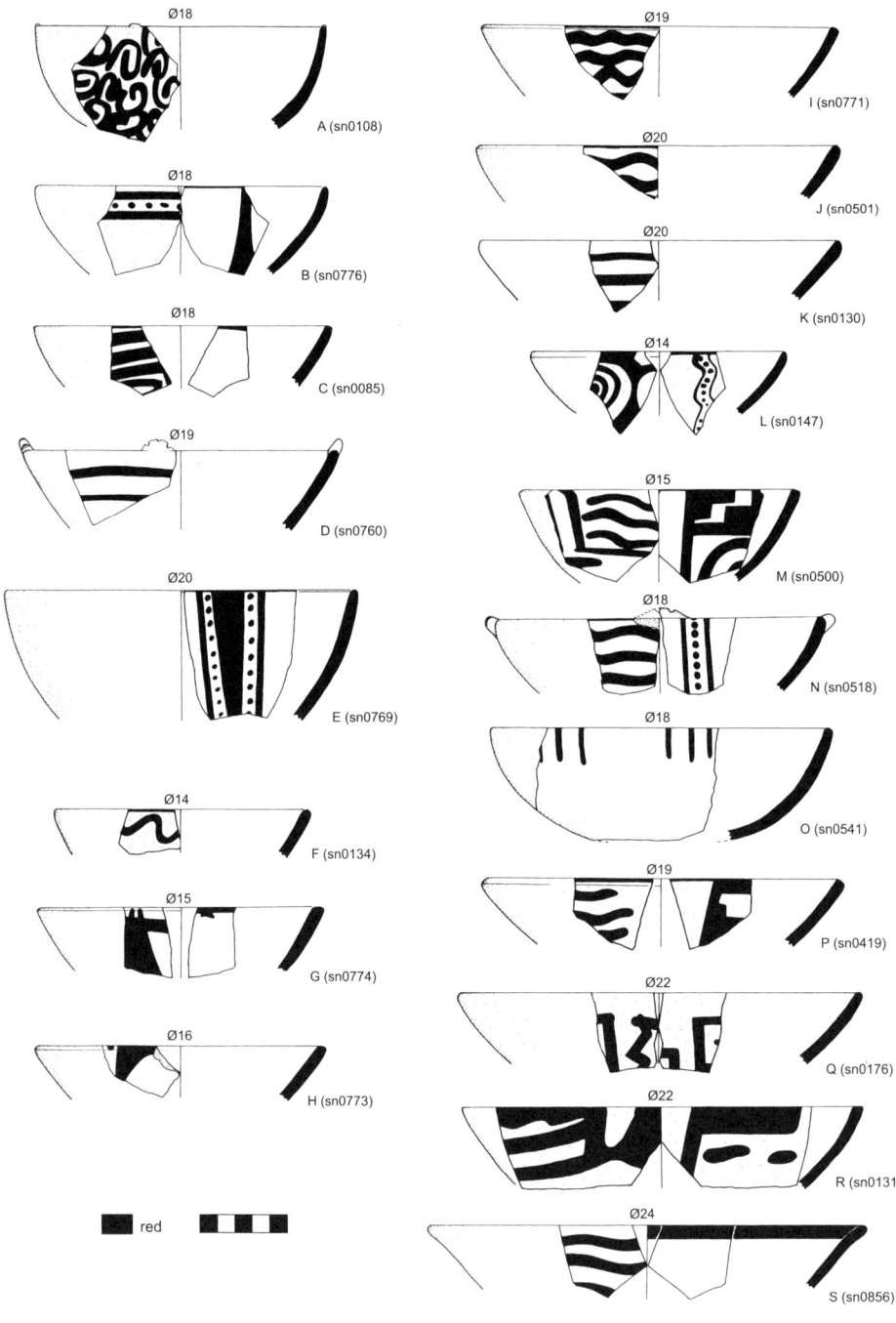

FIGURE 39. Chinchawasi 1 phase Ware A pottery: A–E, Bowl 1a; F–S, Bowl 1b.

commonly, flattening. There is use of rim nubbins in the Bowl 1b category, although it is less frequent.

*Bowl 2.* Bowl 2 is a far less common shape than Bowl 1, representing only 0.6% of all Ware A forms (Figure 41A, B). Bowl 2 is a steep, nearly vertical bowl form, at least near the rim. It is unclear how far the vertical sides extended below the rim, but if classic Recuay bowls can be used as analogies, these may extend 6 to 10 cm down from the lip (Grieder 1978:257; Eisleb 1987, Abb.7). Rim diameters range between 16 and 18 cm, and body sherd thickness measures 0.5 to 0.8 cm. Lip treatment is simple with rounded or slightly thickened and flattened contours (Figure 41A). Painting is executed on the exterior, in typical Chinchawasi 1 designs.

*Bowl 3.* Bowl 3 is an incurving bowl with an uncommon shape (0.6% all Ware A shapes). These are small closed vessels, with rim diameters between 10 and 12 cm and body sherd thickness of 0.6 to 0.8 cm. Examples take a roughly globular or ovoid shape (Figure 41C, D). Lip treatment consists of simple rounding or beveling. Only the exteriors are painted in the Bowl 3 sample.

Cups account for 0.6% of the Ware A formal diagnostics in Chinchawasi 1 deposits.

*Cup 1.* Cup 1 is a vertical or slightly incurving form with exterior painting and was probably used as a special purpose drinking vessel. Cup examples have a mouth diameter between 9 and 10 cm, and a body sherd thickness ranging between 0.6 and 0.8 cm. Lip treatment includes flattening near and inside the lip (Figure 41E, F).

*Cup 2.* Cup 2 is small drinking vessel with a steeply angled profile (Figure 41G), which also may be incurving (Figure 41H). Examples have a mouth diameter between 9 and 10 cm. Like Cup 1, Cup 2 is characterized by exterior painting.

Jars account for 17% (n=56) of the Ware A formal diagnostics in Chinchawasi 1 deposits, including small and regular-sized shapes.

*Jar 1.* Jar 1 is a small, relatively uncommon jar shape with an everted rim profile and a neck that widens towards the body (Figure 42A). It has a mouth diameter of 10 cm. Painted decoration adorns the exterior and is confined primarily to the neck underneath the everted portion of the rim. The rim tapers toward the lip. Lip treatment consists of a simple rounding.

*Jar 2.* Jar 2 (Figure 42B–H) is the most common jar shape in Ware A, Chinchawasi phase 1. The vessel has a short, everted neck that grades from straight to slightly concave in profile. The jar body is probably globular. The intersection between the neck and shoulder ranges from a gradual to sharp angle. There is a wide range of

FIGURE 40. Chinchawasi 1 phase Ware A pottery: A–N, Bowl 1b.

sizes for this jar, with mouth diameters between 10 and 23 cm. Sherd thickness varies between 0.4 and 1 cm. These jars were often equipped with strap handles positioned horizontally, located on or near the shoulder of the vessel (Figure 42F). Lip treatment consists of simple rounding and beveling. The exterior was the preferred surface for painted decoration, although the inner surface of the rim sometimes showed painting, most commonly in the form of rim ticks.

*Jar 3.* This uncommon form has a vertical neck and long, flanged lip (Figure 42I). The few examples have 16 to 20 cm mouth diameters. Painting occurs on the top side of the flange lip as well as the exterior surface. Chinchawasi 1 Ware A Jar 3 resembles the Jar 6 shape in Chinchawasi 1 Ware D.

*Jar 4.* Jar 4 is a small, restricted vessel, with a short everted neck and an ovoid body. Jar 4 specimens have small rim nubbins and vertical strap handles. The only examples (Figure 42K, L) were found in a subterranean tomb offering (OP63) and have 4 to 6 cm mouth diameters.

### Chinchawasi 1 Ware A Surface Treatment

Ware A pottery can be identified through its cream, buff or whitish pink slip. Light-colored pastes are often left unslipped. The pottery also has coarse to fine burnishing to a matte finish or, more commonly, a dull luster. Polishing is rare and surfaces are never lustrous. Despite the burnishing, striations and tiny cavities from the scraping and shaping process are not uncommon, especially on unpainted surfaces.

### Chinchawasi 1 Ware A Painted Decoration

Chinchawasi 1 potters rendered Ware A designs almost exclusively using a dusky red paint over the light cream or whitish pink background. The painted decoration occurs most commonly on vessel exteriors (44.7% of the Chinchawasi 1 decorated sample), especially near the rim register and lips on the bowl and cup forms, and the lips, necks and shoulders on jars. There are several open bowl examples with both interior and exterior painting.

On bowl exteriors, potters preferred repeating lines just below the rim, executed either roughly straight (Figure 39D) or in meanders (Figure 39J, S). Occasionally, a rectangular field encloses the meanders (Figure 39M). Other designs include upward-pointing triangles (Figure 39G), a maze or nested rectangles (Figures 39C and 41B) and curlicues (Figures 39A and 41C). A triangle or maze motif is the primary motif on cups (Figure 41E, F), although there is one example of nested diamonds (Figure 41G). Exterior designs also include band and dot designs (Figures 39B and 42K–L).

Interior painting occurs in 29.9% of the decorated sample. Bowls with only interior painting often portray a grinning face. The face motif consists of concentric circles for eyes, a nose with flaring nostrils that extend around the bottom of each eye, and a rectangular mouth with short strokes for teeth (Figure 40B, H); this motif is also very prominent in the Chinchawasi 2 phase. Concentric circles were also used to decorate bowl exteriors (Figure 39L).

A wide band–dot motif (Figure 40C, G, J, M) is rendered in bichrome. First, the dusky red band is painted and then large creamy white dots are applied over it. These occur as straight bands running the length of the interior surface, or as arcs along the rim, or both. This motif is not found on bowl exteriors.

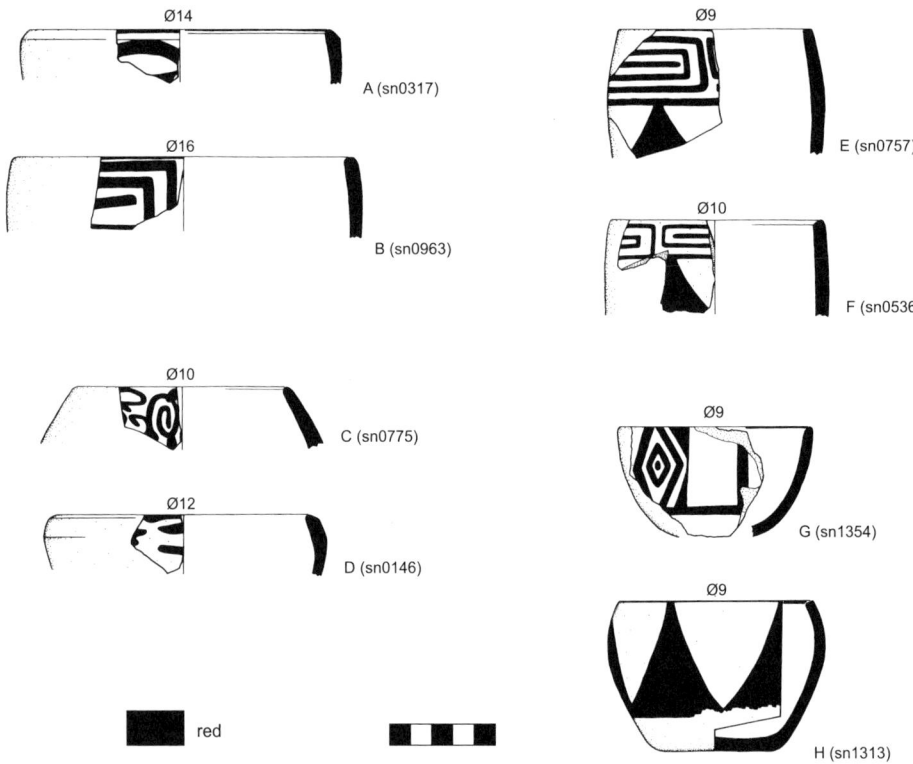

Figure 41. Chinchawasi 1 phase Ware A pottery: A, B, Bowl 2; C, D, Bowl 3; E, F, Cup 1; G, H, Cup 2.

Less frequent interior motifs include dots between two narrow lines (Figure 39L), parallel bands (Figure 40A, N) and pendants with interior geometric designs such as step-motifs (Figure 39M, P), irregular dots (Figure 39R), nested diamonds (Figure 40K) and tapering bands and dots (Figures 39E and 40D). Other less common designs include repeating fields with filler dots (Figure 40E, I, L).

On jar rims and shoulders, the most frequent designs are exterior-painted repeating upward pointing triangles (Figure 42E, F), nested rectangles (Figure 42C, G) and the maze design (Figure 42D). Rim ticks across the lip and bands along the rim are also common features, on both bowls and jars (Figure 42D, I).

### Chinchawasi 1 Ware A Plastic Decoration

Chinchawasi 1 Ware A is characterized by very little plastic decoration. The most common technique under this heading is the use of notched or ribbed nubbins or simple adornos on the rim (1% of the Chinchawasi 1 decorated sample). Nubbins could have had functional properties, such as to aid in holding, but some are too small or not at an ideal angle for such a purpose. Strap handles are common additions to Ware A jars, probably at least two to each vessel. Occasionally they are painted with simple linear strokes or ticks across the width of the handle (0.5 % of the Chinchawasi 1 decorated sample). One strap handle (Figure 42J) shows maze motifs.

Discussion: Chinchawasi 1 Ware A

Ware A is the fancy end of the Chinchawasi 1 spectrum of pottery. The forms are serving in nature, and their recovery from high-status contexts with other prestige artifacts denotes a special function. They were accorded more importance than common plainwares.

Chinchawasi 1 forms and decoration approximate the stylistic repertoire of Kayán Ware A (the fancy class of Recuay period pottery) and suggest possible functional similarities. In particular, the Ware A phase assemblage seems to intentionally imitate certain aspects of Kayán pottery: the light paste, exterior-painted decoration (in red and black) and the focus on open bowl forms.

Chinchawasi 1 Ware A painting draws strongly from the Kayán tradition of painted decoration. Like Kayán pottery, the uppermost exterior register of open bowls provided the design field of choice. Moreover, the designs chosen seem to be derived from the previous Recuay-related repertoire: repeating geometric and linear motifs, rim bands, rim nubbins and the focus on open bowls.

Even the use of the light-colored paste and cream washes may approximate the white paste color and whitish surfaces in Recuay kaolinite pottery. Ware A's use of a light paste suggests that the community of Chinchawas, during the Chinchawasi phase 1, no longer had ready access to the kaolinite clays or pottery of the Callejón de Huaylas, or that it was no longer popular. Second, the preference to produce a lighter surface or paste (either with a thin wash, a combination of clays, or different firing methods), suggests that the lighter color was a stylistic priority.

The use of light-colored clays in Chinchawasi pottery may be analogous to other cases in Andean culture in which technology accommodates preferences in style or value systems. Lechtman (1980), for example, has identified a series of sophisticated metallurgical techniques developed by ancient peoples of the Andes who sought to incorporate certain precious metals, notably gold and silver, into alloys. In so doing, the smiths achieved the desired colors and surfaces of gold and silver, while integrating both the metal and the valued "essence" of the gold and silver within the fabric of the alloy. Making pastes lighter and reformulating older decorative motifs may have preserved certain desired and recognizable qualities of Recuay pottery.

Chinchawasi 1 Ware A pottery has been found in much smaller quantities from other sites in the Callejón de Huaylas, especially near Huaraz. At Shankaiyan, in a series of gallery tombs associated with classic Recuay materials, Bennett (1944:54–59, fig. 17a–c) recovered pottery that show Chinchawasi features: deep everted open bowls, red-on-white decoration, notched rim nubbins and exterior painting in repeating bands or meanders. Many of these pieces use a less fine kaolinite paste that grades to pink. At the Irwá B site (Site 10H, another gallery tomb with Recuay style kaolin sherds) and sites in the vicinity of Ichik Wilkawaín (Site 7H-13, a subterranean gallery tomb) and Site 9H-13 (a "subterranean house"), Bennett (1944) found pottery identical to Chinchawasi 1 Ware A. Shared elements include the convex bowl shapes, ring bases, red paint on cream or buff paste, notched

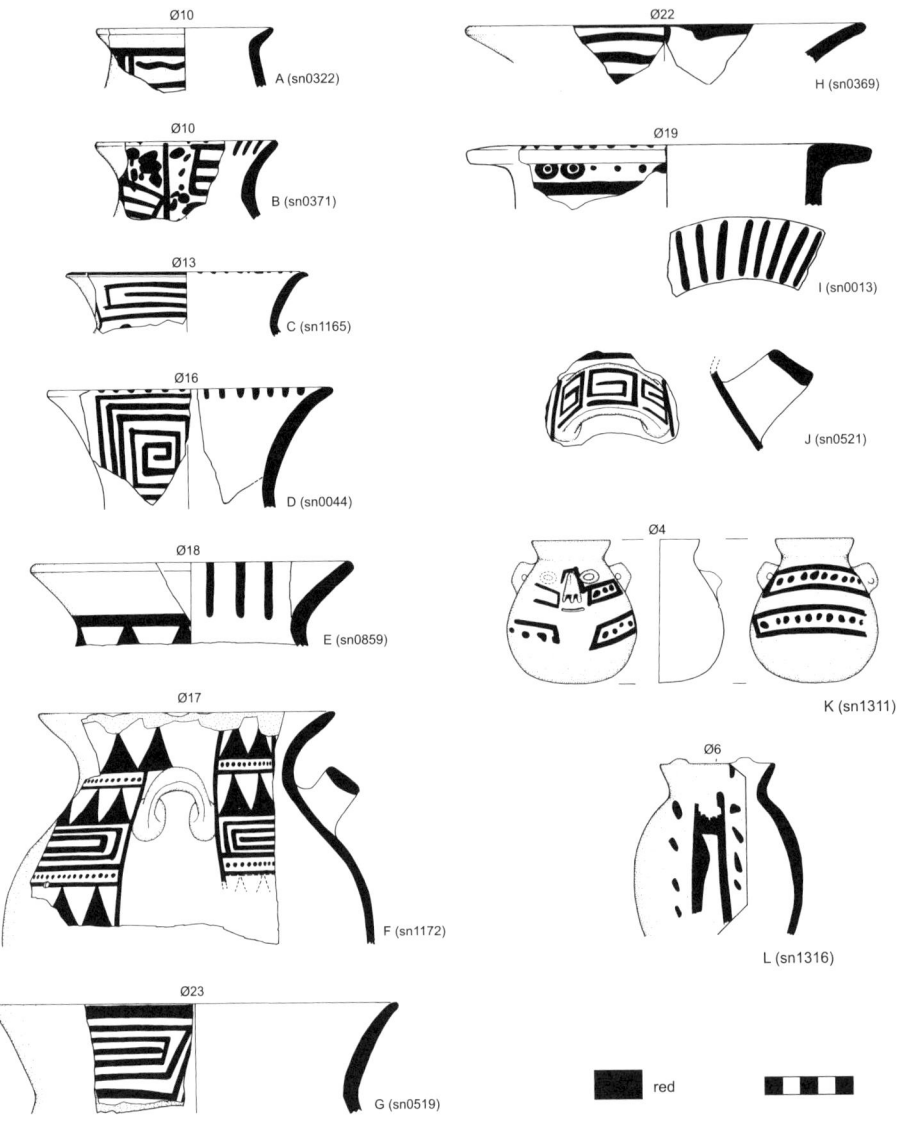

FIGURE 42. Chinchawasi 1 phase Ware A pottery: A, Jar 1; B–H, Jar 2; I, Jar 3; K, L, Jar 4.

rim nubbins, concentric circle eyes and interior bands. On the basis of stylistic criteria, he considered these materials as "slightly earlier than the Tiahuanacoid-influenced collections from other Wilkawaín sites" (Bennett 1944:53).

Other areas of the Callejón de Huaylas have produced ceramics similar to Chinchawasi 1 Ware A. Surface collections from Antajirca (in Museo Arqueológico de Ancash, Huaraz), just south of Huaraz, produced similar sherds in association with Recuay-style stone sculptures and chullpa tombs. In the Pierina mining zone, at the Quitapampa A site (a subterranean tomb underneath a large flat boulder)

Ponte Rosalino (1999a:77–79, lám. 55, 61) recovered several large cups in association with late Recuay ceramics, including kaolin sherds. The vessels bear Chinchawasi-type decoration, especially the maze and triangle motifs.

Outside the greater Huaraz area, ceramics resembling Chinchawasi 1 Ware A decoration occur only sporadically. At Guitarrero Cave, near Mancos on the Cordillera Negra side of the Callejón de Huaylas, Lynch (1980, fig. 9.24b) recovered a ring-based bowl with exterior repeating meanders that resemble Chinchawasi designs. The black and red painting and the interior motif of repeated semicircles and dots are Chinchawasi 1 Ware A conventions. On the recommendation of Gary Vescelius and Hernan Amat, Lynch (1980:230) attributed the vessel to the early Middle Horizon. At Pashash, in Cabana, the Usú phase—the final component in the site's Recuay sequence—has some similarities, including the exclusive use of red paint, linear designs and the nonkaolinite paste (Grieder 1978:70–71, 78). However, unlike Chinchawasi 1 Ware A, Usú pottery relies on plastic decoration (Grieder 1978:78, figs. 40, 50), seen only occasionally in Ware A. Moreover, Usú pottery is left unslipped or is slipped orange, whereas Ware A pottery is typically slipped cream.

Beyond the Recuay zone further north, some general comparisons can be made to Middle Horizon styles of the Huamachuco area. In particular, the Urpay and Tuscan phases, also known as Huamachuco-on-white, focus on dark paint on a light-slipped background, exterior linear designs and painted circle or dot elements (McCown 1945, pl. 22d, h, r, v; Thatcher 1972, figs. 44u, 51–52; Krzanowski 1986a, 1986b; Krzanowski and Tunia 1986, fig. 12). Krzanowski (1986a:251) indicates that "Huamachuco-on-white" includes pottery known also as "black and red on white slip" and "red on white slip" (McCown 1945) and the "Tuscan phase" (Thatcher 1972, figs. 51, 52). The common use of black paint and lack of additional important Ware A diagnostics, however, preclude direct cultural affinities to Chinchawasi 1.

In sum, the stylistic relationships from these northern areas seem more distant than direct analogues of the Huaraz area. The available evidence supports the interpretation that Ware A was a local style that centered around the greater Huaraz area and gained importance at the end of the Recuay tradition (Lau 2004a). Note that, because many of the surface reconnaissance studies conducted on the north–central coast have not extended into the upper valley regions, it is likely that other high elevation sites along the western flanks of the Cordillera Negra will produce pottery of this kind (Richard and Cheryl Daggett, pers. comm. 1998).

## Chinchawasi 1 Ware B

The other principal class of painted Chinchawasi 1 pottery is a white-on-red pottery, referred to as Ware B. Ware B occurs very rarely and is associated primarily with Chinchawasi 1 pottery, accounting for 3% (26 sherds) of the decorated sample. All the fragments of Ware B pottery are technologically and decoratively very similar to one another. This observation seems to indicate: (1) fairly standardized production; (2) a short spurt of popularity and use; or (3) a restricted distribution.

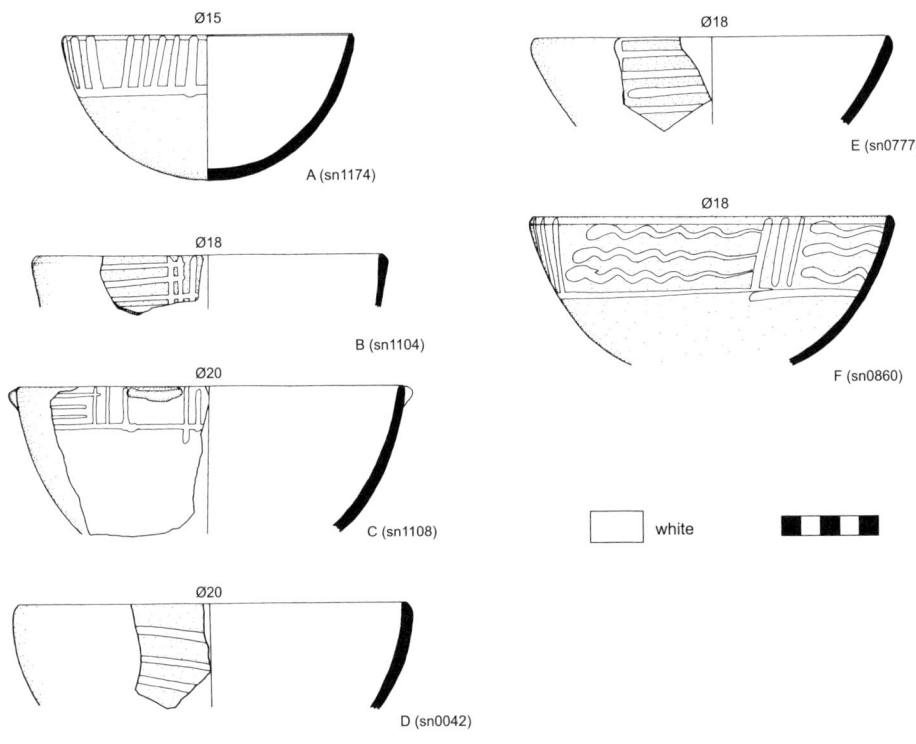

FIGURE 43. Chinchawasi 1 phase Ware B pottery: A–D, Bowl 1a; E, F, Bowl 1b.

CHINCHAWASI 1 WARE B PASTE

Instead of the tan or cream paste, Chinchawasi potters preferred a redware paste. Also, the vessel shapes and the decorative treatments are somewhat different than Ware A. Perhaps because of its use as serving ware, Ware B usually has a better-sorted and finer paste and, typically, fairly thin body thicknesses.

CHINCHAWASI 1 WARE B VESSEL SHAPES

*Bowl 1.* Nearly all Ware B fragments come from globular open bowls (98%). On the basis of vessel profiles, the Bowl 1 form can be categorized into two variants.

The Bowl 1a variant is a deep open bowl with a nearly hemispherical profile (Figure 43A–D). Steep sides characterize the shape (e.g., Figure 43B), with a gentle convexity. Bowl 1a vessels tend to be large bowls with mouth diameters between 15 and 20 cm and an average diameter of 18 cm. Wall thickness tends to be even throughout the vessel, ranging from 0.4 to 0.8 cm. The depth of the bowls provides a consistent curvature to the profile, without any sharp breaks. Thickening sometimes occurs near the lip, which is usually rounded and slightly beveled on the exterior edge. One rim (Figure 43C) features a small, simple appliqué rim nubbin or ledge handle.

The Bowl 1b variant is a shallower bowl, but many of the Bowl 1a attributes are similar to Bowl 1b: even wall thickness, rounded lips and wall thickening near the rim. The only examples measure between 16 and 18 cm in mouth diameter. Like Bowl 1a, potters painted exclusively on bowl exteriors (Figure 43E, F).

### Chinchawasi 1 Ware B Surface Treatment

Ware B pottery is smoothed and burnished to a matte finish, but no example shows polishing. Manufacturing striations are not uncommon. Ware B surfaces either show the paste color or have a thin wash of a deep red slip. In most cases wetting the surface reveals the glittering of small mica inclusions.

### Chinchawasi 1 Ware B Painted Decoration

The open globular bowl is the predominant form for this pottery. As in Ware A, the uppermost rim register of the exterior is the principal decorative field. Designs are fluid, with uneven line weights and inexact intersections. The white paint is thin, so that the red background can sometimes be made out underneath the painting. Designs feature repeating horizontal bands, meandering lines or vertical ticking strokes. These elements can occur in combinations around the entire outer rim.

### Chinchawasi 1 Ware B Plastic Decoration

Like Ware A, Ware B very occasionally shows simple rim nubbins on the exterior of open bowls. These nubbins likely functioned to help grasp the vessel.

### Discussion: Chinchawasi 1 Ware B

Chinchawasi 1 Ware B is a local decorated pottery. Ware B is rare and occurs mainly in association with Ware A in high-status zones. Ware B uses painted designs similar to the repertoire in Recuay pottery, especially along open bowl exteriors, but differs strongly in paste and shape variability. Ware B occurs almost exclusively as open bowls at Chinchawas, indicating that this pottery had limited function or availability, or both.

The closest analogues to Ware B pottery come from the Callejón de Huaylas. From subterranean tombs in the greater Huaraz basin Bennett recovered a series of vessels decorated with white linear and geometric designs, especially on the exterior of open bowl shapes. He designated this pottery "White-on-red" (Bennett 1944:98–99, fig. 12).

White-on-red pottery, known as "Huarás" or "Huaraz," occurs in many parts of the Callejón de Huaylas, but to date there has been very little systematic description and illustration of the style. Vescelius and Amat encountered Huarás materials through settlement surveys in many parts of the Callejón de Huaylas, particularly in the Marcará region, but the results have appeared only in secondhand summaries (Buse 1965; Lanning 1965). Burger (1985a:125–126) reported briefly on Huarás pottery from the post-Early Horizon levels at Huaricoto, contemporary residential architecture, and associated secondary burials within a stone cist. The primary

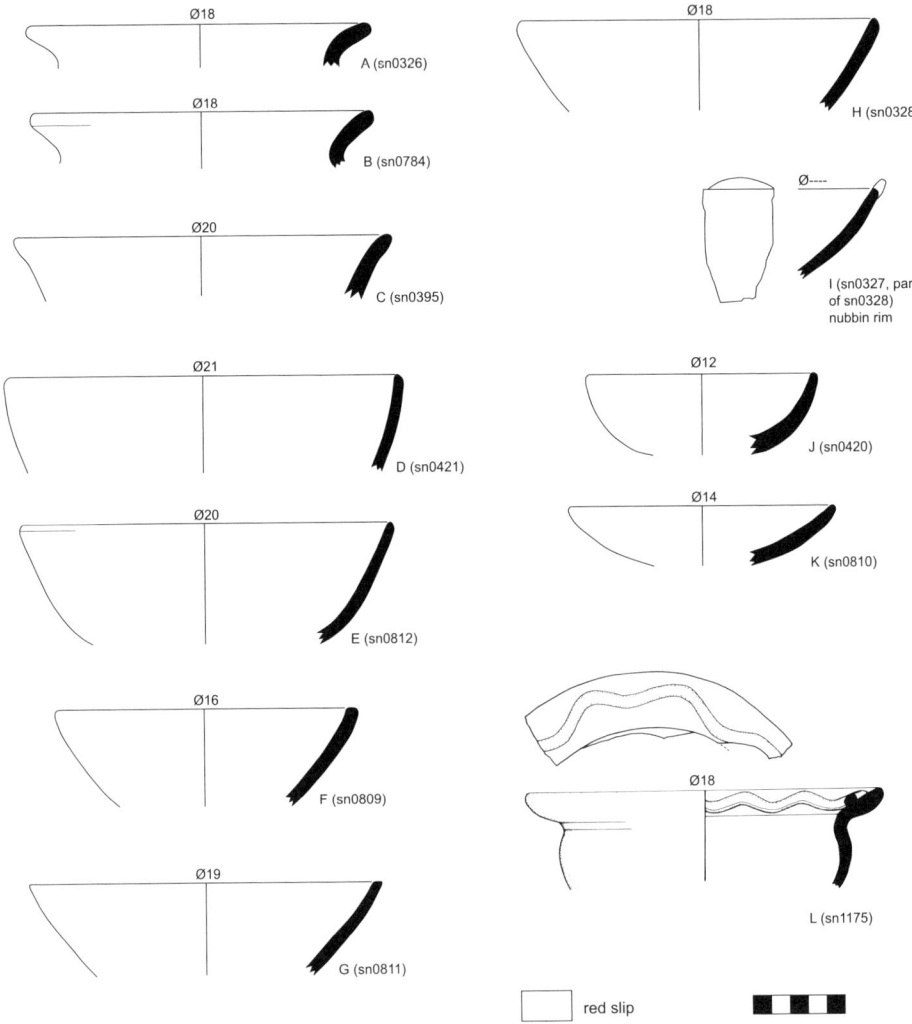

FIGURE 44. Chinchawasi 1 phase Ware C pottery: A, B, Jar 1a; C, Jar 1b; D, E, Bowl 1a; F–I, Bowl 1b; J, K, Bowl 2; L, Bowl 3.

occupation of Queyash Alto, a ceremonial center, seems to be contemporary with Huarás pottery (Gero 1990, 1991, 1992), but the ceramic evidence remains unpublished. From burial contexts at the Amá II site of the Pierina mining zone, Ponte Rosalino (1999a, figs. 2, 8, 21) also reported white-on-red bowls as part of his Cotojirca II phase. White-on-red pottery also occurs at La Pampa as the Tornapampa Thin Brown type; the primary forms are open bowls with exterior painting (Terada 1979:126–127, pl. 99). The Chinchawasi 1 Ware B materials may be most comparable to the white-on-red ceramics found as reworked deposits from looted tombs in Guitarrero Cave; affinities include slightly convex bowl shapes, exterior white painting and the repeating meanders (Lynch 1980:42–43, 230, fig. 9.23b–e).

At a glance, Chinchawasi 1 Ware B pottery resembles Bennett's White-on-red style. The general bowl shape and the exterior painting are the primary similarities. More careful review, however, reveals clear differences. Bennett's (1944:37) vessels have a strongly carinated profile; Chinchawas specimens do not show this feature. Moreover, Bennett's pots are polished to a dull luster, which contrasts with the matte finish of Ware B specimens. Finally, Ware B bowls are, in general, much larger than Bennett's "white-on-red" bowls.

## Chinchawasi 1 Ware C

Chinchawasi 1 Ware C is identified by a distinctive red slip and burnished surface treatment. Red-slipped materials account for 15.1%, or 131 sherds, of the decorated assemblage from Chinchawasi 1 deposits.

### Chinchawasi 1 Ware C Paste

Ware C pottery is typically a redware of medium grade texture. Fine to medium-sized inclusions of angular grit are common. As would be expected, inclusions are better sorted and finer in serving vessels, such as bottles or bowls, when compared to larger storage and cooking vessels.

### Chinchawasi 1 Ware C Vessel Shapes

Bowls constitute the majority of the Chinchawasi 1 Ware C formal diagnostics (77.7%).

*Bowl 1.* Bowl 1 is an open bowl with convex sides. There are two variants as indicated by rim profiles and size. The Bowl 1a variant is a globular open bowl, with a gentle rim convexity and no discernible basal angle (Figure 44D, E). Walls are fairly thin, measuring between 0.6 and 0.75 cm. Deeper bowls commonly have more vertical rim profiles (e.g., Figure 44D). Lips are rounded with the inner lip pinched and more pronounced. Mouth diameters for Bowl 1a range from 18 to 21 cm. The Bowl 1b variant is distinguished by a less convex profile than Bowl 1a, a smaller size and more elaborate lip treatment (Figure 44F–I). Mouth diameters measure 16 to 19 cm. Lips are often beveled horizontally. Walls are generally thicker than Bowl 1a examples, measuring 0.7 to 0.8 cm.

*Bowl 2.* Bowl 2 is small and has relatively thick walls. Some examples have a shallow profile (e.g., Figure 44K), while others have a more globular shape (Figure 44J). Mouth diameters only measure between 12 and 14 cm. Lip treatment consists mainly of a simple rounding.

*Bowl 3.* The Bowl 3 shape consists of a globular bowl and sharply everting flanged lip. In one example (Figure 44L), the body curves inward; an appliqué meandering band resembling a serpent rings the interior surface of the lip.

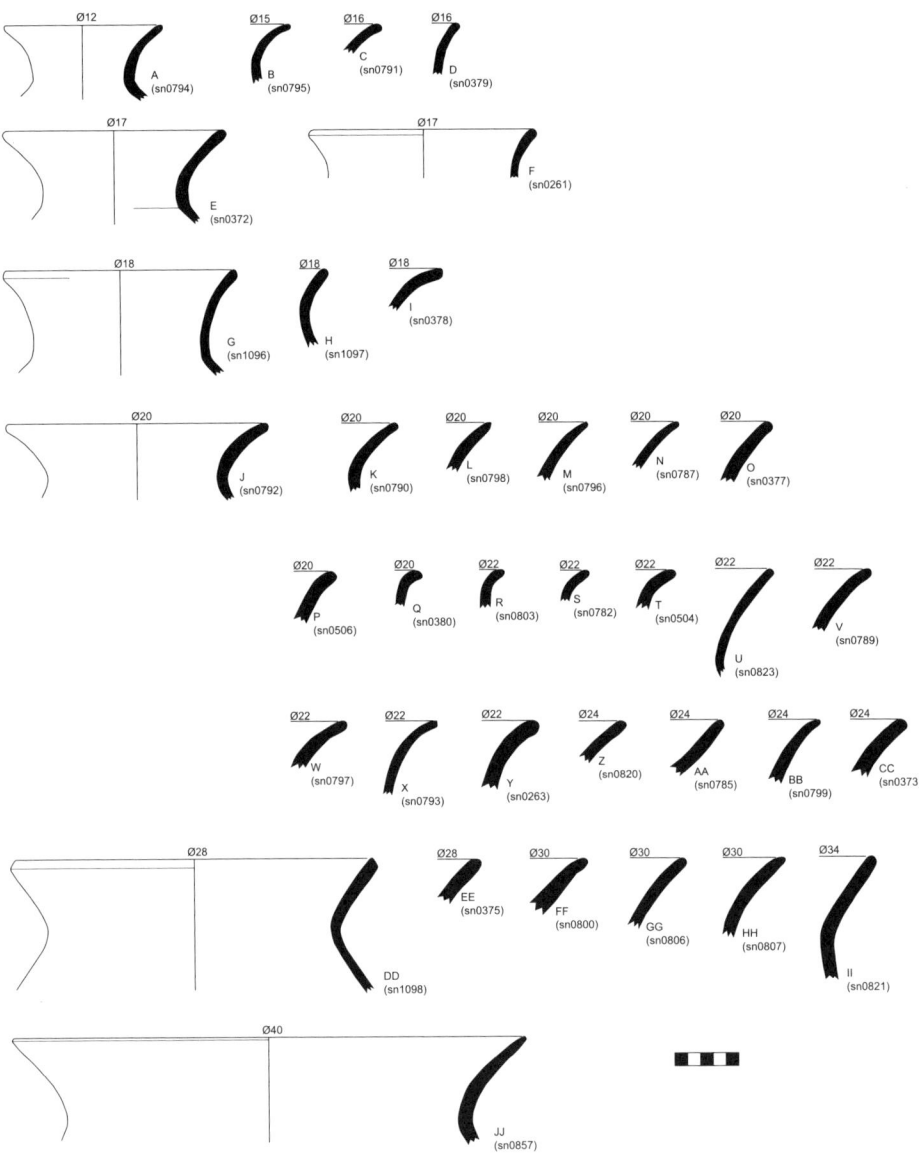

FIGURE 45. Chinchawasi 1 phase Ware D pottery: A–JJ, Jar 1.

Jars represent 18.8% of identified forms; other red-slipped pottery shapes include small cups (2.4%) and bottles (1.2%).

*Jar 1.* Jar 1 is regular-sized closed vessel, with mouth diameters between 18 and 22 cm. There are two main neck treatments. On Jar 1a, the neck treatment is a short, everted profile (Figure 44A, B), with rounded lips. The necks in the Jar 1b shape are longer and have a more vertical flaring profile. Rims may be thickened towards the lip and rounded or pinched (Figure 44C).

CHINCHAWASI 1 WARE C SURFACE TREATMENT AND PAINTED DECORATION

Chinchawasi 1 Ware C pottery is distinguished by the application of a dark red slip. On bowls, the slip covers both interior and exterior surfaces. On jars, exteriors and interiors down to the neck are slipped. Red-slipped pottery commonly has a matte finish and medium burnished surfaces; fine burnishing occurs occasionally. There are no examples of painted decoration on Chinchawasi 1 Ware C beside the slip.

CHINCHAWASI 1 WARE C PLASTIC DECORATION

Plastic decoration is uncommon on Chinchawasi 1 Ware C pottery. There is one example of an appliqué zigzag serpent across the rim of an everted rim bowl (Figure 44L). In later phase wares these appliqué borders are often painted a darker color (usually red) contrasted against a lighter background. Ware C plastic decoration also includes the use of simple ledge nubbins on bowl rims (Figure 44I).

DISCUSSION: CHINCHAWASI 1 WARE C

Like Ware A and Ware B, Chinchawasi 1 Ware C represents a local style of decorated pottery. It has a wider distribution than Ware B, but is less frequent than Ware A.

In shape, Ware C is mainly serving pottery. Bowls, bottles and cups constitute roughly 80% of the formal diagnostics. In addition, there is very little evidence of sooting on Chinchawasi 1 red-slipped pottery that would indicate cooking or repeated use over fire. The red slip and burnishing treatment also represent additional attention given to nonutilitarian functions.

Red-slipped wares have a long tradition in the Callejón de Huaylas, with production as early as the Toril and Huaricoto phases of the Initial Period (Burger 1985b). The most similar examples to Chinchawasi 1 Ware C, however, derive from late Early Intermediate Period and Middle Horizon contexts in the Callejón de Huaylas. Bennett (1944:18–42) referred to a series of polished monochrome redwares found in tombs and subterranean house sites of the Wilkawaín area. Bennett's "deep stone-lined tombs" yielded the largest sample of this ware; most belonged to either "constricted high-collar jars" or "shallow plates" (Bennett 1944:23–24), although other vessel shapes were present (Bennett 1944, fig. 6). At the subterranean house site of 9H-2, red-slipped materials were recovered in association with red-on-buff pottery; as noted, Bennett's red-on-buff is identical to Chinchawasi 1 Ware A materials (Bennett 1944:40–42). Ponte Rosalino (1999a, 1999b:46–50) also reports finding polished red-slipped pottery from sites in the Pierina region belonging to the Cotojirca III and IV phases (corresponding to the late Early Intermediate Period and Middle Horizon, respectively). Similar redware pottery was reported from Honcopampa (Isbell 1989:109, 1991a:34).

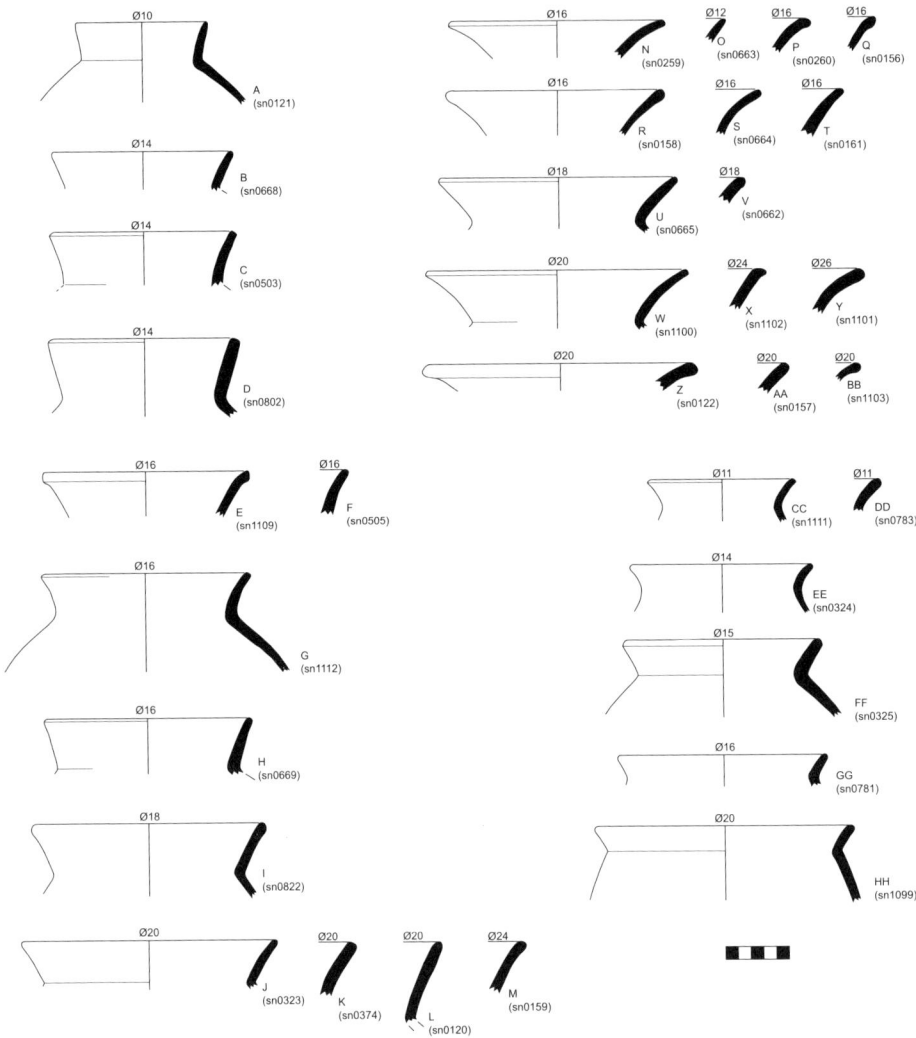

FIGURE 46. Chinchawasi 1 phase Ware D pottery: A–M, Jar 2a; N–BB, Jar 1b; CC–HH, Jar 2b.

## Chinchawasi 1 Ware D

Ware D pottery of Chinchawasi 1 is defined principally on the basis of its red plainware paste and its likely function as kitchenware and everyday utilitarian vessels. The Ware D assemblage consists of 975 formal diagnostic sherds.

### CHINCHAWASI 1 WARE D PASTE

The defining characteristic of Ware D pottery is a redware paste that is typically coarse in texture. Fine to large inclusions of angular grit are common in this ware. Sometimes there are casts of plants, suggesting the addition of fiber inclusions. Compared to thinner-walled vessels, inclusions are coarser and less well sorted in large jars.

### Chinchawasi 1 Ware D Vessel Shapes

Ware D pottery tends to have very thick walls, perhaps as a function of their general utilitarian purpose. There are a variety of Ware D vessel shapes (Figures 45–50), especially in necked jar forms.

Restricted vessels, in addition to their storage uses, probably functioned as cooking vessels as well. Restricted shapes make up 60.4% of the formal diagnostics sample. Of this percentage, jars represent the most common vessel shape in the Chinchawasi 1 Ware D sample, accounting for 59.1% (n=417) of the formal rim diagnostics. There are six major jar shapes.

*Jar 1.* Jar 1 is a restricted jar vessel with a globular body and a flaring (concave), everted neck. Jar 1 examples often have strap handles, probably two to a vessel, located on the shoulder. Lip treatment is basic, with a simple tapering and rounding of the rim. The Jar 1 sample consists of 212 rim sherds. There is wide variability in size, ranging 10 to 40 cm in mouth diameter, and 0.5 to 1.4 cm in rim wall thickness. This variability suggests that the Jar 1 shape was probably used for several functions, including cooking and storage. The large size would have been ideal to collect and store liquids, especially water and *chicha* maize beer. Three arbitrary categories were developed to account for the size variability, mainly on the basis of mouth diameter: size 1 (10 to 16 cm), size 2 (17 to 26 cm) and size 3 (27 to 40 cm). Size 2 dominates the sample, with 163 (out of 212) sherds, or 76.9%. Size 1 and Size 3 accounted for 14.6% and 8.5%, respectively.

There are two variants of Jar 1 indicated by rim stance and wall angle. The shape Jar 1a is the most common jar form in Chinchawasi phase 1 pottery (Figure 45A–JJ). It has an everted rim consisting typically of a concave or flaring profile. Normal wall angles are 20° to 50°. Lips are most commonly tapered (e.g., Figure 45JJ) or rounded (e.g., Figure 45J); lip thickening is rare. Lip beveling occurs in some examples (e.g., Figure 45X, DD). On exterior and interior surfaces, the neck merges with the shoulder typically without a well-defined seam (Figure 45G, DD).

Shape Jar 1b (Figure 46N–BB) resembles Jar 1a in most respects. The main difference is an extremely flaring neck (wall angle exceeding 50°). There is also greater tendency for more elaborate lip modification, such as thickening (e.g., Figure 46Q, BB) and exterior thickening or flanging (e.g., Figure 46P, X).

*Jar 2.* Jar 2 is a restricted jar vessel with a globular body and a short, everted neck. Jar 2 consists of 82 rim sherds and is the second most common shape in Chinchawasi 1 Ware D. Compared with Jar 1, the Jar 2 shape has a smaller size range, as represented by mouth diameters of 10 to 24 cm. Necks are often tapered towards the lip (e.g., Figure 46H). Lip treatment is fairly basic, with simple rounding (Figure 46A) and beveling (Figure 46C) the primary techniques. Although there is one example of slight flanging (Figure 46E), special types of lip treatment, such as thickening, are lacking.

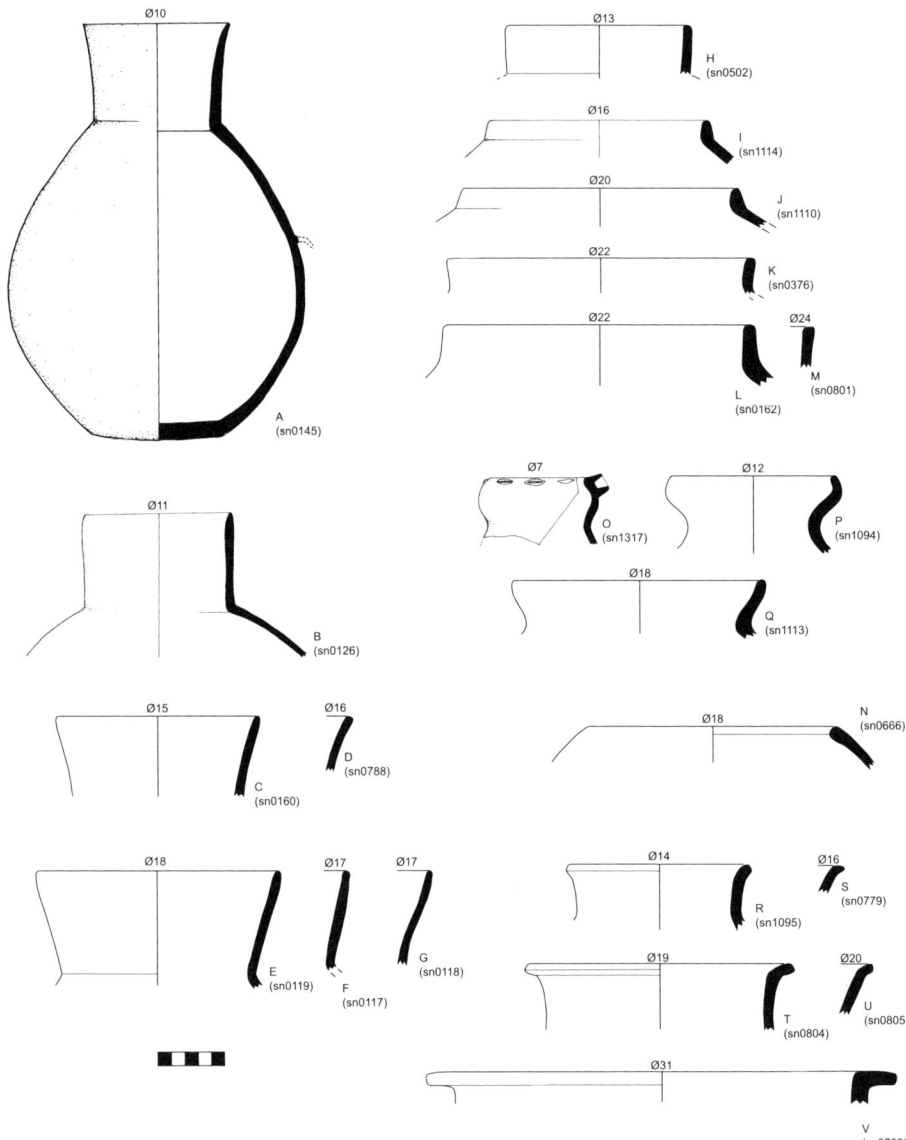

Figure 47. Chinchawasi 1 phase Ware D pottery: A–G, Jar 3; H, Jar 4a; I–M, Jar 4b; O–Q, Jar 5; R–V, Jar 6; N, Neckless Olla 1.

There are two Jar 2 variants. Jar 2a is the more common variant (Figure 46A–M). Necks have either a straight (e.g., Figure 46D) or slightly concave (e.g., Figure 46G) profile. Mouth diameters measure between 10 and 24 cm, and neck–shoulder junctures are typically sharp. The Jar 2b variant has a very short, everted neck (Figure 46CC–HH). Lips are almost always rounded. Mouth diameters measure between 11 and 20 cm. Neck–shoulder junctures can be sharp (Figure 46HH) or smooth (Figure 46CC, EE).

*Jar 3.* Jar 3 is a restricted jar vessel with a straight or slightly everted neck (Figure 47A–G). Compared to Jar 1 and Jar 2, mouth diameters of Jar 3 examples have a more limited range, between 12 and 18 cm. The distinguishing trait is a very steep neck profile (wall angle 0° to 20°). Lip treatment consists of either rounding or slight beveling (Figure 47C, E). This jar shape anticipates a sharp increase in the number and size ranges of straight-necked vessels in later phases. Twelve rims represent the Jar 3 form.

*Jar 4.* Jar 4 is a restricted jar vessel with a short, straight everted neck and probably had a globular body. Fourteen rim sherds represent the Jar 4 shape. Lip treatment is basic, including rounding and beveling.

There are two Jar 4 variants indicated by size and rim stance. Jar 4a (Figure 47H) is a globular vessel with a short vertical neck and mouth diameters of 12 to 15 cm. The Jar 4b shape (Figure 47I–M) has a short neck that extends only several centimeters above the shoulder, more or less vertically. In several examples (e.g., Figure 47I–J), the neck is very short and consists of a thickened portion of the body turned upwards. In contrast to Jar 2a, which probably functioned as a storage and pouring vessel, Jar 2b is larger (mouth diameter 20 to 24 cm) and was probably a cooking vessel, much like a neckless olla.

*Jar 5.* Jar 5 is a restricted jar vessel with a distinctive recurved neck profile (Figure 47O–Q). Examples have either a slight convexity (Figure 47Q) or, more commonly, an incurving lip (Figure 47O, P). Lip treatment is a simple rounding. The Jar 5 sample consists of nine rim sherds. The recurved neck shape is limited to smaller jars, with mouth diameters ranging between 10 and 18 cm. On one example (Figure 47O), there are coffee-bean appliqué adornos along the exterior near the lip and a false short, cylindrical spout.

*Jar 6.* Jar 6 is a restricted jar vessel with a distinctive flanged lip (Figure 47R–V). Examples of Jar 6 have either a straight everted neck (Figure 47S, U) or a nearly vertical profile (Figure 47R, T, V). Lips are rounded, pinched or slightly beveled. Jars with the flanging lips occur in jars with large (19 to 31 cm) and smaller (14 to 16 cm) mouth diameters. Only five rim sherds represent the Jar 6 shape in Chinchawasi 1 Ware D; flanging lips occur only in the Chinchawasi phases.

Less than 1% of the phase total (0.7%) is represented by the Neckless Olla 1 shape (Chinchawasi 1 Ware D).

*Neckless Olla 1.* Olla 1 is a restricted neckless vessel with a globular profile. Olla 1 is large, with a mouth diameter ranging between 18 and 22 cm and wall thickness around 0.7 to 0.9 cm. Rims can be thickened at the lip (Figure 47N). Lip treatment consists of a simple rounding or slight beveling.

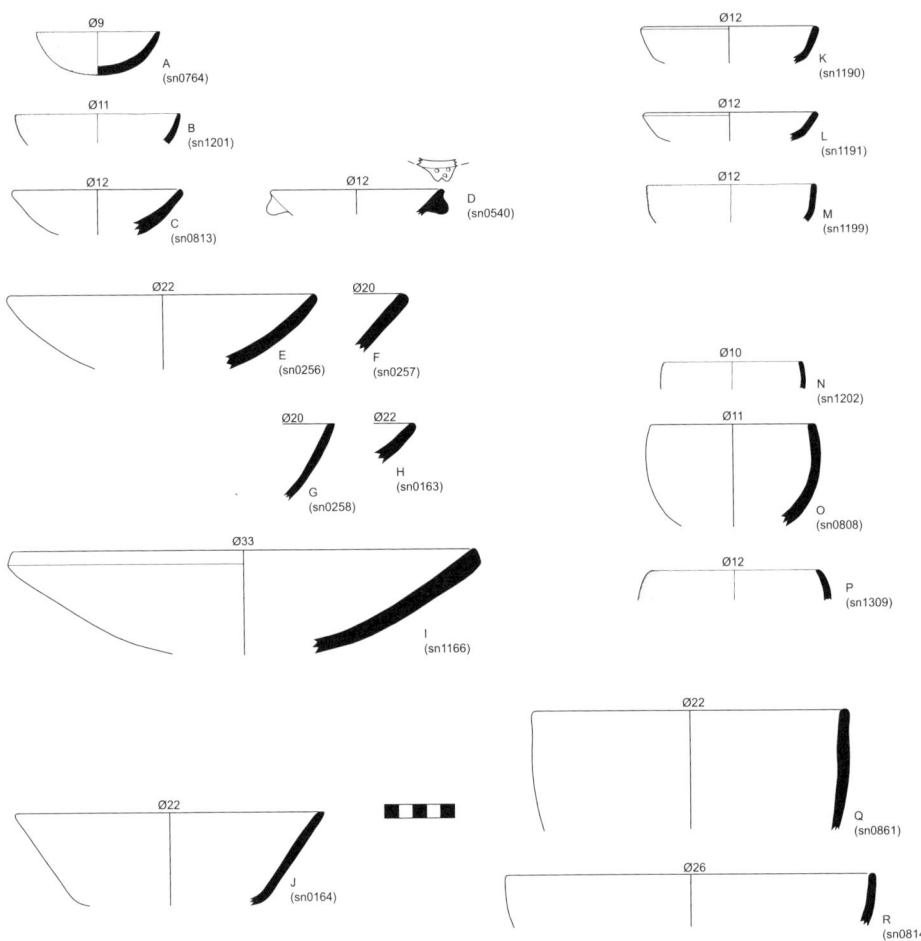

FIGURE 48. Chinchawasi 1 phase Ware D pottery: A–I, Bowl 1a; J, Bowl 1b; K–M, Bowl 1c; N–P, Bowl 2; Q, R, Bowl 3.

Bottles make up 0.6% of the Ware D phase sample.

*Bottles.* Bottle necks typically have a straight, cylindrical profile with an everted lip spout (e.g., Figure 49H). There are three primary bottle forms. Bottle 1 (Figure 49I) has a small lenticular chamber measuring 12 cm across and nearly 6 cm high. For a vessel of its small size, the walls are very thick, up to 1 cm in some areas. Bottle 2 (Figure 49K) has an ovoid chamber with a single vertical strap handle and flat base. The bottle shows fine burnishing. Bottle 3 (Figure 49J) is a single double-chambered, double spout and bridge vessel from a subterranean tomb context (OP63). The chambers taper inwards towards a flat base. The neck and spout are cylindrical, with a slightly flanged lip. For its size, the Bottle 3 specimen has very thick walls, more than 1.2 cm in certain areas.

Open vessels constitute 30.6% of the formal diagnostics sample from the Chinchawasi 1 Ware D sample. Of this total, 29.4% (or 208 rim sherds) consist of bowl shapes, with the remainder composed of cups (1.1%). Open shapes probably functioned mainly as everyday serving vessels. Ring bases (Figure 50I) and conical tripod–handle supports are sometimes added to open vessels (Bennett 1944, fig. 4f).

*Bowl 1.* Bowl 1 is a simple open, shallow dish. Represented by 189 rim sherds, it is categorized into three variants on the basis of rim profile. Bowl 1a is a shallow serving dish (Figure 48A–I). It has convex sides and a curvature without any strong contour breaks. There is wide variability in bowl size, ranging from 9 to 33 cm. Smaller sizes have mouth diameters between 9 and 12 cm, while the most common size has a diameter between 18 and 22 cm. Lip treatment is basic, with a simple tapering (e.g., Figure 48C), rounding (e.g., Figure 48E) or beveling (e.g., Figure 48I).

Bowl 1b has a straight wall and a pronounced basal angle (Figure 48J). Mouth diameters range between 18 and 24 cm. Lips taper and are rounded. The Bowl 1b shape is uncommon in Chinchawasi 1, but becomes very popular during the Chinchawasi 2 and Warmi periods. Bowl 1c is another rare bowl form and is identified by its small size and a distinctive carinated side wall. All examples have either rounded or slightly beveled lips (Figure 48K–M).

*Bowl 2.* Bowl 2 (Figure 48N–P) is a small, incurving bowl with mouth diameters between 10 and 12 cm. It has convex sides and a distinct incurving profile. Lip treatment is basic, with a simple tapering and rounding of the rim. Bowl 2 is a rare form, accounting for only 0.3% of the Ware D total. Bowl 2 and Cup 2 can be considered related shapes, but distinguished on the basis of size.

*Bowl 3.* Bowl 3 is a large deep bowl with steep side walls (Figure 48Q, R). Lip treatment is a simple rounding. Mouth diameters measure between 22 and 26 cm. Straight-sided bowls represent 0.6% of the Ware D sample.

Cups make up 1.4% of the Ware D sample. All examples are small drinking vessels, with three major shapes.

*Cup 1.* Cup 1 is a small open cup, with a semi-oval profile (Figure 49A, B). The mouth diameter measures between 7 and 8 cm. Wall thickness measures between 0.5 and 0.6 cm. Lips are typically rounded over.

*Cup 2.* Cup 2 has a small, globular shape (Figure 49C–F). Side walls are convex and incurving, with no strong contour breaks. Cup 2 has no strongly defined basal angle (Figure 49E). For their size, Cup 2 examples have very thick walls (0.7 to 1 cm). Mouth diameter measures between 5 and 8 cm. One example (Figure 49C) shows a small loop handle that affixes to the rim a few centimeters below the lip.

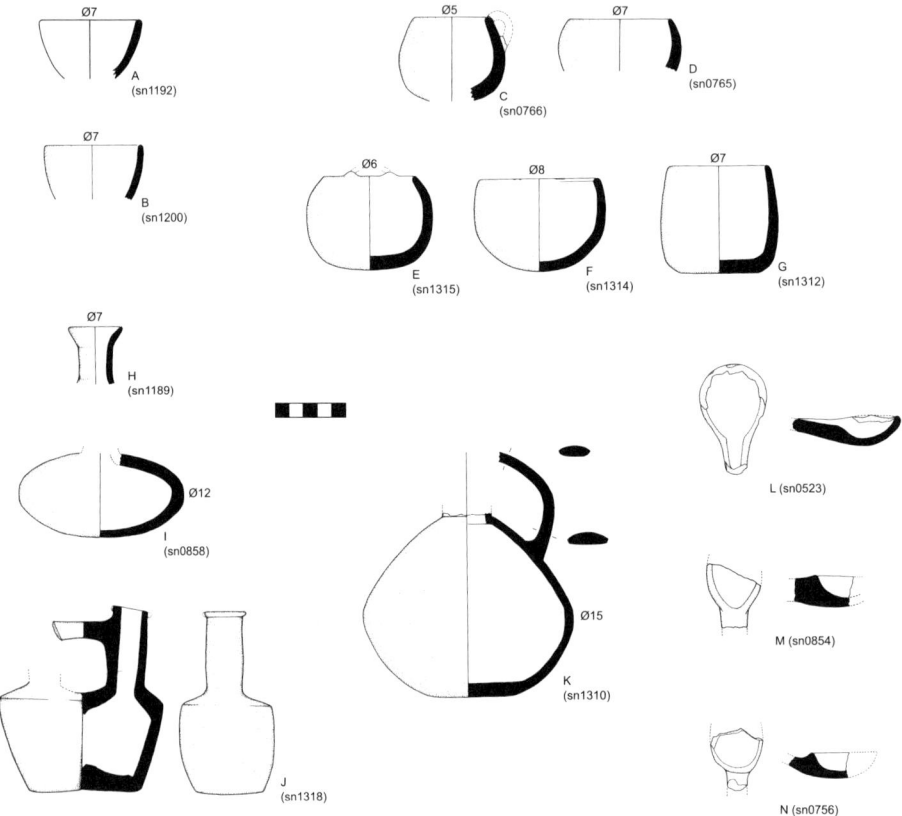

FIGURE 49. Chinchawasi 1 phase Ware D pottery: A, B, Cup 1; C–F, Cup 2; G, Cup 3; H–K, bottles; L–N, spoons.

Lip treatment is a simple rounding or tapering, or both. Cup 2 is very similar in shape to Bowl 2.

*Cup 3.* Cup 3 is a simple vertical sided cup with a flat base (Figure 49G). Walls are slightly convex and incurving. The walls of the base are thick, while the side walls taper towards the lip. Mouth diameter measures 7 cm.

Colanders account for 5.5% (n=39) of the Chinchawasi 1 Ware D sample. These vessels are characterized as open vessels with a series of holes (perforated before firing). In all likelihood, colanders were used for food-related activities such as rinsing, drying and cooking foodstuffs. There are two major forms.

*Colander 1.* The most common colander form (92.3% of the colander sample) is a large, shallow platter (Figure 50A–G). The mouth diameter varies between 20 and 40 cm. All examples have larg circular holes measuring 1.1 to 1.8 cm in diameter. Some examples (Figure 50A, B) have ledge handles extending away from the lip or body to facilitate transport. Lip treatment consists of a simple rounding. Interiors are given preferential treatment, such as smoothing and coarse burnishing. Exteriors often show evidence of the perforation process (Figure 50D, F). In addition, many show signs of burning and sooting, suggesting that Colander 1 shapes were at least sometimes put over fires to facilitate drying or roast certain foods. Colander 1 walls are thick (0.9 to 1.4 cm), which indicate an emphasis on resiliency.

*Colander 2.* Colander 2 is a less common form (7.7% of Ware D sample) and is a regular-sized open bowl with flaring side walls (Figure 50H). Colander 2 can also be identified by its small holes, which measure only 0.3 to 0.5 cm in diameter. Lips show slight beveling or rounding, or both. Unlike Colander 1, Colander 2 examples do not show evidence of burning. Colander bowl shapes become more common in later phases.

*Spoons.* Spoons constitute 0.7% of the Chinchawasi 1 Ware D assemblage (Figure 49L–N). All examples are small. The spoon bowls are oval, with widths of 4 to 5 cm. Handles extend away from the bowl; the joins between handles and bowls are smoothed (Figure 49M) or strongly differentiated (Figure 49N).

### Chinchawasi 1 Ware D Surface Treatment

Ware D surface treatment include smoothing and, less commonly, burnishing to dull matte finishes. A light red slip or wash was sometimes applied, but most Ware D pottery has its fired paste color without additional surface treatment such as fine burnishing or polishing. Striations and tiny cavities from smoothing coils or burnishing are very common. Firing clouds are very common, as is sooting from repeated use over fire.

### Chinchawasi 1 Ware D Painted Decoration

Ware D pottery is characterized by a lack of painted decoration. Exterior surfaces almost always have the redware paste color.

### Chinchawasi 1 Ware D Plastic Decoration

Plastic decoration occurs very rarely in Ware D pottery and consists mainly of modeled handles and appliqué adornos or nubbins. For example, coffee-bean adornos decorate exterior lip edges (Figure 47O). Simple modeled appliqué faces also occur; one example (Figure 50K) shows a person whistling. The adornos sometimes represent animals, such as the profile of a feline (Figure 50O) or leg of a quadruped (Figure 50L). Plastic modeling also occurs on an orangeware figurine fragment (Figure 50M); only the base, represented by two distinct feet or legs, is preserved.

Strap handles, on rare occasions (only 0.1%, or n=3, of the sample), have plastic decoration such as incisions, ticks or dimples, which are common in later Chinchawasi plainwares. A large spoon has a representation of a face on the handle, done through simple incision before firing (Figure 50J). Ledge handles also oc-

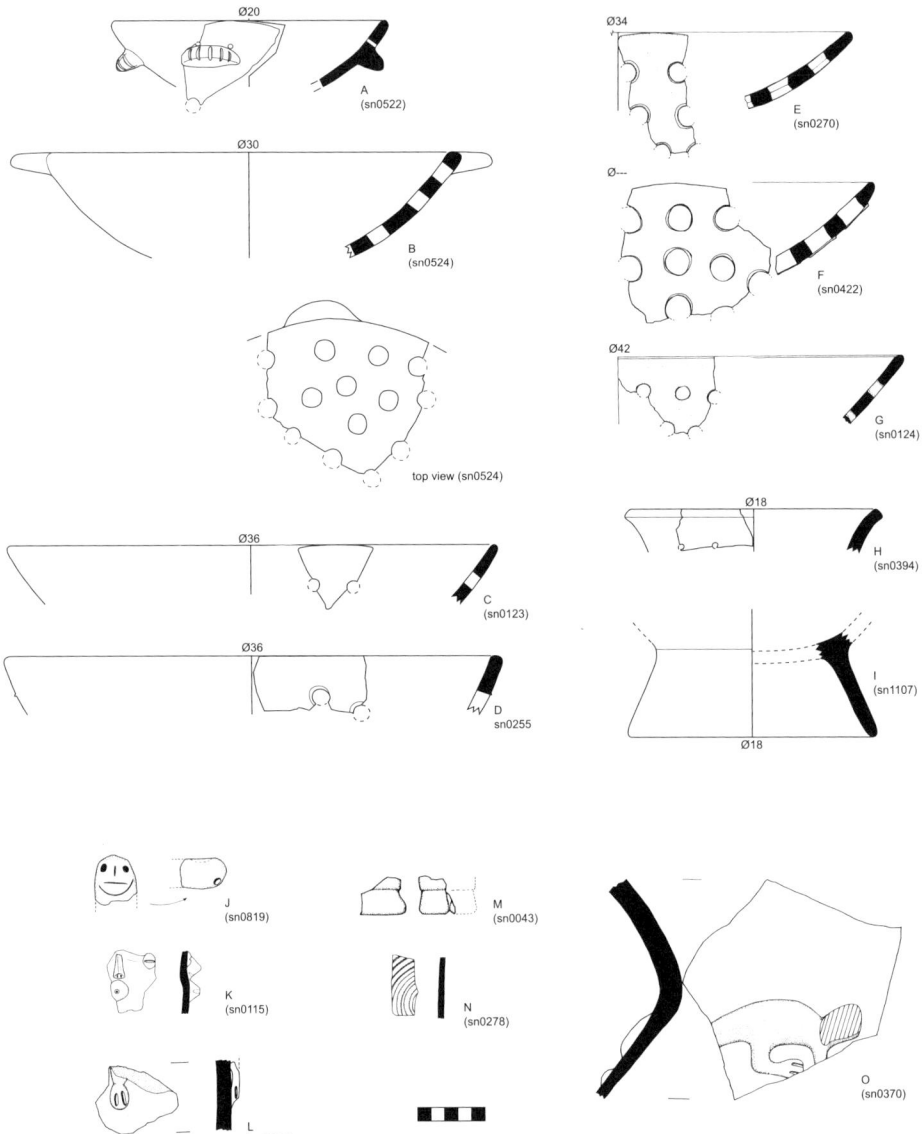

Figure 50. Chinchawasi 1 phase Ware D pottery: A–G, Colander 1; H, Colander 2; I, ring base; J–O, plastic decoration.

casionally have additional decorative treatment, such as ribbing (Figure 50A) or punctation (Figure 48D).

### Discussion: Chinchawasi 1 Ware D

Chinchawasi phase 1 Ware D is a local utilitarian plainware pottery. The commonness of the clay, the frequency and coarseness of inclusions, the vessel forms, and the general lack of decorative attributes all indicate that these ceramics performed,

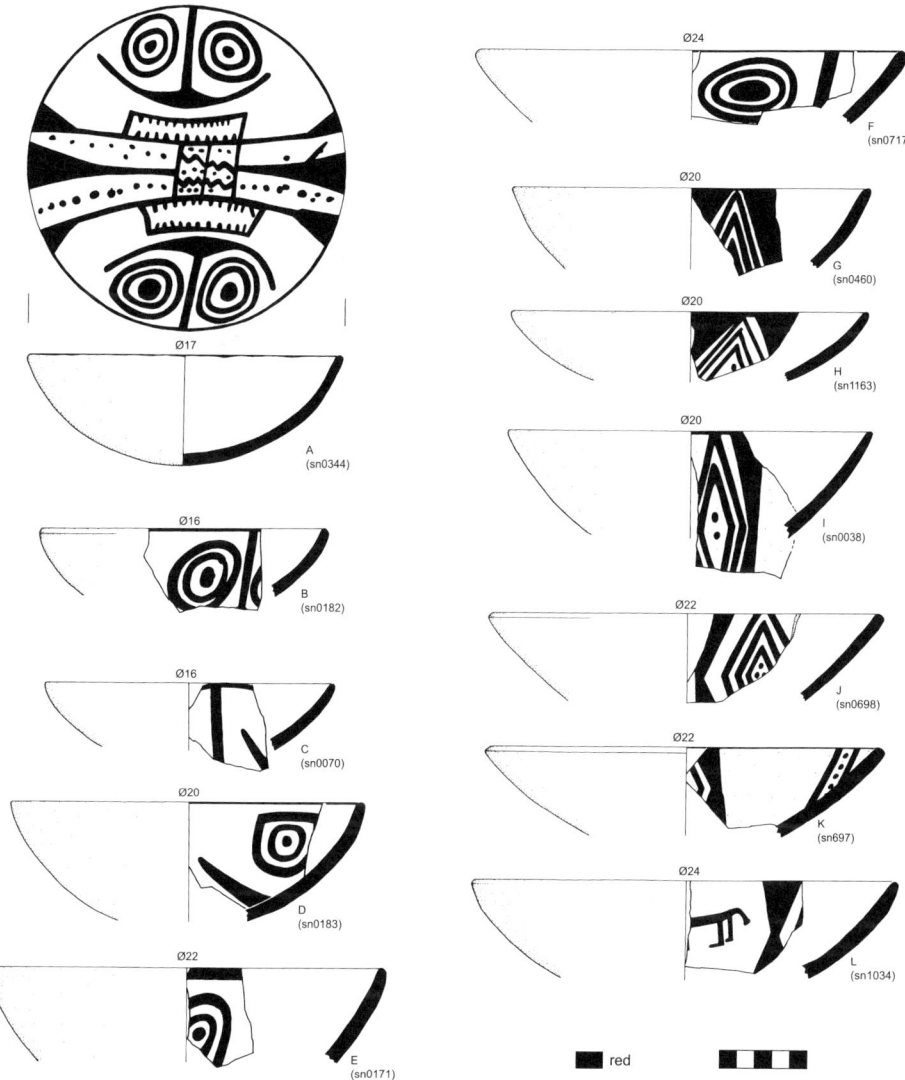

FIGURE 51. Chinchawasi 2 phase Ware A pottery: A–L, Bowl 1a.

in the main, everyday cooking and serving functions. This hypothesis is consistent with the general domestic discard contexts for Ware D.

Plainware pottery of the Callejón de Huaylas has been consistently undertreated in the archaeological literature. For diachronic changes, Bennett's 1944 report remains the best source for plainware inventories and shape comparison. Unfortunately, very few plainware shapes are illustrated, but my examination of the collections from Bennett's Huaraz-area sites, especially from the deep stone-lined tombs and the subterranean house sites, suggest close similarities between the plainware assemblages.

FIGURE 52. Chinchawasi 2 phase Ware A pottery: A–P, Bowl 1a.

Comparable plainware forms occur in many parts of the Callejón de Huaylas. Investigations by Victor Ponte have uncovered similar plainware ceramics belonging to the Cotojirca III and IV phases from various sites in the zone of the Pierina Gold Mine (Ponte Rosalino 1999a, 1999b). Cotojirca III and IV vessel shapes resemble those from Ware D, especially the flaring necked jars and shallow open bowls. Chinchawasi 1's flaring neck jars (regular everted and short everted necks), flange and recurved rims, and several bowl forms are represented in Huacohú and Usú phase material from Pashash (Grieder 1978, figs. 38, 40).

The best-documented assemblage of plainware forms comes from the La Pampa area sites (Terada 1979). Chinchawasi 1 Ware D jars have counterparts especially in the Tornapampa Brown (Terada 1979, pl. 100, nos. 1–13), Tornapampa Grey (Terada 1979, pl. 101, nos. 6–9) and Caserones Orange types (Terada 1979, pl. 96, nos. 7–12, pl. 97, nos. 1, 9, 10, 17–21). Similarly, Chinchawasi 1 bowls have formal counterparts in Tornapampa Thin Orange (Terada 1979, pl. 98, nos. 21, 25–26) and Tornapampa Thin Brown types (Terada 1979, pl. 99, nos. 24, 26, 27). Diachronic comparisons indicate late Early Intermediate Period and Middle Horizon associations.

The colander shapes from Chinchawas are also part of North Highland traditions. Bennett (1944, fig. 11f) encountered colander fragments in many of his tomb excavations; only one is illustrated—a small disc-shaped "sieve" with small holes (8.3 cm in diameter). More closely resembling the larger platter colanders of Chinchawas are examples from Marcahuamachuco, although the Chinchawas artifacts do not have the incurving profile (McCown 1945, fig. 16a, b; also Thatcher 1972, fig. 41i). Colander fragments from Balcón de Judas featured triangular holes (Wegner 2003).

*Chinchawasi 1 Phase Absolute Dating*
Prior to our investigations, Chinchawasi 1 pottery—especially the Ware A diagnostics—has never been isolated from stratigraphic excavations, so there has been no absolute dating of the style. There were three radiocarbon assays from charcoal samples from Chinchawasi 1 contexts (see Table 1). One from OP 19, Level L, measured 1395 ± 45 B.P. (A.D. 555 ± 45 uncalibrated, 2-sigma calibrated range of A.D. 600 to 689). Another sample from OP49, Level D, measured to 1375 ± 45 B.P. (A.D. 575 uncalibrated, 2-sigma calibrated range of A.D. 610 to 763). The final assay, from OP31, Level H, yielded an age of 1305 ± 45 B.P. (A.D. 645 uncalibrated, 2-sigma calibrated range of A.D. 654 to 855). These ages indicate that the Chinchawasi 1 phase coincided with the late part of the Early Intermediate Period, beginning by the mid-6th century A.D. and lasting until about A.D. 700.

## Chinchawasi 2 Phase Ceramics

Chinchawasi 2 continues the Chinchawasi pottery tradition established in phase 1. The pottery shows strong indications of continuity, especially in the local plainware ceramics, but there are also discernible stylistic changes. In particular, the red-on-cream pottery has different configurations, especially of design. White-on-red pottery becomes far less common; its occurrence in Chinchawasi 2, moreover, is in nonprimary contexts, perhaps from mixing or curation. Like phase 1, Chinchawasi 2 pottery occurs throughout Sector 1 of the site and in almost all the excavations. The materials were recovered from a series of archaeological contexts, including large discard or midden deposits (Terrace 1, 3 and 4), ceremonial structures (OP54) and residential activity areas (OP47, OP48 and OP49).

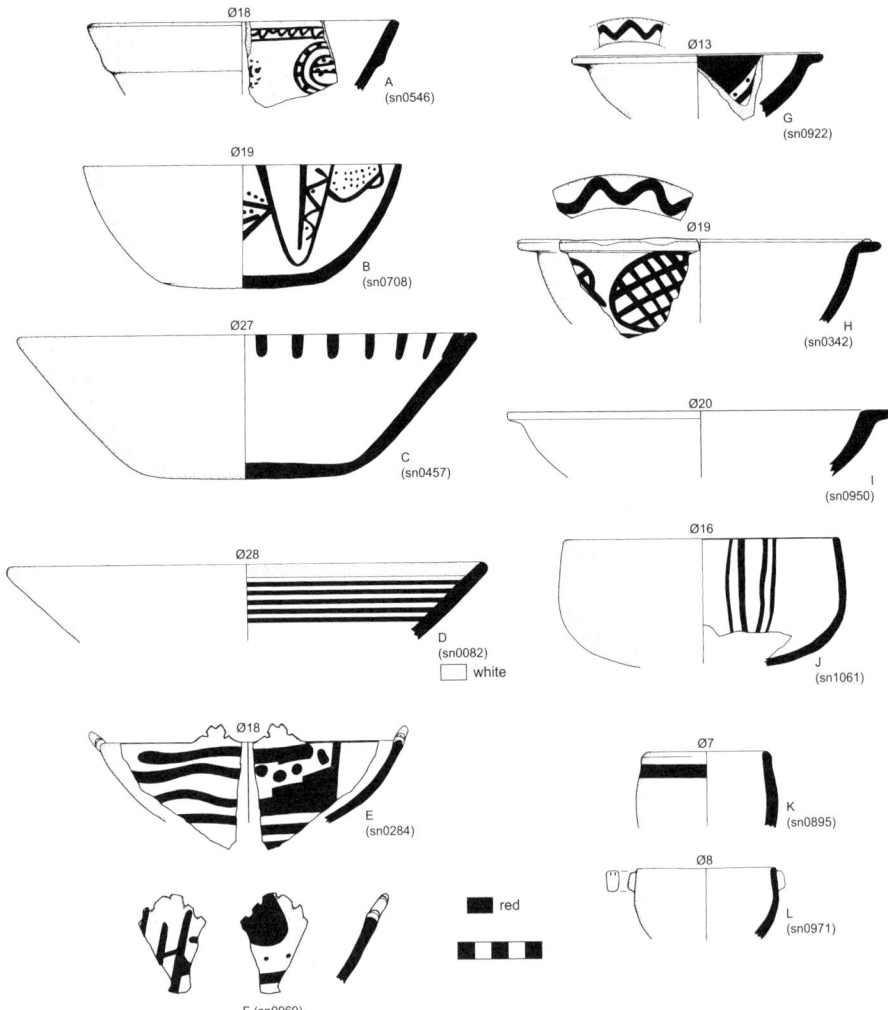

FIGURE 53. Chinchawasi 2 phase Ware A pottery: A–D, Bowl 1b; E, F, Bowl 1c; G–I, Bowl 1d; J, Bowl 2; K, L, Cup 1.

The Chinchawasi 2 sample consists of 6,475 sherds (1,654 decorated sherds and 4,821 plainware form diagnostics). The pottery analysis discerned three major ware groups.

### Chinchawasi 2 Ware A

Chinchawasi 2 Ware A is distinguished from other phase 2 pottery by the use of the red-on-cream painting. Ware A consists of 1,398 sherds.

#### CHINCHAWASI 2 WARE A PASTE

The paste of Chinchawasi 2 Ware A resembles that of Chinchawasi 1 Ware A. Ware A pottery uses an oxidized paste that contains well sorted, regular-sized inclusions of grit and, less frequently, mica. Paste color ranges from tan to whitish pink. In many cases the whitish pink grades into deeper shades of red.

CHINCHAWASI 2 WARE A VESSEL SHAPES

Open vessels make up the majority of the Chinchawasi 2 Ware A sample (78.8%), only slightly less than for Chinchawasi 1 Ware A (83%).

Of the open vessel category, bowls represent the most common shape, comprising 77.2% (n=540) of the formal diagnostics in Chinchawasi 2 deposits.

*Bowl 1.* The most common shape is Bowl 1, a form popularized during phase 1. Bowl 1 is a shallow cumbrous bowl and accounts for over 99% of the bowl sample. There are four variants.

The Bowl 1a shape (Figures 51 and 52) has a fairly shallow profile, with a gently convex curvature that has no prominent breaks. Bowl 1 specimens have painting mainly on the interior surfaces. Bowl 1a specimens have mouth diameters ranging between 10 to 32 cm, with the average size between 16 and 18 cm. Wall thicknesses range from 0.5 to 1.2 cm. Lip treatment is very basic, consisting of either a simple rounding or slight beveling on the upper or exterior edge, or both.

Another common bowl form is the Bowl 1b shape: a simple open bowl or platter with slightly convex walls, a discernible basal angle, and a roughly flat base (Figure 53A–D). Bowl interiors mainly feature painted decoration. Bowl 2 mouth diameters range from 16 to 28 cm.

The Bowl 1c variant has the same shallow globular open bowl form, with the addition of nubbins or adornos along the rim (Figure 53E, F). The nubbins are small pieces of modeled clay joined to the bowl. In all cases, nubbins in Bowl 4 examples are ribbed by pressing down repeatedly across the short dimension of the outer surface. Nubbins most usually take the Chinchawasi phase 1 semicircular shape (e.g., Figure 53F), but can have more elaborate shapes (Figure 53E). Unlike other Bowl 1 examples, Bowl 1c variants are often painted on the exterior as well as the interior.

The Bowl 1d variant has a distinctive flange rim (Figure 53G–I). Examples feature either interior or exterior painting. Bowl mouth diameters are between 14 and 20 cm.

*Bowl 2.* Bowl 2 is an incurving bowl (e.g., Figure 53J). Walls are more vertical than Bowl 1 examples, deepening the interior space of the vessel. Bowl 2 takes an overall globular shape, with bases slightly flattened and a gentle but discernible basal angle. Bowl 2 examples are fairly small containers, with mouth diameters between 8 and 16 cm.

*Cup 1.* Cups represent 1.0% of the Ware A sample (Figure 53K, L). Cup 1 is a small vessel, with mouth diameters between 6 and 8 cm. Walls are nearly vertical. Exte-

FIGURE 54. Chinchawasi 2 phase Ware A pottery: A–D, Jar 1; E–G, Jar 2; H–J, Jar 3; K, Jar 4; N, spoon.

rior surfaces are decorated with simple painted bands (Figure 53K). One example (Figure 53L) shows a small rectangular nubbin on the upper exterior rim.

*Spoons.* One spoon handle had with Chinchawasi type painting (Figure 54N). A small "bump" nubbin is attached to the top surface of the handle; red paint is applied in single long, tapering strokes or as irregular geometric figures.

Restricted vessels constitute 22.2% (n=147) of the Chinchawasi 2 Ware A sample. All examples derive from jar vessels.

*Jar 1.* Jar 1 is a necked vessel with a short, everted rim (Figure 54A–D). Mouth diameter ranges from 16 to 20 cm. Lip treatment consists of simple rounding or slight beveling.

*Jar 2.* Jar 2 is a necked vessel with a flaring (concave) profile (Figure 54E–G). Compared to Jar 1, there is a steeper wall angle (10° to 25°). There is no separate contour for the lip. Mouth diameter ranges from 10 to 20 cm.

*Jar 3.* Jar 3 is a tall, necked vessel with distinctive flanging rim (Figure 54H–J). Necks are nearly vertical or slightly everted in profile. Mouth diameters range from 15 to 22 cm. Unlike many in Chinchawasi 1 (Ware D Jar 6), most necks are not vertical, but are turned slightly outwards.

*Jar 4.* Jar 4 is a necked jar, with a straight, vertical neck profile and no extra lip treatment (Figure 54K). This shape occurs mainly on regular-sized jars and has 12 to15 cm mouth diameters.

CHINCHAWASI 2 WARE A SURFACE TREATMENT
Chinchawasi 2 Ware A pottery is very similar to Chinchawasi 1 Ware A pottery in surface treatment. Ware A pottery can be identified through its cream, buff or whitish pink slip. Light-colored pastes are often left unslipped. The pottery also has coarse to fine burnishing to a matte finish or, more commonly, a dull luster. Polishing is rare and surfaces are never lustrous. Despite the burnishing, striations and tiny cavities from the scraping and shaping process are common, especially on unpainted surfaces.

CHINCHAWASI 2 WARE A PAINTED DECORATION
Chinchawasi 2 potters rendered Ware A designs almost exclusively using a dusky red paint over a light cream or whitish pink background. Supplementary pigments include black and white. Unlike the exterior emphasis in Chinchawasi 1, painted decoration on Chinchawasi 2 open bowls is executed most commonly on vessel interiors (56.9% of the time). Note that this figure is conservative; attributes such as rim "ticking" and rim bands were coded as exterior designs despite the fact that they often occupy interior and exterior surfaces simultaneously. In many cases, Chinchawasi 2 designs cover portions of the entire interior surface with linear, curvilinear and composite motifs (Figure 55B–E). Examples with both interior and exterior painting are also common. There are some examples with a thin white wash covering the interior and exterior surfaces (Figure 52H).

 The major interior designs for phase 2 bowls include the following: a grinning face (Figure 51A–F); repeating lines (e.g., Figures 52A and 53D, J); various bands and filler elements motifs (e.g., Figure 53A, B, E, G); pendants with nested diamonds (Figure 51G–L); filler elements (Figure 52O); or derived chevrons (Figure 52F). Interior rim ticking is another common attribute (Figure 53C).

 There are very few examples of open bowls painted only on the exterior. In such instances, the main designs include repeating meanders (Figure 52M, N). Rare designs include circles with filler elements, such as lines (Figure 52J) or lattices (Figure 53H). Rim ticks (Figure 52I) and cursory, repeating vertical strokes (Figures

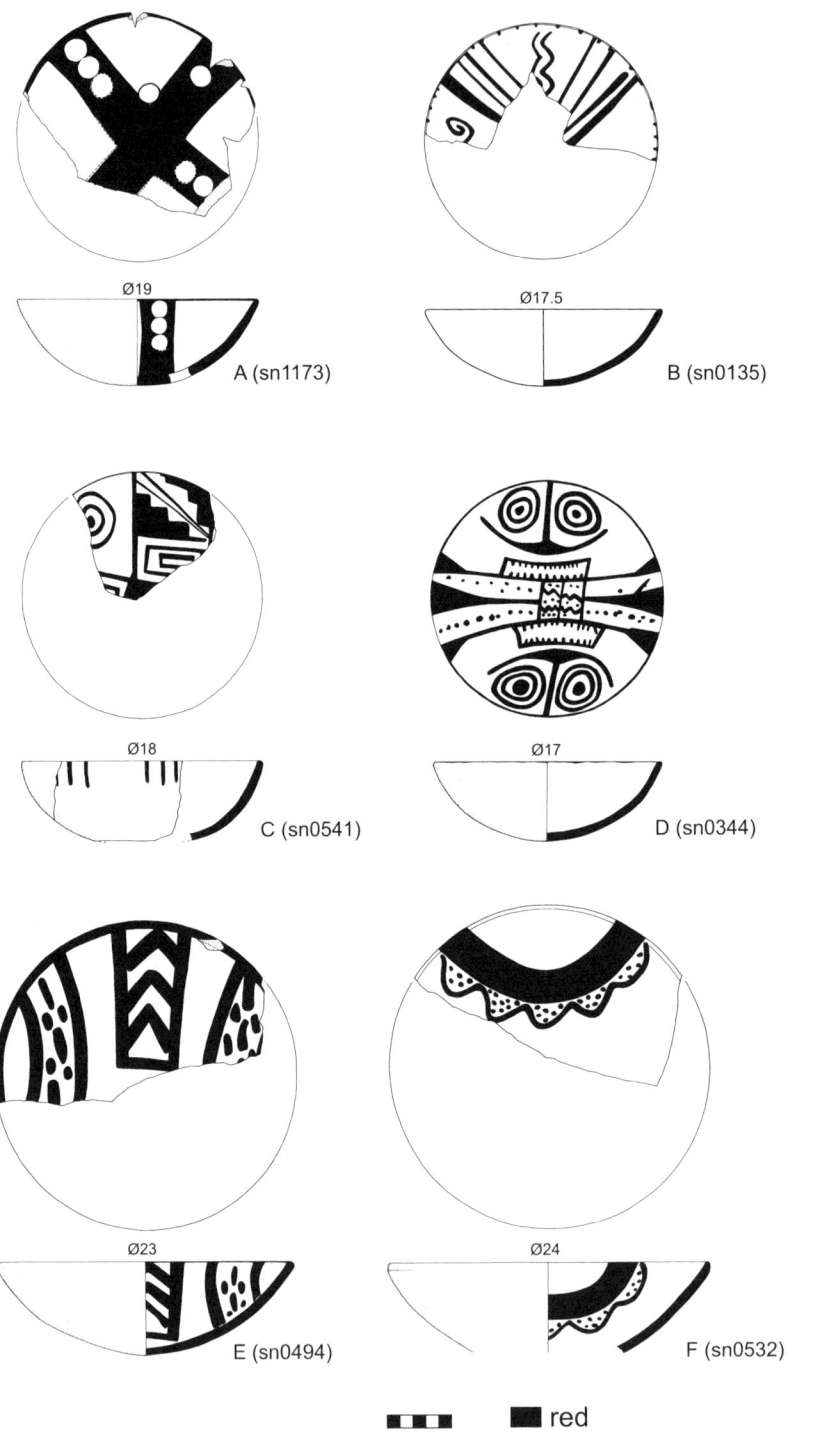

FIGURE 55. Top and profile views of Chinchawasi 1 (A, F) and Chinchawasi 2 phase (B–E) bowls with interior decoration.

52L and 53F) also occur on the exterior. Bowls that have exterior painting typically have interior painting as well.

Phase 2 jars have the exterior decoration popularized in phase 1, especially for the lips, necks and shoulders of jars. Common designs include upward-pointing triangles (Figure 54C, F, G), mazes (Figure 54A) or nested rectangles (Figure 54J). Additional exterior designs include a snarling face (Figure 54M) and a head of a creature that shows characteristics of the Recuay "dragon" or crested feline (Figure 54L) (Bruhns 1976; Menzel 1977; Mackey and Vogel 2003). Rim ticks across the lip, a single band along the rim, or both, are also common features—on bowls or jars.

### Chinchawasi 2 Ware A Plastic Decoration

Plastic decoration occurs seldomly in Chinchawasi 2 Ware A. As in Chinchawasi 1 Ware A, one decorative technique uses ribbed nubbins or simple adornos on the rim. The nubbins are more elaborate in phase 2, often modeled into semicircular and tapered shapes (e.g., Figure 53E, F). Strap handles are common additions to Ware A jars, probably at least two to each vessel. These are often painted with motifs of repeating vertical slashes, mazes, or bands and dots.

There are several examples in the Chinchawasi 2 assemblage of flange rim bowls with meandering serpent-like appliqué (Figure 53G, H). The appliqué adorns the top of the flange rim and is painted in dusky red.

### Discussion: Chinchawasi 2 Ware A

Bowls represent 77.2% of the Chinchawasi 2 Ware A assemblage, compared to 82% in phase 1. Yet phase 2 Ware A manifests greater diversity in bowl shapes than does Chinchawasi phase 1. Open bowls with flat bases or basal angles, or both, become more popular during this phase. Cups and incurving bowls with Chinchawasi designs become less popular. There are more examples of flange rim bowls (Bowl 1d).

Jars are slightly more popular during the Chinchawasi 2 phase, ranging from 16.1% to 21% of the formal sample. Chinchawasi 2 jars maintain most of the same shapes found earlier in Chinchawasi 1. There are some changes, however. The flange rim shape (Chinchawasi 1 Ware A, Jar 3) becomes obsolete. In addition, new jar forms, such as those with straight necks or tall, everted necks, become more predominant.

There was also greater preference for interior-painted open bowls. The nested diamonds motif seen earlier in Chinchawasi 1 remains popular during phase 2. In contrast, there is a decrease in the frequency of the grinning face motif (or constituent elements like the concentric circle eyes), from 4.3% to 1.8% of the decorated sample. Similarly, motifs such as interior step frets (from 0.8% to 0.2%) and wide bands with white dots (1.0% to 0.2%) become less popular. Meanwhile, there is also an increasing emphasis on pendant designs, rim bands and repeating or parallel vertical bands. In addition, stroke widths are, in general, broader.

Exterior designs decrease in popularity from Chinchawasi 1 to Chinchawasi 2. For example, meanders on the upper exterior rim decrease from 4.0% to 1.0% of the

Ware A sample. Also, the occurrence of exterior linear designs drops from 12.5% to 7.3%. Although Chinchawasi 2 Ware A continues to use painted designs from the phase 1 repertoire, there is also an increasing diversity of representations. New designs include circular fields with lattice filler and different band–dot combinations.

Many of stylistic comparisons for Chinchawasi 1 Ware A pottery can be reiterated for Chinchawasi 2 Ware A. The closest associations are from the Huaraz area, especially from Antajirca and the sites in the Wilkawaín area (see Chinchawasi 1 Ware A discussion). Affinities to Huamachuco pottery, such as the Urpay and Tuscan phase (or Huamachuco-on-white) seem stronger, especially in the use of broader stroke widths and a more cursory placement of designs (Thatcher 1972; see also Krzanowski 1986a).

Many stylistic differences between Chinchawasi 1 and Chinchawasi 2 may have broader chronological implications. The stronger emphasis on interior-painted open bowls with basal angles resembles contemporary Middle Horizon Epoch 1 to 2 developments (Kelly 1930; Menzel 1964; Isbell 1977). The presence of these attributes also anticipates their popularity in the next Warmi phase. The increasing frequency of pendant designs is also strongly associated with other local Middle Horizon styles (e.g., Menzel 1964; Anders 1989; González Carré et al. 1999).

Although there is a continuance of certain types of exterior-painted designs (of local Recuay tradition), their proportion decreases sharply in favor of bowls painted only on the interior. This coincides with the Wari expansion into the region. It is likely that the new sociocultural conditions created by Wari influence played a major role in stylistic transformations at Chinchawas during this time.

Diagnostic criteria also indicate a growing break from the Recuay pottery tradition. The decreasing frequency of the grinning face motif—which has connections to contemporary Recuay pottery from throughout the Callejón de Huaylas (Eisleb 1987) and farther north at Pashash (Grieder 1978)—suggests that the representation held less import for local peoples at Chinchawas. In addition, lighter cream-colored clays (associated with the Recuay kaolinite pottery tradition) are replaced by darker pink and red pastes. White-on-red painted pottery (Chinchawasi 1 Ware B) also decreases, by about 37%; note, moreover, that most white-on-red pottery in Chinchawasi 2 can be characterized as less fine in quality. Finally, less emphasis on exterior painting, especially designs such as meanders or horizontal bands across the upper exterior rim, also indicates that Recuay stylistic influence was on the wane by the Chinchawasi 2 phase.

### Chinchawasi 2 Ware B

A distinctive red slip and burnished surface treatment characterize Chinchawasi 1 Ware B. Red-slipped materials account for 11.97%, or 221 sherds, of the decorated assemblage from Chinchawasi 2 deposits.

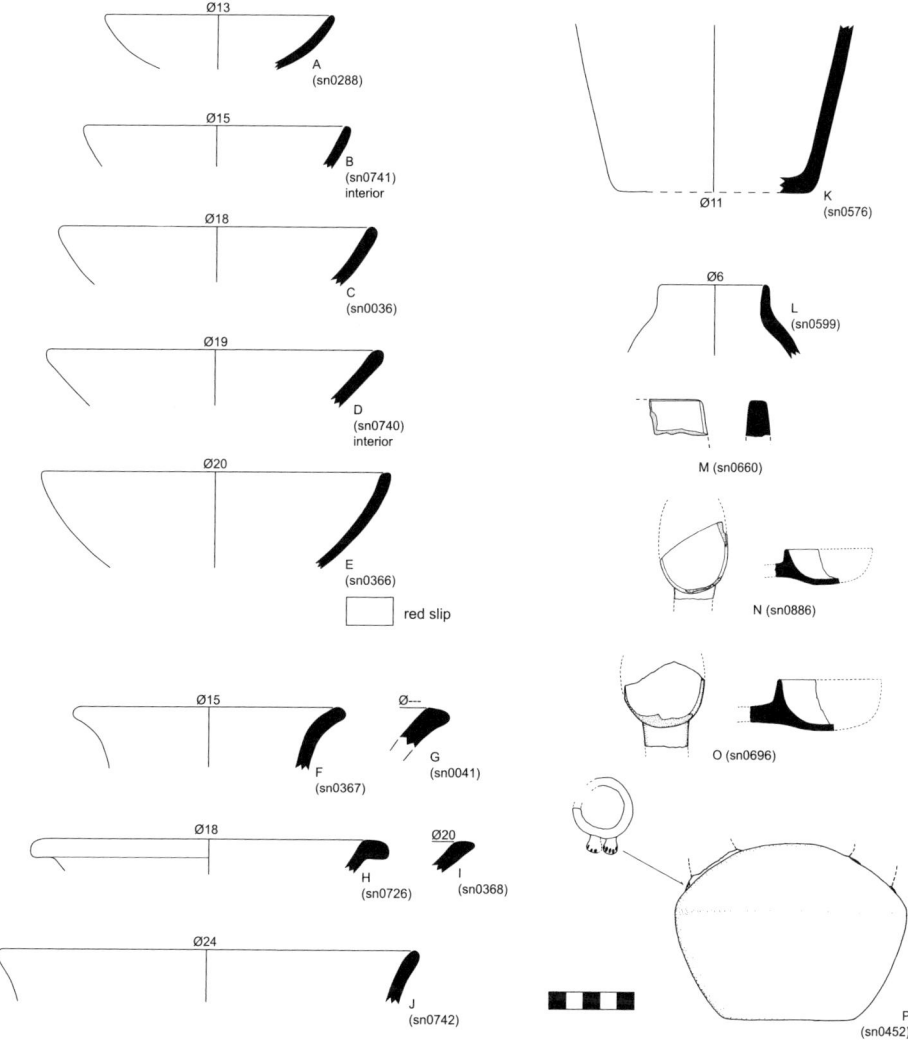

FIGURE 56. Chinchawasi 2 phase Ware B pottery: A–E, Bowl 1; F–I, Jar 1; J, Jar 2; K, Cup 1; L, Jar 3; M, Flat corner; N–O, spoons; P, bottle.

## Chinchawasi 2 Ware B Paste

Ware B is a redware pottery of medium-grade texture. Fine to medium-sized inclusions of angular grit are common.

## Chinchawasi 2 Ware B Vessel Shapes

Bowls make up most of the Chinchawasi 2 Ware B formal diagnostics (72.2%).

*Bowl 1*. Bowl 1 is a globular open bowl with slightly convex sides with no discernible basal angle (Figure 56A–E). Mouth diameter ranges between 12 and 22 cm. Lip treatment includes a slight thickening (Figure 56E), simple rounding (Figure 56C), or on rare occasion slight beveling (Figure 56B).

*Cup 1.* Cup 1 is a large deep vessel (Figure 56K), with steep, straight sides and thick walls (0.9 to 1.0 cm). The base diameter measures approximately 11 cm.

Jars represent 13.6% of the Chinchawasi 2 Ware B sample. There are three principal jar shapes:

*Jar 1.* Jar 1 is a vessel with a sharply everted neck (Figure 56F–I). Mouth diameters vary between 14 and 22 cm. Lip treatment features simple rounding (Figure 56F) or, more commonly, rim thickening (Figure 56G, I) or flanging (Figure 56H).

*Jar 2.* Jar 2 is a short vessel with a slightly everted neck. The neck profile is slightly concave, with lip treatment typically a simple rounding (Figure 56J).

*Jar 3.* Jar 3 is a short-necked restricted globular vessel. One example (Figure 56L) has a mouth diameter of 6 cm.

*Bottles.* The only example of a Ware B bottle is a double spout and bridge vessel (Figure 56P). The bottle has a flat base, with a noticeable carination between the shoulder and body. There are the feet of a small appliqué figure at the base of one of the spouts.

*Spoons.* Spoons take a characteristic shape in Chinchawasi 2 Ware B assemblages (Figure 56N, O). The spoon bowls are oval (width between 4 and 4.5 cm) and fairly deep (between 2 and 2.8 cm).

*Miscellaneous.* Ware B pottery also includes an unidentified tablet-like artifact (Figure 56M). The sherd is flat and thick (1.4 cm at its maximum), probably the corner of a flat ceramic artifact.

CHINCHAWASI 2 WARE B SURFACE TREATMENT AND PAINTED DECORATION
A dark red slip characterizes Chinchawasi 2 Ware B pottery. On bowls, the slip covers both interior and exterior surfaces. On jars, exteriors and interiors down to the neck are slipped. Ware B red-slipped pottery is typically medium burnished to a matte finish. Fine burnishing occurs occasionally. There is no polishing. Besides the red slip, Chinchawasi 2 Ware B is characterized by a lack of painted decoration.

CHINCHAWASI 2 WARE B PLASTIC DECORATION
Plastic decoration is rare on Chinchawasi 2 Ware B pottery. As noted previously, there is one example of modeled feet at the base of a spout on a bottle (Figure 56P).

## Discussion: Chinchawasi 2 Ware B

Chinchawasi 2 Ware B shows strong continuities with red-slipped pottery in Chinchawasi phase 1 (Ware C). As in phase 1, red-slipped wares is a local decorated style of pottery. Red-slipped pottery represents 12.0% of the Chinchawasi 2 decorated sample, decreasing from 15.1% in Chinchawasi 1. This decline anticipates its near disappearance in the subsequent Warmi phase.

The red-slipped pottery shape continued to be used mainly for serving. Bowls, bottles and cups account for 73.9% of the formal diagnostics, a slight decrease from the 80% of Chinchawasi 1 Ware C.

Many of the regional pottery comparisons noted for red-slipped pottery in Chinchawasi 1 can be reiterated for Chinchawasi 2 Ware B. The closest stylistic connections come from the Callejón de Huaylas, especially around the area of Huaraz (Bennett 1944) and Pierina (Ponte Rosalino 1999a, 1999b).

### Chinchawasi 2 Ware C

Ware C pottery of Chinchawasi phase 2 is defined principally on the basis of its coarse redware paste, its general lack of painted or plastic decoration, and a utilitarian function as kitchenware and everyday serving vessels. The Ware C consists of 4,821 formal diagnostics. Of this total, 3,526 were rim sherds useful for identifying vessel shape.

## Chinchawasi 2 Ware C Paste

Chinchawasi phase 2 Ware C pottery is a redware that is typically coarse in paste and texture. Vessels are fired in an oxidizing environment. Paste color includes brick orange to dark reddish brown. Firing clouds are common in Ware C, occurring more frequently on jars than bowls.

Fine to large inclusions of angular grit are common in Chinchawasi 2 Ware C vessels. Sometimes there are casts of plants, suggesting use of fiber temper, or at least as unintentional inclusions. Inclusions are better-sorted and finer (less than 1 mm) in thin-walled vessels, such as bottles or bowls, while in larger vessels such as oversized jars inclusions can be far bigger and less well sorted.

## Chinchawasi 2 Ware C Vessel Shapes

Ware C pottery is dominated by restricted shapes, accounting for 56.9% of the phase sample. Open shapes account for 36.6%. Bowls represent 36.4% of the phase sample. There are four principal bowl shapes.

*Bowl 1.* Bowl 1 is by far the most common shape, accounting for 33.2% of the entire Chinchawasi 2 Ware C assemblage. Bowl 1 is an open bowl form, with convex sides and no discernible basal angle.

There are three variants, categorized primarily by differences in rim stance and profile. The Bowl 1a shape (Figure 57A–I) is distinguished by a very shallow profile, strongly everted (greater than 30°). Lip treatment is usually a simple round-

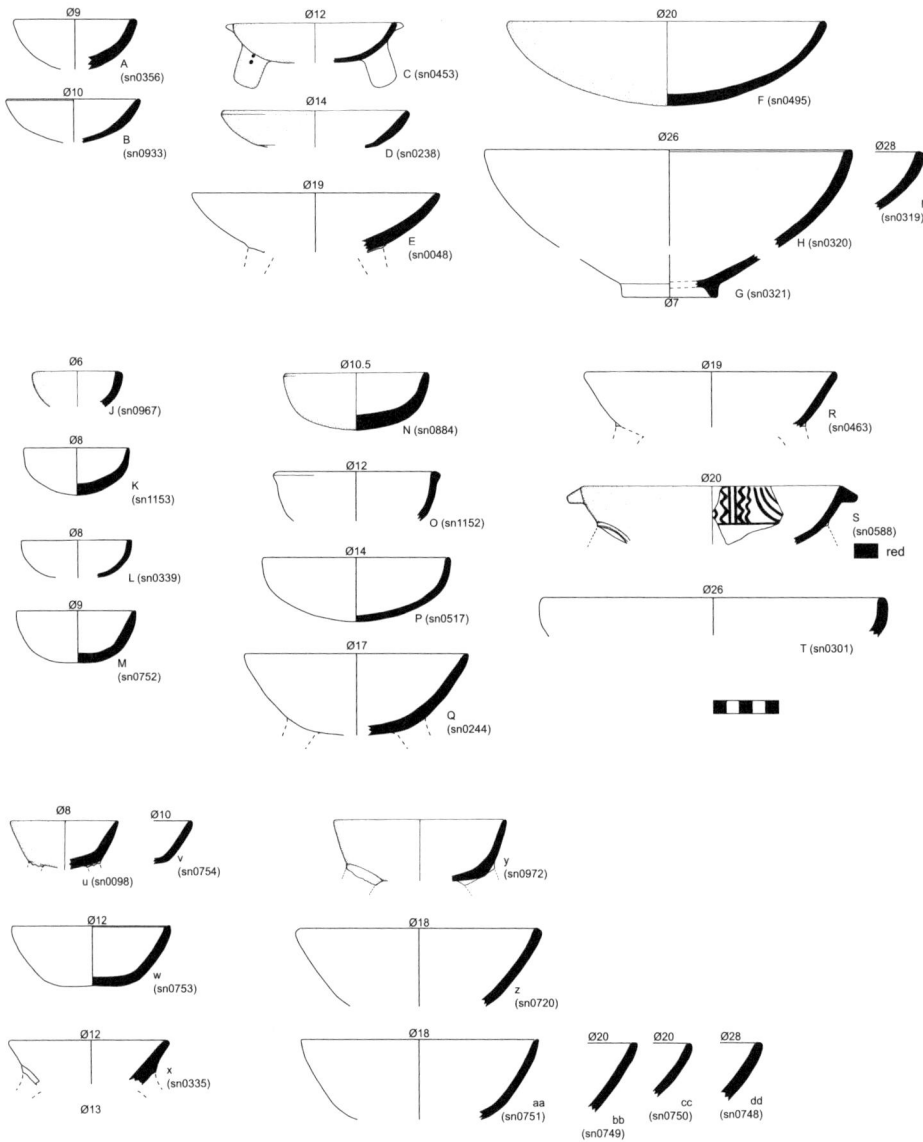

FIGURE 57. Chinchawasi 2 phase Ware C pottery: A–I, Bowl 1a; J–T, Bowl 1b; U–DD, Bowl 1c.

ing, although slight beveling also occurs (Figure 57H). Mouth diameters measure between 8 and 26 cm.

The Bowl 1b shape (Figure 57J–T) has a deeper profile than Bowl 1a and a more vertical rim stance (between 5° and 25°). This bowl variant shows considerable diversity in lip treatment, including simple rounding (Figure 57P), tapering (Figure 57K, M), beveling (Figure 57L) and thickening (Figure 57O). In addition, Bowl 1b shows considerable variability in size, with mouth diameters measuring between 6 and 28 cm. Most examples are small, however, and have diameters of 8 to 14 cm (with a mean of 11.7 cm).

A deeper profile, straighter walls and a flat base distinguish the Bowl 1c shape (Figure 57U–DD). Lip treatment includes simple rounding (Figure 57V), interior edge beveling (Figure 57W, AA) and top edge beveling (Figure 57BB). Mouth diameters range between 8 and 30 cm (with a mean of 18 cm).

There were tripod supports attached to some Bowl 1 vessels. In particular, Bowl 1a (e.g., Figure 57C, E) and Bowl 1c (e.g., Figure 57X, Y) examples have these additions. Tripod bowls (including evidence of support and rim) account for only 0.3% (n=9) of the sample. However, there were 91 individual tripod supports found independent of rims. Of this number, 19.8% were cylindrical with rounded bases (Figure 57C), while the majority consisted of conical examples (62.4%). Ring bases are also occasional add-ons on Ware C Bowl 1 vessels, occurring in 0.4% of the phase sample (e.g., Figures 57G and 58U, V). All are a small strip of clay attached to the base without much additional decorative treatment.

*Bowl 2.* Convex incurving sides distinguish Bowl 2. Bowl 2 accounts for 1.1% (n=38) of the Ware C assemblage. There are two variants, based on ware characteristics. On Bowl 2a examples, mouth diameters range between 5 and 20 cm (with a mean of 13.5 cm). Lip treatment consists most commonly of slight beveling (Figure 58A–H) or simple rounding, or both. Wall thickness is relatively thin and uniform in all vessels, ranging between 0.5 and 0.8 cm, but there is one aberrant example with extremely thick 1.2 to 1.3 cm walls (Figure 58C). A short neck distinguishes Bowl 2b, an incurving bowl variant (Figure 58I–L). Necks are uniformly short, but can be slightly everted (Figure 58J, K), tapering inwards (Figure 58I) or upwards (Figure 58L). Their incurving, squat profile resembles the general Bowl 2 shape.

*Bowl 3.* Bowl 3 is a deep, basin-like vessel with vertical or nearly vertical walls (Figure 58M–O). These bowls are large, with mouth diameters between 24 and 32 cm. Bowl 3 represented only 0.2% of the shape diagnostics.

*Bowl 4.* Bowl 4 is a deep, slightly incurving bowl distinguished by the addition of modeled bulges (Figure 58P–R). These features are hollow ovoid cavities located just below the lip; there were probably multiple bulges in any one bowl (see Eisleb 1987, Abb. 242; Wegner 2000:11). Compared with other bowl shapes in Ware C, Bowl 4 has a finer paste. In addition, bulge bowl surfaces, usually orange to light brown in color, are carefully burnished to a dull matte finish, especially on the exterior. Lips are given a simple rounding. One example shows white rim ticks (Figure 58R). The few examples have mouth diameters of 10 and 14 cm. Bowl 4 accounts for only 0.1% of the shape diagnostics in Chinchawasi 2 Ware C.

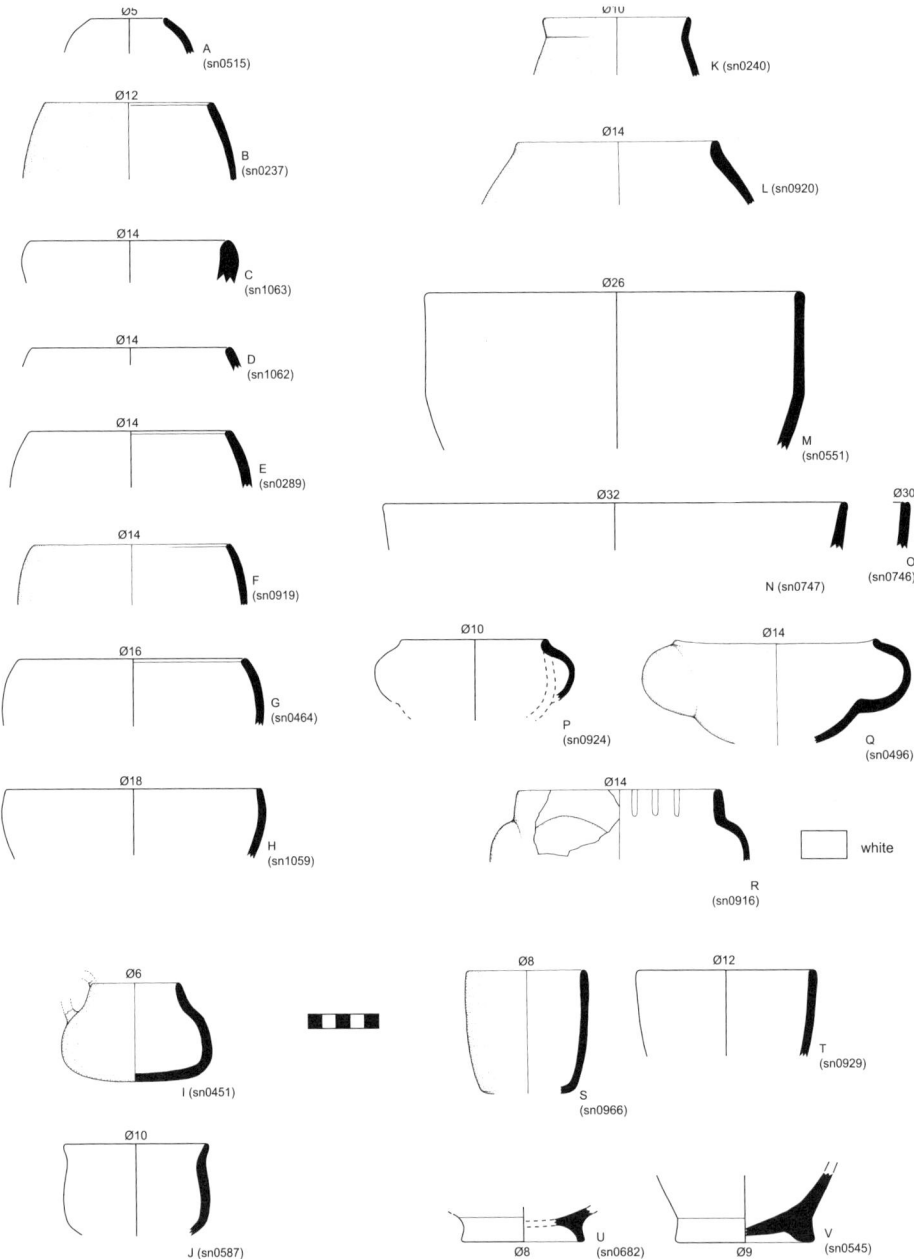

FIGURE 58. Chinchawasi 2 phase Ware C pottery: A–H, Bowl 2a; I–L, Bowl 2b; M–O, Bowl 3; P–R, Bowl 4; S, T, Cup 1; U, V, ring bases.

*Cup 1.* Cups represent 0.1% of the phase shape sample. Cup 1 is a drinking tumbler form with nearly vertical walls, a very slightly convex profile, a flat base and a discernible basal angle (Figure 58S, T). Mouth diameters measure 8 to 12 cm.

Colanders represent 3.6% of the phase sample. These vessels are almost always open vessels with a series of holes perforated before firing. There are three major forms.

*Colander 1.* The Colander 1 shape represents 8.0% of the colander sample. All examples have a basic open bowl shape with rounded lips and no discernible basal angles. Mouth diameters measure between 12 and 16 cm. There are three variants indicated by shape and hole size. The Colander 1a variant is a shallow incurving bowl (Figure 59A) with small holes. Colander 1b (Figure 59B) is a deep globular bowl with a slightly everted lip and small holes. The Colander 1c variant is a globular bowl (Figure 59C, D), with medium-sized holes.

*Colander 2.* The Colander 2 shape takes the form of a neckless olla with a series of small perforated holes starting just below the lip. One example (Figure 59E) has a slightly incurving and rounded lip. Colander 2 accounts for only 0.1% of the colander sample.

*Colander 3.* The Colander 3 shape is a large open platter with a straight (Figure 59F) or slightly convex profile. Colander 3 is the most common colander shape, representing 91.2% (of the shape sample).

*Spoons.* Spoons make up only 0.14% of the formal diagnostics (Figure 59P–S). The spoons have simple ovoid bowls with flattened (Figure 59P) or conical handles (Figure 59Q).

Restricted vessels, in addition to their storage uses, probably also functioned as cooking vessels. Restricted shapes represent 56.9% of the formal diagnostics sample. Of this percentage, jars are the most common vessel shape in the Chinchawasi 2 Ware C sample, accounting for 56.2% of the formal rim diagnostics. There are five major jar shapes.

*Jar 1.* Jar 1 is a restricted jar vessel with a globular body and a flaring (concave) everted neck. Wall angles normally fall between 25° to 50°, but some examples (Jar 1d) approach 70°. Jar 1 examples often have strap handles, probably two to a vessel located on the shoulder. Lip treatment is basic, with a simple tapering and rounding of the rim. Less commonly, there is lip thickening, slight beveling and flanging. The Jar 1 form is represented by 1,220 rim sherds, by far the most common general jar shape. This form is widely variable in size, ranging 10 to 48 cm in mouth diameter and 0.6 to 1.5 cm in rim wall thickness. This variability suggests that the Jar 1 shape was probably used for several functions, including cooking and storage. The large size would have been ideal for collecting and storing liquids, especially water and chicha.

Three arbitrary size categories were developed to account for size variability, on the basis mainly of mouth diameter: size 1 (10 to 17 cm), size 2 (18 to 30 cm)

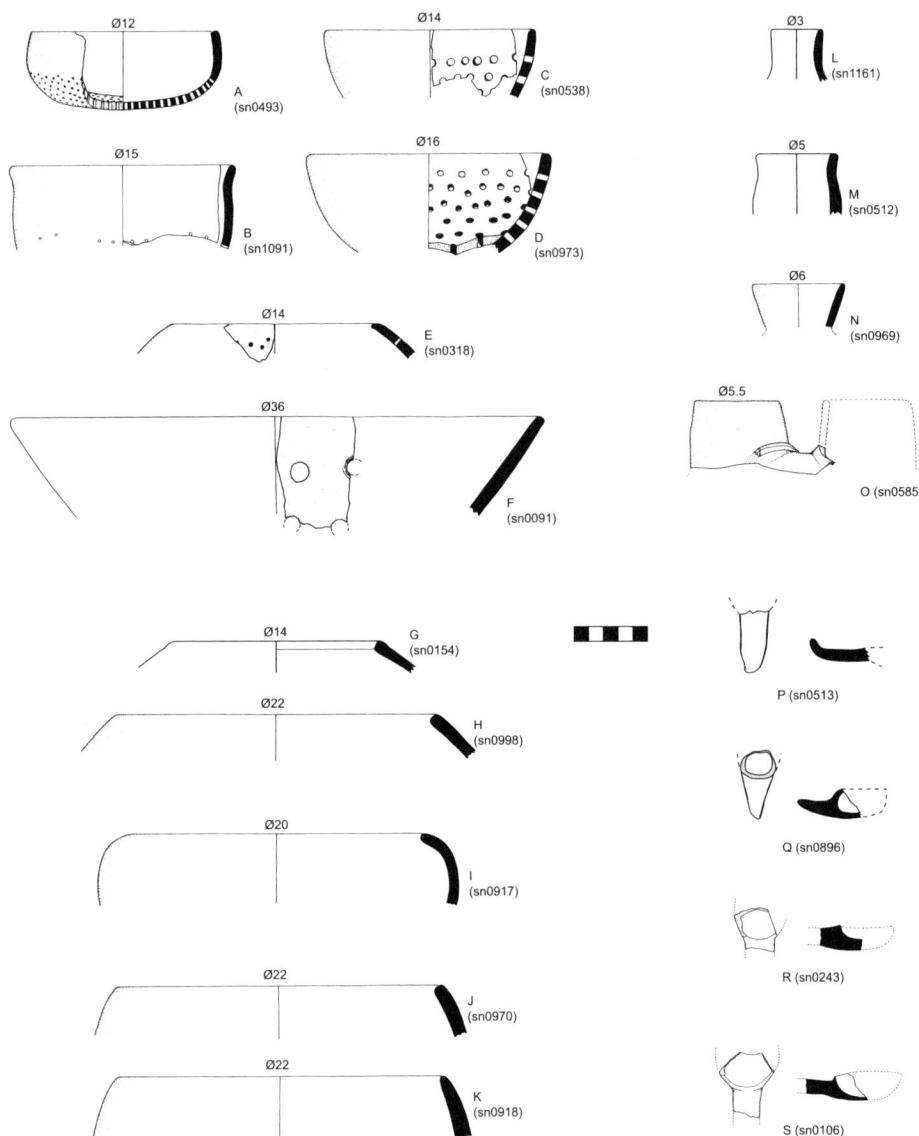

FIGURE 59. Chinchawasi 2 phase Ware C pottery: A, Colander 1a; B, Colander 1b; C, D, Colander 1c; E, Colander 2; F, Colander 3; G, H, Olla 1a; I, Olla 1b; J, K, Olla 1c; L, Bottle 1; M, Bottle 2; N, Bottle 3; O, Bottle 4; P–S, spoons.

and size 3 (30 to 48 cm). Size 2 dominates the sample, including 1,026 out of 1,220 sherds, or 84.1%. Size 1 and Size 3 accounted for 11.1% and 4.8% of the sample, respectively.

There are six variants of Jar 1 indicated by rim stance and wall angle. The Jar 1a shape (Figure 60A–EE) is the most common jar form in Chinchawasi phase 2 pottery. The shape is distinguished by an everted neck that has a flaring or concave

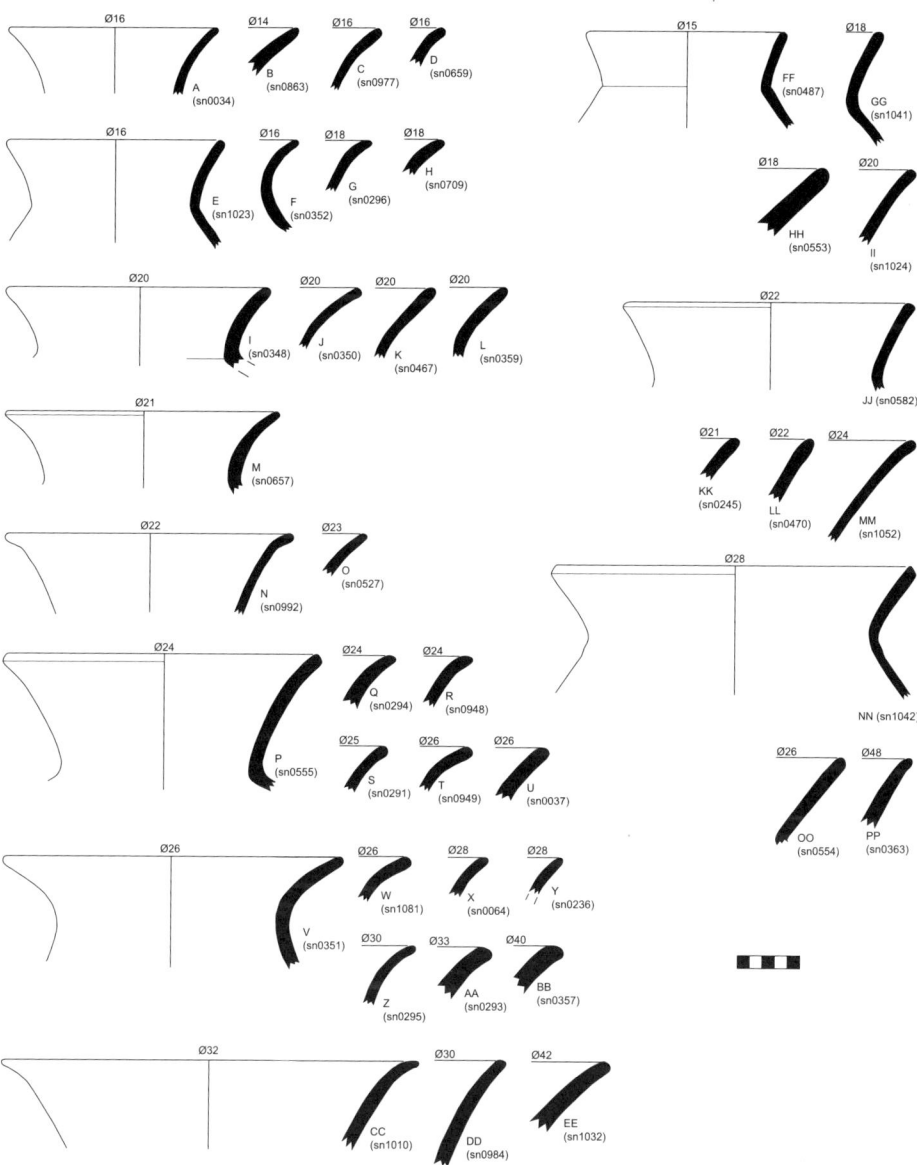

FIGURE 60. Chinchawasi 2 phase Ware C pottery: A–EE, Jar 1a; FF–PP, Jar 1b.

profile. Lips are almost always slightly tapering or rounded. Rims with thickened or beveled (e.g., Figure 60P) lips occur very rarely. Mouth diameters vary from 14 to 42 cm.

Instead of a flaring and concave rim, Jar 1b has direct or straight rims with wall angles typically between 30° and 50° (Figure 60FF–PP). Lips are generally rounded, but beveling is also present (e.g., Figure 60NN). Mouth diameters are

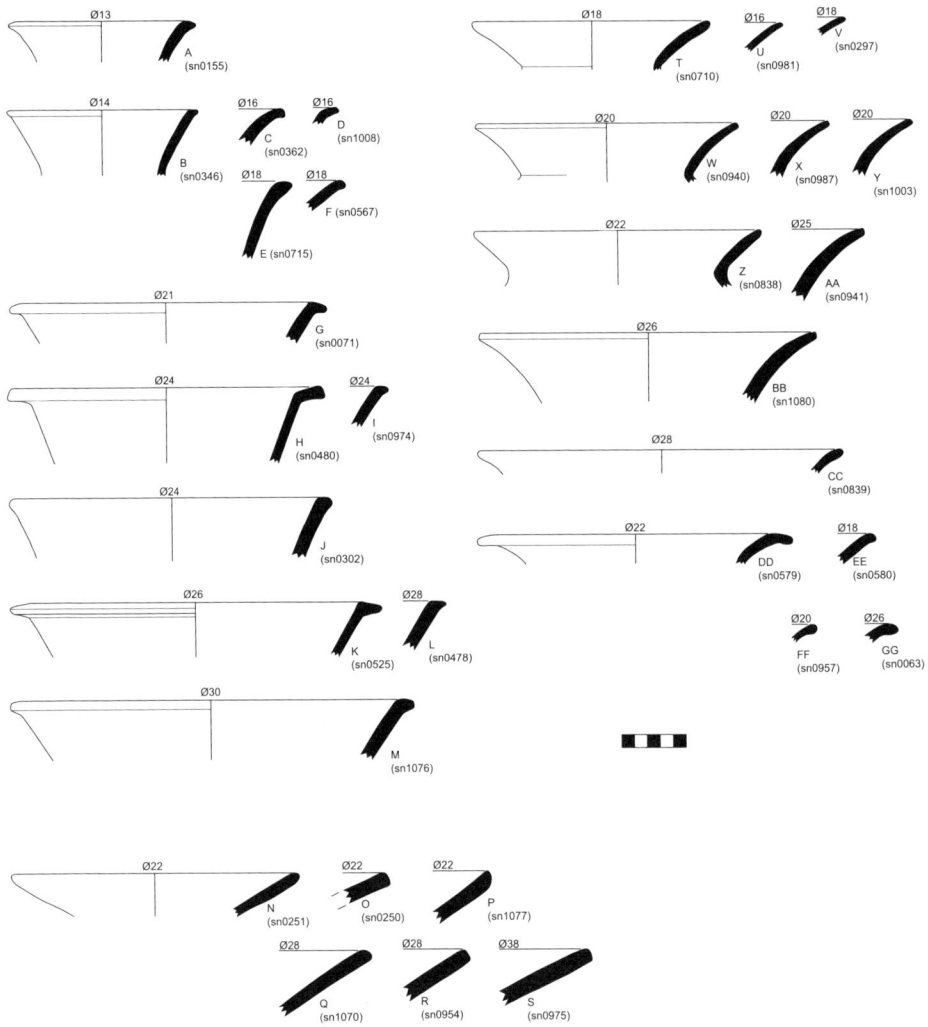

FIGURE 61. Chinchawasi 2 phase Ware C pottery: A–M, Jar 1c; N–GG, Jar 1d.

between 15 and 48 cm. Jar 1c is recognized by its direct everted rim and distinctive thickened and flanged lip (Figure 61A–M). Upper (e.g., Figure 61B, K) and outer (e.g., Figure 61H) lip surfaces are often tapered or beveled. Mouth diameters measure between 13 and 30 cm, with a mean of 21.3 cm.

Jar 1d (Figure 61N–GG) is an everted neck jar with an extremely everted profile and wall angles exceeding 50°. There are three types of neck treatment, including a flaring profile (e.g., Figure 61T–CC), direct profile (e.g., Figure 61N–S) and everted flanged profile (Figure 61DD–GG). Flaring profile examples often have tapered and beveled lips; rounding of the lips is also popular. Direct profile examples have rounding and beveling. Mouth diameters measure between 16 and 38 cm (with a mean of 22.7 cm).

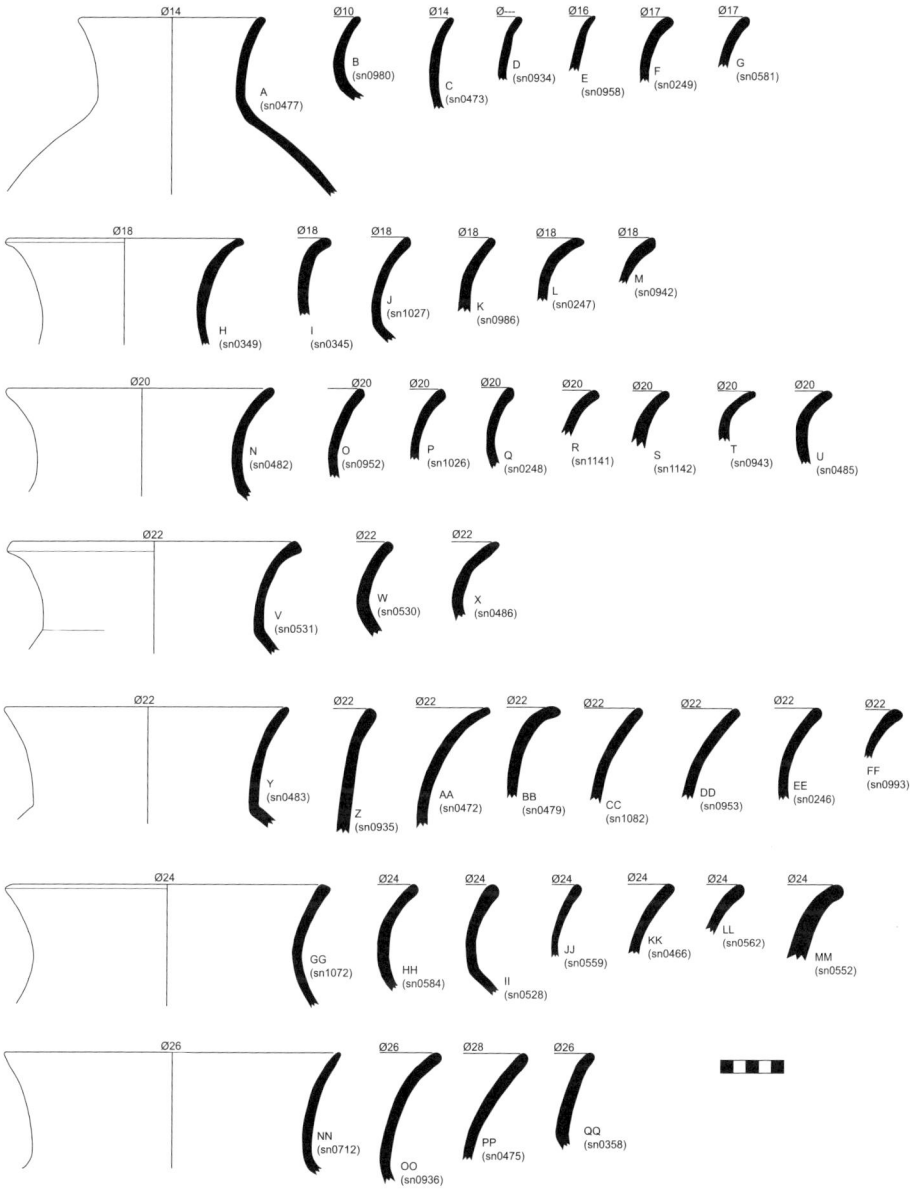

Figure 62. Chinchawasi 2 phase Ware C pottery: A–QQ, Jar 1e.

Jar 1e is distinguished by a slightly tall neck, a steep angle (between 10° and 30°) and a regular flaring profile (Figure 62A–QQ). Lip treatment is almost always a simple rounding or tapering, or both, but there are examples of thickening (e.g., Figure 62V) and beveling (e.g., Figure 62AA, DD). Compared with other Jar 1 variants, there is a more restricted mouth diameter range between 14 and 28 cm, but the mean (21 cm) is roughly similar.

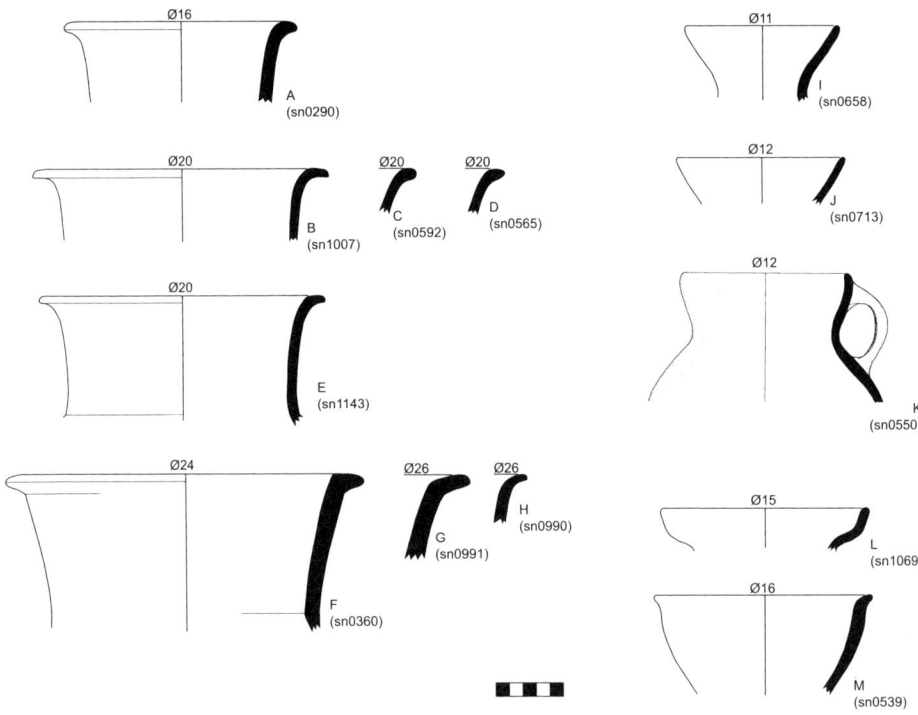

FIGURE 63. Chinchawasi 2 phase Ware C pottery: A–H, Jar 1f; I–M, Jar 1g.

The Jar 1f variant is a tall, steeply angled neck jar with distinctive flanging lips (Figure 63A–H). Wall angles measure typically between 5° and 20°. Near the lip, the rim curves outward. Lips are most commonly pinched and rounded. Mouth diameters range from 16 to 26 cm (with a mean of 21.3 cm). The Jar 1g variant (Figure 63I–M) features everted necks with slightly convex (Figure 63I, J, M) to very convex profiles (Figure 63L). Lip treatment includes simple rounding and slight flanging (Figure 63M). Mouth diameters measure 10 to 16 cm.

*Jar 2.* Jar 2 is a restricted jar vessel with a globular body and a short, everted neck. The Jar 2 shape consists of 362 rim sherds and is the second most common shape in Chinchawasi 2 Ware C, comprising 10.3% of the formal diagnostics. In general, there is a more limited size range, as represented by mouth diameters.

There are five variants indicated mainly by rim profile and lip treatment. The Jar 2a shape is the most common variant and consists of a short, flaring neck (Figure 64A–AA). Lips typically have a simple rounding or tapering towards the lip, or both, but there are instances of slight beveling (Figure 64Z), lip thickening (Figure 64A, B) or recurving with a slightly convex profile (Figure 64Y). Mouth diameters are comparatively small and range from 12 to 23 cm (with a mean of 16.6 cm). Strap handles are sometimes attached vertically, connecting lip and shoulder (Figure 64V). The Jar 2a shape was probably used as a type of small to regular-sized pouring pitcher.

FIGURE 64. Chinchawasi 2 phase Ware C pottery: A–AA, Jar 2a; BB–GG, Jar 2b.

The Jar 2b variant features a short, direct neck (Figure 64BB–GG). Mouth diameters are relatively small, ranging from 10 to 20 cm (with a mean of 14.5 cm). Strap handles are sometimes attached to the jar shoulder. The Jar 2c shape has a very short, flaring neck (Figure 65A–E). Lip treatment includes simple rounding and, less commonly, slight beveling. Compared with other Jar 2 variants, the Jar 2c shape is relatively large, as mouth diameters range from 16 to 28 cm (with a mean of 20 cm). The Jar 2d shape features a very short, direct neck (Figure 65F–P). Typically, the necks are everted, but there are several cases where the neck profile is nearly vertical (Figure 65F, G). Lip treatment includes simple rounding and, less commonly, slight beveling. Mouth diameters range from 8 to 20 cm (with a mean of 15.4 cm).

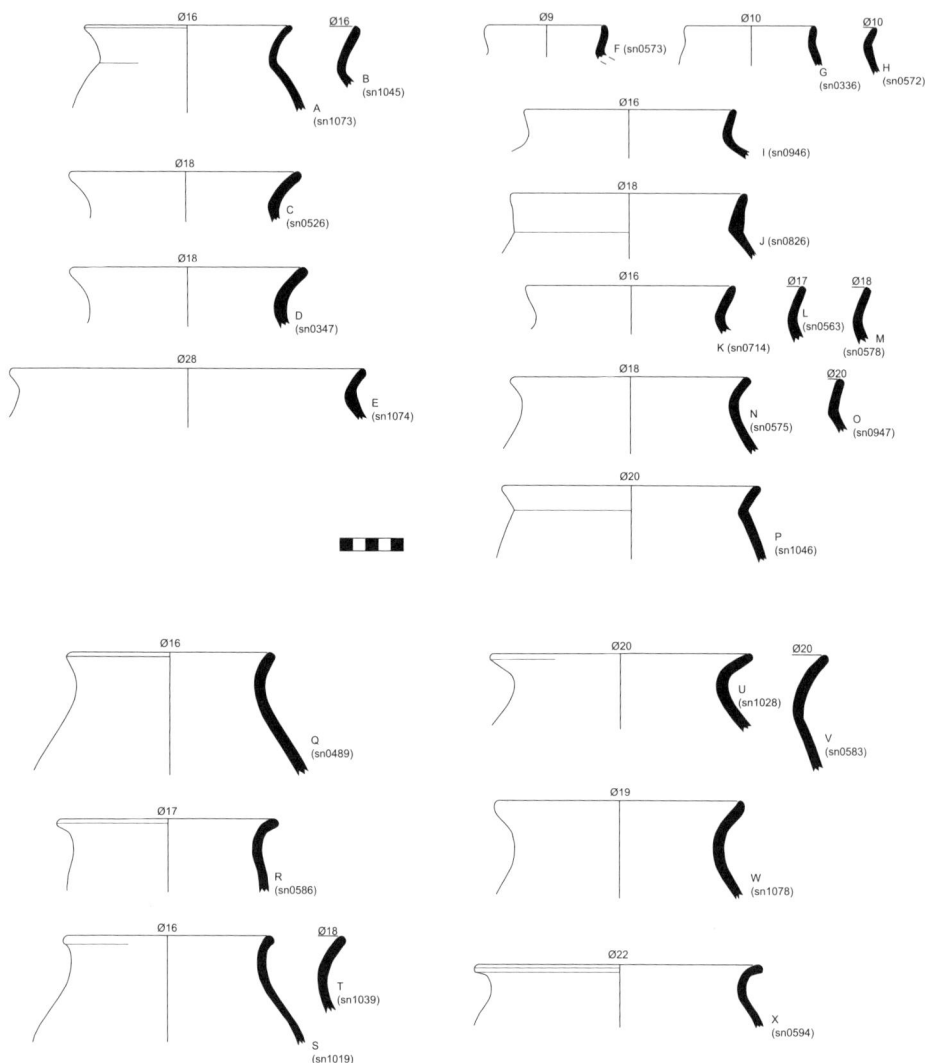

Figure 65. Chinchawasi 2 phase Ware C pottery: A–E, Jar 2c; F–P, Jar 2d; Q–X, Jar 2e.

The Jar 2e variant consists of a very short, flaring everted neck and a steep or low shoulder profile (Figure 65Q–X). Lips are usually given a simple rounding, but can also be slightly thickened (e.g., Figure 65S, X) or recurved with a slight convexity (e.g., Figure 65W). Mouth diameters vary between 16 and 22 cm (with a mean of 18.7 cm). The distinct shoulders, wide orifice and common presence of sooting suggests that the Jar 2e shape could have been used as a cooking olla.

*Jar 3.* Jar 3 has a direct rim, with a nearly vertical to vertical profile. Wall angles measure 5° to 25°. In order of frequency, the most common lip treatments are:

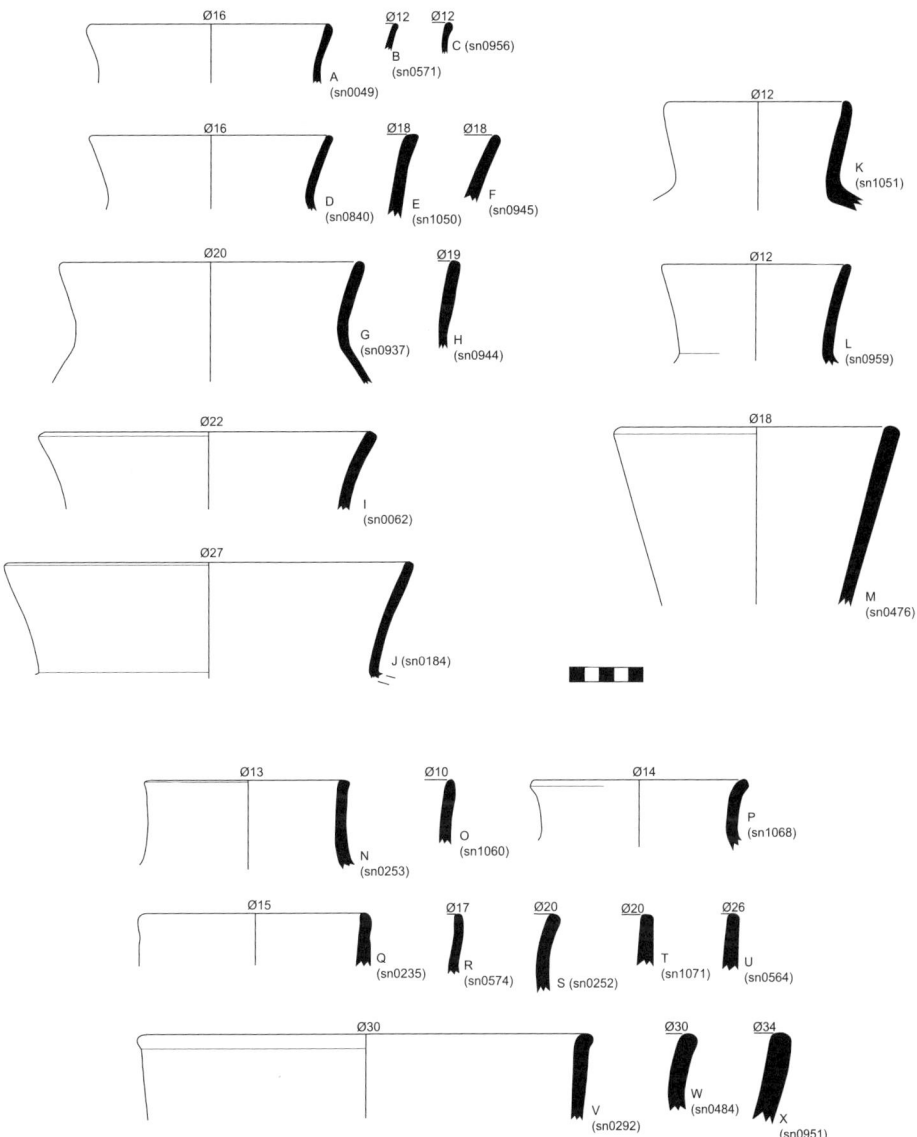

FIGURE 66. Chinchawasi 2 phase Ware C pottery: A–J, Jar 3a; K–M, Jar 3b; N–X, Jar 3c.

simple rounding, slight beveling and thickening. The Jar 3 sample consists of 87 rim sherds (2.5% of the Ware C shape diagnostics).

The Jar 3 shape has three variants. The Jar 3a shape is the most common, with a short to regular-sized neck that is slightly everted (Figure 66A–J). Wall angles measure 15° to 25°. Lip treatment includes simple rounding (Figure 66D) and beveling (Figure 66I), as well as thickening (Figure 66B, C). Mouth diameters range from 12 to 28 cm (with a mean of 18 cm). The Jar 3b variant is distinguished by

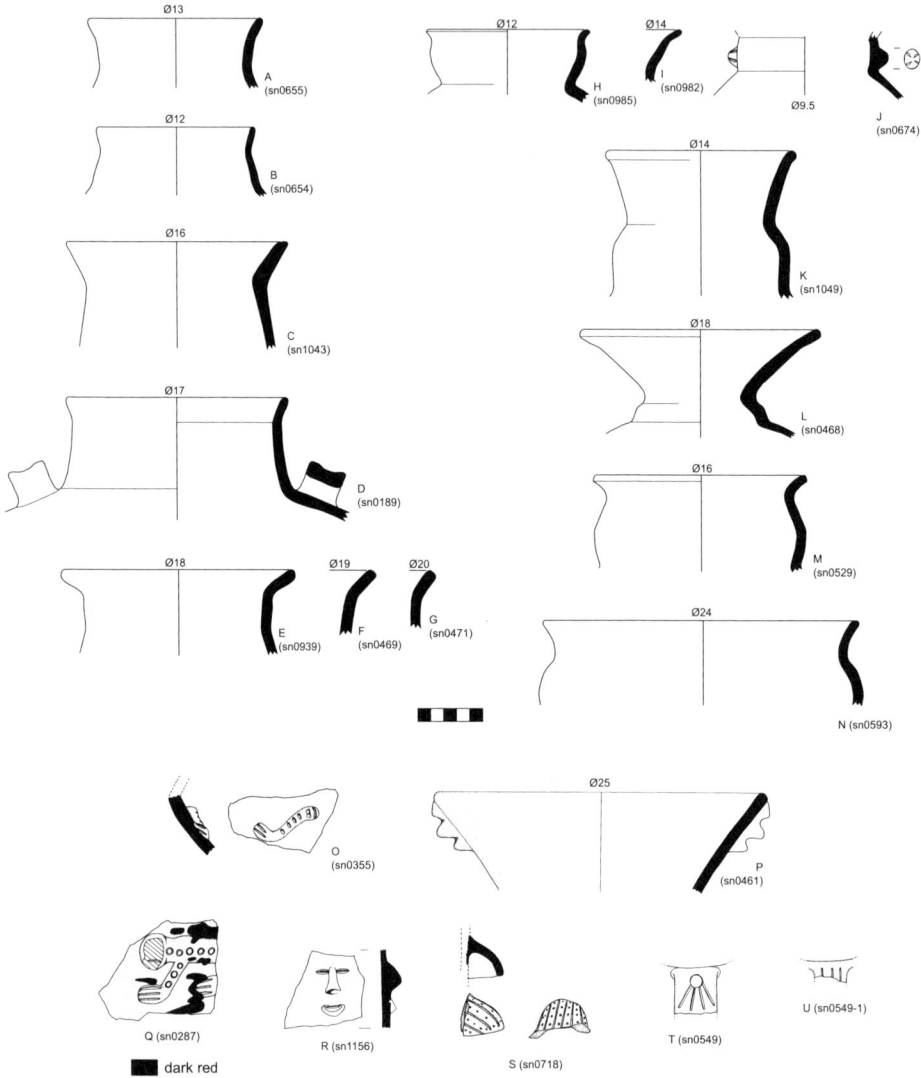

FIGURE 67. Chinchawasi 2 phase Ware C pottery: A–G, Jar 4; H–N, Jar 5; O–U, plastic decoration.

a tall, slightly everted neck with a direct rim profile (Figure 66K–M). Wall angles measure 10° to 20°. Lip treatment is typically a simple rounding. Mouth diameters measure between 12 and 20 cm. The Jar 3c shape has a nearly vertical profile with angles of 0° to 15° (Figure 66N–X). In order of frequency, lip treatment includes rounding (Figure 66U), beveling (Figure 66N, T), thickening (Figure 66V) and one example of slight flanging (Figure 66P). Mouth diameters measure 10 to 34 cm (with a mean of 19.5 cm).

*Jar 4.* Jar 4 shows a neck that is either vertical or tapers slightly inwards, and a mouth orifice that widens towards the lip (Figure 67A–G). Lip treatment is a simple rounding or slight beveling. Mouth diameters measure 12 to 20 cm (with a mean of 16.4 cm). The Jar 4 sample consists of 26 sherds.

*Jar 5.* Jar 5 is distinguished by a recurving of the neck profile (Figure 67H–N). There is substantial variability in recurved neck shapes. Typically, the recurving is applied to the neck or neck–shoulder juncture to regular everted (Figure 67H), tall everted (Figure 67K) and extremely everted jars (Figure 67L). The recurving produces a "bulge" in the profile. Lip treatments include simple rounding and slight beveling. Mouth diameters on recurved neck jars measure 10 to 24 cm (with a mean of 16 cm). The Jar 5 sample consists of 21 sherds (0.6% of the shape diagnostics).

*Olla 1.* Olla 1 is a large, neckless and globular vessel with steep incurving walls. Neckless ollas account for 0.34% of the phase shape sample. Wall thicknesses measure between 0.8 and 1 cm. Lip treatment consists of a simple rounding, tapering or beveling.

There are three variants indicated by rim stance and general profile. Olla 1a is a neckless olla form with a straight direct rim (Figure 59G, H). Examples of this shape have mouth diameters between 14 and 22 cm. The Olla 1b shape is a neckless olla form with a sharply convex profile (Figure 59I). The shoulder to the rim curves almost horizontally. Mouth diameter is approximately 20 cm. The Olla 1c variant is distinguished by a profile that is slightly incurving and convex (Figure 59J, K), compared with the Olla 1a and Olla 1b shapes. Mouth diameters measure between 20 and 22 cm.

*Bottles.* Bottle fragments make up 0.5% of the Chinchawasi 2 Ware C sample. Lip treatment is almost always a simple rounding. There are four shapes as indicated by spout profiles. Bottle 1 is the most common bottle shape and has a short cylindrical spout (Figure 59L).

The Bottle 2 shape has a spout with a slightly incurving neck and a short everted rim (Figure 59M). The Bottle 3 spout is distinguished by a everted, direct rim (Figure 59N). Bottle 4 consists of a single example of a small, dual-chambered vessel with dual spouts (Figure 59O).

*Miniature.* There was also one example of a miniature vessel found in Chinchawasi 2 deposits (Figure 101E) in the shape of a short-necked globular jar with a small, modeled mouth and four punctations on the shoulder. In addition, there is a vertically placed neck-to-shoulder strap handle. Mouth diameter measures 2.5 cm.

CHINCHAWASI 2 WARE C SURFACE TREATMENT
Ware C surfaces include smoothing and, less commonly, burnishing to dull matte finishes. Ware C never shows polishing. A light red slip or wash is sometimes applied, but most Ware C pottery has a fired paste color, which ranges from a dark red to a deep orange. Manufacturing striations and tiny cavities resulting from smooth-

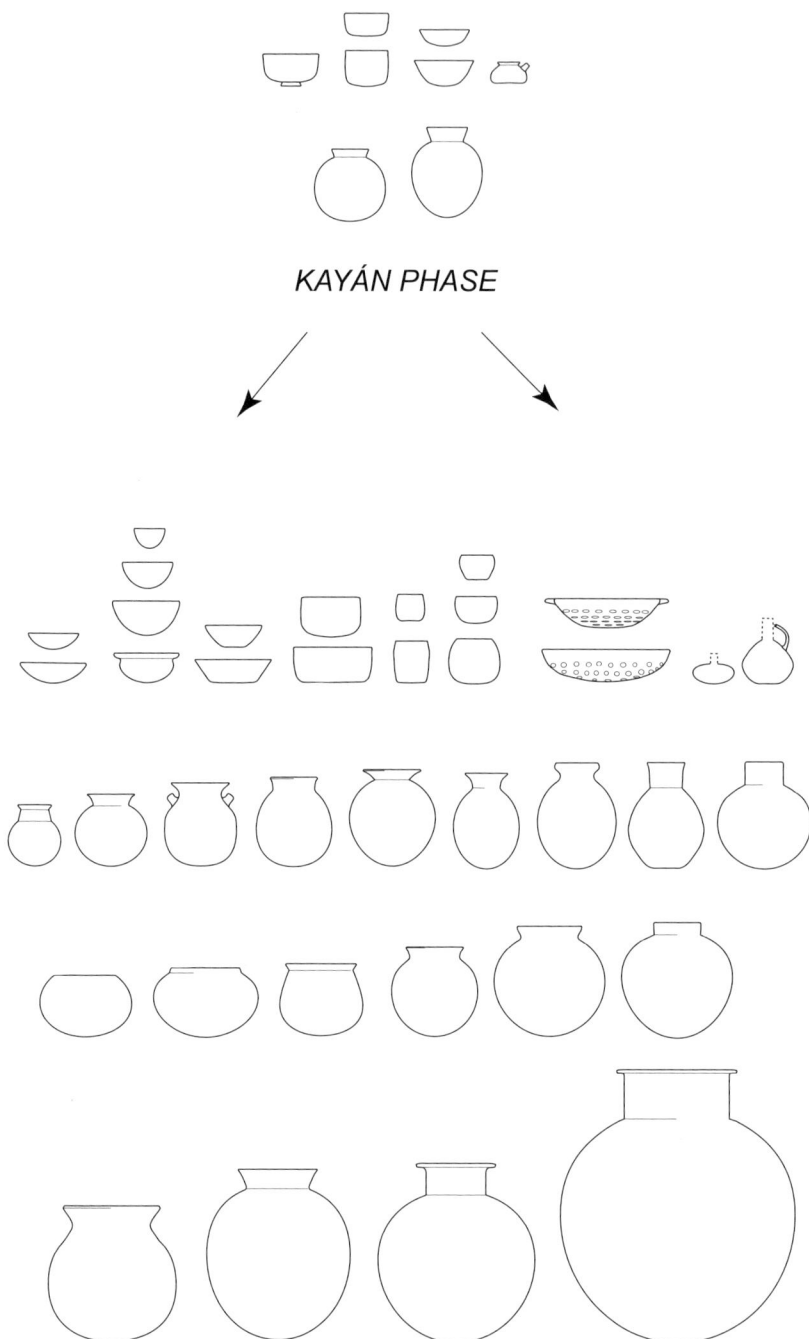

FIGURE 68. Reconstruction of shapes represented in Kayán and Chinchawasi 1 phases.

ing or burnishing are very common. Striations occur primarily on the exterior of bowls and the interiors of jars.

CHINCHAWASI 2 WARE C PAINTED DECORATION
Ware C pottery, as a rule, does not have painted decoration. One notable exception is a dusky red paint typical of Chinchawasi phase painting on a coarse Ware C sherd with a modeled appliqué feline (Figure 67Q).

CHINCHAWASI 2 WARE C PLASTIC DECORATION
Plastic decoration is the most common decoration on Ware C pottery, occurring in 1.4% of the decorated sample (n=33). Appliqué nubbins (e.g., Figure 67J) can be plain or have punctations or striations. Lozenge-like appliqué fillets (Figure 67P) are often ribbed or ticked.

Strap and ledge handles also occasionally show plastic decoration (n=27), including striations (Figure 67U), dimples, ticks at the handle–body juncture, or punctations (Figure 67S). Seven of these examples probably served as maker's marks. Motifs are located in the center or near the base of the strap handles (Figure 103B, E, J, Q, R, T). Center decoration likely occurred on horizontal strap handles (on jar shoulders), while strap handles with offset designs near the handle ends were probably vertical (connecting the lip and neck to the shoulder).

There are a half dozen examples of small appliqué adornos of animals or animal-like representations. One specimen (Figure 67Q) is of a modeled profile feline with aligned punctations across its leg and body. The design and perspective are similar to feline representations in local stone sculpture (Lau 2006b). Other examples of modeled appliqué include feet, paw and snake representations; dot punctations and incisions are the predominant decorative techniques.

DISCUSSION: CHINCHAWASI 2 WARE C
Chinchawasi 2 Ware C is a plainware utilitarian pottery. The constituent shapes, lack of consistent decoration, and evidence for cooking over fire indicate that Ware C pottery was used mainly as daily utilitarian pottery. Functions include storage, cooking, serving, pouring and sieving through colanders.

A comparison with Chinchawasi 1 Ware D pottery reveals significant diachronic patterns. In general, Chinchawasi 2 plainware has greater formal variability than Chinchawasi phase 1 (Figures 68 and 69). Note, however, that the sample size of Chinchawasi 2 plainware is much larger. Restricted vessels continue to predominate, although at a slightly lower percentage—from 60.4% (Chinchawasi 1 Ware D) to 57%. Everted-neck jars constitute the main shape. Tall, vertical-neck jars become more common. Small jars as well as short everted-neck jars occur less frequently. Vertical necks with the thick flanging found in Chinchawasi 1 Ware D (e.g., Jar 6; Figure 47V) disappear. There are more jars with recurved profiles near the neck and shoulder. Open vessels, meanwhile, become more common, representing from 30.6% to 36.6% of the sample. The increasing use of redware for open vessels antici-

### CHINCHAWASI 2 PHASE

FIGURE 69. Reconstruction of shapes represented in Chinchawasi 2 phase.

pates pottery preferences in the Warmi phase. In particular, there are considerably more open cumbrous bowls, tripod bowls and incurving bowls. Cups and small shallow dishes become less common. Bowls with modeled bulges near the rim are new to the Chinchawas sequence.

Both handles and tripod supports become more common. Strap handles (n=823) continue to predominate in Chinchawasi 2; ledge handles, meanwhile,

TABLE 10. Summary of maker's marks by phase.

| Phase | Count | Number of types |
|---|---|---|
| Kayán | 1 | 1 |
| Chinchawasi 1 | — | — |
| Chinchawasi 2 | 7 | 6 |
| Warmi | 17 | 10 |
| Chakwas | — | — |
| Indeterminate phase | 5 | 5 |

show a decline in representation from 5.5% to 2.2% of all handles. Colanders and spoons also become less common. Nevertheless, there is increased shape variability in colanders; different small globular forms supplement the large platter shape common in Chinchawasi 1 Ware D. Maker's marks occur for the first time during the Chinchawasi 2 phase, suggesting that the sources of plainware production and distribution could have been fairly specialized by this time (Table 10).

In regional comparisons, many of the pertinent assemblages, especially on the basis on form, have already been noted for Chinchawasi 1 Ware D (described above). In short, the general repertoire of shapes, especially necked jars and open bowls, has strong similarities to assemblages in highland Ancash, especially the Callejón de Huaylas (Bennett 1944; Grieder 1978; Terada 1979; Ponte Rosalino 1999a, 1999b).

We can draw comparisons for special shapes. Modeled bulge bowls, similar to Bowl 4, have been found in tomb contexts in other parts of the Callejón de Huaylas, including the Huaraz and Katak areas (Bennett 1944, figs. 13i, 17h; Eisleb 1987, Abb. 242). In addition, looted examples of polished blackware are known from the Chacas zone to the east of the Cordillera Blanca (Wegner 2000). The Bowl 2a shape with incurving or inward tapering walls is present in the Tornapampa Thin Brown type from La Pampa (Terada 1979, pl. 99, no. 29). Also, the recurved-neck jars (Ware C Jar 5) are represented in the Usú phase material from Pashash (Grieder 1978, fig. 40), as well as farther north in the Caserones Orange type from the La Pampa area (Terada 1979, pl. 97).

Finally, the use of plastic decoration on Chinchawasi 2 Ware C pottery increases in frequency, if only slightly. A similar pattern is mirrored at Pashash, where plastic decoration becomes more prevalent during the Usú phase, the final component in the site sequence (Grieder 1978). The use of plastic decoration, including maker's marks, anticipates its later importance in the subsequent Warmi and Chakwas phase assemblages. In sum, the stylistic comparisons for Chinchawasi 2 Ware C support an early to middle Middle Horizon association.

## Chinchawasi 2 Phase Absolute Dating

Three radiocarbon assays from charcoal samples from Chinchawasi 2 contexts were performed (see Table 1). One from OP4, Level G, measured to 1290 ± 45 B.P.

(A.D. 660 uncalibrated; 2-sigma calibrated range of A.D. 659 to 875). Another from OP21, Level I, measured to 1255 ± 45 B.P. (A.D. 695 uncalibrated; 2-sigma calibrated range of A.D. 668 to 888). A third sample, from OP26, Level G, yielded an age of 1180 ± 45 B.P. (A.D. 770 uncalibrated; 2-sigma calibrated range of A.D. 726 to 979). On the basis of these ages and associations with local and imported pottery, I estimate that the Chinchawasi 2 phase began by the middle to late 8th century A.D. and lasted until about the beginning of the Warmi phase. After a discussion of the next two ceramic phases, I will review the overall sequence to highlight the changes and continuities of the different pottery styles used at ancient Chinchawas.

CHAPTER SEVEN

# Ceramics of the Warmi and Chakwas Phases

The final two components of the Chinchawas sequence consist of the Warmi and Chakwas phases. After a description of their stylistic features and chronological associations, this chapter provides a general overview of the ceramic sequence and absolute chronology from Chinchawas.

## Warmi Phase Ceramics

The use of a new, distinctive ceramic style marks the beginning of the next occupation at Chinchawas, known as the Warmi phase. Unlike previous components of the sequence, in which there were stylistic continuities (decorative and technological) in local decorated pottery, Warmi painted pottery is strikingly different from its antecedents.

The wide ubiquity of Warmi pottery parallels the distribution of the Chinchawasi phase ceramics, suggesting that the scale of the occupations was comparable. Older Chinchawasi buildings were re-used and dumping activities occurred in similar places. However, there are substantially fewer Warmi sherds, suggesting that the Warmi occupation was of shorter duration.

Our investigations located Warmi pottery in nearly all of the horizontal and test excavations performed in Sector 1. In these, Warmi levels lay directly above Chinchawasi deposits and usually formed the uppermost intact find level. Topmost levels containing Warmi pottery were, on occasion, cut off or disturbed, mainly by plowing, so that the picture of the full occupation is incomplete. In addition, Warmi deposits occasionally contained older materials, especially Chinchawasi 2; we interpret these as curated from the previous phase or part of the mixing of trash deposits and fill during reuse of the architecture. Regardless, the ceramic evidence indicates a very brief but intense Warmi occupation. The radiocarbon measurements discussed below reiterate this observation.

In addition, we located Warmi pottery in chullpa tombs of Sector 2. As in Sector 1, Warmi wares were found in association with exotic Middle Horizon pottery. The pottery includes press-molded and polychrome styles dating to a time late in the Middle Horizon. The Warmi phase occupation at Chinchawas therefore likely falls into this period.

FIGURE 70. Warmi phase Ware A pottery: A–E, Bowl 1a; F–M, Bowl 1b.

Unlike in previous phases, there are fewer major ware categories in local pottery during the Warmi phase. The burnished redware typical of Chinchawasi 1 Ware C and Chinchawasi 2 Ware B disappears. Warmi phase pottery also contrasts with earlier materials, because the local decorated and plain wares use a similar paste. The ceramic analysis defined two major ware categories for the Warmi phase.

### Warmi Ware A

Ware A is the primary diagnostic of Warmi pottery. Ware A consists of 948 sherds, or 17.3% of the total decorated sample from Chinchawas.

## Warmi Ware A Paste

Ware A is identified by a redware paste decorated with a dark paint over an orange to red surface (paste or a light wash). The paste typically shows common medium-sized to coarse inclusions that are generally well sorted.

## Warmi Ware A Vessel Shapes

The predominant shape for Ware A vessels is the open bowl (Figures 70, 71, 72, 73). Bowls represent 91.8% of the total identified decorated forms in Ware A pottery. Some Warmi A bowls have the addition of tripod supports. Eleven examples of rims with tripods were recovered, accounting for 2.1% of the total decorated forms. Tripods are typically conical (Figures 70H and 71A). Similarly, bowls can also have ring bases. Only four examples (0.8% of decorated forms) were recovered; all examples are simple and low (e.g., Figure 72N). This figure is conservative, because only rims with ring bases or tripod supports were counted. There are three principal bowl shapes.

*Bowl 1.* Bowl 1 is an open bowl form distinguished by a straight, everted wall and a discernible basal angle (Figure 70). Bowl 1 walls generally taper toward the lip. Lips have simple rounding or slight beveling treatments. Mouth diameters for Bowl 1 examples range from 16 to 24 cm. There are two variants. The Bowl 1a variant is distinguished by a deep profile (Figure 70A–E). The Bowl 1b variant is distinguished by a shallow profile (Figure 70F–M).

*Bowl 2.* Bowl 2 examples are distinguished by a slightly convex everted walls. Rims generally taper toward the lip. Lip treatments include simple rounding (Figures 71L and 72J), slight beveling (Figures 71D and 72I) and slight thickening (Figure 72L). Most vessels have mouth diameters between 16 and 22 cm.

There are two variants, based on the presence of a basal angle. Bowl 2a is an open bowl with a discernible basal angle (Figure 71A–G). Bowl 2b is an open bowl with a curved convex base and no definite basal angle. These examples seem to be stylistic holdovers from Chinchawasi phase 2 (Figure 71H–P).

*Bowl 3.* Bowl 3 is distinguished by an incurving profile (Figure 72M, N), with convex walls that bend inward near the lip. Rim treatment includes tapering towards the lip and simple rounding. Mouth diameters measure 10 to 20 cm. Bowl 3 is rare in Warmi Ware A, but is very common in Ware B.

Jars account for only 1.5% of the Warmi Ware A sample. One jar form is represented in the sample.

*Jar 1.* Jar 1 is a long-necked jar form with a flaring everted rim (Figure 72O). Lip treatment is a simple rounding, especially on the exterior surface. Jar 1 has a large mouth diameter of 26 cm.

FIGURE 71. Warmi phase Ware A pottery: A–G, Bowl 2a; H–P, Bowl 2b.

## Warmi Ware A Surface Treatment

Ware A pottery has an oxidized redware surface. The surface ranges from a yellowish tan to orange to deep red. In some instances, perhaps through cooking or irregularities with firing, surfaces are blackened (e.g., Figure 71K). Occasionally a light wash of paste-colored slip is applied. The pottery also has coarse to medium burnishing to a dull matte finish with uneven, generally rough surfaces. Polishing is rare and surfaces are never lustrous. Despite the burnishing, striations and tiny cavities from the scraping and shaping process are common, especially on the unpainted surfaces of bowl and jar exteriors.

## Warmi Ware A Painted Decoration

Warmi phase potters rendered Ware A designs almost exclusively using a dark paint over a paste-colored background. Usually the potters painted in a black, dark brown or dark purplish red. White is a minor color. Rarely, there are examples of polychrome sherds, with combinations of red, white and sometimes black. There was quite a bit of latitude in how carefully Warmi phase potters executed the painting. Line weights differ greatly, intersections are casual and motifs, such as nested geometrics, are repeated with considerable variability.

Interior-painted decoration occurs on 83.6% of the Ware A sample. The entire interior surface of open bowls, as well as interior surface of jar rims, are the preferred fields for Ware A painting. Frequent designs include simple, repeating composite motifs within the interior surface, executed either (roughly) straight or in curvilinear designs. Often designs are placed within arc-shaped, V-shaped or rectangular-pendants located along the interior rim.

Band and meander motifs are the most common painted design and account for over 38.2% (n=303) of the sample of interior-decorated Ware A. There are two main band and meander variants: (1) two bands separated by a meander and then repeated with others, but with each band or meander element separate (e.g., Figure 70G), or (2) a series of bands alternating with meanders (e.g., Figure 72J). Band and meander designs are often rendered as nested arcs (Figure 72E), pendants (Figure 72F), or in branching patterns (Figure 71E). Several examples show repeated interior lines or a meander design, or both, running horizontally across the interior rim of open bowls (Figure 72C, N). Finally, polychrome designs also occur in bowl interiors and usually consist of tripartite, multicolored pendant rectangles with meanders (Figure 70F) or multiple meanders (Figure 71P).

Nested geometrics are also popular designs and represent 9.0% of the interior-painted Ware A sample. These almost exclusively occur as pendants and take the form of nested rectangles (Figure 71C), squares (Figure 71G) and triangles (Figures 70J and 72G). While nested squares and rectangles are almost always rendered in black, nested triangles and arcs are executed typically in purple or red.

Designs with arcs are the next major motif category and account for 8.4% of the interior-decorated Ware A assemblage. Arcs occur singly (Figure 71O) or in multiples within a nested arc "pendant" (Figure 71J, K). There is considerable vari-

Figure 72. Warmi phase Ware A pottery: A–L, Bowl 2; M, N, Bowl 3; O, Jar 1.

ability in the quantity, size and line weight of painted arcs.

Ware A also includes a series of minor interior designs. The "tree" motif occurs on 3.2% of all Ware A pottery and consists of a long, thicker band out of which ramify "L"s (Figure 72H) and other lines (Figure 72I). Simple asterisk-like stars (Figure 71B) or stars within pendants (Figure 71F) account for 2.4%. Lattice designs—placed in simple pendants (Figures 70M and 71H) or in more complex composite arrangements (Figure 70B, K)—represent 1.1%.

Compared to the Chinchawasi phase, very few jars have painted decoration. Even simple designs, such as rim ticking and lip and rim bands, decrease markedly in frequency compared with earlier pottery. The predominant design is a series of repeating strokes across the interior rim surface (Figure 72O).

Pottery with exterior-painted decoration is much rarer and represents 12.8% of the Ware A sample. Most are characterized by simple designs of rim bands, repeating bands, lattices and chevrons. Several examples of exterior-painted jars feature polychrome pendant rectangles (band and meander).

## Warmi Ware A Plastic Decoration

As a rule, Ware A vessels do not have plastic decoration, such as the nubbins or adornos common in the Chinchawasi phases. One exception is a series of incised ticks along the exterior base of an open bowl (Figure 71F).

## Discussion: Warmi Ware A

Ware A is the primary decorated ware in Warmi pottery and is the most diagnostic of the phase. It has serving forms and their recovery from contexts with other prestige artifacts denotes a special significance for these ceramics. Certainly, they were accorded more decorative elaboration than the common redwares of Warmi Ware B.

Ware A functioned as serving vessels. By far the most common Ware A shape is the open bowl (Bowls 1 and 2). Add-ons to the basic forms can include ring bases and tripod supports. Moreover, the focus on interior decoration continues the trend seen in Chinchawasi phase 2; interior painting suggests a preference for being viewed from above (Figure 73). Tripod designs are more intricate than Ware A open bowls and suggest the influence of tripod pottery from highland regions to the north, such as Huamachuco, Cajamarca and Celendín (King 1948). The painting appears to be derivative of Cajamarca Tradition cursive styles (Reichlen and Reichlen 1949; Terada and Matsumoto 1985).

Warmi painted decoration shows very little similarity to Chinchawasi 2 painting and breaks discernibly from the earlier Chinchawasi pottery tradition. The emphasis on black or dark brown paint on a redware surface provides the most apparent distinction from the earlier red-on-cream preference. Second, Warmi potters rarely painted on the exteriors of open bowls, which was the design field of choice during the early part of the Chinchawasi phase. Compared with earlier phases, painted bowls make up a far larger percentage of the local decorated style; jars during the Warmi phase are relatively free of painted decoration. Finally, representational emphasis moves to linear (especially band and meander) and geometric patterns that have no obvious antecedents.

These stylistic distinctions show that the long-standing cultural dispositions that characterized Chinchawasi pottery no longer held sway during the Warmi phase. Rather, they point to strong stylistic linkages to other parts of the Central

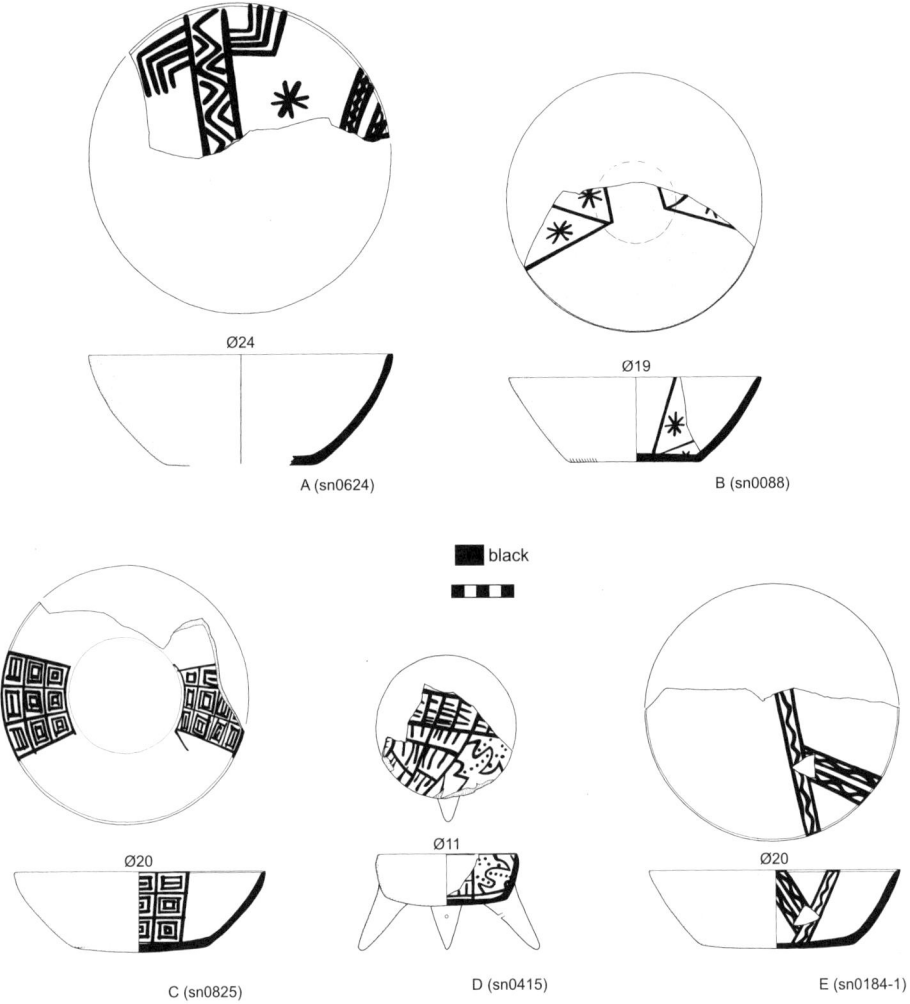

FIGURE 73. Top and profile views of Warmi phase bowls with interior decoration.

Andes. Inspiration for the Warmi style probably derived mostly from external sources.

There have only been a few studies on Middle Horizon pottery from the North Highlands of Peru. Despite some resemblances in pottery, however, there are no direct analogues to the Warmi style elsewhere in the Callejón de Huaylas. In part, this could be due to the lack of related research in the region. Also, very few residential sites of this period have been explored systematically, so that the sample of contemporary pottery from the Callejón de Huaylas is very much biased towards materials from funerary settlements and large centers.

Bennett's research (1944) in the Callejón de Huaylas remains a critical resource. His excavations at chullpa funerary sites around the Wilkawaín area recovered a series of open bowls, tripod bowls and jar necks adorned with polychrome pendant rectangles and meanders (Bennett 1944, fig. 4d, e). He identified the pottery tentatively as "Tiahuanacoid." Similar bowls with pendant rectangle (band and meander) designs from a Middle Horizon offering cache found near the town of Yungay are currently in the town museum of Ranrahirca; the deposit is comparable to other Wari-period offering deposits (Menzel 1964, 1968, 1977; Ravines 1968; Knobloch 1983; Cook 1985). Unprovenienced specimens in the storage collections of the Museo Arqueológico de Ancash in Huaraz also bear Warmi elements.

There is evidence for pottery similar to Warmi Ware A in other parts of the Callejón de Huaylas, but archaeological coverage has been uneven and clear-cut analogues in style, diversity or frequency do not exist. In the area of La Pampa, some painted fragments from the sites of Coronguimarca and Casa de Gallina are similar to Warmi Ware A (Terada 1979, pl. 113, nos. 27, 28, pl. 114, nos. 25, 29). Neither the investigations at Honcopampa nor in the Pierina zone near Huaraz uncovered material that strongly resembles Warmi Ware A. The general conclusion is that there is currently a notable dearth of material analogous to Warmi Ware A from other parts of the Callejón de Huaylas. Thatcher (1972, fig. 35a, b) recovered fine orangeware cumbrous bowls with interior band and meander designs associated with the Amaru phase, or Early Middle Horizon, in Huamachuco (Krzanowski 1986a:250).

In Wilson's lower Santa Valley survey, open bowls with polychrome interior pendant designs (Wilson 1988, fig. 242) appear during the Early Tanguche phase and are associated with the early Middle Horizon and Wari polychrome styles. Cumbrous bowls with interior pendant designs, usually rendered in white paint, also occur along the north-central to central coast under Kroeber's "Middle Period" designation (Kroeber 1925b, pl. 73, 78; Strong 1925, pl. 47; Collier 1955:180–182, fig. 60).

The abovementioned pottery is typically associated with jars bearing black-white-red painted decoration (Tello 1956:312–313, figs. 147–150; Proulx 1973; Donnan and Mackey 1978; Wilson 1995). At Chinchawas, there is very little evidence of such jars. In addition, unlike Warmi Ware A, many of the abovementioned examples often have ring bases or tripod supports. Finally, Ware A pottery is usually painted in dark monochrome pigments, most often black. The above examples often have polychrome painting.

Warmi Ware A, nevertheless, is probably a close relative of these local decorated coastal styles. Many of the surface survey studies conducted on the north-central coast have not extended into the upper valley regions. Because Warmi Ware A may be more characteristic of highland zones, more extensive regional surveys along the western flanks of the Cordillera Negra should locate other high elevation sites that reveal Warmi pottery.

Warmi-related pottery has been found in different parts of the central coast, usually from tomb contexts. Uhle's investigations in Supe (Kroeber 1925b, pl. 73k–o and 78d–f) and Ancón (Strong 1925, pl. 47f, i) recovered interior-painted cum-

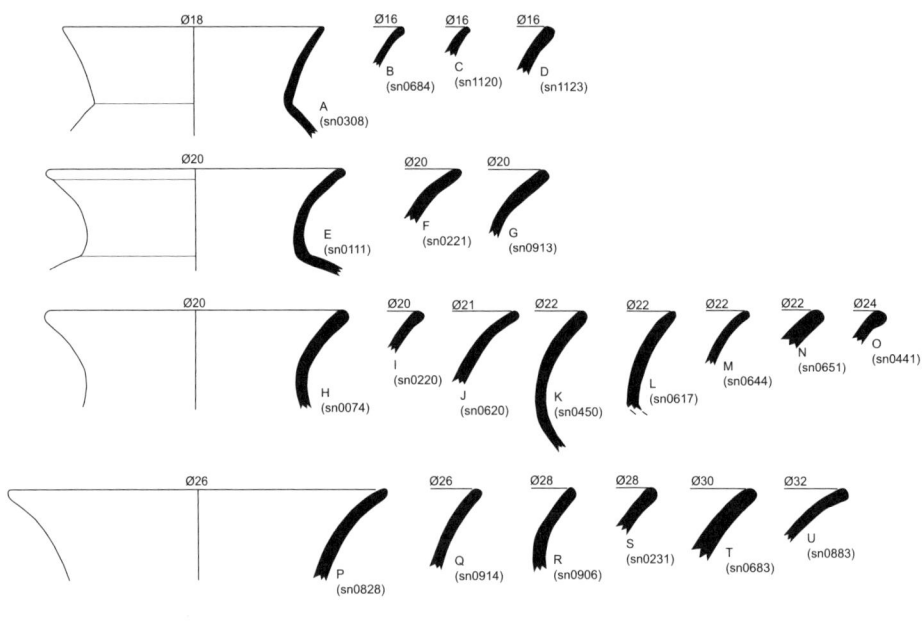
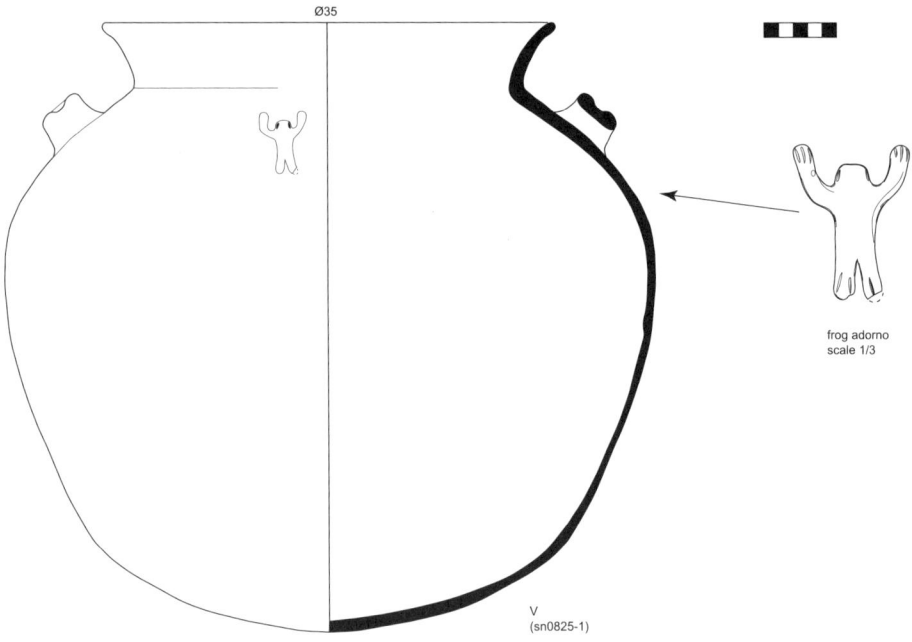

Figure 74. Warmi phase Ware B pottery: A–V, Jar 1a.

brous bowls characterized by direct-everted rims and sharp basal angles. Often, the designs consists of dark-on-light motifs, including pendants, parallel bands and band and meander arcs (Kelly 1930).

Notable parallels to Warmi pottery come from the site of Jargampata, east of Ayacucho in the Central Highlands of Peru (Isbell 1977). Open bowls of the Late Patibamba I and II phase, in particular, provide the most consistent affinities: interior paint, band and meander designs, lattice designs, pendant designs and horizontal band and meander designs (Isbell 1977, figs. 22N, 23U, 24D, 26H, 33A).

The Late Patibamba II phase pertains to the latter part of Middle Horizon Epoch 2, and perhaps partly into Epoch 3. By the end of Late Patibamba II, Jargampata is abandoned and its administrative and provisioning function ceases, probably because of the collapse of Wari political control (Isbell 1977:44–45). This scenario at Jargampata mirrors coeval developments reflected in the cultural inventory at Chinchawas, where a short-lived but intense Warmi occupation is curtailed abruptly. A Late Patibamba I radiocarbon age of 1185 ± 90 B.P. (GX-1933, calibrated A.D. 775 to 968) is consistent with our Warmi measurements and when calibrated correlates to an age at the end the 9th century (Isbell 1977:44; Ziółkowski et al. 1994:292).

Warmi pottery resembles pottery from the area in and around Ayacucho. At the Wari site itself researchers have encountered redware pottery (direct-rim cumbrous bowls and vertical-neck jars) often decorated with simple monochrome or polychrome designs such as pendant rectangles, meanders, the "tree" motif and lattices (e.g., Bennett 1953, fig. 20b; Lumbreras 1960, lám. 6F and 88, 1974b:181–182; Knobloch 1983, pl. 49; González Carré et al. 1999:63–66). The style has been referred to by investigators as "Huamanga" (or "Wamanga") or "Secular Viñaque" and is associated with Middle Horizon Epoch 2 (Menzel 1964, 1968; Anders 1986, 1989; González Carré et al. 1999).

Farther south, Frank Meddens (1985) recovered similar materials in the Chicha–Soras valley. His Middle Horizon Epoch 2 assemblage included interior painted bowls with band and meander designs and nested arcs (Meddens 1985, figs. 81, 86, 99, 43). Gordon McEwan (1984:256) recovered pottery similar to the Warmi style at Pikillacta. In particular, open bowls with polychrome band and meander designs resemble Ware A pottery from Chinchawas.

In short, many of the stylistic elements of Warmi Ware A were widely shared in different parts of the Central Andes and likely resulted from stylistic interaction with Wari. Warmi Ware A seems to have been an innovative, locally produced pottery that emulated the form and design attributes of Wari polychrome styles.

## *Warmi Ware B*

Ware B, a plain redware, is the other principal ware group in Warmi phase pottery. Ware B consists of 2,033 formal diagnostics, mainly rims. In addition, there are 674 nonrim diagnostics in Ware B, including handles, tripod supports and colander body sherds. Ware B materials from the chullpas are included in the discussion.

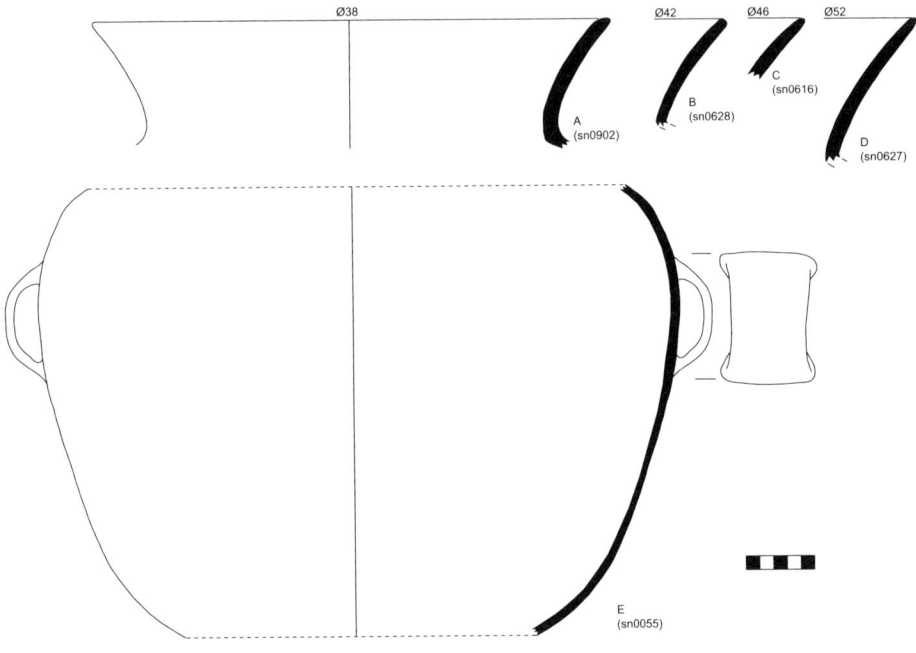

Figure 75. Warmi phase Ware B pottery: A–E, Jar 1a.

Warmi Ware B Paste
The defining characteristic of Ware B pottery is an oxidized redware that is typically coarse in texture. Fine to large inclusions of mica and angular grit are common in this ware. Inclusions are better sorted and finer in thin-walled vessels, such as bottles or bowls. In larger cooking and storage vessels, especially large jars, inclusions can be far larger and less well sorted. On occasion there are casts of plants, suggesting the inclusion of fiber temper. More systematic paste analysis would clarify whether these were intentionally added to the clay during production of Warmi Ware B pottery.

Warmi Ware B Vessel Shapes
The great variety of Ware B pottery shapes reflects both the versatility of the ware as well as its general utilitarian purpose (Figures 74 through 84). Thick-walled fragments most likely derive from large-necked jars and colanders. Thinner-walled vessels include bowls and miscellaneous serving vessels. Necked jars, in addition to their storage uses, probably functioned as cooking vessels as well.

Restricted vessels represent 47.4% (n=963) of the Ware B sample. Aside from a few bottle and olla fragments, jars are predominant. All relevant examples have globular or ovoid body shapes. Strap handles were common additions to jar vessels. These are either vertical (connecting neck to shoulder) or horizontal (typically on the shoulder). There are six major jar shapes.

*Jar 1.* Jar 1 is a restricted jar vessel with an ovoid or globular body and an everted neck. Jar 1 is by far the most common shape, representing 28.3% (n=575) of all identified Ware B vessels. The frequency and diversity of Jar 1 shapes probably reflect their common utility in storage and cooking functions. Jar 1 shows considerable variability in size, with mouth diameters ranging from 9 to 52 cm. There are three size categories, as follows: size 1 (9 to 16 cm), size 2 (18 to 30 cm) and size 3 (31 to 52 cm). The size 2 category was the most popular and accounts for 74.8% of the Jar 1 sample, followed by size 1 (17.2%) and size 3 (8.0%). Although Jar 1 wall angles normally range between 30° and 50°, some necks are nearly vertical (approaching 20°). Strap handles, both vertical and horizontal types, are typical add-ons. Ledge handles are less common.

There are five Jar 1 shape variants, based on rim stance, wall angle and general profile. The Jar 1a variant occurs most frequently. It has a distinct everted neck with a concave, flaring profile (Figures 74 and 75). Rims sometimes taper toward the lip. Lip treatment almost always consists of a simple rounding, although slight beveling (e.g., Figure 74G) and slight thickening (Figure 74O) occur occasionally. Mouth diameter ranges from 12 to 52 cm (with a mean of 25.5 cm).

The Jar 1b variant is distinguished by a more upright profile with wall angles usually between 40° and 25°; the shape maintains a noticeable, if sometimes only slight, concavity (Figure 76A–T). Rims sometimes taper towards the lip. Lip treatment consists of a simple rounding. Beveling (e.g., Figure 76R) is uncommon. Mouth diameters range from 10 to 32 cm (with a mean of 18.2 cm).

The Jar 1c variant evinces a nearly upright neck with a distinctive concave profile (Figure 77A–L). Lip treatment consists almost exclusively of a simple rounding, although slight beveling (Figure 77I) and slight thickening (Figure 77C) occur occasionally. Mouth diameters range from 12 to 24 cm (with a mean of 18.4 cm).

The Jar 1d variant has a direct everted neck, with little concavity (Figure 77M–S). Lip treatment typically includes simple rounding, with some examples of slight beveling (Figure 77O, R). Mouth diameters range between 14 and 34 cm (with a mean of 23.1 cm). The Jar 1e variant is characterized by a tall, slightly everted neck that flanges near the lip (Figure 77T–Y). Lip treatment includes slight thickening (Figure 77U) and beveling (Figure 77Y), but a simple rounding is the most common technique. Mouth diameters range from 16 to 24 cm (with a mean of 20 cm).

*Jar 2.* Jar 2, a globular jar with a short, everted neck, is the next most frequent jar form in Warmi Ware B (13.0% of all restricted vessels, n=125). Compared to Jar 1, Jar 2 shows a much smaller size range, as a rule. The short neck facilitates access to the vessel contents, for example, in cooking.

There are four main variants, based mainly on rim profile. The most common variant is Jar 2a, distinguished by a short, everted neck (Figure 78A–S). Rims often are slightly concave and flaring (Figure 78C) or direct (Figure 78B), and can show tapering towards the lip (Figure 78E). Lip treatment usually involves a simple rounding, although slight beveling and thickening also occur occasionally. Mouth

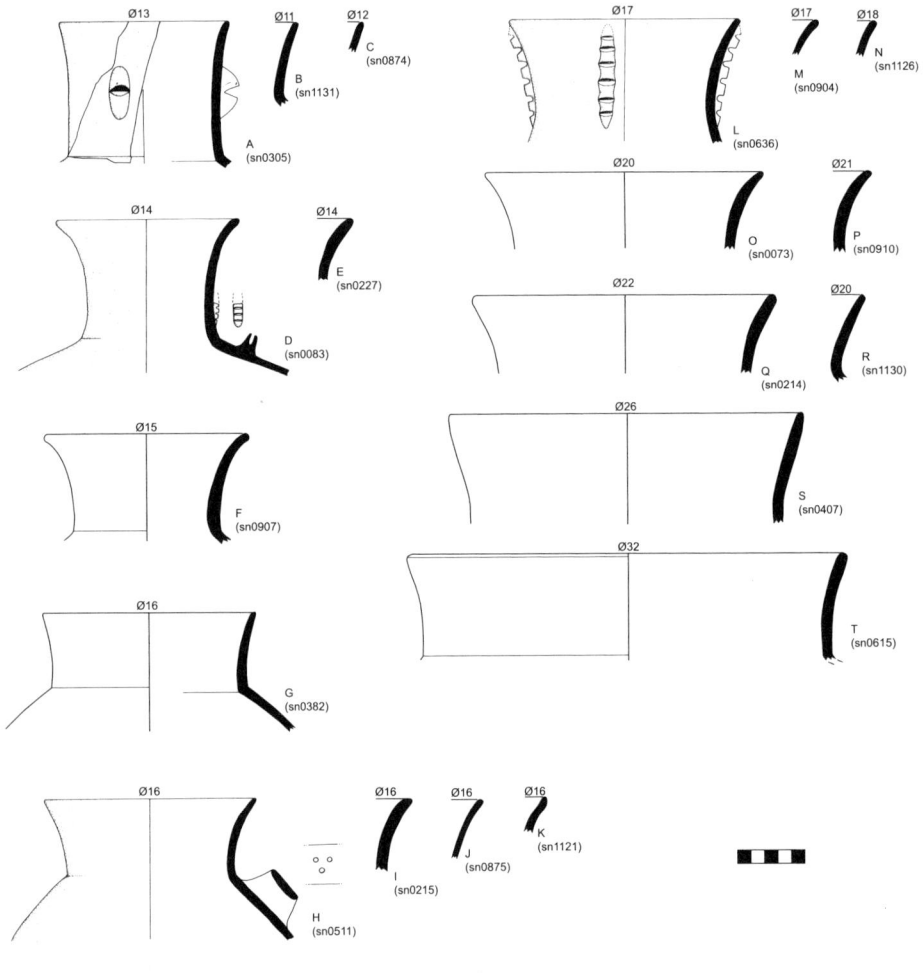

FIGURE 76. Warmi phase Ware B pottery: A–T, Jar 1b.

diameters measure 10 to 24 cm (with a mean of 16.7 cm).

The next most predominant variant is Jar 2b, which is characterized by an extremely flaring neck (Figure 78T–V). Tapering of the rim is very common (Figure 78U). Lip treatment consists typically of a slight beveling (Figure 78V), followed by rounding and thickening (Figure 78T). Mouth diameters range between 16 and 34 cm (with a mean of 22.5 cm).

The Jar 2c variant consists of a very short, concave neck profile. Examples almost always show a simple rounding of the lip, although slight beveling also occurs. Mouth diameters measure from 10 to 22 cm (with a mean of 17.2 cm). The Jar 2d shape is distinguished by a very short everted neck (Figure 79A–F). Lip treatment is commonly simple rounding, but there are several examples of lips with indented profiles (Figure 79C). Mouth diameters measure between 14 and 22 cm (with a mean of 18.7 cm).

*Jar 3.* The Jar 3 sample consists of 63 sherds, representing 6.5% of the restricted vessel sample in Warmi Ware B. Jar 3 is a globular jar with a nearly vertical or vertical neck. All fragments have wall angles that measure between 0° and 20°. The shape often shows a straight, direct rim, with little convex or concave curvature.

There are three variants, based on rim profile. The Jar 3a shape (Figure 79G–O) is distinguished by a steep, nearly vertical neck profile (wall angles usually between 0° and 10°). Some necks are longer than others (e.g., Figure 79G). Lip treatment consists almost always of a simple rounding. Mouth diameters range between 12 and 34 cm (with a mean of 18.7 cm).

The Jar 3b shape is distinguished by a slightly more everted neck profile (wall angles between 10° and 20°), but, like Jar 3a, has the straight direct rim (Figure 79P–V). Lip treatment is usually a simple rounding, but there are occasional examples of slight beveling. Mouth diameters measure 10 to 20 cm (with a mean of 16 cm). The Jar 3c variant shows a very short neck with a direct rim (Figure 80A–D). Lip treatment consists mainly of the simple rounding technique. Mouth diameters measure 12 to 20 cm (with a mean of 15.2 cm).

*Jar 4.* The Jar 4 shape is distinguished by a recurving of the neck profile (Figure 80E–H). There are two main types. The first is characterized by a recurving at the neck–shoulder juncture (Figure 80E, H). There are several examples from the chullpa tombs (Figure 83J, K). The other type recurves near the lip, where it is slightly convex; near the shoulder it is usually concave (Figure 80G). Lip treatment consists mainly of a simple rounding. Jar 4 recurved shapes are relatively rare, accounting for only 2.5% (n=24) of Ware B restricted vessels.

*Jar 5.* The Jar 5 shape is distinguished by an incurving neck profile (Figure 80I) and is rare in the Warmi Ware B sample. It occurs mostly as small pouring jars, with either upright convex necks (Figure 80I), slightly everted convex necks or inward-tapering necks (e.g., Figure 83L). Lip treatment is typically a simple rounding.

*Jar 6.* Jar 6 is a restricted necked jar form, probably a pitcher (Figure 80J). The shape occurs infrequently (n=4) and is typified by a straight, somewhat tapering neck with a simple rounded lip. The neck is connected to the shoulder with a strap handle, which would have facilitated pouring.

*Olla 1.* Olla 1 is a restricted globular vessel, with an inward-tapering neck (Figure 80L, M). There are only a few examples of this shape. The vessel is fairly large and was probably used for storage or cooking; mouth diameters measure between 19 and 22 cm. Lip treatment consists of a simple rounding, with some subtle beveling.

*Bottles.* Bottles are very rare in the Ware B sample. The available specimens have short, slightly outcurving spouts. The spout examples are fairly small, measuring only 4 to 4.5 cm in diameter (Figure 80K; see also Figure 83M, N).

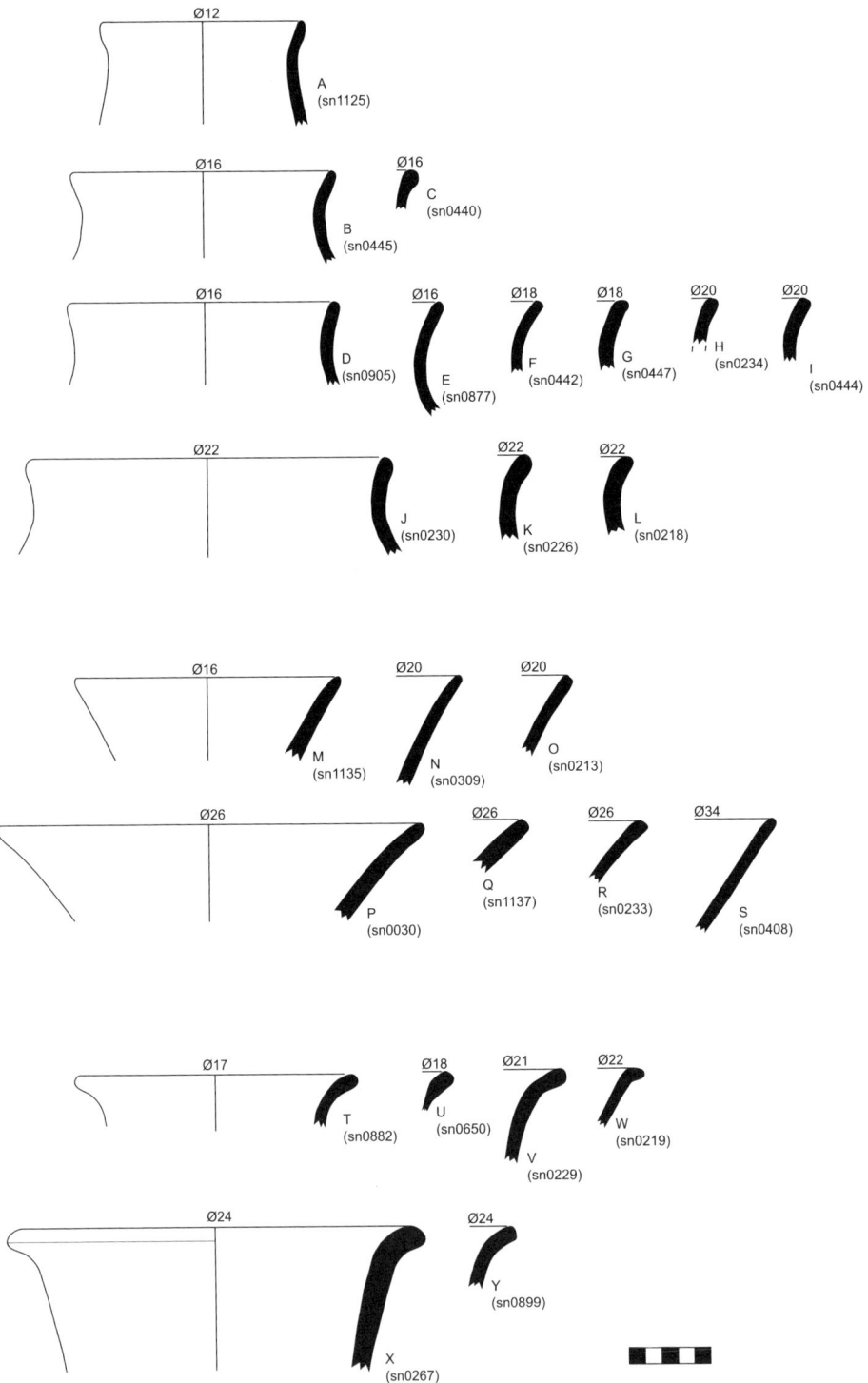

FIGURE 77. Warmi phase Ware B pottery: A–L, Jar 1c; M–S, Jar 1d; T–Y, Jar 1e.

Open shapes represent 46.4% (n=944) of Warmi Ware B formal sample. Of this total, most are rim fragments of bowls.

*Bowl 1*. Bowl 1 is the predominant open shape, accounting for 92.7% of the sample. Many open bowls may have had tripod supports or ring bases. Only a small percentage of rim sherds with evidence of tripod supports or ring bases were recorded: four and eight observations, respectively. Some bowls have ledge handles near the lip.

There are four Bowl 1 variants. The Bowl 1a shape is a simple open bowl, with roughly straight everted walls and a prominent basal angle (Figures 81A–G and 83O–W). Rims may taper towards the lip (Figure 81B). Lip treatment usually consists of a simple rounding; occasionally slight beveling is present (Figure 81E). Bowl 1a is especially frequent in the assemblage recovered from the chullpas. In these examples lips show more frequent beveling. Mouth diameters measure 9 to 22 cm (with a mean of 15.2 cm). Warmi Ware B Bowl 1a is directly comparable to Ware A Bowl 1a.

The Bowl 1b shape is a shallow open bowl, with a convex curving rim and no discernible basal angle (Figures 81H–L and 84A–G). Wall thickness varies greatly, between 0.4 and 1.0 cm. Lips are either given a simple rounded treatment or are beveled with slight thickening (Figure 84G). In some instances, the lips have an indented or notched profile (Figure 84E). Ledge handles are occasionally attached to the exterior rim just below the lip (Figure 81I, K). Ring bases may also be attached (Figure 84B). In the chullpa assemblages, there is a preference for beveled lip edges (Figure 84F). The Bowl 1b examples are typically very small; mouth diameters for the Bowl 1b variant measure between 7 and 24 cm (with a mean of 12.8 cm).

The Bowl 1c shape is similar to Bowl 1b, with convex walls and no basal angle; however, Bowl 1c has a deeper profile (Figure 84H–R). Lip treatment is typically a simple rounding, but beveling (Figure 84N) and thickening (Figure 84J) also occur. Bowl 1c can have ring bases (Figure 84R). Mouth diameters range from 7 to 20 cm (with a mean of 16.4 cm).

The Bowl 1d variant is an open bowl distinguished by a sharp upcurved or incurved profile near the lip (Figures 81M–N and 84S–Z). Lip treatment includes simple rounding, beveling (Figure 84T) and slight thickening (Figures 81M and 84W). Mouth diameters vary from 10 to 22 cm (with a mean of 15.4 cm). Like Bowl 1c, Bowl 1d examples come mainly from chullpa excavations.

*Bowl 2*. Bowl 2 is an incurving bowl form. The sample consists of 42 sherds, or 4.4% of the open shape sample. There are two variants based on wall angle and profile. The Bowl 2a shape shows incurving sides with wall angles between −15° and −30° (Figure 81O–T). The side walls are often thin (Figure 81O, Q), averaging 0.5 to 0.7 cm in width. Rims sometimes taper toward the lip. Ledge handles, affixed on the exterior just below the lip, are common additions to Bowl 2a examples. Lip treatment consists of a simple rounding. One nearly complete vessel had an oval mouth plan (Figure 81O). Hence, mouth "diameter" measurements should only be consid-

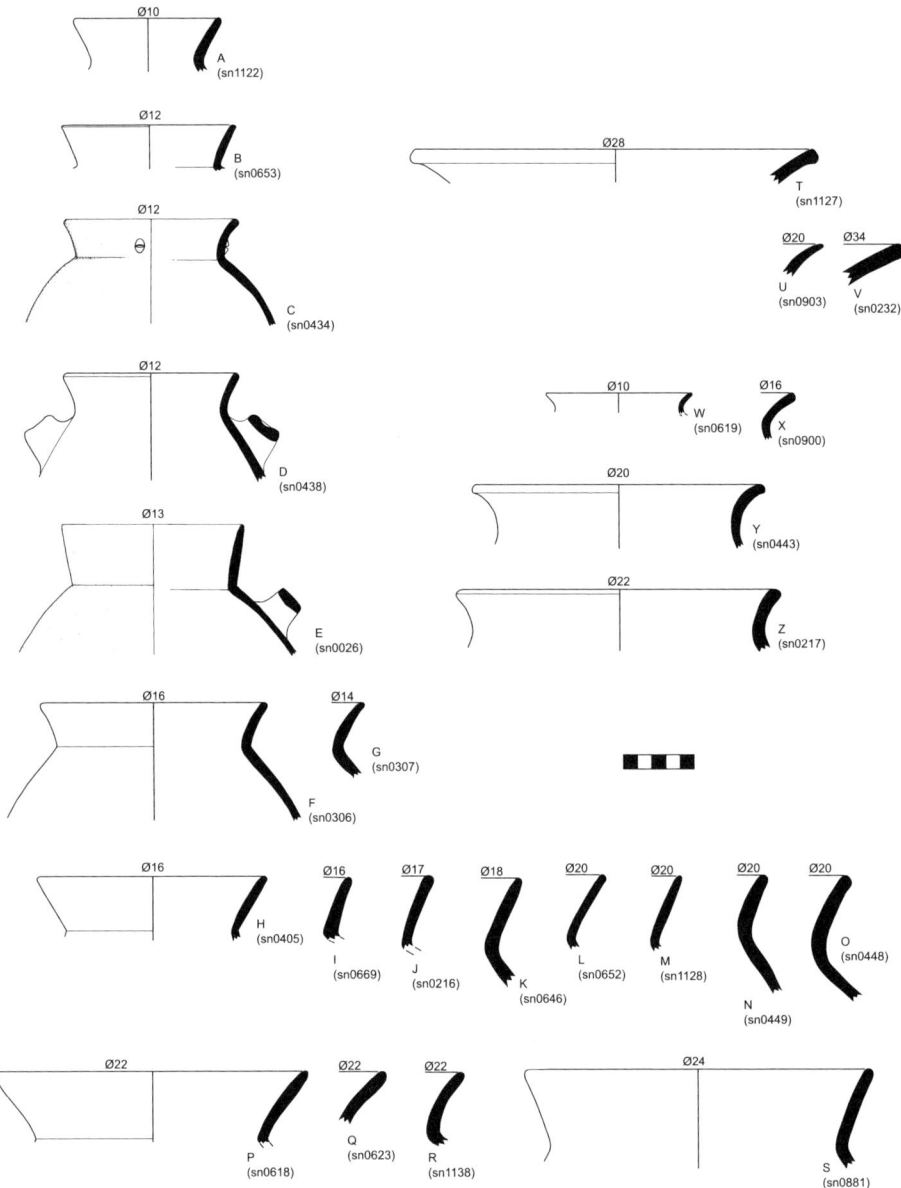

FIGURE 78. Warmi phase Ware B pottery: A–S, Jar 2a; T–V, Jar 2b; W–Z, Jar 2c.

ered general sizing. Bowl 2a mouth diameters range between 12 and 20 cm (with a mean of 15.7 cm). Most examples of this form show evidence of sooty, carbonized exteriors, suggesting that they were put over fires for cooking. Tripod supports and ledge handles facilitated such purposes. The Bowl 2a shape occurred only in Sector 1 pits, reiterating their general domestic function.

Bowl 2b is a rarer shape, with only a few examples (Figures 81U and 83X). The shape evinces a sharply incurving wall (wall angles between −40° and −50°). Lip treatment favors a simple tapering or rounding.

*Bowl 3.* Bowl 3 is a deep, vertical-sided bowl (Figure 81V, W), which could have been a large drinking vessel. The shape occurs in only a few examples. Lip treatment consists of simple rounding. Mouth diameter is 12 cm.

*Bowl 4.* Bowl 4 is an extremely shallow dish with a large hole perforated in the center of the base (Figure 81X). It is a rare shape, with only three examples and found only in Sector 1. They measure between 20 and 22 cm in mouth diameter. Hole diameter is 3.2 to 3.6 cm. The vessel has a slightly convex profile and a simple rounded lip treatment. This form was possibly a lid, funnel or sieve, or a turning plate for potters.

Colander fragments (n=38) account for only 1.9% of the total Ware B assemblage, a sharp decrease from the previous Chinchawasi 2 phase. Despite the decrease in frequency, however, there is considerable formal diversity represented in the Warmi Ware B colander sample. The underside of colanders frequently show evidence of soot, suggesting that they may have been used over fires. All colander fragments were found in Sector 1; there were none in the funerary zone (Sector 2).

*Colander 1.* Colander 1 forms can be called colander bowls. These are fairly small vessels, with variants using typical Ware B shapes. Each example has multiple, small to medium perforations that facilitate the draining of liquid from contents within the bowl.

There are four variants based on formal differences. Colander 1a is a simple open bowl sieve form with everted sides and a rounded lip (Figure 82A). Perforated holes are medium-sized (0.3 to 0.4 cm) and occur as high as 1 cm from the lip. Colander 1a is fairly small, with a mouth diameter of only 14 cm. Colander 1b is a colander bowl with straight or slightly convex sides. Holes can range from small (Figure 82C) to medium-sized (Figure 82D), and occur several centimeters below the lip. Mouth diameters range from 14 to 16 cm.

Colander 1c has flaring sides and is distinguished by a recurved profile (Figure 82E). Holes are typically small (below 0.3 cm) and occur consistently farther down on the bowl body, more than 4 cm from the lip. Mouth diameters range between 15 and 19 cm. Colander 1d is distinguished by an incurving profile (Figure 82B). Holes are medium-sized. Mouth diameter is 13 cm.

*Colander 2.* Colander 2 takes the form of a large colander platter seen earlier in Chinchawasi 2 Ware C. The holes are typically large and circular, but there is also an example with large quadrangular holes (Figure 82F). Lip treatment includes thick-

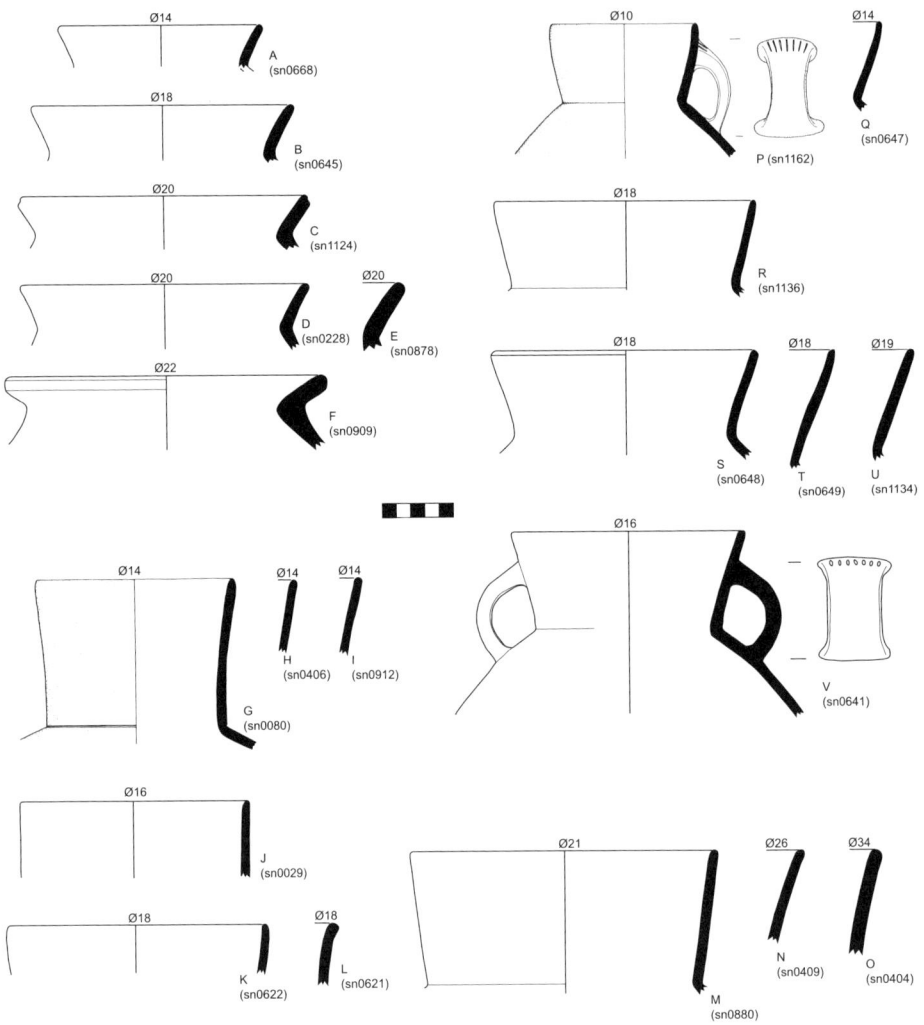

FIGURE 79. Warmi phase Ware B pottery: A–F, Jar 2d; G–O, Jar 3a; P–V, Jar 3b.

ening and rounding. Mouth diameters measure between 30 and 44 cm. Several examples were more oval than circular in plan view. Rim diameter measurements, therefore, should only be considered estimates.

Spoons, though present, are extremely rare in Warmi Ware B pottery, with only seven examples. There are several types of spoons represented in the sample.

*Spoon 1.* Spoon 1 has a circular or ovoid bowl and handle. Size differences indicate two Spoon 1 variants. The Spoon 1a variant has a round or ovoid bowl (Figure 82G) and a long handle. The spoon bowls measure about 3 or 4 cm across. Spoon 1b is essentially the same shape as Spoon 1a, but is far larger and so can be considered a ladle (Figure 82I). There are two examples from Warmi deposits. No example was found complete, but the bowl of these spoons could have measured 7 or 8 cm across.

*Spoon 2.* Spoon 2 has a circular bowl and a short flat or conical handle (Figure 82H, J). There is one example (Figure 82H) with multiple short incisions executed across the top surface of the spoon that resemble the incisions on the base of a Ware A cumbrous bowl (e.g., Figure 71F). One specimen (Figure 82J) could be a miniature.

Ware B pottery also includes miniatures of full size vessels. The sample shows variability in form as well as in craftsmanship. Several show better care in manufacture. Curiously, some miniatures feature forms absent in our entire diagnostic sample.

*Miniatures.* Miniature 1 is a common open bowl, with straight everted walls, a pronounced basal angle and beveled lips (Figure 101G, H, J). Mouth diameters range between 5 and 11 cm. Miniature 2a is a common tripod bowl form (Figure 101I). Mouth diameter measures about 7 cm. Miniature 2b is an olla or a deep globular bowl with tripod supports (Figure 101D). It is relatively small compared to the other miniatures, with a mouth diameter of 2.6 cm. This form in full size does not exist in our ceramic sample from Chinchawas.

Miniature 3a is a long-necked jar form with a pronounced neck convexity near the rim (Figure 101C). Mouth diameter is 1.4 cm. This form in full size is very rare in the Warmi phase. Miniature 3b is a short-necked jar with tapering sides (Figure 101A). The vessel is very small and has thin walls. Mouth diameter measures only 1 cm. This form in full size is not found in the Warmi phase repertoire of forms. Miniature 3d is a short-necked olla (Figure 101B). There are two perforated nubbins that probably represent strap handles. Mouth diameter measures 4 cm. This form occurs in full size during the Warmi phase. Miniature 4 is a double chambered spout and bridge vessel (Figure 101F). Only one chamber functions in the miniature (Figure 101F, right chamber); the other chamber is solid. Maximum dimension is 7.9 cm across the length of both chambers. This form in full size is not found in the entire Chinchawas assemblage (Kroeber 1925a, pl. 67f).

## Warmi Ware B Surface Treatment

Although a light red slip or wash can be present, most of Ware B pottery was left with its fired paste color. There is substantial variability in paste color, ranging from brown to bright orange and red. This seems to be the result of a combination of factors, including the position of the pot during firing, reheating when used in cooking, and other burning activities. Moreover, the great variation in surface color extends to sherds from the same vessel. In many cases oxidized surfaces have been blackened through cooking. Fire clouds are very common. Ware B surfaces were smoothed and, less commonly, burnished to dull matte finishes. They were not pol-

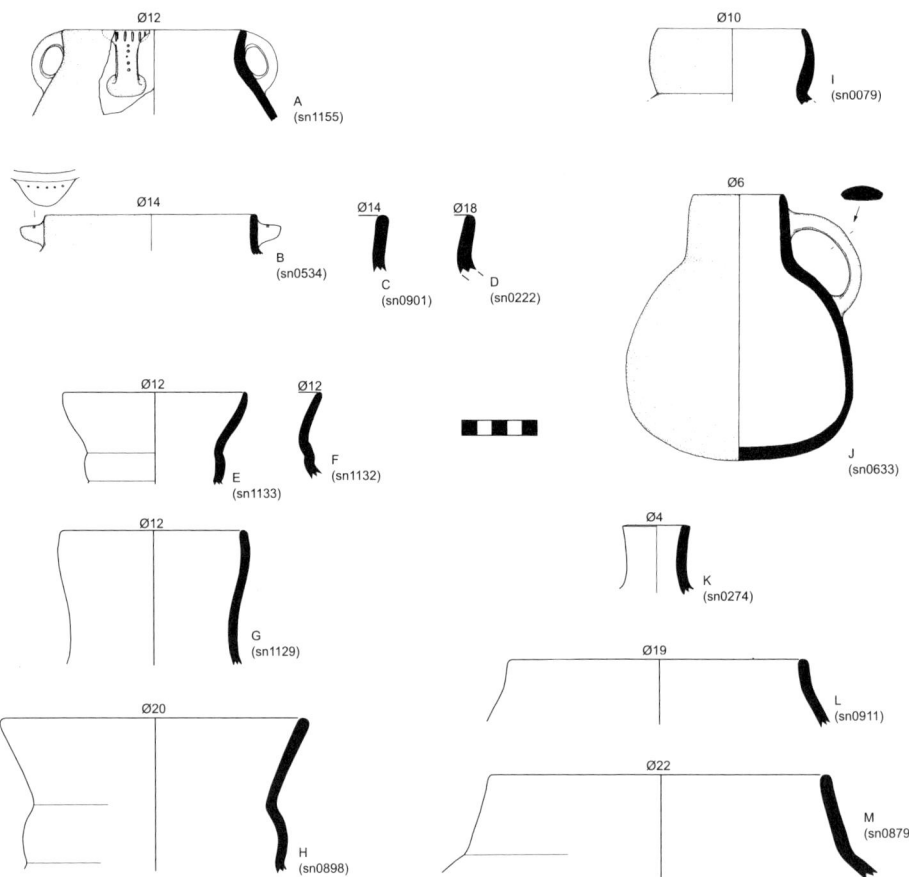

Figure 80. Warmi phase Ware B pottery : A–D, Jar 3c; E–H, Jar 4; I, Jar 5; J, Jar 6; K, Bottle 1; L, M, Olla 1.

ished to a high luster. Striations resulting from smoothing or burnishing are very common, especially on bowl exteriors.

Warmi Ware B Painted Decoration
Warmi Ware B pottery is characterized by a lack of painted decoration. In rare instances, there may be examples of white or black rim ticks on jar rims. There is no polychrome painting in Ware B pottery.

Warmi Ware B Plastic Decoration
Plastic decoration becomes more popular during the Warmi phase and is especially apparent in Ware B pottery, with 68 observations (about 6.5% of the total decorated sample in Warmi deposits). There is also a greater range of methods in how plastic decoration was applied. Plastic decoration is found mainly on jars, but instances on bowls and spoons also occur.

Punctations and incisions are the most common decorative elements, especially on jars. Strap handles or raised bands of jars were common media for the decoration. Strap handles are sometimes decorated with short, repeating incisions (Figures 79P and 80A) or long alignments of punctations (Figures 79V and 80A). Long incisions may be combined with aligned punctations to form decorative bands (Figure 82L). The neck and shoulder seam of jars may be delimited by a fine incised groove (Figure 79G). Appliqué strips or bands with punctated circles are sometimes attached to the shoulder–neck juncture of jar and bottle vessels (Figure 82N, O). Like strap handles, some ledge handles of bowls and spoon handles show aligned punctations (Figure 80B) or short repeating incisions (Figure 82H). Ledge handles of bowls may also be modeled (Figure 81I, K).

Many simple designs are repeated on strap handles, indicating that they may be maker's or potter's marks. There are 17 examples and 13 designs in the Warmi sample. The marks can be directly in the center of the handle, but also occur on either side of the handle, near the seams where the handle attaches to the vessel body. All the marks were made with techniques of shallow incision, dimpling or punctation, or some combination of these, to form simple abstract designs, often very cursory (Figure 103). They include simple crosses, irregular strokes and short alignments of punctations (Figure 103A, D, F–I, M–Q, S, U).

Nubbins and appliqué fillets are occasionally applied to Warmi Ware B pottery. Notched or ribbed fillets are attached vertically to jar necks (Figures 76D, L and 83K), but there are also horizontal examples on bowls (Figure 81K). In addition to their decorative accent, the ribbed fillets could have provided a grip or traction for securing rope to vessels for transport or hanging purposes. Notched or perforated, beak-like nubbins are also prevalent in the Warmi Ware B phase. These adorn jars and are located on the neck (Figures 76A, 78C, 82M and 83J) or on the shoulder (Figure 76D).

Modeling is also prevalent in the Ware B sample, which contains several examples of modeled animal adornos. These are affixed occasionally to the shoulders of jars. The only recognizable figure is a frog-like creature (Figure 74V), but there are several fragments representing lower leg elements of animals. There are also several facial representations located typically on the neck area of jars. Facial parts, such as mouths or noses, are usually rendered through appliqué, modeling and incision. They range from rather schematic (Figure 82K) to more realistic (Figure 82P) and whimsical (Figure 82Q) faces. There is one example of a press-molded face on a jar neck (Figure 82R), showing cheeks, a notched forehead and distinctive lines incised across the nostrils, perhaps indicating scars or tattoos.

Drilled perforations represent another type of plastic modification of vessels in Warmi Ware B. The few examples have small holes measuring less than 1 cm in diameter and occur on bowls near the rims (Figure 81L, N), perhaps as repair attempts.

## Discussion: Warmi Ware B

Ware B pottery can be characterized as the utilitarian line of pottery during the

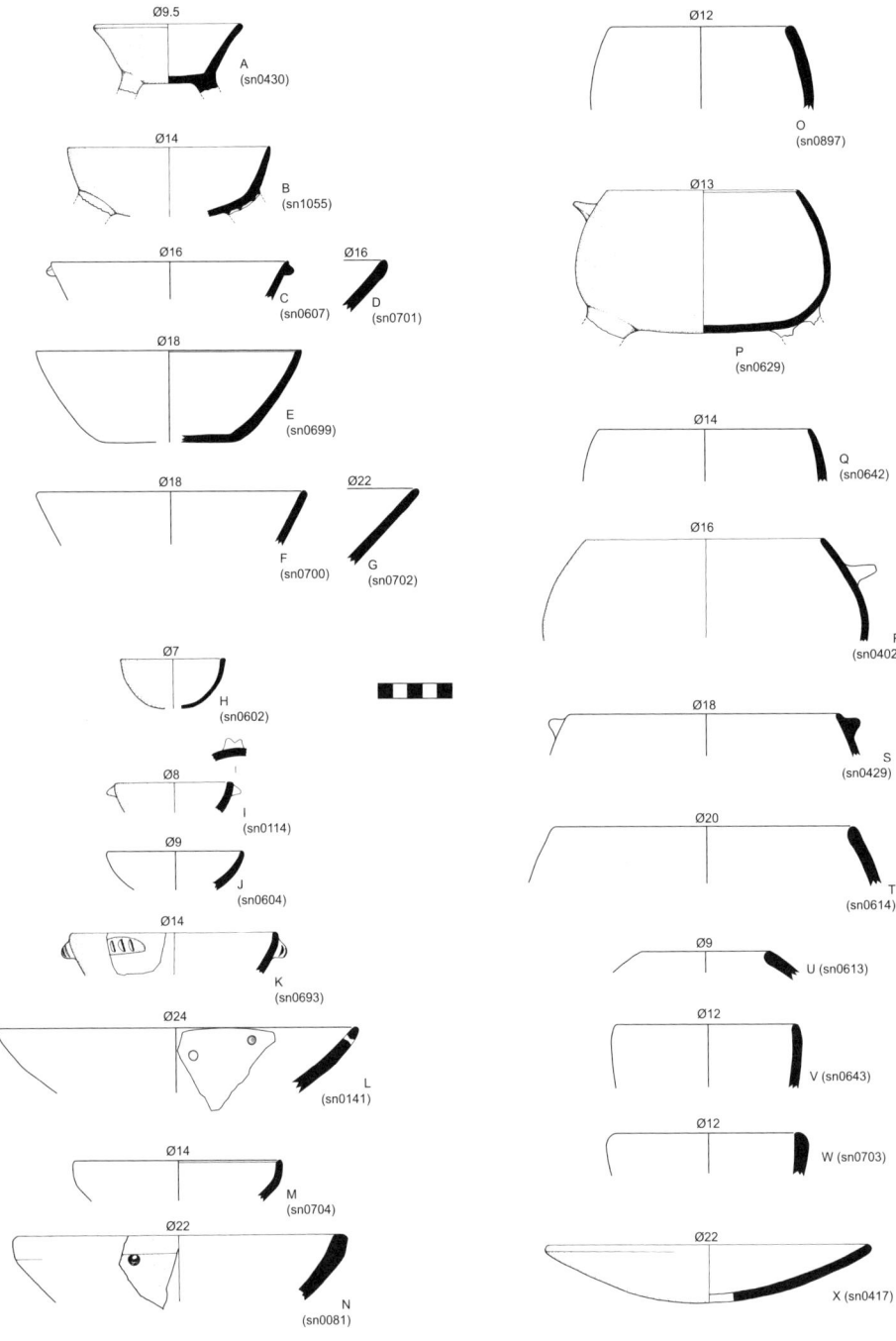

FIGURE 81. Warmi phase Ware B pottery: A–G, Bowl 1a; H–L, Bowl 1b; M, N, Bowl 1d; O–T, Bowl 2a; U, Bowl 2b; V, W, Bowl 3; X, Bowl 4.

Warmi phase. With the exception of some plastic decoration, Ware B shows very little decorative treatment and is represented by shapes used for quotidian purposes, especially for cooking food, storage and consumption. The paste is generally coarse and fragments often shows signs of being placed over fire. As in earlier phases, Warmi plainware pottery is dominated by bowls and necked jars.

Despite considerable continuity in vessel shapes, there are also important diachronic patterns that distinguish the Warmi plainware from the earlier plainware components. First is the increase in the representation of open shapes (mainly bowls, from 36.5% in Chinchawasi 2 to 46.4% in Warmi) and the corresponding decrease in restricted vessels (mainly jars, from 57.0% to 47.4%). There are several hypotheses that could account for this shift. The different percentages may indeed reflect the continuing trend starting in the Chinchawasi 1 phase of using and discarding more serving equipment (i.e., bowls). On the other hand, Warmi restricted vessels (i.e., jars) are generally fairly large, which could have obviated the need for more jars. Compared to Chinchawasi 2, the sample of Warmi plainware pottery shows less shape diversity (Figure 85).

Specific shapes have discernible patterns. First, large neckless ollas disappear. Colanders drop in popularity, from 3.6% to 1.9% of the phase assemblages. Large platter colanders especially diminish in frequency. Cups also decline, perhaps related to the boom in imported drinking goblets (see Chapter 8). Bulge-rim bowls also disappear. Shapes that increase in frequency are incurving bowls and very short-necked jars. Tall, direct-neck jars become more frequent, perhaps reflecting Wari-related influence on the use of the shape, especially for jar vessels with face-necks or polychrome pendants, or both (Bennett 1944, fig. 9; Isbell 1977).

There are also noticeable differences in rim treatment. The flanging of rims, especially at sharp angles, becomes less common. Wide flanging of vertical necks does not occur during the Warmi phase. In addition, beveling of lips, especially on bowls, becomes more prevalent. Indenting or notching of the lip, in profile, is introduced.

Nonshape diagnostics (handles, tripod supports and colanders) also show different frequency patterns. Ledge handles become much more common during the Warmi phase compared with Chinchawasi 2, from 2.0% to 5.1% of all handles. Loop handles and *kanchero* (corn popper) handles are no longer represented in the sample. There is also a greater percentage of tripod support fragments, especially conical ones, from 7.0% to 11.0% of all nonshape diagnostics. Meanwhile, the percentage of colander sherds (nonrims) drops slightly, from 26.3% to 22.0% of the Warmi nonshape diagnostics.

In general function, the two sectors of the site show notable differences in Ware B use. Ancient activities in Sector 1 resulted in the discard of open and restricted vessels in relatively equal frequencies (roughly 47% each). In contrast, the plainware pottery sample from the chullpas manifests a strong bias toward open shapes (72.3%), underscoring the importance of serving pottery in the funerary areas. Furthermore, the corpus of restricted shapes in the chullpa assemblages is represented mainly by unusual bottles and small decorated jars; colanders and large jars are rare.

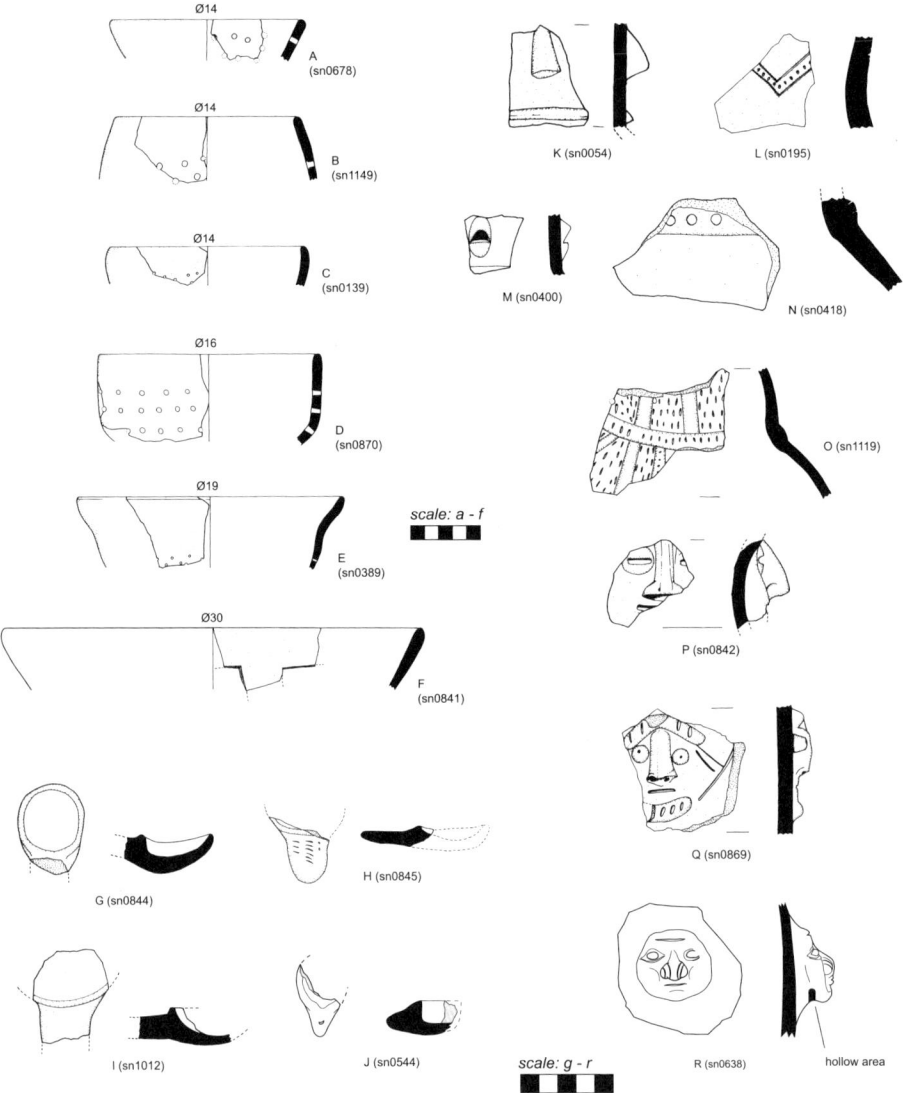

Figure 82. Warmi phase Ware B pottery: A–F, colanders; G–J, spoons; K–R, plastic decoration.

The sources and mechanisms of production and distribution of Warmi Ware B pottery are unclear. Our investigations did not encounter evidence of Warmi pottery production at the site, such as kilns; one waster was documented. The lack of appropriate clay sources and water at the site probably precluded intensive production at Chinchawas. However, the sheer quantity of plain utilitarian pottery at Chinchawas would indicate a nearby source, probably in the Callejón de Huaylas or in other parts of the upper Casma Valley.

The repertoire of Ware B vessel shapes has strong similarities to Middle Horizon period ceramics from North Highland sites (Bennett 1944; Isbell 1989; Ponte Rosalino 1999a). As an assemblage, the formal diversity of Ware B is best compared to pottery recovered by the Japanese investigations at La Pampa. In particular, Ware B necked-jar forms have analogues in the Caserones Orange type (Terada 1979, pl. 96, nos. 7–12, pl. 97, nos. 1, 9, 17, 18) and Tornapampa Brown type (Terada 1979, pl. 100, nos. 1–13), while Ware B bowls show strong similarities to the Tornapampa Brown (Terada 1979, pl. 100, nos. 14–16), Tornapampa Thin Brown (Terada 1979, pl. 99, nos. 24–30) and Tornapampa Thin Orange (Terada 1979, pl. 98, nos. 21, 25, 26) types. The Tornapampa and Caserones phases extend from the Early Intermediate Period to the early part of the Late Horizon (Terada 1979).

Ware B also has stylistic affinities to coastal cultures. Ware B shapes would not be out of place in many Middle Horizon plainware assemblages from the north coast (Strong and Evans 1952; Collier 1955; Donnan 1973; Wilson 1988, 1995). In addition, the example of a press-molded face (Figure 82R) at Chinchawas pertains more to ceramic traditions of the north coast. Shimada (1994:171–173, fig. 7.32) commonly finds similar jar necks in the urban sector of Pampa Grande and associates them with lower status residential groups.

A notable change in ceramic patterns is the increasing frequency of maker's marks (Figure 103; see Table 10). Although some examples were found in Chinchawasi 2 deposits, most of the sample pertains to the Warmi phase. In technique and design, the Warmi marks strongly resemble the maker's marks found on pottery from the north coast, specifically from Late Moche and Middle Horizon contexts (Donnan 1973, fig. 164–201; Wilson 1988, fig. 226, 236). The main difference, however, is that in the coastal examples the marks occurred predominantly on jar and olla necks, whereas all the specimens from Chinchawas are located on strap and ledge handles. Nevertheless, the increase in maker's marks could reflect a growing specialization of production or distribution, or both, of common plainware pottery during Warmi times. Both Chinchawasi 2 and Warmi phases share the single dimple design, suggesting possible continuity of production from one source.

Some observations should also be made about the use of miniature ceramic vessels at Chinchawas (Figure 101). All the miniatures are of a plain redware without painted decoration and pertain to Ware B. Of the 10 examples from the site, nine were recovered from Warmi contexts. And of these, all but one were from chullpa tombs. I surmise that these miniatures saw final use as small dedicatory offerings in funerary ceremonies during Warmi times. It is not clear, though, whether they were produced solely for this purpose (an interpretation supported by their limited spatial distribution) or whether they also circulated as toys, ornaments or something else. The other Warmi specimen was recovered from OP53, a room in a high-status residence. The use of miniatures is not uncommon at funerary sites in the Callejón de Huaylas and there are also cases from coastal mortuary and non-mortuary contexts (Bennett 1944; Donnan 1973:103; Paredes 2005).

In sum, Ware B is a plain redware that functioned largely as the utilitarian pottery for Warmi phase peoples at Chinchawas. Vessels for everyday use dominate

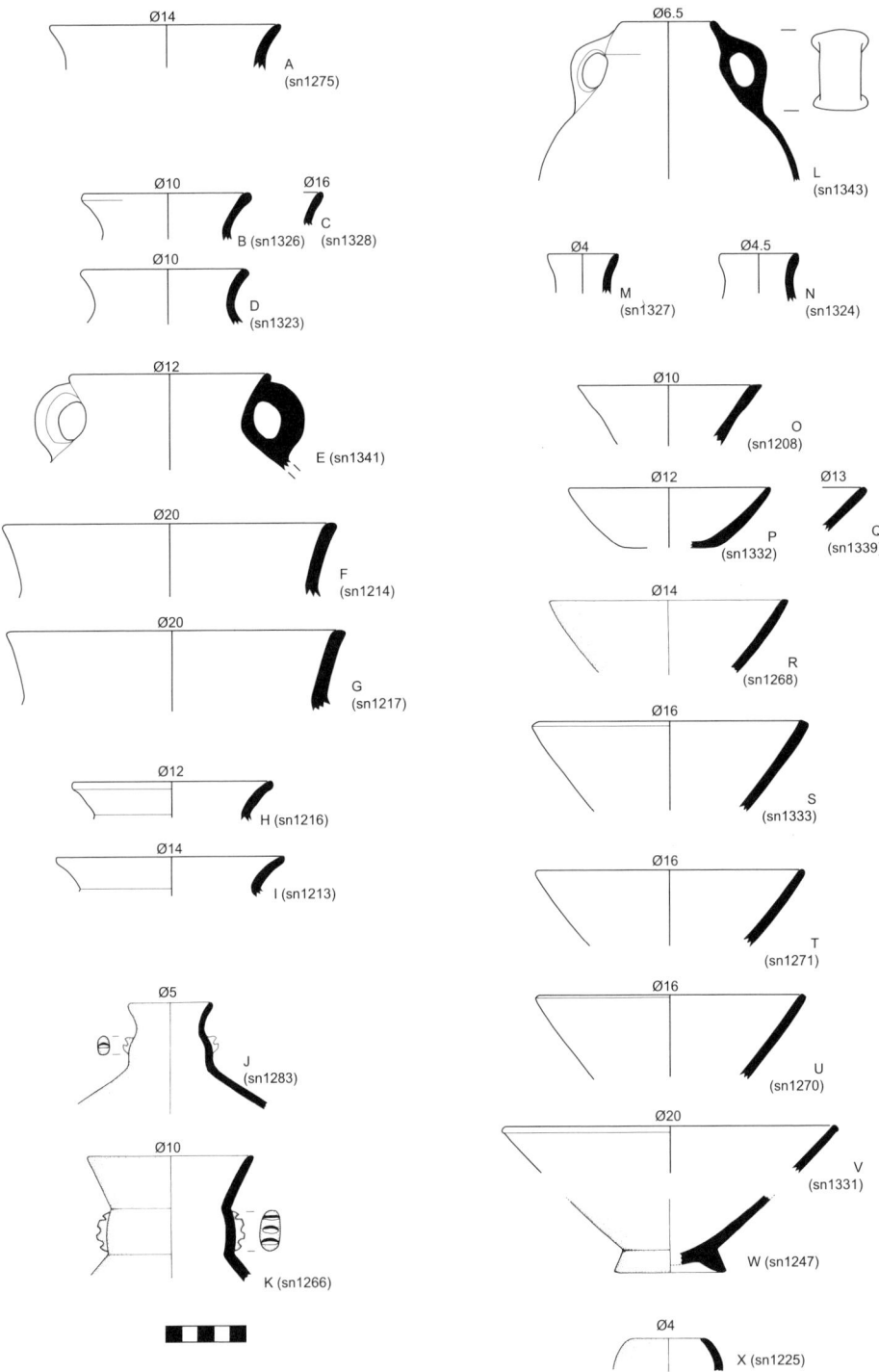

FIGURE 83. Warmi phase Ware B pottery from Sector 2 chullpas: A, Jar 1a; B–G, Jar 2a; H, I, Jar 2b; J, K, Jar 4; L, Jar 5; O–W, Bowl 1a; X, Bowl 2b.

the variety of shapes: storage jars, cooking jars, and open bowls. There are strong affinities to North Highland assemblages, but coastal influences are also present.

*Warmi Phase Absolute Dating*
Although similar pottery has been found before in the Callejón de Huaylas, Warmi phase pottery of the Callejón de Huaylas has never been systematically identified in the literature. Warmi contexts, moreover, have never been dated using the radiocarbon method. Three AMS radiocarbon assays of charcoal samples were performed (see Table 1). One from OP36, Level G, measured to 1170 ± 55 B.P. (A.D. 780 uncalibrated; 2-sigma calibrated range of A.D. 718 to 998). Another from OP43, Level I, measured to 1160 ± 45 B.P. (A.D. 790 uncalibrated; 2-sigma calibrated range of A.D. 778 to 991). The final radiocarbon assay, from OP20, Level F, yielded an age of 1150 ± 50 B.P. (A.D. 800 uncalibrated; 2-sigma calibrated range of A.D. 778 to 1006).

These measurements form a coherent set of calibrated dates (A.D. 886, 888 and 891), especially given that the carbon samples were taken from excavations in different parts of the site. The radiocarbon evidence mirrors the sharp distinction between Chinchawasi and Warmi assemblages and suggests that a rapid change in material culture occurred at the end of the 9th century A.D. On the basis of ages for the Chinchawasi 2 phase and associations with local and imported pottery, I estimate that the Warmi phase was popular by the mid-9th century A.D. and lasted only about a century.

## Chakwas Phase Ceramics

The Chakwas phase is the final major pottery style in the Chinchawas chronology. Chakwas pottery was found in certain parts of the site, particularly in the uppermost levels of the excavations. Because many of these deposits have been disturbed, we can only discuss components of the ceramic style in general terms, without much association to architectural or stratigraphic context.

Apart from its general placement after the Warmi phase, there is little good evidence to firmly situate the Chakwas phase in an absolute chronology. However, because the Chakwas style does not resemble Inka pottery, and because of stylistic relationships to pre-Inka potteries of the Callejón de Huaylas, it seems that the Chakwas phase represents a Late Intermediate Period occupation of Chinchawas.

*Characteristics of Chakwas Phase Ceramics*
The Chakwas phase consists of 180 decorated and plainware sherds. The small size of the sample and lack of good contextual information preclude a precise understanding of the Chakwas occupation at Chinchawas. Nevertheless, Chakwas cultural characteristics can be outlined.

CHAKWAS PASTE
Chakwas phase pottery is characterized by an oxidized redware that is typically

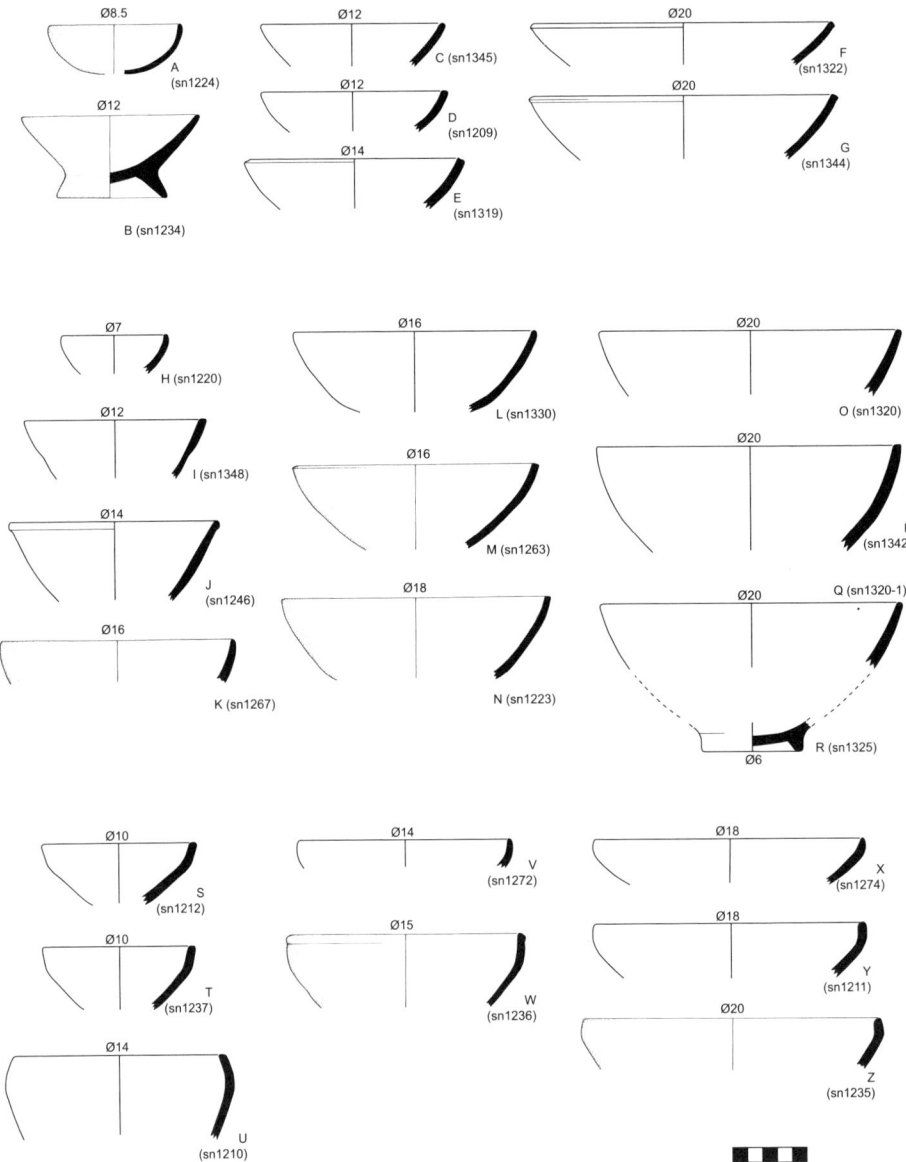

FIGURE 84. Warmi phase Ware B pottery from Sector 2 chullpas: A–G, Bowl 1b; H–R, Bowl 1c; S–Z, Bowl 1d.

coarse. Like all local plainware pottery throughout the Chinchawas sequence, Chakwas ware has fine to large inclusions of mica and angular grit. The size and sorting of these inclusions largely depended on the size and function of the vessel.

CHAKWAS VESSEL SHAPES
In contrast to the previous Warmi phase, in which there were equal percentages of

open and closed vessels, the Chakwas phase is distinguished by more open vessels (43.2%) than closed vessels (34.4%).

*Bowl 1.* Open shapes consist of 54 sherds, all from bowl forms. The most common shape is Bowl 1, a simple convex-sided open bowl with no discernible basal angle. There are two variants based on wall angle and profile. Bowl 1a is a shallow globular bowl with a slightly convex profile (Figure 86A–F). Wall angles typically measure between 30° and 50°. Lip treatment consists of simple rounding, notching (in profile) (Figure 86F) and slight beveling, especially on the interior lip (Figure 86D, E). Mouth diameters range from 8 to 22 cm (with a mean of 13.3 cm). These bowls can have rim adornos or ledge handles, or both.

The Bowl 1b variant has a deeper profile, with wall angles usually between 30° and 20° (Figure 86G–L). Lip treatment consists most commonly of beveling (e.g., Figure 86J), especially on the interior edge, followed by simple rounding (Figure 86G). In general, Bowl 1b examples are larger, with mouth diameters between 14 and 20 cm (with a mean of 16.1 cm). Rim adornos can be present. One complete example has a ring base (Figure 86L).

*Bowl 2.* Bowl 2 is an open bowl distinguished by direct-everted walls and a discernible basal angle (Figure 86M–Q). There are two variants based on rim stance and profile. The more common variant (Bowl 2a) shows direct-everted walls, with a wall angle between 35° and 50° (Figure 86M–P). Lip treatment is a simple pinching and rounding, or beveling, especially on the top edge (e.g., Figure 86M, O). Mouth diameters range between 10 and 22 cm. The rarer variant is Bowl 2b, a shallow version of Bowl 2a (Figure 86Q). Wall angle measures approximately 30°. The top edge of the lip is beveled flat. Mouth diameter is 20 cm.

*Bowl 3.* Bowl 3 is a slightly incurving bowl (Figure 86R–S). Toward the lip, the rim angles inwards, as in Warmi Ware B, Bowl 1d. Lip treatment consists of a simple rounding. Mouth diameters measure approximately 16 cm.

Restricted vessels account for 34.4% of the formal diagnostics. Nearly all are from jars. There are four main jar categories.

*Jar 1.* Jar 1 is short-necked jar with a globular body. There are two variants based on rim stance and profile. The Jar 1a variant has a short and direct-everted rim (Figure 87A–E). Rims taper toward the lip; lip treatment consists of a simple rounding. Vertical strap handles attach from the neck to shoulder (Figure 87E). Mouth diameters range from 4.5 to 20 cm. The Jar 1b variant has a short and flaring everted rim (Figure 87F–I). Lip treatment consists of rounding, but beveling (Figure 87F) and slight thickening (Figure 87H) also occur. Mouth diameter ranges from 6 to 24 cm.

*Jar 2.* The Jar 2 shape is a regular-necked jar with a globular body (Figure 87J–R).

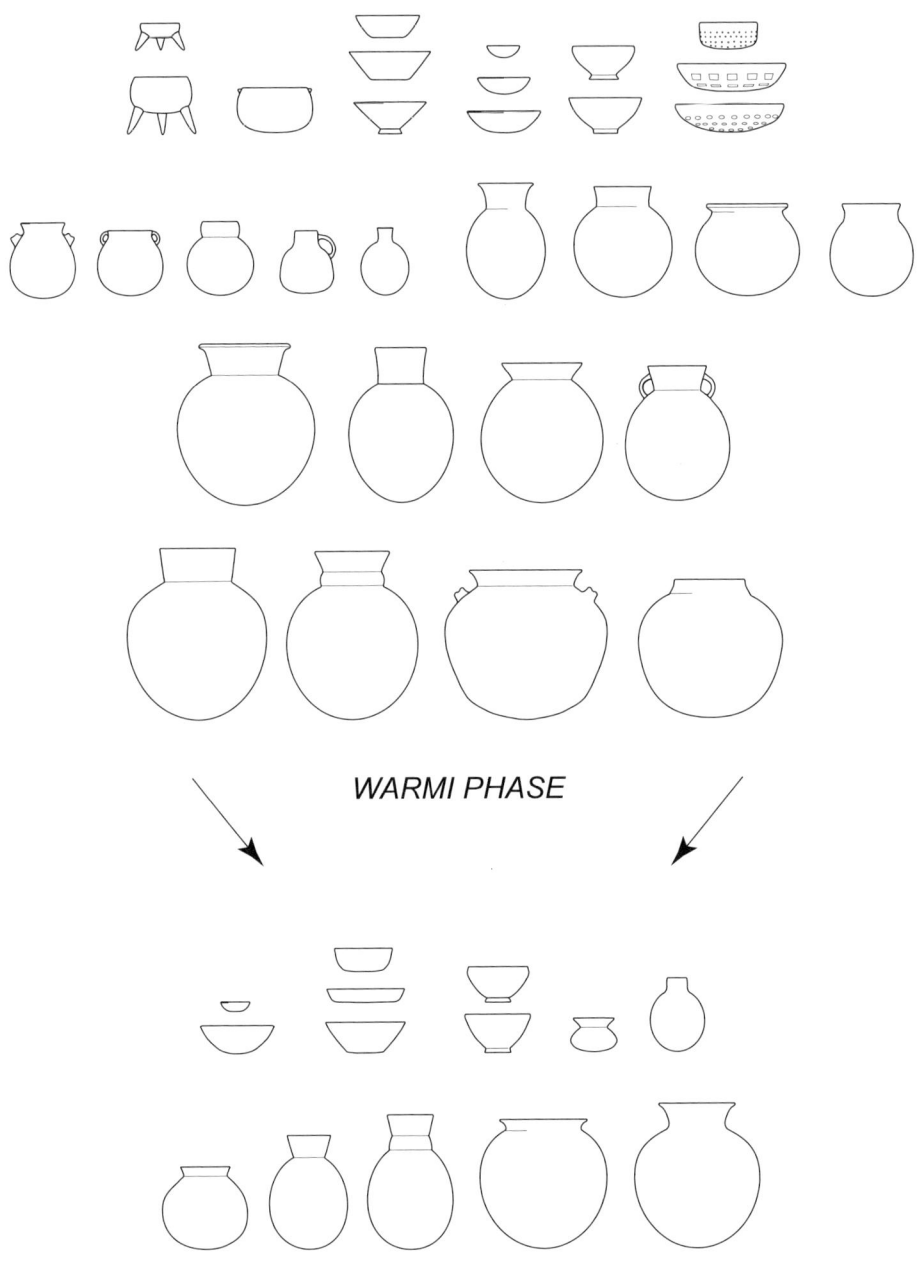

FIGURE 85. Reconstruction of shapes represented in Warmi and Chakwas phases.

There are two variants based on rim profile. The Jar 2a variant has a flaring and concave-everted neck (Figure 87J–O). Lip treatment consists of a simple rounding, although beveling and slight thickening (Figure 87O) also occur. Examples have mouth diameters of 11 to 30 cm. The Jar 2b shape shows a direct-everted rim (Figure 87P–R). Lip treatment includes a simple rounding. Mouth diameters measure 12 to 14 cm.

*Jar 3.* Jar 3 is a restricted jar form, with a recurved neck profile (Figure 88A–D). In all cases, the recurving occurs at the neck–shoulder juncture. Rims are sometimes more everted (Figure 88B) or more vertical (Figure 88C). Lip treatment features simple rounding or slight beveling. Examples have mouth diameters between 8 and 13 cm. There is a large-sized example, in which a rim diameter estimate was not possible (Figure 88D).

*Bottle 1.* The Chakwas bottle sample has only two sherds. Both are spout sherds, measuring 5 cm in mouth diameter, and are from vertical necked bottles. One example has a simple direct rim, with rounded lips (Figure 88E). The other shows a slight recurved profile (Figure 88F); the rim tapers towards the lip, which is also rounded.

### CHAKWAS SURFACE TREATMENT

A light red slip or wash is occasionally applied, but most Chakwas pottery is the color of its fired paste, which ranges from a light brown to bright orange and red. Like Warmi Ware B, the variability in paste color probably results from several factors, including firing, use and position of the sherd on the vessel. In many cases, oxidized surfaces have been blackened through cooking. Fire clouds are very common. Chakwas pottery surfaces include smoothing and, less commonly, burnishing to dull matte finishes. Striations resulting from smoothing are very common. There is no polishing.

### CHAKWAS PAINTED DECORATION

Chakwas phase ware is characterized by a lack of painted decoration. However, in one example, there is an interior-painted nested rectangles motif in black (Figure 86D). Another example, a jar neck, has red exterior bands (Figure 87R).

### CHAKWAS PLASTIC DECORATION

Chakwas phase ware is distinguished mainly by its plastic decoration. Plastic decoration modes can be both functional and purely decorative. Strap and ledge handles are common add-ons to Chakwas vessels. Punctation and incision are the most common techniques. Size variations in the punctations range from small dots to larger circles. They occur commonly in large fields of multiple punctations, but were also used more sparingly (e.g., Figure 86E, J). Incised grooves can be shallow and thin to deep and broad. Incised designs include simple lines, meanders (Figure 88M) and lattices (Figure 87C).

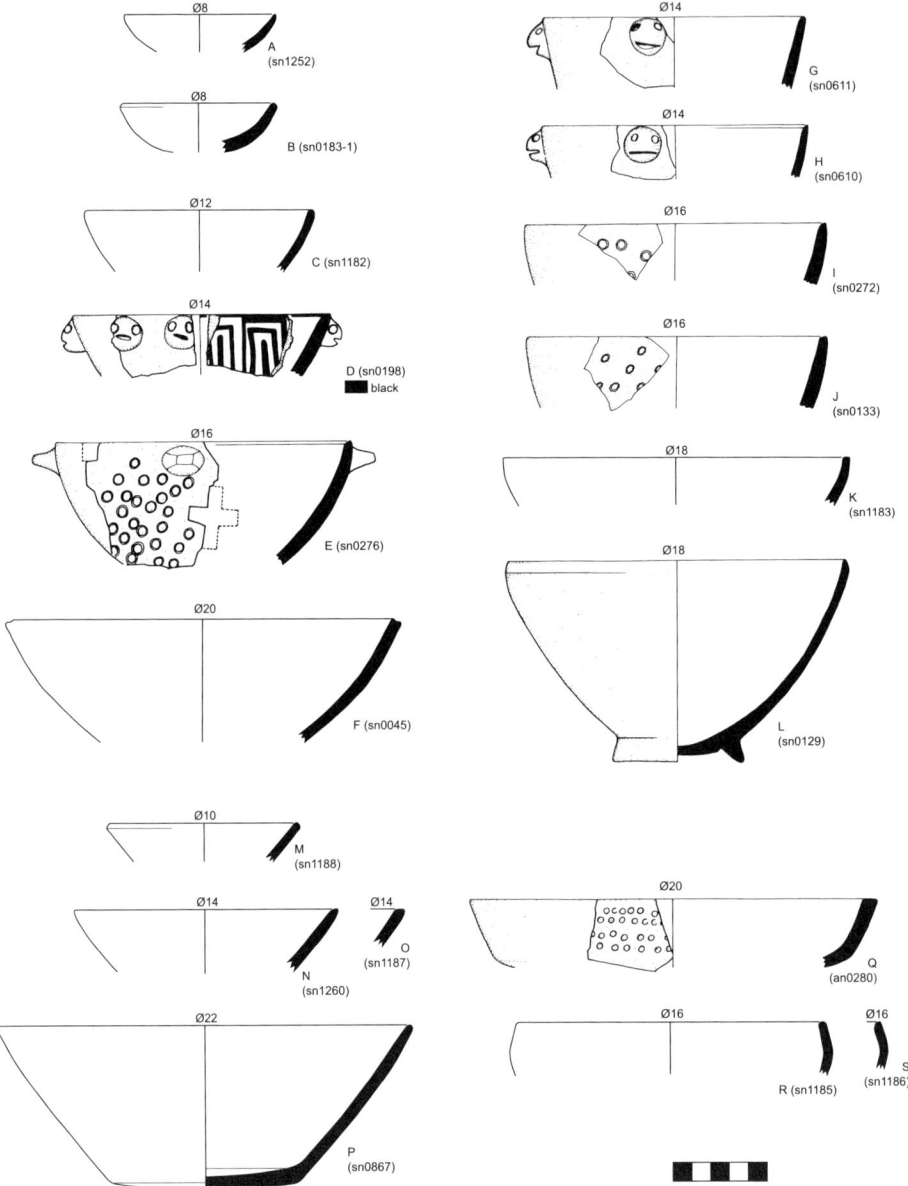

FIGURE 86. Chakwas phase pottery: A–F, Bowl 1a; G–L, Bowl 1b; M–P, Bowl 2a; Q, Bowl 2b; R, S, Bowl 3.

The application of punctations and incisions is often very liberal and casual. They occur typically on strap handles of jars (Figure 87E), jar necks (Figure 87J) or the exterior sides of open bowls (Figure 86E, J, Q). Punctations and incisions occur independently, but often they are combined to achieve lattice and punctate row patterns (Figure 88G–L) and zoned punctate fields (Figure 87E, J). A simple incised cross on one fragment (Figure 87O; see also Figure 103A) may be a potter's mark. As in the Chinchawas example, jar necks were common areas to place simple maker's marks, such as crosses, in coastal Moche pottery (Donnan 1973). There are no other similar marks on the Chakwas phase sample.

Chakwas pottery is also distinguished by the addition of simple appliqué nubbins, adornos and fillets. Nubbins are often placed on jar shoulders and necks, and are usually punctated (Figures 87D and 88D). There are several examples of convex bowls with repeating face nubbins on the exterior rim just below the lip (Figure 86D, G, H). Each face nubbin has two punctate circles for eyes and a short incision for a mouth; based on small differences in these features, the examples have some variability in expression. Ribbed appliqué fillets are typically lozenge-shaped and oriented vertically on the necks of jars (Figures 87O, R and 88A). There are also examples of small neck adornos, often notched and punctated to resemble a beak or mouth (Figure 87Q).

Plastic modification also includes selective removal of clay. On one bowl fragment sections of the clay were cut out before firing to produce rim notching and a cross shape (Figure 86E). Drilled perforations are also present in Chakwas pottery (Figure 88A). They were perhaps used to hang vessels, for repair, or for some sieving function.

Discussion: Chakwas Phase

The Chakwas style of pottery is substantially different from the previous Warmi style at Chinchawas. The near-exclusive preference for plastic decoration in lieu of painted decoration is a strong break from Warmi conventions. Many of the distinctive Warmi attributes are no longer present. The pottery, in general, lacks the quality and diversity characteristic of the Warmi style.

In addition, there is a trend towards smaller shapes (Figure 85). Small jars (those with diameters less than 15 cm), for example, represent 45.2% of all jars, followed by those that are regular size (16 to 26 cm, 42.9%) and oversize (greater than 27 cm, 9.5%). Small, shallow bowls are also common and make up 33.3% of the total bowl assemblage.

Despite the stylistic gulf between Warmi and Chakwas pottery, there are some interesting continuities. First, there are strong formal similarities in jar and bowl shapes, as there is throughout the Chinchawas sequence. For example, Bowl 1a and Bowl 2a could be holdovers from Warmi Ware B conventions. In addition, the recurved profiles of jars seem to have been derived from Warmi antecedents. Whereas Warmi examples are associated with face–neck or human effigy depictions, Chakwas recurved-neck jars are plain; perhaps the recurved shape alludes to the prior face–neck tradition. The use of punctation is also a shared trait, but the technique is performed on different parts of the vessel in the two styles. Finally, ribbed fillets on jar necks or upper shoulders are another shared decorative technique.

At Chinchawas, Chakwas-type plastic decoration had been established as early as the Chinchawasi 1 phase, but was comparatively rare. For example, incisions and

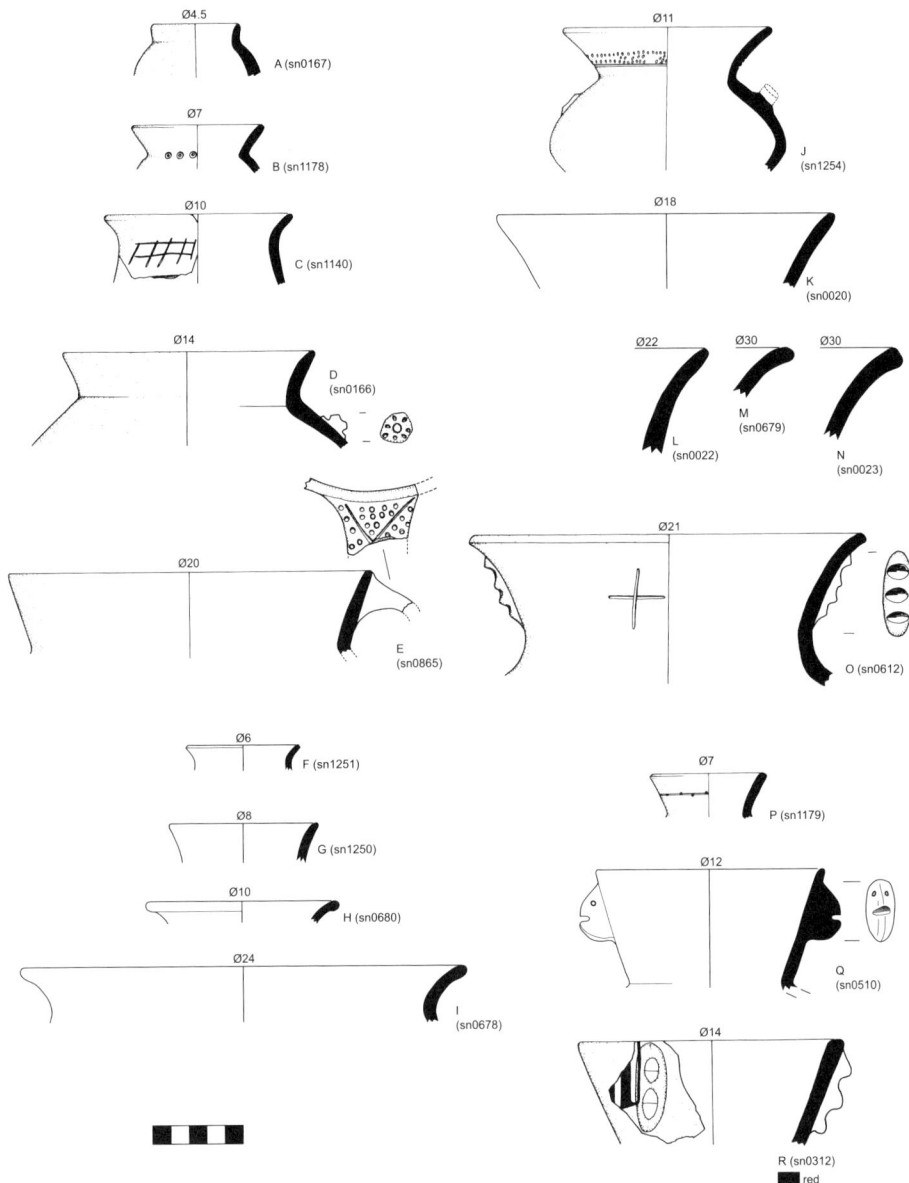

FIGURE 87. Chakwas phase pottery: A–E, Jar 1a; F–I, Jar 1b; J–O, Jar 2a; P–R, Jar 2b.

punctation were used as accents on modeled animal adornos (e.g., felines), face representations, nubbins and appliqué strips in the earlier phases, especially Warmi. During the Chakwas phase, techniques of plastic decoration are more intensively used, perhaps an intentional rejection of the previous Wari cultural associations. As noted, the dark-on-plain (Ware A) pottery of the Warmi phase has stylistic counterparts in many parts of the Central Andes and is associated with Wari period socioeconomic interaction. The decline of Wari stylistic elements in favor of more local traditions suggests that Wari influence at Chinchawas weakened. No longer interested in Warmi stylistic ties, Chakwas peoples withdrew from this sphere of interaction sometime after A.D. 900.

The Chakwas style strongly resembles the late, pre-Inka pottery that occurs in many parts of the North Highlands. In the Callejón de Huaylas, the ceramics are known as the Aquilpo style. Gary Vescelius and Hernan Amat coined the style designation, named after the Quebrada Aquilpo (Cordillera Blanca), during their archaeological research in the Callejón de Huaylas, especially in the region near the towns of Marcará and Carhuaz (Buse 1965; Lanning 1965; Bonavia 1966). Like Chakwas pottery, Aquilpo wares consist of plain redwares, emphasize plastic decoration on exteriors of small jars and bowls, and lack painted or slip decoration. Punctate circles and incised grooves are the most common decorative techniques. Besides the work by Vescelius and Amat, Chakwas-like pottery has been found throughout the Callejón de Huaylas. At sites of the Pierina region, Ponte Rosalino (1999a) recovered Chakwas-like pottery through surface survey and excavations, at sites such as Maquellouán (Ponte Rosalino 1999a, lám. 2, 34, 36), Ancosh Punta (Ponte Rosalino 1999a, lám. 9, 15), Carhuac Punta (Ponte Rosalino 1999a, lám. 19, 21) and Marenayoc (Ponte Rosalino 1999a, lám. 50). Specific stylistic affinities include incised and punctate dots and circles on jar necks of the Ancosh style, as well as punctate circles on bowl exteriors (Ponte Rosalino 1999a, foto 13, 24). Lane (2006) identified Aquilpo-related pottery in the upper reaches of the Nepeña valley. Zaki (1987, Abb. 9) reported pottery from sites in the Santa Cruz area, near Caraz; some jar neck fragments show punctate circles common on Aquilpo pottery. Aquilpo material has also been reported at Honcopampa (Isbell 1988a:14–15, 1991a:34), but the pottery from the site has yet to be fully published. Aquilpo style pottery can be found in the Museo Arqueológico de Ancash (in Huaraz) as well as in the Museo Histórico in Ranrahirca.

Across the Cordillera Blanca to the southeast, at the sites of Pójoc and Waman Wain in the upper Mosna drainage, Burger (1982) identified a late prehistoric pottery referred to as the Pójoc style. Like coeval styles of the North Highlands, Pójoc ceramics constituted a rustic style distinguished principally on the basis of plastic decoration (see also Ibarra 2003b, fig. 39). Incisions and punctate dots and circles adorn jar necks and appliqué strips; recurving of jar necks is another shared feature (Burger 1982, figs. 9–15, 22–25, 50–59). In contrast to Chakwas pottery, punctation in Pójoc pottery sometimes includes smaller circles offset within larger circles.

Other archaeological investigations in the North Highlands have recovered comparable plainwares that emphasize plastic decoration. At sites in the La Pampa region, Terada (1979, pl. 95, no. 6, pl. 97, no. 2, 7) encountered a series of jars with ribbed fillets and punctate circles, in addition to a bowl with face nubbins belonging to the Caserones period. Farther north, in the highland areas around Huamachuco and the Alto Chicama zone, research has encountered Late Intermediate Period wares that rely on punctation and notching on jar necks and shoulders and on ap-

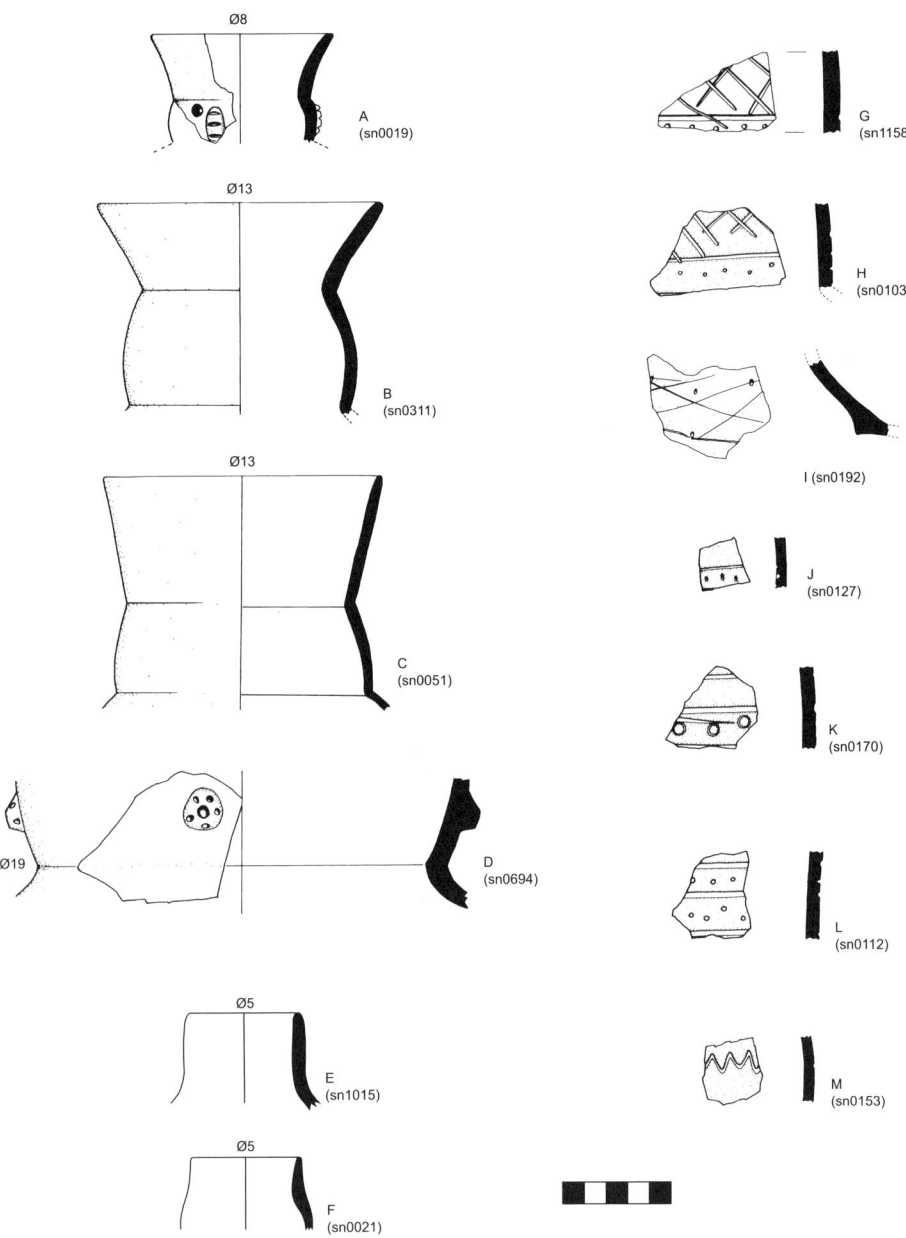

FIGURE 88. Chakwas phase pottery: A–D, Jar 3; E, F, Bottle 1; G–M, plastic decoration.

pliqué strips ("Late Huamachuco," McCown 1945, fig. 14; "Toro phase," Thatcher 1972, fig. 58; Krzanowski 1977, figs. 14, 17, 1986a). Krzanowski (1986a:250–253) agrees on the general ceramic characterization, but argues that plastic techniques used in "Huamachuco Impressed" pottery were probably in circulation by the Middle Horizon as a component of the Yuraccama tradition—a cultural tradition in the

Alto Chicama zone that became prominent only after the Middle Horizon (see also Krzanowski and Pawlikowski 1980). Krzanowski's hypothesis is consistent with the periodization of occasional finds of punctated ceramics in the pre-Chakwas phases at Chinchawas (Zaki 1978b, figs. 21–25).

To the south of the Callejón de Huaylas, in the highlands of the Huaura drainage, investigations at the site of Andamarca and other sites in the Cayash archaeological zone recovered pottery decorated with punctate circles and punctate dots (Krzanowski and Tunia 1986, figs. 13–21). The decoration, typical of the Quillahuaca type of the Cayash phase, occurred almost exclusively on jar exteriors, especially along thickened lips. In all these cases the pottery derives from pre-Inka contexts of the Late Intermediate Period.

There are also related materials from the coast, especially in the lower Casma Valley. In upper levels of excavations at sites like Cerro Sechín, Tello (1956) identified an "Estilo Casma" that is characterized by plastic decoration, including circular punctations, ribbed nubbins and incision, especially on plainware necked jars with strap handles. Kroeber (1944:51) termed the ceramics "Sechín pottery." On the basis of surface surveys, Thompson (1962:416) modified the designation to "Casma Incised" and called attention to possible highland sources for the style. More recent surveys have encountered related variants in Santa (see Late Tanguche and Early Tambo Real assemblages in Wilson 1988, figs. 259–261, 266, 272) as well as in Nepeña (Proulx 1973, pl. 15). The frequency and density of sites indicate that lower Casma was intensively occupied at this time. Based on the strong stylistic similarity, Wilson (1995:203–206) postulates that during the heyday of the Casma Incised style, the late Middle Horizon, the three valleys may have been sociopolitically integrated.

The ubiquity of plastic-decorated redwares throughout the northern highlands and parts of the coast has important sociocultural implications, but has drawn relatively little attention. The artistic and technological achievements of the Early Intermediate Period and Middle Horizon in the North Highlands, especially in pottery and architecture, by and large eclipse later material cultures. Material cultures of the Late Intermediate Period are usually characterized as simple and derivative. Unfortunately, these terms have also been taken to describe the complexity of contemporary social and political arrangements. Archaeological details about the political landscape during the late Middle Horizon and subsequent Late Intermediate Period are little known, but ethnohistorical accounts relate that Inka expansion encountered large chiefdoms and independent cultural groups associated by region, such as the Huaylas and Pincos nations (Rowe 1946; Ibarra 2003b; Herrera 2005). Although far from complete, the ceramic evidence could reflect more cultural interaction or lack of pottery distinctions between regional groups than previously assumed for late Middle Horizon and the subsequent Late Intermediate Period.

Directly pertinent or fully reported radiocarbon measurements are currently unavailable. Vescelius analyzed a series of radiocarbon dates from the Marcará area

(Ravines 1982b:179–180; Ziółkowski et al. 1994:320–321), but their exact contexts and associations have never been reported. Several additional dates, with Late Intermediate Period ages, have been produced for the Pierina mining impact studies (Ponte Rosalino 1999a:106; Lau 2004a:195).

In summary, the chronological placement of Chakwas and Chakwas contemporary pottery is based on relative dating. Where available, the stylistic evidence indicates that Chakwas and associated Aquilpo materials are late in the Callejón de Huaylas sequence and should correspond to local highland peoples living in the region before the Inka. The unsophisticated quality of the Aquilpo pottery and other material remains have contributed to the interpretation that the culture reflects a period of return to more rustic local highland adaptations, after the socioorganizational and artistic achievements before and during the period of Wari influence (Lanning 1965:140).

At Chinchawas, the Chakwas phase contemporary with Aquilpo seems to reinforce this view. Though our sample of Chakwas is limited both in quantity and by context, no substantial building program can be identified with Chakwas pottery. Further, Chinchawas was never re-used by Chakwas peoples as intensively or in the ways established earlier during the Chinchawasi or Warmi phases. Rather, the character and general contexts of Chakwas remains reflect a much lighter, ephemeral occupation at Chinchawas. The lack of associated architecture and dense occupational refuse suggests that Chakwas pottery was probably used by small transient groups, perhaps composed of semi-sedentary farmers or herders, or both, who used the site for temporary shelter and corral areas. This is the current use pattern now for the site, with no permanent residences.

## Post-Chakwas Occupation

The prehistoric occupation of Chinchawas ended some time during the Chakwas phase. We did not recover discernible evidence for intensive occupation during the Inka period at Chinchawas. This seems consistent with the paucity of Inka pottery in the lower Casma valley (Collier 1962:416–417; Wilson 1995), indicating that the use of Inka pottery was not frequent, perhaps reflecting a light Late Horizon influence on material culture in both the coastal and highland zones of the valley. Colonial and more recent occupations are mainly reflected in sporadic surficial finds of broken domestic refuse.

## Overview of the Ceramic Chronology of Chinchawas

The foregoing discussion characterized the pottery assemblages of Chinchawas to reconstruct their history of use. The Chinchawas sequence is set within the general chronological framework proposed by John H. Rowe (1962). Building on Wendell Bennett's influential conception (1948) of the "Peruvian Co-tradition," Rowe's scheme partitions general cultural units for the Andean region through which local sequences can be related stylistically to the master ceramic sequence from Ica. Under this framework, the Chinchawas sequence commences during the Early Intermediate Period, spans the Middle Horizon, and concludes during the Late Intermediate Period.

The local ceramics from Chinchawas, especially the decorated wares, evince similarities and differences with more familiar regional styles. In this way, the pottery indicates shifting cultural ties and relates the community uniquely to different regions and sociopolitical processes of the Central Andes through time.

In general, the local plain utilitarian wares are characterized by little marked stylistic change, either in form or in fabric. General shapes, especially necked jars and cumbrous bowls, continue throughout the sequence with only slight stylistic variations. There is no evidence to suggest that there was a complete replacement of local plainware styles. Rather, the patterns of utilitarian ceramics at Chinchawas reflect strong continuity and resiliency in the local tradition of plainware pottery.

In contrast, considerable stylistic transformations typify the local decorated wares. The Kayán phase can be characterized as a local North Highland style and representative of the Huaraz area of the Callejón de Huaylas. Chinchawas, at this time, was a small provincial settlement.

During Chinchawasi 1, the local pottery retained many elements of earlier North Highland styles. But the frequency and character of local pottery indicate a more intensive and diverse functional use of Chinchawas. Early Wari influence at Chinchawas was felt at this time in the form of imported goods (see Chapter 8) as well as some stylistic elements, but was fairly indirect. During Chinchawasi 2 outside influence was broadened, with stylistic ties to the coast as well as the Central Highlands. Nevertheless, on the basis of phase 1 antecedents, Chinchawasi 2 remained a distinct, local North Highland style.

Completely new stylistic conventions were adopted during the Warmi phase that indicate significant local stylistic changes prompted by new sociocultural conditions created by Wari state influence. Finally, Chakwas phase pottery represents a return to a simpler, more regional North Highland style.

## Conclusions

The two Chinchawasi ceramic phases are consistent with other lines of data showing strong continuities in the character and use of residential, public and mortuary architecture, stone sculpture, and stone tools. As late as A.D. 800, local traditions managed to thrive at Chinchawas, even as Wari expanded into the region. Such evidence suggests that the community of Chinchawas was largely autonomous during Middle Horizon 1. Local peoples probably accommodated new ideas and benefits from Wari affiliations, but relied heavily on local stylistic and technological traditions.

Wari culture initially appeared as a prestige style, co-opted by local leaders for personal and communal prerogatives. Only during Middle Horizon 2 and immediately after did Wari influence affect local painted pottery significantly, indicating perhaps that foreign styles and ideas were more pervasive at the community level. People during this time began to use pottery that emulated pottery with associations to Central Highland sources. In addition to local decorated ceramics, changes in mortuary practice, stone sculptural iconography, long distance trade and economic production at Chinchawas indicate that major sociocultural transformations were occurring locally as responses to regional Andean processes.

In sum, the stylistic analyses of local pottery at Chinchawas, especially when combined with additional lines of evidence, provide indices of how local peoples negotiated internal and external cultural affiliations through time. The research underscores the utility of ceramic chronology for distinguishing diachronic change at the community level.

CHAPTER EIGHT

 FANCY AND IMPORTED CERAMICS

The association of fancy and imported pottery with local styles furnishes one of the most basic tools for chronological comparison in archaeology (Rowe 1962). Its basic premise is that if a known style of pottery is found with another style of pottery, there is a great likelihood that both were produced or used during the same general time frame. While there are often natural and anthropogenic factors (such as depositional processes, curation, breakage, among others) that blur this relationship, the assumption of contemporaneity through co-occurrence facilitates the temporal association of lesser known styles with better-documented styles.

At the same time that imported pottery clarifies chronological concerns, its study also provides a measure to gauge the character of relationships that local peoples had with groups in other regions of the Andes. Long distance exchange often has special functional and symbolic roles in many societies of ancient America (e.g., Burger 1992; Helms 1993); its practice at Chinchawas was no different.

After a summary of the assemblages from the mortuary excavations in Sector 2, I will describe the nonlocal ceramics of Sector 1 by phase and by category, followed by a discussion of cultural comparisons, source regions and likely relative dating. This chapter concludes with a discussion, based on spatial and temporal variability in imported pottery styles, of the history of pottery exchange and interregional contacts at Chinchawas and its implications for Central Andean archaeology.

## Fancy Pottery in Subterranean Tombs, Sector 2

Excavations in the subterranean tombs of Sector 2 found fancy wares of local and foreign origin. In OP56 and OP65 only small fragments remained, but in OP63 our research recovered some whole and nearly complete vessels from a cache of burial offerings left in the tomb's entry vestibule. The category of fancy pottery includes local styles of the Casma headwaters as well as from the Callejón de Huaylas zones, examples from the North Central and North Coast, and unidentified vessels. The pottery is associated especially with late Early Intermediate Period and early Middle Horizon styles.

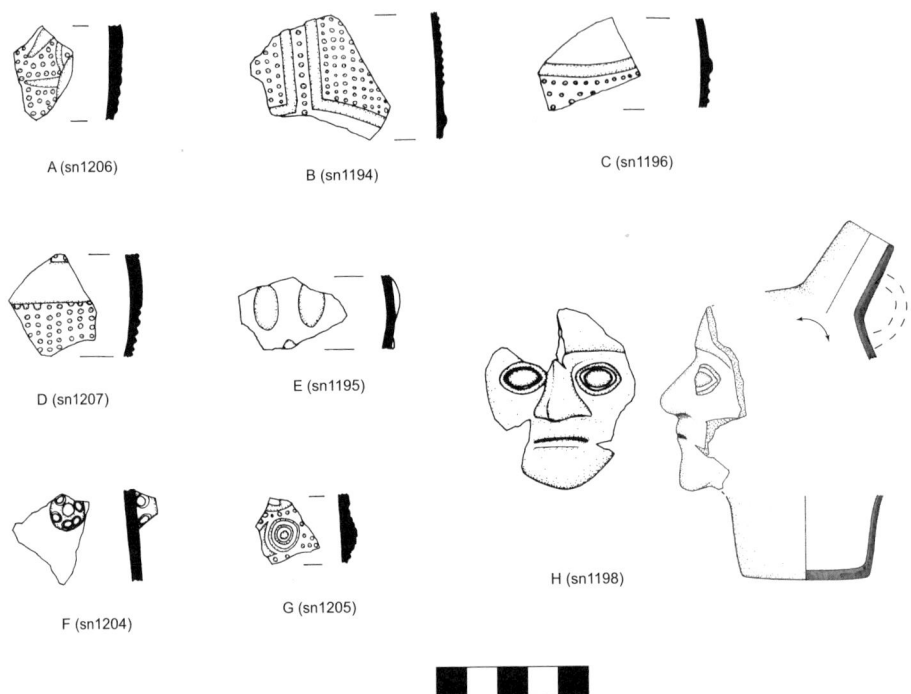

FIGURE 89. Fancy pottery from subterranean tombs, Sector 2.

## Fancy Pottery Styles

### CHINCHAWASI 1 STYLE

Small bowls, with convex or incurving forms and general exterior red-painted decoration (Figure 41G, H), are typical forms of the Chinchawasi 1 phase. However, the designs are unusual for the form. The nested diamonds (Figure 41G), for example, are more common in Chinchawasi phase 2 interior bowls, and the upward-pointing triangles (without mazes; see Figure 41H) are more typical of exterior decorated jars. Nevertheless, their shape and decoration are consistent with the Chinchawasi phase 1 style.

Two small exterior-painted decorated jars were also found in OP63 (Figure 42K, L). In general shape they resemble, in much smaller size, the short-necked jars of Chinchawasi phase 1 in Sector 1 (e.g., Figure 42B, F). The use of an effigy face and the banded and dot designs are unusual in the Chinchawasi sample.

### RECUAY STYLE

This form is a small short-necked squat jar (Figure 38E) that features a short cylindrical spout. It is of redware and shows no discernible decoration because the exterior surface is badly spalled and eroded. The shape and spout are characteristic of the Recuay style of the Callejón de Huaylas (e.g., Bennett 1944, fig. 17g; Eisleb 1987, pl. 38).

## Late Moche Style

In OP56, we recovered fragments of a Moche IV or V effigy vessel: a very small bottle with a short, slightly tapering spout (Figure 89H). The spout shows evidence of the base of a small loop handle that extended from the spout to the body. The bottle has a flat base. The fabric is a thin brown ware and in some parts retains a fine exterior polish, while the interior is rough and gritty. The vessel depicts a man with features rendered in the typical Moche style: prominent ovoid eyes, a high brow ridge, a broad nose and a stoic, if stern, expression.

## Polished Blackware

Also in OP56, we encountered 13 small sherds of a highly polished and reduced blackware with raised designs: small dots, bands, ovals and concentric circles (Figure 89A–G). The paste is very fine, with common and well-sorted, fine white grit inclusions. The sherds seem to be from a single fancy North Coast bottle, possibly Moche V or later.

## Small Jar with Appliqué Nubbins

The vessel fragment is of a small cambered rim jar (Figure 47O) made of redware. It is decorated with repeating small, notched appliqué strips placed just below the lip. In addition, a false spout was positioned near the lip of the vessel. There is a similar appliqué treatment on the shoulder of a jar found in a Recuay gallery tomb at Shankaiyan, near Huaraz (Bennett 1944, fig. 18e).

## Plain Burnished Bottles

One vessel (Figure 49J) is a nearly complete dual chamber, double spout and bridge bottle. For a vessel of its size, the walls, of a dull orangeware, are very thick. It is unslipped and, other than a burnished matte finish, does not have more elaborate decoration. A single-chambered bottle (Figure 49K), with a strap handle connecting a spout (no longer extant) and the shoulder of the bottle body, is of orangeware, burnished to a dull, matte finish, and has a large fire cloud on its exterior surface.

Dual-chambered bottles have a wide, if limited, distribution both in time and space in north-central and northern Peru. They have been documented both in the highlands for the Recuay and Cajamarca styles and on the coast, at least for Gallinazo and Moche cultures. But there are no direct analogues to the tomb example (Figure 49J). The general form of the bottle (Figure 49K) resembles single-spouted bottles found from the north-central to north coasts and associated with late Early Intermediate Period styles, especially those of Moche phase IV and Gallinazo (Strong and Evans 1952, fig. 69.4; Donnan 1973, figs. 42, 43; Proulx 1973, pl. 6c; Donnan and Mackey 1978:109, fig. 32; Wilson 1988, fig. 240e).

### *Discussion: Subterranean Tomb Pottery*

The Chinchawasi 1 style materials were probably derived from nearby local sources, probably from in and around the site of Chinchawas and the upper Casma head-

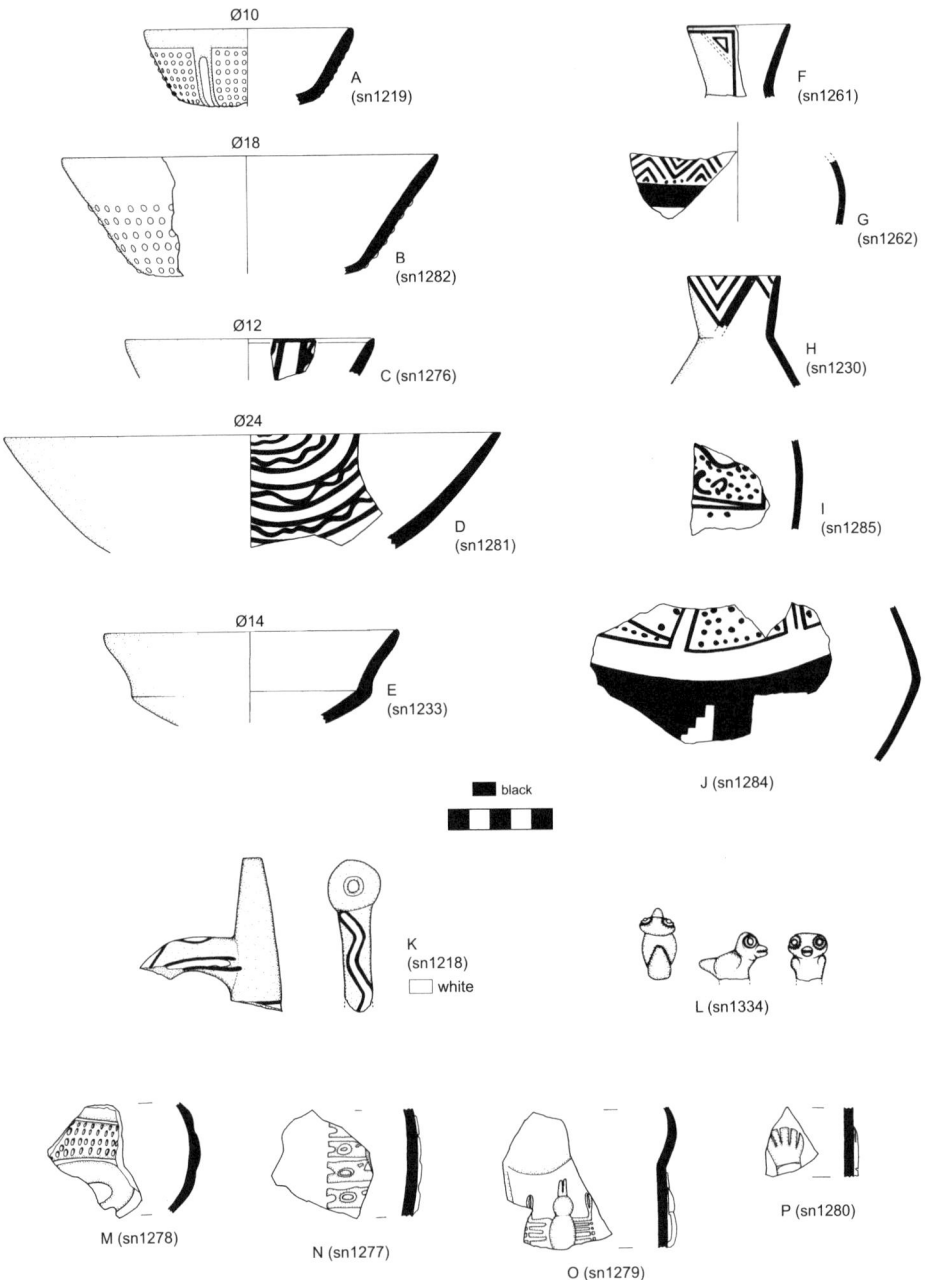

FIGURE 90. Fancy pottery from chullpa tombs, Sector 2.

waters zone. The Recuay-like material most likely drew inspiration from sources in the Callejón de Huaylas. The late Moche materials, meanwhile, come from the southern Moche culture zone (Castillo and Donnan 1994a, 1994b; Shimada 1994; Bawden 1996). Given the stylistic evidence, then, the pottery and primary use of the subterranean tombs can be attributed to the Chinchawasi 1 phase, dating around A.D. 500 to 700.

## Fancy Pottery in Chullpa Tombs, Sector 2

In nearly all of the chullpa tombs of Sector 2, excavations recovered fragments of decorated ceramics in association with human bones and other miscellaneous artifacts. The pottery forms a corpus of material coherent both in stylistic and temporal terms, pertaining mainly to the Warmi phase occupation of the Chinchawas site.

*Fancy Pottery Styles*

WARMI STYLE
In two of the chullpas (OP61 and OP64), we recovered fragments of Warmi Ware A bowls (Figure 90C, D). Mouth diameters range in size between 12 and 24 cm. Decoration includes black bands and meanders in arcs or bands over a red unslipped surface. These are Warmi style materials from Sector 1, Chinchawas, and have associations with the middle to late Middle Horizon.

HUARI NORTEÑO B
In chullpas OP57, OP59 and OP61, fragments of canteens and bottles were recovered (Figure 90F–J). These thin redware sherds feature a creamy white–tan slip, fine burnishing and black painted designs (featuring steps, dots, sausages, nested triangles and Vs). Pottery of this type, common beginning by the middle portion of the Middle Horizon sites of the North Central Coast, is referred to as the "Huari Norteño B" or "Red, White and Black" style (Kroeber 1925a, pl. 62a; Tello 1956, fig. 150a; Proulx 1973, pl. 11, 12; Wilson 1988, figs. 243–246). The nested Vs on a flaring neck may be more common in Nievería wares, however (Shady 1982, figs. 3d, 21c).

PRESS-MOLDED BLACKWARE
A blackware open bowl decorated with press-molded raised bands and dots (Figure 90A) was recovered in OP57. It has a fine reduced paste with scarce mica inclusions and is unpolished. Its mouth diameter measures 10 cm. Such mold-made material is known from the North Central Coast and pertains to the Middle Horizon (Kroeber 1925b, fig. 75h; Collier 1955, fig. 55). According to Collier (1955:169–171), such bowls were especially popular during the Middle Horizon 2 contemporary Tomaval Period. There is also a blackware adorno of a bird (Figure 90L). It is broken at the base, but could have decorated a bottle spout or shoulder, or perhaps the rim of a bowl.

Press-molded Unslipped Redware

In OP61 we recovered evidence for a redware open bowl (Figure 90B) with aligned raised dots along the lower side of the vessel. The paste is oxidized and light brownish red; the surface treatment includes a burnishing to a semi-lustrous finish. Its rim diameter measures 18 cm. The closest pottery resemblance comes from the North Central Coast and farther north. Wilson identified an analogous specimen as part of his Early Tanguche collection from Santa (Wilson 1988, fig. 241g). Such pottery in Virú, referred to as "San Nicolás Molded," began during the late Moche occupation of Virú and became most popular during the subsequent Middle Horizon contemporary Tomaval Period (Collier 1955:111, 172, fig. 57). Similar pottery also occurs farther north in funerary settings, such as from Moche (Donnan and Mackey 1978:265, fig. 2).

Press-molded Slipped Redware

We recovered press-molded fragments of an oxidized redware (Figure 90M–P) in OP61. These differ from the other press-molded wares by having a fine burnished surface, a deep red slip and more elaborate depictions. All of the fragments are unworked in the interior, indicating that this sample (molded only on convex-sided exteriors) probably derived from jars or bottles. Comparative pottery has been documented by Wilson (1988, fig. 249) for the Santa Valley, Proulx (1973, pl. 9a, b) for the Nepeña Valley, and also Donnan and Mackey (1978:255, fig. 1) for the Moche Valley. Whether called Huari Norteño B or Early Chimu, they seem to belong to the post-Middle Horizon 1 styles of those respective valleys. However, reduced blackwares and press-molding became established in the Moche Valley during Moche V (Bawden 1996). In Virú, Collier (1955:111) also observed that San Nicolás Molded, a red oxidized press-molded ware, was first used in late Huancaco (or Moche-contemporary) pottery.

Press-molded Painted Redware

In OP59, we recovered a badly eroded press-molded sherd of an oxidized redware that is thinly coated with a red and white wash. The sherd comes from a straight-sided everted drinking cup that has better preserved stylistic counterparts in Sector 1 (Figure 93). The sherd carries four different images on two registers, divided by a vertical band of incised lines that form chevrons. The wider, lower register takes up about two-thirds of the pressed-molded band and depicts (left to right) a front-face figure with a headdress of serpentine or feline heads and a profile feline with feline or serpentine heads emerging from its paws and mouth.

Nievería

Excavations in OP57 recovered a conical spout and bridge fragment (Figure 90K). It is from a Nievería style bottle, which used a fine oxidized paste, fine burnishing to a dull luster and black and white paint over a light greenish brown slip. The cream–white between black painted design occurs on the bridge as meanders or bands and also on the bottom of the spout near the fracture. Similar spouts are common in Nievería style pottery, especially the general conical form and round (in section) bridges (Gayton 1927, pl. 94a, 97c, e; Tello 1956, fig. 153d).

*Discussion: Chullpa Tomb Pottery*

The remains from the chullpa tombs form a coherent set of stylistic and temporal materials. Warmi phase materials were found in a several of the chullpas; radiocarbon associations from deposits in Sector 1 suggest a middle to late Middle Horizon occupation. This accords with the press-molded and Huari Norteño styles linked to coastal groups. The strong preference for coastal imports in the Chinchawas chullpas is interesting and is consistent with other chullpa tomb gravelots in the Callejón de Huaylas (Bennett 1944; Paredes et al. 2000; Ponte Rosalino 2000).

# Fancy and Imported Pottery in Sector 1

A wide range of imported and fancy pottery was found during stratigraphic excavations in Sector 1 of Chinchawas. The materials can be associated to late Early Intermediate Period and Middle Horizon styles. Their distributions across the Chinchawas site will be discussed, followed by general considerations of fancy pottery at Chinchawas, including relative dating, function and cultural interaction.

*Fancy and Imported Pottery Styles*

CAJAMARCA STYLE

In various operations of Sector 1, our investigations recovered Cajamarca and Cajamarca-related pottery (Figure 91A–O). The materials are contemporary with Chinchawasi 2 and Warmi phase materials. Some (Figure 91A–G, L) are likely direct imports: they are of a fine white kaolinite paste, painted in a dark brown over a dull matte paste surface. Spoon fragments (Figure 91E–G) belong to the Cajamarca spoon tradition, particularly of form C-2 or A-1 (Terada and Onuki 1982, fig. 62). One sherd (Figure 91B) comes from the base of an open bowl and has either a classic or floral cursive design (Terada and Matsumoto 1985, lám. 5, 6).

Excavations also recovered fragments of Cajamarca-related pottery (e.g., Figure 91J–K, M). They are almost certainly imports, but differ slightly from documented Cajamarca styles by having a less fine grittier paste, broader line weights or derivative cursive painting. Another difference is the use of red instead of, or in conjunction with, black or dark brown paint. These specimens could be comparable to specimens of Bennett's "Geometric on Light" or the "cursive" variant of his Wari Polychrome pottery from the Wari site (Bennett 1953, pl. 9, fig. 13). But the Chinchawas specimens are much finer than these locally made derivations of Cajamarca pottery and probably represent lesser known Cajamarca imports.

Given its distinctive characteristics, Cajamarca pottery has been identified in special Middle Horizon contexts outside of the Cajamarca area and is commonly

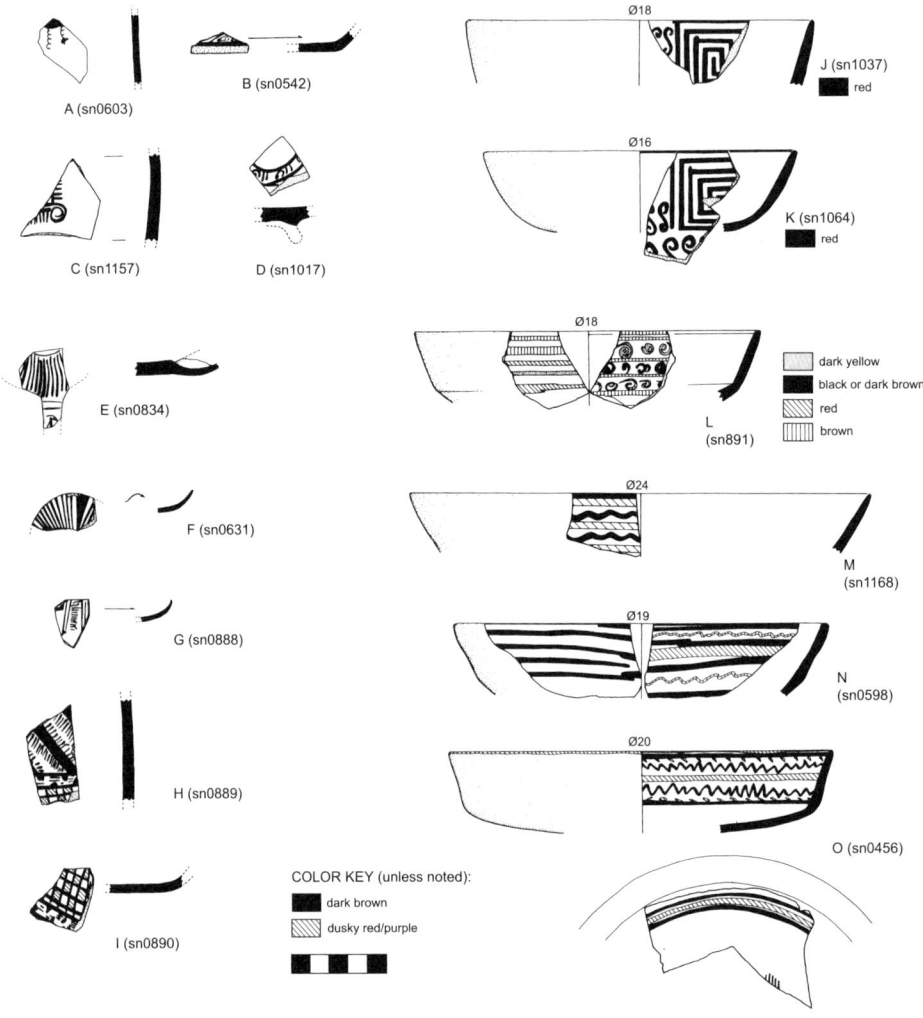

Figure 91. Fancy kaolinite pottery, Cajamarca and Cajamarca-related.

regarded as a prestige ware (Menzel 1964:71–72; Lanning 1967; Shady 1988). Lanning (1967:138), for example, declares: "The middle Marañon region, especially the area of Cajamarca, also seems to have enjoyed special prestige in the Huari Empire."

In the Callejón de Huaylas, Cajamarca pottery occurs rarely, but typically in ceremonial contexts. At Tornapampa (Terada 1979), a site consisting of a series of chullpas, surface collections recovered several pieces of kaolinite ware, including one open bowl fragment with exterior Rectilinear or Floral Cursive designs characteristic of the Middle Cajamarca period (Terada 1979). Bennett (1944) documented Cajamarca ceramics, mainly spoons, from a "subterranean house site," deep stone-lined tomb, and other sites in the zone around Huaraz. There has been mention of "Marañon" pottery from the chullpa sector of Honcopampa (Bennett

1953; Lanning 1965; Amat Olazábal 1976b), as well as at Chavín de Huántar (Tello 1960). Cajamarca materials were also found at the area of Antaraká, near Carhuaz (Lau 2006a).

Great concentrations and diversity of known cursive pottery outside Cajamarca proper occur in the Huamachuco area, just south of the Cajamarca zone (McCown 1945; Thatcher 1972, 1975, 1977). Max Uhle found cursive painted specimens in Huamachuco, which have stylistic analogues at Chinchawas (compare Figure 91D with ceramics illustrated in Kroeber 1930, pl. 11, fig. 5, and McCown 1945:308–309, pl. 19f). Additionally, John and Theresa Topic identified Cajamarca Cursive spoons and a pedestal bowl in the funerary goods of an early Middle Horizon mausoleum at Cerro Amaru (T. Topic and J. Topic 1984; J. Topic and T. Topic 1992).

Cajamarca pottery distribution follows a general clinal pattern outside the North Highlands, but is more prominent in settlements with Wari presence. There have also been finds of Cajamarca pottery farther south in Ayacucho (Bennett 1953; Menzel 1964; Benavides 1991; Cook 1994), Huancavelica (Ravines 1968, 1977), Andahuaylas (Menzel 1964) and Pikillacta (McEwan 1996). Ravines's discovery at Ayapata is notable because his Cajamarca material has counterparts (Figure 91D, H, I) at Chinchawas (Ravines 1968, fig. 32, 34). The offering deposit at Ayapata was dated to Middle Horizon 2A (Menzel 1968; Ravines 1968, 1977).

Cajamarca styles, not surprisingly, also figure prominently as prestige wares in the North Coast, and are not uncommon to Late Moche sites (Shimada 1994; Castillo 2001; Bernuy and Bernal 2005). Cajamarca peoples were in intense contact with their coastal counterparts throughout the Early Intermediate Period and Middle Horizon (Leonard and Russell 1993; Montenegro 1993; Shimada 1994). The current data on distribution indicate that Cajamarca pottery, at least in the highlands, is almost always found in special use contexts (whether in mortuaries, offering deposits or public spaces) and in association with Wari or Wari-related fancy pottery.

Polychrome and Indeterminate Kaolinite

In several excavations we encountered fragments of a fancy polychrome kaolinite pottery (Figure 91N, O) not of the Kayán (Recuay kaolinite) style, that we grouped as "indeterminate kaolinite" (Table 11). All reconstructible vessels of this ware were from bowls (Figure 91N, O). The paste is a hard kaolinite and fires white or, more typically, a grayish white. It is characterized by common but small inclusions of dark angular grit, but no mica. Polychrome painting on both the interior and exterior of the vessels distinguishes this ware. Interior designs are rendered in red, black, purple, brown or black paint and include bands, rows of repeating short strokes, curlicues and irregular meanders running the entire interior circumference near the lip. Only bands, also near the lip, characterize exterior decoration. The interior base of these vessels was also painted; designs include circular bands and groups of cursive strokes farther towards the center (Figure 91O).

TABLE 11. Summary of fancy and imported pottery by architectural contexts, all phases.

| | Huari Norteño | Viñaque | Fine red burnished | Fine gray | Purple iridescent | Wilkawaín resist | Cajamarca | Cajamarca-related | Nievería | Fine orange | Wari polychrome |
|---|---|---|---|---|---|---|---|---|---|---|---|
| *Kayán* | | | | | | | | | | | |
| Residential | — | — | — | — | — | — | — | — | — | — | — |
| Midden or refuse | — | — | — | — | — | — | — | — | — | — | — |
| Patio or enclosure | — | — | — | — | — | — | — | — | — | — | — |
| Terrace | — | — | — | — | — | — | — | — | — | — | — |
| Phase count (n) | — | — | — | — | — | — | — | — | — | — | — |
| Percentage | — | — | — | — | — | — | — | — | — | — | — |
| *Chinchawasi 1* | | | | | | | | | | | |
| Residential | — | — | — | — | — | — | — | — | — | — | — |
| Midden | — | — | — | — | — | — | — | — | — | — | — |
| Room complex | — | — | — | — | — | — | — | — | — | — | — |
| Patio or enclosure | — | — | — | — | — | — | — | — | — | — | — |
| Terrace | — | — | — | — | — | — | — | — | — | — | 1 |
| Torréon | — | — | — | — | — | — | — | — | — | — | 1 |
| Mortuary | — | — | — | — | — | — | — | — | — | — | — |
| Phase count (n) | — | — | — | — | — | — | — | — | — | — | 2 |
| Percentage | — | — | — | — | — | — | — | — | — | — | 3.2 |
| *Chinchawasi 2* | | | | | | | | | | | |
| Residential | — | — | — | — | — | — | 2 | — | — | 3 | — |
| Midden or refuse | — | — | — | 12 | 7 | — | 11 | — | 7 | — | 7 |
| Room complex | — | — | — | — | — | — | 1 | — | — | 4 | — |
| Patio or enclosure | — | — | — | — | — | — | — | — | — | — | — |
| Terrace | — | — | 1 | 1 | 2 | 18 | — | 1 | — | 2 | 9 |
| Mortuary | — | — | — | — | — | — | — | — | — | — | — |
| Torréon | — | — | — | — | — | — | — | — | — | — | 1 |
| Phase count (n) | — | — | 1 | 13 | 9 | 18 | 14 | 1 | 7 | 9 | 17 |
| Percentage | — | — | 0.5 | 6.8 | 4.7 | 9.4 | 7.3 | 0.5 | 3.6 | 4.7 | 8.9 |
| *Warmi* | | | | | | | | | | | |
| Residential | — | — | — | — | — | — | — | — | — | — | — |
| Midden or refuse | — | 4 | 1 | 1 | 2 | — | 2 | 2 | 1 | 13 | 29 |
| Room complex | — | — | — | — | — | 1 | — | — | — | 1 | — |
| Patio or enclosure | — | — | 1 | — | — | — | — | — | — | — | — |
| Terrace | 1 | — | — | — | 1 | — | — | 3 | — | 2 | 4 |
| Mortuary | 35 | — | 1 | — | — | — | — | — | 1 | — | — |
| Fill | — | — | — | — | — | — | — | — | — | 1 | 1 |
| Phase count (n) | 36 | 4 | 3 | 1 | 3 | 1 | 2 | 5 | 2 | 17 | 34 |
| Percentage | 10.2 | 1.1 | 0.9 | 0.3 | 0.9 | 0.3 | 0.6 | 1.4 | 0.6 | 4.8 | 9.7 |
| *Chakwas* | | | | | | | | | | | |
| Percentage | — | — | — | — | — | — | — | — | — | — | — |
| Plowzone or mixed (n) | — | — | 3 | — | — | — | — | — | — | 5 | 3 |
| Percentage | — | — | 2.8 | — | — | — | — | — | — | 4.7 | 2.8 |

TABLE 11 CONTINUED.

| | Press-molded redware | Fine pink, nonspoon | Fine pink, spoon | Face-neck ware | Polished blackware, decorated | Polished blackware | Late Moche | Indeterminate kaolinite | Recuay | Total | Context percentage |
|---|---|---|---|---|---|---|---|---|---|---|---|
| *Kayán* | | | | | | | | | | | |
| Residential | 2 | — | — | — | — | — | — | 8 | 10 | 20 | 27.8 |
| Midden or refuse | — | — | — | — | — | — | — | — | 1 | 1 | 1.4 |
| Patio or enclosure | — | — | — | — | — | — | — | 3 | 12 | 15 | 20.8 |
| Terrace | — | — | — | — | — | — | — | 14 | 22 | 36 | 50.0 |
| Phase count (n) | 2 | — | — | — | — | — | — | 25 | 45 | 72 | 100.0% |
| Percentage | 2.8 | — | — | — | — | — | — | 34.7 | 62.5 | 100% | |
| *Chinchawasi 1* | | | | | | | | | | | |
| Residential | 1 | — | — | 1 | — | 1 | — | 1 | 2 | 6 | 9.5 |
| Midden | — | — | — | — | — | — | — | — | — | 0 | 0.0 |
| Room complex | — | — | 1 | — | — | — | — | — | — | 1 | 1.6 |
| Patio or enclosure | — | — | — | — | — | — | — | 4 | — | 4 | 6.3 |
| Terrace | — | 1 | 1 | — | — | 5 | 2 | 10 | 8 | 28 | 44.4 |
| Torréon | — | — | — | — | — | — | — | 1 | 2 | 4 | 6.3 |
| Mortuary | — | — | — | — | 10 | 3 | 7 | — | — | 20 | 31.7 |
| Phase count (n) | 1 | 1 | 2 | 1 | 10 | 9 | 9 | 16 | 12 | 63 | 100.0% |
| Percentage | 1.6 | 1.6 | 3.2 | 1.6 | 15.9 | 14.3 | 14.3 | 25.4 | 19.0 | 100% | |
| *Chinchawasi 2* | | | | | | | | | | | |
| Residential | — | — | — | — | — | 3 | — | 3 | — | 11 | 5.7 |
| Midden or refuse | — | 3 | 1 | 27 | — | 5 | — | 1 | 2 | 83 | 43.2 |
| Room complex | 3 | — | — | 2 | 1 | — | — | 1 | — | 12 | 6.3 |
| Patio or enclosure | — | — | — | — | — | — | — | — | — | 0 | 0.0 |
| Terrace | 9 | 2 | 17 | 4 | 1 | 3 | — | 10 | 3 | 83 | 43.2 |
| Mortuary | — | — | — | — | — | — | — | — | — | 0 | 0.0 |
| Torréon | — | — | 1 | — | — | — | — | — | 1 | 3 | 1.6 |
| Phase count (n) | 12 | 5 | 19 | 33 | 2 | 11 | — | 15 | 6 | 192 | 100.0% |
| Percentage | 6.3 | 2.6 | 9.9 | 17.2 | 1.0 | 5.7 | — | 7.8 | 3.1 | 100% | |
| *Warmi* | | | | | | | | | | | |
| Residential | — | — | — | — | — | — | — | — | — | — | 0.0 |
| Midden or refuse | 27 | 2 | 9 | 18 | — | 10 | — | 1 | 3 | 125 | 35.5 |
| Room complex | 16 | — | 1 | — | — | — | — | — | — | 19 | 5.4 |
| Patio or enclosure | — | — | — | — | 1 | — | — | — | — | 2 | 0.6 |
| Terrace | 62 | 7 | 8 | 9 | 13 | 18 | — | 2 | — | 130 | 36.9 |
| Mortuary | 16 | — | — | — | 4 | 11 | — | — | — | 68 | 19.3 |
| Fill | — | — | — | — | 2 | 4 | — | — | 8 | | 2.3 |
| Phase count (n) | 121 | 9 | 18 | 27 | 19 | 44 | — | 3 | 3 | 352 | 100% |
| Percentage | 34.4 | 2.6 | 5.1 | 7.7 | 5.4 | 12.5 | — | 0.9 | 0.9 | 100% | |
| *Chakwas* | | | | | | | | | | | |
| Percentage | — | — | — | — | — | — | — | — | — | 0% | — |
| Plowzone or mixed (n) | 12 | 3 | 8 | 6 | 2 | 4 | — | 36 | 25 | 107 | 100.0% |
| Percentage | 11.2 | 2.8 | 7.5 | 5.6 | 1.9 | 3.7 | — | 33.6 | 23.4 | 100% | |

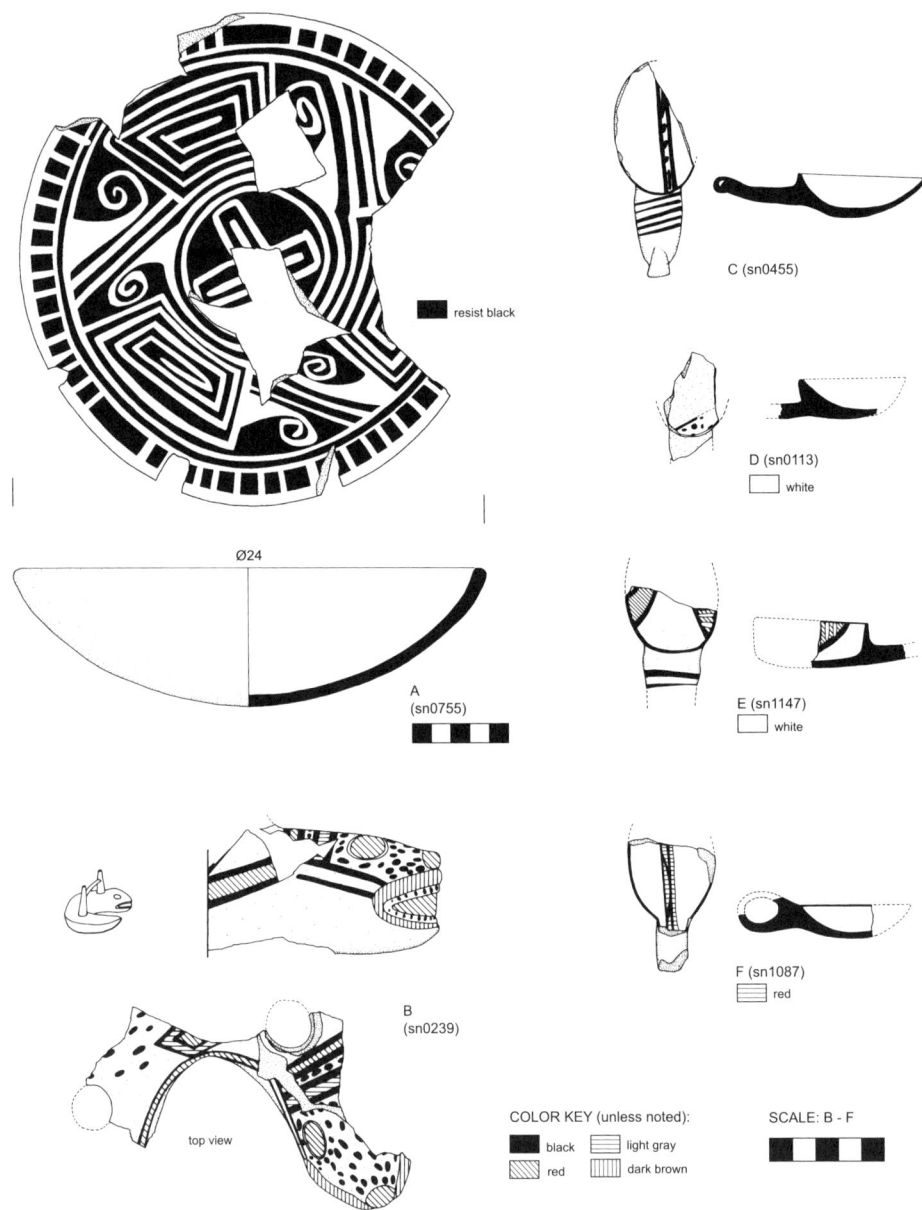

FIGURE 92. Wilkawaín resist-painted bowl (A), Nievería effigy bottle (B) and fine pinkware spoons (C–F).

Polychrome kaolinite ceramics were recovered only in Chinchawasi phase 1 and 2 contexts, with no overlap in Warmi deposits. This ware resists definitive comparison to known regional styles. It resembles Recuay pottery, especially in the use of kaolinite clays, the open bowl form, and exterior polychrome or monochrome painting, but in form and decoration most closely resembles Cajamarca and

Cajamarca-related pottery in the collection. Similar pottery has also been found at Huari in association with early Middle Horizon pottery (Bennett 1953; Lumbreras 1960, lám. 13h; Menzel 1964; Cook 1994, lám. 27e–h). Bennett (1953:68–69) drew comparisons to Cajamarca wares called the "Marañon style," a white-paste pottery with cursive painting that he considered to be imported wares.

## Wilkawaín Resist-painted

In OP46, Level E, we recovered fragments of a plate with a distinctive resist design (Figure 92A). The vessel was 80% reconstructible, made of a redware with well-sorted uncommon inclusions of grit and mica flecks. Mouth diameter is 24 cm. Areas of the base have been burnt; nevertheless, the exterior shows burnishing striations and retains, for the most part, the red paste surface. The interior shows a much finer treatment. It has a medium luster finish and no striations. The design is rendered in negative; that is, the background is in black and the design is in the paste color of the surface. Beginning from the lip toward the center, the complex design shows (1) a pattern of cross-ticks dividing concentric bands, (2) maze pendants alternating with wave designs ending in curlicues and (3) a central cruciform image.

Bennett (1944:26, fig. 8) recovered two very similar plates from a deep stone-lined tomb in the Ichik Wilkawaín complex, near Huaraz in the Callejón de Huaylas. The plates are generally finer than the Chinchawas specimen, with a thinner body thickness, a finer paste and more brilliant surface finish. The form and the quality of the resist painting, however, are nearly identical in the three examples. Bennett's plates were found in association with "Tiahuanacoid" materials, including Chakipampa B specimens (Menzel 1964:68, 75). Tello (1956, fig. 134) illustrates a pyroengraved gourd fragment with a similar curlicue and maze design from surface collections of looted tombs at the site of San Diego, in Casma. Tello (1956:298) associated the fragment with "período último" ceramics with plastic decoration (Pozorski and Pozorski 1987b:53).

## Nievería

During the course of the excavation of Terrace 4 in Sector 1, fragments from a polychrome effigy vessel (Figure 92B) were found in the lower layers, associated with Chinchawasi phase 2 materials. The vessel is a double spout and bridge bottle, of which only a portion of the body remains. These fragments show the remnants of two holes where the spouts and body were joined. The vessel is made of a hard grayish redware with well-sorted common white grit inclusions. The exterior is finely burnished and slipped orange, while the interior was left rough. The vessel depicts a mythical creature with a serpent form but feline characteristics. The lack of legs and the vessel's shape denote a general serpent body, while the eyes, nose, spots and mouth with teeth resemble feline attributes. Designs are rendered in polychrome (black, dark brown, gray, red and white) and include typical Middle Horizon elements (the polychrome pendant rectangle and polychrome diamond).

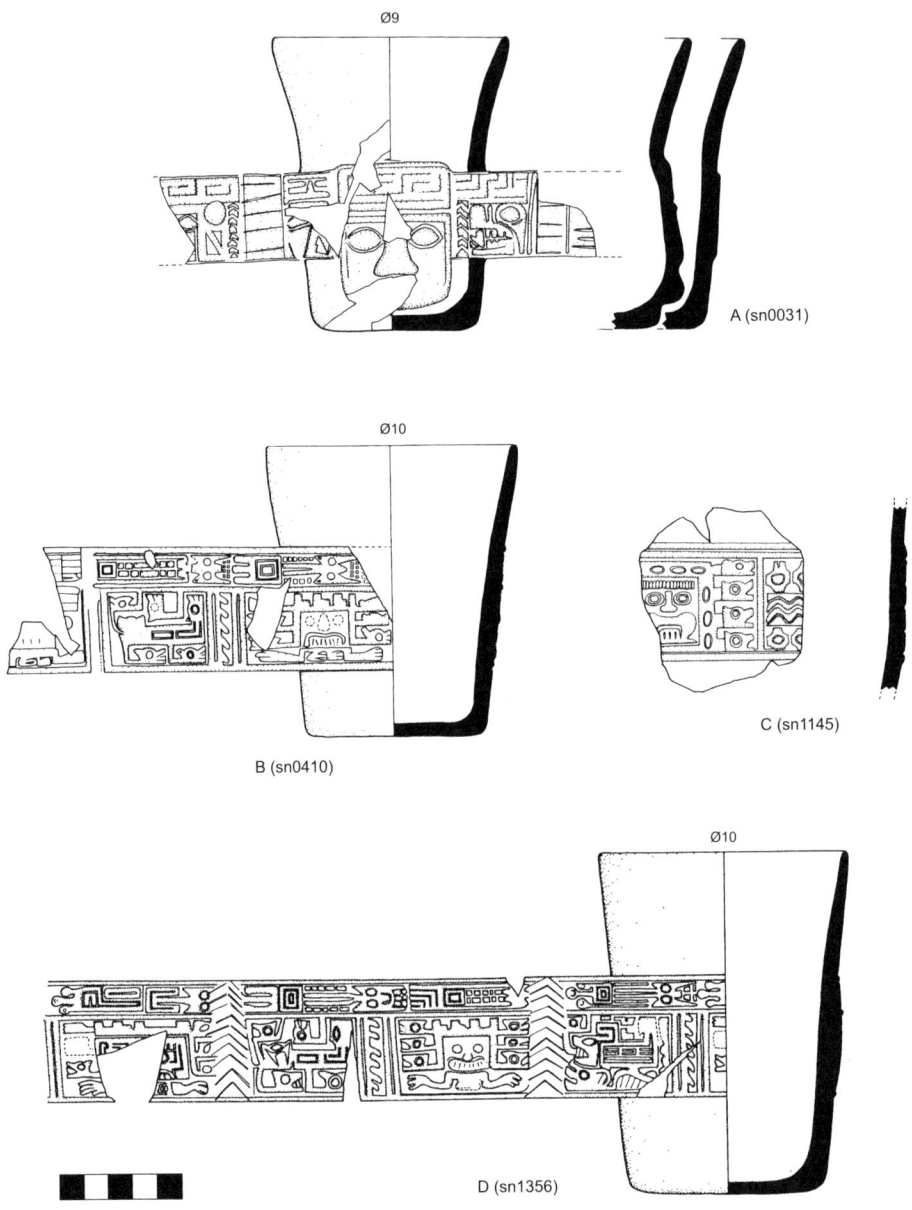

FIGURE 93. Press-molded tumblers.

In decoration and form, the effigy vessel resembles Nievería serpent effigy bottles from the Central Coast (e.g., de Lavalle 1984:142).

PRESS-MOLDED TUMBLERS, SUPE STYLE

Another imported ceramic type includes press-molded cups or tumblers (Figures 93A–D and 94C). These are sometimes referred to as "keros." The general shape consists uniformly of straight or slightly flaring everted sides and a flat base. The specimens measure between 11 and 13 cm in height with mouth diameters between 9 and 10 cm. The vessels are of a redware of medium hardness and fabric (well-sorted, common small and medium grit, and mica inclusions). Unmolded surfaces are treated to a fine burnish, leaving a dull luster. In one example (Figure 93D), the vessel surface is covered in a thin red wash, while the molded surface is painted white.

Several tumbler specimens were found in good, nearly complete condition. Only occasionally are they found in fragmentary condition, suggesting that, in general, most were disposed of intact or as offerings. One specimen (Figure 93D) was recovered in excavations of a northern construction on Sector 1 (OP66), probably a house or mausoleum, but the rest of the sample comes from refuse or residential contexts (Figures 93A–C and 94C). Most of the press-molded tumblers are Warmi phase contemporary.

A register of complex press-molded designs distinguishes the tumblers. Prefire incisions that form chevrons or horizontal bands were applied to blank vertical strips of the vessel, probably to conceal the joins of the mold (Figure 93A, D). The design band is positioned 4 or 5 cm below the lip, wraps around the entire vessel and measures 3.4 to 4.6 cm in width. The depictions can be categorized into three design groups.

*Design A.* The best example of Design A is the fragment (Figure 93A) with the dominant image of a human face in high relief. The face, measuring 5.8 cm in height and 4.4 cm in width, is somewhat larger than the remaining press-molded band (3.3 cm in width). The face consists of a headdress adorned with a dual greco-maze pattern, a raised band along the edge of the face and a broad nose. The pressed band is less clear, but seems to present iconic panels of attendant figures often seen in Wari painted pottery (Cook 1994). Between panels are blank spaces filled with horizontal, prefire incisions. On one side is a panel of an avian profile facing a vertical row of chevrons. The dominant elements here are the mouth with teeth (the front interlocking), a flap or band wrapping below the eye band distinctive to hawks (Yacovleff 1932) and a prominent curving nose or beak. The other panel is less well preserved but shows the front of the face of another figure with more human characteristics, such as an ovoid eye; the circle above the triangles could be an ear or ear spool. Like the avian image, chevrons border the face. A greco-maze band tops both figures on the panel, like the principal face. The panel juxtaposed directly to the principal image is broken and is blurry because of incomplete molding.

*Design B.* Design B is more common than Design A in our limited sample (Figure 93B–D). In contrast to Design A, which focuses on a very human-like frontal face image, Design B depicts alternating panels of two mythical figures. One is a front-face figure. The other is a profile of a feline (the lower third of the press-molded register). The panels are topped by a band of legless creatures seen from above (the upper third).

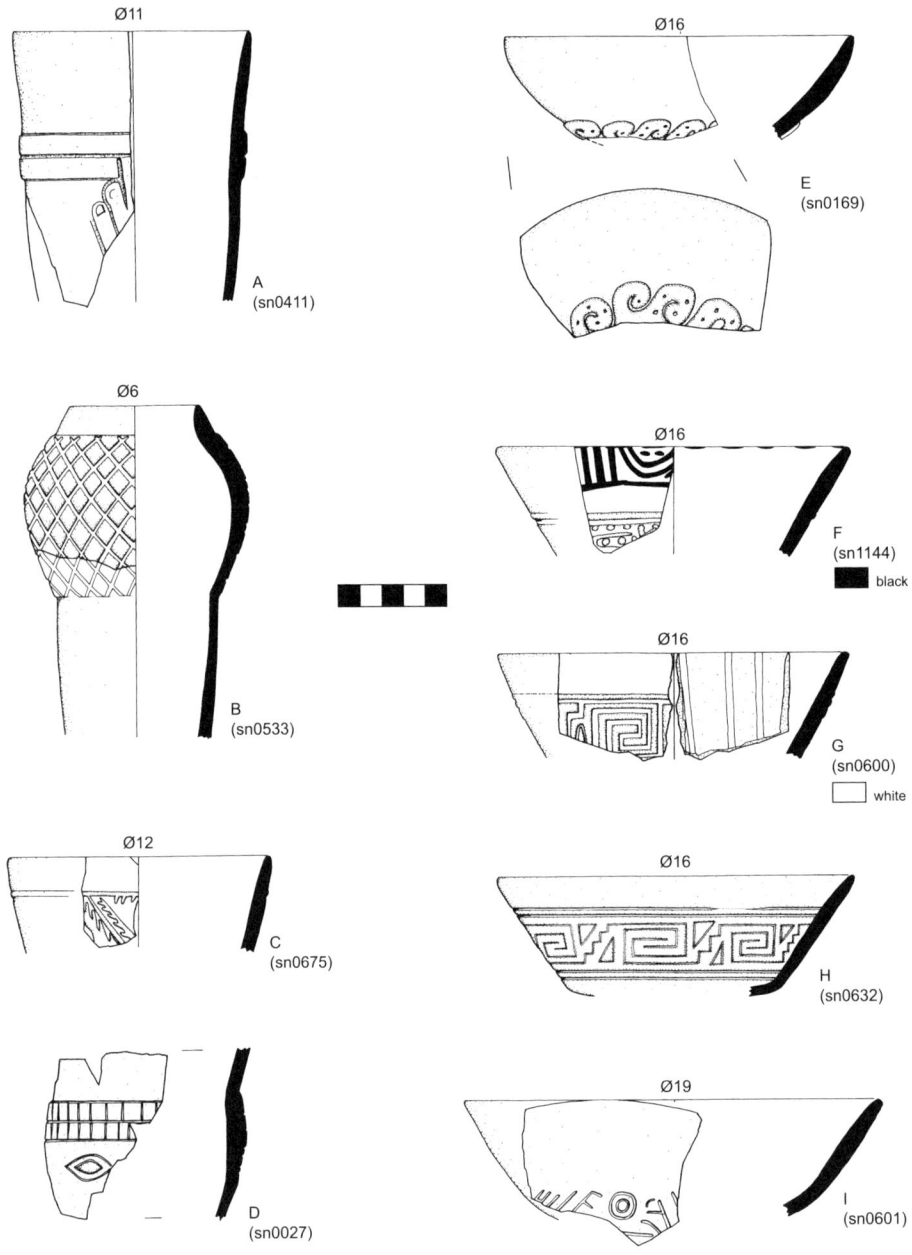

Figure 94. Press-molded tumblers (A–D) and bowls (E–I).

The front-face figure, without a lower jaw (agnathic), has a distinctive headdress crowned with step motifs and terminating in stylized appendage heads of serpents or felines, three or four to a side (Figure 93C, D) (Menzel 1977:34). The figure is also portrayed without a torso, although commonly has elongated "hands" and protruding "feet" (Figure 93B). The alternate panel depicts the profile of a feline figure, with its tail, legs and mouth terminating in serpent or feline heads similar to the ends of the agnathic figure's headdress. The feline has rectangular forms in its torso and tail area.

Images of legless creatures with different configurations decorate the upper register. The creatures are seen from above and are distinguished by a two-prong head with teeth and a prominent nose, and typically end with a design of nested rectangles and three circular "star" finials on the tail. The torso can have (1) internal rectangular blocks, (2) a bifurcate tine design with rectangular blocks on either side or (3) a maze-like design. There is one press-molded fragment (Figure 93C) that shows the agnathic face without the feline profile panel and the upper legless creature register. Instead, the alternate panel has meander designs between groups of cruciform shapes (formed by indented corners) with a central circle.

*Design C.* This decoration is the least common in the Chinchawas sample, represented by one sherd (Figure 94C). This sherd has press-molding identical to vessels carrying Designs A and B, but the content of the pressed image is different. The only discernible imagery consists of barb-like extensions, which also occur in Design B examples as borders separating the alternating panels of the lower register. However, because these protrusions (in Design C) are located on the topmost part of the design band and run diagonally, they are not typical borders. Design C should be considered a provisional category until a more complete image can be identified.

*Comparisons.* As part of his Early Tanguche assemblage, Wilson (1988, fig. 255c) documents a press-molded fragment with the Design B front-face image. Press-molded redware vessels are also known from Virú, but not usually in the tumbler form or with similar motifs (Collier 1955:172–175). The best known comparative pottery comes from coastal burials excavated by Uhle in Supe, attributed stylistically to the "Supe Middle Period" (Kroeber 1925b, figs. 73a, 75f, 78m). Menzel (1964:36, 1977) identified "Supe Middle Period" pottery as belonging to Middle Horizon Epochs 2 and 3. The technique of press-molding, although established earlier on the North Coast, grew increasingly popular in Epoch 2 in certain areas of the north central and central coasts and became the predominant decorative mode in Epoch 3 (Menzel 1977:31–32).

The Chinchawas tumblers, however, show strong stylistic links with Wari pottery and Wari religious iconography. In particular, these connections can be attributed to themes depicted in Central Highland pottery during the Middle Horizon. In several Supe tumblers (Kroeber 1925b, figs. 78m, 73a), the identical legless mythical animal with "star" finials appears, placed similarly on the top register. Menzel (1977:33–34, note 107) observes that the circular tail designs occur widely in Wari-influenced painted pottery and textiles. She likens them to stars that mark the creatures as "Star Animals." Rowe identified these figures as supernatural animal spirits in Inca religion (Menzel 1977:33–34, note 107). In Wari culture, they seem to be part of the Wari pantheon of mythical beings associated with celestial or supernatural phenomena (Menzel 1977:34).

Design A's avian profile head may approximate Viñaque-style profile heads with feline attributes (Bennett 1953, pl. 3k). The style of rendering feline appendage heads, moreover, is a stylistic crossover between Central Coast press-molded pottery and Middle Horizon 2B Wari painted pottery (Menzel 1977:34). Finally, the tumbler form and design position, especially, are shared elements between the Supe and Chinchawas specimens. They suggest participation in a Wari religious tradition among the local cultures. In this way, Menzel (1977:35) states: "Tumblers are an important emblem of the gods in Huari religion, and also appear as secular prestige vessels in Huari culture."

The depiction of front-face images on coastal-style tumblers is noteworthy. For one thing, this is not common in the Central Coast examples. Front-face images, however, are familiar designs in highland Wari fancy pottery. The bodiless human head was an important motif that had broad appeal in Wari provinces and was especially common in Middle Horizon Epoch 2B pottery throughout the Central Andes (Menzel 1964:41–42). Our investigations at Chinchawas did not recover depictions of the Pachacamac griffin, the religious icon of the Central Coast "branch" of Wari religion (Menzel 1964). During the period of interaction with Wari culture, then, Chinchawas peoples obtained vessels that used a coastal decorative technology, but which bore highland Wari iconography. Front-face images do not appear in contemporary painted wares at Chinchawas; our sample contained only molded versions.

Despite strong technological similarities and some design parallels, the specimens from Supe and Chinchawas are not identical. For example, the illustrated Supe materials do not have the central agnathic image or the feline profile panel of Design B. And the Chinchawas tumblers do not show themes important in the Supe repertory, such as the "sky scene" (Menzel 1977). There is, therefore, probably another source for the Chinchawas tumblers, perhaps in Casma, Huarmey or Nepeña. Another possibility is that the religious content prominent in the tumbler style at Chinchawas (Figure 93) had changed by the time the press-molded imagery became dominant along the Central Coast.

Tumblers, Non-Supe Style

A set of distinctive pottery tumblers, also found at Chinchawas in the same contexts as the Supe press-molded specimens, is associated with the Warmi occupation. They neither feature the same iconography as the Supe-type tumblers, nor do they use the same press-mold technology (Figure 94A, B, D). Rather, they are either incised or combine press-molding and incision.

One vessel (Figure 94A) is a tumbler with the same general shape as the Supe type. It has a hard, unslipped pinkish orange paste with frequent gritty inclusions and small amounts of mica. The vessel was burnished to a dull matte finish. A press-molded design of at least three appendages, perhaps of feathers or the tail appendages of the "Huari Star Animal," connects with two raised bands, the uppermost located 4.4 cm below the lip. The appendages have circular or semicircular figures on their ends.

Two other tumblers seem to have Middle Horizon Epoch 2B connections to the North Coast. The first is of an unusual tumbler form (Figure 94B), with nearly vertical sides interrupted by a bulging profile near the rim. It is made of a gritty yellowish orange paste, with common small- to medium-sized mica inclusions. It is unslipped and was burnished only to a dull but smooth matte finish. A series of incised, criss-crossing diagonals, which form a lattice pattern, decorate the bulging band. The other tumbler (Figure 94D) has incision and modeling. The sherd, of a grayish brown paste with many small mica flecks, derives from a unslipped tumbler form with everted sides. Unlike the rougher interior, the exterior surface is finely burnished with sharp and deep patterned incisions. The vessel depicts the face and headband of a human. The eye, cheek and "forehead" are raised through modeling. These latter two vessels resemble modeled Wari (Middle Horizon 2B) provincial pottery found by Uhle on the North Coast (Kroeber 1925a, pl. 65b; Menzel 1977, fig. 52). Although the forms are very different, elements of the design (such as lattice bands and an effigy) and decorative technique (modeling and incision) are similar. Press-molded orangeware material was also recovered from the deep stone-lined tombs (Site 7H-1) of Ichik Wilkawaín (Bennett 1944).

Press-molded Ware, North Central Coast Style
In various operations in Sector 1, we identified fragments of oxidized press-molded redwares (Figure 94E–I) in the ceramic sample. The vessels are of a redware of medium hardness and fabric (well sorted, with many common small- and medium-sized grit and mica inclusions). The open bowl represents the only vessel form for this group. Vessels have straight or slightly convex sides and, where evident, a flat base. Lip treatment consists of a simple tapering and rounding. The bowls are of medium size and have mouth diameters range from 16 to 19 cm. Surfaces are unslipped and unmolded surfaces are treated to a medium burnish, leaving little (e.g., Figure 94E) or a slight dull luster (e.g., Figure 94H), especially in the interior.

Molded designs are located on the vessel exteriors, either near or on the base (e.g., Figure 94I) or several centimeters below the lip (e.g., Figure 94H). Unlike the Supe-like material, these open bowls emphasize curvilinear and geometric designs: mazes, the step-triangle motif, curlicues, or waves and repeating raised dots. There are two examples with painting: one (Figure 94G) has white interior lines, while the other (Figure 94F) has black painted vertical ticks and a nested arcs-and-dots design.

The sample resembles ceramics from the Nepeña, Santa and Virú valleys from the north central coast. In particular, San Nicolás Molded pottery, from Virú, is very similar, with oxidized firing, the predominant form (open bowl), lack of elaborate surface treatment, painted interiors and the use of raised dots (Collier 1955:172–175). Designs between San Nicolás Molded and the Chinchawas vessels are not identical. Chinchawas designs are more intricate. The press-molding is clearer and more orderly. And certain designs do not occur identically in the San Nicolás sample, such as repeating curlicues with punctations and the maze and step-triangle motifs.

Similar pottery has been found most commonly along the north-central and north coast, although in low frequencies. Redware bowls with press-molded designs occur in the Early Tanguche pottery in Santa (see Wilson 1988, fig. 255d) and Huari Norteño B collections in Nepeña (curlicues in Proulx 1973, pl. 8g). There are parallels in pottery found by Uhle farther north at Huaca del Sol in Moche (Kroeber 1925a, pl. 65c, e, g, h). In particular, the design band with alternating step-triangle and maze panels (Figure 94H) is repeated in some of the sherds (Kroeber 1925a, pl. 65c, e). Press-molded pottery of this style does not occur as frequently outside this region.

In temporal terms, the best estimate for the imported examples from Chinchawas is a general association with the middle to late Middle Horizon. It should be noted that several specimens (Figure 94E, H) were found in association with local Warmi phase diagnostics. On review of Uhle's notes, Kroeber (1925a:212) considered that the press-molded material from Site A, Huaca del Sol, at Moche were contemporaneous with "Tiahuanacoid" materials from adjacent tombs. Menzel (1977:38) later confirmed this hypothesis and added that they resulted from the deliberate smashing of artifacts common in Wari offering deposits during Middle Horizon 2.

## Polished Decorated Blackware

This category consists of a blackware, usually with a polished surface or press-molded design, or both (Figure 95). Vessels have a reduced, soft gray paste characterized by well-sorted inclusions of small-sized grit, perhaps sand and occasional mica. The paste is medium-hard and gray.

Most of the fragments are from bottles or jars (e.g., Figure 95F, G, I, L). Exterior surfaces are colored black or, less commonly, a brownish gray. Polished exterior surfaces show press-molding; additional techniques include incision (Figure 95M) and modeling (Figure 95G). Interior surfaces, meanwhile, were left unworked and rough. There are also some examples of blackware bowls (Figure 95C, E, K). While bowl interiors can also show polishing, the focus of elaboration is on the exteriors, which feature press-molded and modeled designs. Bowls can be incurving (e.g., Figure 95E), but everted profiles (e.g., Figure 95C, D, K) are more common.

Despite the general similarity in paste and plastic decoration, more careful examination of the decorative technique and design suggests that the fragments probably correspond to multiple traditions and sources from the north and north-central coasts. First, the techniques of decoration differ. Press-molded designs are slightly rounded with raised areas grading into the background (Figure 95N, I). In others, the designs are sharp and flat. The press-molded designs also differ in depth of execution, with some in very low relief (e.g., Figure 95K, L). There are also examples of prefire incision (Figure 95M) and modeling (Figure 95E, G, H) that contrast with the molded specimens. Second, the designs differ considerably

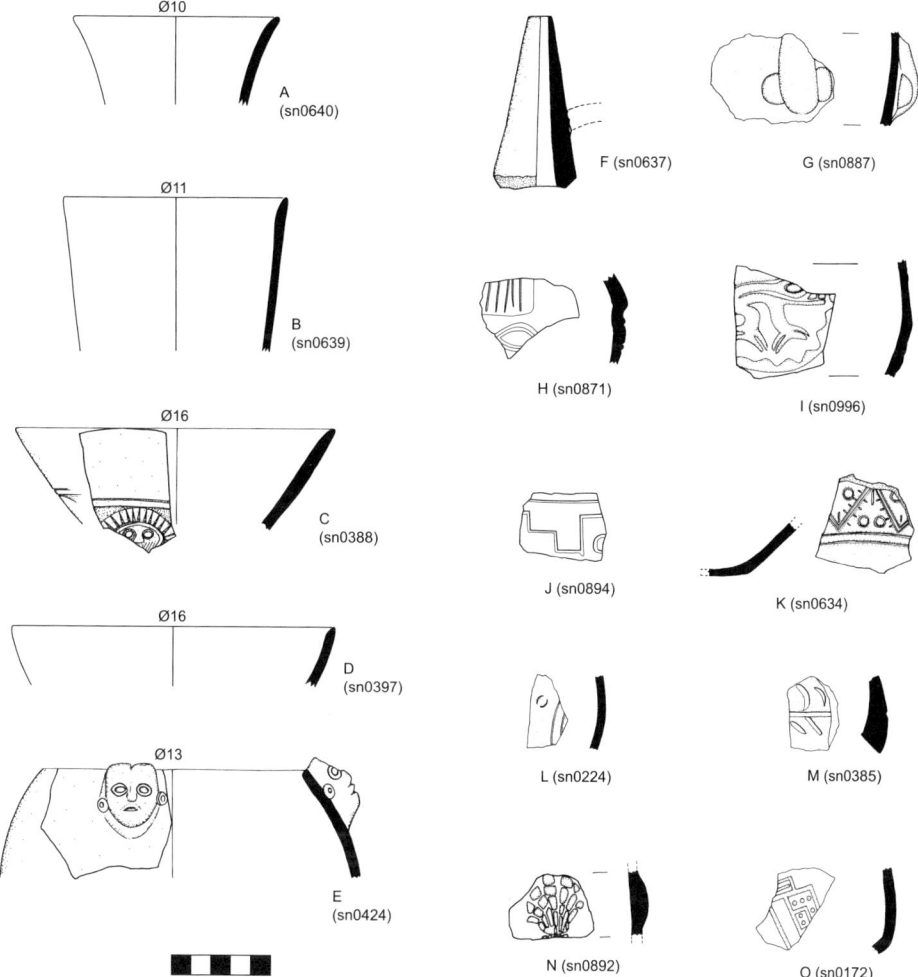

FIGURE 95. Polished blackware pottery: A, B, tumblers; C–E, bowls; F, spout; G–O, exterior plastic decoration.

from one another. One fragment (Figure 95N) represents a marine shell, perhaps *Spondylus* sp. Another shows an image of a mythical animal (Figure 95I), perhaps a feline, that seems stylistically similar to the shell depiction, as does a polished sherd with a monkey image. However, these contrast with the front-face image (Figure 95C) with a corona headdress and modeled facial depictions (Figure 95E, G). The triangle face motif (Figure 95K) is another distinctive design that does not occur again in our ceramic sample.

The fragmentary condition of the sample and the long duration of polished blackware pottery traditions preclude precise stylistic associations. The Chinchawas specimens can be best compared to pottery from the north coast, especially from between the Virú and Moche valleys. For example, the conical spout (Figure 95F) can correspond just as well to Moche V (Shimada 1994) as to provincial Wari styles

(Menzel 1977, fig. 51) and Chimu culture (e.g., Kroeber 1925a, pl. 62e). Nevertheless, there is stylistic rationale to associate some of the polished blackware from Chinchawas to the Middle Horizon. First, the repeated triangle face motif (Figure 95K), which probably has roots in central coast styles of the Early Intermediate Period (e.g., Kroeber 1926, pl. 89A; Patterson 1966), appears as a press-molded element in Moche V pottery (Bawden 1996:275–276, fig. 9.1). Bawden (1994, 1996) also notes that production of pressed blackware became increasingly prevalent during Moche V. The triangle face motif is also prevalent in Supe press-molded wares (Kroeber 1925b, pl. 75i) and could have variants in the central highland wares of the Middle Horizon (Lumbreras 1960, lám. 7h; Knobloch 1983, pl. 53f). Second, Menzel (1977:32) observes that press-molded designs during Middle Horizon Epoch 2, at least in Supe, are very low in relief. Several blackware sherds from Chinchawas (e.g., Figure 95E, L) could therefore fall under this category.

Finally, polished blackware also occurs, if sporadically, in the highlands (Bennett 1944, 1953; Lumbreras 1960). Like the examples from Chinchawas, Bennett's tomb material has objects that emphasize figural representations, especially of anthropomorphic faces, animals (especially birds) and marine shells. Specimens with available contexts often indicate stratigraphic and iconographic associations to the Middle Horizon (Bennett 1944, fig. 6; Topic and Topic 1984). Some of Bennett's material from his Wilkawaín sites, in particular, can be dated to the Middle Horizon Epoch 1B on the basis of associations with Chakipampa B pottery. It is unknown whether the greater Huaraz region was also a locus of blackware pottery production. Relevant decorated examples and their iconography indicate that a foreign, probably coastal, source is more likely.

The sample of polished blackware could also have late Middle Horizon associations. The press-molded creature (see Figure 95I) is probably mythical. It seems to have composite features of both felines (general profile and teeth) and semireptilian characteristics (dual-opposed feet). The image can be associated with two coastal iconographic traditions: the "moon animal" in northern Peru art, common during the late Early Intermediate Period, and the "sky scene" feline of the central coast, prevalent during Middle Horizon 3 (Carrión Cachot 1959; Bruhns 1976; Menzel 1977; Mackey and Vogel 2003), or both. The front-face image with a corona headdress (Figure 95C) could be an elaborate version of a simple repeating face image found on a pressed-molded bowl from an "Early Chimu" burial at Moche (Donnan and Mackey 1978:255, fig. 3).

Fancy Polychrome Pottery, Wari Style

The investigations recovered Wari style fancy polychrome pottery from Sector 1 (Figures 96 and 97). Such pottery was not found in the Sector 2 tombs. These vessels are made of a common to medium-fine redware (ranging from dark dusky red to orange), with common inclusions of grit of variable size and mica. In several cases the paste is fired very hard (Figure 96A, C). Polychrome painting occurs only on a small number of vessel forms categorized as bowls, jars and tumblers.

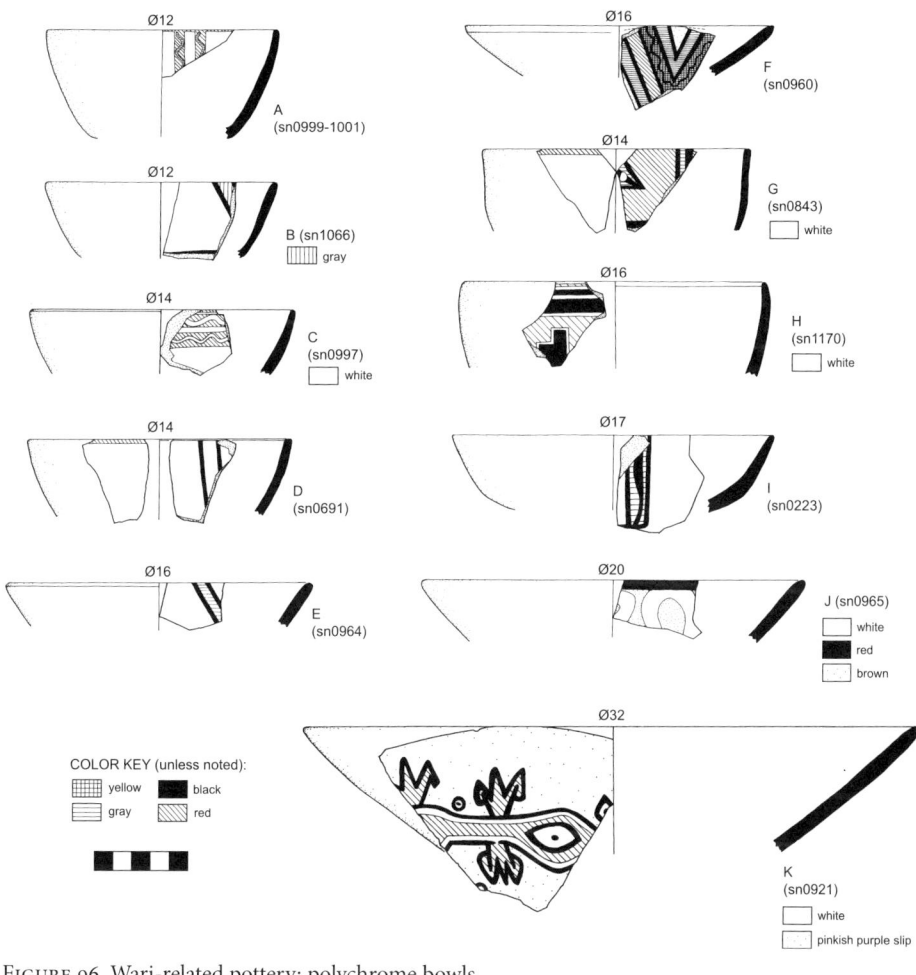

FIGURE 96. Wari-related pottery: polychrome bowls.

*Tumblers.* Tumblers make up the smallest group, with only a few examples (Figure 97G, H). These were found in Sector 1, in Warmi phase deposits. One example (Figure 97H) derives from a provincial Wari style tumbler typical for Middle Horizon Epoch 2B (Menzel 1977, fig. 46A–C). Its painted designs include a lattice pattern (a black and white on red) broken by a panel of three white dots over which are black crosses.

*Jars.* Jars are the second most abundant form category for Wari style polychrome ware (Figure 97A–E). This category consists primarily of larger vessels (e.g., Figure 97B). One jar sherd (Figure 97D) shows design affinities to Middle Horizon Epoch 1 styles of the central highlands. The design is executed in polychrome over a dark red slipped and polished surface. It lies just below the neck on the shoulder of the jar and has two panels separated by three vertical bands, one of which contains a meander; the others are painted. The clearest panel shows two S-shaped figures, which are common in Wari Chakipampa B pottery. The general form also resembles the "Tiahuanacoid" pottery found in the deep stone-lined tombs at Ichik Wilkawaín, attributed to Middle Horizon 1B (Bennett 1944, fig. 9; Menzel 1964).

Other jar sherds with polychrome designs are from vertical-neck jars (Figure 97A, B) and are much more simply painted with less elaborate surface treatment. Neck designs include band and meander pendants and lines across the base of the neck. Body designs include rows of white crosses. While there are formal resemblances to Epoch 1 jars, the character of these designs suggests a Middle Horizon 2 position.

*Bowls.* The sample of Wari style polychrome painted pottery consists principally of bowls (Figure 96A–K). Most pieces in this category are interior-painted open bowls. The bowls, generally, have fairly vertical sides, but some are shallower. They are small, with mouth diameters ranging between 12 and 17 cm. There is some variation in the paste used, between a common orangeware to a lighter, very hard and fine oxidized ware, divided into "Wari polychrome," "fine orange" and "fine red burnished." Surfaces are generally burnished to a dull matte finish, although one (Figure 96F) is burnished to a fine matte, almost chalky, finish and another (Figure 96G) retains a dull but discernible luster. Designs focus on single or multiple bands of different colors, sometimes with meanders (e.g., Figure 96A) or organized as pendants (Figure 96I).

*Unidentified form.* There are also several Wari polychrome fragments that cannot be identified to form. However, they all have polychrome painting on the exterior and slipped or burnished interiors typical of small bowls or tumblers. Common designs include triple recurved ray appendages, chevrons and polychrome bands. These designs can be of Middle Horizon 1B or Middle Horizon Epoch 2 style (Menzel 1964).

*Comparisons.* Comparative material comes from the Central Highland zones showing a strong Wari influence. The Middle and Late Patibamba I phases at Jargampata (Isbell 1977) and materials recovered in the Chicha–Soras Valley (Meddens 1985) are comparable styles dating to Middle Horizon, Epoch 2. From the Wari type site, "Wamanga" or "Huamanga" style pottery provides possible analogues in form and decoration. Interior bands and meanders, tree designs, repeated white loops, pendant rectangles and filler elements (dots, crosses and "sausage" curls) are common shared elements. The Wamanga style is often synonymous with Menzel's "secular Viñaque" and pertains to Middle Horizon 2 (Lumbreras 1960, 1974b; Anders 1989; González Carré et al. 1999; Pozzi-Escot 1999).

There are several exceptional exterior-painted examples (Figures 96H, K and 97F) that show strong Wari affinities. One unique polychrome fragment from a small, highly polished incurving bowl (Figure 97F) depicts a portion of a mythical

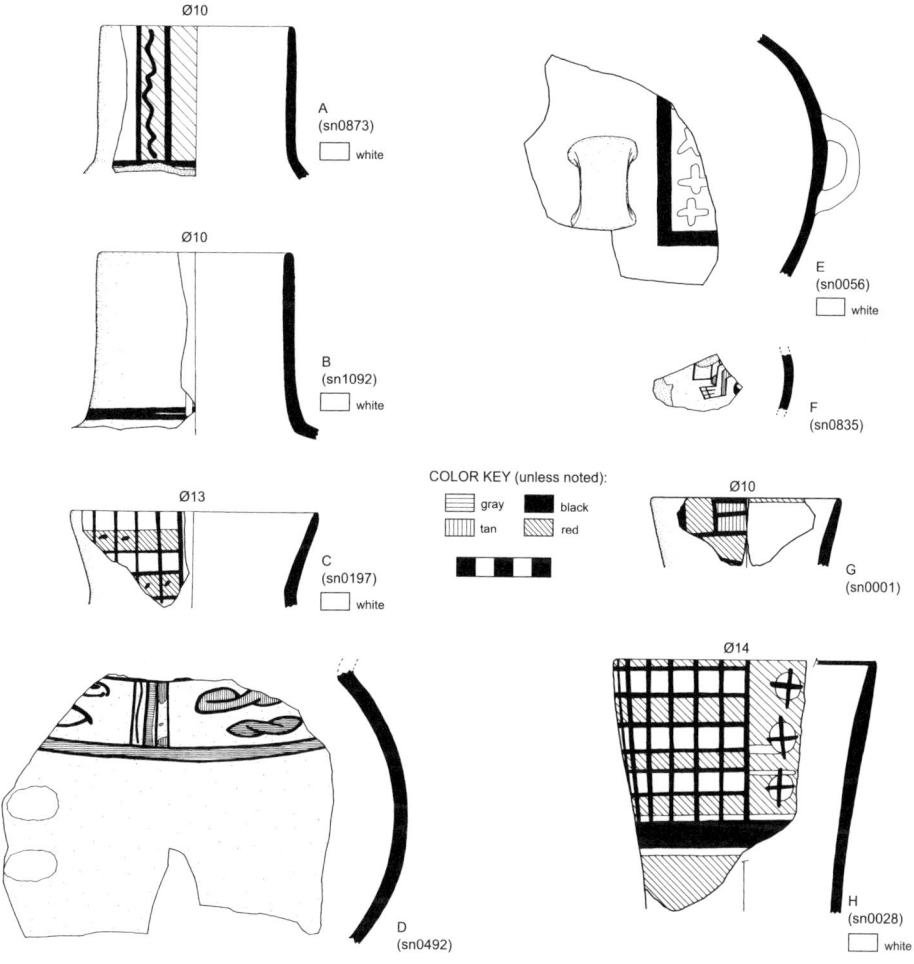

FIGURE 97. Wari-related pottery: A–E, polychrome jars; F, bottle; G, H, tumblers.

figure. The figure has probable counterparts in Chakipampa B pottery of the central highlands (Bennett 1953, figs. 17C, 18Q, pl. 6F; Menzel 1964, 1977, fig. 63, bottom right).

Several fragments from a large open bowl (Figure 96K) show portions of a Wari style mythical creature. The bowl has a redware paste, with common grit but no mica. Both the interior and exterior are slipped with a pinkish brown slip and polished to a dull luster; both surfaces become iridescent when wet. The mythical creature has a large eye, a long body of uneven width and tripartite rayed appendages. Dotted white dots are supplementary elements. The recurved ray appendages resemble identical elements in Chakipampa B designs (Bennett 1953, fig. 18M). The creature, with the single eye, could be a variant of Menzel's "three-fillet band" figure (Menzel 1964:11, fig. 3). Patricia Knobloch (1983, pl. 58g, see also pl. 51c)

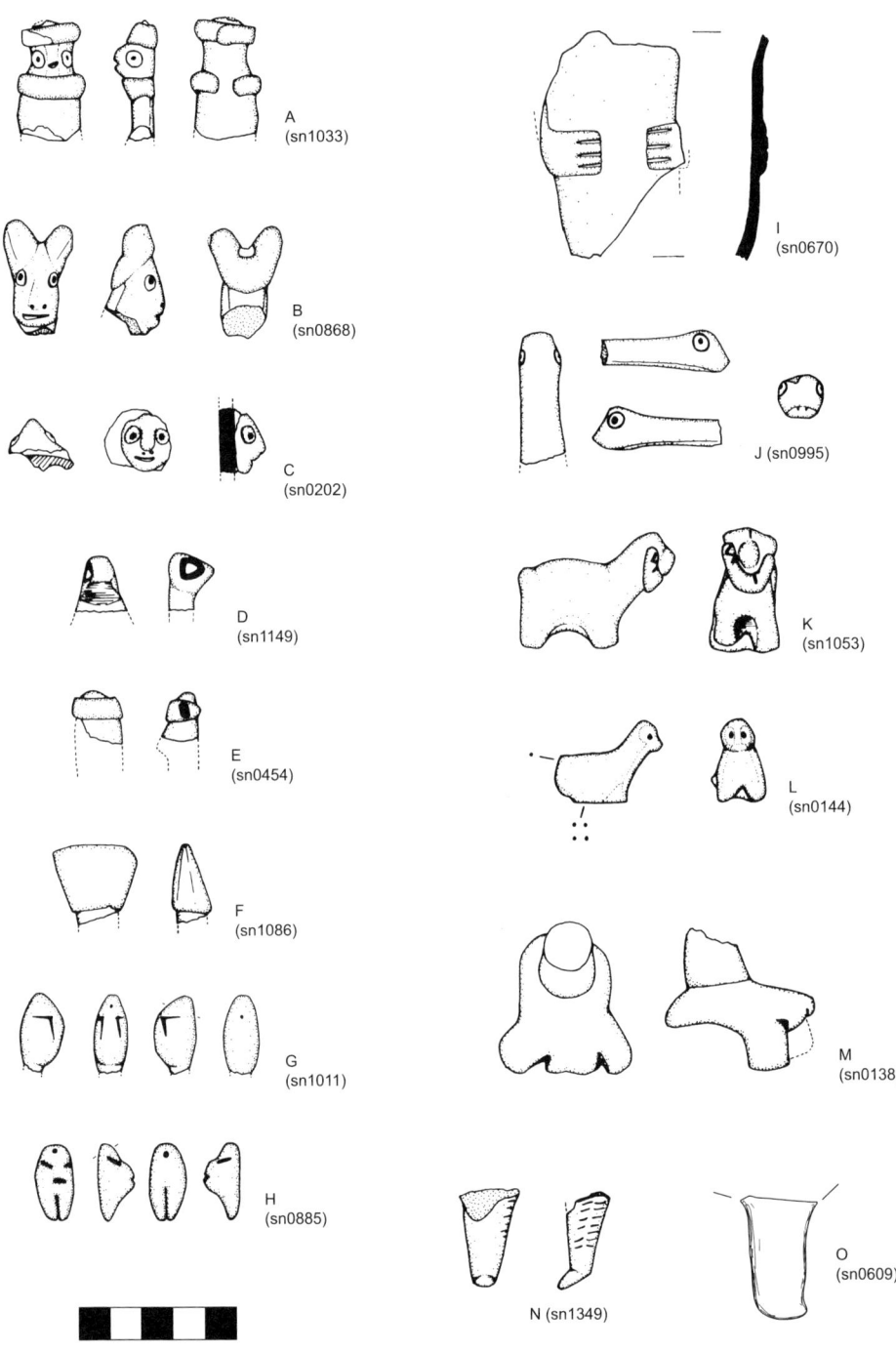

FIGURE 98. Modeled figurines and adornos.

also identified a similar "3-fillet band" creature in a Middle Horizon Epoch 1 deposit, also from a large open bowl or dish.

Finally, there is one exterior decorated sherd (Figure 96H) of an open bowl, with slightly convex incurving sides and a burnished, matte surface. The design includes several horizontal bands with white borders near the lip and a step motif, also bordered in white. The step motif, thin white borders, small modular widths and matte finish all characterize Chakipampa B pottery from Ayacucho (Menzel 1964:16; e.g., Bennett 1953, pl. 4D). The design also carries over into Viñaque (e.g., Bennett 1953, fig. 11A–E), but in larger modular widths.

FINE PINKWARE

There is another large corpus of imported pottery, distinguished by a very fine pink or light reddish orange clay. The clay has few inclusions of very small grit and fired to a brittle, chalky consistency. This ware was used exclusively to manufacture small artifacts, for which there are three categories: spoons, figurines and miscellaneous or indeterminate artifacts.

*Spoons.* Spoons (e.g., Figure 92C–F) were recovered during our excavations in Sector 1, but are absent in our sample from Sector 2. Compared with other imports, fine pinkware spoon sherds occur frequently and typically in very small fragments, probably a function of their thin walls and brittleness. They occur as early as the Chinchawasi 1 phase, but are most popular during the Chinchawasi 2 and Warmi phases.

The spoons have a fairly standardized bowl form but differ in handle shape. They are small, with the longest example measuring just over 9 cm in length. Bowls are oval in plan and relatively shallow. Handles, meanwhile, can be simple (Figure 92E), truncate and flattened (Figure 92C), or looped (Figure 92F). The handles often have convex profiles, with the end curving upward prominently.

Spoons also differ in their painted decoration. Fink pinkware spoons are slipped red and, less commonly, orange and are finely burnished to a matte or dull luster finish. Designs are painted in combinations of white, black and dark red paints and include familiar motifs: dots within bands, bands and meanders, arcs and repeating "tick" lines.

Such spoons appear in other highland zones. Menzel (1968, fig. 54) illustrates a Chakipampa B spoon from Wari that is identical in form and size to some Chinchawas specimens. Closer to Chinchawas, Bennett (1944, fig. 13F) identified examples from sites 9H-1 ("Subterranean House site") and 7H-1 (a deep stone-lined tomb). Both are Middle Horizon tombs in the vicinity of Huaraz. Similar spoons exist in private collections in highland Ancash.

*Figurines.* Several figurine and adorno fragments have the same fine pink or orange paste (Figure 98A–C, F). All the figurines depict anthropomorphic figures or faces and are carefully modeled. The fine clay, apparently, worked well for modeling small, delicate pottery objects such as spoons and figurines.

One sherd, from a hollow figurine effigy (Figure 98I), depicts the torso of an anthropomorphic figure. Crude hands are positioned over the stomach. The exterior surface is burnished to a matte finish and has a bright reddish orange slip, while the interior is unworked and shows the fingerprints of the potter. Such figurines appear occasionally in the archaeological record. All fit within Middle Horizon contexts (e.g., Kauffmann Doig 1980:287; Topic and Topic 1984, fig. 11B; Meddens 1985, fig. 85; Wilson 1988, fig. 252; Paredes, et al. 2000:259).

In other fine pinkware fragments, potters paid careful attention to the eyes and headdresses of the figures. Eyes are formed by modeling a small, circular and flattened piece of clay, punctated in or near the middle, bordered occasionally by incision around the eye. Headdresses are elaborate and seem to mimic "turbans" (Figure 98E, F) on minor and statue-like figures on Recuay pots (e.g., Eisleb 1987, pl. 183, 185, 206). One example (Figure 98B) seems to represent an anthropomorph with animal-like ears or an unusual headdress. There are few comparative diagnostics with which to associate these pinkware and orangeware figurines. Nevertheless, because of their provenience and technological similarity to the spoons, we can safely attribute them to the Chinchawasi 2 and Warmi phases.

*Miscellaneous.* The fine pinkware paste was also used in a few miscellaneous objects for which there is no intact specimen. The category includes tubular fragments that resemble slip cast panpipe fragments found by Bennett (1944) at sites in the Huaraz area (see Dawson 1964). These fragments are generally very thin and occur as a single tube or, in one instance, as two connected tubes. There are also several small, flat sherds of unknown purpose that use the fine pinkware paste.

### Red-on-cream, Moche Style

Excavations in Terrace 4 in Chinchawasi 1 levels recovered two sherds of a Moche style red-on-cream pottery. The fragments were unlike the red-on-cream pottery of the Chinchawasi styles. The sherds are very thin and derive from the shoulder of a bottle, as the interior is unworked and rough. The paint is thicker, the surface has more of a luster, and the slip covers a deep red paste that is rarely found in Chinchawasi phase pottery. The design consists of red dots on a cream (off-white) background. This pottery is more common on the coast during the Moche period (e.g., Strong and Evans 1952, fig. 71L), and a similar design and color scheme often decorate the shoulders of Moche stirrup spout bottles and small jars (e.g., Donnan and Mackey 1978:106, 119).

### Figurine Pendants

These are two modeled plainware fragments depicting anthropomorphs (Figure 98G, H). Both are made of regular red clay, with no slip or elaborate surface treatment besides the modeling. Each figurine is perforated through the forehead, probably for hanging as a pendant. One fragment is broken at the neck (Figure 98G) and shows the head with a distinctive eye design formed by two incisions, one across

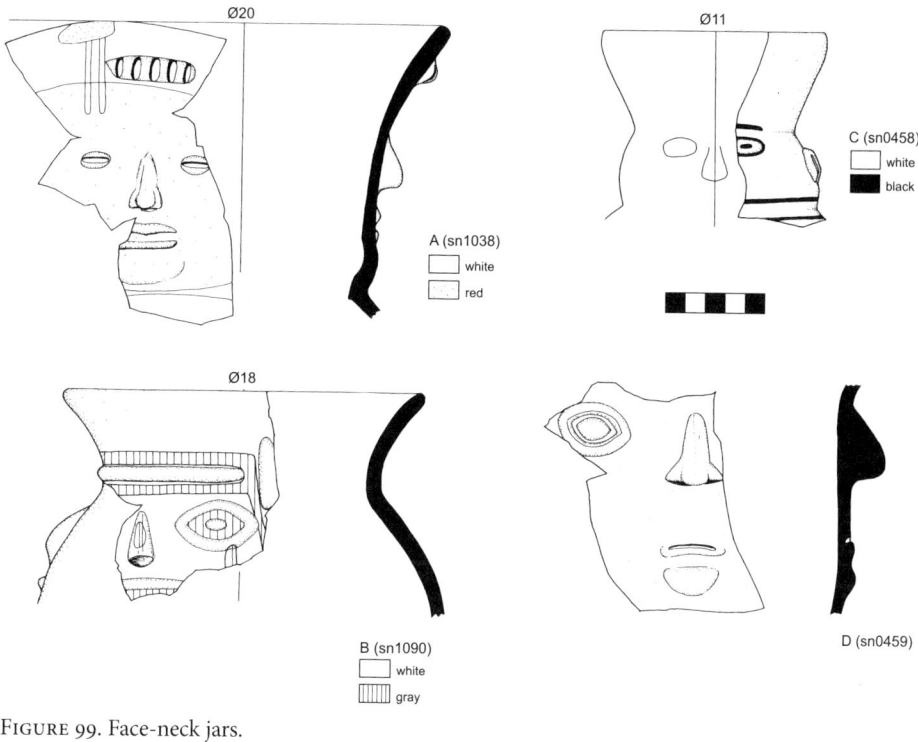

FIGURE 99. Face-neck jars.

and one down. The other figurine (Figure 98H) is complete and portrays a biped figure. Incisions and modeling detail two legs and the features of the face. Both specimens were found in Middle Horizon refuse deposits.

ANIMAL FIGURINES

These are plainware fragments depicting animals, probably camelids (Figure 98K, L, N, O). All are made of common red clay, with no slip or elaborate surface treatment besides the modeling. Features of the animal are rendered through incisions or sculpting, such as the leg and foot of a mammal, probably a camelid (see Figure 98N). Small, horizontal incisions decorate the upper leg, perhaps mimicking the texture of the animal's coat. The repeated incisions resemble the incision technique prominent in Warmi phase plastic decoration (Figures 71F and 82H). In Andahuaylas, Grossman (1983, figs. 96, 97) encountered similarly modeled camelid miniatures at the site of Waywaka. They were found in cistern fill, dating to the Qasawirka phase of the Early Intermediate Period.

PAINTED FACE-NECK VESSELS

Face-neck vessels (Figure 99) also form part of the fancy, decorated pottery assemblage at Chinchawas. All examples use common redware clay, with common grit and sometimes mica inclusions. They are almost exclusively from Middle Horizon contexts and are associated with Chinchawasi 2 and Warmi phase de-

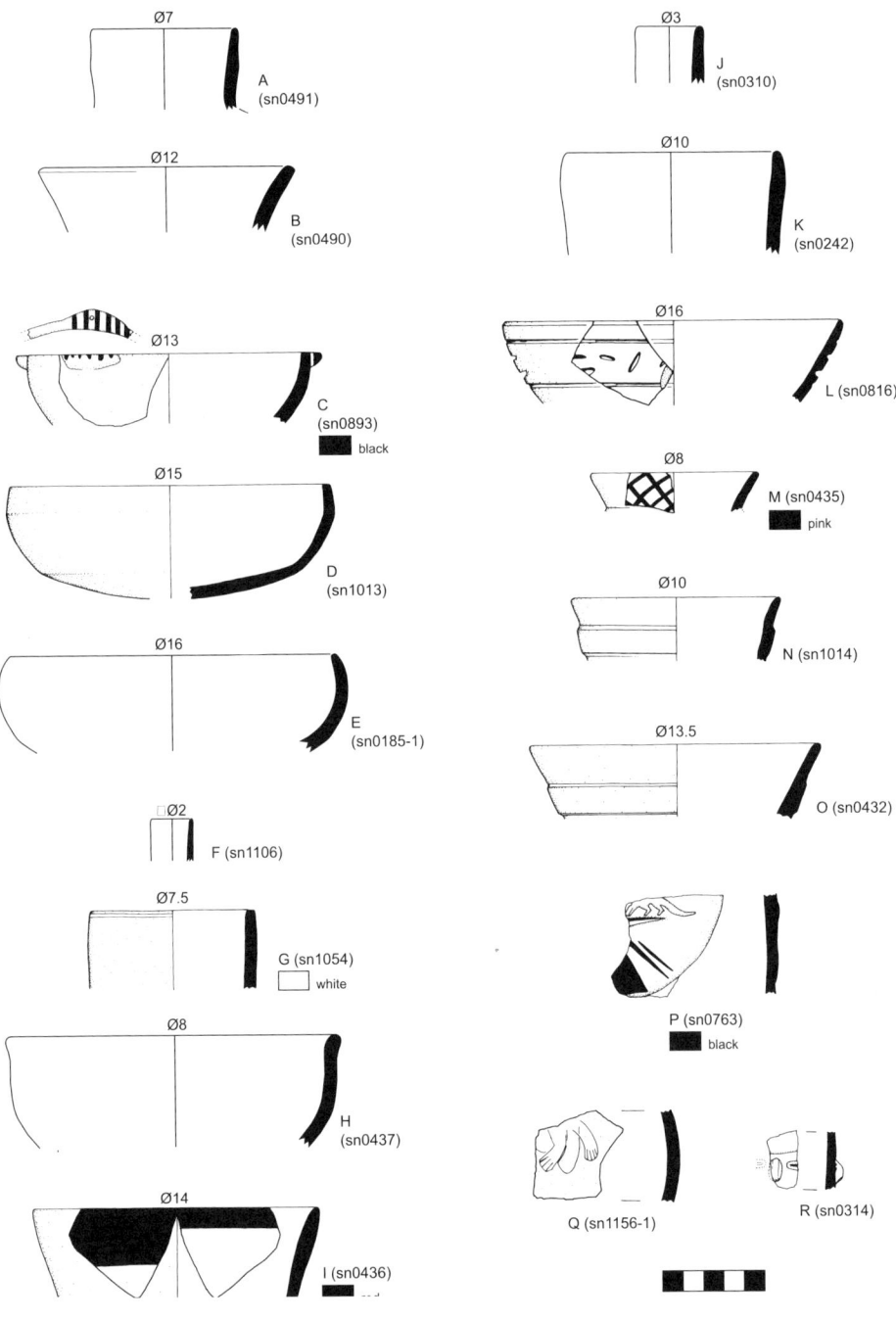

FIGURE 100. Other fancy wares: A, B, Fine Orange; C–E, Purple Iridescent; F–I, Fine Pink; J–R, Fine/Polished Brown.

posits. Unpainted face-neck vessels are discussed in the next section. Considerable heterogeneity characterizes the form and decoration of the painted face-neck specimens.

A rim fragment from a necked vessel with a very everted rim (Figure 99A) has "coffee-bean" eyes, a carefully modeled nose and slightly raised lips and chin. The area around these facial features is painted red, while the neck and two lines are in white. There is also a ribbed appliqué fillet above the nose. Another (Figure 99B) derives from a flaring neck vessel with a globular body profile or one with a cambered neck. Simple facial features, including a forehead band and mouth, are formed using long bands of clay. Gray paint accentuates these features. Another sherd (Figure 99C) derives from a flaring neck vessel with a cambered profile. Modeled facial areas include the eye interior and ear. Additional features are painted in black lines. Black lines border the white neck band. One fragment (Figure 99D) is slipped in matte red and uses the modeling technique present also in another fragment (see Figure 99B). Facial features are far apart, but special attention was given to a very protruding nose and slightly raised lower lip and chin.

Vessels decorated with faces and necks are common features in Middle Horizon Wari and post-Wari ceramic assemblages throughout the Central Andes. It is difficult to identify definite stylistic ties, especially since the Chinchawas face–neck decorations themselves differ greatly from one another in form and design.

Unpainted Modeled Face–neck Decoration

There are also several unpainted face-neck fragments (Figures 67R and 82P, Q, R). All examples use a common redware paste and show very little burnishing on a paste-colored surface. The faces can be fairly simple, with small appliqué strips (e.g., Figure 67R) or more elaborate decorative modes, such as ribbed fillets, incision and modeling (e.g., Figure 78Q). Like the painted face-neck decoration, it is difficult to determine the source of these more simple face-neck fragments. From their stratigraphic contexts, however, unpainted face-neck vessels seem to have been most prevalent during the Warmi phase of occupation. Their source is not yet identified, although given the character of the paste, local production cannot be ruled out.

Purple Iridescent Style

Purple iridescent is an oxidized ware characterized by a very polished, lustrous dark reddish brown or purple surface (Figure 100C–E). The paste is fine and hard, with occasional but well-sorted inclusions of small- to medium-sized angular grit and mica. Surfaces are smooth and polished to a medium luster. The pottery has a very dark brown or dark purple slip. The purple, especially, can be iridescent, particularly when damp. There is a very little painted decoration on purple iridescent pottery, usually limited to black rim ticks or simple linear patterns on vessel exteriors. Of the sample, only a few show plastic decoration. This seems to be restricted to formal additions, such as rim nubbins and nubbin holes. Lip treatment is simple

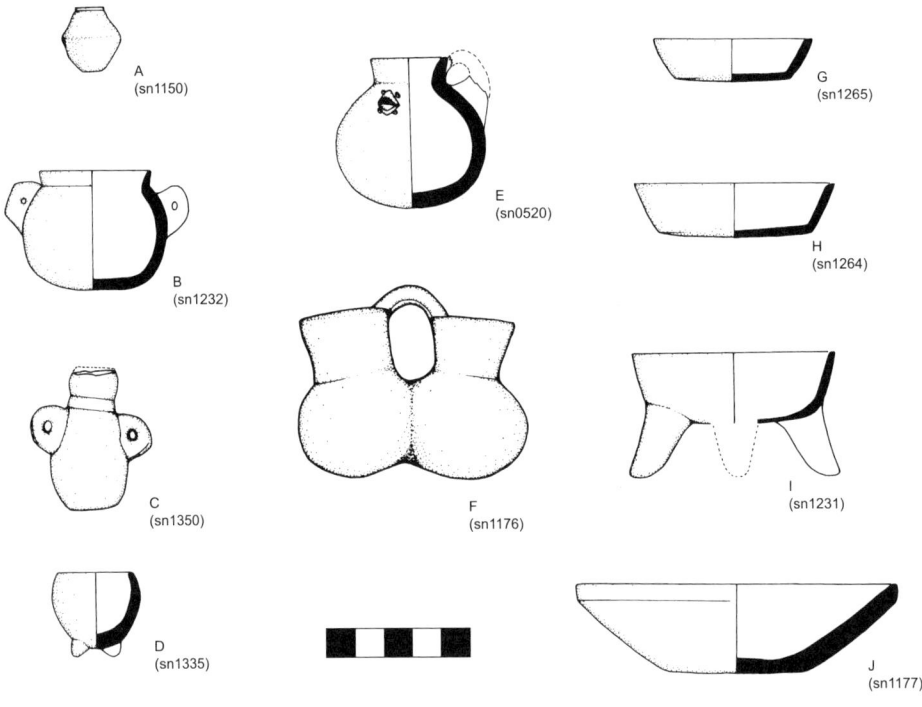

FIGURE 101. Miniature vessels.

and includes a basic rounding or slight beveling. Purple iridescent shapes include a convex open bowl form and a shallow incurving bowl.

Purple iridescent ware is a rare fancy pottery that occurs mainly in the Chinchawasi 2 phase, but survived at least to Warmi times. Moreover, it was used principally for small and fairly delicate serving vessels. The quality of surface treatment, moreover, supports an argument that purple iridescent ware functioned as a low-use prestige ceramic from as yet an unknown source.

### Fine Gray Wares

Fine grayware is a partly reduced, partly oxidized redware characterized by a low luster brownish gray exterior surface. The paste is fine and hard, with regular well-sorted inclusions of small angular grit and mica. The paste color grades from a light gray to brownish gray. Exterior surfaces are smooth and burnished to a low luster, and several sherds showed hand modeling. Only a small open bowl and bottle shape were represented in the sample. Fine grayware appears almost exclusively during the Chinchawasi 2 phase and seems to have been an imported fancy pottery type.

### Fine Polished Brown

Fine polished brown (Figure 100J–R) is an oxidized ware. Its paste ranges from medium-fine to fine, but is relatively hard, with a light brown exterior surface.

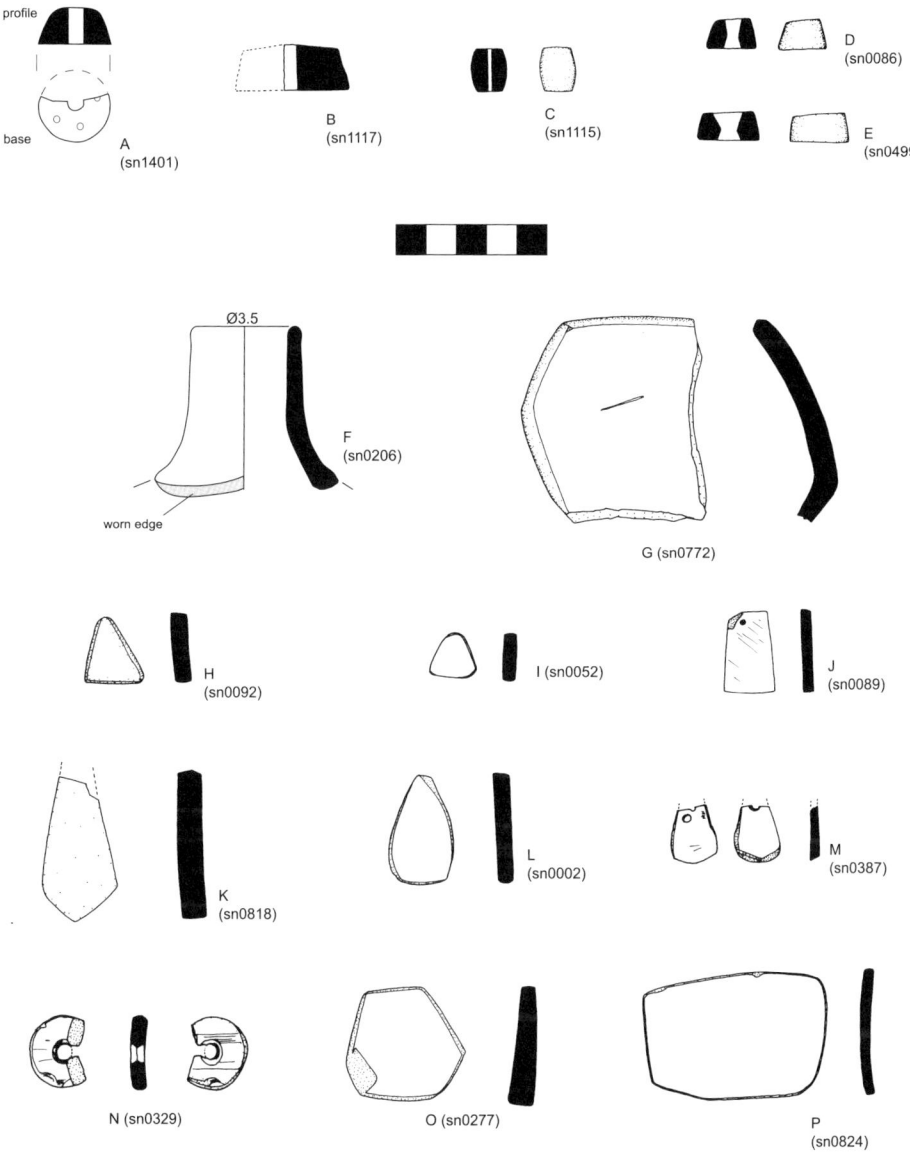

FIGURE 102. Fired pottery whorls and ground ceramic objects.

Surfaces show polishing to low lusters (Figure 100M, R). The ware often has plastic decoration, nearly always on the exterior. Techniques used include incision (Figure 100Q), zoned punctation (Figure 100L) and modeling (Figure 100P, R). Forms include drinking cups (Figure 100M–O), bowls and bottles. One exceptional piece in the form of a modeled face, very likely Moche in origin, comes from a finely burnished bottle or jar (Figure 100P). A band with two stripes painted in thin black paint extends away from the mouth to the chin, perhaps representing facial hair, tattooing or painted decoration. Above the mouth, resembling half of a moustache, is a modeled design in the form of quadrupedal animal with a tail, perhaps a fox, lizard or viscacha. The sherd may have had warfare associations (Lau 2004b:179).

Miscellaneous Ceramic Objects
(Fired Whorls and Ground Sherds)
The investigations also recovered a series of fired whorls (Figure 102A–E). One may have also been a type of bead (Figure 102C). Although of different sizes and shapes, most feature a truncate profile. One of the whorls has punctations on the wide base (Figure 102A). These whorls are more elaborate than those that reuse broken ceramics. Finally, we also encountered recycled ceramic sherds (Figure 102F–P) shaped into specific geometric forms, including teardrops, triangles, circles, trapezoids and other angular forms. Some have been partly perforated, presumably to hang as a pendant, while others are large enough to have been used as scrapers and scoops.

## Distributions of Fancy and Imported Ceramics at Chinchawas

This section, organized by phase, discusses the spatial and temporal distributions of the fancy and imported pottery from Chinchawas (see Table 11), with a focus on diachronic transformations in the evidence for long-distance interaction and regional stylistic influences at Chinchawas.

*Kayán Phase*
The Kayán kaolinite pottery is most similar in style to Recuay ceramics. It is an imported ware probably derived from the Callejón de Huaylas, most likely from a pottery-producing center near Huaraz. Wegner (2003) documented this style in quantity at the site of Balcón de Judas. Of the 72 fancy sherds in Kayán deposits at Chinchawas, 70 (or 97%) belonged to kaolinite styles, 62.5% were of the Recuay style of the Huaraz area, and 34.7% were of kaolinite wares that could not be identified (without decoration or with eroded decoration). Nevertheless, the unidentified sherds were almost certainly produced in the North Highlands.

Recuay kaolinite was found in both special-use and residential areas. About 21% of the Kayán Recuay sample was recovered in patio–enclosure contexts. As described earlier, these provided integral spaces for public, communal activities. About 28% of the sample came from the residential context of OP45. Half of the Kayán Recuay sample came from "terrace" areas. "Terrace" here is a misnomer, because the first identifiable terrace walls date to Chinchawasi 1. Most of this group can be categorized as materials located in peripheral zones (Terrace 1, Terrace 2 and Terrace 3) that immediately flank and are downslope from the Kayán patio–enclosures and the OP45 residence. Given their stratigraphic location, most of the Kayán sample in the Terrace category represents surface scatter eroding away from the upper, central zone of Sector 1.

The ceramic evidence indicates that the Kayán occupation was part of larger Recuay developments in the Huaraz area of the Callejón de Huaylas (Lau 2005). Local groups shared a highland-based background that enabled appreciation of the iconography in Recuay material culture.

### Chinchawasi 1 Phase

Compared to the Kayán phase, a wider range of external contacts prevailed during the Chinchawasi 1 phase. Certainly by the end of Chinchawasi 1 the community at Chinchawas was actively participating in an exchange network connecting the central highlands to the north highlands and to the north coast.

Of the sample (n=63), our data show that Chinchawas peoples imported pottery from the North Highlands (19% Recuay style, 25% indeterminate kaolinite, 4.8% fine pinkware), the Central Highlands (3.2% Wari style) and the North Coast (14% Late Moche style). In addition, polished blackware (30%) belonging to North Highland or North Coast traditions, or both, became important. There is one press-molded piece, probably from the north-central and north coast.

In addition, there were important changes in the distributions and use patterns of imported pottery between the Kayán and Chinchawasi 1 phases. Imported pottery occurred in mortuary contexts and represented 31.7% of the Chinchawasi 1 phase total. The only styles identified include Late Moche (Moche V) and polished blackware.

About 11% of the fancy pottery was found in excavations of room complexes and residences. The sample includes Recuay and indeterminate kaolinite sherds, polished blackware, fink pinkware, a face-neck style and press-molded redware. All categories are represented only by trace amounts occurring predominantly as fragments on beaten dirt floors and surface refuse scatter. Compared to the Kayán phase, fancy pottery had a less significant presence in residential and domestic contexts during Chinchawasi 1. Fancy pottery within patio–enclosures decreases sharply to 6.3% of the phase sample. Only indeterminate kaolinite sherds are represented, which suggests that earlier activities in the patio–enclosures diminished in frequency and importance.

Terrace areas contained about 44% of the phase sample. Activities using imported pottery within the areas cordoned off by the perimeter walls apparently became more important. The pottery is fragmentary and occurs as light refuse and surface scatter. Fine pinkware, Wari polychrome (Chakipampa-related), polished blackware, and Late Moche (probably Moche IV red-on-cream) styles are represented in small quantities. Indeterminate and Recuay kaolinite form most of the phase sample from terraces (64.3%).

Fancy pottery also occurs in the Torreón structure. Three kaolinite fragments and one fancy Wari polychrome are represented in the foundation deposits of the building (6.3% of the phase). From its inception during Chinchawasi 1, then, activities inside the Torreón structure included high-status goods.

*Chinchawasi 2 Phase*

The importation of pottery of different regional styles intensified greatly during the Chinchawasi 2 phase (see Table 11). A greater abundance and expanded repertoire of foreign fancy pottery indicate more intensive participation in existing trade networks and a broadening of regional connections by the Chinchawas community. Notably, the diversity of trade wares coincided with the resurgence of Wari culture in the Central Highlands during Middle Horizon Epoch 2 and later expansion to areas outside the Wari heartland, including the Callejón de Huaylas (Menzel 1964).

As in the Chinchawasi 1 phase, the imported pottery sample of 192 sherds comes from both highland and coastal sources. Not surprisingly, Chinchawasi 2 peoples continued to have strong connections to the nearby Huaraz area and the rest of the Callejón de Huaylas. Compared to Chinchawasi 1, fine pinkware, usually in the form of spoons, increases strongly—from 3.8% to 12.5% of the respective phase totals. As expected, Recuay kaolinite decreases in popularity (3.1%), as does indeterminate kaolinite (7.8%).

New styles of the North Highlands appeared for the first time during the Chinchawasi 2 phase. The small sample available suggests that the "Wilkawaín resist" style (9.4%) had a limited distribution within the Callejón de Huaylas. In addition, presence of Cajamarca (0.5%) and Cajamarca-related styles (7.3%) shows a preference for prestigious kaolinite wares.

Middle Horizon pottery from the Central Highlands was also popular, with Wari polychrome styles accounting for 8.9% of the phase total of imported ceramics during Chinchawasi 2. Additional Wari influence also is manifested in the fine orange (4.7%) and fine red burnished styles (0.5%). As described previously, these bear close affinities to "secular" wares produced in the Central Highlands during Middle Horizon Epoch 2, such as the Wamanga style or secular Viñaque style of the Wari site (Lumbreras 1960, 1974b; Menzel 1964, 1968) and the Middle and Late Patibamba style of Jargampata (Isbell 1977).

Small amounts of imported pottery came from the Central Coast in the form of Nievería style pottery (3.6%). In addition, press-molded wares typical of the north-central and north coasts, especially of Supe and Virú, became increasingly common (6.3%) and are precursors to their maximum popularity in later Warmi contexts.

Several classes of fancy wares can be categorized as foreign wares, but cannot be identified to source with any certainty. Polished blackware represents just less than 7% of the phase total and therefore decreased in popularity. In general, the blackwares show affinities to both nearby highland areas (Huaraz and Wilkawaín) and coastal regions, particularly the north and north-central coasts. Face-neck vessels also increase in frequency, accounting for 17% of the phase total. Finally, there are several unidentified categories with fine pastes and a diagnostic slipped surface: fine gray (6.8%) and purple iridescent (4.7%).

The intrasite distributions of fancy pottery show continuities and changes. The patio–enclosures, which were so vital in the Kayán period and which continued to function during the Chinchawasi 1 phase, did not contain much fancy pottery during Chinchawasi 2. Excavations in residential and room complex contexts recovered 12% of the imported phase sample. This percentage is comparable to the Chinchawasi 1 phase. Fine orange, Cajamarca-related, indeterminate kaolinite and press-molded redware are the most frequent styles. The Torreón continued to be used during Chinchawasi 2 as a high-status area. Excavations revealed limited quantities of Wari polychrome, fine pinkware and Recuay style kaolinite in and around the structure.

Imported pottery continued to be very significant within terrace spaces, making up 43.2% of the phase sample. The most common wares included Wilkawaín resist, Wari polychrome, press-molded redware, fine pinkware and indeterminate kaolinite. Other styles are represented by smaller frequencies. As would be expected, Recuay style kaolinite nearly disappeared in importance, and probably occurs only because of inadvertent mixing. Wari-related iconography is a common denominator among the usual imported styles in the terrace spaces. The greater abundance and variability in imported pottery indicate that local leaders were both investing more and diversifying the range of cultural materials used in public display in open, communal areas. If, as is argued, the activities included functions such as commensal events and corporate gatherings, using new Wari-inspired icons with older imagery could have been a useful strategy for local leaders. The diversity and sheer quantity of such pottery enhanced the conspicuous displays.

Finally, midden accumulations figured prominently in the provenience of fancy and imported pottery, accounting for 43.2% of the phase total. At least one midden (Terrace 4) could be the result of large and concentrated feasting events. Another, the uppermost layers in OP48 in Room Complex 3, seems to represent the locus or receptacle for repeated trash deposition during Chinchawasi 2 (and Warmi) times. By far the most common fancy type is that of decorated face-neck vessels, followed by fine gray, Cajamarca-related, Nievería, Wari polychrome and purple iridescent. The occurrence of these specialized styles indicates that imported pottery functioned contemporaneously with the accumulation of the midden. In the case of the large concentrated trash deposit of Terrace 4, the fancy pots were likely used and broken, perhaps purposefully, during the feasting events. Moreover, the common occurrence of face-necks in such contexts suggests that face-neck vessels were integral elements in consumption activities. Adding to the variability of face-neck vessel function, the evidence for use of face-necks in feasting at Chinchawas complements their well-documented roles in Middle Horizon offering traditions (Menzel 1964, 1968; Ravines 1968; Cook 1985).

We can make several important observations about the fancy pottery repertoire during Chinchawasi phase 2. First, Chinchawasi 2 contexts contained more than a threefold increase in the total number of imported sherds compared with the previous phase. The greater frequency suggests that Chinchawasi peoples acquired and used imports more frequently. Second, the exchange network expanded to include the Cajamarca, North Central Coast and Central Coast regions. Many of the

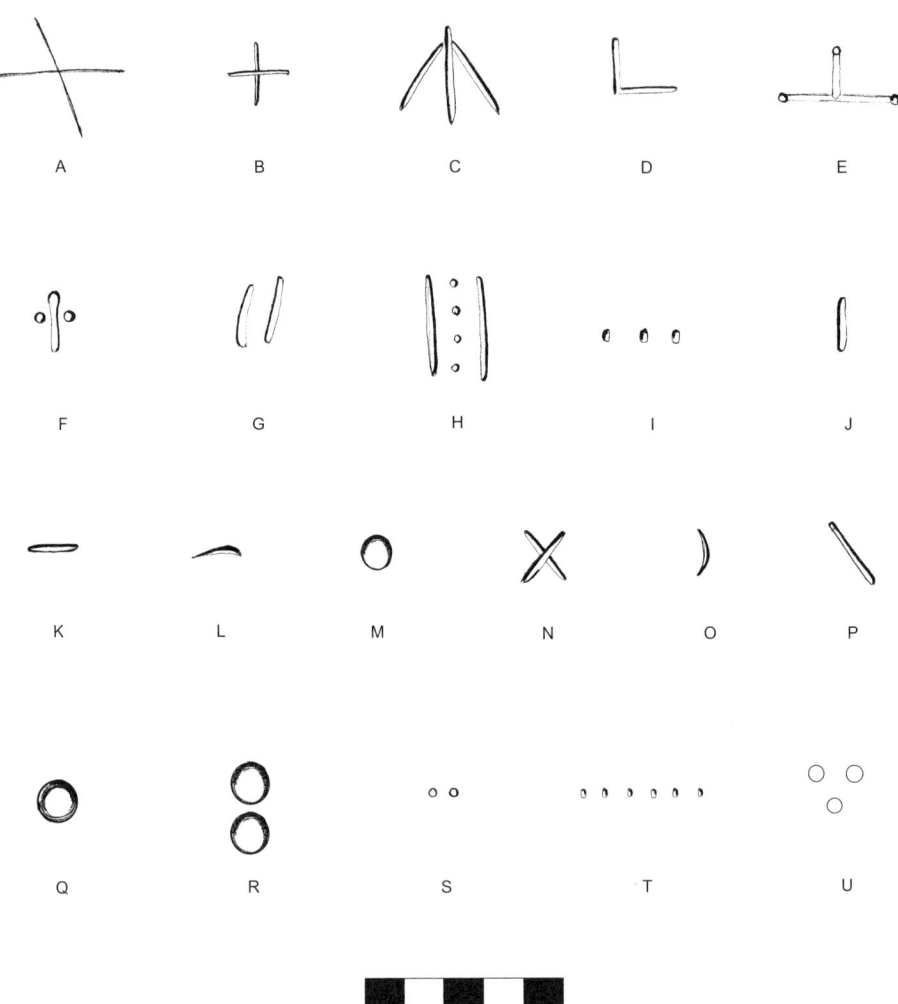

FIGURE 103. Strap handle marks: A–M, marks on handle center; N–U, marks on handle end.

unidentified fancy styles suggest that other cultures and regions participated in the network. In sum, not only were existing long-distance exchange routes being exploited more intensively, but new interregional ties were being cultivated. Chinchawasi 2 peoples, apparently, became increasingly interested in using luxury goods and iconography to exploit their attendant ideological references and status.

Overall, the intensification of trade relations supports other material evidence indicating intensified forms of local economic production and interaction, such as (1) the acquisition of obsidian (discussed in Chapter 9), (2) use of ceramic whorls and associated fiber production and (3) the greater frequency and variety of maker's marks (see Figure 103) on plainware vessels. All the evidence suggests a wider range of sources for pottery and raw materials (Lau 2005). In short, Chinchawasi 2 was a major growth period for the Chinchawas site and for its economy.

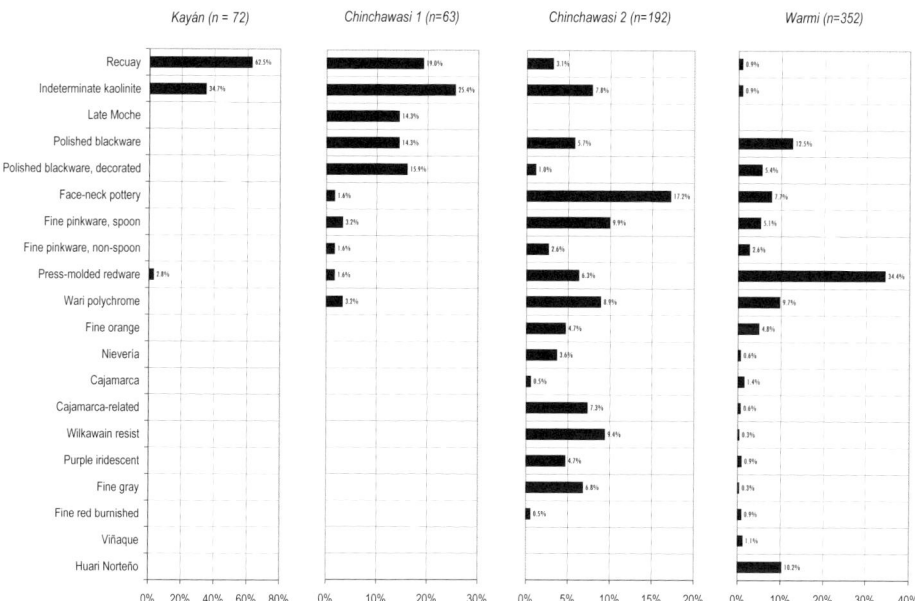

FIGURE 104. Comparison of fancy and imported frequencies by phase.

## *Warmi Phase*

Long-distance commerce for imported pottery reached unprecedented levels during the Warmi phase. The phase total of imported sherds (n=352) is greater than the previous three phases combined (see Table 11). Moreover, not only did volume increase, but there was greater diversity in available styles and range of interregional contacts (Figure 104).

The Callejón de Huaylas diminished in importance as a region for prestige pottery. Fine pinkware decreases to 7.7% of the phase sample. And the frequency of Wilkawaín resist reduces to only 0.3%. Recuay style kaolinite and indeterminate kaolinite categories occur at 0.9% each and, most likely, are the result of redeposition in the terrace areas. There are greater numbers of Cajamarca sherds (1.4%). Meanwhile, Cajamarca-related pottery decreases to only 0.6%. Despite the small sample, compared with the Chinchawasi 2 phase, it seems that local peoples at Chinchawas were better able to acquire true Cajamarca pottery during the Warmi phase.

The substantial presence of fancy Wari styles emphasizes the continued cultural importance of the Central Highlands. Wari polychrome, fine orange and fine red burnished occur in roughly the same percentages, at 9.7%, 4.8% and 0.9%, respectively. In sheer quantity, however, these import types nearly double. Examples of Viñaque style pottery (1.1%) also support the picture of strong Central Highland relationships during the Middle Horizon.

A few pottery wares lost popularity during the Warmi phase. Fine gray (0.3%) and purple iridescent (0.9%) ceramics decline sharply. Face-neck pottery decreases

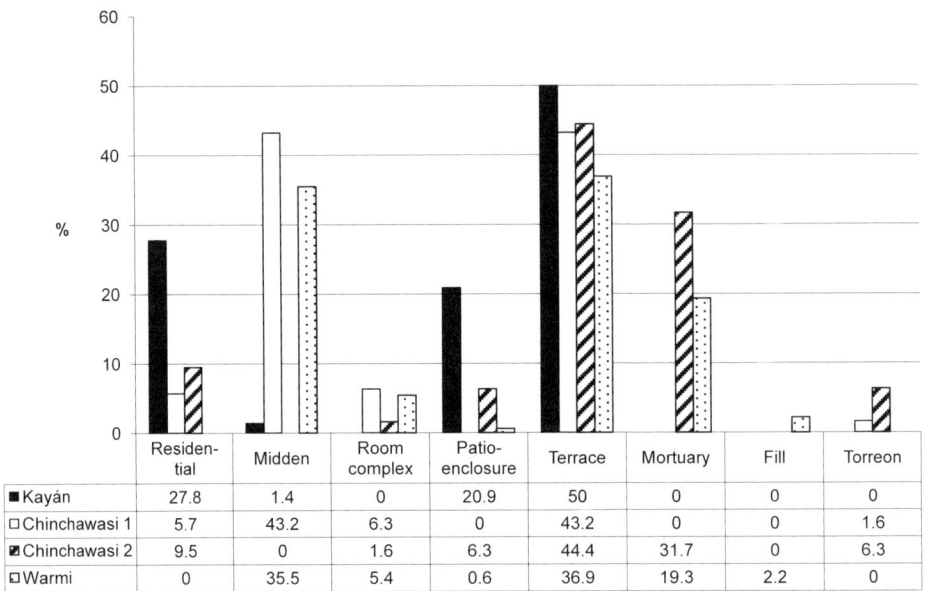

FIGURE 105. Distribution of fancy and imported styles by context.

in importance, to 7.7%. Finally, Nievería (0.6%) of the Central Coast lost importance in the Warmi phase.

Polished blackware and modeled polished blackware frequencies rose sharply, to approximately 18.4% of the total imports in the Warmi phase. Some of the modeled blackware can be attributed to North Coast styles (lenticular forms, figural representations) as well as to highland and Central Coast traditions (banded keros). However, a large percentage of the blackware category, especially undecorated pieces and body sherds, could not be attributed stylistically.

Like Viñaque, Huari Norteño B represents another new style of pottery that emerged for the first time during the Warmi phase. In total, there were 36 sherds of Huari Norteño B pottery, making up 10.2% of the phase sum. Of these, 35 were found in the Warmi phase chullpas of Sector 2. Only one sherd was found in Sector 1.

The Warmi phase is distinguished by a high percentage of coastal style press-molded pottery (34%, n=121). This pottery has its origins in different valleys of the north (Virú and Santa) and north-central coasts (Supe, probably Huarmey). In sheer number and percentage, press-molded pottery dwarfs any other import category and signals a dramatic shift towards cultural linkages with the coast.

The distributions of imported pottery by context generally follow the pattern established during the Chinchawasi 2 phase (Figure 105). On the other hand, there is strong variation in terms of where a particular style may be located at the intra-site functional level. Just over 5% of the phase sample occurred in room complexes. The small percentage is comparable to the preceding Chinchawasi 2 phase, and suggests that imported pottery maintained a minor role in the activities of the room complexes, compared to other areas excavated. By far the predominant style is the press-molded redware.

Imported pottery occurred in midden proveniences 35.5% of the time. Of this total, Wari polychrome was the most represented, followed by press-molded redware, face-neck vessels, fine orange (n=13), fine pinkware and polished blackware. In addition, considerable diversity is denoted by small amounts of 10 other imported wares. In sum, the data indicate that a wide range of imported pottery was commonly used and disposed of in midden areas, especially as residential refuse or debris from feasting activities.

A total of 130 imported sherds, or 36.9% of the phase sample, came from terrace excavations. Of this amount, nearly half (47.7%) were press-molded redware, followed by polished blackware, fine pinkware and face-neck vessels. The press-molded redware consisted primarily of keros and press-molded bowls. Their considerable numbers in the terrace excavations suggest that these serving vessels were especially important in terrace activities. Finally, 0.6% of the imported sample of pottery during the Warmi phase occurred in the abandoned patio-enclosures, probably as miscellaneous reworked debris. And 2.2% occurred in fill deposits.

Perhaps the most notable change is the use of fancy exotic pottery in the mortuary contexts of Sector 2. About 19.3% of the imported pottery during the Warmi phase came from the chullpas. All but two sherds pertain to four pottery categories; in decreasing importance, they include Huari Norteño (n=35), press-molded redware (n=16), polished blackware (n=11) and modeled polished blackware (n=4). The other two sherds can be attributed to fine red burnished and Niebería. One salient observation is that nearly all of the Huari Norteño sample (35 out of 36 sherds) found came from the chullpa excavations. Apparently, certain styles were favored over others as funerary goods during Warmi times.

Compared with previous phases, imported pottery during the Warmi phase is of higher quality. Some of the most elaborate pieces, such as the press-molded tumblers, show considerable investment in labor and transaction. Furthermore, the new forms and pottery technology, combined with familiar yet reworked imagery, charged the imported pottery with symbolic value. The new exotics and their importance in different cultural practices made the pottery attractive to local groups during the Warmi occupation.

## Cultural Interaction at Chinchawas

The data from imported pottery at Chinchawas reveal a long history of exchange and interregional contact during the latter part of the Early Intermediate Period and the Middle Horizon. In this section I provide a brief chronological description of the interregional relationships (see Figure 104), followed by a discussion of their implications.

## Kayán Phase

Little can be said about the degree of interaction of Kayán phase peoples with groups outside the Callejón de Huaylas. The current evidence indicates that this phase at Chinchawas reflects a light occupation characterized by strong insularity of cultural interaction, with little pretensions to wealth or status.

## Chinchawasi 1 Phase

The strong North Highland bias of the Kayán imported sample continued during the subsequent Chinchawasi 1 occupation. Long-distance commerce remained largely focused on the highlands, but, in addition to the Recuay and other wares of the Callejón de Huaylas, we see Central Highland influences for the first time. Moreover, there were some limited coastal connections, such as a few examples of Late Moche wares. The available sample, though small compared with later phases, indicates that Chinchawas peoples had a greater range of economic and cultural ties during the Chinchawasi 1 phase.

The evidence of exotic wares suggests sporadic trade relations with neighboring regions with strong independent cultural traditions. As noted, Chinchawasi 1 peoples were already participating in Recuay traditions and exchange interests. But by the 7th century A.D. we see the emergence of powerful polities in the Central Highlands (Isbell and Schreiber 1978; Isbell 1988b), the North Coast (Shimada 1994; Bawden 1996), the North Highlands (T. Topic 1991) and other regions (Shady 1988; Schreiber 1992). The increasing presence of prestige goods from these regions at Chinchawas probably resulted from the growing sociopolitical dynamism and interaction of the age.

Greater access reflected a greater desire of local leaders at Chinchawas to acquire precious commodities. As anthropologists have pointed out, the acquisition of strange and rare goods from distant areas often enhances the prestige of leaders. The ability to acquire an object—its history, special properties or the ideas packaged in it—and the exhibition of the object in public circumstances all play a role in this process.

By the end of the Chinchawasi 1 phase, the first early Middle Horizon imports began to appear (Chakipampa-related, Moche V, polished blackware). The terminal portion of the Chinchawasi 1 phase would correspond to the initial Wari expansion during Middle Horizon Epoch 1 (Menzel 1964). During this time architectural, iconographic and technical elements in material culture throughout the Andes are seen as archaeological correlates of Middle Horizon state expansionism extending from the site of Wari, Ayacucho, in the central highlands (Menzel 1964; Lumbreras 1974b; Isbell and Schreiber 1978; Benavides 1984).

Other than the Wari-polychrome pottery, however, none of these elements is present at Chinchawas. As reflected by other aspects of the material culture at the site, the local occupation was not characterized by military conquest, reorganization of settlement layout, or by known Wari administrative architectural forms (Isbell and McEwan 1991). Moreover, as the local painted and plain wares show, local Chinchawasi 1 pottery manifested little influence from Wari styles, either in form or iconography.

The initial Wari presence at Chinchawas seems to have centered on long-distance, commercial interests. Our data are consistent with models in which Wari culture by Middle Horizon 1B extended initially to parts of the Central Andes as a result of exchange interests (Shady 1982; T. Topic 1991). The focus seems to have been special goods of limited circulation. Moreover, as represented by fine pinkware and Chakipampa-related ceramics, initial Wari influence on Chinchawas during the early Middle Horizon seems to have been a highland-based and highland-inspired strategy.

In sum, like many sites of highland Ancash, the community of Chinchawas began to manifest growing exchange ties by the 7th century AD. The end result was that peoples of small provincial villages like Chinchawas were, at the very least, cognizant of regional cultural traditions, as expressed in exotic pottery and other rare items. Among these, Wari-affiliated commodities and iconography were key parts of several prestige cultures that local leaders used to negotiate their social status within the Chinchawas community.

*Chinchawasi 2 Phase*

There was much more foreign pottery as well as an expanded range of sources during Chinchawasi phase 2 (see Figure 104). In addition to already established highland networks, exotic coastal pottery became increasingly popular, with sources along the central, north-central and north coasts. Chinchawas's emergence as a participant in a far-ranging exchange network coincided with Wari expansion into other parts of Peru (Menzel 1964).

During the Chinchawasi 2 occupation, Chinchawas never seems to be fully integrated into Wari's administrative infrastructure. There are some stylistic affinities between Chinchawasi 2 and Wari styles and also limited evidence for products imported from the Central Highlands. Chinchawasi 2 peoples, however, felt the influence of several regional cultures, including Wari, Cajamarca, the North Coast and Huaraz-based groups in the Callejón de Huaylas. The influence took the form of imported objects as well as of stylistic emulation in local decorated ceramics.

These data from Chinchawas shed light on the dynamic nature of the early Middle Horizon cultural and political landscape. During Chinchawasi 2, Wari's effect at the site is seen most prominently in its imported commodities and iconography. Motivation for adopting these new patterns at Chinchawas could have had a strong economic and ideological undertone.

*Warmi Phase*

During the Warmi phase, Wari culture had a more profound influence on Chinchawas. As they did in earlier times, the local leaders of Chinchawas acquired foreign pottery to display in public functions to reaffirm their status.

Fancy pottery is found in the highest percentages in terrace areas and domestic refuse accumulations. Nearly all fancy vessels have a serving focus: serving bowls, spoons or face-neck jars. Notably, their use also crossed over into mortuary ritual as grave offerings. Chinchawas's economic status was probably increasingly competitive in the region during the Warmi phase.

Foreign pottery was most common during the Warmi occupation. At this time, coastal imports, especially press-molded wares of the north-central and north coasts, predominate in the assemblage. Either prestige associations with these areas became more desirable or these regions exerted more cultural influence. In addition, more impressive craftsmanship characterizes the imports. Warmi peoples, therefore, not only intensified Chinchawas's role in long-distance commerce, but achieved unprecedented access to higher quality products.

At the same time that the imported pottery during the Warmi phase held a predominately coastal flavor, Warmi peoples preferred a distinct style of local painted secular pottery that had Central Highland roots. These ceramics, or Warmi Ware A, are of a common redware, typically flat-based open bowls with or without ring-bases, with simple interior painted designs in monochrome or polychrome: parallel bands, bands and meanders, nested arcs, nested geometrics and pendants. In nearly all aspects, Warmi Ware A represented a drastic transformation from the earlier local ceramic tradition. Moreover, the change occurred quickly and definitively.

Ware A style pottery had developed widely by the end of Middle Horizon Epoch 2 (Menzel 1964). This wide distribution and its local pastes and local stylistic mixing indicate that they were probably not imports. Rather, they seem to be material correlates for Wari stylistic influence down to the domestic level. In sum, the imported pottery corroborates other lines of evidence that show that Chinchawas underwent significant cultural transformations during the Warmi phase. Sharp changes in the reception of material culture, including new dispositions for emulating Wari styles, indicate that the overall community was more receptive toward Wari cultural influence by the 9th century A.D.

## Discussion

The long history of interregional interaction at Chinchawas raises a series of questions about the role and importance of rural communities, in general, within the wider Andean world. For one thing, it is unclear what sorts of goods Chinchawas had to exchange. A pottery-for-pottery swap seems unlikely, because its local fancy pottery had a very limited distribution outside the greater Chinchawas area. More likely, Chinchawas peoples exchanged agricultural products, such as high-altitude grains and tubers. Potatoes could have been transported raw or processed, as in freeze-dried *chuño*. In addition, Chinchawas almost certainly derived commercial leverage from its herding economy. Camelids could have been traded on the hoof or processed as freeze-dried *ch'arki*. Moreover, camelid fiber would have been valued, either as raw material, or perhaps as woven textiles and clothes in the local tradition. The location of Chinchawas, near the pass (Punta Kallán, or Kayánpunta) of a major coastal–highland corridor, would have promoted local interest in cultural interaction. The Wari presence at Chinchawas, ultimately, could have also been instigated by the site's strategic location.

Unlike other areas under Wari influence, there are no images of the Pachacamac griffin in any medium at Chinchawas, suggesting that this dimension of Wari religion was not favored in the Chinchawas zone. Indeed, the focus seems to be more on front-face icons, which are more representative of highland Wari religion, as expressed in Viñaque wares (Menzel 1964, 1977). Profile felines with transforming appendages and Wari mythical creatures belonged to earlier highland traditions. It seems, then, that ancient Chinchawasinos preferred highland Wari religious iconography on vessels using a coastal technology.

An accommodating and inclusive ideology was an integral part of the early Wari expansion process (Menzel 1964; Lumbreras 1974a; Isbell 1988b). At the most general level, Wari iconography emphasized universalizing themes of fertility and creator worship (Cook 1994). These precepts have a long history in the Andes and probably resonated with most societies of the Central Andes during the period immediately before Wari expansion (Tello 1923; Carrión Cachot 1955, 1959; Sherbondy 1992; Cook 1994). Local peoples of the Recuay tradition felt at home with these themes and easily adopted them to fit within their own ideological system.

A dialectical relationship therefore characterizes the iconographies of Wari and regional cultures by the early Middle Horizon. Wari religion was configured in such a way as to accommodate and absorb local traditions. Meanwhile, regional cultures were autonomous enough to appropriate Wari stylistic elements to forge new, but familiar and comprehensible, religious imagery. In addition to pottery, the stone sculpture at Chinchawas, which brings together Wari and Recuay elements, provides another instance of syncretism that combined local practices with exotic imagery (Lau 2006b).

Wari interests at Chinchawas also probably construed an ethos of communalism. In many ethnohistoric and ethnographic accounts, themes of fertility and abundance often relate intimately with the concern for agropastoral production in small-scale farming communities (e.g., Allen 1988; Sherbondy 1992). A generalized Wari religion that promoted cooperation through communalism would also have been attractive for local leaders trying to mobilize labor. In this way, for local leaders and communities, the cross-cultural connections so evident in the Wari sphere of influence may have been used to establish and maintain relations of production at the local level.

Bawden (1996) refers to the iconography of Moche pottery as the "language of power." Through a state-sanctioned religion that imbued a higher, supernatural status to its practitioners, Moche elites derived political and economic status through ideology. According to Bawden, Moche rulers could maintain their exploitative relationship with commoners as long as the integrity of the language remained intact. Moche elite material culture, in this scheme, directly reflected the success and failure of their social system. Bawden (1996:317) points out that the growing importance of foreign goods and non-Moche iconography promoted the demise of Late Moche societies (see also Castillo 1993). In effect, Moche religion, the state's "language of power," became increasingly denatured by exotic elements. The political authority that had once adhered to strict Moche iconographic orthodoxy began to introduce exotic elements to sustain their status. Ultimately, the foreign ideology invested in imported goods grew out from Moche elite control and became a destabilizing force. Hence, Bawden (1996:317) believes that the "elite had to look beyond the borders of the North Coast region for support for the first time. This shift inevitably eroded absolute elite control, encouraged lower-status groups to share in the production and use of local copies, and promoted the process of decline that in a surprisingly short time resulted in the end of the Moche system."

It may be instructive to compare the initial boom in imported pottery at Chinchawas during the Chinchawasi 2 occupation. Certainly, the diversity of imported pottery at sites such as San José de Moro (Castillo 2001) is mirrored somewhat by the Chinchawas evidence. However, the scale and contexts of imported pottery differ. Not only was Chinchawas a small site compared to the best known Late Moche settlements, but most of the imported materials during the Chinchawasi 2 phase occurred as refuse in terrace, habitations and patio spaces, with no direct associations to mortuary ritual. Rare imported pottery therefore probably circulated mainly in residential and public activities. This pattern contrasts with the mortuary focus of imported pottery use at San José de Moro (Castillo 2001).

In addition, there are no signs of imminent collapse or abandonment during the Chinchawasi 2 occupation. On the contrary, the character of the settlement and intrasite artifact patterning is quite vigorous. During Chinchawasi 2, then, people were importing pottery not so much to reinforce a crumbling ideology, but rather by intensifying long-distance contacts, they marshaled foreign cultural connections for personal and group-level gain in activities such as household or kin-based rituals and public gatherings. In doing so, individuals reaffirmed their own status opportunistically under the context of community well-being.

Interestingly, by the early Middle Horizon at Chinchawas the acquisition of exotics, especially in fancy ceramics, privileged diversity. Local inhabitants at Chinchawas had the ability as well as the interest to acquire fancy ceramics from multiple sources, suggesting a burgeoning awareness of the widely disparate regions and cultures of the Central Andes. Elsewhere I have suggested that this was a type of cosmopolitanism, found in certain settlements across northern Peru, which was facilitated by Wari expansion and trade networks during the Middle Horizon (Lau 2005).

CHAPTER NINE

LOCAL ECONOMY AND TRADE:
EVIDENCE FROM
OTHER ARTIFACTS

Lithic, bone, shell and metal remains were also recovered during the archaeological investigations at Chinchawas. This chapter describes important features useful for discerning artifact function, cultural affiliation and significance. Following a brief review of methodology, the chapter presents a summary for each artifact class, archaeological contexts and associations by phase. The section concludes with a general consideration of the artifact classes and their sociocultural significance in the Chinchawas sequence.

By identifying patterns of artifact use, popularity and discard, the artifact analyses aim to provide diachronic insights on local economic activities, craft production and interregional exchange at Chinchawas. The analyses facilitate further insights on cultural patterns and transformations at Chinchawas. In particular, there was a sharp intensification of local economic specializations during the Chinchawasi 2 phase, such as in camelid fiber processing, stone and bone tool production and long-distance trade. Acquisition of rare materials, such as metal artifacts and obsidian, also increased noticeably during this time.

Artifact distributions across the site will also be detailed. The intrasite patterns of various artifact categories reinforce status distinctions between special ceremonial zones and domestic areas. Like the ceramic and stone sculptural data, the evidence shows that the site underwent strong cultural and social changes during the Middle Horizon, probably a result of conditions prompted by interaction with the Wari state.

## Methodology

Before review, artifacts were cleaned and labeled. Observations on basic characteristics such as material, artifact type, dimensions, and color, among others, were entered onto a spreadsheet to facilitate comparison and provide basic descriptive statistics. Selected artifacts were illustrated and photographed. We conducted laboratory analyses throughout the period of field investigations (from August 1996 to October 1997) and during the summer of 1998. Subsequently, Richard L. Burger (Yale University) and Heather Lechtman (Massachusetts Institute of Technology) coordinated technical analyses for 27 obsidian samples and seven metal artifacts, respectively, to examine chemical composition and provide insights on local trade and technology. The results of these analyses are included in this text.

TABLE 12. Summary of lithic artifacts.

| Forms | Kayán Count | % | Chinchawasi 1 Count | % | Chinchawasi 2 Count | % | Warmi Count | % | Chakwas Count | % | Total Count | % |
|---|---|---|---|---|---|---|---|---|---|---|---|---|
| *Silex (chert)* | | | | | | | | | | | | |
| Black-brown (debitage) | 20 | 33.3 | 183 | 36.7 | 513 | 42.6 | 166 | 47.3 | 9 | 37.5 | 1153 | 40.6 |
| Black-brown (core) | 1 | 1.7 | 15 | 3.0 | 29 | 2.4 | 1 | 0.3 | — | — | 62 | 2.2 |
| Black-brown (tool) | — | — | 27 | 5.4 | 34 | 2.8 | 5 | 1.4 | — | — | 76 | 2.7 |
| Light brown (debitage) | 3 | 5.0 | 48 | 9.6 | 97 | 8.1 | 31 | 8.8 | 2 | 8.3 | 267 | 9.4 |
| Light brown (core) | — | — | 3 | 0.6 | 4 | 0.3 | — | — | — | — | 7 | 0.2 |
| Light brown (tool) | — | — | 8 | 1.6 | 10 | 0.8 | 3 | 0.9 | — | — | 28 | 1.0 |
| Red (debitage) | 10 | 16.7 | 76 | 15.2 | 137 | 11.4 | 45 | 12.8 | 7 | 29.2 | 386 | 13.6 |
| Red (core) | — | — | 7 | 1.4 | 5 | 0.4 | — | — | — | — | 13 | 0.5 |
| Red (tool) | 1 | 1.7 | 17 | 3.4 | 12 | 1.0 | 7 | 2.0 | — | — | 41 | 1.4 |
| Yellow (debitage) | 6 | 10.0 | 40 | 8.0 | 66 | 5.5 | 21 | 6.0 | 2 | 8.3 | 201 | 7.1 |
| Yellow (core) | 2 | 3.3 | 5 | 1.0 | 5 | 0.4 | 1 | 0.3 | — | — | 15 | 0.5 |
| Yellow (tool) | 2 | 3.3 | 7 | 1.4 | 14 | 1.2 | 12 | 3.4 | — | — | 34 | 1.2 |
| Miscellaneous (debitage) | 1 | 1.7 | 7 | 1.4 | 4 | 0.3 | 1 | 0.3 | — | — | 18 | 0.6 |
| Miscellaneous (tool) | 1 | 1.7 | 4 | 0.8 | 1 | 0.1 | 1 | 0.3 | — | — | 7 | 0.2 |
| *Siliceous andesites and quartzites* | | | | | | | | | | | | |
| Fine gray (debitage) | — | — | 15 | 3.0 | 19 | 1.6 | 2 | 0.6 | — | — | 50 | 1.8 |
| Fine gray (tool) | 1 | 1.7 | 1 | 0.2 | 4 | 0.3 | 1 | 0.3 | — | — | 8 | 0.3 |
| Coarse gray (debitage) | — | — | 5 | 1.0 | 29 | 2.4 | 8 | 2.3 | — | — | 63 | 2.2 |
| Coarse gray (core) | 1 | 1.7 | 2 | 0.4 | 2 | 0.2 | — | — | — | — | 6 | 0.2 |
| Coarse gray (tool) | — | — | — | — | 6 | 0.5 | — | — | — | — | 6 | 0.2 |
| Green (debitage) | — | — | — | — | 12 | 1.0 | 1 | 0.3 | — | — | 14 | 0.5 |
| Fine white (debitage) | — | — | 2 | 0.4 | 13 | 1.1 | 4 | 1.1 | — | — | 22 | 0.8 |
| Fine white (tool) | — | — | 1 | 0.2 | — | — | — | — | — | — | 1 | 0.0 |
| White (debitage) | — | — | 2 | 0.4 | 8 | 0.7 | 3 | 0.9 | 1 | 4.2 | 23 | 0.8 |
| Brown (fragments) | 1 | 1.7 | 5 | 1.0 | 2 | 0.2 | — | — | — | — | 8 | 0.3 |
| Brown (tool) | — | — | 1 | 0.2 | — | — | — | — | — | — | 2 | 0.1 |
| Fine black (debitage) | — | — | 2 | 0.4 | 14 | 1.2 | 4 | 1.1 | — | — | 25 | 0.9 |
| Fine black (tool) | — | — | — | — | 5 | 0.4 | 1 | 0.3 | — | — | 7 | 0.2 |
| Coarse black (debitage) | 5 | 8.3 | 3 | 0.6 | 17 | 1.4 | 3 | 0.9 | — | — | 36 | 1.3 |
| Coarse black (tool) | — | — | 2 | 0.4 | 2 | 0.2 | — | — | — | — | 4 | 0.1 |
| Pink (debitage) | 1 | 1.7 | 1 | 0.2 | 59 | 4.9 | 2 | 0.6 | — | — | 80 | 2.8 |
| Pink (tool) | — | — | — | — | 9 | 0.7 | — | — | — | — | 13 | 0.5 |
| Red (debitage) | — | — | — | 0.6 | 7 | 0.6 | 3 | 0.9 | — | — | 20 | 0.7 |
| Red (tool) | — | — | — | — | 4 | 0.3 | 1 | 0.3 | — | — | 5 | 0.2 |
| *Obsidian* | | | | | | | | | | | | |
| Flake | — | — | — | — | 17 | 1.4 | 8 | 2.3 | — | — | 32 | 1.1 |
| Tool | — | — | — | — | 16 | 1.3 | 4 | 1.1 | — | — | 24 | 0.8 |
| *Chalcedony* | — | — | — | — | 3 | 0.2 | 1 | 0.3 | — | — | 4 | 0.1 |
| *Quartz* | 1 | 1.7 | 5 | 1.0 | 15 | 1.2 | 8 | 2.3 | 1 | 4.2 | 41 | 1.4 |
| *Quartz crystal* | 2 | 3.3 | 2 | 0.4 | 2 | 0.2 | 3 | 0.9 | 2 | 8.3 | 18 | 0.6 |
| *Slate* | | | | | | | | | | | | |
| Miscellaneous | — | — | — | — | 7 | 0.6 | — | — | — | — | 9 | 0.3 |
| Tool | 1 | 1.7 | — | — | 1 | 0.1 | — | — | — | — | 2 | 0.1 |
| *Slag* | — | — | — | — | — | — | — | — | — | — | 6 | 0.2 |
| Total | 60 | 100.0% | 499 | 100.0% | 1204 | 100.0% | 351 | 100.0% | 24 | 100.0% | 2837 | 100.0% |

# Chipped Stone Artifacts

The corpus of lithic artifacts divides into two general categories: chipped stone tools and ground stone tools. Investigations recovered 2,837 chipped stone artifacts from Chinchawas (Tables 12 and 13). Of this total, most is debitage. Many of the identifiable fragments are from broken tools. The research recovered very few complete specimens. Despite the quantity of materials, in general, most of the chipped stone tools share in a simple production technology characterized by an interest in expediency over elaboration or formal consistency. The corpus reflects regular and nonspecialized chipped stone production at the site.

## *Materials*

The Cordillera Negra offers a wide array of quality raw materials for lithic production (Lynch 1980; Gero 1983). Ancient peoples at Chinchawas, however, used a fairly small range. The most popular raw materials were chert, known as locally as silex, and siliceous andesites and quartzites. More uncommon materials include, in decreasing frequency: quartz, obsidian, slate and chalcedony. With the exception of obsidian, the materials occur naturally in the Cordillera Negra (Lynch 1980).

### Silex

Of the total chipped stone assemblage, silex (81.4%) is, by far, the most common raw material. The crypto-crystalline structure of silex allows for sharp cutting edges. However, local silex is very brittle and often contains natural flaws that hinder removal of long blades, especially from the black–dark brown variety. Thus, despite its general ubiquity and the capability of producing sharp edges, very few large silex tools were found. Most of the silex sample can be characterized as small unworked flakes, chips and miscellaneous waste debris. Of the silex cores found, typically large round nodules, some showing evidence of flaking. Cutting activities probably included the use of small flakes removed as needed from cores.

There are four main color varieties in the silex category. The most popular were black or very dark brown (45.5%), red (15.5%), light brown (10.6%) and yellow (8.8%). There is also a minor category, "Miscellaneous Silex" (0.8%), composed of white, gray or tan varieties. The black and light brown types are opaque, while the red and yellow are not. Large fragments, nodules or cores, on occasion manifest two, maybe three, colors on the same object. The most frequent combinations are black and red, and yellow and red.

Silex artifacts are fairly small. The most popular are simple cutting flakes (some with retouch). Unifacial scrapers, blade tools and several points are also represented in the silex assemblage.

Most of the identified tools and cores from Chinchawas used black–dark brown silex. Of the major silex varieties, however, yellow silex was used for the greatest proportion of tools and cores, accounting for 19.6% of the total assemblage. Red silex is next at 12.3%, followed by light brown silex (11.6%) and black–

TABLE 13. Summary of lithic artifacts by architectural contexts, all phases.

| | Kayán | | | Chinchawasi 1 | | | | | Chinchawasi 2 | | | | |
| --- | --- | --- | --- | --- | --- | --- | --- | --- | --- | --- | --- | --- | --- |
| | Terrace | Room | Enclosure | Midden | Terrace | Room | Torreón | Tomb | Midden | Terrace | Room | Enclosure | Torreón |
| *Silex (chert)* | | | | | | | | | | | | | |
| Black-brown (debitage) | 9 | 7 | 4 | 41 | 73 | 56 | 11 | 2 | 185 | 193 | 118 | 10 | 7 |
| Black-brown (core) | — | 1 | — | 9 | 1 | 5 | — | — | 7 | 13 | 9 | — | — |
| Black-brown (tool) | — | — | — | 10 | 11 | 4 | 2 | — | 10 | 11 | 13 | — | — |
| Light brown (debitage) | — | 3 | — | 11 | 20 | 12 | 5 | — | 33 | 37 | 23 | — | 4 |
| Light brown (core) | — | — | — | 2 | — | 1 | — | — | 2 | — | 2 | — | — |
| Light brown (tool) | — | — | — | 5 | 3 | — | — | — | 1 | 6 | 3 | — | — |
| Red (debitage) | 3 | 5 | 2 | 22 | 33 | 14 | 6 | 1 | 32 | 61 | 37 | 2 | 5 |
| Red (core) | — | — | — | 2 | 3 | 2 | — | — | 4 | — | 1 | — | — |
| Red (tool) | — | — | 1 | 11 | 3 | 3 | — | — | 3 | 6 | 2 | — | 1 |
| Yellow (debitage) | 2 | — | 4 | 17 | 14 | 9 | — | — | 27 | 19 | 18 | 1 | 1 |
| Yellow (core) | — | 2 | — | 4 | — | 1 | — | — | 2 | 1 | 2 | — | — |
| Yellow (tool) | 2 | — | — | 1 | 6 | — | — | — | 2 | 9 | 2 | — | 1 |
| Miscellaneous (debitage) | 1 | — | — | 5 | 1 | — | 1 | — | — | — | 3 | — | 1 |
| Miscellaneous (tool) | 1 | — | — | 3 | 1 | — | — | — | — | 1 | — | — | — |
| *Siliceous andesites and quartzites* | | | | | | | | | | | | | |
| Fine gray (debitage) | — | — | — | 9 | 5 | 1 | — | — | 7 | 8 | 4 | — | — |
| Fine gray (tool) | 1 | — | — | 1 | — | — | — | — | — | 4 | — | — | — |
| Coarse gray (debitage) | — | — | — | 1 | 4 | — | — | — | 21 | 5 | 3 | — | — |
| Coarse gray (core) | — | — | 1 | 1 | — | 1 | — | — | — | — | 2 | — | — |
| Coarse gray (tool) | — | — | — | — | — | — | — | — | 4 | 1 | 1 | — | — |
| Green (debitage) | — | — | — | — | — | — | — | — | 6 | 2 | 3 | 1 | — |
| Fine white (debitage) | — | — | — | — | — | 2 | — | — | 3 | 3 | 7 | — | — |
| Fine white (tool) | — | — | — | 1 | — | — | — | — | — | — | — | — | — |
| White (debitage) | — | — | — | — | 1 | 1 | — | — | 5 | 3 | — | — | — |
| Brown (fragments) | — | — | 1 | — | 4 | 1 | — | — | — | 1 | 1 | — | — |
| Brown (tool) | — | — | — | 1 | — | — | — | — | — | — | — | — | — |
| Fine black (debitage) | — | — | — | 2 | — | — | — | — | 3 | 2 | 9 | — | — |
| Fine black (tool) | — | — | — | — | — | — | — | — | 3 | — | 2 | — | — |
| Coarse black (debitage) | 5 | — | — | — | 2 | — | 1 | — | 4 | 8 | 4 | — | 1 |
| Coarse black (tool) | — | — | — | 1 | 1 | — | — | — | — | 2 | — | — | — |
| Pink (debitage) | 1 | — | — | — | — | 1 | — | — | 45 | 3 | 9 | — | 2 |
| Pink (tool) | — | — | — | — | — | — | — | — | 5 | 1 | 3 | — | — |
| Red (debitage) | — | — | — | 3 | — | — | — | — | 1 | 3 | 3 | — | — |
| Red (tool) | — | — | — | — | — | — | — | — | — | 3 | 1 | — | — |
| *Obsidian* | | | | | | | | | | | | | |
| Flake | — | — | — | — | — | — | — | — | 9 | 4 | 1 | — | 3 |
| Tool | — | — | — | — | — | — | — | — | 7 | 2 | 5 | — | 2 |
| *Chalcedony* | — | — | — | — | — | — | — | — | 1 | 2 | — | — | — |
| *Quartz* | — | 1 | — | 2 | 3 | — | — | — | 2 | 4 | 6 | — | 3 |
| *Quartz crystal* | 2 | — | — | 1 | 1 | — | — | — | 1 | 1 | — | — | — |
| *Slate* | | | | | | | | | | | | | |
| Miscellaneous | — | — | — | — | — | — | — | — | — | 7 | — | — | — |
| Tool | 1 | — | — | — | — | — | — | — | — | 1 | — | — | — |
| *Slag* | — | — | — | — | — | — | — | — | — | — | — | — | — |
| Total | 28 | 19 | 13 | 166 | 190 | 114 | 26 | 3 | 435 | 427 | 297 | 14 | 31 |
| Percentage | 46.7% | 31.7% | 21.7% | 33.3% | 38.1% | 22.8% | 5.2% | 0.6% | 36.1% | 35.5% | 24.7% | 1.2% | 2.6% |

TABLE 13 CONTINUED.

|  | Warmi | | | | | Chakwas | | |
|---|---|---|---|---|---|---|---|---|
|  | Midden | Terrace | Room | Enclosure | Tomb | Terrace | Room | Tomb |
| *Silex (chert)* | | | | | | | | |
| Black-brown (debitage) | 38 | 104 | 10 | 14 | — | 3 | 6 | — |
| Black-brown (core) | — | 1 | — | — | — | — | — | — |
| Black-brown (tool) | 1 | 2 | 1 | 1 | — | — | — | — |
| Light brown (debitage) | 14 | 14 | 1 | — | 2 | — | 2 | — |
| Light brown (core) | — | — | — | — | — | — | — | — |
| Light brown (tool) | 1 | 2 | — | — | — | — | — | — |
| Red (debitage) | 8 | 33 | 2 | 2 | — | 2 | 5 | — |
| Red (core) | — | — | — | — | — | — | — | — |
| Red (tool) | — | 5 | 1 | 1 | — | — | — | — |
| Yellow (debitage) | 3 | 13 | 3 | 2 | — | — | 2 | — |
| Yellow (core) | — | 1 | — | — | — | — | — | — |
| Yellow (tool) | — | 12 | — | — | — | — | — | — |
| Miscellaneous (debitage) | — | 1 | — | — | — | — | — | — |
| Miscellaneous (tool) | — | — | — | — | 1 | — | — | — |
| *Siliceous andesites and quartzites* | | | | | | | | |
| Fine gray (debitage) | — | 2 | — | — | — | — | — | — |
| Fine gray (tool) | — | 1 | — | — | — | — | — | — |
| Coarse gray (debitage) | 7 | 1 | — | — | — | — | — | — |
| Coarse gray (core) | — | — | — | — | — | — | — | — |
| Coarse gray (tool) | — | — | — | — | — | — | — | — |
| Green (debitage) | — | 1 | — | — | — | — | — | — |
| Fine white (debitage) | — | 3 | 1 | — | — | — | — | — |
| Fine white (tool) | — | — | — | — | — | — | — | — |
| White (debitage) | — | 3 | — | — | — | — | 1 | — |
| Brown (fragments) | — | — | — | — | — | — | — | — |
| Brown (tool) | — | — | — | — | — | — | — | — |
| Fine black (debitage) | 4 | — | — | — | — | — | — | — |
| Fine black (tool) | — | 1 | — | — | — | — | — | — |
| Coarse black (debitage) | — | 1 | 1 | 1 | — | — | — | — |
| Coarse black (tool) | — | — | — | — | — | — | — | — |
| Pink (debitage) | 1 | 1 | — | — | — | — | — | — |
| Pink (tool) | — | — | — | — | — | — | — | — |
| Red (debitage) | 2 | 1 | — | — | — | — | — | — |
| Red (tool) | — | 1 | — | — | — | — | — | — |
| *Obsidian* | | | | | | | | |
| Flake | 4 | 4 | — | — | — | — | — | — |
| Tool | 2 | 1 | — | — | 1 | — | — | — |
| *Chalcedony* | — | 1 | — | — | — | — | — | — |
| *Quartz* | 2 | 4 | — | — | 2 | — | 1 | — |
| *Quartz crystal* | 1 | 2 | — | — | — | — | 1 | 1 |
| *Slate* | | | | | | | | |
| Miscellaneous | — | — | — | — | — | — | — | — |
| Tool | — | — | — | — | — | — | — | — |
| *Slag* | — | — | — | — | — | — | — | — |
| Total | 88 | 216 | 20 | 21 | 6 | 5 | 18 | 1 |
| Percentage | 25.1% | 61.5% | 5.7% | 6.0% | 1.7% | 20.8% | 75.0% | 4.2% |

dark brown (10.7%). At 28%, miscellaneous silex (white and gray) also shows up in a high proportion of tools and cores in the total assemblage. Especially given the general brittle quality of black–dark brown material, the relative proportions indicate that yellow and red silex were better suited and preferred for tool production.

### Siliceous Andesites and Quartzites

The second most common category consists of siliceous andesites and quartzites, with 393 artifacts. Compared to silex, these raw materials are coarser-grained and furnish poorer cutting edges. However, tools made of siliceous andesites and quartzites are larger and less brittle.

Siliceous andesites and quartzites can be categorized by their color and general graininess. Fine varieties include, in order of frequency: gray (n=58), black (n=32), white (n=23) and green (n=14). Coarser varieties consist of pink (n=93), gray (n=75), black (n=40), red (n=25), white (n=23) and brown (n=10).

Of the 393 specimens, about 13.2% (n=52) are tools. The proportion of tools to debitage is roughly the same as for the silex assemblage. Most of the siliceous andesite tools are large unifacial or bifacial scrapers. Several points are also represented in the assemblage.

### Obsidian

The investigations at Chinchawas recovered 56 obsidian artifacts, all of which share a black, opaque color and uniform good quality with few natural imperfections. Obsidian does not occur naturally locally in the Cordillera Negra. Throughout Peru only of handful of sources furnished obsidian to prehistoric Andean peoples in antiquity (Burger and Asaro 1977; Burger and Glascock 2000). Twenty-seven samples of the Chinchawas assemblage were analyzed using neutron activation analysis done at the University of Missouri Research Reactor Center. All samples yielded chemical signatures consistent with the Quispisisa source near Huanca Sancos, Ayacucho, Peru (Burger and Glascock 2000). The analysis strongly suggests that the Quispisisa source was the major, if not exclusive, supplier of obsidian to the ancient peoples of Chinchawas (Burger et al. 2006).

The assemblage consists nearly exclusively of small unmodified flakes and small flake tools. The tool sample is made up primarily of projectile points, especially broken tip and basal portions. Several complete points were also recovered. Of the total obsidian assemblage, a large proportion are modified tools (42.9%), the largest group of all the lithic materials at Chinchawas. The high percentage indicates that obsidian was particularly prized for its utility in tool-making and that production optimized use of the raw material.

### Slate

The research identified 11 slate artifacts. Most of the slate assemblage consists of flat fragments of unknown function. Their presence at Chinchawas is notable, because slate must have been brought to the ridgetop intentionally. In addition, a pendant and two complete ground stone points, most likely of slate, were recovered.

CHALCEDONY

The four fragments of chalcedony found are all characterized by a fine-grained texture and a white or light tan opaque surface. Several have orange streaks. The assemblage includes several flakes and one relatively long blade, perhaps a knife.

QUARTZ AND QUARTZ CRYSTALS

An ancillary category of quartz and quartz crystal remains consists of 59 artifacts. Most of these artifacts are unworked, although a few show deliberate modification, like polish or slight flaking. The quartz crystals could have been used as symbolic curiosities (Burger 1984a: 217). One specimen was found in Chullpa Tomb 6 (OP58).

*Phase Descriptions: Chipped Stone Tools*

This discussion does not attempt a formal typology of the lithics at Chinchawas. The summaries below aim to provide useful descriptions of cultural elements, by phase, for additional research and comparisons.

KAYÁN PHASE

The Kayán phase assemblage consists of 60 specimens (see Table 12 and Figure 106). The small size of the sample precludes a detailed understanding of Kayán lithic production and use. Nevertheless, we can make some salient observations about the available data.

The sample contains a large proportion of silex artifacts (78.3%), including debitage and cores. One important locus for lithic materials was the floor of a Kayán phase house structure (e.g., OP45). Another was the floor of Enclosure 2. We found several quartz crystals in Kayán levels in OP12 and OP19 of Terrace 1. Finally, a ground-slate point (Figure 106A) was found in OP12n.H and resembles similar points found in Huarás White-on-Red and Recuay contexts (e.g., Lavallée 1970; Lumbreras 1974c:47–51; Amat Olazábal 1976a).

The Kayán data are patterned as work and discard scatters located throughout the Sector 1 ridgetop of Chinchawas. Lithic artifacts, including core and flake scrapers, were collected in house structures (Figure 106E) as well as on open terraces of the ridgetop (Figure 106B–D). Debitage and tools from Enclosure 2 show that cutting activities also occurred in public architectural spaces, perhaps for butchering and cutting of meat in special feasting occasions. No evidence of lithics was recovered in Kayán deposits of Sector 2.

CHINCHAWASI 1 PHASE

The subsequent phase, Chinchawasi 1, contains a much larger sample of lithics (n=499). The large percentage of silex material (n=447, or 89.6% of the phase col-

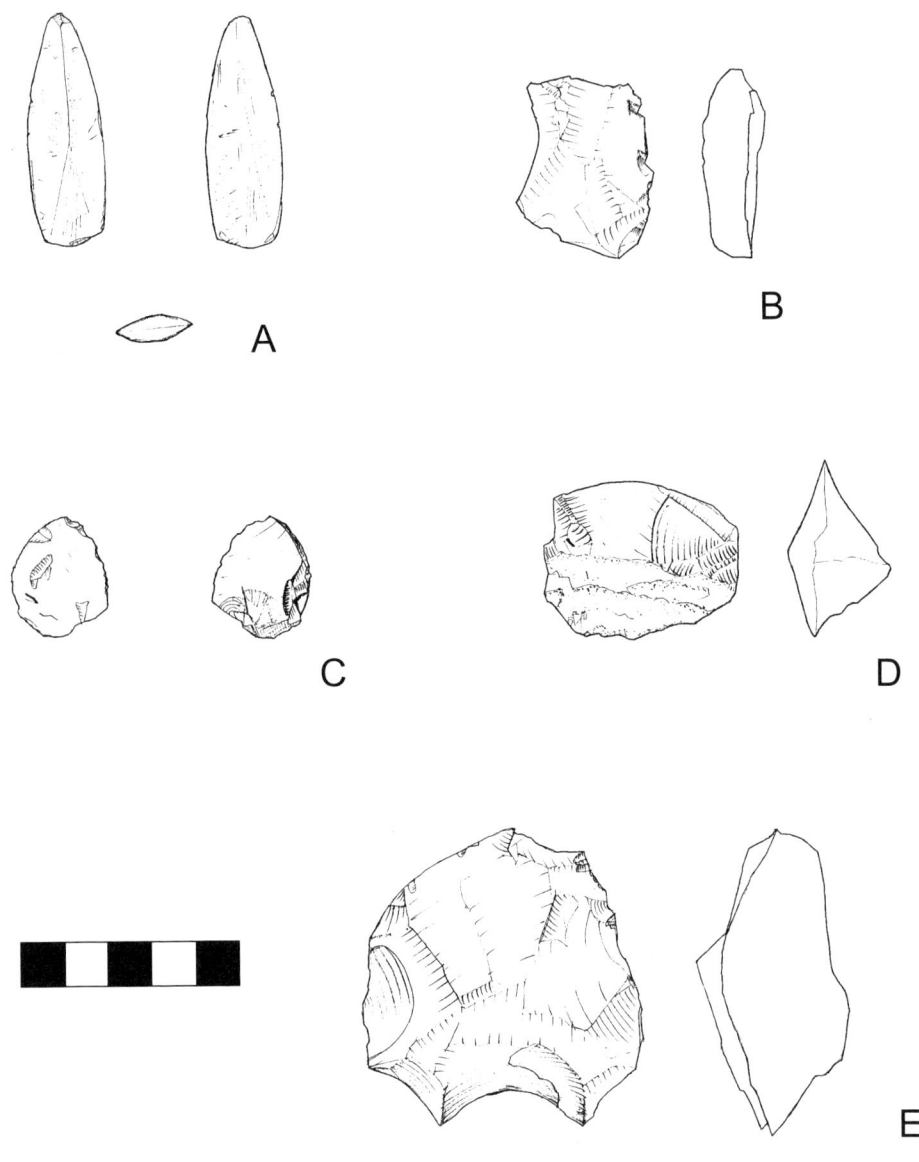

FIGURE 106. Kayán phase lithics.

lection) indicates that silex, a reliance on which was established earlier in the Kayán phase, continued as the primary raw material. Flaked andesite and quartzite tools represent 9.0% (n=45) of the phase total. Although there are quartz and quartz crystals (altogether, 1.4%) in some Chinchawasi 1 deposits, there is a notable absence of obsidian, chalcedony and slate tools.

Chinchawasi 1 lithics appear most frequently in terrace (38.1%) and midden (33.3%) areas of Sector 1 (see Table 13), followed by common occurrence in room interiors (22.8%). The highest proportion of coarser materials (siliceous andesites

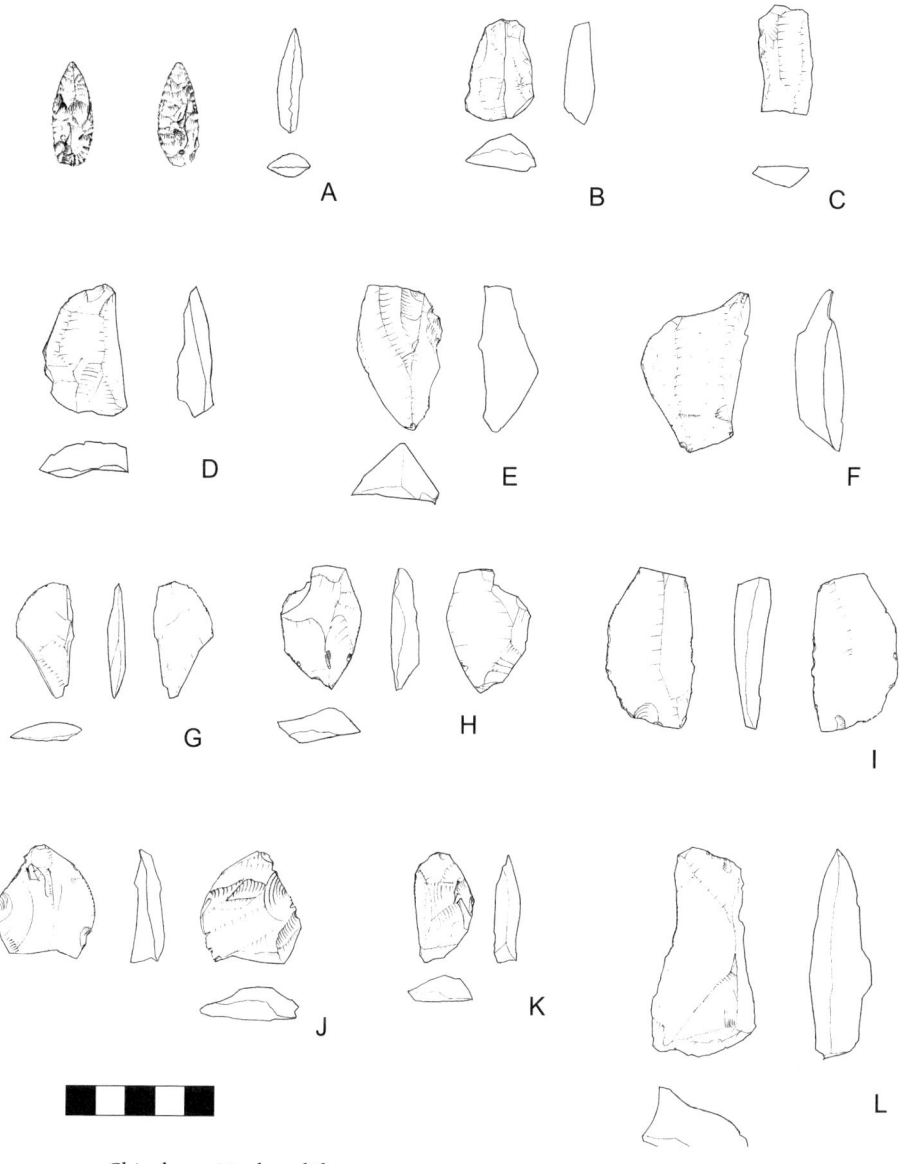

FIGURE 107. Chinchawasi 1 phase lithics.

and quartzites) occurs in the midden excavations, especially Terrace 1 (OP46). Silex occurs in greater proportions in the operations within the terraces (especially OP35) and room interiors (notably OP47 and OP49). Local artisans may have preferred producing and using sharper silex tools at these loci. Coarser materials, meanwhile, tend to be slightly more associated with use and discard activities that accumulated in midden deposits. There is a very minor representation of lithic materials within the Torreón structure (OP54) and within Chinchawasi phase tombs; with one exception, all artifacts (n=28) from these zones are of finer silex.

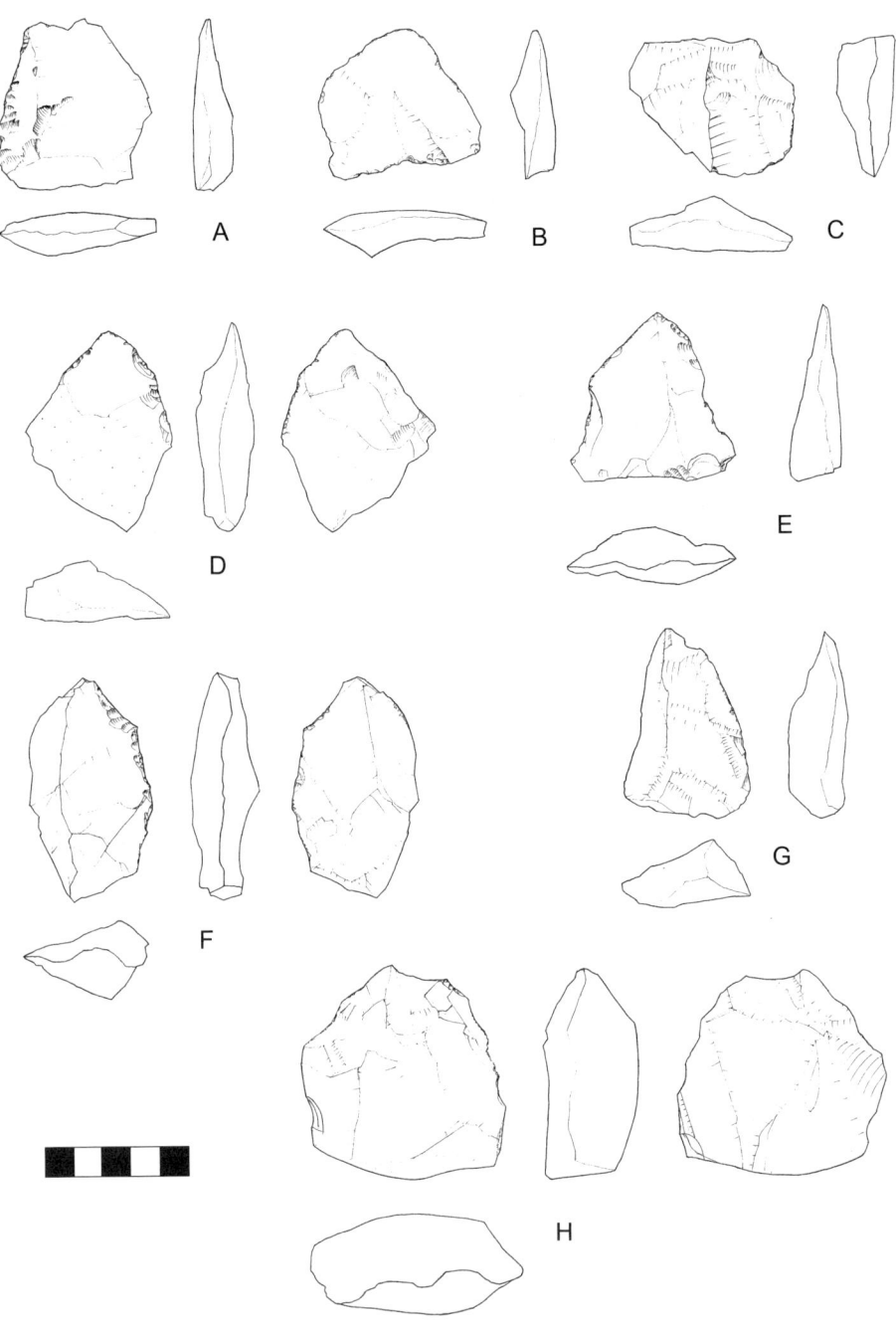

FIGURE 108. Chinchawasi 1 phase lithics.

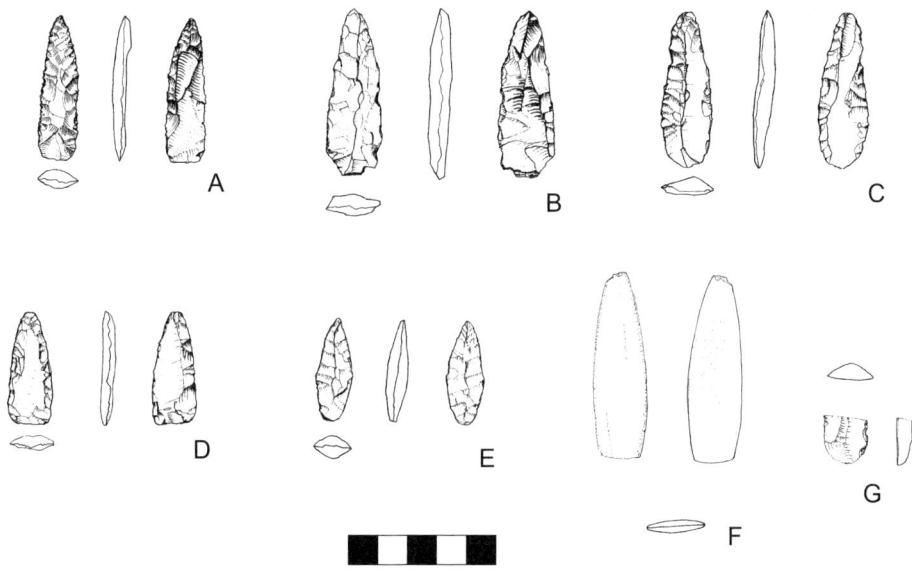

FIGURE 109. Chinchawasi 2 phase lithics.

The Chinchawasi 1 lithics can be divided into four major categories: projectile points, blade tools, flake scrapers and cores. The only complete point (Figure 107A), has a willow-leaf foliate shape, with a rounded base and a thick lenticular cross-section, comparable to forms in pottery-bearing levels at Quishqui Puncu and Guitarrero Cave (Lynch 1970:23–24, 1980:178–179). Blade artifacts (Figure 107C, D, F, I) were produced for cutting and scraping activities. Very few show retouch, suggesting that most were made, used and discarded without intensive additional modification. Scrapers also show such opportunism; typically, they use small, irregularly shaped flakes (Figures 107H, J and 108A.). Larger, more elaborate scrapers often have a triangular form for modified edges (Figure 108D, E) and occasionally may be worked bifacially (Figure 108F, H).

CHINCHAWASI 2 PHASE

The Chinchawasi 2 phase (see Table 12) shows a dramatic increase in the sheer quantity of lithic artifacts (n=1,204). Although varieties of silex (chert) continue to make up the majority (77.3%) of the phase sample, the figure represents a decrease of 12.3%. Other raw materials compensate for the reduction, including siliceous andesites and quartzites (17.6%), quartz (1.4%) and very small amounts of slate. The increased use of siliceous andesites and quartzites, as expressed by an 8.6% jump in proportion, indicates that coarser materials were exploited and used more frequently.

New materials occur at Chinchawas for the first time. Three specimens of an opaque whitish orange material, probably chalcedony, were recovered. More important, obsidian appears for the first time at Chinchawas, comprising 2.7% (n=33) of the phase sample. Neutron activation analysis (NAA) of 17 samples from this

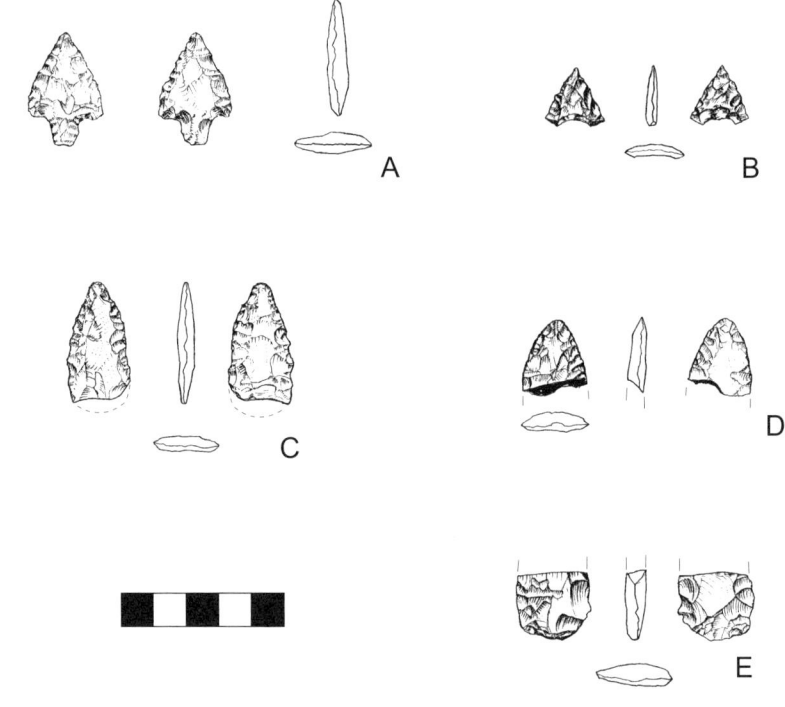

FIGURE 110. Chinchawasi 2 phase lithics.

phase all show the signature of the Quispisisa source (Burger and Glascock 2000; Burger et al. 2006). The sudden and substantial presence of obsidian indicates the opening of an important long-distance trade network to the Central Highlands during the Chinchawasi 2 phase.

The distribution of lithics occurs at roughly the same proportions as Chinchawasi 1 (see Table 11). Midden areas form the most common context (36.1%), followed by terraces (35.5%), interiors of rooms (24.7%), interiors of enclosures (1.2%) and the Torreón structure (2.6%). The relative frequencies indicate a general continuity in the patterns of chipped stone tool production, use and discard at the Chinchawas site.

Several notable changes occur in relative distributions of chipped stone materials (see Table 13). In particular, there is a dramatic increase in the frequency of coarser lithic materials (such as siliceous andesites and quartzites) in midden excavations—from 12.0% in Chinchawasi 1 to 24.6% in Chinchawasi 2.

Obsidian occurs throughout Sector 1, but is absent in the sample from excavation units within enclosures. Despite the small sample size, obsidian accounts for 16.1% (n=5) of the chipped stone artifacts from the Torreón structure (OP54); for the rest of the site, obsidian represents only 2.4% of the total phase assemblage. Together with other lines of evidence, including pottery, metal artifacts (see below) and architectural arrangement, the ratio suggests that peoples using the Torreón structure had greater access to rare goods or the activities inside required the use or

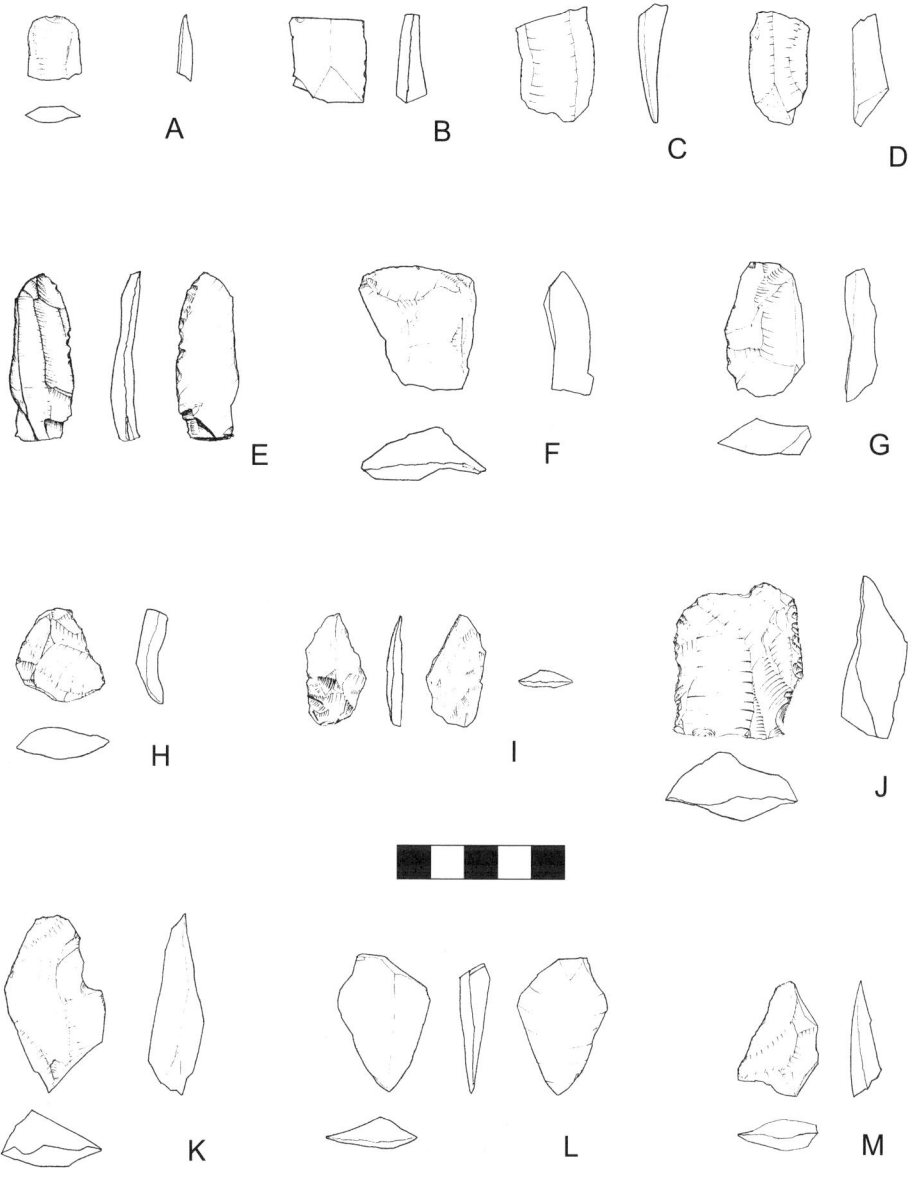

FIGURE 111. Chinchawasi 2 phase lithics.

display of obsidian, or both; the architectural arrangement and stone carving (s41) also reiterate the structure's special purpose, probably ceremonial, character.

The Chinchawasi 2 toolkit (Figures 109 to 113) also shows greater variety than Chinchawasi 1, although the categories are largely similar (projectile points, blade tools, flake scrapers and cores).

Projectile points occur in greater number and diversity. In general, they are also of better craftsmanship. In addition to older forms such as ground-slate (Fig-

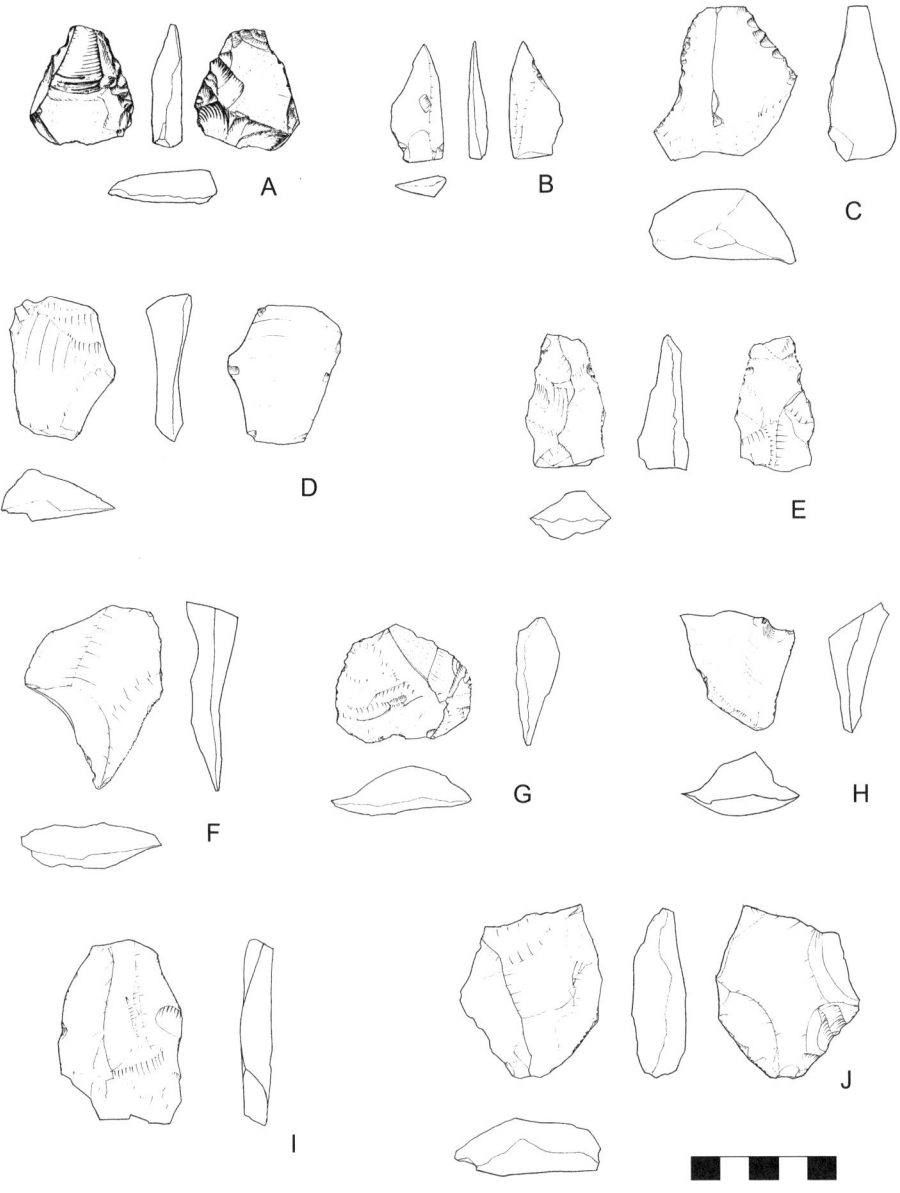

FIGURE 112. Chinchawasi 2 phase lithics.

ure 109F) and willow-leaf (Figure 109E) types, new forms characterize the phase, including flat lanceolate (Figure 109A) and elongated, triangular varieties (Figure 109B–D). Flat (see Figure 109A) and rounded bases (see Figure 109G) are evident in the same assemblage.

Completely new forms occur in the sample of obsidian projectile points (Figure 110A–E), such as a triangular shape with a short stem (Figure 110A). Another smaller triangular point has a concave-notched base and concave cross section

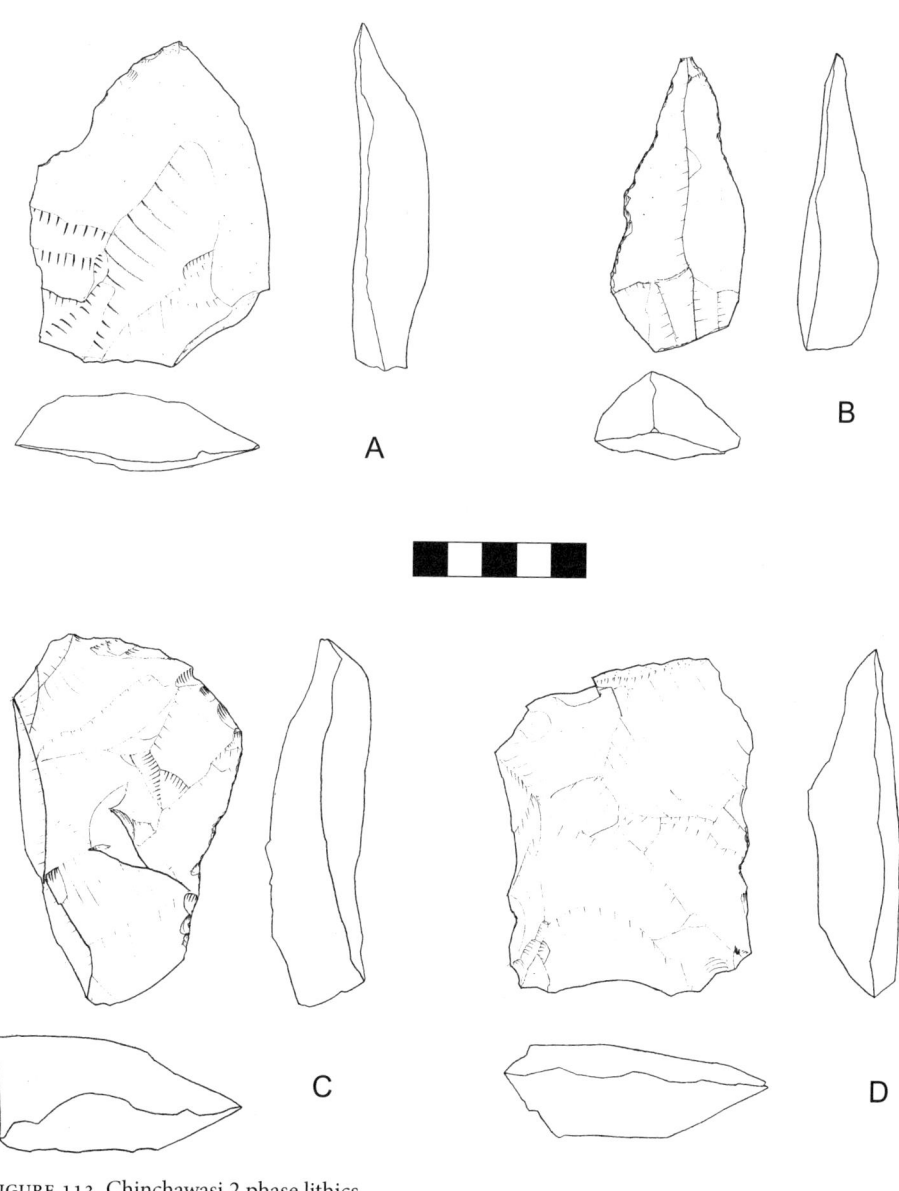

FIGURE 113. Chinchawasi 2 phase lithics.

(Figure 110B). The remaining specimens, all fragments, share a teardrop shape, with rounded base and flat, lozenge-shaped cross section (Figure 110C–E). All the specimens are highly unusual in the local Chinchawas formal repertoire and strongly suggest that obsidian was imported both as prepared projectile points and as raw material.

Blade tools (Figure 111A–G) and irregular flake scrapers (see Figures 111J and 112A, C, J) continue to be produced without strong formal consistency. Some flaked artifacts are quite large (Figure 113A, C, D) compared with other phases.

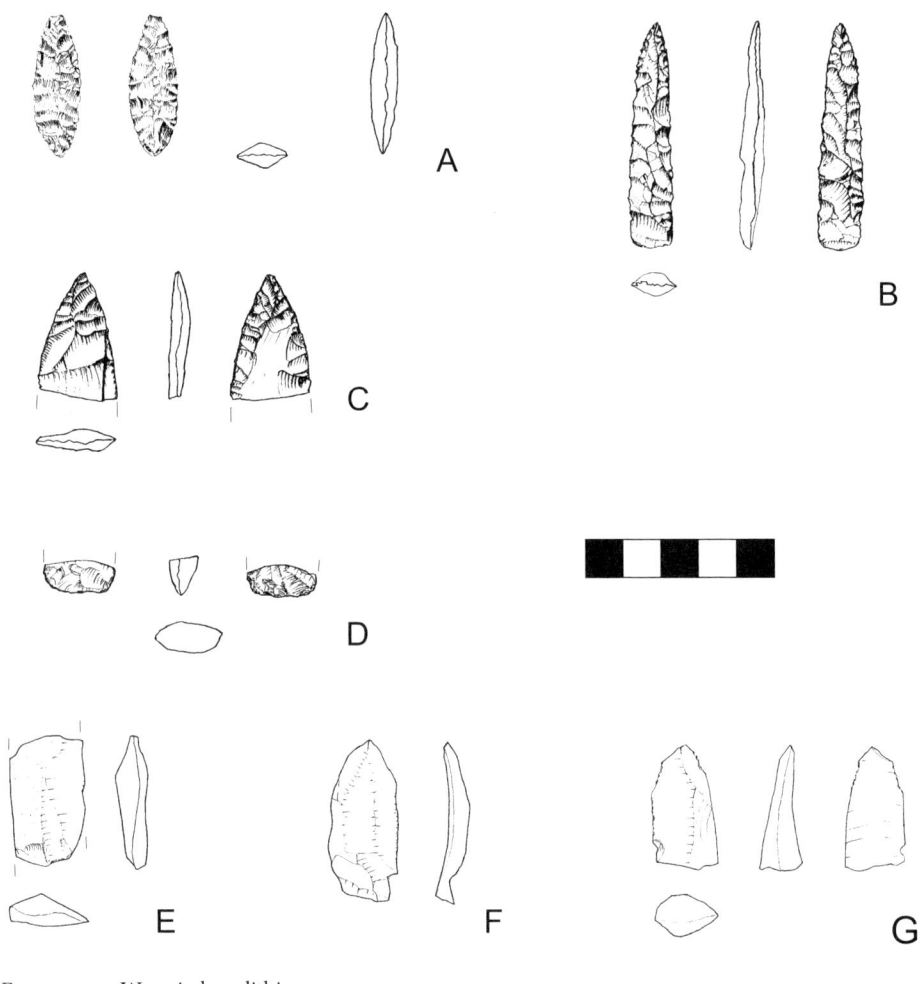

FIGURE 114. Warmi phase lithics.

## Warmi Phase

The Warmi phase sample of chipped stone material consists of 351 artifacts (Table 12). Of this sample, 83.8% are silex artifacts. The remaining materials include, in descending order: siliceous andesites and quartzites (9.4%), obsidian (3.4%), quartz and quartz crystals (3.1%), and one example of chalcedony. No slate tools were identified. Compared with the preceding phase, silex increases in representation at the expense of the andesites, which drop noticeably, by 8.2%. With the notable exception of obsidian, the relative proportions of the Warmi sample resemble most strongly those of Chinchawasi phase 1. Seven neutron activation analysis assays indicate that long-distance exchange for Quispisisa obsidian continued at least into the Warmi phase (Burger et al. 2006).

Compared with the preceding phase, there are differences in the archaeological contexts of Warmi chipped stone artifacts (see Table 13 and Figure 116). The

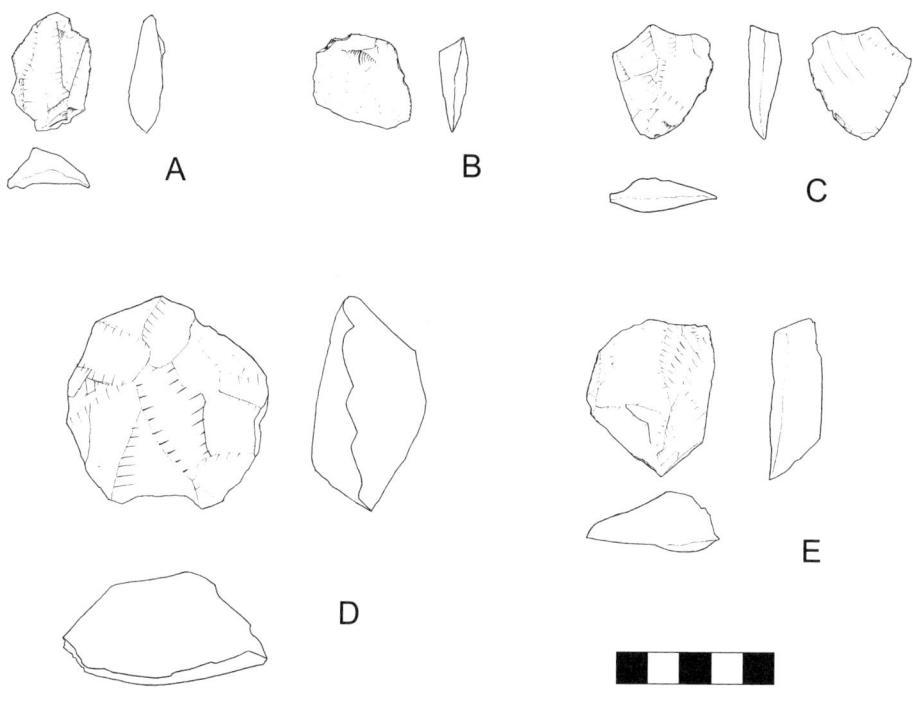

FIGURE 115. Warmi phase lithics.

representation of chipped lithics decreases markedly in room excavations (24.7% to 5.7%) as well as in midden deposits (36.1% to 25.1%). In contrast, Warmi lithics are much more common along the terraces of Chinchawas, increasing from 35.5% to 61.5%. In other words, the older patterns of chipped stone use and discard in rooms and midden fall out of favor; in lieu, the open terraces witnessed far more intensive activities using lithics. The data suggest that different economic patterns that emerged at the close of the Chinchawasi 2 phase parallel strong contemporary stylistic changes in ceramics and stone sculpture.

The formal diversity of Chinchawasi phase 2 does not continue into the Warmi phase (Figures 114 and 115). There are fewer types of projectile points, for example (Figure 114A–D). A typical willow-leaf (foliate) type is made of red silex, with a pointed base (Figure 114A). A long, lanceolate point, also of red chert, shows careful bifacial reduction and an eye-shaped cross section (Figure 114B). The obsidian sample includes two point fragments: one tip of a teardrop-shaped point and the other a rounded-corner base (Figure 114C–D). All the points were found in terrace excavations. Blade tools (Figure 114E–G) include at least one knife-like implement (Figure 114F). Scrapers take irregular forms, utilizing flakes (Figure 115A–C) as well as larger bifaces (Figure 115D, E). Compared with the Chinchawasi 2 phase, there was a notable decrease in the density and general quality of the chipped stone lithics.

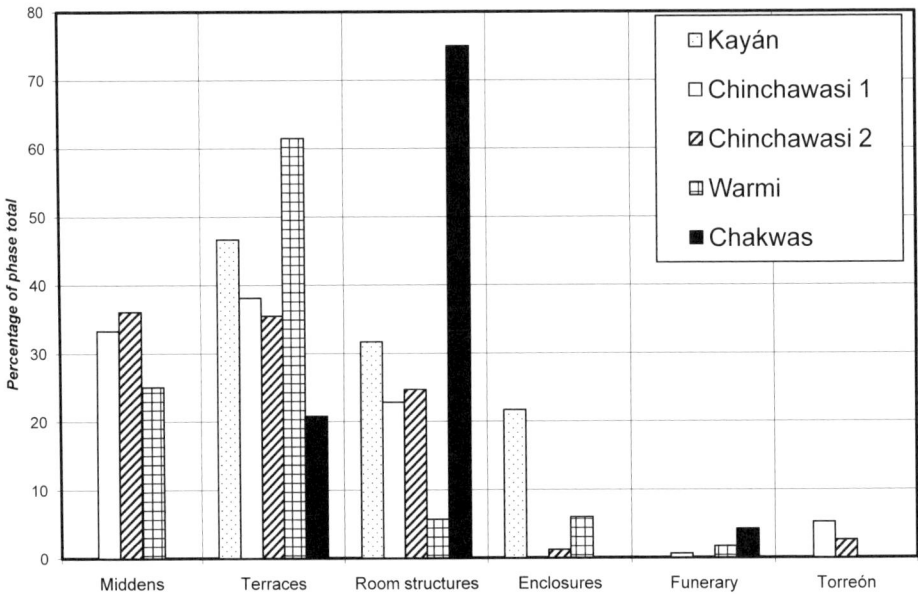

FIGURE 116. Distributions of chipped stone artifacts at Chinchawas, by context and phase.

CHAKWAS PHASE

The Chakwas phase sample of chipped stone material consists of 24 artifacts. Despite the small sample size, we can make some general observations. First, the local dependence on silex raw material (83.3% of the sample) extends into the Chakwas phase (Figure 117), and indicates that traditional sources for raw material continued to be exploited, even as obsidian exchange ceases. Several quartz crystals were identified in Chakwas deposits, one from Chullpa Tomb 6 (OP58).

## Groundstone Artifacts

During the course of the Chinchawas project, the excavations recovered a large sample of groundstone objects. Most of the artifacts were waterworn pebbles and cobbles. Given the ridgetop location of Chinchawas, probably most, if not all, of the objects discussed in the following section were collected from valley bottoms to the north and west of the site.

As a preliminary characterization of the groundstone tools, this discussion emphasizes general artifact function, archaeological contexts and chronological relationships. Analyses of wear patterns, identification and sourcing of specific raw materials and tool production remain for future research. Three general categories make up the assemblage (1) grinding stones (mortars, pestles and grinding slabs), (2) hammerstones and (3) rounded pebble objects (slingstones, polishers and miscellaneous).

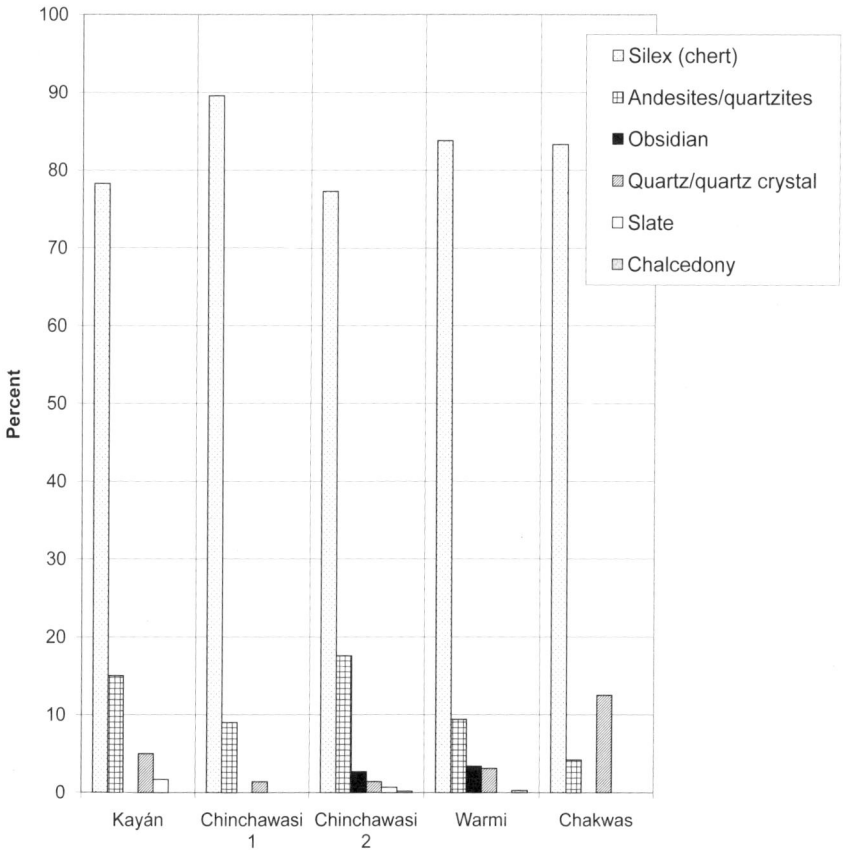

FIGURE 117. Summary of materials used at Chinchawas in chipped stone assemblage.

*Grinding Stones*

The excavations recovered 105 grinding stones (Table 14). Grinding stones were identified by the presence of one or more worked surface resulting from human modification. Identifiable materials include varieties of granite, andesite and basalt. There is also a wide range of color, including white, pink, grays and black.

The corpus can be grouped into four general formal types. The first type are hand grinding tools, or *manos* (n=79); these take various forms, using truncated (Figure 118A–E), discoidal (Figure 118Q–T) and spheroid (Figure 118U–CC) shapes, and can be used with one hand. Some hand grinding tools, considered "pestles," are cylindrical or ovoid and have wear on the outer ends (Figure 118DD, EE). Another tool type consists of large and elongate grinding tools (n=8) meant to be used with two hands in a rocking or back and forth motion (Figure 119G–I). The third type are mortars (n=15), typically, large cobbles with central depressions from pestle wear (Figure 119A–D, F). Finally, the investigations documented several large and flat grinding slabs, locally known as *batánes* (n=3); all examples were identified within room structures.

TABLE 14. Summary of grinding stones by phase.

| | Hand-sized | Large | Mortar | Batán | Total |
|---|---|---|---|---|---|
| Kayán | — | — | — | 1 | 1 |
| Chinchawasi 1 | 15 | — | 2 | 1 | 18 |
| Chinchawasi 2 | 32 | 4 | 7 | 1 | 44 |
| Warmi | 18 | 4 | 5 | — | 27 |
| Chakwas | 3 | — | — | — | 3 |
| Indeterminate phase | 11 | — | 1 | — | 12 |
| Total | 79 | 8 | 15 | 3 | 105 |

### Kayán Phase

The Kayán phase is represented by only one groundstone object, a large flat grinding slab found in the central room of OP45. The small number of groundstone tools in the Kayán assemblage should be considered, at least in part, a result of the small size of sampled Kayán contexts.

### Chinchawasi 1 Phase

The Chinchawasi 1 phase features a marked increase in the number of grinding stones. The phase assemblage consists of 15 hand grinding stones, two mortars and one batán. Groundstone artifacts are especially concentrated in midden deposits (OP46, OP47 and OP31) and in the cooking area of OP49. As percentages by architectural context, the distributions within midden and room interior contexts are identical at 44.4%, followed by several artifacts in terraces (11.1%). As would be expected, no grinding tools were recovered in the Sector 2 funerary area.

On the basis of the present evidence, grinding activities during Chinchawasi phase 1 centered within room interior contexts primarily, and perhaps also along the open terraces. As a tradition established earlier in Kayán times, large batánes were situated in room interiors, likely used to process grain and other foods for the local household. Grinding activities within individual structures also seems reasonable given the frequent and strong winds that scour the Sector 1 ridgetop. None of the ground stone artifacts discarded in midden deposits was broken.

### Chinchawasi 2 Phase

An increase in grinding stone frequency and use characterizes the Chinchawasi 2 phase, mirroring patterns of intensification and diversification in other dimensions of local material culture. The phase assemblage (n=44) consists of 32 hand grinding tools, seven mortars, one batán and the first appearance of large elongate grinding stones. There is strong representation of grinding tools in midden contexts, accounting for about 59.1% of the phase total (n=26); many are from the dense refuse deposits in OP38 and OP48. Only seven of the 26 midden specimens are broken, indicating that even complete and still usable implements were discarded. Open terrace areas and room structures continue to show grinding tools, at proportions of 25% (n=11) and 13.6% (n=6), respectively.

As in Chinchawasi 1 times, the distributional patterns suggest that grinding activities occurred mainly within room structures and secondarily in terrace areas. The data also show that there was considerable discard of grinding stones, even of complete specimens. As expected, grinding stones are rare in special ceremonial areas. They are absent in the Sector 2 cemetery area. A fragment of a large ground stone object (Figure 119E) was found in Chinchawasi 2 deposits of the Torreón structure; the specimen is unusual because it combines a general mortar form and a hole perforation shaped into the center.

Warmi Phase

In the Warmi phase, the sample shows a reduction in the overall number of grinding stones, with only 27 examples. The assemblage includes 18 hand grinding stones, four large (elongate) grinding stones and five mortars. No batánes were found in Warmi deposits. The general representation of grinding stone types is comparable to previous phases.

New patterns emerged, however, for contexts of grinding tool use and discard during the Warmi phase. In particular, a greater proportion of groundstone tools occurs along the open terraces, at 62.9% (n=17) of the phase sample; the sample shows a corresponding deemphasis of tools in room (n=3) and midden (n=4) deposits. As noted earlier, only 23.8% of the preceding Chinchawasi 2 sample was recovered from the terraces. Therefore, Warmi peoples at Chinchawas seem to have preferred the open terrace areas to perform grinding activities as well as for general discard of groundstone implements. Five of the examples from the terrace areas are broken fragments, rendering them unserviceable.

Chakwas Phase

The Chakwas phase assemblage consists of only three hand grinding stones. The small amount is consistent with the other Chakwas remains that indicate a light, ephemeral occupation after the Warmi phase.

## Hammerstones

The research recovered 31 hammerstones at Chinchawas, 26 with phase associations (Tables 15 and 16). Hammerstones were identified by the presence of pecking on one or more ends of the stone objects. In general, local peoples produced hammerstones from small river cobbles and stones. Identifiable materials include granite and basalt, usually black, dark gray and reddish brown. Although there are several large examples, most of the hammerstones fit comfortably in one hand (Figure 120A–C). The mean dimensions (see Table 15) of the artifacts are 6.1 cm in length ($s=2.5$, $n=30$), 4.7 cm in width ($s=2.1$, $n=25$) and 3.3 cm in thickness ($s=1.9$, $n=30$).

All the hammerstones come from excavations in Sector 1 (Table 16). For the Kayán phase, only one hammerstone was identified, in Enclosure 2. In the succeed-

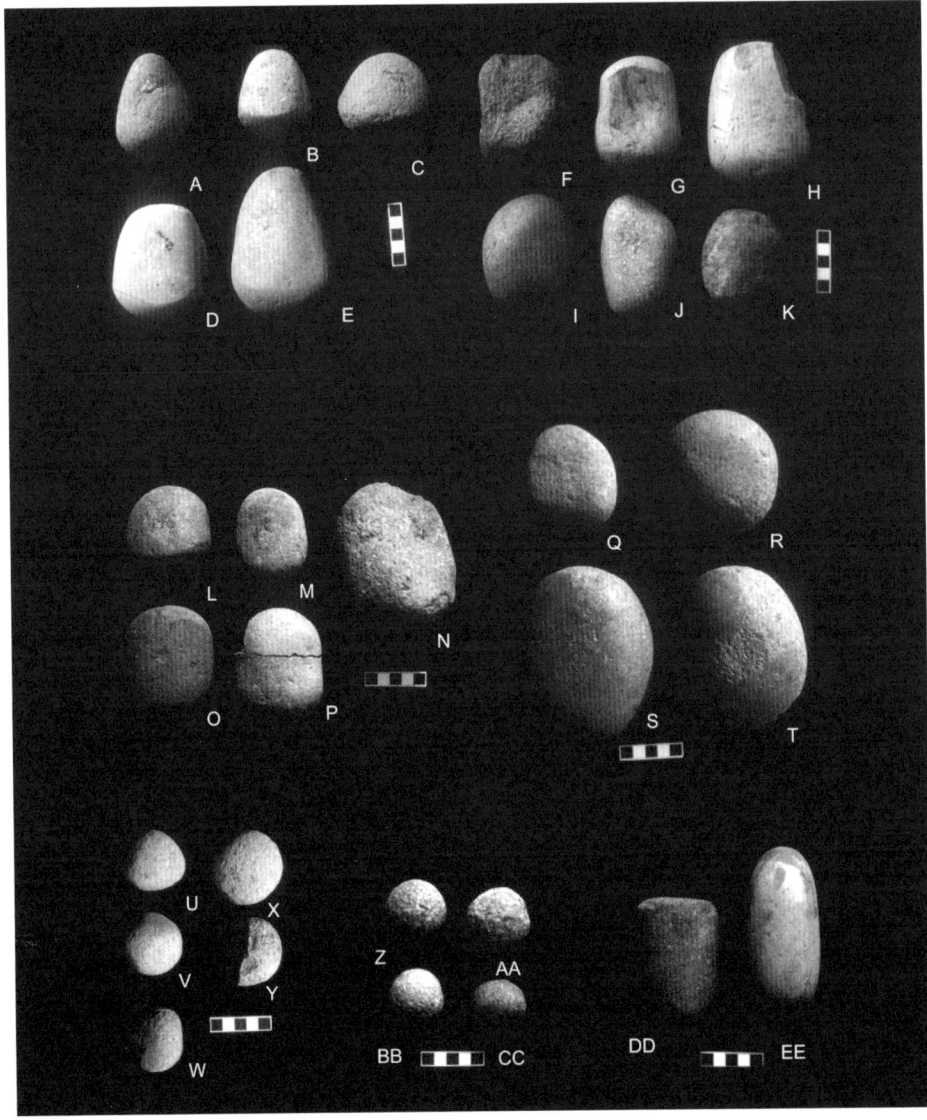

Figure 118. Hand grinding stones (A–EE), Sector 1.

ing Chinchawasi 1 phase, we found five: four from midden deposits and one from a terrace area. There is a large increase in hammerstones during the Chinchawasi 2 phase, with 16 examples. Of this total, 11 were from midden areas, four from room contexts and one from terrace areas. Finally, only four hammerstones were recovered from Warmi deposits: two from refuse deposits, one from room interiors and one from a terrace excavation.

The distributional patterns are somewhat different than those of the chipped stone artifacts. As noted above, representation of flaked lithics was often very common in room structures and floors. The hammerstones, in contrast, are

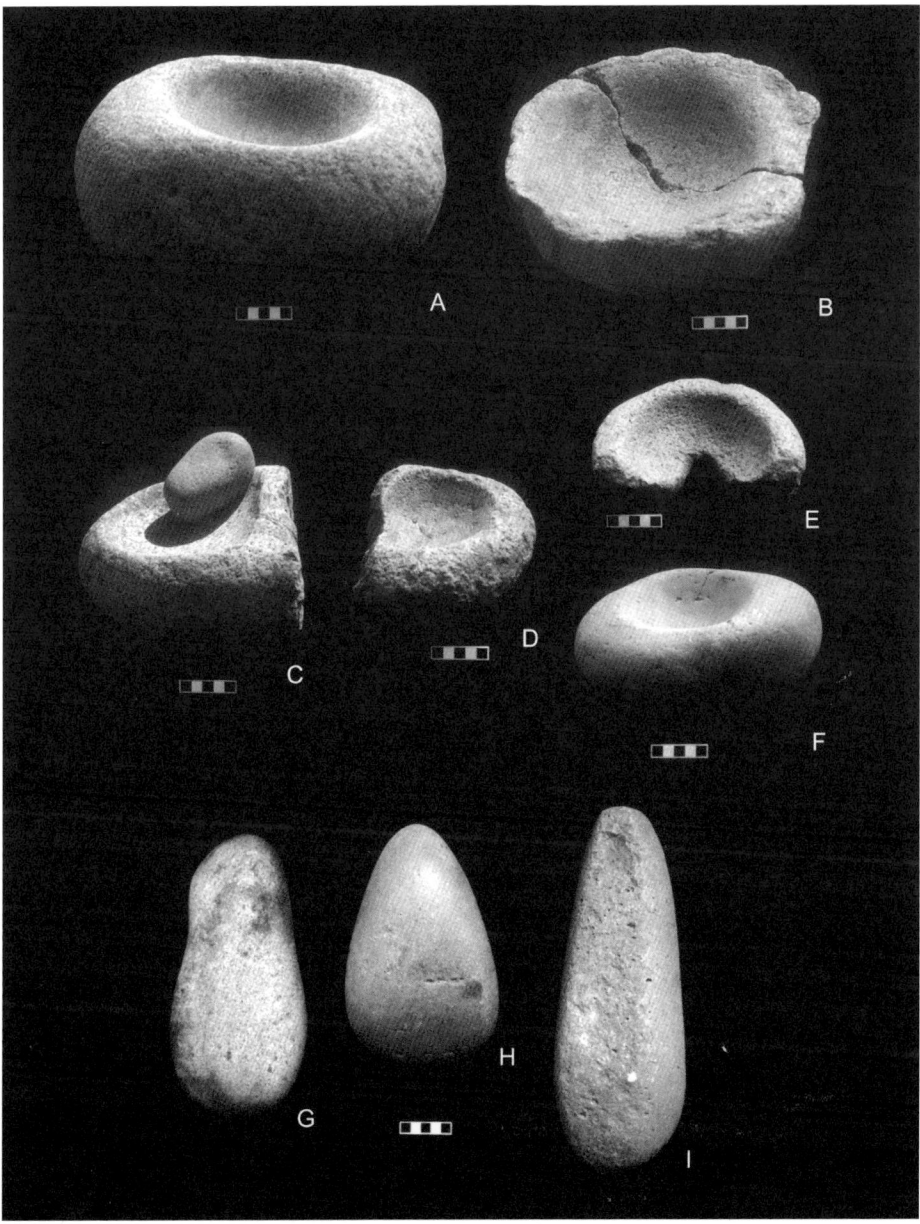

FIGURE 119. Mortars (A–F) and large grinding stones (G–I), Sector 1.

found mainly as midden debris, especially in the Chinchawasi 1 and 2 phases. There are two plausible interpretations for the data. One is that while tools could have been chipped within room structures, clean-up frequently included unwanted hammerstones as part of the refuse removal. The other possible alternative is that local peoples flaked lithics and discarded manufacturing tools on top of refuse heaps.

TABLE 15. Summary statistics of hammerstones.

|  | Midden | Terrace | Rooms | Enclosures | Total |
|---|---|---|---|---|---|
| Kayán | — | — | — | 1 | 1 |
| Chinchawasi 1 | 4 | 1 | — | — | 5 |
| Chinchawasi 2 | 11 | 1 | 4 | — | 16 |
| Warmi | 2 | 1 | 1 | — | 4 |
| Total | 17 | 3 | 5 | 1 | 26 |

TABLE 16. Summary of hammerstones by phase. All measurements are in centimeters.

|  | Length | Width | Thickness |
|---|---|---|---|
| Mean | 6.1 | 4.7 | 3.3 |
| Standard error | 0.5 | 0.4 | 0.3 |
| Standard deviation | 2.5 | 2.1 | 1.9 |
| Sample variance | 6.3 | 4.3 | 3.6 |
| Range | 9.9 | 7.2 | 9.6 |
| Minimum | 3.1 | 1.8 | 1.4 |
| Maximum | 13.0 | 9.0 | 11.0 |
| Sum | 183.5 | 116.5 | 99.9 |
| Total | 30 | 25 | 30 |

Two very small specimens resemble hammerstones used for working metal sheets (Grossman 1972). Both examples take the form of a small hand-held truncate forms, with rounded corners (Figure 120C). The basal surface is flat or slightly convex to facilitate the hammering of thin and even metal sheets, or laminas. It is unclear whether these tools played a role in the manufacture of the copper-metal lamina artifacts (discussed below) found at the site.

## Pebble and Slingstone Objects

The excavations also recovered a series (n=170) of small round pebble artifacts (Tables 17 and 18). The assemblage of artifacts can be largely characterized as unmodified pebbles or small, rounded stones. Because of the location of the site, the artifacts do not occur naturally near Chinchawas. More likely, they were collected from river deposits and brought to the site for their utility as polishers and as slingstone projectiles (Figure 121A–E), given their large numbers. Twenty specimens seem to be polishing stones on the basis of very smooth surfaces and discoidal shape (Figure 120D–E).

All the stones have a uniform character. Most are gray, black, brown or white. They are mostly spheroid or irregular spheroid shapes, but also occur with ovoid

TABLE 17. Summary of pebble and slingstone objects by phase.

|  | Midden | Terrace | Rooms | Enclosures | Funerary | Total |
|---|---|---|---|---|---|---|
| Kayán | — | 1 | 2 | — | — | 3 |
| Chinchawasi 1 | 13 | 6 | 7 | — | — | 26 |
| Chinchawasi 2 | 24 | 21 | 24 | 1 | — | 70 |
| Warmi | 8 | 12 | 4 | 5 | 3 | 32 |
| Total | 45 | 40 | 37 | 6 | 3 | 131 |

TABLE 18. Summary statistics of pebble and slingstone objects. All measurements are in centimeters.

|  | Length | Width | Thickness |
|---|---|---|---|
| Mean | 3.1 | 2.5 | 1.8 |
| Standard error | 0.1 | 0.1 | 0.1 |
| Standard deviation | 1.3 | 1.0 | 0.6 |
| Sample variance | 1.6 | 0.9 | 0.4 |
| Range | 6.8 | 5.8 | 3.6 |
| Minimum | 1.3 | 1.1 | 0.5 |
| Maximum | 8.1 | 6.9 | 4.1 |
| Sum | 513.2 | 225.7 | 241.6 |
| Total | 168 | 89 | 138 |

or lozenge shapes. The mean dimensions (see Table 18) of the pebbles are 3.1 cm in length ($s$=1.3, n=168), 2.5 cm in width ($s$=1.0, n=89) and 1.8 cm in thickness ($s$=0.6, n=138). All are small and can be accommodated in hand-held slings.

Pebble and slingstone objects occur throughout the site sequence. Kayán phase deposits produced three slingstones, two from the rooms in OP45 and one from a terrace excavation. The Chinchawasi 1 phase assemblage consists of 26 specimens, found in the following archaeological contexts: midden deposits (n=13), room interiors (n=7) and terrace areas (n=6). By far the largest inventory comes from the Chinchawasi 2 phase, with 70 specimens recovered from the following contexts: midden deposits (n=24), room interiors (n=24), terrace areas (n=21) and enclosures (n=1). Six of these artifacts could be polishing stones. During the Warmi phase, 32 specimens were recovered from the following archaeological contexts: terrace areas (n=12), midden deposits (n=8), enclosures (n=5), room interiors (n=4) and funerary (n=3). One Warmi specimen, from a fill deposit in Enclosure 2, may be a polishing stone.

Several inferences can be made about the distributional patterns. First, the use of slingstones occurred throughout the occupation of Chinchawas, especially during the Chinchawasi 2 phase. Second, most of the slingstones were recovered

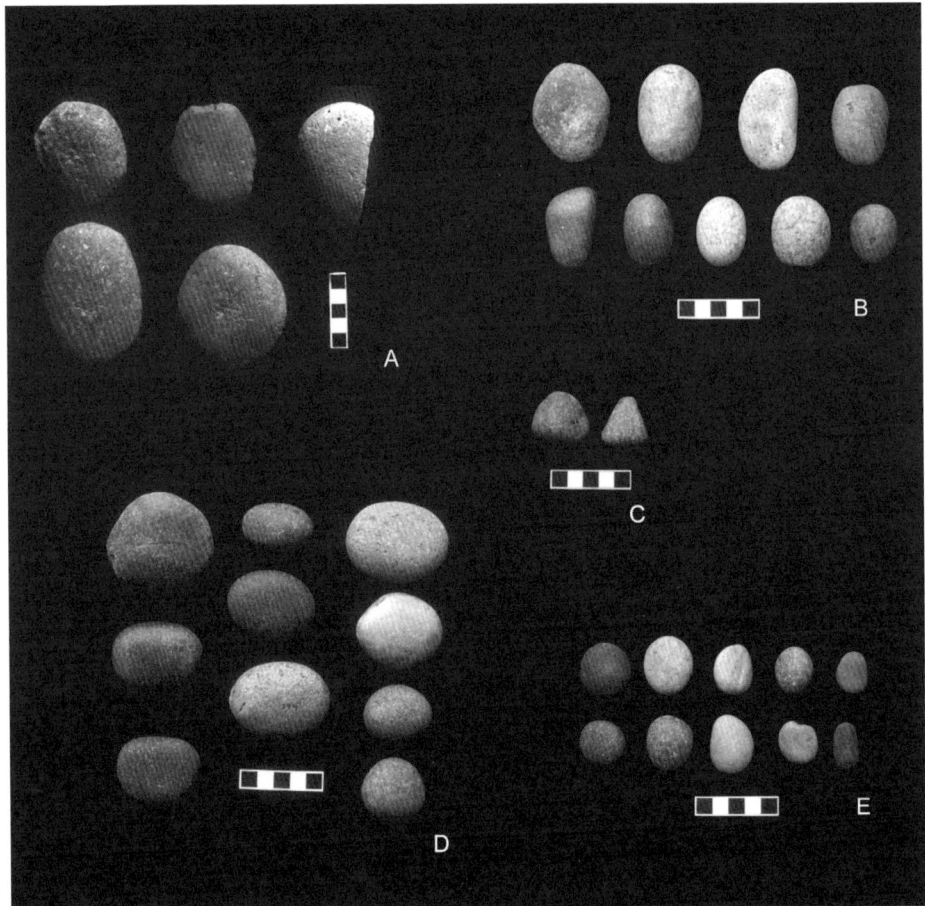

FIGURE 120. Hammerstones (groups A–C) and stone polishers (groups D, E), Sector 1.

in the primary residential zone of Sector 1, indicating that the stones were largely reserved for use or stored in this zone. The only evidence for slingstones in Sector 2 consists of three examples found in Warmi phase chullpa tombs; specifically, CT-6 and CT-12. Two of the specimens are irregular spheroids of metal, probably iron, each measuring about 2.5 cm in diameter (Figure 121E). As part of the general innovative program in mortuary practice during Warmi times, the metal objects likely were grave offerings within the chullpas. Another was found in the plowzone levels of OP46.

It is currently unclear, though, what targets the slingstones were meant for in practice. Their common occurrence within walled terrace areas indicates that at least some, especially the larger examples, could have been defensive weapons against human attackers. There is no evidence for intact piles of slingstones, however, as in contemporary fortified settlements in the lower and middle Moche valley (Topic 1982; Topic and Topic 1987). Smaller slingstones could have been used to hunt small birds and highland mammals, such as viscacha and fox.

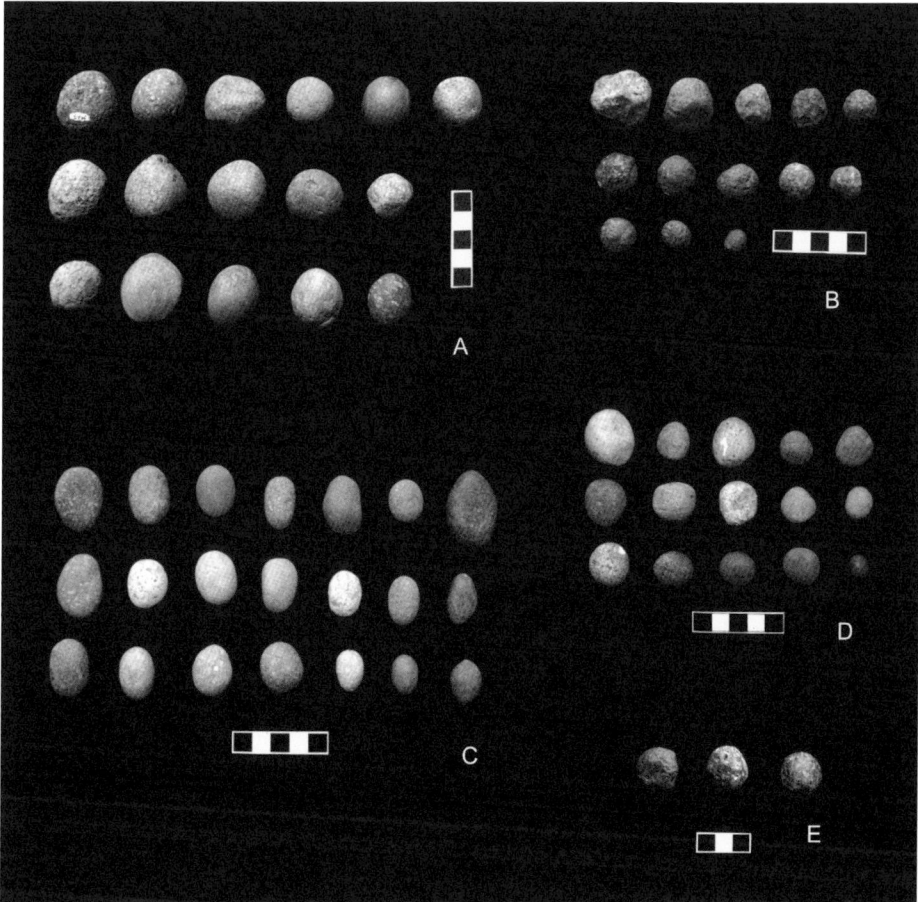

FIGURE 121. Pebble and slingstone objects (groups A–E).

## Miscellaneous Stone Artifacts

This section describes miscellaneous stone objects, including figurines, small carved objects, hafted implements, beads and pendants.

### Figurines

Four stone figurines were recovered at Chinchawas. Two, stylized representations of camelids, are made out of a waxy, white stone. Details are rendered through careful incision, although features are schematic, like the rectangular noses, ears and legs. The smaller object (Figure 122B) was found in the refuse fill within OP49 and can date to Chinchawasi 2 or later. Subtle incisions represent a short tail. A small perforation through the body facilitates hanging, probably as a necklace pendant. The larger specimen (Figure 122A) was found in OP37, Level E east, and is associated with mixed remains directly above a Chinchawasi 2 stratum. Simple notches between the front and hind legs portray the animal's penis.

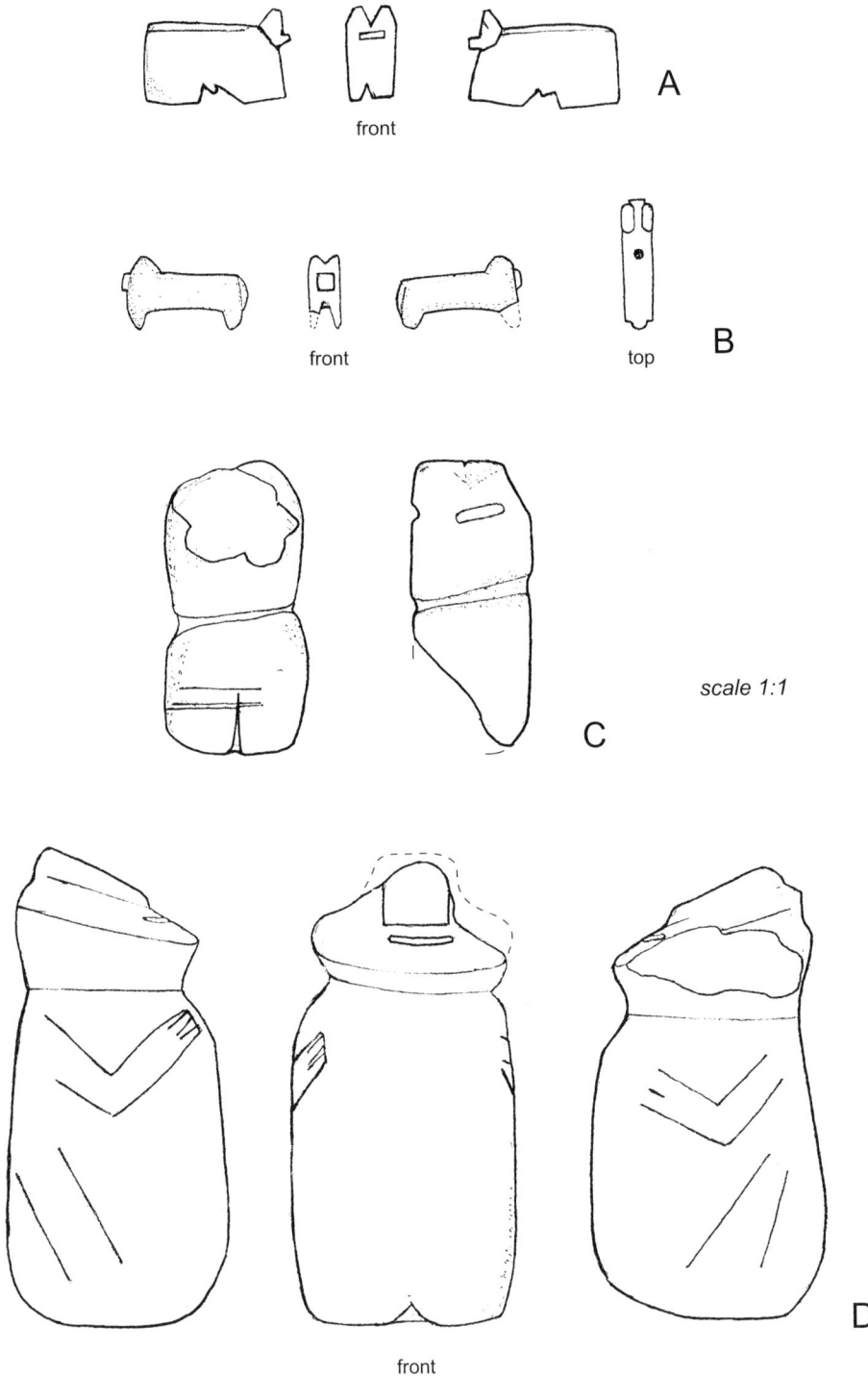

FIGURE 122. Carved stone figurines (A–D), Sector 1.

Another figurine, found in OP35E (terrace area, Chinchawasi 2 phase) is of a seated or squatting anthropomorph (Figure 122D). The figurine, made out of a white, rough stone with many small cavities, is very poorly preserved. In some areas the incised detail and part of the head have spalled off. The anthropomorph shows a large sloping face, with a rectangular nose, groove mouth and sharp relief between the chin and body. Post-cranial features are incised: bent arms, extended fingers, upper legs (thighs) and a grooved notch to separate the legs. Given the posture and mask-like representation of the head, the figurine resembles anthropomorphic depictions in Recuay tradition stone sculpture, especially of the Huaraz area (Schaedel 1948a; Lau 2006b). As in sculptural iconography, the figurine could be an ancestor representation in the form of a seated mummy bundle.

The final miniature carving (Figure 122C) was found in OP23H, a midden deposit dating to Chinchawasi 2. The object shows two rounded ends divided by a narrow center groove. The ends of the front and back show vertical notches reminiscent of the notch feature (Figure 122D). Several linear incisions cut across the front and top aspects.

## Carved Objects

The excavations also recovered two carved plaque-like objects. The first, from the surface level of OP29 (terrace), is a broken fragment (Figure 123A), measuring 10.1 cm in length, of a rough gray material. On the top surface a series of small circular depressions forms an outer ring; a large circular gouge separates a central depression with two shallow pecked holes opposite one another within the center. This design at Chinchawas is mirrored by a large copper-metal repoussé adornment found nearby in OP40 within an intact Chinchawasi 2 stratum of refuse or fill (Level D). The ring of circular depressions also resembles monolithic stone Sculpture s28 found in Sector 2 (Lau 2006b:222).

Nearby, in OP41, another carved rock was uncovered, laying flat on top of sterile (Figure 123B). The object, made of a dark gray shale-like stone, was part of an aligned series of rocks that formed the basal row of a Chinchawasi 1 stone wall. The carving (20 by 13 cm) shows deliberate incisions on both flat sides. The top image, as found, shows a large portion of an oval-shaped feature. Within the oval are a series of incisions, several of which form an irregular rectangular element. There is at least one partly drilled hole within the square. On the back side (Figure 123B, reverse), there is another series of incisions that form a rough lattice pattern on one end. As part of the wall, the carving on either (flat) side would have been hidden from view. Presumably it was worked, discarded and then collected as general construction material.

## Large Hafted Implements

We found three stone implements in the Sector 1 area, probably agricultural tools, dating to the Chinchawasi and Warmi phases. The first specimen (Figure 124A) is flat and has a long, trapezoidal shape (24.2 by 10.5 by 1.6 cm). It is made of a silver-

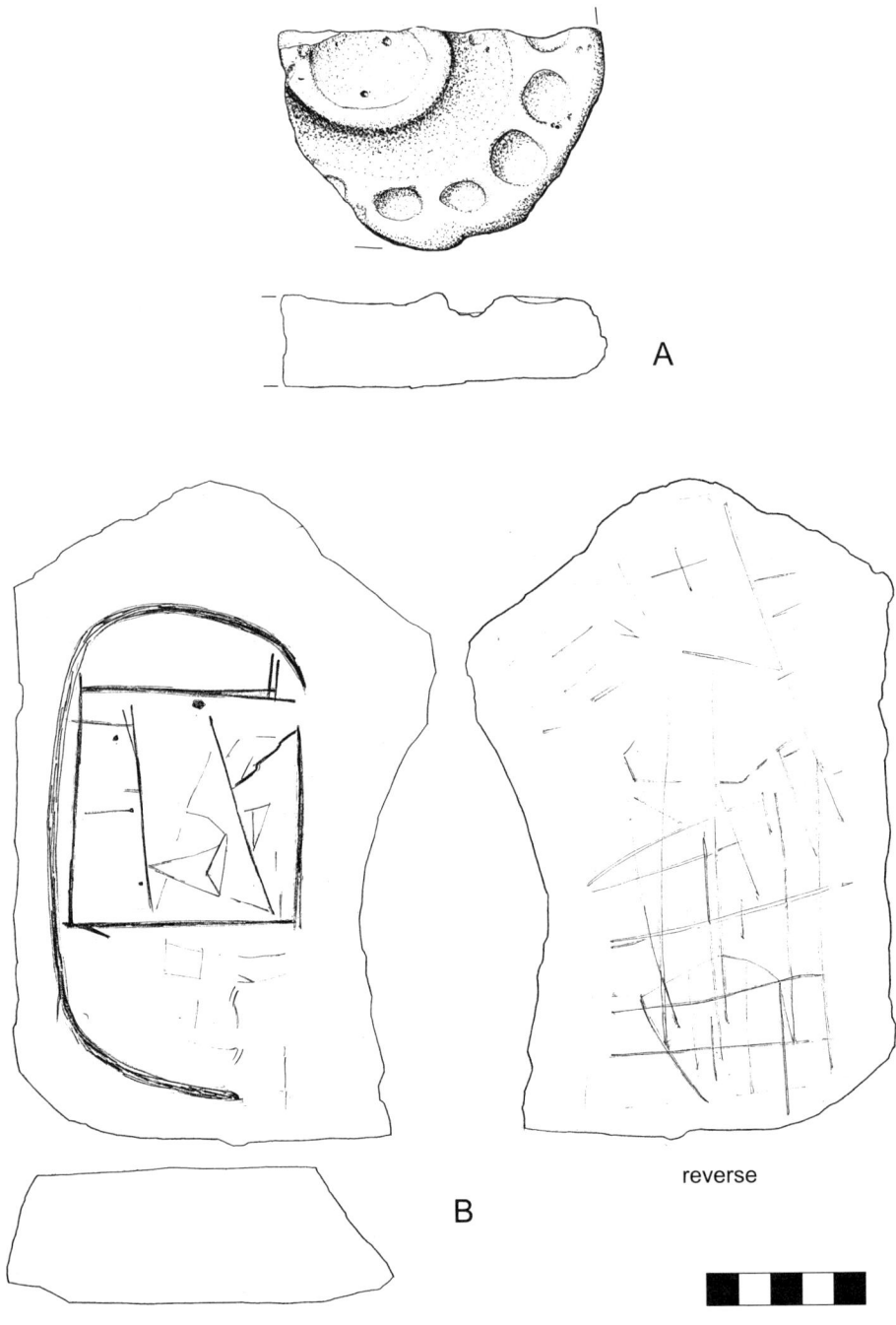

FIGURE 123. Small stone carvings (A, B), Sector 1.

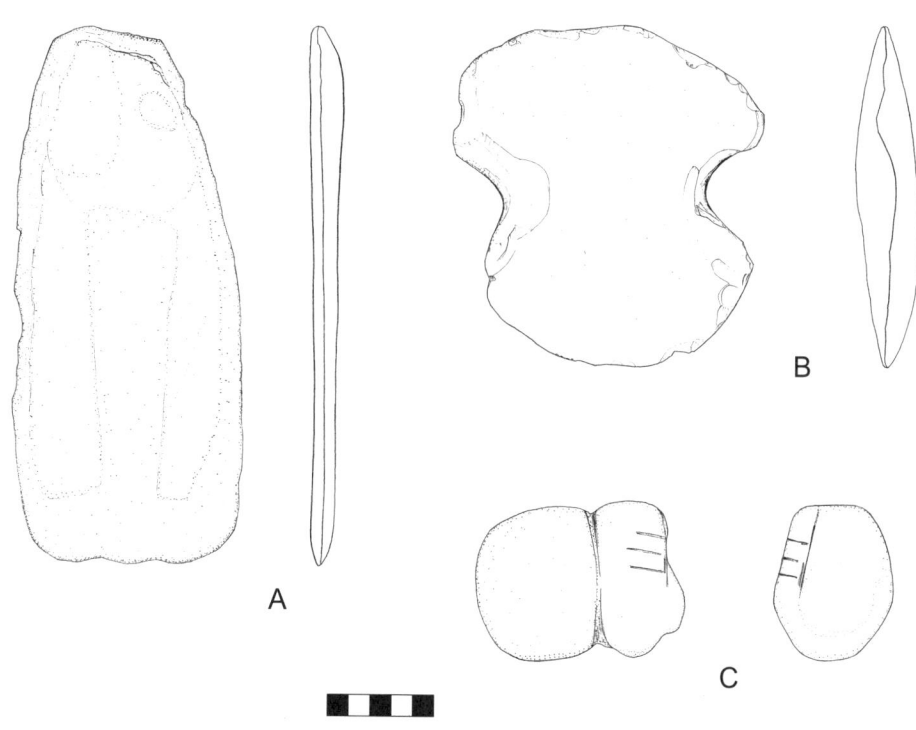

FIGURE 124. Large hafted stone implements.

gray, partly iridescent rock with planar cleavage, tentatively identified as a type of schist. The object was in a Warmi level of OP43 and was probably the blade portion of a hoe-like tool. There is wear on the wide end as well as a shallow groove along the central portion of the long axis, probably to facilitate hafting.

Another stone object (Figure 124C), found in the lowermost level of OP48 (room interior), is of poorly preserved and porous white rock. The object is grooved towards the center to facilitate hafting. On the narrower portion, a series of three short grooves nearly crosses with two vertical incisions at the end. The tool is suitable for use as a mallet, small clod-breaker, or perhaps weapon.

The final hafted tool (Figure 124B) is a large, roughly discoidal axe blade (15.5 by 14.3 cm). The axe makes use of a large cortical fragment of a fine dark gray stone, with deep side notches for hafting. The wide convex end was the primary work edge. The axe comes from Chinchawasi 1 deposits of the Torreón structure (OP54).

## Beads and Pendants

The investigations recovered 12 bead and pendant objects (Figure 125A–K). The artifacts with secure associations date to occupations between the Kayán and Warmi phases. Several of the specimens have holes that have only been partly drilled (Figure 125J, K). These may be considered pendants in process, or "blanks." Most of the pendants are made from trapezoidal or flat, rounded (discoidal or ovoid) stones

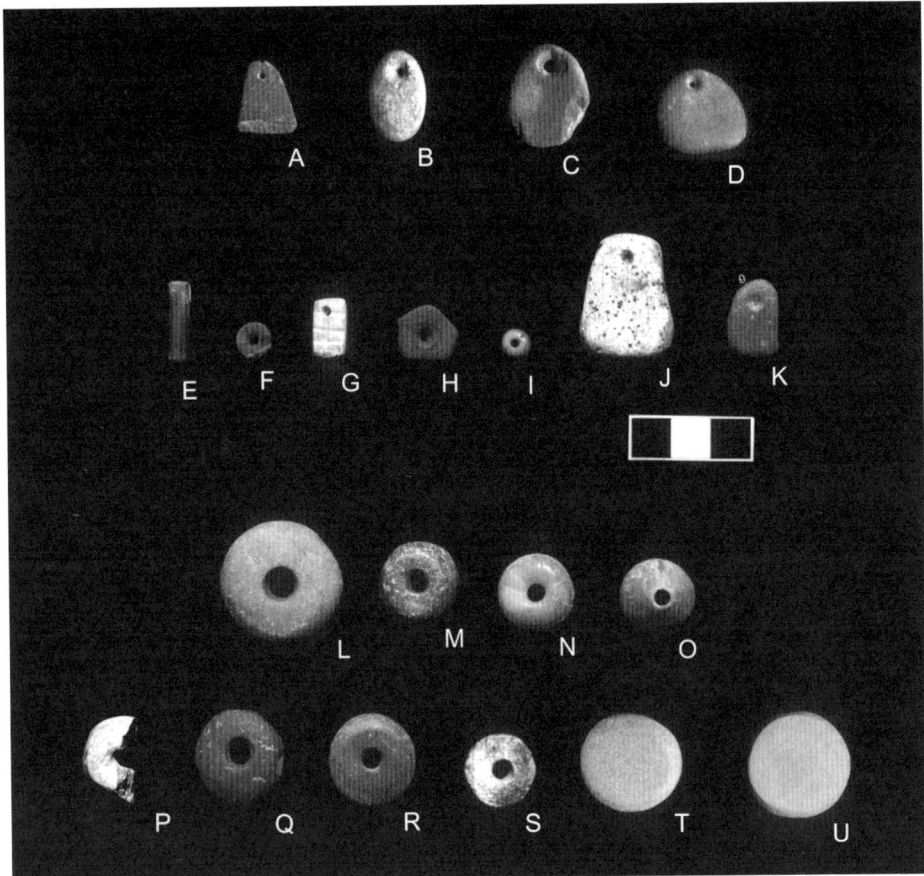

FIGURE 125. Stone beads and pendants (A–K), spindle whorls (L–S) and small stone discs (T, U).

with perforations in the upper hanging end; these preferences were apparently the local tradition in lapidary use.

Kayán Phase

The only Kayán example, found in OP3 of Enclosure 2 has a trapezoidal shape and is made from a grayish white stone with orange streaks (Figure 125J). There are partly drilled holes on either side of the pendant.

Chinchawasi 1 Phase

The Chinchawasi 1 phase sample consists of three examples. One is a small turquoise-colored bead (Figure 125I) found in Subterranean Tomb 3 (ST-3). Another specimen, made of whitish tan stone, was recovered from the refuse deposit in OP46 east, Level G; the front of the rectangular bead shows three horizontal incisions (Figure 125G). The other specimen, of dark gray stone with white speckles, comes from the Chinchawasi 1 floor of OP40; the hole on the front face is only partly drilled (Figure 125K).

CHINCHAWASI 2 PHASE

Five examples were from Chinchawasi 2 contexts. Three beads were recovered in terrace areas (OP14, 35 and 37), one from midden refuse (OP40) and another from a room floor (OP48). Two use flat, rounded pebbles (Figure 125B, D). Another is a flat, trapezoidal black slate fragment (Figure 125A). The most elaborate bead in the sample, made of a black stone, is long and cylindrical (Figure 125E). The final specimen is a flat perforated ornament made of an iridescent fragment of golden brown mica.

WARMI PHASE

The Warmi sample consists of two examples: illustrates a black, flat discoidal pendant (Figure 125C) from a terrace excavation (OP39) and a flat circular stone bead (Figure 125F) found in Chullpa Tomb 5 (OP59). The bead has a single central hole and is made from a reddish brown rock with white and deep red streaks.

## Spindle Whorls and Discs

The archaeological investigations recovered many spindle whorls and whorl-type artifacts in the process of manufacture, or whorl "blanks." As finished artifacts, spindle whorls were counterweights on the ends of narrow rods (such as spindles) to facilitate the spinning of thread, probably the hair of camelids, especially of alpaca. Together with bone and ceramic varieties, the spindle whorls show that fiber processing and textile production were a vital component of the local economy throughout Chinchawas's occupation. Ancient peoples at Chinchawas used spindle whorls made from three different types of material: ceramics, bone and groundstone.

*Ceramic Spindle Whorls*

By far, ceramic is the most common material used for the recovered spindle whorls. Although there are five examples of whorls that have been fired (Figures 102A, B, D, E, and 126E), most of the sample (n=84) are of recycled broken potsherds that have been ground down, at least roughly, into discs and drilled for the insertion of a spindle (Figure 126D). Many discarded examples were broken from use (Figure 126B). In addition, the excavations recovered a large assemblage of whorls in preparation, which were termed "blanks" (n=162).

*Perforated Whorls*

Perforated ceramic whorls (Figure 126B, D) occur throughout the Chinchawas sequence (Table 19). Kayán deposits revealed two examples, both from terrace excavations (OP21 and OP43). During Chinchawasi 1 times, surprisingly, the sample shows only a slightly greater abundance, with six examples: three from refuse deposits, one from a room structure (OP47) and two identified within the Torreón structure (OP54). The presence of spindle whorls in the Torreón structure suggests that activities within the structure included spinning, perhaps by women.

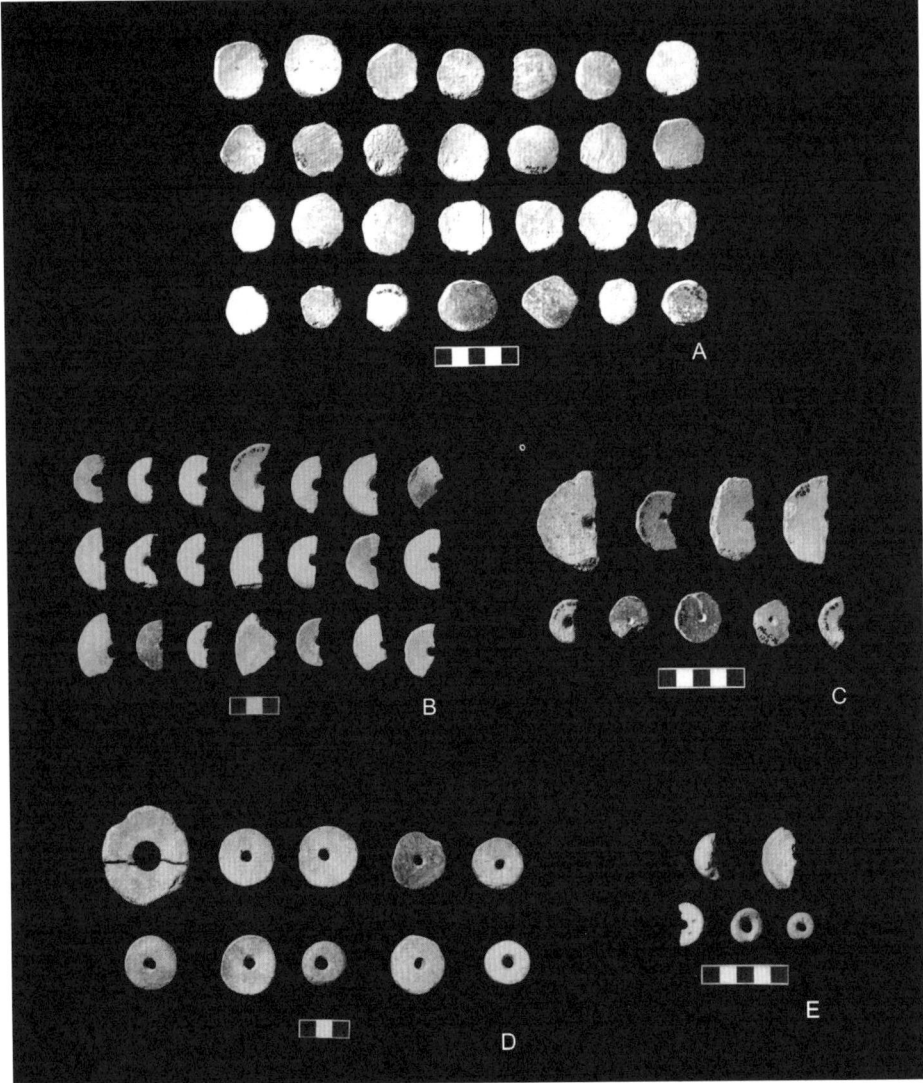

FIGURE 126. Ceramic spindle whorls and blanks: group A, whorl blanks; group B, broken whorls; group C, partly perforated whorls; group D, complete whorls; group E, fired ceramic whorls.

The general scarcity of spindle whorls in Chinchawasi 1 contrasts starkly with the subsequent occupation. There were 40 whorls found in Chinchawasi 2 deposits, in the following cultural contexts: terrace areas (n=16), midden deposits (n=14), room floors (n=9) and one specimen from the Torreón structure. The Warmi occupation saw a reduction in the abundance of spindle whorls (n=15) found in terrace (n=8) midden (n=5), funerary (n=1) and enclosure (n=1) contexts.

The strong representation in terrace areas during the Chinchawasi 2 and Warmi occupations suggests that spinning activities frequently occurred in open air contexts, as is common today. The remaining frequencies seem to reflect pat-

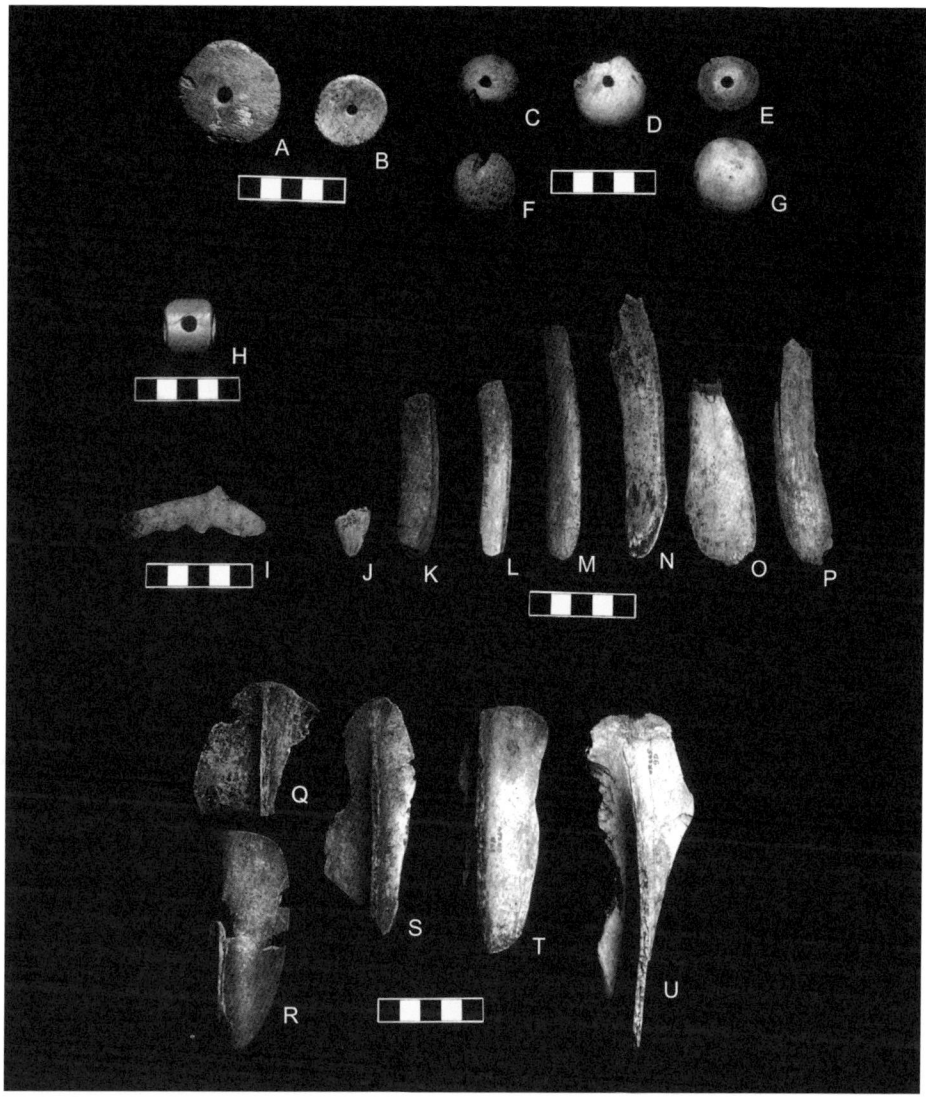

FIGURE 127. Bone implements: A–H, spindle whorls and blanks; I, ornament; J–P, rib tools; Q–U, scapula scrapers.

terns in general discard and domestic storage of common everyday items. The great surge in whorl frequency during the Chinchawasi 2 phase seems to be evidence of an intensification of camelid fiber processing and probably local textile production, in general.

The mean dimensions of the ceramic whorls support the trend of textile production intensification (see Table 19). Chinchawasi 2 whorls are, on average, 3.5 mm wider and slightly thicker (0.1 mm) than in previous phases. The larger whorl size could indicate an interest in heavier weights to process greater or thicker quantities of thread. In the subsequent Warmi phase, whorl diameter decreases slightly

TABLE 19. Summary statistics and chart of mean dimensions (in millimeters) of perforated ceramic spindle whorls.

| | Total sample-(all phases) | | Kayán | | Chinchawasi 1 | | Chinchawasi 2 | | Warmi | |
|---|---|---|---|---|---|---|---|---|---|---|
| | Diameter | Thickness | Diameter | Thickness | Diameter | Thickness | Diameter | Thickness | Diameter | Thickness |
| Mean | 31.7 | 7.5 | 28.5 | 6.9 | 29.6 | 7.2 | 33.1 | 7.3 | 32.0 | 7.5 |
| Standard error | 0.8 | 0.3 | 0.5 | 1.5 | 1.8 | 0.7 | 1.3 | 0.4 | 1.5 | 0.8 |
| Standard deviation | 6.5 | 2.4 | 0.7 | 2.1 | 4.5 | 1.7 | 7.6 | 2.3 | 5.1 | 3.0 |
| Sample variance | 42.6 | 6.0 | 0.5 | 4.2 | 20.1 | 2.7 | 58.4 | 5.3 | 25.9 | 8.7 |
| Range | 38 | 11.1 | 1 | 2.9 | 11.1 | 4.2 | 35 | 11.1 | 18 | 10.6 |
| Minimum | 17 | 4.4 | 28 | 5.4 | 26.3 | 4.8 | 20 | 4.4 | 24 | 4.9 |
| Maximum | 55 | 15.5 | 29 | 8.3 | 37.4 | 9 | 55 | 15.5 | 42 | 15.5 |
| Sum | 2126.7 | 629 | 57 | 13.7 | 177.7 | 43.4 | 1092.1 | 291.6 | 383.6 | 113.2 |
| Count | 67 | 84 | 2 | 2 | 6 | 6 | 33 | 40 | 12 | 15 |

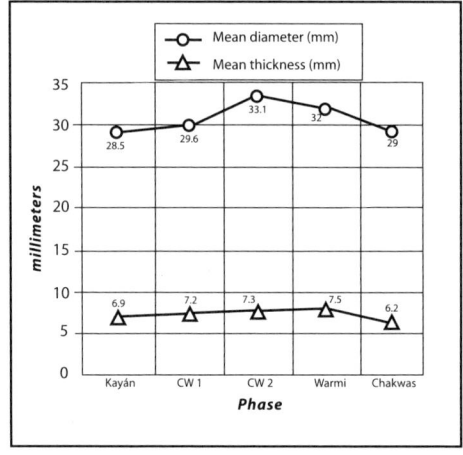

(by about 1 mm), but there is an increase in thickness (0.3 mm), on average. The dimensions of whorls from the Chakwas phase drop to pre-Chinchawasi 2 levels. Finally, eight of the perforated whorls use decorated or painted sherds, including blackware, white kaolinite and polychrome Wari examples.

SPINDLE WHORL BLANKS

The assemblage contains 162 blanks (Figure 126A, C), all roughly disc-shaped, with one or more edges that have been intentionally ground down. About a third of the sample (31.5%, n=51) consists of broken fragments. Many blanks (16%, n=26) also have partly drilled holes (Figure 126C). These artifacts can be understood to be spindle whorl blanks that were broken during manufacture or lost or discarded

TABLE 20. Summary statistics and chart of mean dimensions (in millimeters) of ceramic spindle whorl blanks.

| | Total sample (all phases) | | Warmi | |
|---|---|---|---|---|
| | Diameter | Thickness | Diameter | Thickness |
| Mean | 37.2 | 7.5 | 38.4 | 7.0 |
| Standard error | 0.8 | 0.3 | 2.3 | 0.4 |
| Median | 35.8 | 7.0 | 38.3 | 6.9 |
| Mode | 35.5 | 6.6 | 35.5 | 6.8 |
| Range | 49.2 | 39.3 | 34.2 | 7.9 |
| Minimum | 16.1 | 3.1 | 24.0 | 3.1 |
| Maximum | 65.3 | 42.4 | 58.2 | 11.0 |
| Sum | 5094.7 | 1213.0 | 767.3 | 182.7 |
| Count | 137 | 162 | 20 | 26 |

| | Kayán | | Chinchawasi 1 | | Chinchawasi 2 | | Chakwas | |
|---|---|---|---|---|---|---|---|---|
| | Diameter | Thickness | Diameter | Thickness | Diameter | Thickness | Diameter | Thickness |
| Mean | 41.7 | 7.7 | 40.0 | 7.9 | 37.1 | 7.3 | 32.6 | 5.5 |
| Standard error | 0.2 | 0.9 | 3.3 | 0.5 | 1.2 | 0.2 | 6.0 | 0.7 |
| Standard deviation | 0.3 | 1.5 | 11.6 | 1.9 | 9.8 | 1.8 | 8.4 | 1.5 |
| Sample variance | 0.1 | 2.2 | 133.5 | 3.6 | 95.7 | 3.4 | 70.8 | 2.1 |
| Range | 0.5 | 2.8 | 41.6 | 6.7 | 45.7 | 9.4 | 11.9 | 3.3 |
| Minimum | 41.5 | 6.6 | 22.2 | 4.8 | 19.6 | 4.6 | 26.6 | 3.3 |
| Maximum | 42.0 | 9.4 | 63.8 | 11.5 | 65.3 | 14.0 | 38.5 | 6.6 |
| Sum | 125.1 | 23.2 | 479.5 | 110.5 | 2482.5 | 532.7 | 65.1 | 27.3 |
| Count | 3 | 3 | 12 | 14 | 67 | 73 | 2 | 5 |

in mid-preparation. Certainly, given the ubiquity of potsherds at Chinchawas, it is unlikely that such objects were either considered irreplaceable or curated assiduously.

Blanks occur throughout the Chinchawas sequence. The Kayán phase sample includes three examples, two from Enclosure 2 (OP3) and one from a terrace area (OP25). The Chinchawasi 1 phase sample has 14 examples from terrace (n=7), midden (n=4) and room (n=3) contexts. The distributional patterns again point to the open terrace areas as the likely locales for whorl manufacture, which was probably a fairly casual activity, done when needed.

During the Chinchawasi 2 phase, the frequency of whorl blanks (n=73) increased sharply. The majority of the sample (52%, n=38) was recovered from refuse strata, and probably were discards from the manufacturing process. Their presence in terraces continued at a lower proportion (19.2%, n=14). Eighteen of the blanks (24%) came from room interiors. The Torreón structure contained two specimens, as well as one blank each in Enclosure 1. The dramatic increase in blanks during the Chinchawasi 2 phase mirrors the greater numbers of finished whorls (bone, ceramics and stone) in general. The pattern in spindle whorl blanks reinforces the argument that local peoples intensified textile production during Chinchawasi phase 2.

For the subsequent Warmi phase, fewer blanks (n=26) make up the sample, distributed as follows: midden (n=12), terrace (n=9), room interiors (n=3) and one each in Enclosure 2 and in Chullpa Tomb 2. Finally, the Chakwas phase sample consists of five spindle whorl blanks.

Local peoples at Chinchawas used smaller and thinner blanks in the latter occupations (Table 20). The blanks are the largest in diameter (41.7 cm) during Kayán times and decrease fairly steadily to an average diameter of 32.6 cm during the Chakwas phase. Similarly, the blanks from the early phases (Kayán and Chinchawasi 1) are, on average, thicker than the later examples.

Bone Spindle Whorls

There are seven specimens in the assemblage of bone spindle whorls. A Chinchawasi 1 specimen (Figure 127H), recovered from a room interior context (OP47e), shows a central perforation through a hollow tube segment of bone. The whorl has rounded corners and tapers towards the top in cross section; the outer surfaces show abrasion and are waxy smooth.

The Chinchawasi 2 sample has four specimens, all made from the ball joint of the proximal femur (Figure 127C–E, G). Two were found in midden contexts (OP38 and OP40) and one each was found in a terrace area and within the Torreón structure. The whorl specimens show a roughly hemispherical cross section; bases are flattened through abrasion. All have clean central perforations, except the Torreón example, which only has a partly drilled hole (Figure 127G). The Torreón specimen also has an additional bevel at the base. The objects are fairly large, between 2.9 and 3.5 cm in maximum diameter, suggesting that the femoral elements were probably from camelids.

The two Warmi bone spindle whorls were recovered from midden deposits in OP50 and OP49. The whorls are nearly perfectly circular, measuring 3.2 cm and 4.8 cm in maximum diameter. Unlike the Chinchawasi 2 specimens, the Warmi whorls are made from flat bone segments, probably from scapulas (Figure 127A, B).

Stone Spindle Whorls

The excavations recovered eight complete groundstone stone spindle whorls (Figure 125L–S). Each is made of hard, sometimes opaque, stone and all are worked to a smooth or polished surface. None exceeds 3 cm in diameter. Stone spindle whorls are commonly found in the graves of ancient coastal populations and are often associated with the spinning of cotton fiber. The stone whorls at Chinchawas can be considered modest sumptuary items, because of their rarity and craftsmanship. In addition, the provenience of several groundstone whorls indicates their importance as grave offerings as well as items of status display in public structures. A fragment of a whorl, with a trapezoidal cross section, was recovered in a stratum with mixed cultural remains, in OP11.

There are two whorls in the Chinchawasi 1 sample. One black stone specimen (Figure 125R) found in a midden deposit (OP46eG) has a flat, discoidal shape and measures 2.2 cm in diameter. In cross section, the top surface slopes outward slightly near the sides, whereas the basal surface is largely flat. Finer craftsmanship distinguishes the other Chinchawasi 1 whorl (Figure 125O), found in the Torreón structure of Sector 1. The conical whorl is made from a fine, light gray, opaque stone and truncates towards the top and base.

The Chinchawasi 2 assemblage consists of four whorls. Two were found in floor levels of rooms (OP48 and OP52) and two others were recovered from midden refuse (OP23 and OP46). In cross section, one whorl shows a rounded trapezoid shape (Figure 125M), while others bear half-lozenge shapes with flat bases (Figure 125Q, S). Several are made from opaque beige stones and are highly polished. One of these examples is carved with decorative radial incisions, with a circular ring border (Figure 125N). The other two are made from black and speckled light brown stones and are less finely made.

Only one example was found in a Warmi context—in Chullpa Tomb 2 (OP57). The whorl, the widest in diameter of the entire Chinchawas assemblage, is made from a light brown stone and is ground smooth (Figure 125L).

*Small Circular Discs*
In addition to whorls, several small circular stone discs were recovered (Figure 125T, U). Both were found in terrace areas; one with Chinchawasi 2 remains (Figure 125U) and the other in mixed strata. The items take the form of spindle whorls, but do not have drilled perforations. Each measures about 2.5 cm in diameter and between 0.4 and 0.9 cm in thickness; they are made from brown stones smoothed to a matte finish.

## Bone Artifacts

The assemblage of bone artifacts consists of 108 specimens, including the seven bone spindle whorls described earlier. All show intentional modification using a variety of manufacturing and decorative techniques, including grinding, polishing, incision, perforation and carving. The summaries below describe the bone artifact categories: spatulas, needles, awls and perforators, cranial spoons, pelvic trowels, rib tools, scapula scrapers, ornaments, tool production debris and Antler artifacts.

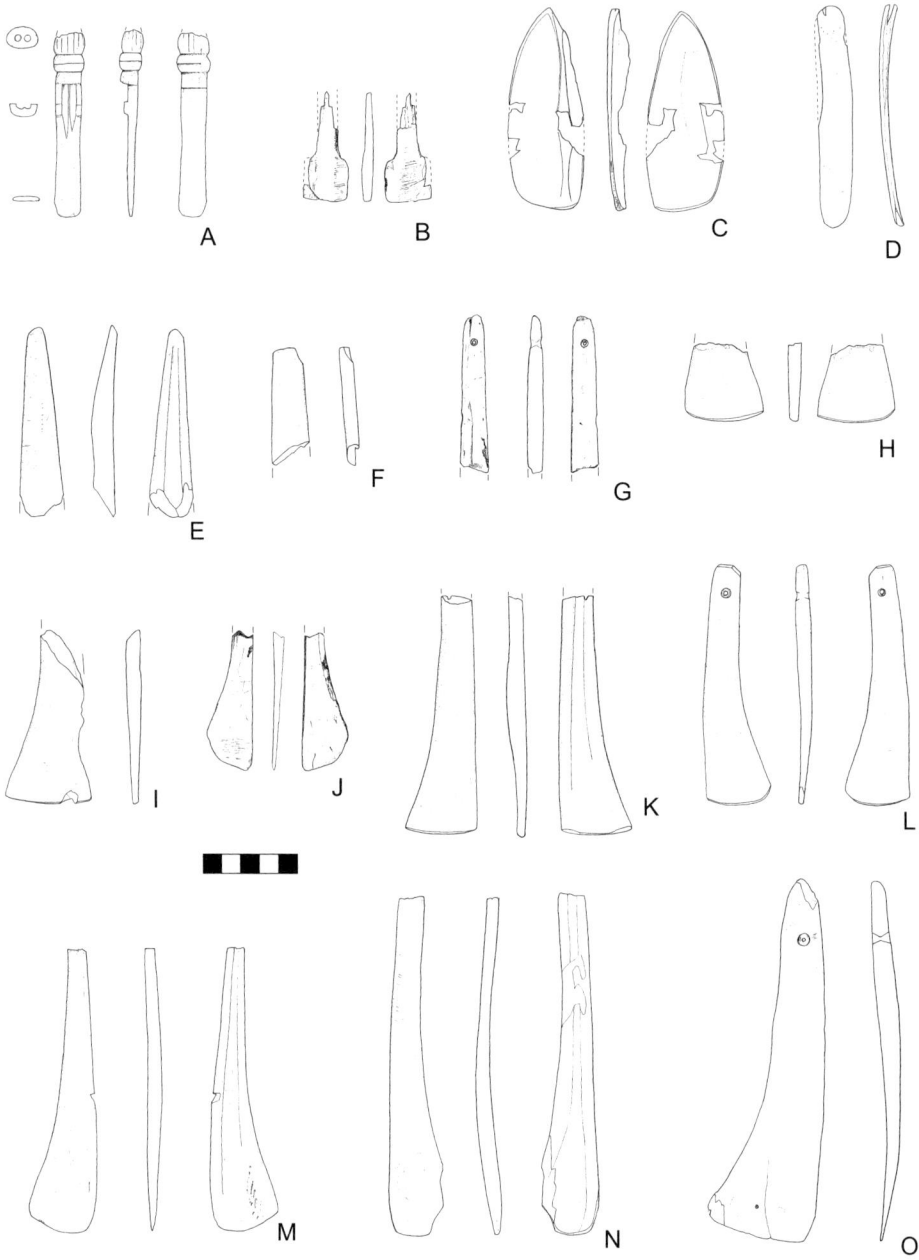

FIGURE 128. Bone implements: A, B, small spatulas; C–O, scraping tools.

TABLE 21. Summary of bone spatula artifacts by phase and architectural context.

| | Midden | Terrace | Rooms | Enclosures | Torreón | Funerary | Total |
|---|---|---|---|---|---|---|---|
| Kayán | — | — | — | — | — | — | — |
| Chinchawasi 1 | 1 | 1 | 6 | — | 2 | — | 10 |
| Chinchawasi 2 | 4 | 2 | 4 | — | — | — | 10 |
| Warmi | 1 | — | 1 | — | — | — | 2 |
| Chakwas | — | — | — | — | — | — | — |
| Total | 6 | 3 | 11 | — | 2 | — | 22 |

## Spatulas

Spatulas, or handled scrapers, are a popular tool category, with 22 specimens (Table 21). Most are made from long bone segments (such as the camelid humerus), with the narrow bone shaft as the handle and a wider articular end for the scraping edge (Figure 128E–O). Less commonly, spatulas use metapodials or other postcranial elements (Figure 128A, B). Broken handles (n=8) and edge fragments (n=5) are represented in the sample in addition to complete specimens (n=9). The scraping edge commonly shows a convex shape from grinding and scraping activity, and the handle nearly always manifests hand use polish. In addition, four of the handles are perforated to hang the tools (e.g., Figure 128G).

The use of spatulas became established during the Chinchawasi 1 phase and are common equipment in room inventories. Six of the 10 phase artifacts are from room interiors, including two complete spatulas. Terrace and midden deposits yielded one artifact each, while the excavation of the Torreón structure revealed a complete specimen as well as one handle fragment.

The presence of spatulas in room interiors continued in the Chinchawasi 2 phase, including one complete example. Four other spatulas were recovered from midden contexts, including a finely worked specimen (Figure 128A) with a long blade that tapers in cross section, two raised lateral tabs, and an elaborate finial rendered by carving and incision. The blade end features hand polish. Finally, in the Chinchawasi 2 sample, two spatula end fragments were recovered in terrace areas, including one small specimen with a squarish work surface (Figure 128B). Warmi phase deposits contained two spatula specimens; both are handle fragments made from metapodials.

In all likelihood, the spatulas were used in cooking and serving activities. The distributional patterns suggest that spatulas were commonly used and stored in room interiors, consistent with their domestic functions. The smaller, finely crafted bone implements (Figure 128A, B) could have been used for weaving or ritual purposes.

## Needles

There are 13 bone needles, including six complete examples (Figure 129A–H and Table 22). All the needles are made from bone fragments and have been abraded to

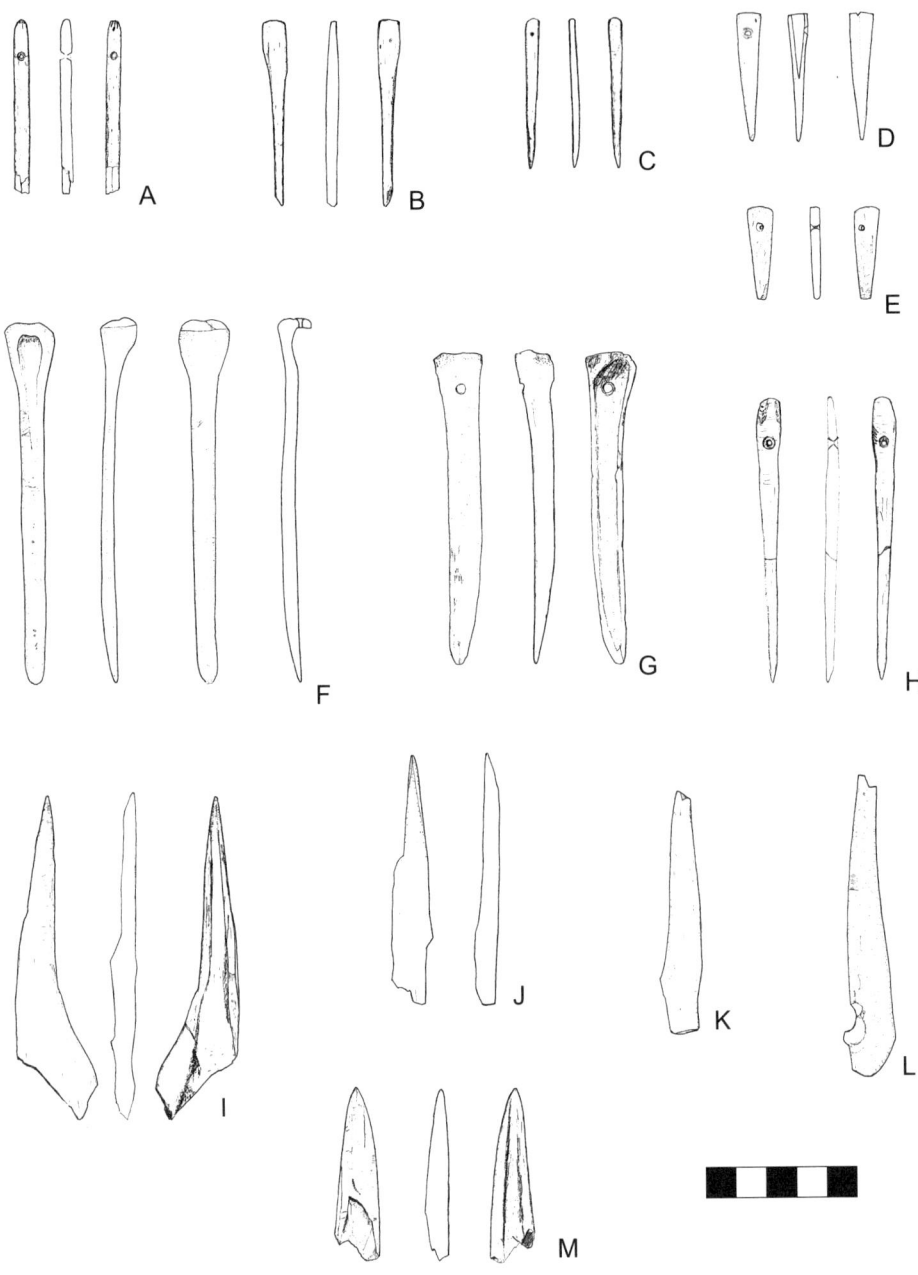

FIGURE 129. Bone implements: A–H, needles; I–M, awls and perforators.

TABLE 22. Summary of bone needle artifacts by phase and architectural context.

|  | Midden | Terrace | Rooms | Enclosures | Torreón | Funerary | Total |
|---|---|---|---|---|---|---|---|
| Kayán | — | 1 | — | — | — | — | 1 |
| Chinchawasi 1 | 1 | 1 | — | — | — | — | 2 |
| Chinchawasi 2 | 1 | 1 | 5 | — | — | — | 7 |
| Warmi | 1 | 2 | — | — | — | — | 3 |
| Chakwas | — | — | — | — | — | — | — |
| Total | 3 | 5 | 5 | — | — | — | 13 |

shape and sharpen the shaft. Use polish is common. Two needles were heat-treated and charred before polishing (Figure 129E, H). Both techniques provide for harder and more resilient surfaces that resist splintering. Two of the needles have only partly drilled holes (Figure 129B, C).

There are three general types of needles. The first type is characterized by a flat or round head connected to a long thin shaft that is circular in cross section (Figure 129A, B, H). The second type has a flattened and elongated triangular shape with a rectangular or oval cross section (Figure 129D, E). The other distinctive type typically has a perforated needle head and a long flat or concave shaft (Figure 129F, G).

The Kayán phase is represented by one example, found in a terrace area (OP43). There were two Chinchawasi 1 specimens, one each in midden (OP46) and terrace (OP35) excavations. During the Chinchawasi 2 phase, single needles were found in terrace (OP35) and midden (OP40) deposits. The major change in distribution is the occurrence of five needle artifacts in room structures, three of them intact. The Warmi phase saw a return to general discard patterns seen prior to Chinchawasi 2, in midden (n=1) and terrace areas (n=2).

The distribution patterns indicate that needlework occurred throughout the occupation of Chinchawas. Most likely, such activities were organized at the household level and conducted in open terrace areas and within house structures. Broken needles were often discarded. The smaller triangular needles and thin-shafted examples would have been ideal for finer stitching, such as for apparel. The larger needles with sizeable heads could have been more useful for coarser textiles or those with widely spaced threads, such as mesh bags; their long flat shafts (e.g., Figure 129F) could have also had utility in weaving.

### Awls and Perforators

The excavations recovered eight awls (Table 23) characterized by long tapering shafts, abraded surfaces and worn tips, usually with polished surfaces (Figure 129I–M). Two similar awls were found in Chinchawasi 1 contexts (Figure 129K, L); one specimen was fabricated from the ulna of a small mammal. The Chinchawasi 2 sample consists of three examples, all from midden deposits. Two of the three specimens are simple bone splinters with sharpened tips (Figure 129I, J); the other

TABLE 23. Summary of bone awl and perforator objects by phase and architectural context.

|  | Midden | Terrace | Rooms | Enclosures | Torreón | Funerary | Total |
|---|---|---|---|---|---|---|---|
| Kayán | — | — | — | — | — | — | — |
| Chinchawasi 1 | 1 | — | 1 | — | — | — | 2 |
| Chinchawasi 2 | 3 | — | — | — | — | — | 3 |
| Warmi | 1 | 1 | 1 | — | — | — | 3 |
| Chakwas | — | — | — | — | — | — | — |
| Total | 5 | 1 | 2 | — | — | — | 8 |

TABLE 24. Summary of cranial spoon artifacts by phase and architectural context.

|  | Midden | Terrace | Rooms | Enclosures | Torreón | Funerary | Total |
|---|---|---|---|---|---|---|---|
| Kayán | — | 1 | — | — | — | — | 1 |
| Chinchawasi 1 | 3 | 2 | — | — | — | — | 5 |
| Chinchawasi 2 | 1 | 4 | 2 | — | 1 | — | 8 |
| Warmi | 1 | 4 | — | — | — | — | 5 |
| Chakwas | — | — | — | — | — | — | — |
| Indet. phase | — | — | — | — | — | — | 1 |
| Total | 5 | 11 | 2 | — | 1 | — | 20 |

seems to be the tip fragment of a more elaborately fashioned tool (Figure 129M). Three examples are from the Warmi phase assemblage.

### Cranial Spoons

Twenty artifacts made from animal crania were recovered (Table 24). Distinctive wear on the fragments, deliberate rounding of edge surfaces and the general shape indicate that these artifacts were used as spoons or general scooping implements (Figure 130A–S). There are both complete specimens and fragments in the sample. Complete objects (Figure 130J, O, P, S) include large versions made from both left and right frontals and smaller examples (Figure 130A–I, K) made from only one side of the frontals. In the complete examples, the back portion of the cranium serves as the spoon bowl and shows the greatest degree of edge wear. In some cases (Figure 130J, O, S), the extension toward the nasal area is the handle. At least one example uses a deer cranium, but most of the artifacts seem to be made from camelid bone.

Cranial spoons and spoon fragments are most numerous during the Chinchawasi and Warmi phases. The total distribution of the cranial objects strongly favors deposition in the terrace areas, followed by representation in midden deposits, and occasional examples from room interiors and the Torreón structure. The pattern

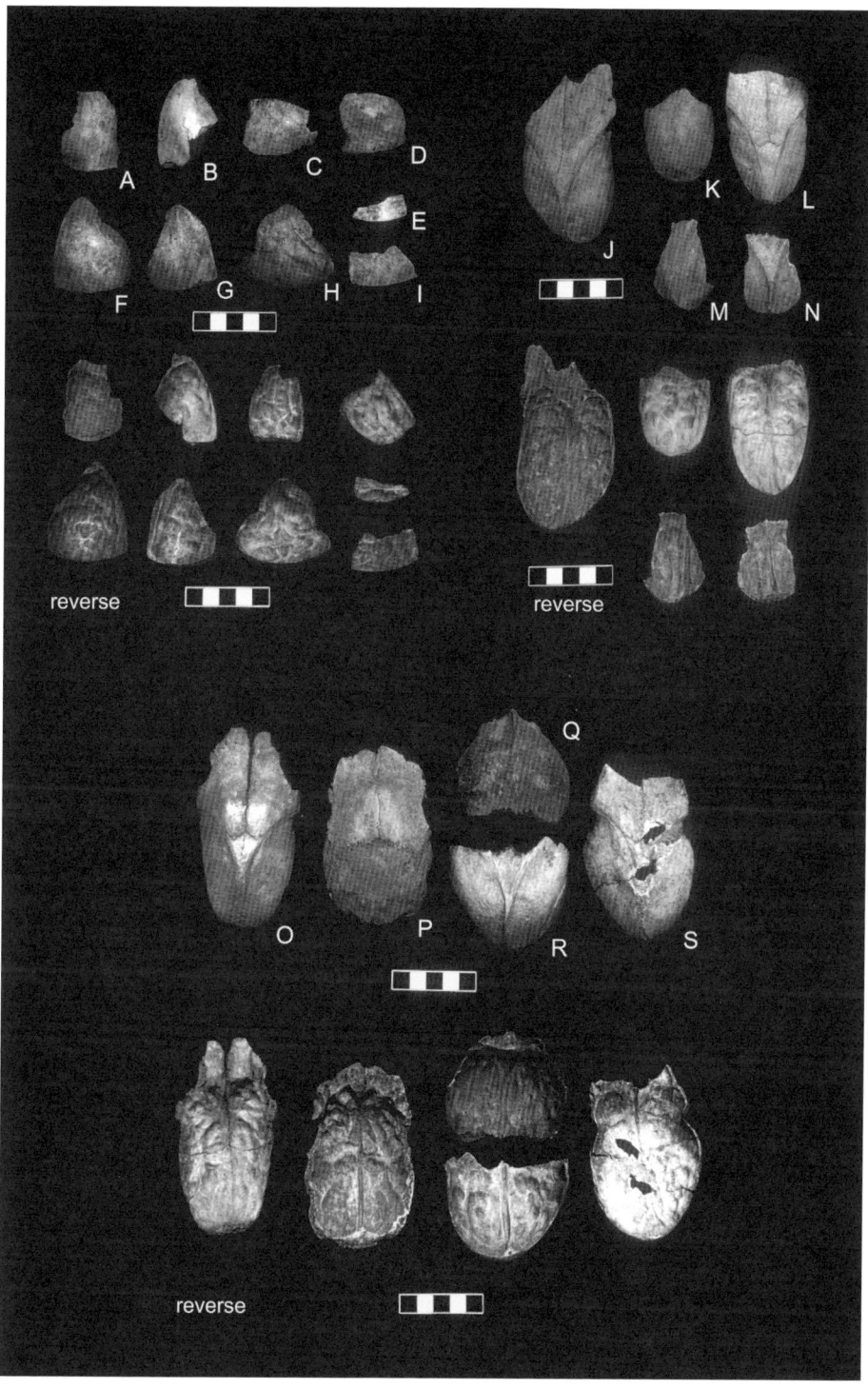

FIGURE 130. Bone implements: A–S, cranial spoons.

TABLE 25. Summary of pelvic trowel artifacts by phase and architectural context.

|  | Midden | Terrace | Rooms | Enclosures | Torreón | Funerary | Total |
|---|---|---|---|---|---|---|---|
| Chinchawasi 1 | 1 | — | — | — | — | — | 1 |
| Chinchawasi 2 | 1 | — | 1 | — | — | — | 2 |
| Total | 2 | — | 1 | — | — | — | 3 |

TABLE 26. Summary of rib tools by phase and architectural context.

|  | Midden | Terrace | Rooms | Enclosures | Torreón | Funerary | Total |
|---|---|---|---|---|---|---|---|
| Chinchawasi 1 | 3 | — | — | — | — | — | 3 |
| Chinchawasi 2 | 7 | — | — | — | — | — | 7 |
| Total | 10 | — | — | — | — | — | 10 |

TABLE 27. Summary of scapula scrapers by phase and architectural context.

|  | Midden | Terrace | Rooms | Enclosures | Torreón | Funerary | Total |
|---|---|---|---|---|---|---|---|
| Chinchawasi 1 | 1 | 1 | — | — | — | — | 2 |
| Chinchawasi 2 | 2 | 1 | — | — | — | — | 3 |
| Warmi | 3 | 1 | — | — | — | — | 4 |
| Indeterminate | — | — | — | — | — | — | 1 |
| Total | 6 | 3 | — | — | — | — | 10 |

crosscuts the phases, suggesting general continuity of use and discard of cranial spoons across the occupation of Chinchawas, especially in domestic contexts. Analogous artifacts were reported from highland sites (e.g., Gero 1991; Rowe 1944). In sum, it seems that cranial spoons were common eating and serving utensils for local peoples.

### Pelvic Trowels

The three scraping implements recovered from Chinchawasi 1 and Chinchawasi 2 domestic contexts (Table 25) are made from camelid pelvises (Miller 2003:55–57). The tools, called "pelvic trowels," use the wide portion of the iliac blade as the work surface and the iliac neck as the handle (Figure 131A, B). In all examples, the work edges show evidence of wear and abrasion and the handles of hand use polish.

### Rib Tools

The excavations recovered 10 objects made from rib elements, probably from camelids or deer (Table 26). The artifacts were identified on the basis of evi-

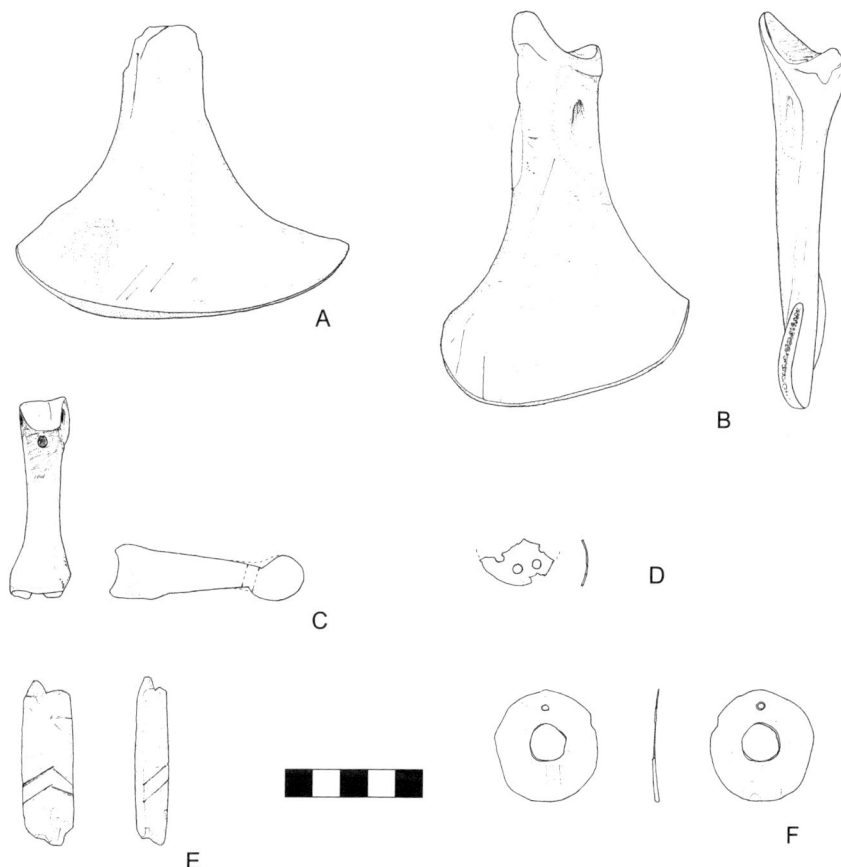

FIGURE 131. Bone implements: A, B, pelvic trowels; C–F, miscellaneous modified bone objects.

dence for hand polish, deliberate rounding or sharpening of one or both ends (Figures 127J–P and 128D). All the tools were encountered in midden refuse, notably of OP38 and OP40, and were associated with Chinchawasi 1 (n=3) and Chinchawasi 2 (n=7) materials. These artifacts probably constitute makeshift implements for cooking and eating activities. Elsewhere I have interpreted the rib tools as the discarded remains of nearby feasting episodes in Enclosure 2 (Lau 2002).

## Scapula Scrapers

The bone artifact assemblage also consists of 10 scapula tools (Table 27) identified as scapula scrapers (Figure 127Q–U). Many of the tools show hand use polish on the wide posterior edge, indicating their use as handles. Other specimens (e.g, Figures 127R and 128C) use the spine of a scapula element to help provide a grip for the tool. General wear often characterizes the anterior and, less frequently, medial edges. The spine, acromion and glenoid cavity were often reduced or removed, or both, during manufacture. Scapula scrapers occur during the Chinchawasi 1 (n=2),

TABLE 28. Summary of bone ornament objects by phase and architectural context.

|  | Midden | Terrace | Rooms | Enclosures | Torreón | Funerary | Total |
|---|---|---|---|---|---|---|---|
| Kayán | — | — | — | — | — | — | — |
| Chinchawasi 1 | 1 | — | — | — | — | — | 1 |
| Chinchawasi 2 | 1 | — | — | — | — | — | 1 |
| Warmi | 1 | 1 | — | — | — | — | 2 |
| Chakwas | — | 1 | — | — | — | — | 1 |
| Total | 3 | 2 | — | — | — | — | 5 |

TABLE 29. Summary of bone tool production debris by phase and architectural context.

|  | Midden | Terrace | Rooms | Enclosures | Torreón | Funerary | Total |
|---|---|---|---|---|---|---|---|
| Chinchawasi 1 | 3 | — | — | — | — | — | 3 |
| Chinchawasi 2 | 4 | — | 2 | — | — | — | 6 |
| Warmi | — | 1 |  |  |  |  | 1 |
| Total | 7 | 1 | 2 | — | — | — | 10 |

TABLE 30. Summary of antler artifacts by phase and architectural context.

|  | Midden | Percentage | Terrace | Percentage | Rooms | Percentage | Total |
|---|---|---|---|---|---|---|---|
| Chinchawasi 1 | 4 | 36.4 | 1 | 9.1 | 6 | 54.5 | 11 |
| Chinchawasi 2 | 15 | 62.5 | 7 | 29.2 | 2 | 8.3 | 24 |
| Warmi | 3 | 37.5 | 5 | 62.5 | 0 | 0.0 | 8 |
| Total | 22 |  | 13 |  | 8 |  | 43 |

TABLE 31. Summary of antler artifacts by type and phase.

|  | Tine | Base | Indeterminate | Other | Tool | Total |
|---|---|---|---|---|---|---|
| Chinchawasi 1 | 1 | 6 | 2 | — | 2 | 11 |
| Chinchawasi 2 | 5 | 10 | 4 | 2 | 3 | 24 |
| Warmi | — | 2 | — | 1 | 5 | 8 |
| Total | 6 | 18 | 6 | 3 | 10 | 43 |

Chinchawasi 2 (n=3) and Warmi (n=4) phases. All examples are from midden or terrace contexts, indicating a general domestic function.

## Ornaments

The sample of bone artifacts also includes five objects (Table 28) probably intended as ornaments or personal effects. One object, from a Chinchawasi 1 refuse level (OP46), is a short segment of a long bone that has four prominent incisions forming a simple chevron pattern (Figure 131E). A thin bone fragment in the shape of a fish (Figure 127I) was found in the refuse deposit of OP40, associated with Chinchawasi 2 materials. Two specimens from Warmi deposits are made from thin circular bone sheets and are perforated, probably as pendants or ornamentation (Figure 131D, F). Finally, from a Chakwas association, a camelid first phalange (Figure 131C) is perforated through the bone near the distal articular surface; the shaft area on either side of the hole shows evidence of having been abraded. The phalange could have been worn as a pendant, or used as a whistle.

## Tool Production Debris

Ten waste fragments from bone tool production were identified from midden, terrace and room contexts (Table 29). Chinchawasi 1 (n=3), Chinchawasi 2 (n=6) and Warmi (n=1) phases are represented. In all specimens, bones have been scored, sawn for removal of desired segments of the bone shaft, or both. Cuts are most frequently along lateromedial dimensions. Ancient peoples preferred camelid long bones and metapodials (although one metapodial is of deer). The data set suggests that bone tool production certainly occurred locally and was probably organized at the level of each individual household.

## Antler Artifacts

The final bone artifact category consists of 43 deer antler objects (Tables 30 and 31). Most of the identifiable specimens (20 out of 26, or 76.9%) are made from taruca (*Hippocamelus antisensis*) antler; the remaining six came from white-tailed deer (*Odocoileus virginianus*) (identification by Javier Barrio, who conducted a conservation-based research project on deer populations in the Parque Nacional Huascarán, personal communication 1998). Large antler fragments show cut marks or have had their tines removed (Figure 132A, E). The assemblage includes 10 modified antler tools, mainly tine awls and perforators (Figure 132C, D, G). Other implements include a shaft straightener (Figure 132F) and several possible retouch tools (Figure 132B).

The evidence for the production and use of antler tools occurs exclusively during the Chinchawasi and Warmi phases. The sample shows suggestive diachronic patterns in distribution. Eleven antler artifacts make up the Chinchawasi 1 phase sample, with a little more than half of the specimens (54.5%) found in the interior deposits of room structures. In the succeeding Chinchawasi 2 phase, their presence in rooms, at only 8.3%, decreases sharply in favor of midden (62.5%) and terrace (29.2%) areas. Many of the specimens of this phase seem to be debris from antler

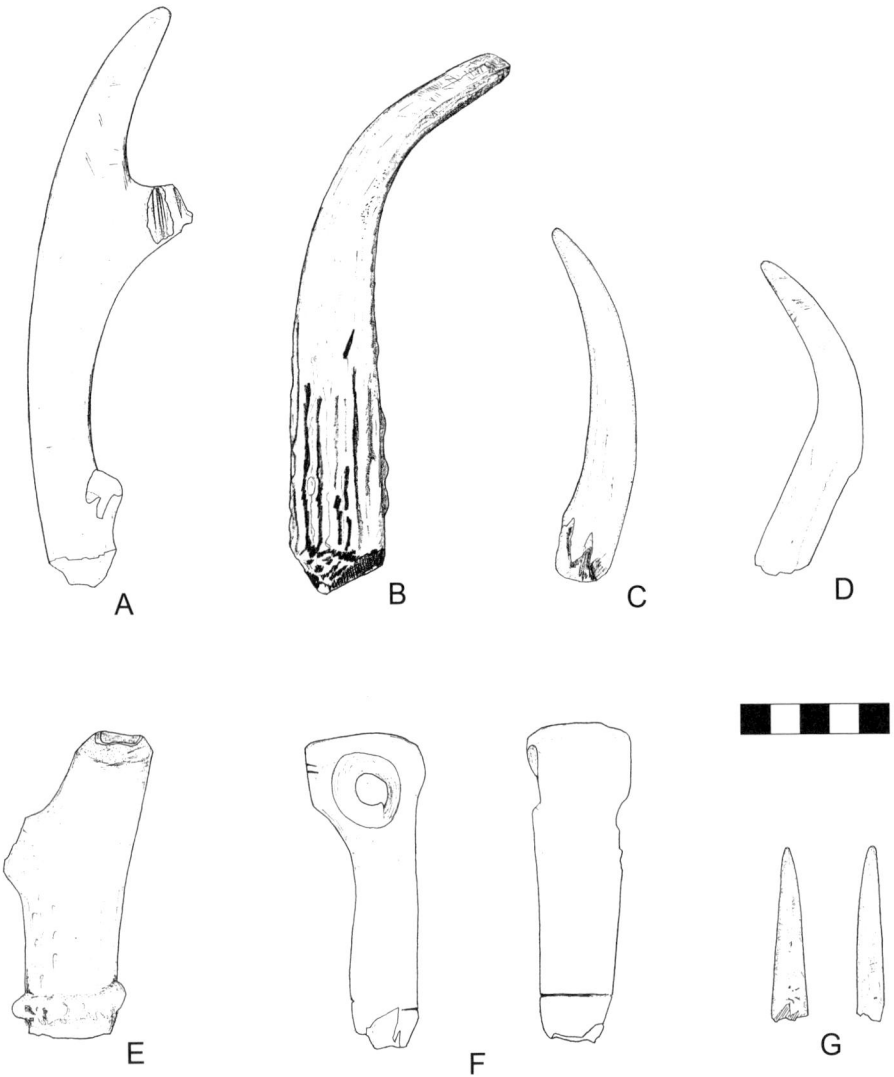

FIGURE 132. Antler objects: A–D, G, awl and reaming tools; E, worked base; F, shaft straightener.

tool manufacture; that is, cut unwanted fragments and discarded antler bases. In the succeeding Warmi phase, none of the antler objects is found in room structures. The Warmi sample contains the highest ratio of tools, while the Chinchawasi 2 phase has the greatest proportion of manufacturing debris.

## Shell Artifacts

The small corpus of marine shell artifacts at Chinchawas consists of nine specimens. Three are from Chinchawasi 1 deposits within the Torreón structure of Sector 1 (OP54). All three are perforated and were meant to be worn or hung, probably

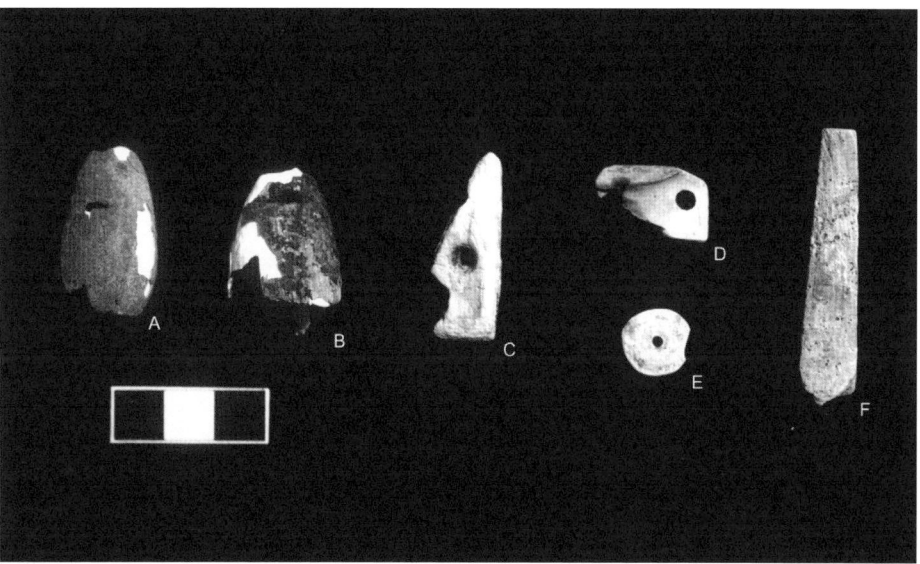

Figure 133. Shell ornaments.

as pendants. A long, trapezoidal fragment (Figure 133F) probably formed one of a series of wedge-like segments for a full-collar neck adornment; pottery and sculptural representations of important Recuay individuals frequently show this collar adornment (Lumbreras 1974a, fig. 128). Another is a thin circular disk with a center hole (Figure 133E). The final Chinchawasi shell artifact is a broken fragment of an irregular trapezoidal ornament with two drilled perforations (Figure 133D).

The remaining six specimens are from Warmi contexts. One, a small rectangular shell object of indeterminate function, was found in the terrace excavation of OP43. The five other artifacts were recovered in chullpa tomb contexts. A large fragment of a triangular shell pendant (Figure 133C) is from Chullpa Tomb 7 (OP61); it is perforated in the center and partly drilled on the side. Two other shell fragments, discovered in Chullpa Tomb 6 and 8 (OP58 and OP60, respectively), show no modification. The final two shell objects are nearly complete, but badly spalled, *Conus* sp. specimens (Figure 133A, B). Both show saw marks near the tip that facilitate hanging as pendants or stringing together as musical instruments.

We can make several important observations about the distribution of the shell artifacts. First, all the identifiable shell objects clearly represent rare adornments or pendants intended to be worn or hung. In addition, all were recovered from special architectural contexts. Their proveniences reiterate their status as rare and imported luxury goods. Finally, shell artifacts are conspicuously absent in the Chinchawasi 2 phase sample; this is notable because other important goods, such as exotic coastal pottery, local decorated pottery, obsidian and metal artifacts witnessed a surge in abundance or appeared for the first time during the Chinchawasi 2 phase.

TABLE 32. Summary of copper-metal objects by phase and architectural context.

|  | Midden | Terrace | Rooms | Enclosures | Torreón | Funerary | Total |
|---|---|---|---|---|---|---|---|
| Kayán | — | — | — | — | — | — | — |
| Chinchawasi 1 | — | — | 2 | — | 3 | 2 | 7 |
| Chinchawasi 2 | 17 | 3 | 4 | — | 3 | — | 27 |
| Warmi | — | 4 | 1 | 1 | — | 8 | 14 |
| Chakwas | — | — | — | — | — | — | — |
| Indeterminate phase | — | — | — | — | — | — | 9 |
| Total | 17 | 7 | 7 | 1 | 6 | 10 | 57 |

TABLE 33. Summary of copper-metal objects by type and phase.

|  | Shawl pin | Pin head | Pin shaft | Lamina object | Loop ring | Tool | Total |
|---|---|---|---|---|---|---|---|
| Kayán | — | — | — | — | — | — | — |
| Chinchawasi 1 | 3 | — | 1 | 2 | — | 1 | 7 |
| Chinchawasi 2 | 4 | 5 | 3 | 13 | — | 2 | 27 |
| Warmi | 7 | 1 | 1 | 2 | 2 | 1 | 14 |
| Chakwas | — | — | — | — | — | — | — |
| Indeterminate phase | — | 2 | 4 | 3 | — | — | 9 |
| Total | 14 | 8 | 9 | 20 | 2 | 4 | 57 |

# Metal Artifacts

Finally, 57 metal artifacts were recovered during the course of the investigations (Table 32) and fall into three general categories: shawl pins, hammered sheet adornments and tools (Table 33). Given their corroded surfaces, all the artifacts evidently contain at least some copper. Eight samples have been analyzed for their metal content; the results will be presented in the general phase descriptions below.

## *Chinchawasi 1 Phase*

The Chinchawasi 1 phase consists of seven artifacts (Figure 134A–D). From room contexts (OP25 and OP49), two lamina ornaments were found, including a perforated rectangular example. Chinchawasi 1 deposits of the Torreón structure produced three artifacts: a pointed tool (perhaps a small awl), a perforated rectangular lamina ornament and a complete nail-head shawl pin. On either side of the perforation near the pin head is a series of incisions. Finally, the subterranean tombs in Sector 2 yielded a complete pin and the shaft of a broken pin. The complete pin likely had a nail-type head.

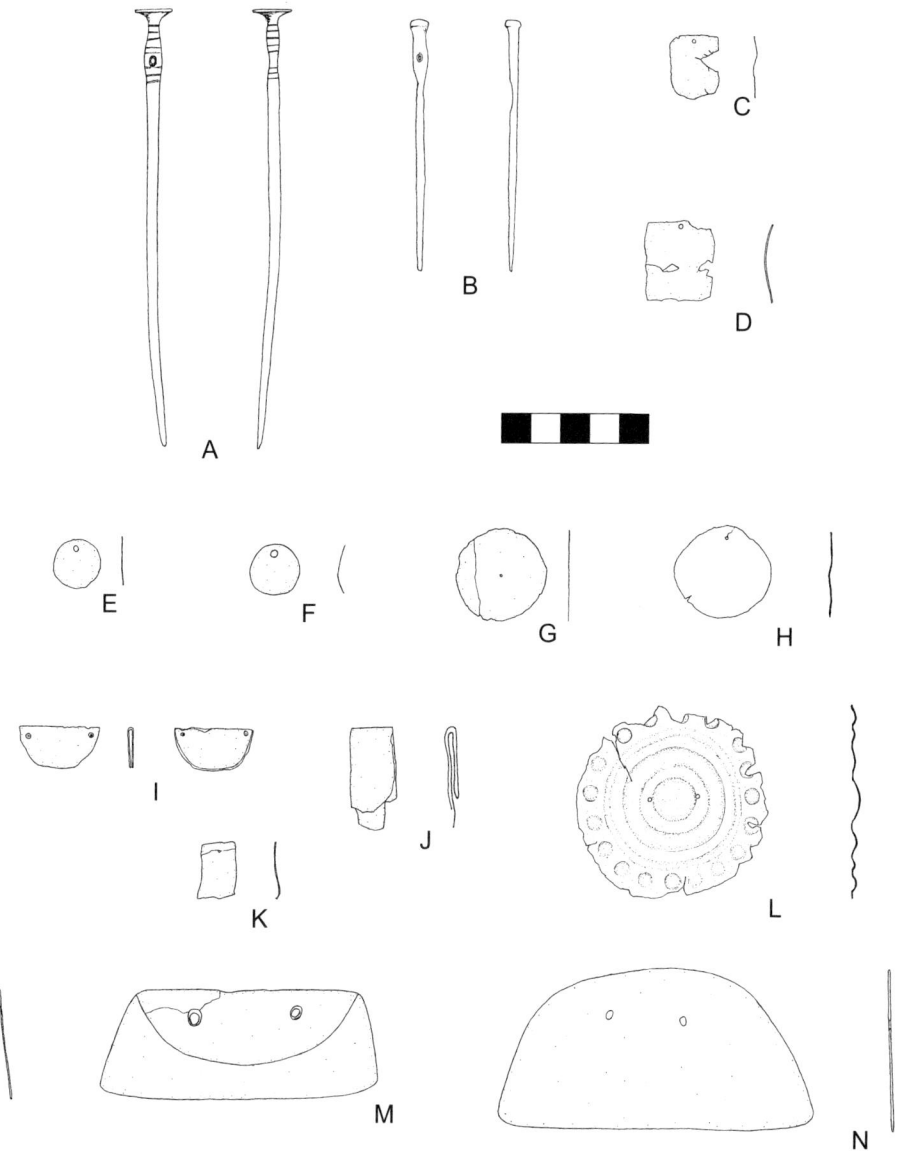

FIGURE 134. Metal artifacts: A–D, Chinchawasi 1 phase; E–N, Chinchawasi 2 phase.

The pin shaft and pointed tool were analyzed under a scanning electron microscope. Both were nearly pure copper (Heather Lechtman, personal communication 2000).

## Chinchawasi 2 Phase

The Chinchawasi 2 phase shows a sharp increase in the use of copper-metal artifacts, with 27 specimens (Figures 134E–N and 135A–L). Midden contexts yielded most of the sample (n=17). Of this total, nine artifacts are hammered lamina

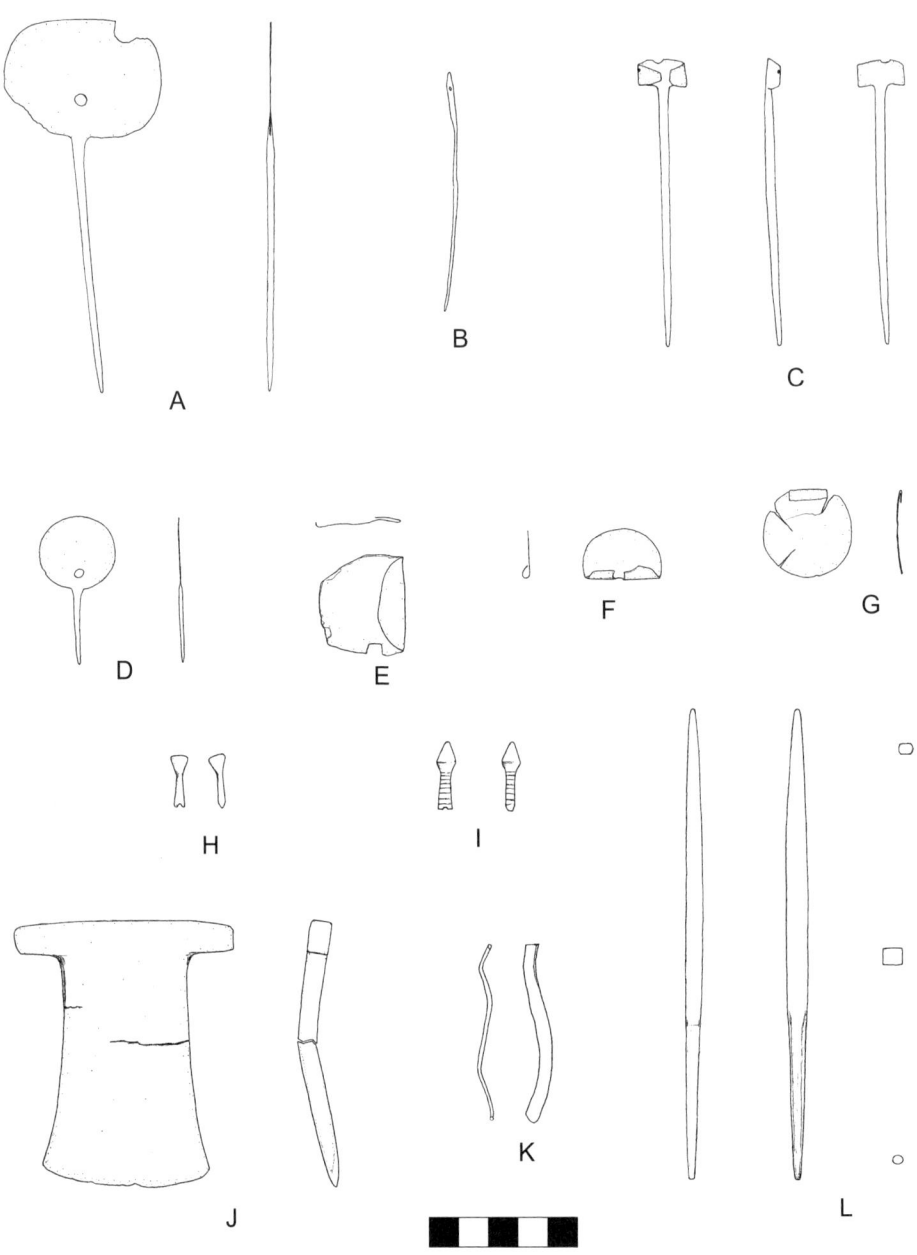

Figure 135. Metal artifacts: A–L, Chinchawasi 2 phase.

objects, including five complete perforated circular ornaments, one perforated rectangular ornament, one narrow band folded over several times, one irregularly shaped fragment and one semicircular adornment. One circular specimen is particularly large (with a diameter of 6.5 cm) and has repoussé dots and concentric circles (Figure 134L); two holes were used to attach the ornament to a garment or headdress. The semicircular specimen (Figure 134I) is folded along one axis; two crimping punch-holes could have been used to affix the ornament to the edge of a garment. Midden contexts also yielded three discoidal-head shawl pins, two broken pin heads with bulbous finials (Figure 135H–I), one discoidal pin head and one pin shaft. The discoidal head pins, commonly with at least one perforation near the shaft–head juncture, appear for the first time in the Chinchawasi sequence. Finally, the midden fill deposit of OP48 revealed a T-shaped copper-metal axe head (Figure 135J); the axe was apparently discarded after failure along the center portion, presumably from use.

Three pin broken pin fragments were recovered from the terraces: one discoidal head broken at the perforation and two pin shafts. The room structures yielded more intact artifacts, including a circular lamina, a broken pin and two large trapezoidal plates, perhaps knife blades or adornments (Figure 134M, N). Each of the trapezoidal plates has two holes, maybe also for attaching to garments or necklaces; one example is folded over.

Finally, three copper-metal artifacts were found within Chinchawasi 2 deposits of the Torreón structure. In addition to a complete pin and a fragment of a narrow band (Figure 135K), excavations recovered a long awl or punch tool. In cross section, the implement is circular on one end, oval on the other, and square in the center (Figure 135L).

Four specimens from Chinchawasi 2 were analyzed under a scanning electron microscope, including two pin shafts, one lamina fragment and a narrow strip (Figure 135K). All the artifacts are of pure copper, except for the lamina fragment, which contains 0.5% arsenic.

## *Warmi Phase*

Most Warmi phase metal artifacts came from the chullpa funerary contexts of Sector 2. Three complete shawl pins were recovered, two with nail-type heads (Figure 136A, B) and one with a discoidal head with two perforations (Figure 136F). Chullpa excavations also yielded two folded, rectangular lamina objects. OP57 in Chullpa Tomb 2 recovered an atlatl hook (Figure 136H), similar to Wari period examples (e.g., Benavides 1984, lám. 28, no. 38). And finally, two loop rings (Figure 136I, J) were encountered in the cyst tombs underneath the floor of Chullpa Tomb 11 (OP64).

Warmi remains in Sector 1 are more fragmentary. Along the terraces, four pin artifacts were recovered, including one complete specimen with a round finial, two discoidal head pin shafts and one discoidal pin head. A pin shaft was recovered in room contexts. And finally, an open enclosure area (OP15) yielded a complete discoidal pin. Two circular embossed punctations seem to represent the eyes of discoidal head, with the perforation as the mouth.

One Warmi phase lamina fragment (Figure 136K) is composed of a copper–silver alloy (72.7% Cu, 27.3% Ag). Another lamina fragment manifests similar microstructure and similar copper-silver composition (Heather Lechtman, personal communication 2000).

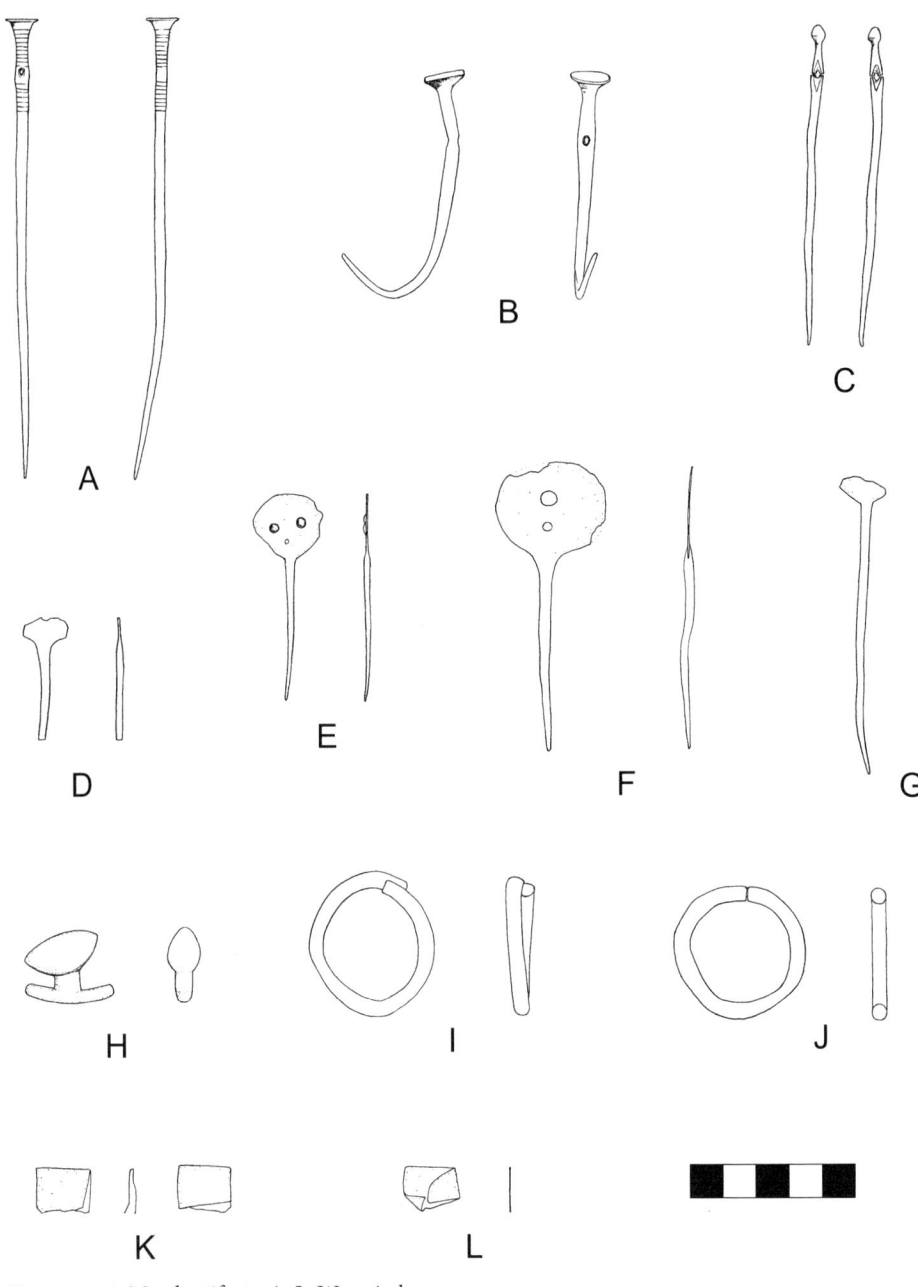

FIGURE 136. Metal artifacts: A–L, Warmi phase.

In sum, the copper-metal artifacts at Chinchawas are interpreted as rare, luxury goods. Most were adornments, but several were also tools. During Chinchawasi phases 1 and 2, distribution patterns indicate that Sector 1 was the primary locale for the use and discard of metal objects. As would be expected, the items frequently survived intact in room interiors and the Torreón structure. Along the terraces and middens, the artifacts often tended to be broken. During the Warmi phase, the distribution of metal artifacts shifted towards the chullpa funerary structures and coincided with the use of new copper-silver alloys.

Although definitive stylistic patterns in metal artifacts cannot be established given the small sample, suggest some trends using the current data. Shawl pins with nail or finial heads seem to be produced or curated throughout the sequence. Discoidal head shawl pins appeared by the subsequent Chinchawasi 2 phase and predominated until the end of the Warmi occupation. The Warmi mortuary program shows important innovations in grave offerings, including the copper–silver ornaments and a spearthrower hook.

## Conclusions

This chapter describes the lithic, bone, shell and metal artifacts from the Chinchawas site. As expected, the artifact distributions emphasize strong functional distinctions between different parts of the site, as defined by architectural arrangements, especially between domestic (midden, open terrace areas and room structures), public–ceremonial (Torreón and enclosures) and funerary contexts.

Most of the chipped stone, groundstone and bone artifacts make up the equipment for economic production at the residential level. Not surprisingly, the use, storage and discard of these artifacts are most commonly associated with domestic contexts. Common domestic tools occur very infrequently in funerary or special purpose contexts.

Currently the data do not inform clearly about whether economic practices or activity areas can be differentiated on the basis of gender. Typically, in traditional highland groups documented ethnographically and ethnohistorically, textile production and food preparation are often considered responsibilities of women, while other activities, such as hunting, building construction and involvement in corporate work projects are commonly associated with men. If these generalizations hold true for ancient Chinchawas, then the gear for economic activities associated with women are amply represented in the cultural remains, especially in the toolkits for weaving and food preparation.

The data show that small-scale craft production occurred throughout the occupational sequence. In general, there is strong continuity in the overall character of local economic activities. Household and community reproduction relied on high altitude agriculture and camelid pastoralism. The cultural remains reflect craft activities geared for processing the products of these economic practices. Local peoples collected waterworn stones of various dimensions for use in food preparation, hunting and perhaps also local site defense. Other types of stone performed as agricultural implements or as the raw material for figurines and carvings. Chipped stone lithic production provided the key implements for cutting and scraping activities, likely associated with camelid meat and fiber production.

Because of the difficulties of preservation or sampling biases, bone tools have seen very little treatment in the archaeological record of the North Highlands. At Chinchawas, animal bones, especially of camelids, were abundant and readily available throughout the occupational sequence as a raw material. The data display a rich diversity of bone artifacts geared towards fiber processing, needlework, food preparation and serving, chipped stone tool production and ornamentation. Because many of the bone implements can be used for scraping and perforating, the processing of hides cannot be ruled out as another important economic activity. Future research focused on use-wear should clarify the functions of different types of bone implements.

Multiple lines of evidence, including that from spindle whorls, whorl blanks, bone needles and other weaving implements, indicate that textile production was a key component of the local economy. In particular, the surge in artifact frequencies as well as overall increases in the metrical data of weaving tools may reflect a growing interest in the intensification of fiber processing during the Chinchawasi 2 phase. These data mirror the dramatic increase in the overall number of camelid individuals represented by faunal remains at the site (Lau 2007). Together with agricultural resources, camelid-based products, such as portable dried meat ch'arki, textiles and fiber material, probably constituted the community's capital in exchange ventures for nonlocal goods (for example, obsidian, fancy ceramics and copper-metal). It is not surprising, then, that local peoples garnered unprecedented access to exotic goods at the same time that camelid production intensified.

Sumptuary items, including metal, shell and groundstone objects, appear frequently in funerary and public architectural contexts. Such goods likely were symbols of prestige and unequal access. In a small community like Chinchawas, in which there seems to have been little internal differentiation, such rare items would have figured prominently in episodes of status display. The distribution of Chinchawasi phase metal artifacts indicates that public displays occurred most frequently in Sector 1. In some instances, local peoples removed sumptuaries from circulation by including them as grave offerings. This practice became especially prominent by the Warmi phase, as part of the overall makeover in local funerary practices and material culture.

In conclusion, the artifact classes discussed here contributed to the prehistoric economy at Chinchawas. Overall, the data allow for a general reconstruction of local productive activities in a small highland community and their change through time. The economic activities at Chinchawas were remarkably diverse; some specialization can be documented especially for local camelid production. The major socioeconomic transformations occurred at Chinchawas during and after the Chinchawasi 2 occupation. In particular, the intensification of local economic production and long-distance exchange coincided with the period of Wari expansion.

CHAPTER TEN

# REVIEW AND CONCLUSIONS

By drawing together the insights from these investigations and different analyses, I conclude here with a diachronic review of Chinchawas's history of occupation to outline the growth and decline of the ancient community and discern socio-economic developments that can be understood alongside broader chronological and sociopolitical patterns in Andean prehistory. On the basis of the Chinchawas evidence, I end with general considerations of Recuay culture and its transformations in the Central Andes.

## Results of the Chinchawas Research

### Chronology

Perhaps the most fundamental contribution of this research is to the local chronological sequence for Chinchawas's ancient occupation. Ceramic data enabled the reconstruction of five cultural phases that can be positioned chronologically using relative dating and radiocarbon evidence.

The initial occupation at Chinchawas began with the Kayán phase (around A.D. 300 to 600) and is associated with Recuay culture during the Early Intermediate Period. The subsequent Chinchawasi 1 phase (about A.D. 600 to 700) constituted a late Recuay style, which began during the late Early Intermediate Period. The subsequent Chinchawasi 2 phase (around A.D. 700 to 850) was the florescence of the Chinchawasi style and belonged to the early part of the Middle Horizon.

By the middle of the 9th century A.D., the development of the Warmi phase (ca. A.D. 850 to 950) was a significant break in local cultural continuity. Unlike earlier occupations, which were linked by discernible stylistic continuity, fancy Warmi ceramics were fundamentally different from their antecedents and apparently drew their inspiration from foreign styles, probably with Central Highland roots. The Warmi phase was the last major phase of occupation at the site and is associated with the middle to latter part of the Middle Horizon. Finally, the Chakwas phase belonged to the Late Intermediate Period, which began around A.D. 1000; it is unclear when use of Chakwas style pottery ended.

### Paleoclimate and Ancient Settlement

The ancient community of Chinchawas, at 3,850 masl, flourished at the transition between the upper limits of sustainable intensive agriculture and higher grasslands ideal for pastoralism. Chinchawas also benefited from its strategic location on a defensible hilltop, which overlooked the most directly accessible route and lowest pass connecting the highland basin area of Huaraz and the coastal valley of Casma. Given its high location, it stands to reason that long-term patterns of significant paleoclimatic change could alter the productive capacities of the local environment.

Paleoenvironmental conditions in northern Peru during the Holocene are poorly known, especially in relation to changing economic practices and animal resources in the highlands. But glacial ice cores are beginning to furnish important evidence for local climate change (Thompson et al. 1995; Thompson 2001). Ice core data from Nevado Huascarán, in the heart of the Callejón de Huaylas, indicate that mean temperatures in highland Ancash dropped markedly during the latter half of the 1st millennium A.D., as reflected in gross one-hundred-year averages of oxygen isotope ratios. Colder weather began near the middle of the millennium, but mean averages were lowest between the 6th and 8th centuries A.D. (Thompson 2001).

Because of colder conditions, Chinchawas's economic focus by mid-millennium probably turned increasingly toward camelid herding. The important belt of land between 3,700 and 3,900 masl, where modern farmers cultivate potatoes and other high altitude cultigens, would have probably been shifted to lower altitudes in cold weather periods during Chinchawas's occupation. Furthermore, the retreat downward of arable lands probably enlarged the area of natural pasturage in and around the Chinchawas site. The dense quantities of camelid remains, the general infrequency of agricultural and hunting implements, the presence of large ancient corrals and abundant spindle whorls throughout the site sequence support the hypothesis that stockraising, in benefiting from nearby pasture lands, played a key economic role in the prosperity of Chinchawas.

Despite the sharp climatic fluctuations evident in ice core records, especially in the Quelccaya ice cores, the archaeological record indicates steady occupation of Chinchawas from about A.D. 500 to 900 (Thompson et al. 1984, 1992; Thompson and Mosley-Thompson 1987, 1989; reviewed in Lau 2001). Paleoclimatic regimes do not seem to have caused any site-level abandonment or major gaps in use of the site. The stability of occupation at Chinchawas may underscore the flexibility and adaptive character of economic practices among North Highland agropastoral groups.

Paleoenvironmental fluctuations therefore likely helped to create different conditions in which local groups maneuvered to improve their economic standing. As more paleoclimatic data become available, notably the annual records from the Huascarán glacier, it will be possible to examine some of the hypotheses provided here with finer chronological precision.

### Spatial Organization and Architecture

The documentation of Recuay tradition settlement organization through mapping and excavation is another contribution to the archaeological literature. Excavation sampling revealed significant subsurface remains, including earlier buildings, features and activity contexts, which are not inferrable from the surficial reconnaissance.

Chinchawas was a small hilltop settlement. All the architecture documented at Chinchawas was constructed from stone masonry. Bedrock outcrops available for quarrying are found throughout the site, but are most prominent in the southwest portion. Tall, perimeter walls protected the core community, but also formed large and walled interior terrace spaces. In these spaces, especially to the north and west, local peoples built rectangular agglutinated room structures, identified as permanent residences. Some structures opened into terrace areas that also functioned as the loci for domestic activities. It is likely that farther down the slopes we will find more domestic residences underneath erosional deposits.

Throughout the village, stone-covered drainage canals diverted the wet season rainwater, keeping it from accumulating in open terrace areas and in room complexes. Contemporary irrigation canals flow past Chinchawas, but none could be associated with ancient diagnostic materials.

The central portion of the site was partitioned into several walled, open-air enclosures that were public meeting areas. Local peoples adorned the public constructions with monolithic stone sculpture. To the east of the enclosures, on the highest part of the site, was an elaborate building with concentric walls built directly atop bedrock. Given its placement, construction and artifacts, this Torreón structure was certainly of paramount importance to the local community from its earliest inception. While the research identifies activities such as intensive meat consumption, burning and offerings in and around the structure, determination of the Torreón's specific function remains for future research.

Through time, the Chinchawas community also developed its own cemetery, located to the east and southeast of the main ridgetop. Here subterranean and aboveground chullpa mortuary constructions were built to house important individuals and groups of individuals. The most elaborate stonemasonry at the site was reserved for some of these tombs. Many of the chullpa constructions are clustered together, probably reflecting an interest in nested social affiliations between descent groups.

The Kayán phase at Chinchawas constituted a light occupation at a small hamlet settlement. Kayán phase materials were limited to the topmost part of Sector 1, with evidence only for small-scale residential functions and intermittent public gatherings within special enclosures.

The Chinchawasi 1 phase occupation covered a larger portion of the ridgetop, reflecting a larger settlement and population. The Chinchawasi 1 occupation was also more diverse in function. Residential and public activities continued at the site, but were more widespread and occurred in greater intensity. In addition, we see the first evidence for mortuary ritual in Sector 2, as well as for corporate architectural projects. Large perimeter walls and a circular tower structure (Torreón) were major constructions of this occupation. During Chinchawasi 2, the village reached its greatest size and intensity of occupation. Although the nucleation in architecture continued during this phase, there were no major changes in settlement planning or character. Sector 1 continued to be the focus of residential and public activities.

The Warmi occupation, the last phase of intensive use of Chinchawas, precipitated significant changes in architectural arrangement and use. First, patio enclosures within the main sector of the site were no longer the focus of community ceremony. Ceremonial activity shifted away from Sector 1 to chullpa burial monuments in Sector 2. Subterranean tombs became obsolete. There was also widespread disregard for earlier buildings, even important constructions such as the Torreón structure, as shown by their destruction or reuse under different contexts, especially dumping. Finally, later reoccupations by Chakwas and historical groups were relatively small-scale, fairly light, and without any major new construction programs.

*Local Economy and Material Culture*
Throughout the site's history of occupation, household and community reproduction relied on high altitude agriculture and camelid pastoralism. The cultural remains also reflect small group activities around products from these enterprises: food preparation, camelid meat processing and consumption, and fiber processing for textiles and weaving.

The large ceramic assemblage from the site is evidence of both domestic and special purpose functions. By far the largest component of the sample consists of cooking and storage vessels, which show that there was an intensive occupation of the site, especially around A.D. 500 to 900. The lack of a permanent water source on Sector 1 indicates that the collection, transport and storage of water would have been a continual priority for the community. Evidence of maker's marks, especially in the Chinchawasi 2 and Warmi phase deposits, shows that the inhabitants had wider access to a greater range of pottery products during the Middle Horizon.

We can characterize the local material culture as conservative, practical and resourceful. Bone tools were common components of domestic toolkits and included cooking, serving, weaving and scraping implements. Spindle whorls (of ground stone, fired and recycled ceramics and bone) show that fiber preparation was a prominent economic activity throughout the sequence. Ground stone and flaked lithic tools also indicate the importance of domestic activities in different portions of the settlement. Many implements were made at the site.

Analysis of the faunal remains indicates that camelids were the principal animals exploited throughout the prehistoric occupation of Chinchawas. Camelids constituted a regular and dependable source of protein, but also furnished hair fiber, sinew and bone for various implements. Possibly they were also used as transport animals for the inhabitants of Chinchawas. In general, very few species are represented. Not surprisingly, the faunal sample is dominated by domestic animals (camelids and guinea pig); hunting was of minor importance for provisioning meat. By phase, the greatest diversity of animal species occurred during Chinchawasi 2. The low faunal diversity underscores that there was reliable access to camelids in the community, most likely through local herding.

The overall character of local economic activities—in location and activity types—shows strong continuity, especially at the domestic level. Most activities are understood in the context of room complexes, defined as a group of individual structures, most often linked functionally to an enclosed open space. The room complex was likely the basic living and work area of the small domestic groups that made up the community of Chinchawas throughout its history. The major changes in economic patterns occurred during the Chinchawasi 2 phase, which shows a greater abundance and density of artifact remains at the site. These data are interpreted to reflect a larger population as well as an intensification of economic production, especially of camelid production, textile fiber processing and trade.

*Interaction and Exchange*

The project recovered substantial evidence for changing patterns of trade and cultural interaction between the Chinchawas community and other regions of the Central Andes. The interpretations rely on data from stylistic analyses of local decorated pottery as well as of imported goods, especially fancy ceramics, obsidian, shell and metal artifacts.

Chinchawas's favorable location along a major coast–highland trade route was a main reason for the establishment and prosperity of the ancient community. The Kayán phase ceramic evidence shows that, from the onset of their occupation, local peoples of Chinchawas participated within the Recuay cultural tradition based in the Callejón de Huaylas.

For Chinchawasi 1, the data evince a strong continuation of cultural interchange with Recuay in the North Highlands, but with new long-distance connections with Late Moche and, by the end of the occupation, with Wari-related groups. Chinchawas's relationships to these areas seem principally centered around the limited exchange of fancy ceramics; there is no evidence for hostilities or military takeover. During Chinchawasi phase 2, the scale and range of exchange contacts widened. Connections with the Central Highlands (Wari-related), North Highlands (Cajamarca), North Coast (Late Moche) and Central Coast (Nievería) cultures reflect an interest and capacity for intensified interregional trade. Also at this time, Quispisisa obsidian from the Central Highlands became widely available to groups at Chinchawas. Analyses of metal samples indicate that local inhabitants also had access to copper, copper–arsenic and silver–copper materials.

By the Warmi phase, the earlier focus on highland exchange shifted substantially to networks with the coast. As sumptuary goods, Central Coast (press-molded styles) and North Coast (Huari Norteño) styles seem to have been preferred over Wari-related, Cajamarca and other North Highland products. Overall, the changes in local economic production and long-distance exchange at Chinchawas seem to have been facilitated by broader sociopolitical transformations associated with Wari cultural expansion (Lau 2005).

*Social Organization at Chinchawas*
The investigations at Chinchawasi recovered limited evidence for social inequality, namely in architecture, luxury goods and mortuary practices. Variability in rare imported goods—such as fancy imported ceramics, metals and shell—indicates some wealth differentiation, especially in specific architectural spaces, such as Terrace 4, Room Complex 3, the Torreón structure and in several of the mortuary constructions. Status differences could also be indicated by the architectural elaboration and use of both residential and funerary structures, specifically through differences in size, masonry quality, layout, presence of stone sculpture and contents.

However, these indices do not show the wide disparities in access or cultural elaboration that we would expect to be commensurate with highly ranked societies or permanent social inequality. For example, while there are residential structures and tombs of different sizes and elaboration, none could be interpreted as categorically different than others in size, quality or contents. In other words, we do not have data to argue the existence of a "palace" or "royal" grave. Similarly, while the ancient inhabitants of Chinchawas had considerable access to rare long-distance goods, the materials did not amass in one residential structure or tomb; the materials were dispersed across the site and clustered most often in special purpose or ceremonial areas.

The data from Chinchawas are consistent with a model of a community of multiple coexisting corporate groups, probably based on descent or co-residence, or both. The evidence for social differentiation in trade goods and architecture likely reflects the specific socioeconomic resources and prerogatives of each group. Further, leadership roles at Chinchawas do not seem to have been inherited, but were probably based on the capacity of certain individuals to marshal political capital or prestige. The Chinchawas investigations suggest that unequal economic production, public display of sumptuaries and festive hospitality made this possible (Lau 2002).

Corporate building projects included elaborate mortuary buildings and ceremonial enclosures, but political authority likely also extended to community-wide civil and ritual domains, especially in the agricultural calendar and distribution of herd and water resources. Defense of community territory, as reflected in Chinchawas's large perimeter walls and defensive posture, was probably also an important responsibility of local leaders (e.g., Espinoza Soriano 1978; Mayer 2002). Overall, segmented group or kin-based organization seems to have provided the ancient Chinchawas community flexible sociopolitical arrangements and the milieu for remarkable cultural developments without permanent hierarchy.

*Ceremonial Practices and Local Complexity*
Evidence for Chinchawas social differentiation manifested especially in local cer-

emonial practices. The investigations discerned two distinct religious programs rooted in ancestor veneration (Lau 2001, 2002). The initial Chinchawasi phase occupations stressed ceremonies held within patio–enclosures on the main ridgetop of Sector 1. Because of their association to higher status residences and proximity to rich midden deposits, the enclosures were special places for commensal activities sponsored by local leaders interested in augmenting prestige through wealth display and festive generosity (e.g., Morris 1979; Murra 1980; Gero 1990; Clark and Blake 1994; Dietler 1996). Refuse was cleared from these ceremonial spaces and disposed of in adjacent rooms and terraces. The analysis of this material suggests that the main activities included the display of rare or sumptuary items and the eating of camelid meat. Fine ceramics, mainly locally decorated open bowls that had been broken, were likely used for serving food and drink.

Graves of this period were relatively modest subterranean chamber tombs. Most labor investment, apparently, was directed at elaborating the ceremonial enclosures with fine masonry, drainage canals and stone sculpture. Featuring images of felines and ancestor figures, the sculptures were references to descent and authority as well as aggrandizing expressions of political leadership (Lau 2002).

By the Warmi phase, ceremonial practices at Chinchawas underwent a series of notable transformations. Mortuary architecture, in the form of chullpas, was emphasized over the building and intensive use of elaborate patio–enclosures in Sector 1. Many stone sculptures were incorporated into chullpa structures, most depicting single anthropomorphic figures. And wealth, in the form of grave goods, was taken out of general circulation by their placement, as offerings, in the mausolea.

The chullpa tombs and their sculptures formed the basic elements of religious ceremony during the Warmi phase. Low walls demarcated boundaries between tombs and clusters of tombs. And it is within these enclosures that local cult activities persisted, consisting of offerings and probably ritual drinking, but apparently very little camelid meat consumption. Overall, the ceremonial practices therefore shifted from inclusive wide-scale events in Sector 1 to smaller-scale, probably more segmented, cult activities in Sector 2.

Chinchawas was part of a much broader pattern in the Early Intermediate Period in which art and architecture were integral components of leadership ideology. There was a basic association between Recuay artworks and funerary contexts (Lau 2000, 2002, 2006b). Many Recuay representations on ceramics and stone sculpture cannot be separated from their functions in ancestor ceremonies and displays of important male leaders. By expressing the legitimacy of local leaders (pedigree and access to goods, labor and special knowledge), Recuay stone sculpture, pottery and corporate architecture were important instruments of political authority.

## Transformations in the Recuay Tradition and Community at Chinchawas

Finally, the Chinchawas investigations elicit important implications for the prehistory of the North Central Highlands during the 1st millennium A.D. Specifically, the Chinchawas research enables an understanding of Recuay social and cultural transformations during the period of Wari expansion, the first pan-Andean state.

As the territory dividing major culture areas in northern Peru, highland Ancash was a vital zone for sociocultural interaction and trade during the 1st millennium A.D. During the Early Intermediate Period, the Recuay heartland adjoined flourishing coastal societies, such as the Moche, Gallinazo and Lima (Bennett 1939:133–136; Strong and Evans 1952:242–244; Patterson 1966:94–95; Proulx 1982), Central Highland and Huamachuco–Cajamarca groups in the highlands (Topic and Topic 1985, 2000; Matsumoto 1988, 1994) and the tropical montane forest peoples to the east (Church 1996:494–497). Cultural interaction within and between these regions—in the form of stylistic affinities as well as trade goods—suggests that Recuay groups drew economic advantage through its intermediate geographic position. The Chinchawas community, for example, prospered from its favorable location along a major corridor for movement of goods between the coast and the highlands.

A collateral effect of Recuay's central geographic location was that Recuay culture drew selectively from many representational styles. The appropriation of important elements from different symbol systems, such as the Recuay feline (Moche and Gallinazo), the frontal face motif with four head appendages (Cajamarca) and interlocking serpents (Lima), indicates that Recuay iconography was mutable and could be recast for different purposes. Certainly, one likely reason would be to claim exotic sources of religious or cultural faculty in displays of leadership ideology.

Chinchawas developed during a period of Andean prehistory characterized by warfare and considerable sociopolitical unrest. Despite its residential and economic functions, the site still took the form of a well-defended hilltop settlement, with multiple perimeter walls enclosing tightly agglutinated residences. This spatial configuration emerged by Chinchawasi phase 1, around A.D. 600, and is part of a generalized defensive pattern for Recuay communities. The investigations also documented slingstones, club heads and projectile points, which could have been used as weapons in combat, beyond their principal use in hunting and farming. The emphasis on warfare and leadership also manifested in the imagery of Recuay tradition stone sculpture (Schaedel 1948a). Several monoliths at Chinchawas, as is common in Recuay artworks, depict males with clubs as well as trophy head and hand motifs (Lau 2006b); these were images of heroic ancestors and mythical "conquerors."

Although there was general continuity in the general character of local economic practices at Chinchawas, new patterns became established during the 7th century A.D. Chinchawasi 1 peoples emphasized long-distance exchange, indicating new, if limited, interaction with Late Moche and Wari peoples. The exchange was primarily for luxury items used for display and cult purposes, apparently showing a local interest in referencing affiliations with exotic emblems and iconographies of powerful, stratified societies.

Promoted by colder climatic conditions, the local herding economy of Chinchawas prospered during the latter portion of the Chinchawasi 2 occupation (about A.D. 800) and resulted in concomitant developments in increased site size and diversification of material culture. There was a surge of long-distance exchange, in particular, during this time. Both the range of sources and the frequency of exotics increased markedly, reflecting the growing interest and capacity of local leaders at Chinchawas to acquire rare sumptuary items from different areas of the Central Andes.

Significant changes in the economy and material culture at Chinchawas occurred during the early portion of the Middle Horizon, the period associated with expansion of the Wari state, by around A.D. 700. Wari culture and precepts reached many parts of the Callejón de Huaylas and the Central Andes, more generally, at this time (e.g., Menzel 1964, 1977; Isbell 1989; Schreiber 1992).

It is unclear whether Chinchawas was ever integrated into the Wari state apparatus. Chinchawas's interaction with Wari is characterized mainly by importation of rare items from Wari area sources, especially pottery and obsidian. Further, the stylistic evidence from local decorated pottery suggests that early Wari influence at Chinchawas was fairly indirect, even as late as A.D. 800. It is probable that exchange was the principal motivation for initial Wari presence during Chinchawasi 1 and during the intensified interaction of Chinchawasi 2.

Later Wari influence in the Callejón de Huaylas coincided with sharp transformations in the Recuay tradition (Lau 2004b). At Chinchawas, the stylistic makeover in local decorated pottery mirrored notable changes in mortuary practice, stone sculptural iconography and long-distance exchange. The intensity of site occupation and local economic activities also declined during the Warmi phase. Nevertheless, the occupation manifested cultural forms that are typically highland (local redware pottery, chullpas and use of stone sculpture), but bearing very strong stylistic influence from the coast (in iconography and especially in trade items— imported pottery and shell). By the end of the period of Wari expansion in the Callejón de Huaylas, cultural dispositions at Chinchawas favored intensification of trade and cultural interaction with coastal groups.

Considerable variability therefore characterized Wari influence in the Callejón de Huaylas. By the early Middle Horizon, different sites in the Callejón de Huaylas maintained different levels of interaction with Wari. Unlike the case at Chinchawas, some sites, such as Queyash Alto and Pashash, which have post-Recuay occupations, show very little Wari influence (Grieder 1978; Gero 1991), either in trade or stylistic interaction. Meanwhile, other sites, such as Honcopampa, had more functional relationships to Wari, specifically in architectural forms (Isbell 1991a). But overall, Wari culture in the Callejón de Huaylas was particularly prominent in contexts for ostentation (e.g., Chinchawas), offering deposits and funerary ritual (e.g., Wilkawaín, Honcopampa, Chinchawas and Pierina).

Even small rural communities, such as Chinchawas, managed to acquire objects bearing Wari and Wari-related motifs. Indeed, for its small size, the archaeological record at Chinchawas is remarkable for the long history of interest, diversity and demonstrated consumption of exotic goods (Lau 2005). The Chinchawas research also helps to show that Wari influence on Callejón de Huaylas groups changed through time. Early in the Middle Horizon, Chinchawasi peoples claimed new ideas and benefits from Wari affiliation, usually in the form of highland trade goods, but relied heavily on local cultural and technological traditions. Later (Warmi phase) there was greater importation of coastal exotics while local decorated pottery emulated secular Wari styles.

More data are required to assess whether similar diachronic patterns prevailed at large political centers in the Recuay heartland, such as at Honcopampa or Yayno, in addition to the small village case provided by Chinchawas. Such research would illuminate how groups of different political complexity responded to new socioeconomic conditions during the Early Intermediate Period and Middle Horizon.

## Chinchawas and the Late Middle Horizon

The investigations at Chinchawas have produced evidence of cultural transformations at the single-site level, which can be compared to patterns found in other regions of northern Peru. One of the crucial findings of the work is the record of profound changes at the site during the middle to later Middle Horizon, when Central Highland Wari power was thought to be either in decline or had already ceased (Rowe and Menzel 1967).

This transformation is manifested in four principal ways at Chinchawas. The first was the community-wide adoption of a local decorated pottery, known as Warmi Ware A. This pottery has little to do with the previous Chinchawasi 2 style and marked the close of any recognizable links to the older Recuay tradition. Second, new architectural arrangements characterized the site, where Warmi phase peoples constructed over or integrated Chinchawasi buildings into new arrangements. Third, there were major changes in corporate ritual. The use of chullpas and the veneration of associated stone sculptures in Sector 2 supplanted earlier practices focused on Sector 1 and subterranean tombs (Lau 2002). Finally, there were new patterns in long-distance trade that highlighted different interregional contacts, with a newfound emphasis on coastal sources (Lau 2005).

Menzel (1964) contended that the demise of the Wari empire occurred at the end of Middle Horizon 2, usually placed around A.D. 800. She characterized the period immediately following as a time when there was less stylistic "integration" and a trend, or subsidence of Wari, into regional diversification. The Chinchawas data certainly fit the pattern. One could argue, however, that more seems to have been happening than a simple reversion to local ways—Wari seems to have left its mark, culturally, at the site.

A comparable process occurred in the pottery assemblages of Jequetepeque (for example, Transitional Period at San José de Moro) and in Nepeña and Santa (called various styles such as Huari Norteno B, Black-White-Red, Santa). The highlands were marked by similar transformations, namely at Huamachuco (Amaru to Tuscan phase) and the Cajamarca region (Late Cajamarca or Cajamarca IV). Essentially, each of these areas saw the displacement of earlier, very strong and distinctive pottery-making traditions. For each of these cases, the local pottery production had been vigorous and was a model of regional corporate identity (for example, Recuay, Moche and Cajamarca, among others). The passing of Wari in each of these regions, however, resulted in the adoption of new painted design motifs and color combinations (such as pendant designs, interior open bowl decoration, polychrome painting, and bands and meanders), which had been distinctive parts of the Wari stylistic vocabulary.

While the implications of these patterns can only be hinted at provisionally at this stage, there emerge some interesting avenues for further research. At the very least, the evidence suggests that Wari stylistic influence did not end with the demise of the state, if we follow the Menzel timeline. We have yet to determine whether late Middle Horizon imagery held some type of religious significance, referred to Wari insignia or had anything to do with Wari at all. This is a crucial question, because the enduring quality of these once-alien elements hints at the nature and timing of Wari expansion itself and its reception across the provinces.

One would expect that, if Wari culture spread through military conquest and ruled through subjugation, its cultural expressions would have been evacuated once its political power ended. This does not need to have been an even process. But in fact we see, in core areas (for example, at Pachacamac, Lima, Nasca and Ica) as well as in peripheral areas of the Wari state (Moche, Recuay and Cajamarca), widespread cultural hybridization following the collapse of the Huari capital. Rather than rejecting the style, local pottery production actively integrated Wari formal and design attributes, such as beaker and bowl forms, pendant designs, mythical figures, band and meander motifs and polychrome combinations, among others.

The process may be somewhat akin to the long-lasting effects the distribution of Chavín art and religion had on later Andean cultures, what Rowe referred to as a "long shadow in ancient Peru" (Rowe 1967:87). If the Wari state collapsed at the end of Middle Horizon 2, often believed to have occurred around A.D. 800 to 850, Wari expansion continued to leave an indelible mark on many of the groups in the Central Andes. Wari, like Chavín, also had a long shadow in ancient Peru.

The best documented case for this process comes from San José de Moro, where years of investigation have resulted in a large sample of associated ceramics for Moche to post-Moche funerary practices (Castillo and Donnan 1994b; Castillo 2000, 2001; Rucabado and Castillo 2003). The research has identified a sequence of interregional interactions during the Late Moche (around A.D. 600 to 800) and Transitional (around A.D. 800 to 950) periods, in which local elites obtained exotics and directed pottery production to emulate regional styles, especially of contemporary prestige wares. One of the most important source cultures was Wari, especially of the Central Highlands and Central Coast. Even in the latter period, Middle Horizon 2 Viñaque, Pachacamac and Atarco style materials continued to be found with Cajamarca and Casma press-molded styles (Castillo 2000:164, 2001:327).

Foreign wares were first imported by Moche elites and then later emulated later on for widespread consumption by lower status groups (Castillo 2000:174, 2001:325). This is also the pattern we see at Chinchawas, where importation of objects (Chinchawasi 1 and Chinchawasi 2, ending around A.D. 800 to 850) was followed by a phase (Warmi) of derived local pottery production and a reconfigured exchange network privileging styles from the coast (Huari Norteño and press-molded styles). Like San José de Moro, among the most prominent emulated styles at Chinchawas were Wari and Cajamarca. Finally, like the Warmi occupation and its ceramic style, the Transitional period lasted only a relatively brief time and seems to have ended abruptly, around A.D. 950 to 1000 (Castillo 2001:327).

Another possibility that has not been explored systematically is whether Wari political or religious power continued to be prominent even up until the last centuries of the 1st millennium A.D., despite the demise of the Huari capital. Menzel proposed that Wari expansion ended at the end of Middle Horizon 2, but recent investigations at Conchopata indicate that, even in the Wari heartland, Chakipampa and Ocros pottery, thought mainly to be expansion-related Middle Horizon 1 styles (Menzel 1964), continued to be used well into the late Middle Horizon (Isbell 2000:46). A review of calibrated radiocarbon determinations from Wari provincial sites suggest that state building programs, some associated with early Middle Horizon pottery, continued up to around A.D. 1000 (Williams 2001:80–81).

The forms of pottery importation and stylistic emulation that are seen in Northern Peru (for example, Chinchawas and San José de Moro) may be more understandable if Wari authority, however configured, was still operative during the 9th and 10th centuries A.D. Warmi painted pottery was largely a derivative style based on Wari designs and forms, suggesting that Warmi peoples suscribed to their cultural meanings. What these were is unclear, but it is not implausible that interior geometric and pendant designs constituted Wari-related religious or political references. Unlike San José de Moro, Warmi peoples do not seem to have been characterized by great differences in wealth or status. So the adoption of Wari elements in local pottery were important for both elites as well as nonelites.

Ultimately, the dynamic cultural interactions during the early and late Middle Horizon require additional research, especially the local chronology and material correlates of state–local encounters. The relations between identity and culture in any colonial situation are obviously complex, but these are often mediated through objects, their use and imagery (e.g., Thomas 1991; Cummins 2002; Gosden 2004). The cultural remains at Chinchawas suggest that the close of the Middle Horizon was not simply a time when peoples reverted to previous lifeways or relied on foreign influences. Wari interaction contributed to the new pottery style and patterns of exchange, but these represented only parts of the local cultural dynamism during the period. New things were happening across the Central Andes by the end of the first millennium A.D., and the people at Chinchawas were active participants in the developments.

## Concluding Comments

This study describes the results of the archaeological investigations at the small rural community of Chinchawas, Department of Ancash, Peru. The principal objective has been to reconstruct local cultural patterns to illuminate what a typical settlement of the Recuay cultural tradition might have looked like, operated, been organized and changed through time.

The research adopted a community-wide approach and a methodology of site mapping, local surface survey and excavation sampling in different parts of a Recuay tradition village. Analysis of different classes of artifacts and architectural contexts considered diachronic patterns in economic activities, ceremonial practices and local settlement organization. I argued that the data manifest shared cultural dispositions and practices, held or performed in common, which are fundamental for distinguishing the character of ancient communities. Focusing on a single site enabled a detailed analysis of how different dimensions of the Chinchawas community may have been constituted, persisted and changed in antiquity.

This research also shows the utility of a rural perspective in the study of prehistoric social complexity. At the same time that rural communities provide the empirical basis for reconstructing local cultural patterns and change, they facilitate the understanding of how larger political systems interact with provincial groups. The evidence from the study furnished, in essence, valuable measures to gauge the timing and trajectory of the first pan-Andean state. By providing balance to archaeological models based on coastal research and regional centers, further study of rural highland communities will enrich our knowledge of the cultural and social diversity in Andean prehistory.

*APPENDIX*

# Provenience Information

FIGURE 37
    A (9J); B (54B ceniza); C (3C); D (5A); E (46e.H); F (5A); G (48D); H (3C); I (7A); J (9I); K (3C); L (21J); M (28B); N (46F); O (9I); P (35H); Q (49A amb2); R (29B); S (40c.C); T (54A); U (6B); V (40c.C); W (6C).

FIGURE 38
    A (3C); B (33sf); C (35B); D (19K); E (65B).

FIGURE 39
    A (11F); B (46e.G); C (8I); D (46e.G); E (46e.g.); F (14C); G (46e.G); H (46e.G); I (46e.G); J (38F); K (12n.H); L (17C); M (38F); N (40E); O (40c.E); P (36H); Q (19L); R (12n.H); S (47e.G).

FIGURE 40
    A (54D); B (46e.G); C (54D); D (46e.G); E (46e.G); F (19L); G (46e.G); H (46e.G); I (19K); J (46e.G); K (49D); L (40E); M (46e.G); N (46e.G).

FIGURE 41
    A (29E); B (48D); C (46e.G); D (17C); E (46e.G); F (40c.C); G (65C); H (63A).

FIGURE 42
    A (29F); B (31F); C (54C); D (4G); E (47e.G); F (54D); G (40E); H (31F); I (3C); J (40E); K (63A); L (63A).

FIGURE 43
    A (54D); B (49D); C (49D); D (4G); E (46e.G); F (47e.G).

FIGURE 44
    A (29F); B (46e.G); C (35G); D (36H); E (46e.G); F (46e.G); G (46e.G); H (29F); I (29F); J (36H); K (46e.G); L (54E).

FIGURE 45
    A (46e.G); B (46e.G); C (46e.G); D (31F); E (31F); F (23I); G (49D); H (49D); I (31F); J (46e.G); K (46e.G); L (46e.G); M (46e.G); N (46e.G); O (31F); P (38F); Q (31F); R (46e.G); S (46e.G); T (38F); U (46e.H); V (46e.G); W (46e.G); X (46e.G); Y (23I); Z (46e.H); AA (46e.G); BB (46e.G); CC (31F); DD (49D); EE (31F); FF (46e.G); GG (46e.G); HH (46e.G); II (46e.H); JJ (47e.G).

FIGURE 46
    A (12F); B (43L); C (38F); D (46e.G); E (49E); F (38F); G (49E); H (43L); I (46e.H); J (29F); K (31F); L (12F); M (19K); N (23I); O (43K); P (23I); Q (19K); R (19K); S (43K); T (19K); U (43K); V (43K); W (49D); X (49D); Y (49D); Z (12F); AA (19K); BB (49D); CC (49E); DD (46e.G); EE (29F); FF (29F); GG (46e.G); HH (49D).

FIGURE 47
    A (17B); B (12F); C (19K); D (46e.G); E (12F); F (12F); G (12F); H (38F); I (49E); J (49E); K (31F); L (19K); M (46e.G); N (43K); O (63A); P (49D); Q (49E); R (49D); S (46e.G); T (46e.G); U (46e.G); V (46e.G).

FIGURE 48
    A (46e.G); B (56A); C (46e.G); D (40c.E); E (23I); F (23I); G (23I); H (19L); I (54C); J (19L); K (56A); L (56A); N (56A); N (56A); O (46e.G); P (63sf); Q (47e.G); R (46e.G).

FIGURE 49
    A (56A); B (56A); C (46e.G); D (46e.G); E (63A); F (63B); G (63A); H (56A); I (47e.G); J (63A); K (63A); L (40E); M (47e.F); N (46e.G).

FIGURE 50
    A (40E); B (40E); C (12F); D (23I); E (24I); F (36H); G (12F); H (35G); I (49D); J (46e.H); K (12F); L (23I); M (4G); N (25E); O (31F).

FIGURE 51
A (30G); B (20F); C (6F); D (20F); E (19H); F (46E); G (38D); H (54B); I (4F); J (46E); K (46E); L (49A).

FIGURE 52
A (53A); B (31D); C (23H-I); D (49C); E (41C); F (38D); G (41C); H (46H); I (38D); J (21H); K (31E); L (9G); M (30F); N (20G); O (26G); P (26H).

FIGURE 53
A (41C); B (46E); C (38D); D (8I); E (26G); F (6F); G (48C); H (30F); I (48C); J (49B); K (48B); L (48D).

FIGURE 54
A (9G); B (12F); C (6F); D (26G-H); E (35F); F (23E); G (6F); H (48C); I (6F); J (48D); K (6F); L (9G); M (4E); N (48D).

FIGURE 55
A (54D); B (14C); C (40c.E); D (30G); E (38D); F (40E).

FIGURE 56
A (26H); B (46F); C (4E); D (46F); E (31E); F (31E); G (4F-G); H (46F); I (31E); J (46F); K (41C); L (42A); M (43J); N (48B); O (46E); P (38D).

FIGURE 57
A (31E); B (48C); C (38D); D (23H); E (5E); F (38D); G (29E); H (29E); I (29E); J (48D); K (53A); L (30E); M (46F); N (48B); O (53A); P (40C); Q (23H); R (38D); S (41E); T (26I); U (9H); V (46F); W (46F); X (30D); Y (48D); Z (46F); AA (46F); BB (46F); CC (46F); DD (46F).

FIGURE 58
A (40C); B (23H); C (49B); D (49B); E (26H); F (48C); G (38D); H (49B); I (38D); J (41D); K (23H); L (48C); M (41C); N (46F); O (46F); P (48C); Q (38D-E); R (48C); S (48D); T (48C); U (46B); V (41C).

FIGURE 59
A (38D); B (49C); C (40c.D); D (48D); E (29E); F (9G); G (19D); H (48E); I (48C); J (48D); K (48C); L (54B); M (40C); N (48D); O (41D); P (40C); Q (48B); R (23H); S (11D).

FIGURE 60
A (4E); B (47w.E); C (48D); D (43J); E (49A); F (31D); G (26H); H (46E); I (31D); J (31D); K (38D); L (31E); M (43J); N (48D); O (40E); P (41C); Q (26H); R (48C); S (26H); T (48C); U (4F); V (31D); W (49C); X (6E); Y (23G); Z (26H); AA (26H); BB (31E); CC (48E); DD (48D); EE (49A); FF (38D); GG (49B); HH (41C); II (49A); JJ (41D); KK (23H); LL (38D); MM (49B); NN (49B); NN (41C); PP (31E).

FIGURE 61
A (19H); B (31D); C (48E); D (31E); E (41C); F (46E); G (6F); H (38D); I (48D); J (26I); K (40F); L (38D); M (49C); N (23H); O (23H); P (49C); Q (49C); R (48C); S (48D); T (46E); U (48D); V (26H); W (48C); X (48D); Y (48E); Z (48w.J); AA (48C); BB (49C); CC (46w.J); DD (41D); EE (41D); FF (48C); GG (6E).

FIGURE 62
A (38D); B (48D); C (38D); D (48C); E (48C); F (23H); G (41D); H (31D); I (31D); J (49A); K (48D); L (23H); M (48C); N (38D); O (48C); P (49A); Q (23H); R (50w.A); S (50w.A); T (48C); U (38D); V (40E); W (40E); X (38D); Y (38D); Z (48C); AA (38D); BB (38D); CC (49C); DD (48C); EE (23H); FF (48D); GG (49C); HH (41D); II (40E); JJ (14C); KK (38D); LL (41C); MM (41C); NN (46E); OO (48C); PP (38D); QQ (31E).

FIGURE 63
A (26H); B (48E); C (41E); D (41C); E (50w.A); F (31E); G (48D); H (48D); I (43J); J (46E); K (41C); L (49C); M (40c.D).

FIGURE 64
A (49A); B (49A); C (31E); D (49B); E (30D); F (46F); G (48D); H (38D); I (48E); J (48D); K (38D); L (46E); M (18F); N (18F); O (4E); P (41C); Q (18F); R (48D); S (48C); T (38E);

# Appendix

U (48E); V (40C); W (38D); X (49B); Y (49C); Z (49C); AA (41C); BB (43J); CC (48D); DD (9G); EE (41C); FF (48C); GG (41C).

## Figure 65
A (49C); B (49B); C (40E); D (31D); E (49C); F (41C); G (30D); H (41C); I (48C); J (46w.I); K (46E); L (41C); M (41D); N (41C); O (48C); P (49B); Q (38D); R (41D); S (49A); T (49B); U (49A); V (41D); W (49C); X (41E).

## Figure 66
A (5E); B (41C); C (48C); D (46w.J); E (49B); F (48C); G (48C); H (48C); I (6E); J (20F); K (49B); L (48C); M (38D); N (23H); O (49B); P (23H); Q (49C); R (23G); S (23H); T (49C); U (41C); V (26H); W (38D); X (48C).

## Figure 67
A (43J); B (43J); C (49B); D (21H); E (48C); F (38D); G (38D); H (48D); I (48D); J (44C); K (49B); L (38D); M (40E); N (41E); O (31E); P (38D); Q (26H); R (53A); S (46F); T (41C); U (41C).

## Figure 70
A (52A); B (44A); C (34D); D (37e.E); E (36G); F (40B); G (20D); H (23D-E); I (6C); J (20E); K (43I); L (36G); M (36G).

## Figure 71
A (36G); B (43E); C (43E); D (23E); E (21E); F (9E); G (46w.H); H (15B); I (46C); J (8C); K (23F); L (38C); M (46C); N (36G); O (23F); P (23F).

## Figure 72
A (8C); B (15B); C (6C); D (9F); E (6C); F (36G); G (4C); H (6D); I (19H); J (26F); K (40B); L (25B); M (36G); N (20sf); O (23F).

## Figure 73
A (43E-F); B (9E); C (46w.H); D (36G); E (21E).

## Figure 74
A (27B); B (48B); C (50A); D (50A); E (12B); F (23F); G (48B); H (8C); I (23F); J (43E); K (38C); L (43E); M (43I); N (43I); O (38C); P (46w.I); Q (48B); R (48B); S (23F); T (43I); U (48A); V (46w.H).

## Figure 75
A (48B); B (43F); C (43E); D (43F); E (6D).

## Figure 76
A (27B); B (50A); C (48A); D (8E); E (23F); F (48B); G (32B); H (40C); I (23F); J (48A); K (50A); L (43I); M (48B); N (50A); O (8C); P (48B); Q (23F); R (50A); S (36G); T (43E).

## Figure 77
A (50A); B (38C); C (38C); D (48B); E (48A); F (38C); G (38C); H (23F); I (38C); J (23F); K (23F); L (23F); M (50A); N (27B); O (23F); P (4D); Q (50A); R (23F); S (36G); T (48A); U (43I); V (23F); W (23F); X (24E); Y (48B).

## Figure 78
A (50A); B (43I); C (38C); D (38C); E (4D-E); F (27B); G (27B); H (36G); I (43E); J (23F); K (43I); L (43I); M (50A); N (38C); O (38C); P (43E); Q (43E); R (50A); S (48A); T (50A); U (48B); V (23F); W (43E); X (48B); Y (38C); Z (23F).

## Figure 79
A (43E); B (43I); C (50A); D (23F); E (48A); F (48B); G (8D-E); H (36G); I (48B); J (4D); K (43E); L (43E); M (48A); N (36G); O (36G); P (54B); Q (43I); R (50A); S (43I); T (43I); U (50A); V (43I).

## Figure 80
A (53A); B (40c.B); C (48B); D (23F); E (50A); F (50A); G (50A); H (48B); I (8D); J (43I); K (25B); L (48B); M (48A).

FIGURE 81
    A (38B); B (49B); C (43D); D (46E); E (46E); F (46E); G (46E); H (42A); I (12D); J (43D);
    K (46C); L (15B); M (46E); N (8E); O (48B); P (43H); Q (43I); R (36G); S (38A); T (43E);
    U (43F); V (43I); W (46E); X (36G).

FIGURE 82
    A (46A); B (52B); C (15B); D (48A); E (34F); F (47A); G (47C); H (47C); I (49sf); J (41A);
    K (6C); L (22B); M (36E); N (36G); O (50A); P (47B); Q (48A); R (43I).

FIGURE 83
    A (61A); B (64B); C (64B); D (64B); E (64C); F (57sf); G (57A); H (57A); I (57sf); J (61A.n2);
    K (59sf); L (64C); M (64B); N (64B); O (57sf); P (64B); Q (64C); R (59A); S (64B); T (60A);
    U (60A); V (64B); W (57x); X (57A).

FIGURE 84
    A (57A); B (57x); C (64C); D (57sf); E (64sf); F (64B); G (64C); H (57A); I (64D); J (57x);
    K (59A); L (64B); M (59sf); N (57A); O (64sf); P (64C); Q (64B); R (64B); S (57sf); T (57x);
    U (57sf); V (60A); W (57sf); X (61A); Y (57sf); Z (57sf).

FIGURE 86
    A (58A); B (21B); C (55A); D (23C); E (25C); F (5A); G (43E); H (43E); I (25B); J (13A);
    K (55A); L (12n.C); M (55sf); N (58B); O (55sf); P (48sf); Q (26B); R (55sf); S (55sf).

FIGURE 87
    A (19E); B (55A); C (50w.A); D (19D); E (48sf); F (58A); G (58sf); H (46A); I (46A); J (58sf-B);
    K (4B); L (4B); M (46A); N (4B); O (43E); P (55A); Q (40B); R (28A).

FIGURE 88
    A (4B); B (28A); C (6B-C); D (46C); E (49sf); F (4B); G (54A); H (10A); I (22A); J (12n.C);
    K (19H); L (12B); M (19sf).

FIGURE 89
    A (56B); B (56A); C (56A); D (56B); E (56A); F (56B); G (56B); H (56A-B).

FIGURE 90
    A (57A); B (61A); C (61A); D (61A); E (57x); F (59sf); G (57x); H (59sf); I (61A.n2);
    J (61A.n2); K (57A.g2); L (64C); M (61A); N (61A); O (61A); P (61A).

FIGURE 91
    A (43D); B (41sf); C (53B); D (49A); E (46w.I); F (43I); G (48B); H (48B); I (48B); J (49B-C);
    K (49C); L (48B); M (54C); N (41F); O (38D+).

FIGURE 92
    A (46F-G); B (23H); C (38D); D (12C); E (52A); F (49C).

FIGURE 93
    A (4D-E); B (36G); C (51A); D (66A).

FIGURE 94
    A (36G); B (40c.B); C (45B); D (4D); E (19H); F (51A); G (42A); H (43I); I (42A).

FIGURE 95
    A (43I); B (43I); C (34E); D (35J); E (37w.D); F (43I); G (48B); H (48A); I (48D); J (48B);
    K (43I); L (23G); M (33A); N (48B); O (19K).

FIGURE 96
    A (48E); B (49C); C (48D); D (46C); E (48D); F (48D); G (47C); H (54C.t); I (23G); J (48D);
    K (48C).

FIGURE 97
    A (48A); B (49C); C (23B); D (38D); E (6D); F (46w.I); G (1B); H (4D).

FIGURE 98
    A (49A); B (48A); C (23D); D (54C.t); E (38D); F (49C); G (49sf); H (48B); I (43c.1); J (48D);
    K (49B); L (16C); M (15B); N (64D); O (43E).

FIGURE 99
  A (49B); B (49C); C (38D); D (38D).

FIGURE 100
  A (38D); B (38D); C (48B); D (49sf); E (21E); F (49D); G (49B); H (38C); I (38C); J (27C); K (23H); L (46e.G); M (38C); N (49sf); O (38B); P (46e.G); Q (53B); R (28B).

FIGURE 101
  A (53A); B (57x); C (64D); D (64C); E (40E); F (55A); G (59sf); H (59sf); I (57sf); J (55A).

FIGURE 102
  A (38C); B (50A); C (49E); D (9C); E (38E); F (23E); G (46e.G); H (9G); I (6C); J (9F); K (46e.G); L (3sf); M (34D); N (30B); O (25D); P (47w.D).

FIGURE 106
  A (12n.H); B (19M); C (12n.H); D (9I); E (45A).

FIGURE 107
  A (12F); B (46e.G); C (35G); D (43K); E (21I); F (46e.G); G (54D); H (46e.G); I (49D); J (46e.G); K (46e.G); L (29F).

FIGURE 108
  A (46e.G); B (29F); C (29F); D (46e.G); E (46e.G); F (43K); G (43K); H (31G).

FIGURE 109
  A (39F); B (40D); C (48E); D (48E); E (41C); F (29D); G (54A);

FIGURE 110
  A (8G); B (49C); C (49C); D (44C); E (46w.I).

FIGURE 111
  A (28B); B (40c.D); C (24H); D (43J); E (40C); F (48E); G (46w.I); H (9H); I (9H); J (49C); K (9G); L (41C); M (11D).

FIGURE 112
  A (38E); B (42C); C (20F); D (20F); E (22D); F (40D); G (48E); H (14B); I (54B); J (40C).

FIGURE 113
  A (41C); B (40C); C (53A); D (40D).

FIGURE 114
  A (12B); B (41A); C (48B); D (23F); E (34E); F (47w.D); G (50A).

FIGURE 115
  A (36C); B (43E); C (46C); D (48B); E (48B).

FIGURE 118
  A (48C); B (49D); C (46E); D (9C); E (48A); F (22B); G (15A); H (48B); I (54A); J (48E); K (38D); L (47C); M (38E); N (40c.B); O (47C); P (23H); Q (49D); R (9H); S (43c.2); T (39C); U (47e.G); V (48D); W (46e.G); X (31G); Y (12C); Z (50A); AA (40c.B); BB (15A); CC (35E); DD (49C); EE (9C).

FIGURE 119
  A (15A); B (38D); C (48E); D (49D); E (54B); F (9C); G (36G); H (30E); I (40w.F-G).

FIGURE 120
  A [top row, left to right: (38C), (46w.J), (40c.D); bottom row: (46e.G), (38D)]; B [top row: (40C), (48B), (48C), (53A); bottom row: (40C), (40E), (27sf), (3C), (46e.G)]; C [(46E), (49A)]; D [left column, top to bottom: (46e.G), (48B), (48B); middle column: (48A), (46e.G), (54sf); right column: (48A), (49D), (38D), (46e.G)]; E [top row, left to right: (46F), (48D), (43c.2), (37A), (43J); bottom row: (43C), (43I), (10sf), (43D), (37w.E)].

FIGURE 121
  A [top row, left to right: (54sf), (40sf), (48D), (39w.E), (23H), (49B); middle row: (51A), (4F), (48B), (40D), (48B); bottom row: (54A), (43E), (35A), (49D), (46e.G)]; B [top row: (9C), (46e.G), (18B), (23G), (43w.E); middle row: (32C), (40D), (20F), (30G), (40c.B); bottom row:

(41F), (46e.H), (41sf)]; C [top row: (46B), (46e.G), (46E), (40C), (49B), (38F), (46e.G); middle row: (49A), (26H), (48D), (12n.C), (62E), (19E), (8D); bottom row: (39B), (30F), (43K), (15B), (49A), (47e.G), (31E)]; D [top row: (48E), (49D), (41sf), (36H), (48E); middle row: (38C), (40B), (20C), (54A), (45B); bottom row: (54A), (38C), (46w.I), (42C), (9E)]; E [(46C), (64C), (58B)].

FIGURE 122
A (37e.E); B (49sf); C (23H); D (35E).

FIGURE 123
A (29/30sf); B (41D).

FIGURE 124
A (43E); B (54C); C (48E).

FIGURE 125
A (35F); B (37w.E); C (39C); D (40C); E (48E); F (59B); G (46e.G); H (30B); I (65B); J (3C); K (40F); L (57sf); M (48E); N (46F); O (54C); P (11A); Q (52A); R (46e.G); S (23H); T (37w.D); U (39F).

FIGURE 126
A [top row, left to right: (49sf), (54A), (47B), (36B), (48D), (48D), (50A); second row: (49sf), (31D), (37w.D), (9H), (40c.C), (38E), (40D); third row: (40B), (23C), (40B), (62C), (48C), (10E), (49sf); bottom row: (46sf), (47C), (35H), (48B), (48E), (48C), (38D)]; B [top row: (24D), (40c.A), (43E), (47e.D), (42A), (41C), (26H); middle row: (21D), (48C), (9C), (37B), (48C), (48D), (9H); bottom row: (8A), (1B), (62C), (46w.I), (43L), (48C), (17A)]; C [top row: (50A), (19D), (40A), (48B): bottom row: (48B), (40D), (48C), (17A), (48B)]; D [top row: (38D), (48B), (47e.G), (58B), (8D); bottom row: (38F), (39E), (46e.G), (48B), (53B)]; E [top row: (n/a), (50A); bottom row: (38C), (38E), (9C)].

FIGURE 127
A (50A); B (49B); C (37w.E); D (40E); E (38E); F (9G); G (54B); H (47e.G); I (40D); J (38C); K (38C); L (46e.H); M (17C); N (40D); O (46e.G); P (38C); Q (40D); R (47e.E); S (40C); T (27B); U (9D).

FIGURE 128
A (48C); B (27C); C (47e.E); D (54C); E (47e.F); F (54C); G (29F); H (48E); I (48C); J (20F); K (47e.G); L (40D); M (47w.E); N (49D); O (48D).

FIGURE 129
A (34E); B (35H); C (35E); D (50w); E (40C); F (49C amb1); G (4F); H (36G); I (23G); J (46w.I); K (49D); L (46e.G); M (23G).

FIGURE 130
A (36H); B (46e.G); C (43K); D (41F); E (46e.G); F (46e.G); G (47e.E); H (6F); I (46w.I); J (43E); K (54B); L (43I); M (43J); N (38C); O (17A); P (43F); Q (6F); R (9D); S (12n.H).

FIGURE 131
A (47e.E); B (40D); C (39B); D (38C); E (46e.G); F (43F).

FIGURE 132
A (44C); B (23E); C (41D); D (50A); E (49E); F (48D); G (50A).

FIGURE 133
A (55A); B (55A); C (61A); D (54D); E (54C); F (54C).

FIGURE 134
A (54C); B (65B); C (49D); D (54D); E (30C); F (40C); G (30C); H (38C); I (48B); J (48C); K (48B); L (40D); M (47e.E); N (53B).

FIGURE 135
A (48C); B (54B); C (48B); D (48C); E (46w.I); F (39w.E); G (49B); H (40D); I (48B); J (48B); K (54B); L (54B).

FIGURE 136
A (57A); B (57A); C (27B); D (11C); E (15B); F (59B); G (9E); H (57A); I (64cam3); J (64cam3); K (58B); L (55A).

# REFERENCES

ALLEN, CATHERINE J. 1988. *The Hold Life Has: Coca and Cultural Identity in an Andean Community*. Washington, DC: Smithsonian Institution Press. 283 pp.

ALLEY, RICHARD B. 2000. Ice-core evidence of abrupt climate changes. *Proceedings of the National Academy of Sciences* 97(4):1331–1334.

ALDENDERFER, MARK S., ed. 1993. *Domestic Architecture, Ethnicity and Complementarity in the South Central Andes*. Iowa City: University of Iowa Press. 178 pp.

AMAT OLAZÁBAL, HERNÁN. 1976a. Estudios arqueológicos en la cuenca del Mosna y en el Alto Marañon. *Actas del XLI Congreso Internacional de Americanistas* [Proceedings of the 41st International Congress of Americanists], Volume 3; 1974 Sept 2–7; Mexico City, Mexico. Mexico City: Instituto Nacional de Anthropologia e Historia. pp. 532–544.

—1976b. *Las formaciones agropecuarias de los períodos Formativo, Desarrollo Regional, Imperio Huari y Estados Regionales de Ancash* [dissertation]. Arequipa, Peru: Universidad Nacional de San Agustín, Programa Académico de Historia y Antropología. 340 pp.

—2003. Huarás y Recuay en la secuencia cultural del Callejón de Conchucos: Valle del Mosna. In: Bebel Ibarra, ed. *Arqueología de la sierra de Ancash: propuestas y perspectivas*. Lima: Instituto Cultural Runa. pp. 97–120.

ANDERS, MARTHA B. 1986. Wari experiments in statecraft: a view from Azángaro. In: Ramiro Matos, Solveig Turpin and Herbert Eling, eds. *Andean Archaeology: Papers in Memory of Clifford Evans*. Los Angeles: University of California, Los Angeles, Institute of Archaeology. pp. 163–188.

—1989. Wamanga pottery: Symbolic resistance and subversion in Middle Horizon Epoch 2 ceramics from the planned Wari site of Azángaro (Ayacucho, Peru). In: Diana Tkaczuk and Brian Vivian, eds. *Cultures in Conflict: Current Archaeological Perspectives*. Calgary, Alberta, Canada: University of Calgary Archaeological Association. pp. 7–18.

ANTÚNEZ DE MAYOLO, SANTIAGO. 1935. Las ruinas de Tinyash (Exploración arqueológica). *Boletín de la Sociedad Geográfica de Lima* 58:193–220.

BANKMANN, ULF. 1973. Bemerkungen zu einigen Skulpturen aus dem nordperuanische Hochland. *Atti del XL Congresso Internazionale degli Americanisti* [Proceedings of the 40th International Congress of Americanists], Volume 1; 1972 Sept 3–10; Rome and Genoa, Italy. Genova: Tilgher. pp. 285–291.

—1979. Moche und Recuay. *Baessler-Archiv, Neue Folge* 27:253–271.

—1981. Zwei skulpturen aus dem Callejón de Huaylas, Peru im Museum zu Basel. *Verdhandlungen der Naturforschenden Gesellschaft in Basel* 92:39–46.

—1988. Recuay–Studien, I: Früheste Abbildung einer Keramik des Recuay-Stils. *Baessler-Archiv Neue Folge* 36(1):99–108.

BAWDEN, GARTH. 1994. Nuevas formas de ceramica Moche V: procedentes de Galindo. In: Santiago Uceda and Elías Mujica, eds. *Moche: Propuestas y Prospectivas*. Lima: l'Institut Francais d'Etudes Andines. pp. 389–414. (Travaux de l'Institut Francais d'Etudes Andines 79.)

—1996. *The Moche*. Oxford: Blackwell Publishers. 375 pp.

BENAVIDES C., MARIO. 1984. *Carácter del Estado Wari*. Ayacucho, Peru: Universidad Nacional de San Cristóbal de Huamanga. 189 pp.

—1991. Cheqo Wasi, Huari. In: William H. Isbell and Gordon F. McEwan, eds. *Huari Administrative Structure: Prehistoric Monumental Architecture and State Government*. Washington, DC: Dumbarton Oaks. pp. 55–69.

BENNETT, WENDELL C. 1939. *Archaeology of the North Coast of Peru: An Account of Excavation in Virú and Lambayeque Valleys*. New York: American Museum of Natural History. 153 pp. (Anthropological Papers 37(1).)

—1944. *The North Highlands of Peru: Excavations in the Callejón de Huaylas and at Chavín de Huántar*. New York: American Museum of Natural History. 114 pp. (Anthropological Papers 39(1).)

—1948. The Peruvian co-tradition. In: Wendell C. Bennett, ed. *A Reappraisal of Peruvian Archaeology*. Menasha, WI: Society for American Archaeology. pp. 1–7. (Memoirs 4.)

—1953. *Excavations at Wari, Ayacucho, Peru*. New Haven: Yale University Press. 126 pp. (Yale University Publications in Anthropology 49.)

BERMANN, MARC. 1994. *Lukurmata: Household Archaeology in Prehispanic Bolivia*. Princeton, NJ: Princeton University Press. 307 pp.

BERNUY, KATIUSHA AND VANESSA BERNAL. 2005. Influencia Cajamarca en los rituales funerarios del Período Transicional en San Jose de Moro. In: Claudio César Olaya and Marina Romero Bernales, eds. *Muerte y Evidencias Funerarias en los Andes Centrales: Avances y Perspectivas*. Lima: Universidad Nacional Federico Villareal. pp. 61–77. (Corriente Arqueológica 1.)

BILLMAN, BRIAN R. 1996. *The Evolution of Prehistoric Political Organizations in the Moche Valley, Peru* [dissertation]. Santa Barbara: University of California, Santa Barbara, Department of Anthropology. 385 pp. Available from: ProQuest Dissertations & Theses [database online]; http://www.proquest.com (publication AAT 9708060).

BODENLOS, ALFRED J. AND GEORGE L. ERICKSEN. 1955. *Lead-Zinc Deposits of the Cordillera Blanca and Northern Cordillera Huayhuash, Peru*. Washington, DC: United States Geological Survey. 166 pp. (USGS Bulletin 1017.)

BODENLOS, ALFRED J. AND JOHN A. STRACZEK. 1957. *Base-Metal Deposits of the Cordillera Negra Departamento de Ancash, Peru*. Washington, DC: United States Geological Survey. 165 pp. (USGS Bulletin 1040.)

BONAVÍA, DUCCIO. 1966. *Sitios Arqueológicos del Perú*. Lima: Museo Nacional de Antropología y Arqueología. 71 pp. (Arqueológicas 9.)

—1991. *Perú: Hombre e Historia*. Volume 1, De los orígenes al siglo XV. Lima: EDUBANCO. 586 pp.

BONNIER, ELISABETH, ROSALEEN HOWARD, LAWRENCE KAPLAN AND CATHERINE ROZENBERG. 1983. Recherches archéologiques, paléobotaniques et ethnolinguistiques dans une vallée du Haut Maranon (Pérou): le projet Tantamayo Piruru. *Bulletin de l'Institut français d'études andines* 12:103–133.

BRUHNS, KAREN O. 1976. The moon animal in northern Peruvian art and culture. *Ñawpa Pacha* 14:21–40.

BUENO MENDOZA, ALBERTO. 1989. Arqueología de Ancash: nuevas perspectivas. In: Camila Estremadoyro R., ed. *Ancash: Historia y Cultura*. Lima: CONCYTEC. pp. 31–43.

BURGER, RICHARD L. 1982. Pójoc and Waman Wain: two Early Horizon villages in the Chavín heartland. *Ñawpa Pacha* 20:3–40.

—1984a. *The Prehistoric Occupation of Chavín de Huántar, Peru*. Berkeley: University of California Press. 403 pp. (University of California Publications in Anthropology 14.)

—1984b. Archaeological areas and prehistoric frontiers: the case of Formative Peru and Ecuador. In: Richard L. Burger, Mario Rivera and David Browman, eds. *Social and Economic Organization in the Prehistoric Andes*. Oxford: British Archaeological Reports. pp. 33–71. (BAR International Series 194.)

—1985a. Archaeological investigations at Huaricoto, Ancash, Peru: 1978–1979. *National Geographic Society Research Reports* 19:119–127.

—1985b. Prehistoric stylistic change and cultural development at Huaricoto, Peru. *National Geographic Research* 1(4):505–534.

—1992. *Chavín and the Origins of Andean Civilization*. London: Thames and Hudson. 248 pp.

BURGER, RICHARD L. AND FRANK ASARO. 1977. *Trace Element Analysis of Obsidian Artifacts from the Andes: New Perspectives on Pre-Hispanic Economic Interaction in Peru and Bolivia*. Berkeley: University of California, Lawrence Berkeley Laboratory, Technical Information Department. 88 pp. (Report LBL–6343.)

BURGER, RICHARD L., KAREN L. CHÁVEZ AND SERGIO J. CHÁVEZ. 2000. Through the glass darkly: prehispanic obsidian procurement and exchange in Southern Peru and Northern Bolivia. *Journal of World Prehistory* 14(3):267–362.

BURGER, RICHARD L. AND MICHAEL GLASCOCK. 2000. Locating the Quispisisa obsidian source in the Department of Ayacucho, Peru. *Latin American Antiquity* 11:258–268.

BURGER, RICHARD L., GEORGE F. LAU, VICTOR M. PONTE R. AND MICHAEL D. GLASCOCK. 2006. The history of prehispanic obsidian procurement in highland Ancash. In: Alexander Herrera, Carolina Orsini and Kevin Lane, eds. *La Complejidad Social en la Sierra de Ancash: Ensayos Sobre Paisaje, Economía y Continuidades Culturales*. Milan: Civiche Raccolte d'Arte Applicata del Castello Sforzesco. pp. 103–120.

BURGER, RICHARD L. AND LUCY C. SALAZAR-BURGER. 1980. Ritual and religion at Huaricoto. *Archaeology* 33:26–32.

—1986. Early organizational diversity in the Peruvian highlands: Huaricoto and Kotosh. In: Ramiro Matos, Solveig Turpin and Herbert Eling, eds. *Andean Archaeology: Papers in Memory of Clifford Evans*. Los Angeles: University of California, Los Angeles, Institute of Archaeology. pp. 65–82.

BUSE, HERMANN. 1965. *Introducción al Peru*. Lima: Imprenta del Colegio Militar "Leoncio Prado." 393 pp.

CANUTO, MARCELLO AND JASON YAEGER, eds. 2000. *The Archaeology of Communities: A New World Perspective*. New York: Routledge. 271 pp.

CAPRA, ALESSANDRO, STEFANO GANDOLFI, LAURA LAURENCICH, FRANCESCO MANCINI, ALBERTO MINELLI, CAROLINA ORSINI AND AURELIO RODRÍGUEZ. 2002. Multidisciplinary approach for archeological survey: exploring GPS method in landscape archaeology studies. *Journal of Cultural Heritage* 2:93–99.

CARDICH, AUGUSTO. 1985. The fluctuating upper limits of cultivation in the Central Andes and their impact on Peruvian prehistory. *Advances in World Archaeology* 4:293–333.

CARRIÓN CACHOT, REBECA. 1955. El culto de agua en el antiguo Peru. La paccha elemento cultural pan-andino. *Revista del Museo Nacional de Antropología y Arqueología* 2(2):50–140.

—1959. *La Religión en el Antiguo Peru (Norte y Centro de la Costa, Período Post-clásico)*. Lima: Published by the author. 151 pp.

CASTILLO, LUIS JAIME. 1993. Prácticas funerarias, poder e ideología en la sociedad Moche Tardía. *Gaceta Arqueológica Andina* 7(7):67–73.

—2000. La presencia Wari en San José de Moro. *Boletín de Arqueología PUCP* 4:143–179.

—2001. Last of the Mochicas: a view from the Jequetepeque Valley. In: Joanne Pillsbury, ed. *Moche Art and Archaeology in Ancient Peru*. Washington, DC: National Gallery of Art. pp. 307–332. (Studies in the History of Art 63.)

CASTILLO, LUIS JAIME AND CHRISTOPHER B. DONNAN. 1994a. Los Mochicas del norte y los Mochicas del sur. In: Krzysztof Makowski, ed. *Vicús*. Lima: Banco de Crédito. pp. 143–182.

—1994b. La ocupación Moche de San José de Moro, Jequetepeque. In: Santiago Uceda and Elías Mujica, eds. *Moche: Propuestas y Prospectivas*. Lima: l'Institut Francais d'Etudes Andines. pp. 93–146. (Travaux de l'Institut Francais d'Etudes Andines 79.)

CHRISTIANSEN, JORGE G. 1967. *El cultivo de papa en el Peru*. Lima: Editorial Jurídica. 351 pp.

CHURCH, WARREN B. 1996. *Prehistoric Cultural Development and Interregional Interaction in the Tropical Montane Forests of Peru* [dissertation]. New Haven: Yale University, Department of Anthropology. 895 pp. Available from: ProQuest Dissertations & Theses [database online]; http://www.proquest.com (publication AAT 9712763).

CLARK, JOHN E. AND MICHAEL BLAKE. 1994. The power of prestige: competitive generosity and the emergence of rank in Lowland Mesoamerica. In: Elizabeth Brumfiel and John W. Fox, eds. *Factional Competition and Political Development in the New World*. Cambridge: Cambridge University Press. pp. 17–30.

CLOTHIER, WILLIAM J. II. 1943. Recuay pottery in the lower Santa Valley. *Revista del Museo Nacional* 12(2):239–242.

COBBING, E. J., W. S. PITCHER, J. J. WILSON, J. W. BALDOCK, W. P. TAYLOR, W. MCCOURT AND N. J. SNELLING. 1981. *The Geology of the Western Cordillera of Northern Peru*. London: H.M.S.O., Institute of Geological Sciences. 143 pp. (Overseas Memoir 5.)

COLLIER, DONALD. 1955. *Cultural Chronology and Change as Reflected in the Ceramics of the Virú Valley, Peru*. Chicago: Field Museum. 226 pp. (Fieldiana: Anthropology 43.)

—1962. Archaeological Investigations in the Casma Valley. Akten des 34. *Internationalen AmerikanistenKongresses Wien* [Proceedings of the 34th International Congress of Americanists]; 1960 July 18–25; Vienna, Austria. Vienna: Ferdinand Berger, Horn. pp. 411–417.

COOK, ANITA G. 1985. The Middle Horizon ceramic offerings from Conchopata. *Ñawpa Pacha* 22–23:49–90.

—1994. *Wari y Tiwanaku: Entre el Estilo y Imagen*. Lima: Pontificia Universidad Católica del Peru. 344 pp.

—2001. Huari D-shaped structures, sacrificial offerings and divine rulership. In: Elizabeth P. Benson and Anita G. Cook, eds. *Ritual Sacrifice in Ancient Peru*. Austin: University of Texas Press. pp. 137–163.

COOK, NOBLE DAVID. 1981. *Demographic Collapse: Indian Peru, 1520–1620*. Cambridge: Cambridge University Press. 310 pp.

COSSIO, A. 1964. *Geología de los Cuadrángulos de Santiago de Chuco y Santa Rosa, Peru*. Lima: Servicio de Geología y Minería. 69 pp. (Boletín 8.)

CUMMINS, THOMAS B. 2002. *Toasts with the Inca: Andean Abstraction and Colonial Images on Kero Vessels*. Ann Arbor: University of Michigan Press. 377 pp.

CZWARNO, R. MICHAEL. 1983. *Ceramic Indications of Cultural Interaction: Evidence from Northern Peru* [master's thesis]. Peterborough, Ontario, Canada: Trent University, Department of Anthropology. 247 pp.

DAGGETT, RICHARD E. 1985. The Early Horizon–Early Intermediate Period transition: a view from the Nepeña and Virú Valleys. In: D. Peter Kvietok and Daniel H. Sandweiss, eds. *Recent Studies in Andean Prehistory and Protohistory*. Ithaca, NY: Cornell University, Latin American Studies Program. pp. 41–65.

—1987. Toward the development of the state on the north central coast of Peru. In: Jonathan Haas, Shelia Pozorski and Thomas Pozorski, eds. *The Origins and Development of the Andean State*. Cambridge: Cambridge University Press. pp. 70–82.

D'ALTROY, TERENCE N. 1992. *Provincial Power in the Inka Empire*. Washington, DC: Smithsonian Institution Press. 272 pp.

DAWSON, LAWRENCE E. 1964. Slip casting: a ceramic technique invented in ancient Peru. *Ñawpa Pacha* 2:107–111.

DE LAVALLE, JOSE ANTONIO, ed. 1984. *Culturas Precolombinas: Huari*. Lima: Banco de Crédito del Peru. 195 pp.

DELEONARDIS, LISA AND GEORGE F. LAU. 2004. Life, death and ancestors. In: Helaine Silverman, ed. *Andean Archaeology*. Oxford: Blackwell Publishers. pp. 77–115.

DIETLER, MICHAEL. 1996. Feasts and commensal politics in the political economy: food, power and status in prehistoric Europe. In: Polly Weissner and Wulf Schiefenhövel, eds. *Food and the Status Quest: An Interdisciplinary Perspective*. Providence, RI: Berghahn Books. pp. 87–125.

DILLEHAY, TOM D. 2001. Town and country in Late Moche times: a view from two northern valleys. In: Joanne Pillsbury, ed. *Moche Art and Archaeology in Ancient Peru*. Washington, DC: National Gallery of Art. pp. 259–283. (Studies in the History of Art 63.)

DISSELHOFF, HANS-DIETRICH. 1956. Hand-und kopftrophäen in plastischen Darstellung der Recuay-keramik. *Baessler Archiv, Neue Folge* 4:25–32.

DONNAN, CHRISTOPHER B. 1968. An association of Middle Horizon Epoch 2A specimens from the Chicama Valley, Peru. *Ñawpa Pacha* 6:15–18.

—1973. *Moche Occupation of the Santa Valley, Peru*. Berkeley: University of California Press. 144 pp. (University of California Publications in Anthropology 8.)

—1978. *Moche Art of Peru: Pre-Columbian Symbolic Communication*. Los Angeles: University of California, Los Angeles, Museum of Cultural History. 206 pp.

DONNAN, CHRISTOPHER B. AND CAROL J. MACKEY. 1978. *Ancient Burial Practices of the Moche Valley, Peru*. Austin: University of Texas Press. 412 pp.

DRUC, ISABELLE C. 1998. *Ceramic Production and Distribution in the Chavín Sphere of Influence (North-central Andes)*. Oxford: J. and E. Hedges. 121 pp. (BAR International Series 731.)

DUVIOLS, PIERRE. 1986. *Cultura Andina y Represión: Procesos y Visitas de Idolatrías y Hecherías Cajatambo, siglo XVII*. Cuzco: Centro de Estudios Rurales Andinos "Bartolomé de las Casas." 570 pp.

EISLEB, DIETER. 1960. Bemerkungen zu einem Recuay-Gefäss aus der sammlung des Berliner Völkerkunde–Museums. *Baessler-Archiv, Neue Folge* 8:83–87.

—1987. *Altperuanische Kulturen*. Volume 4, Recuay. Berlin: Staatliche Museen Preussischer Kulturbesitz, Museum für Völkerkunde. 61 pp.

ESPEJO NUÑEZ, JULIO. 1957. Primeros indicios arqueológicos del estilo cultural Huaylas (Recuay) en la cuenca del Pukcha (Peru). *Cuadernos Americanos* 91:137–150.

—1959. Katayok y Molle–Ukru. *Peru Indígena* 8(18–19):91–98.

ESPINOZA SORIANO, WALDEMAR. 1978. *Huaraz: Poder, Sociedad y Economía en los Siglos XV y XVI—Reflexiones en Torno a las Visitas de 1558, 1594 y 1712*. Lima: Seminario de Historia Rural Andina, Universidad Nacional Mayor de San Marcos. 165 pp.

FORD, JAMES A. AND GORDON R. WILLEY. 1949. *Surface Survey of the Virú Valley, Peru*. New York: American Museum of Natural History. 89 pp. (Anthropological Papers 43(1).)

GAMBINI ESCUDERO, WILFREDO. 1984. *Santa y Nepeña: Dos Valles, dos Culturas*. Lima: Imprenta M. Castillo. 196 pp.

GAYTON, ANNA H. 1927. The Uhle collections from Nievería. *University of California Publications in American Archaeology and Ethnology* 21(8):305–329.

GERO, JOAN M. 1983. *Material Culture and the Reproduction of Social Complexity: A Lithic Example from the Peruvian Formative* [dissertation]. Amherst, MA: University of Massachusetts, Department of Anthropology. 254 pp. Available from: ProQuest Dissertations & Theses [database online]; http://www.proquest.com (publication AAT 8317466).

—1990. Pottery, power, and…parties! *Archaeology* 43(2):52–56.

—1991. Who experienced what in prehistory?: A narrative explanation from Queyash, Peru. In: Robert W. Preucel, ed. *Processual and Postprocessual Archaeologies: Multiple Ways of Knowing the Past*. Carbondale, IL: Southern Illinois University. pp. 126–139. (Center for Archaeological Investigations Occasional Paper 10.)

—1992. Feasts and females: gender ideology and political meals in the Andes. *Norwegian Archaeological Review* 25(1):15–30.

—1999. La iconografía Recuay y el estudio de género. *Gaceta Arqueológica Andina* 25:23–44.

—2001. Field knots and ceramic beaus: interpreting gender in the Peruvian Early Intermediate Period. In: Cecelia Klein, ed. Gender in Pre-hispanic America. Washington, DC: Dumbarton Oaks. pp. 15–55.

GLOWACKI, MARY. 2002. The Huaro archaeological site complex: rethinking the Huari occupation of Cuzco. In: William H. Isbell and Helaine Silverman, eds. *Andean Archaeology*. Volume 1, Variations in Sociopolitical Organization. New York: Kluwer Academic/Plenum Publishers. pp. 267–285.

GODELIER, MAURICE. 1977. *Perspectives in Marxist Anthropology*. Cambridge: Cambridge University Press. 243 pp.

GONZÁLEZ CARRÉ, ENRIQUE, ENRIQUE BRAYGARAC DAVILA, CIRILO VIVANCO POMACANCHARI, VERA TIESLER BLOS AND MÁXIMO LOPEZ QUISPE. 1999. *El Templo Mayor en la Ciudad de Wari: Estudios Arqueológicos en Vegachayoq Moqo-Ayacucho*. Ayacucho, Peru: Universidad Nacional de San Cristóbal de Huamanga. 135 pp.

GOSDEN, CHRIS. 2004. *Archaeology and Colonialism: Cultural Contact from 5000 BC to the Present*. Cambridge: Cambridge University Press. 186 pp.

GRIEDER, TERENCE. 1978. *The Art and Archaeology of Pashash*. Austin: University of Texas Press. 268 pp.

—1992. Signs of an ideology of authority in Ancash. In: A. Sean Goldsmith, Sandra Garvie, David Selin and Jeannette Smith, eds. Ancient Images, Ancient Thought: The Archaeology of Ideology. Calgary: University of Calgary Archaeological Association. pp. 181–185.

GRIEDER, TERENCE, ALBERTO BUENO MENDOZA, C. EARLE SMITH JR. AND ROBERT M. MALINA. 1988. *La Galgada, Peru: A Preceramic Culture in Transition*. Austin: University of Texas Press. 282 pp.

GRIMALDO G., CLAUDIA. 1999. Apéndice D: Análisis de los artefactos líticos. In: Victor M. Ponte Rosalino. *Análisis de los Asentamientos Arqueológicos en el área de Influencia de la Mina*

*Pierina*. Huaraz: Mina Barrick. Report submitted to Mina Barrick Misquichilca and Instituto Nacional de Cultura, pp. 205–306.

GROSSMAN, JOEL W. 1972. An ancient gold worker's toolkit: the earliest metal technology in Peru. *Archaeology* (25)4:270–275.

—1983. Demographic change and economic transformation in the south-central highlands of pre-Huari Peru. *Ñawpa Pacha* 21:45–126.

HASTORF, CHRISTINE A. 1993. *Agriculture and the Onset of Political Inequality before the Inka*. Cambridge: Cambridge University Press. 298 pp.

HELMS, MARY W. 1993. *Craft and the Kingly Ideal*. Austin: University of Texas Press. 287 pp.

HERNÁNDEZ PRÍNCIPE, RODRIGO. 1923. Mitología andina. *Inca* 1:25–78.

HERRERA, ALEXANDER. 1999. Proyecto de exploración arqueológica Conchucos. *Boletín del Museo de Arqueología y Antropología* 2:8–13.

—2003. Patrones de asentamiento y cambios en las estrategias de ocupación en la cuenca sur del río Yanamayo. In: Bebel Ibarra, ed. *Arqueología de la Sierra de Ancash: Propuestas y Perspectivas*. Lima: Instituto Cultural Runa. pp. 221–249.

—2005. *Territory and Identity in the Pre-Columbian Andes of Northern Peru* [dissertation]. Cambridge: Cambridge University, Department of Archaeology. 454 pp.

HERRERA, ALEXANDER, KEVIN LANE AND CAROLINA ORSINI, eds. 2006. *La Complejidad Social en la Sierra de Ancash*. Milan: Castello Sforzesco. 197 pp.

HOLLISTER, V. F. AND SIRVAS B. E. 1978. The Calipuy Formation of northern Peru, and its relation to volcanism in the Northern Andes. *Journal of Volcanology and Geothermal Research* 4:89–98.

HYSLOP, JOHN. 1990. *Inka Settlement Planning*. Austin: University of Texas Press. 377 pp.

IBARRA, BEBEL, ed. 2003a. *Arqueología de la Sierra de Ancash: Propuestas y Perspectivas*. Lima: Instituto Cultural Runa. 545 pp.

—2003b. Arqueología del Valle del Puchca: economía, cosmovisión y secuencia estilística. In: Bebel Ibarra, ed. *Arqueología de la Sierra de Ancash: Propuestas y Perspectivas*. Lima: Instituto Cultural Runa. pp. 251–330.

ISBELL, WILLIAM H. 1977. *The Rural Foundation for Urbanism: Economic and Stylistic Interaction between Rural and Urban Communities in Eighth-century Peru*. Urbana, IL: University of Illinois Press. 188 pp. (Illinois Studies in Anthropology 10.)

—1988a. Report on the 1987 research season, and an evaluation of Huari influence at the Peruvian North Highland archaeological site of Honcopampa. Paper presented at: 28th Annual Meeting of the Institute of Andean Studies; 1988 January 8–9; Berkeley, CA.

—1988b. City and state in Middle Horizon Huari. In: Richard W. Keatinge, ed. *Peruvian Prehistory*. Cambridge: Cambridge University Press. pp. 164–189.

—1989. Honcopampa: Was it a Huari administrative centre? In: Robert M. Czwarno, Frank M. Meddens and Alexandra Morgan, eds. *The Nature of Wari: A Reappraisal of the Middle Horizon in Peru*. Oxford: British Archaeological Reports. pp. 98–114. (BAR International Series 525.)

—1991a. Honcopampa: monumental ruins in Peru's North Highlands. *Expedition* 33(3): 27–36.

—1991b. Huari administration and the orthogonal cellular architecture horizon. In: William H. Isbell and Gordon F. McEwan, eds. *Huari Administrative Structure: Prehistoric Monumental Architecture and State Government*. Washington, DC: Dumbarton Oaks. pp. 397–315.

—1997. *Mummies and Mortuary Monuments.* Austin: University of Texas Press. 371 pp.

—2000. Repensando el Horizonte Medio: el caso de Conchopata, Ayacucho, Peru. *Boletín de Arqueología PUCP* 4:9–68.

—2001. Reflexiones finales. *Boletín de Arqueología PUCP* 5:455–479.

ISBELL, WILLIAM H. AND GORDON F. MCEWAN. 1991. A history of Huari studies and introduction to current interpretations. In: William H. Isbell and Gordon F. McEwan, eds. *Huari Administrative Structure: Prehistoric Monumental Architecture and State Government.* Washington, DC: Dumbarton Oaks. pp. 1–17.

ISBELL, WILLIAM H. AND KATHARINA J. SCHREIBER. 1978. Was Huari a state? *American Antiquity* 43:372–389.

JENNINGS, JUSTIN. 2006a. Cores, peripheries, and regional realities in Middle Horizon, Peru. *Journal of Anthropological Archaeology* 25:346–370.

—2006b. Understanding Middle Horizon Peru: hermeneutic spirals, interpretative traditions and Wari administrative centers. *Latin American Antiquity* 17:265–285.

JENNINGS, JUSTIN AND NATHAN CRAIG. 2001. Politywide analysis and imperial political economy: the relationship between valley political complexity and administrative centers in the Wari empire of the Central Andes. *Journal of Anthropological Archaeology* 20:479–502.

JULIEN, DANIEL G. 1988. *Ancient Cuismancu: Settlement and Cultural Dynamics in the Cajamarca Region of the North Highlands of Peru, 200 B.C-A.D. 1532* [dissertation]. Austin: University of Texas, Austin Department of Anthropology. 415 pp. Available from: ProQuest Dissertations & Theses [database online]; http://www.proquest.com (publication AAT 8909683).

KAUFFMANN DOIG, FEDERICO. 1956. Las ruinas de Chopijirca (Vicos, Ancash). *Revista del Museo Nacional* 25:120–139.

—1966. *Mochica-Nazca-Recuay en la Arqueología Peruana.* Lima: Universidad Nacional Mayor de San Marcos. 96 pp.

—1980. *Manual de Arqueología Peruana.* 7th ed. Lima: Ediciones PEISA. 800 pp.

KAULICKE, PETER, ed. 1997. *La Muerte en el Antiguo Peru: Contextos y Conceptos Funerarios.* Lima: Pontificia Universidad Católica del Peru. 387 pp. (Boletín de Arqueología PUC 1.)

KELLY, ISABEL T. 1930. Peruvian cumbrous bowls. *University of California Publications in American Archaeology and Ethnology* 24(6):325–341.

KING, ARDEN R. 1948. Tripod pottery in the Central Andean area. *American Antiquity* 2:103–116.

KNOBLOCH, PATRICIA J. 1983. *A Study of the Andean Huari Ceramics from the Early Intermediate Period to the Middle Horizon Epoch 1* [dissertation]. Binghamton, NY: State University of New York, Binghamton, Department of Anthropology. 436 pp. Available from: ProQuest Dissertations & Theses [database online]; http://www.proquest.com (publication AAT 8321223).

KOLATA, ALAN. 1993. *The Tiwanaku.* Cambridge, MA: Blackwell Publishers. 317 pp.

—1996. *Tiwanaku and Its Hinterland: Archaeology and Paleoecology of an Andean Civilization.* Volume 1, Agroecology. Washington, DC: Smithsonian Institution Press. 323 pp.

KROEBER, ALFRED L. 1925a. The Uhle pottery collections from Moche. *University of California Publications in American Archaeology and Ethnology* 21:191–234.

—1925b. The Uhle pottery collections from Supe. *University of California Publications in American Archaeology and Ethnology* 21:235–264.

—1926. Archaeological explorations in Peru, pt. I: ancient pottery from Trujillo. *Anthropological Memoirs, Field Museum of Natural History* 2(1):1–43.

—1930. Archaeological explorations in Peru, pt. 2: the Northern Coast. *Anthropological Memoirs, Field Museum of Natural History* 2(2):47–115.

—1944. *Peruvian Archeology in 1942*. New York: Viking Fund. 151 pp. (Viking Fund Publications in Anthropology 4.)

—1950. A local style of lifelike sculptured stone heads in ancient Peru. In: Ilse Tönnies, ed. *Beiträge zur Gesellungs-und Völkerwissenschaft: Professor Dr. Richard Thurnwald zu seinem achtzigsten Geburtstag gewidmet*. Berlin: Gebr. Mann. pp. 195–198.

Krzanowski, Andrzej. 1977. Yuraccama: the settlement complex in the Alto Chicama region (Northern Peru). In: Janusz Kozlowski, ed. *Polish Contributions in New World Archaeology, Part I*. Krakow: Polska Academia Nauk–Oddzial w Krakowie. pp. 29–58. (Prace Komisji Archeologicznej 16.)

—1986a. The cultural chronology of Northern Andes of Peru (the Huamachuco–Quiruvilca–Otuzco region). *Acta Archaeologica Carpathica* 25:231–264.

—1986b. Editor. *Cayash Prehispánico*. Krakow: Polska Academia Nauk–Oddzial w Krakowie. 227 pp. (Prace Komisji Archeologicznej 25.)

Krzanowski, Andrzej and Maciej Pawlikowski. 1980. North Peruvian ceramics in the aspect of petrographic analysis. In: Janusz Koslowski, ed. *Polish Contributions in New World Archaeology, Part II*. Krakow: Polska Academia Nauk–Oddzial w Krakowie, Komisja Archeologizna. pp. 63–101. (Prace Komisji Archeologicznej 19.)

Krzanowski, Andrzej and Krzysztof Tunia. 1986. Cerámica de la región Cayash. In: Andrzej Krzanowski, ed. *Cayash Prehispánico*. Krakow: Polska Academia Nauk–Oddzial w Krakowie. pp. 49–186. (Prace Komisji Archeologicznej 25.)

Lane, Kevin J. 2006. *Engineering the Puna: Hydraulics of Agro-pastoral Communities in a North Central Peruvian Valley* [dissertation]. Cambridge: Cambridge University, Department of Archaeology. 261 pp.

Lanning, Edward P. 1965. Current research: highland South America. *American Antiquity* 31:139–140.

—1967. *Peru Before the Incas*. Englewood Cliffs, NJ: Prentice-Hall. 216 pp.

Larco Hoyle, Rafael. 1948. *Cronología Arqueológica del Norte de Peru*. Buenos Aires: Sociedad Geográfica Americana. 87 pp.

—1960. La cultura Santa. In: Semana de Arqueología Peruana. *Antiguo Peru: Espacio y Tiempo; trabajos presentados a la Semana de Arqueología Peruana, 9–14 de noviembre de 1959*. Lima: Librería-Editorial Juan Mejía Baca. pp. 235–239.

—1962. *La Cultura Santa*. Lima: Litografía Valverde S.A. 29 pp.

Lau, George F. 2000. Espacio ceremonial Recuay. In: Krzysztof Makowski, ed. *Los Dioses del Antiguo Peru*. Lima: Banco de Crédito del Peru. pp. 178–197.

—2001. *The Ancient Community of Chinchawas: Economy and Ceremony in the North Highlands of Peru* [dissertation]. New Haven: Yale University, Department of Anthropology. 667 pp. Available from: ProQuest Dissertations & Theses [database online]; http://www.proquest.com (publication AAT 3007374).

—2002. Feasting and ancestor veneration at Chinchawas, North Highlands of Ancash, Peru. *Latin American Antiquity* 13:279–304.

—2004a. The Recuay Culture of Peru's North-central Highlands: a reevaluation of chronology and its implications. *Journal of Field Archaeology* 29:177–202.

—2004b. Object of contention: an examination of Recuay-Moche combat imagery. *Cambridge Archaeological Journal* 14:163–184.

—2005. Core–periphery relations in the Recuay hinterlands: economic interaction at Chinchawas. *Antiquity* 79:78–99.

—2006a. Northern exposures: Recuay-Cajamarca boundaries and interaction. In William H. Isbell and Helaine Silverman, eds. *Andean Archaeology III: North and South*. New York: Plenum/Kluwer Publishers. pp. 143–170.

—2006b. Recuay Tradition sculptures of Chinchawas, North Highlands of Ancash, Peru. *Zeitschrift für Archäeologie Aussereuropäischer Kulturen* 1:183–250.

—2007. Animal resources and Recuay cultural transformations at Chinchawas, North Highlands, Peru. *Andean Past* 8:449–476.

Lau, George F. and Gabriel Ramón. 2007. Yayno, cima del mundo: ciudadela fortificada de la tradición Recuay. *Gaceta Cultural del Peru* 27:26–28.

Laurencich, Laura and Steven Wegner, eds. 2001. *El Museo de Chacas*. Bologna: Editrice Compositori. 110 pp.

Lavallée, Danièle. 1970. Industrias líticas del Período Huaráz, procedentes de Chavín de Huántar. *Revista del Museo Nacional* 36:193–233.

Lechtman, Heather N. 1980. The Central Andes: metallurgy without iron. In: Theodore A. Wertime and James D. Muhly, eds. *The Coming of the Age of Iron*. New Haven: Yale University Press. pp. 267–334.

—2003. Tiwanaku period (Middle Horizon) bronze metallurgy in the Lake Titicaca Basin. In: Alan L. Kolata, ed. *Tiwanaku and Its Hinterland: Archaeology and Paleoecology of an Andean Civilization*. Volume 2, Urban and Rural Archaeology. Washington, DC: Smithsonian Institution Press. pp. 404–434.

Leonard, Banks S. and Glenn S. Russell. 1993. Cerámica Cajamarca de la parte baja del Valle de Chicama. In: Segundo Arréstegui, ed. *IX Congreso Peruano del Hombre y la Cultura Andina: Cajamarca-perú, 2-6 junio 1992*. Cajamarca, Peru: Universidad Nacional de Cajamarca. pp. 151–166.

Lumbreras, Luis G. 1960. La cultura de Wari, Ayacucho. *Etnología y Arqueología* 1:130–227.

—1970. *Los templos de Chavín: Guia para el Visitante*. Lima: Corporación Peruana de Santa. 165 pp.

—1974a. *The Peoples and Cultures of Ancient Peru*. Washington, DC: Smithsonian Institution Press. 248 pp.

—1974b. *Las Fundaciones de Huamanga*. Lima: Editorial Nueva Edición. 238 pp.

—1974c. Informe de labores del Proyecto Chavín. *Arqueológicas* 15:37–55.

—1977. Excavaciones en el templo antiguo de Chavín (sector R): informe de la sexta campaña. *Ñawpa Pacha* 15:1–38.

—1989. *Chavín de Huántar en el Nacimiento de la Civilización Andina*. Lima: INDEA. 245 pp.

Lynch, Thomas F. 1970. *Excavations at Quishqui Puncu in the Callejón de Huaylas, Peru*. Pocatello, ID: Idaho State University Museum. 61 pp. (Occasional Papers of the Idaho State University Museum 26.)

—1971. Preceramic transhumance in the Callejon de Huaylas, Peru. *American Antiquity* 36:139–48.

—1977. Current research: Andean South America. *American Antiquity* 42:284–286.

—1980. Editor. *Guitarrero Cave: Early Man in the Andes*. New York: Academic Press. 328 pp.

MacEachern, Scott, David J. W. Archer and Richard D. Garvin, eds. 1989. *Households and Communities*. Calgary, Alberta, Canada: University of Calgary Archaeological Association. 550 pp.

MACKEY, CAROL J. 1982. The Middle Horizon as viewed from the Moche Valley. In: Michael E. Moseley and Kent C. Day, eds. *Chan Chan: Andean Desert City*. Albuquerque: University of New Mexico Press. pp. 321–332.

MACKEY, CAROL J. AND MELISSA VOGEL. 2003. La Luna sobre los Andes: una revisión del animal lunar. In: Santiago Uceda and Elias Mujíca, eds. *Moche: Hacia el Final del Milenio*. Volume 1. Lima: Pontificia Universidad Católica del Peru. pp. 325–342.

MAKOWSKI, KRZYSZTOF, ed. 1994. *Vicús*. Lima: Banco de Crédito. 381 pp.

MAKOWSKI, KRZYSZTOF AND JULIO RUCABADO YONG. 2000. Hombres y deidades en la iconografía Recuay. In: Krzysztof Makowski, ed. *Los Dioses del Antiguo Peru*. Lima: Banco de Crédito. pp. 199–235.

MALPASS, MICHAEL. 1983. The Preceramic Occupations of the Casma Valley, Peru [dissertation]. Madison, WI: University of Wisconsin, Department of Anthropology. 281 pp. Available from: ProQuest Dissertations & Theses [database online]; http://www.proquest.com (publication AAT 8316223).

—1985. Two Preceramic and Formative occupations in the Cordillera Negra: preliminary report. In: Daniel H. Sandweiss and D. Peter Kvietok, eds. *Recent Studies in Andean Prehistory and Protohistory*. Ithaca, NY: Cornell Latin American Studies Program. pp. 15–40.

MANRIQUE P., ELBA. 1999. Textilería Recuay. In: José Antonio de Lavalle and Rosario de Lavalle de Cárdenas, eds. *Tejidos Milenarios del Peru*. Lima: AFP Integra. pp. 251–258.

MATSUMOTO, RYOZO. 1988. The Cajamarca Culture: its evolution and interaction with coastal peer polities. Paper presented at: 53rd Annual Meeting of the Society for American Archaeology; 1988 April 27–May 1; Phoenix, AZ.

—1994. Dos modos de proceso sociocultural: el Horizonte Temprano y el Periodo Intermedio Temprano en el valle de Cajamarca. In: Luis Millones and Yoshio Onuki, eds. *El Mundo Ceremonial Andino*. Lima: Editorial Horizonte. pp. 167–197.

MAYER, ENRIQUE. 2002. *The Articulated Peasant: Household Economies in the Andes*. Boulder, CO: Westview Press. 390 pp.

MCCOWN, THEODORE D. 1945. Pre-Incaic Huamachuco: survey and excavations in the region of Huamachuco and Cajabamba. *University of California Publications in American Archaeology and Ethnology* 39(4):223–399.

MCEWAN, GORDON F. 1984. *The Middle Horizon in the Valley of Cuzco, Peru: The Impact of the Wari Occupation of Pikillacta in the Lucre Basin (Andes)* [dissertation]. Austin: University of Texas, Department of Anthropology. 311 pp. Available from: ProQuest Dissertations & Theses [database online]; http://www.proquest.com (publication AAT 8508311).

—1996. Archaeological investigations at Pikillacta, a Wari site in Peru. *Journal of Field Archaeology* 23:169–186.

—2005. ed. *Pikillacta: The Wari Empire in Cuzco*. Iowa City: University of Iowa Press. 182 pp.

MEDDENS, FRANK M. 1985. *The Chicha/Soras Valley during the Middle Horizon: Provincial Aspects of Wari* [dissertation]. London: University College London, Institute of Archaeology. 397 pp.

MEDDENS, FRANK AND ANITA G. COOK. 2001. La administración Wari y el culto a los muertos: Yako, los edificios en forma "D" en la sierra sur-central del Peru. In: Pedro Bazán, ed. *Wari: Arte Precolombino Peruano*. Lima: Fundación El Monte. pp. 213–228.

MEJÍA XESSPE, TORIBIO. 1941. Walun y Chinchawas: dos nuevos sitios en la Cordillera Negra. *Chaski* 1(1):18–24.

—1948 Jan 7. Soterrados de Katak. *El Comercio.*

—1957. Chullpas precolombinas en el área andina. *Revista de la Universidad Nacional de la Plata* 2:101–108.

—1965–1966. Técnica negativa en la decoración de la cerámica peruana. *Revista del Museo Nacional* 34:28–32.

MENZEL, DOROTHY. 1964. Style and time in the Middle Horizon. *Ñawpa Pacha* 2:1–105.

—1968. New data on the Huari Empire in Middle Horizon Epoch 2A. *Ñawpa Pacha* 6:47–114.

—1977. *The Archaeology of Ancient Peru and the Work of Max Uhle.* Berkeley: University of California, Berkeley, Lowie Museum of Anthropology. 135 pp.

MIDDENDORF, ERNST W. [1893–1895]. *Peru: Beobachtungen und Studien über das Land und seine Bewohner während eines 25 Jährigen Aufenthalts.* Berlin: R. Oppenheim. 3 volumes.

MILLER, GEORGE R. 1979. *An Introduction to the Ethnoarchaeology of the Andean Camelids* [dissertation]. Berkeley: University of California, Berkeley, Department of Anthropology. 319 pp. Available from: ProQuest Dissertations & Theses [database online]; http://www.proquest.com (publication AAT 8014808).

—2003. Food for the dead, tools for the afterlife: zooarchaeology at Machu Picchu. In: Richard L. Burger and Lucy C. Salazar, eds. *The 1912 Yale Peruvian Scientific Collections from Machu Picchu: Human and Animal Remains.* New Haven: Yale University, Department of Anthropology, and Peabody Museum of Natural History. pp. 1–63. (Yale University Publications in Anthropology 85.)

MILLER, GEORGE R. AND RICHARD L. BURGER. 1995. Our father the cayman, our dinner the llama: animal utilization at Chavín de Huántar, Peru. *American Antiquity* 60:421–458.

MILLONES, LUIS. 1979. Religion and power in the Andes: idolatrous curacas of the Central Sierra. *Ethnohistory* 26:243–263.

MONTENEGRO C., JORGE. 1993. El estilo Cajamarca Costeño: una aproximación. In: Segundo Arréstegui, ed. *IX Congreso Peruano del Hombre y la Cultura Andina: Cajamarca-perú, 2-6 junio 1992.* Cajamarca, Peru: Universidad Nacional de Cajamarca. pp. 137–150.

MONTOYA VERA, MARIA DEL ROSARIO. 1989. Estudio preliminar sobre uso del espacio en un asentamiento Recuay y secuencia ocupacional: Sitio VS 103:6 Quebrada El Silencio, Valle Medio del Santa: informe final [research report]. Trujillo, Peru: Universidad Nacional de Trujillo, Facultad de Ciencias Sociales. 65 pp.

MORRIS, CRAIG. 1979. Maize beer in the economics, politics, and religion of the Inca Empire. In: Clifford Gastineau, William Darby and Thomas Turner, eds. *Fermented Food Beverages in Nutrition.* New York: Academic Press. pp. 21–34.

MORRIS, CRAIG AND DONALD E. THOMPSON. 1985. *Huánuco Pampa: An Inca City and its Hinterland.* London: Thames and Hudson. 181 pp.

MOSELEY, MICHAEL E. 1975. Prehistoric principles of labor organization in the Moche Valley, Peru. *American Antiquity* 40:191–196.

—1983. The good old days were better: agrarian collapse and tectonics. *American Anthropologist* 85:773–799.

—1992. *The Incas and their Ancestors.* London: Thames and Hudson. 272 pp.

—1999. Preposterism: oxymorons of post-modern prehistory. *Review of Archaeology* 20:1–11.

MURRA, JOHN V. 1980. *The Economic Organization of the Inka State.* Greenwich, CT: JAI Press. 208 pp.

OAKLAND RODMAN, AMY AND ARABEL FERNANDEZ. 2000. Huari and Tiwanaku textiles: comparisons and contexts. *Boletín de Arqueología PUCP* 4:119–30.

[ONERN] OFICINA NACIONAL DE EVALUACIÓN DE RECURSOS NATURALES, PERU. 1972. *Inventario, Evaluación y Uso Racional de los Recursos Naturales de la Costa: Cuencas de los Ríos Casma, Culebras y Huarmey*. Lima: República del Perú, Presidencia de la República, ONERN. 445 pp. (Estudios ONERN 36.)

—1973. *Estudio de suelos del Callejón de Huaylas*. Lima: República del Perú, Presidencia de la República, ONERN y Comisión de Reconstrucción y Rehabilitación de la Zona Afectada. 140 pp.

OFFLER, R., L. AGUIRRE, B. LEVI AND S. CHILD. 1980. Burial metamorphism in rocks of the Western Andes of Peru. *Lithos* 13(1):31–42.

ONUKI, YOSHIO. 1998. Ocho tumbas especiales de Kuntur Wasi. *Boletín de Arqueología PUC* 1:79–114.

ORSINI, CAROLINA. 2003. Transformaciones culturales durante el Intermedio Temprano el valle de Chacas: hacia el desarrollo de asentamientos complejos en un área de la sierra nor-central del Peru. In: Bebel Ibarra, ed. *Arqueología de la Sierra de Ancash: Propuestas y Perspectivas*. Lima: Instituto Cultural Runa. pp. 161–174.

—2007. *Pastori e Guerrieri: I Recuay, un Popolo Preispanico delle Ande del Peru*. Milan: Jaca Books. 159 pp.

PAREDES, JUAN. 2005. Redescubriendo Willkawaín e Ichic Willkawaín. *Boletín Informativo Mensual* 3(2):2–3.

PAREDES, JUAN, BERENICE QUINTANA AND MOISÉS LINARES. 2000. Tumbas de la época Wari en el Callejón de Huaylas. *Boletín de Arqueología PUC* 4:253–288.

PATTERSON, THOMAS C. 1966. *Pattern and Process in the Early Intermediate Period Pottery of the Central Coast of Peru*. Berkeley: University of California Press. 180 pp. (University of California Publications in Anthropology 3.)

—1971. Chavín: an interpretation of its spread and influence. In: Elizabeth P. Benson, ed. *Dumbarton Oaks Conference on Chavín*. Washington, DC: Dumbarton Oaks. pp. 29–48.

PAULSEN, ALLISON C. 1974. The thorny oyster and voice of God: *Spondylus* and *Strombus* in Andean prehistory. *American Antiquity* 39:597–607.

PILLSBURY, JOANNE, ed. 2001. *Moche Art and Archaeology in Ancient Peru*. Washington, DC: National Gallery of Art. 343 pp. (Studies in the History of Art 63.)

PONTE ROSALINO, VICTOR M. 1999a. Análisis de los asentamientos arqueológicos en el área de influencia de la Mina Pierina. Huaraz, Peru: Mina Pierina. Report submitted to Mina Barrick Misquichilca and Instituto Nacional de Cultura.

—1999b. Excavaciones arqueológicas en el área de Marenayoc. Huaraz, Peru: Report submitted to Mina Barrick Misquichilca and Instituto Nacional de Cultura.

—2000. Transformación social y política en el Callejón de Huaylas, siglos III–X d.C. *Boletín de Arqueología PUCP* 4:217–252.

PORTER, KATHERINE N. 1992. Recuay style painted textile. *Textile Museum Journal* 31:71–81.

POZORSKI, SHELIA AND THOMAS POZORSKI. 1987a. Chavín, the Early Horizon and the Initial Period. In: Jonathan Haas, Shelia Pozorski and Thomas Pozorski, eds. *The Origins and Development of the Andean State*. Cambridge: Cambridge University Press. pp. 36–46.

—1987b. Early Settlement and Subsistence in the Casma Valley, Peru. Iowa City: University of Iowa Press. 149 pp.

POZZI-ESCOT, DENISE. 1999. Una visión de contexto. In: Denise Pozzi-Escot, Marleni Alarcón and Cirilo Vivanco, eds. *Etnografía Alfarera Wari: Los Artesanos de Conchopata*. Ayacucho: Universidad Nacional de San Cristóbal de Huamanga. pp. 10–32.

Proulx, Donald A. 1968. *An Archaeological Study of the Nepeña Valley, Peru*. Amherst, MA: University of Massachusetts, Department of Anthropology. 189 pp. (Research Report 2.)

—1973. *Archaeological Investigations in the Nepeña Valley, Peru*. Amherst, MA: University of Massachusetts, Department of Anthropology. 292 pp. (Research Report 13.)

—1982. Territoriality in the Early Intermediate Period: the case of Moche and Recuay. *Ñawpa Pacha* 20:83–96.

—1985. *An Analysis of the Early Cultural Sequence in the Nepeña Valley, Peru*. Amherst, MA: University of Massachusetts, Department of Anthropology. 359 pp. (Research Report 25.)

Pulgar Vidal, Javier. 1972. *La Geografía del Peru: Los Ocho Regiones Naturales del Peru*. Lima: Editorial Universo. 256 pp.

Raimondi, Antonio. 1873. *El Departamento de Ancachs y sus Riquezas Minerales*. Lima: Imprenta El Nacional. 651 pp.

Rasnake, Roger. 1988. *Domination and Cultural Resistance: Authority and Power among an Andean People*. Durham, NC: Duke University Press. 321 pp.

Ravines, Rogger. 1968. Un depósito de ofrendas del Horizonte Medio en la sierra central del Peru. *Ñawpa Pacha* 6:19–46.

—1977. Excavaciones en Ayapata, Huancavelica, Peru. *Ñawpa Pacha* 15:49–100.

—1982a. *Arqueología del Valle Medio del Jequetepeque*. Lima: Proyecto de Rescate Arqueológico Jequetepeque, Instituto Nacional de Cultura, Lima. 225 pp.

—1982b. *Panorama de la Arqueología Andina*. Lima: Instituto de Estudios Peruanos. 334 pp.

Reichert, Raphael X. 1977a. *The Recuay Ceramic Style—A Re-evaluation* [dissertation]. Los Angeles: University of California, Los Angeles, Department of Art History. 372 pp. Available from: ProQuest Dissertations & Theses [database online]; http://www.proquest.com (publication AAT 7719644).

—1977b. Pre–Columbian ceramics: the problem of partial counterfeits. In: Alana Cordy-Collins and Jean Stern, eds. *Pre-Columbian Art History: Selected Readings*. Palo Alto, CA: Peek Publications. pp. 393–406.

—1982a. Moche iconography—the highland connection. In: Alana Cordy-Collins, ed. *Pre-Columbian Art History: Selected Readings*. Palo Alto, CA: Peek Publications. pp. 279–291.

—1982b. A counterfeit Moche-Recuay vessel and its origins. In: Elizabeth Boone, ed. *Falsifications and Misreconstructions of Pre-Columbian Art*. Washington, DC: Dumbarton Oaks. pp. 51–62.

—1989. A Moche battle and the question of identity. In: Diana C. Tkaczuk and Brian C. Vivian, eds. *Cultures in Conflict: Current Archaeological Perspectives*. Calgary, Alberta, Canada: University of Calgary Archaeological Association. pp. 86–89.

Reichlen, Henry and Paule Reichlen. 1949. Recherches archeologiques dans les Andes de Cajamarca. *Journal de la Société des Américanistes de Paris* 38:137–174.

Rice, Prudence. 1987. *Pottery Analysis: A Sourcebook*. Chicago: University of Chicago Press. 559 pp.

Rowe, John H. 1944. *An Introduction to the Archaeology of Cuzco*. Cambridge, MA: Peabody Museum of Archaeology and Ethnology. 69 pp. (Papers of the Peabody Museum of Archaeology and Ethnology 27(2).)

—1946. Inca culture at the time of the Spanish Conquest. In: Julian H. Steward, ed. *Handbook of South American Indians*. Volume 2: The Andean Civilizations. Washington, DC: US Government Printing Office. pp. 183–330. (Bulletin, Smithsonian Institution, Bureau of American Ethnology Bulletin 143.)

—1956. Archaeological explorations in southern Peru. *American Antiquity* 22:120–137.

—1962. Stages and periods in archaeological interpretation. *Southwestern Journal of Anthropology* 18(1):40–54.

—1961. Stratigraphy and seriation. *American Antiquity* 26:324–330.

—1967. Form and meaning in Chavín art. In: John H. Rowe and Dorothy Menzel, eds. *Peruvian Archaeology: Selected Readings*. Palo Alto, CA: Peek Publications. pp. 72–103.

Rowe, John H. and Dorothy Menzel, eds. 1967. *Peruvian Archaeology: Selected Readings*. Palo Alto, CA: Peek Publications. 320 pp.

Rucabado Yong, Julio and Luis Jaime Castillo. 2003. El período Transicional en San José de Moro. In: Santiago Uceda and Elías Mujica, eds. *Moche: Hacia el Final del Milenio*. Volume 1. Lima: Pontificia Universidad Católica del Peru. pp. 15–42.

Salomon, Frank. 1991. Introductory essay: the Huarochirí manuscript. In: Frank Salomon and George Urioste, eds. *The Huarochirí Manuscript: A Testament of Ancient and Colonial Religion*. Austin: University of Texas Press. pp. 1–38.

—1995. "Beautiful grandparents": Andean ancestor shrines and mortuary ritual as seen through colonial records. In: Tom Dillehay, ed. *Tombs for the Living: Andean Mortuary Practices*. Washington, DC: Dumbarton Oaks. pp. 315–353.

Sawyer, Michael J. 1985. *An Analysis of Mammalian Faunal Remains from the Site of Huaricoto, PAN3-35* [master's thesis]. Hayward: California State University, Hayward, Department of Anthropology. 139 pp.

Schaedel, Richard P. 1948a. Stone sculpture in the Callejón de Huaylas. In: Wendell C. Bennett, ed. *A Reappraisal of Peruvian Archaeology*. Menasha, WI: Society for American Archaeology. pp. 66–79. (Memoirs of the Society for American Archaeology 4.)

—1948b. The Callejón de Huaylas of Peru and its monuments. *Archaeology* 1(4):198–202.

—1952. *An Analysis of Central Andean Stone Sculpture* [dissertation]. New Haven: Yale University, Department of Anthropology. 495 pp. Available from: ProQuest Dissertations & Theses [database online]; http://www.proquest.com (publication AAT 6612635).

—1966. Incipient urbanization and secularization in Tiahuanacoid Peru. *American Antiquity* 31:338–344.

—1993. Congruence of horizon with polity: Huari and the Middle Horizon. In: Don S. Rice, ed. *Latin American Horizons*. Washington, DC: Dumbarton Oaks. pp. 225–262.

Schindler, Helmut. 2000. *The Norbert Mayrock Art Collection from Ancient Peru*. [Munich]: Staatliche Museum für Völkerkunde München. 384 pp.

Schreiber, Katharina J. 1992. *Wari Imperialism in Middle Horizon Peru*. Ann Arbor: University of Michigan Museum of Anthropology. 332 pp. (Museum of Anthropology Anthropological Papers 87.)

—2001. The Wari empire of Middle Horizon Peru: the epistemological challenge of documenting an empire without documentary evidence. In: Susan Alcock, Terence D'Altroy, Kathleen Morrison and Carla Sinopoli, eds. *Empires: Perspectives from Archaeology and History*. New York: Cambridge University Press. pp. 70–92.

—2004. Sacred landscapes and imperial ideologies: the Wari empire in Sondondo, Peru. In: Kevin Vaughn, Dennis Ogburn and Christina Conlee, eds. *Foundations of Power in the Prehispanic Andes*. Arlington, VA: American Anthropological Association. pp. 131–150.

—2005. Imperial agendas and local agency: Wari colonial strategies. In: Gil Stein, ed. *The Archaeology of Colonial Encounters: Comparative Perspectives*. Santa Fe, NM: School of American Research. pp. 237–262.

Schuler-Schömig, Immina von. 1979. Die "Fremdkrieger" in Darstellungen der Moche-Keramik. Eine ikonographische Studie. *Baessler Archiv, Neue Folge* 27:135–213.

Schwartz, Glenn M. and Steven E. Falconer. 1994. Rural approaches to social complexity. In: Glenn M. Schwartz and Steven E. Falconer, eds. *Archaeological Views from the Countryside: Village Communities in Early Complex Societies*. Washington, DC: Smithsonian Institution Press. pp. 1–9.

Shady, Ruth. 1982. La cultura Nievería y la interacción social en el mundo andino en la época Huari. *Arqueológicas* 19:5–108.

—1988. La época Huari como interacción de las sociedades regionales. *Revista Andina* 6 (1):67–99.

—1989. Cambios significativos occuridos en el mundo andino. In: R. Michael Czwarno, Frank M. Meddens and Alexandra Morgan, eds. *The Nature of Wari: A Reappraisal of the Middle Horizon Period in Peru*. Oxford: British Archaeological Reports. pp. 146–165. (BAR International Series 525.)

Shady, Ruth and Hermilio Rosas. 1976. *Enterramientos en chullpas de Chota (Cajamarca)*. Lima: Museo Nacional de Antropología y Arqueología. 35 pp.

Sherbondy, Jeannette E. 1992. Water ideology in Inka ethnogenesis. In: Robert Dover, Katharine Seibold and John McDowell, eds. *Andean Cosmologies through Time: Persistence and Emergence*. Bloomington: Indiana University Press. pp. 46–66.

Shimada, Izumi. 1987. Horizontal and vertical dimensions of prehistoric states in north Peru. In: Jonathan Haas, Shelia Pozorski and Thomas Pozorski, eds. *The Origins and Development of the Andean State*. Cambridge: Cambridge University Press. pp. 130–144.

—1994. *Pampa Grande and the Mochica Culture*. Austin: University of Texas Press. 323 pp.

Shimada, Izumi, Crystal B. Schaff, Lonnie G. Thompson and Ellen Mosley-Thompson. 1991. Cultural impacts of severe droughts in the prehistoric Andes: application of a 1,500 year ice core precipitation record. *World Archaeology* 22:247–270.

Sievers, Wilhelm. 1914. *Reise in Peru und Ecuador, Ausgeführt 1909*. Munich and Leipzig: Duncker and Humblot. 411 pp.

Silverman, Helaine. 1993. *Cahuachi in the Ancient Nasca World*. Iowa City: University of Iowa Press. 371 pp.

Silverman, Helaine and Donald A. Proulx. 2002. *The Nasca*. Malden, MA: Blackwell. 339 pp.

Smith, John W. Jr. 1977. Recuay gaming boards: a preliminary study. *Indiana* 4:111–137.

—1978. *The Recuay Culture: A Reconstruction Based on Artistic Motifs* [dissertation]. Austin: University of Texas, Austin, Department of Anthropology. 377 pp. Available from: ProQuest Dissertations & Theses [database online]; http://www.proquest.com (publication AAT 7900636.)

Soriano Infante, Augusto. 1940. Algo sobre la arqueología de Ancash. In: *Actas y Trabajos Científicos del XXVII Congreso Internacional de Americanistas*, Volume 1 [Proceedings and Scientific Works of the 27th International Congress of Americanists]; 2nd session, Lima, Peru; 1939. Lima: International Congress of Americanists. pp. 473–483.

—1941. Monografía de Ancash, Nepeña (Provincia de Santa). *Revista del Museo Nacional* 10(2):263–277.

STANISH, CHARLES. 1992. *Ancient Andean Political Economy*. Austin: University of Texas Press. 195 pp.

—2003. *Ancient Titicaca: The Evolution of Complex Society in Southern Peru and Northern Bolivia*. Berkeley: University of California Press. 354 pp.

STERN, STEVE J., ed. 1987. *Resistance, Rebellion, and Consciousness in the Andean Peasant World: Eighteenth to Twentieth Centuries*. Madison: University of Wisconsin Press. 446 pp.

STRONG, WILLIAM D. 1925. The Uhle Pottery Collections from Ancón. *University of California Publications in American Archaeology and Ethnology* 21:135–190.

STRONG, WILLIAM D. AND CLIFFORD EVANS. 1952. *Cultural Stratigraphy in the Virú Valley, Northern Peru: The Formative and Florescent Epochs*. New York: Columbia University Press. 373 pp. (Columbia Studies in Archeology and Ethnology 4.)

STUIVER, MINZE AND REIMER, PAULA J. 1993. Extended $^{14}$C data base and revised CALIB 3.0 $^{14}$C age calibration program. *Radiocarbon* 35(1):215–230. Available from: http://calib.qub.ac.uk/calib/

TELLO, JULIO C. 1923. Wira Kocha. *Inca* 1(1):93–320; 1(3):583–606.

—1929. *Antiguo Perú: Primera Época*. Lima: Comisión Organizadora del Segundo Congreso de Turismo. 183 pp.

—1930. Andean civilization: some problems of Peruvian archaeology. In: IAC. *Proceedings of the 23rd International Congress of Americanists*; New York, NY, USA; 1928. New York: Science Press Co. pp. 259–290.

—1940. Origen y desarrollo de las civilizaciones prehistóricas andinas. In: *Actas y Trabajos Científicos del XXVII Congreso Internacional de Americanistas*, Volume 1 [Proceedings and Scientific Works of the 27th International Congress of Americanists]; 2nd session, Lima, Peru; 1939. Volume 1. Lima: International Congress of Americanists. pp. 589–720.

—1942. *Origen y desarrollo de las civilizaciones prehistóricas andinas*. Lima: Librería e Imprenta Gil, S.A. 132 pp.

—1956. *Arqueología del Valle de Casma*. Lima: Editorial San Marcos. 344 pp. (Universidad Nacional Mayor de San Marcos, Publicación Antropológica del Archivo "Julio C. Tello" 1.)

—1960. *Chavín: Cultura Matriz de la Civilización Andina*. Lima: Impr. de la Universidad de San Marcos. 425 pp. (Universidad Nacional Mayor de San Marcos, Publicación Antropológica del Archivo "Julio C. Tello" 2.)

TERADA, KAZUO. 1979. *Excavations at La Pampa in the North Highlands of Peru, 1975*. Tokyo: University of Tokyo Press. 194 pp.

TERADA, KAZUO AND RYOZO MATSUMOTO. 1985. Sobre la cronología de la tradición Cajamarca. In: Fernando Silva Santiesteban, Waldemar Espinoza Soriano and Rogger Ravines, eds. *Historia del Cajamarca*. Cajamarca, Peru: Instituto Nacional de Cultura, Cajamarca. pp. 67–89.

TERADA, KAZUO AND YOSHIO ONUKI. 1982. *Excavations at Huacaloma in the Cajamarca Valley, Peru, 1979*. Tokyo: University of Tokyo Press. 351 pp.

—1985. *The Formative Period in the Cajamarca Basin, Peru: Excavations at Huacaloma and Layzón, 1982*. Tokyo: University of Tokyo Press. 345 pp.

THATCHER, JOHN P. 1972. *Continuity and Change in the Ceramics of Huamachuco, North Highlands, Peru* [dissertation]. Philadelphia: University of Pennsylvania, Department of Anthropology. 272 pp. Available from: ProQuest Dissertations & Theses [database online]; http://www.proquest.com (publication AAT 7225679).

—1975. Early Intermediate Period and Middle Horizon 1B ceramic assemblages of Huamachuco, North Highlands, Peru. *Ñawpa Pacha* 10–12:109–127.

—1977. A Middle Horizon 1B cache from Huamachuco, North Highlands, Peru. *Ñawpa Pacha* 15:101–110.

—1979. Early ceramic assemblages from Huamachuco, North Highlands, Peru. *Ñawpa Pacha* 17:91–106.

THOMAS, NICHOLAS. 1991. *Entangled Objects*. Cambridge: Harvard University Press. 259 pp.

THOMPSON, DONALD E. 1962. The problem of dating certain stone-faced, stepped pyramids on the north coast of Peru. *Southwestern Journal of Anthropology* 18(4):291–301

THOMPSON, DONALD E. AND ROGGER RAVINES. 1973. Tinyash: a prehispanic village in the Andean puna. *Archaeology* 26(2):94–100.

THOMPSON, LONNIE G. 2001. Huascarán, Peru Ice Core Data [internet]. IGBP PAGES/World Data Center for Paleoclimatology Data Contribution Series #2001–008. Boulder, CO: NOAA/National Climate Data Center Paleoclimatology Program; [accessed 2001 October]. Available from: http://www.ngdc.noaa.gov/paleo/icecore/trop/huascaran/huascaran_data.html

THOMPSON, LONNIE G. AND ELLEN MOSLEY-THOMPSON. 1987. Evidence of abrupt climatic change during the last 1500 years recorded in ice-cores from the tropical Quelccaya ice cap. In: Wolf H. Berger and Laurent D. Labeyrie, eds. *Abrupt Climate Change*. Norwell, MA: D. Reidel. pp. 99–110. (NATO ASI Series C, Volume 216.)

—1989. One-half millennia of tropical climate variability as recorded in the stratigraphy of the Quelccaya ice cap, Peru. *Geophysical Monograph* 55:15–31.

THOMPSON, LONNIE G., ELLEN MOSLEY-THOMPSON, WILLI DANSGAARD AND PIETER GROOTES. 1986. The Little Ice Age as recorded in the stratigraphy of the tropical Quelccaya ice cap. *Science* 234:361–364.

THOMPSON, LONNIE G., ELLEN MOSLEY-THOMPSON, MARY E. DAVIS, PING-NAN LIN, KEITH A. HENDERSON, JIHONG COLE-DAI, JOHN F. BOLZAN AND KAM-BIU LIU. 1995. Late glacial stage and Holocene ice core records from Huascarán, Peru. *Science* 269:46–50.

THOMPSON, LONNIE G., ELLEN MOSLEY-THOMPSON, MARY E. DAVIS, PING-NAN LIN, KEITH A. HENDERSON AND TRACY A. MASHIOTTA. 2003. Tropical glacier and ice core evidence of climate change on annual and millennial time scales. *Climate Change* 59:37–155.

THOMPSON, LONNIE G., ELLEN MOSLEY-THOMPSON, PIETER GROOTES, MICHEL POURCHET AND STEFAN HASTENRATH. 1984. Tropical glaciers: potential for ice-core paleoclimatic reconstructions. *Journal of Geophysical Research* 89(D3):4638–4646.

THOMPSON, LONNIE G., ELLEN MOSLEY-THOMPSON AND P. A. THOMPSON. 1992. Reconstructing interannual climatic variability from tropical and subtropical ice-core records. In: Henry F. Diaz and Vera Markgraf, eds. *El Niño: Historical and Paleoclimatic Aspects of Southern Oscillation*. Cambridge: Cambridge University Press. pp. 295–322.

TOPIC, JOHN R. 1991. Huari and Huamachuco. In: William H. Isbell and Gordon F. McEwan, eds. *Huari Administrative Structure: Prehistoric Monumental Architecture and State Government*. Washington, DC: Dumbarton Oaks. pp. 141–164.

—1998. Ethnogenesis in Huamachuco. *Andean Past* 5:109–127.

TOPIC, JOHN R. AND THERESA L. TOPIC. 1978. Prehistoric fortification systems in northern Peru. *Current Anthropology* 19:618–619.

—1983. Coast-highland relations in northern Peru: some observations on routes, networks, and scales of interaction. In: Richard Leventhal and Alan Kolata, eds. *Civilization in the Ancient Americas*. Albuquerque: University of New Mexico Press. pp. 237–259.

—1985. El Horizonte Medio en Huamachuco. *Revista del Museo Nacional* 47:13–52.

—1987. The archaeological investigation of Andean militarism: some cautionary observations. In: Jonathan Haas, Shelia Pozorski and Thomas Pozorski, eds. *The Origins and Development of the Andean State*. Cambridge: Cambridge University Press. pp. 47–55.

—1992. The rise and decline of Cerro Amaru: an Andean shrine during the Early Intermediate Period and Middle Horizon. In: A. Sean Goldsmith, Sandra Garvie, David Selin and Jeannette Smith, eds. *Ancient Images, Ancient Thought: The Archaeology of Ideology*. Calgary, Alberta, Canada: University of Calgary Archaeological Association. pp. 167–180.

—2000. Hacia la comprensión del fenómeno Huari: una perspectiva norteña. *Boletín de Arqueología PUCP* 4:181–217.

TOPIC, THERESA L. 1982. The Early Intermediate Period and its legacy. In: Michael E. Moseley and Kent C. Day, eds. *Chan Chan: Andean Desert City*. Albuquerque: University of New Mexico Press. pp. 255–284.

—1985. The kaolin ceramic tradition in the Northern Sierra. Paper presented at: Fourth Annual Meeting of the Northeast Conference on Andean Archaeology and Ethnohistory; 1985 November 2–3; State University of New York, Albany, NY.

—1991. The Middle Horizon in northern Peru. In: William H. Isbell and Gordon F. McEwan, eds. *Huari Administrative Structure: Prehistoric Monumental Architecture and State Government*. Washington, DC, Dumbarton Oaks. pp. 233–246.

TOPIC, THERESA L. AND JOHN R. TOPIC. 1984. *Huamachuco Archaeological Project: Preliminary Report of the Third Season, June–August 1983*. Peterborough, Ontario, Canada: Trent University. 80 pp. (Trent University Occasional Papers in Anthropology 1.)

TOSI, JOSEPH A. JR. 1960. *Zonas de vida natural en el Peru*. Lima: Instituto de Ciencias Agrícolas de la OEA. 207 pp. (Zona Andina, Boletín Técnico 5.)

TSCHAUNER, HARTMUT. 2003. Honco Pampa: arquitectura de élite del Horizonte Medio del Callejón de Huaylas. In: Bebel Ibarra, ed. *Arqueología de la Sierra de Ancash: Propuestas y Perspectivas*. Lima: Instituto Cultural Runa. pp. 193–220.

UCEDA, SANTIAGO AND ELÍAS MUJICA, eds. 1994. *Moche: Propuestas y Perspectivas*. Lima: l'Institut Francais d'Etudes Andines 79. 549 pp. (Travaux de l'Institut Francais d'Etudes Andines 79.)

UHLE, MAX. 1903. *Pachacamac: Report of the William Pepper, M.D., L.L.D., Peruvian Expedition of 1896*. Philadelphia: Department of Archaeology of the University of Pennsylvania. 103 pp.

VARÓN GABAI, RAFAEL. 1980. *Curacas y Encomenderos: Acomodamiento Nativo en Huaraz, siglos XVI y XVII*. Lima: P. L. Villanueva. 103 pp.

WEGNER, STEVEN A. 1982. Hacia una definición de la cultura Recuay. *Serie Investigaciones* 5:1–8.

—1988. *Cultura Recuay*. Lima: Banco Continental and Museo Arqueológico de Ancash. 9 pp. (Exhibition, Lima, September–October 1988.)

—2000. *Arqueología y arte antiguo de Chacas*. Huaraz, Peru: Instituto Cultural Ancashwain. 19 pp.

—2003. Identificando el área de dominio Recuay: un extendido inventario cerámico para la identificación de asentamientos Recuay. In: Bebel Ibarra, ed. *Arqueología de la Sierra de Ancash: Propuestas y Perspectivas*. Lima: Instituto Cultural Runa. pp. 121–134.

WIENER, CHARLES. 1880. *Pérou et Bolivie. Récit de voyage suivi d'études archéologiques et ethnographiques et de notes sur l'écriture et les langues des populations indiennes*. Paris: Librairie Hatchette. 796 pp.

WILLEY, GORDON R. 1945. Horizon styles and pottery traditions in Peruvian archaeology. *American Antiquity* 11:49–56.

—1953. *Prehistoric Settlement Patterns in the Virú Valley, Peru.* Washington, DC: US Government Printing Office. 453 pp. (Smithsonian Institution, Bureau of American Ethnology Bulletin 155.)

WILLIAMS, CARLOS AND JOSE PIÑEDA. 1985. Desde Ayacucho hasta Cajamarca: formas arquitectónicas con filiación Wari. *Boletín de Lima* 7:55-61.

WILLIAMS, PATRICK RYAN. 2001. Cerro Baúl: a Wari center on the Tiwanaku frontier. *Latin American Antiquity* 12:67–83.

WILSON, DAVID J. 1988. *Prehispanic Settlement Patterns in the Lower Santa Valley, Peru.* Washington, DC: Smithsonian Institution Press. 590 pp.

—1995. Prehispanic settlement patterns in the Casma Valley, North Coast of Peru: preliminary results to date. *Journal of the Steward Anthropological Society* 23(1–2):189–227.

WILSON, JOHN, LUIS REYES AND JULIO GARAYAR. 1967. *Geología de los Cuadrángulos de Mollebamba, Tayabamba, Huaylas, Pomabamba, Carhuaz y Huari.* Lima: Servicio de Geología y Minería. 69 pp. (Servicio de Geología y Minería Boletín 16.)

YACOVLEFF, EUGENIO. 1932. Las falcónidas en el arte y en las creencias de los antiguos peruanos. *Revista del Museo Nacional* 1(1):33–111.

ZAKI, ANDRZEJ. 1978a. El mausoleo de piedra con decoracion plastica en Santa Cruz, Callejón de Huaylas. In: Ramiro, Matos M., ed. *III Congreso Peruano del Hombre y La Cultura Andina*; 1977 January 3–February 5; Lima, Peru. Volume 2. [Lima]: Editora Lasontay. pp. 443–448.

—1978b. *Ayangay.* London: Polish Archaeological Discoveries in Peru. 140 pp.

—1987. Zoomorphe Steinskulpturen aus Santa Cruz (Peru): Ein Beitrag zum Raubtiermotiv in der vorkolumbischen Kunst. *Schweizerische Amerikanisten-Gesellschaft Bulletin* 51:7–18.

ZIÓŁKOWSKI, MARIUSZ S., MIECZYSLAW F. PAZDUR, ANDRZEJ KRZANOWSKI AND ADAM MICHCZYNSKI. 1994. *Andes: Radiocarbon Database for Bolivia, Ecuador and Peru.* Warsaw: Andean Archaeological Mission of the Institute of Archaeology, Warsaw University and Gliwice Radiocarbon Laboratory of the Institute of Physics, Silesian Technical University. 604 pp.

ZUIDEMA, R. TOM. 1973. Kinship and ancestor cult in three Peruvian communities: Hernandez Príncipe's account of 1622. *Bulletin de l'Institut Français d'Ètudes Andines* 2(1):16–33.

—1978. Shaft-tombs and the Inca empire. *Journal of the Steward Anthropological Society* 9:133–178.

—1988. Dynastic structures in Andean culture. In: Michael E. Moseley and Alana Cordy-Collins, eds. *The Northern Dynasties: Kingship and Statecraft in Chimor.* Washington, DC: Dumbarton Oaks. pp. 483–505.

# Index

## A

agglutinated rooms
   see room complexes
agricultural production, 15–16,
   17–18, 22, 354
alpacas, 101
Alto Chicama zone, 243–245
Amá II site, 162
Ancash
   geographic location, 11
   interregional interactions,
      360–361
   paleoclimate, 354
   prehistoric records, 21–23
   Recuay culture, 23–29
   sociocultural complexity,
      27–29
   Wari expansion, 29–32
ancestor veneration, 9, 22, 26, 28,
   135–137, 323, 358–359
Ancón, 215, 217
Ancosh Punta, 243
Andahuaylas, 257
Andamarca, 245
animal figurines, 277
Antajirca, 33, 158
antler artifacts, 343–344
Aquilpo-style ceramics, 243, 246
archaeological fieldwork
   excavations methodology,
      39–41
   site mapping, 39
   stratigraphic excavations, 39
architectural characteristics
   Chinchawas, 354–356
   mortuary constructions,
      115–118
   Recuay culture, 26
   Wari culture, 31–32
Atarco-style ceramics, 363
awls and perforators, 337–338
Ayacucho highlands, 29–34, 257
Ayapata, 257
Azángaro, 31

## B

Balcón de Judas, 148–149, 282
barley, 17
batán, 46, 314
beads and pendants
   characteristics, 325–326
   Chinchawasi 1 phase, 326
   Chinchawasi 2 phase, 327
   Kayán phase, 326

   Warmi phase, 327
beans, 17
Bennett, Wendell C., 24–25, 31,
   117, 147–148, 214–215
blackware
   fancy and imported ceramics,
      251, 268–270, 283, 284
   Operation 9 (OP9), 75
   Operation 23 (OP23), 95
   Operation 48 (OP48), 51–52
   Operation 56 (ST-1), 119
   Operation 57 (CT-2), 125
   Operation 64 (CT-12), 129
   spatiotemporal distributions,
      283, 284
   Warmi phase ceramics,
      288–289
blade tools
   Chinchawasi 1 phase, 305
   Chinchawasi 2 phase, 309
   Warmi phase, 311
bone artifacts
   antler artifacts, 343–344
   awls and perforators,
      337–338
   bone spindle whorls, 332
   characteristics, 333–335
   cranial spoons, 338–340
   domestic patterns, 356
   economic trade, 351–352
   needles, 335–337
   Operation 38 (OP38), 100,
      102–103
   Operation 40 (OP40), 100,
      102–103
   Operation 41 (OP41), 100,
      102–103
   Operation 42 (OP42), 100,
      102–103
   Operation 46 (OP46), 83, 84
   Operation 52 (OP52), 61
   Operation 54 (OP54), 63
   ornaments, 343
   pelvic trowels, 340
   rib tools, 340–341
   scapula scrapers, 341, 343
   spatulas, 335
   tool production debris, 343
bone spindle whorls, 332
bottles
   Chakwas phase ceramics, 239
   Chinchawasi 1 Ware D, 170
   Chinchawasi 2 Ware B, 186
   Chinchawasi 2 Ware C, 201

   fancy ceramics, 251
   plain burnished bottles, 251
   subterranean tombs, 251
   Warmi Ware B, 221
bowls
   Chakwas phase ceramics, 237
   Chinchawasi 1 Ware A,
      151–153
   Chinchawasi 1 Ware B,
      160–161
   Chinchawasi 1 Ware C, 163
   Chinchawasi 1 Ware D, 171
   Chinchawasi 2 Ware A, 179
   Chinchawasi 2 Ware B,
      185–186
   Chinchawasi 2 Ware C,
      187–189
   chullpa tombs, 125, 127
   Kayán Ware A, 141, 143
   Kayán Ware B, 147
   subterranean tombs, 119
   Wari polychrome ceramics,
      272
   Warmi Ware A, 209
   Warmi Ware B, 223–225
brown ware, 280–282
burial practices
   see mortuary constructions
burnt materials
   Operation 11 (OP11), 70
   Operation 15 (OP15), 86
   Operation 20 (OP20), 92
   Operation 22 (OP22), 71
   Operation 23 (OP23), 95
   Operation 31 (OP31), 97
   Operation 35 (OP35), 107
   Operation 37 (OP37), 110
   Operation 43 (OP43), 79
   Operation 46 (OP46), 83
   Operation 47 (OP47), 90
   Operation 48 (OP48), 51
   Operation 53 (OP53), 55

## C

*cacicazgos*, 28
Cajamarca pottery tradition
   fancy and imported ceramics,
      255–257, 284
   interregional interactions, 360
   Operation 23 (OP23), 95
   Operation 46 (OP46), 84
   Recuay culture, 27
   sociocultural transformations,
      363

spatiotemporal distributions, 284
Wari expansion, 30, 287
Warmi phase ceramics, 287
Calipuy Formation, 13
Callejón de Conchucos, 34
Callejón de Huaylas
 Aquilpo-style ceramics, 243, 246
 Cajamarca pottery tradition, 256–257
 Chakwas phase ceramics, 243
 Chinchawasi 1 Ware A, 157–159
 Chinchawasi 1 Ware B, 161
 Chinchawasi 1 Ware C, 165
 Chinchawasi 2 Ware C, 205
 fancy and imported ceramics, 284–286
 geographic location, 11
 Kayán phase ceramics, 147–150, 282–283
 mortuary constructions, 117
 paleoclimate, 354
 plainware ceramics, 174–176
 prehistorical records, 21–23
 seasonal characteristics, 15–16
 soil characteristics, 16
 Wari expansion, 30–34, 361–364
 Warmi Ware A, 214–215
camelids
 chullpa tombs, 132
 economic trade, 292–293, 351–352
 functional roles, 356–357
 Operation 15 (OP15), 86
 Operation 23 (OP23), 95
 Operation 37 (OP37), 110
 Operation 38 (OP38), 101
 Operation 40 (OP40), 101
 Operation 41 (OP41), 101
 Operation 42 (OP42), 101
 Operation 46 (OP46), 83
 Operation 54 (OP54), 63
 Recuay culture, 26
 stockraising activities, 354
canals
 Operation 4 (OP4), 87
 Operation 18 (OP18), 78
 Operation 22 (OP22), 71
 Operation 32 (OP32), 43–44
 Operation 46 (OP46), 83
 settlement organization, 355
 terrace areas, 113–114
*Canis* sp., 101
Caraz, 243
Carhuac Punta, 243
carved objects, 323

Casa de Gallina, 215
*caserío*, 16
Casma, 25, 261, 266, 354
Casma–Huaraz road, 18–19, 69
Casma Valley, 245
*Cavia* sp., 101
Cayash phase ceramics, 245
ceramic spindle whorls, 327
ceremonial practices, 3–5, 65-67, 358–359
Cerro Baúl, 32
Cerro Sechín, 245
Chacas zone, 205
Chakipampa style pottery, 31, 33, 261, 270, 275
Chakwas phase ceramics
 characteristics, 235, 241–246
 Chinchawas occupation, 356
 chipped stone artifacts, 312
 chronology, 353
 chullpa tombs, 133
 Operation 21 (OP21), 74
 Operation 25 (OP25), 46
 Operation 48 (OP48), 51, 53
 Operation 49 (OP49), 57
 Operation 52 (OP52), 61
 Operation 54 (OP54), 63
 painted decoration, 239
 paste characteristics, 235–236
 plastic decoration, 239–241
 research methodology, 139–141
 stylistic features, 38
 surface treatment, 239
 vessel shapes, 236–239
chalcedony, 301
 *see also* chipped stone artifacts
Chavín cult, 23, 24
Chavín de Huántar, 23, 117–118, 149, 257
*Chenopodium quinoa*, 17
chert, 14, 297, 300
 *see also* chipped stone artifacts
Chicha–Soras valley, 217, 272
Chimu culture, 270
Chinchawas ceramic sequence
 chronology, 1–3, 246–247, 353
 fancy ceramics, 250, 283–286
 Operation 56 (ST-1), 119
 stylistic features, 37–38
 Wari cultural influences, 247
Chinchawas community
 ancestor veneration, 135–137, 358–359
 ancient settlement, 35, 353–354
 architectural characteristics, 354–356
 artwork, 359

ceremonial practices, 358–359
Chakwas phase, 356
Chinchawasi 1 phase, 355
Chinchawasi 2 phase, 355–356
community studies, 9–10
defensive patterns, 360
domestic functions, 356–357
economic patterns, 18–19, 356–357
fancy and imported ceramics, 292–294
human skeletal remains, 134–135
interregional interactions, 289–292, 357–358, 360–361
Kayán phase, 355
Late Middle Horizon, 362–364
material culture, 356–357
modern settlement, 16–19
post-Chakwas occupation, 246
religious practices, 293–294
settlement organization, 354–356, 360
social organization, 358
sociocultural transformations, 359–364
Wari expansion, 293–294, 361–364
Warmi phase, 356, 362
 *see also* mortuary constructions
Chinchawasi 1 phase ceramics
 Chinchawasi 1 Ware A, 151–159
 Chinchawasi 1 Ware B, 159–163
 Chinchawasi 1 Ware C, 163–165
 Chinchawasi 1 Ware D, 166–177
 Chinchawas occupation, 355
 chipped stone artifacts, 301–305
 chronology, 353
 chullpa tombs, 133
 Enclosure 2 operations, 44–45
 fancy and imported ceramics, 250, 283
 interregional interactions, 290–291, 357
 Operation 4 (OP4), 87
 Operation 9 (OP9), 75
 Operation 12 (OP12), 77
 Operation 18 (OP18), 78
 Operation 24 (OP24), 72–73
 Operation 25 (OP25), 46, 346
 Operation 28 (OP28), 112
 Operation 29 (OP29), 96

Operation 31 (OP31), 97–99
Operation 36 (OP36), 108–109
Operation 43 (OP43), 81
Operation 46 (OP46), 83
Operation 47 (OP47), 90, 91
Operation 54 (OP54), 63
Operation 63 (ST-2), 119–120
radiocarbon dating measurements, 177
research background, 151
research summary, 113
spatiotemporal distributions, 283
stylistic features, 38
subterranean tombs, 133
Terrace 4, 105
Chinchawasi 1 Ware A
  characteristics, 157–159
  painted decoration, 155–156
  paste characteristics, 151
  plastic decoration, 156
  surface treatment, 155
  vessel shapes, 151–155
Chinchawasi 1 Ware B
  characteristics, 159, 161–163
  painted decoration, 161
  paste characteristics, 160
  plastic decoration, 161
  surface treatment, 161
  vessel shapes, 160–161
Chinchawasi 1 Ware C
  characteristics, 163, 165
  painted decoration, 165
  paste characteristics, 163
  plastic decoration, 165
  surface treatment, 165
  vessel shapes, 163–165
Chinchawasi 1 Ware D
  characteristics, 166, 174–177
  painted decoration, 173
  paste characteristics, 166
  plastic decoration, 173–174
  surface treatment, 173
  vessel shapes, 167–173
Chinchawasi 2 phase ceramics
  Chinchawasi 2 Ware A, 178–184
  Chinchawasi 2 Ware B, 184–187
  Chinchawasi 2 Ware C, 187–205
  Chinchawas occupation, 355–356
  chipped stone artifacts, 305–309
  chronology, 353
  face-neck vessels, 277, 279, 285

fancy and imported ceramics, 284–286
interregional interactions, 291, 357
Operation 4 (OP4), 87
Operation 8 (OP8), 89
Operation 9 (OP9), 75
Operation 11 (OP11), 70
Operation 14 (OP14), 86
Operation 18 (OP18), 77–78
Operation 20 (OP20), 92–93
Operation 22 (OP22), 71
Operation 23 (OP23), 95
Operation 24 (OP24), 72
Operation 26 (OP26), 46, 47–48
Operation 27 (OP27), 112
Operation 29 (OP29), 96
Operation 30 (OP30), 96–97
Operation 31 (OP31), 97
Operation 35 (OP35), 107
Operation 37 (OP37), 110
Operation 38 (OP38), 99–101
Operation 39 (OP39), 111
Operation 40 (OP40), 99–101
Operation 41 (OP41), 99–101
Operation 42 (OP42), 99–101
Operation 46 (OP46), 82–83
Operation 47 (OP47), 90
Operation 48 (OP48), 51–53, 285
Operation 49 (OP49), 57
Operation 52 (OP52), 61
Operation 53 (OP53), 55
Operation 54 (OP54), 63
Operation 62 (OP62), 113
radiocarbon dating measurements, 205–206
research background, 177–178
spatiotemporal distributions, 284–286
stylistic features, 38
Terrace 4, 105
Chinchawasi 2 Ware A
  characteristics, 178, 183–184
  painted decoration, 181–183
  paste characteristics, 178–179
  plastic decoration, 183
  surface treatment, 181
  vessel shapes, 179–181
Chinchawasi 2 Ware B
  characteristics, 184, 187
  painted decoration, 186
  paste characteristics, 185
  plastic decoration, 186
  surface treatment, 186
  vessel shapes, 185–186
Chinchawasi 2 Ware C
  characteristics, 187, 203–205

  painted decoration, 203
  paste characteristics, 187
  plastic decoration, 203
  surface treatment, 201, 203
  vessel shapes, 187–201
chipped stone artifacts
  Chakwas phase, 312
  chalcedony, 301
  Chinchawasi 1 phase, 301–305
  Chinchawasi 2 phase, 305–309
  economic trade, 351
  Kayán phase, 301
  obsidian, 300
  quartzites, 300
  quartz/quartz crystals, 301
  raw materials, 297, 300–301
  silex (chert), 297, 300
  siliceous andesites, 300
  slate, 300–301
  Warmi phase, 310–311
chullpa tombs
  ancestor veneration, 135–137
  burial pits, 131
  ceremonial practices, 359
  characteristics, 121–122, 131–132
  cultural associations and functions, 133–134, 355
  fancy ceramics, 253–255
  Huari Norteño, 253
  human skeletal remains, 134–135
  interment changes, 137
  Operation 55 (CT-13), 122–123
  Operation 57 (CT-2), 123–125
  Operation 58 (CT-6), 126–127, 345
  Operation 59 (CT-5), 127
  Operation 60 (CT-8), 127–129, 345
  Operation 61 (CT-7), 129, 345
  Operation 64 (CT-12), 129, 131
  redware ceramics, 254
  research background, 115–118
  research summary, 131–132
  Warmi phase ceramics, 133, 253
  Wilkawaín area, 31–33
climatic conditions, 20–21
colanders
  Chinchawasi 1 Ware D, 172–173
  Chinchawasi 2 Ware C, 191
  Warmi Ware B, 225–226

community, definition of, 5–6
Conchopata, 364
Conchucos, 24, 32, 34
*Conus* sp., 123, 345
copper-metal artifacts
    Operation 15 (OP15), 86
    Operation 38 (OP38), 100, 103
    Operation 40 (OP40), 100, 103
    Operation 41 (OP41), 100, 103
    Operation 42 (OP42), 100, 103
    Operation 46 (OP46), 84
    Operation 47 (OP47), 90
    Operation 48 (OP48), 51
    Operation 49 (OP49), 57
    Operation 54 (OP54), 63
    Operation 55 (CT-13), 123
    Operation 57 (CT-2), 125
    Operation 58 (CT-6), 127
    Operation 59 (CT-5), 127
    Operation 64 (CT-12), 131
    Operation 65 (ST-3), 120
    ornaments, 347–349
Cordillera Blanca, 13
Cordillera Negra, 11, 13–14, 15
cores
    Chinchawasi 1 phase, 305
    Kayán phase, 301
Coronguimarca, 215
Cotojirca III and IV ceramic phases, 176
cranial spoons
    characteristics, 338–340
    Operation 38 (OP38), 100
    Operation 40 (OP40), 100
    Operation 41 (OP41), 100
    Operation 42 (OP42), 100
    Operation 43 (OP43), 81
    Operation 44 (OP44), 79
    Operation 46 (OP46), 83
    Operation 54 (OP54), 63
Cretaceous, 13
cups
    Chinchawasi 1 Ware A, 153
    Chinchawasi 1 Ware D, 171–172
    Chinchawasi 2 Ware A, 179–180
    Chinchawasi 2 Ware B, 186
    Chinchawasi 2 Ware C, 190
    Operation 4 (OP4), 87
*curacazgos*, 28
cuy, 101, 110

# D

debitage
    *see* chipped stone artifacts

decorative motifs
    Chakwas phase ceramics, 239
    Chinchawasi 1 Ware A, 155–156
    Chinchawasi 1 Ware B, 161
    Chinchawasi 1 Ware C, 165
    Chinchawasi 1 Ware D, 173
    Chinchawasi 2 Ware A, 181–183
    Chinchawasi 2 Ware B, 186
    Chinchawasi 2 Ware C, 203
    Kayán Ware A, 145
    Kayán Ware B, 147
    Warmi Ware A, 211–213
    Warmi Ware B, 228
deer, 101, 103, 110, 343–344
defensive architecture, 25–26, 69, 86, 320, 354, 358, 360
drinking cups, 87
D-shaped structures, 32

# E

Early Horizon Period, 23
Early Intermediate Period
    animal figurines, 277
    blackware, 270
    Cajamarca pottery tradition, 257
    Chinchawas ceramic sequence, 38, 246–247
    Chinchawasi 1 Ware C, 165
    chronology, 353
    Enclosure 2 operations, 44–45
    Operation 7 (OP7), 43
    Recuay culture, 23–29, 359
    research background, 1, 3, 6
    subterranean tombs, 119–120
Early Tanguche ceramic phase, 215, 254, 268
economic trade
    bone artifacts, 333–344
    Casma–Huaraz road, 18–19, 69
    Chakwas phase, 315
    chipped stone artifacts, 297–312
    domestic patterns, 356–357
    Early Horizon Period, 23
    fancy and imported ceramics, 289–292
    groundstone artifacts, 312–321
    interregional interactions, 289–292, 357–358
    metal artifacts, 346–351
    Middle Horizon, 133
    miscellaneous stone artifacts, 321–327
    modern settlements, 18–19
    research background, 295
    research methodology, 295
    research objectives, 3
    research summary, 351–352
    shell artifacts, 344–345
    spindle whorls and discs, 327–333
    Wari cultural influences, 357–358
effigy vessels, 251, 261–262
employment, 19
Enclosure 1, Sector 1
    characteristics, 66–67
    Operation 1 (OP1), 41
    Operation 2 (OP2), 41–42
Enclosure 2, Sector 1
    characteristics, 42, 44–45, 66–67
    Operation 3 (OP3), 42–43
    Operation 7 (OP7), 43
    Operation 32 (OP32), 43–44
enclosures, 41–45, 66–67, 355, 360
environmental diversity, 14–15

# F

face-neck vessels, 277, 279, 285, 287–288
fancy ceramics
    animal figurines, 277
    blackware, 251, 253, 268–270, 283, 284
    bottles, 251
    Cajamarca pottery tradition, 255–257
    Chinchawasi 1 phase ceramics, 250, 283
    Chinchawasi 2 phase ceramics, 284–286
    chullpa tombs, 253–255
    face-neck vessels, 277, 279, 285, 287–288
    figurine pendants, 276–277
    fine grayware, 280, 285, 287
    fine polished brown ware, 280–282
    fired whorls, 282
    Huari Norteño, 253
    interregional interactions, 289–292
    jars, 251
    Kayán phase ceramics, 282–283
    Late Moche style, 251
    Nievería, 254–255, 261–262, 288
    non-Supe-style tumblers, 266–267
    North Central Coast-style redware, 267–268
    Operation 54 (OP54), 63
    painted redware, 254

pinkware, 275–276, 283
polychrome kaolinite pottery, 257, 260–261
press-molded ceramics, 262–266
purple iridescent-style ceramics, 279–280, 285, 287
Recuay culture, 250
recycled ceramic sherds, 282
red-on-cream Moche-style ceramics, 276
redware ceramics, 254
research background, 249
resist-painted ceramics, 261
Sector 1 excavations, 255–282
Sector 2 excavations, 249–251, 253
significance, 292–294
slipped redware, 254
spatiotemporal distributions, 282–289
subterranean tombs, 249–251, 253
Supe-style tumblers, 262–266
unpainted face-neck fragments, 279
unslipped redware, 254
Wari polychrome ceramics, 270–273, 275, 284, 287
Warmi phase ceramics, 253, 287–289
faunal remains
Operation 12 (OP12), 77
Operation 15 (OP15), 86
Operation 23 (OP23), 95
Operation 35 (OP35), 107
Operation 37 (OP37), 110
Operation 38 (OP38), 100–101
Operation 40 (OP40), 100–101
Operation 41 (OP41), 100–101
Operation 42 (OP42), 100–101
Operation 46 (OP46), 83
Operation 47 (OP47), 90
Operation 54 (OP54), 63, 65
feasting activities
ancestor veneration, 9
chipped stone tools, 301
corporate feasts, 67, 105
fancy and imported ceramics, 285, 289
Kayán Ware A, 149
midden accumulations, 66, 285, 289, 341
fieldwork methodology
Sector 1 excavations, 37–67

Sector 2 excavations, 115
figurines
animal figurines, 277
characteristics, 321–323
figurine pendants, 276–277
Kayán phase ceramics, 149
Operation 38 (OP38), 100
Operation 40 (OP40), 100
Operation 41 (OP41), 100
Operation 42 (OP42), 100
Operation 49 (OP49), 57
Operation 57 (CT-2), 125
Operation 64 (CT-12), 131
pinkware, 275–276
Wari culture, 33
fine grayware, 280, 285, 287
fine polished brown ware, 280–282
fired whorls, 282
flagstone pavement floors
Operation 5 (OP5), 91
Operation 37 (OP37), 110
Warmi phase, 85
flake scrapers
Chinchawasi 1 phase, 305
Chinchawasi 2 phase, 309
Kayán phase, 301
Warmi phase, 311

## G
Gallinazo, 27, 360
geological processes, 13–14, 19–20
grayware, 280, 285, 287
grinding stones
Chakwas phase, 315
Chinchawasi 1 phase, 314
Chinchawasi 2 phase, 314–315
Kayán phase, 314
Operation 15 (OP15), 86
Operation 21 (OP21), 74
Operation 22 (OP22), 71
Operation 24 (OP24), 72
Operation 30 (OP30), 97
Operation 31 (OP31), 97
Operation 43 (OP43), 79
Operation 46 (OP46), 82, 84
Operation 47 (OP47), 90
Warmi phase, 315
groundstone artifacts
characteristics, 312
economic trade, 351
grinding stones, 312–315
hammerstones, 315–318
pebble and slingstone objects, 318–321
guinea pigs, 101, 110
Guitarrero Cave, 22, 149, 159

## H
hammerstones, 315–318
highland Ancash
geographic location, 11
interregional interactions, 360–361
paleoclimate, 354
prehistoric records, 21–23
Recuay culture, 23–29
sociocultural complexity, 27–29
Wari expansion, 29–32
*Hippocamelus antisensis*, 101, 103, 343
Honcopampa, 31–32, 150, 165, 256–257, 361
Huaca del Sol, 268
Huamachuco, 27, 30, 159, 243–245, 257, 360, 362–363
Huancavelica, 257
Huarás style pottery, 25, 27, 161–163
Huaraz
Cajamarca pottery tradition, 256–257
Chinchawasi 1 Ware A, 157–159
Chinchawasi 1 Ware B, 161–162
Chinchawasi 2 Ware C, 205
economic trade, 18–19
Kayán phase ceramics, 282–283
mortuary constructions, 117
paleoclimate, 354
Wari expansion, 32–33
Huaricoto, 23, 27, 117, 150, 161
Huari Norteño, 33, 129, 253, 268, 288
Huaura area, 245
human skeletal remains, 134–135
*see also* mortuary constructions
hydrological patterns, 19–20

## I
ice core records, 20–21, 354
Ichik Wilkawaín, 31, 157, 261
imported and fancy ceramics
animal figurines, 277
blackware, 268–270, 283, 284
Cajamarca pottery tradition, 255–257
Chinchawasi 1 phase ceramics, 283
Chinchawasi 2 phase ceramics, 284–286
face-neck vessels, 277, 279, 285, 287–288
figurine pendants, 276–277
fine grayware, 280, 285, 287

fine polished brown ware,
    280–282
fired whorls, 282
interregional interactions,
    289–292, 363–364
Kayán phase ceramics,
    282–283
Niervería, 261–262, 288
non-Supe-style tumblers,
    266–267
North Central Coast-style
    redware, 267–268
painted redware, 254
pinkware, 275–276, 283
polychrome kaolinite pottery,
    257, 260–261
press-molded ceramics,
    262–266
purple iridescent-style
    ceramics, 279–280, 285,
    287
recycled ceramic sherds, 282
red-on-cream Moche-style
    ceramics, 276
research background, 249
resist-painted ceramics, 261
Sector 1 excavations,
    255–282
significance, 292–294
slipped redware, 254
spatiotemporal distributions,
    282–289
Supe-style tumblers, 262–266
unpainted face-neck
    fragments, 279
Wari polychrome ceramics,
    270–273, 275, 284, 287
Warmi phase ceramics,
    287–289
Inca period, 117
indeterminate kaolinite pottery,
    257, 283
Initial Period, 23
Inka pottery, 246
interregional interactions
    Chinchawasi 1 phase,
        290–291
    Chinchawasi 2 phase, 291
    fancy and imported ceramics,
        289–292
    Kayán phase, 290
    research methodology, 6–8
    Wari culture, 290–291
    Warmi phase, 291–292
irrigation systems, 19–20
Irwá B site, 157

## J

Jancu tomb, 117
Jargampata, 8, 217, 272

jars
    Chakwas phase ceramics,
        237, 239
    Chinchawasi 1 Ware A,
        153–155
    Chinchawasi 1 Ware C,
        164–165
    Chinchawasi 1 Ware D,
        167–169
    Chinchawasi 2 Ware A,
        180–181
    Chinchawasi 2 Ware B, 186
    Chinchawasi 2 Ware C,
        191–201
    chullpa tombs, 125, 127
    fancy ceramics, 251
    Kayán Ware B, 147
    subterranean tombs, 119
    Wari polychrome ceramics,
        271–272
    Warmi Ware A, 209
    Warmi Ware B, 219–221
Jequetepeque, 362
Jincamocco, 31

## K

kaolinite ceramics
    see Cajamarca pottery
        tradition; Kayán phase
        ceramics
Karachuko, 16
Katak, 149, 205
Kayán phase ceramics
    characteristics, 147–150
    Chinchawas occupation, 355
    chipped stone artifacts, 301
    chronology, 353
    Enclosure 2 operations,
        43–45
    fancy and imported ceramics,
        282–283
    functional roles, 149–150
    interregional interactions,
        290, 357
    Kayán Ware A, 141–145
    Kayán Ware B, 145–147
    Operation 5 (OP5), 91
    Operation 9 (OP9), 75–76
    Operation 14 (OP14), 86
    Operation 28 (OP28), 112
    Operation 29 (OP29), 96
    Operation 38 (OP38), 100
    Operation 41 (OP41), 100
    Operation 43 (OP43), 81
    Operation 46 (OP46), 83
    Operation 54 (OP54), 63
    radiocarbon dating
        measurements, 150
    research summary, 113
    Room Complex 1, 46

Room Complex 5, 59
spatiotemporal distributions,
    282–283
stylistic features, 38
Kayán Ware A
    kaolin/kaolinite paste, 141
    painted decoration, 143, 145
    plastic decoration, 145
    surface treatment, 143
    vessel shapes, 141–143
Kayán Ware B
    nonkaolinite redware pastes,
        145
    painted decoration, 147
    plastic decoration, 147
    surface treatment, 147
    vessel shapes, 145–147
kin-based organization, 358
Kishwar, 16
Kotosh Religious Tradition, 23

## L

La Galgada, 23
*Lagidium* sp., 101
land use, 15–16
La Pampa, 65, 150, 162, 177, 205,
    215, 243
lapis lazuli, 34
Larco Hoyle, Rafael, 24
large hafted implements, 323,
    325
Late Intermediate Period,
    243–245, 246, 353
Late Middle Horizon, 362–364
Late Patibamba I and II ceramic
    phase, 217, 272, 284
Late Preceramic Period, 22–23
Lima, 27, 360
line painting
    Chinchawasi 2 Ware A, 184
    Kayán Ware A, 145
lithic artifacts, 296–312
local economy and trade
    bone artifacts, 333–344
    Chakwas phase, 315
    chipped stone artifacts,
        297–312
    domestic patterns, 356–357
    groundstone artifacts,
        312–321
    interregional interactions,
        289–292, 357–358
    metal artifacts, 346–351
    miscellaneous stone artifacts,
        321–327
    research background, 295
    research methodology, 295
    research objectives, 3
    research summary, 351–352
    shell artifacts, 344–345

spindle whorls and discs, 327–333
Wari cultural influences, 357–358

# M

maize, 17
Maquellouán, 243
"Marañon" pottery, 256, 261
Marcahuamachuco, 177
Marcará area, 26, 245
Marenayoc, 243
material culture, 356–357
meat, usable, 101–102
metal artifacts
    characteristics, 346
    Chinchawasi 1 phase, 346–347
    Chinchawasi 2 phase, 347–349
    economic trade, 352
    Operation 48 (OP48), 51
    Recuay culture, 25
    Warmi phase, 349–351
Middle Horizon
    blackware, 253, 269–270
    Cajamarca pottery tradition, 257
    Chinchawas ceramic sequence, 38, 246–247
    Chinchawasi 1 Ware A, 159
    Chinchawasi 1 Ware C, 165
    Chinchawasi 2 phase ceramics, 284–286
    Chinchawasi 2 Ware A, 184
    chronology, 353
    chullpa tombs, 127, 133
    economic trade, 133
    face-neck vessels, 277, 279
    fancy and imported ceramics, 284–286
    interregional interactions, 289–292
    non-Supe-style tumblers, 266–267
    North Central Coast-style redware, 268
    Operation 4 (OP4), 87
    Operation 11 (OP11), 70
    Operation 20 (OP20), 92
    Operation 23 (OP23), 95
    Operation 24 (OP24), 72
    Operation 25 (OP25), 46
    Operation 27 (OP27), 112
    Operation 30 (OP30), 97
    Operation 36 (OP36), 108
    Operation 38 (OP38), 99–101
    Operation 40 (OP40), 99–101
    Operation 41 (OP41), 99–101
    Operation 42 (OP42), 99–101
    Operation 43 (OP43), 79
    Operation 46 (OP46), 84
    Operation 48 (OP48), 51–52
    Operation 49 (OP49), 57
    Operation 54 (OP54), 63
    redware ceramics, 244–245, 254
    research background, 1, 3, 6–7
    Wari expansion, 6–7, 29–34, 293–294, 361–364
    Wari polychrome ceramics, 272
    Warmi Ware A, 214–215, 217
    Warmi Ware B, 233
mineral deposits, 13
miniature vessels
    Chinchawasi 2 Ware C, 201
    Warmi Ware B, 227, 233
miscellaneous stone artifacts
    beads and pendants, 325–327
    carved objects, 323
    figurines, 321–323
    large hafted implements, 323, 325
Moche
    blackware, 269–270
    Cajamarca pottery tradition, 257
    fancy ceramics, 251, 254
    interregional interactions, 357, 360–361, 363
    North Central Coast-style redware, 268
    Operation 56 (ST-1), 119
    Recuay culture, 25, 28–29
    red-on-cream ceramics, 276
    religious practices, 293–294
    sociocultural transformations, 363–364
    Warmi Ware B, 233
monolithic stonecarvings, 25, 360
mortars and pestles
    Operation 43 (OP43), 81
    Operation 48 (OP48), 52
mortuary constructions
    ancestor veneration, 135–137
    burial pits, 131
    Chinchawasi 1 Ware B, 161
    chullpa tombs, 121–132, 355, 359
    cultural associations and functions, 133–134, 355
    human skeletal remains, 134–135
    interment changes, 137
    Operation 55 (CT-13), 122–123
    Operation 56 (ST-1), 118–119
    Operation 57 (CT-2), 123–125
    Operation 58 (CT-6), 126–127
    Operation 59 (CT-5), 127
    Operation 60 (CT-8), 127–129
    Operation 61 (CT-7), 129
    Operation 63 (ST-2), 119
    Operation 64 (CT-12), 129, 131
    Operation 65 (ST-3), 119–121
    Recuay culture, 26
    research background, 115–118
    research summary, 121, 131–132
    social organization, 358
    subterranean tombs, 118–121, 355, 359
    Wari culture, 33–34
Mosna area, 26
mummies, 135

# N

neckless ollas
    Chinchawasi 1 Ware D, 169
    Chinchawasi 2 Ware C, 201
needles, 335–337
Nepeña, 25, 243, 254, 267–268, 362
Nevado Huascarán, 13, 354
Nievería
    fancy ceramics, 254–255, 261–262, 284, 288
    Operation 57 (CT-2), 125
    spatiotemporal distributions, 284
    Wari culture, 33
non-Supe-style tumblers, 266–267
North Central Coast-style redware, 267–268
North Highlands
    Cajamarca pottery tradition, 257
    Chinchawasi 1 Ware D, 177
    fancy and imported ceramics, 283, 284–286
    interregional interactions, 360–361
    Kayán phase ceramics, 149
    plainware ceramics, 243–245
    pre-Inca pottery, 243
    Recuay culture, 149, 357
    Wari expansion, 29–34
    Warmi Ware A, 214

# O

obsidian artifacts
    chipped stone artifacts, 300

economic trade, 357
Middle Horizon, 133
Operation 8 (OP8), 89
Operation 38 (OP38), 100
Operation 40 (OP40), 100
Operation 41 (OP41), 100
Operation 42 (OP42), 100
Operation 46 (OP46), 84
Operation 49 (OP49), 57
Operation 54 (OP54), 63
sources, 7
Wari culture, 34
oca, 17, 18
Ocros pottery, 364
*Odocoileus virginianus*, 101, 103, 343
ollas
    Chinchawasi 1 Ware D, 169
    Chinchawasi 2 Ware C, 201
    Warmi Ware B, 221
*Ollucus tuberosus*, 17
Operation 1 (OP1), 41
Operation 2 (OP2), 41–42
Operation 3 (OP3), 42–43
Operation 4 (OP4), 87
Operation 5 (OP5), 91–93
Operation 6 (OP6), 91–94
Operation 7 (OP7), 43
Operation 8 (OP8), 89
Operation 9 (OP9), 73–76
Operation 10 (OP10), 70–71
Operation 11 (OP11), 70
Operation 12 (OP12), 76–77
Operation 13 (OP13), 85
Operation 14 (OP14), 85–86
Operation 15 (OP15), 86
Operation 16 (OP16), 48–49
Operation 17 (OP17), 49
Operation 18 (OP18), 77–78
Operation 19 (OP19), 73–76
Operation 20 (OP20), 91–93
Operation 21 (OP21), 73–76
Operation 22 (OP22), 71–72
Operation 23 (OP23), 95–96
Operation 24 (OP24), 72–73
Operation 25 (OP25), 45–47, 346
Operation 26 (OP26), 46, 47–48
Operation 27 (OP27), 111–112
Operation 28 (OP28), 112
Operation 29 (OP29), 96
Operation 30 (OP30), 96–97
Operation 31 (OP31), 97–99
Operation 32 (OP32), 43–44
Operation 33 (OP33), 106
Operation 34 (OP34), 106–107
Operation 35 (OP35), 107–108
Operation 36 (OP36), 108–109
Operation 37 (OP37), 109–110
Operation 38 (OP38), 99–103
Operation 39 (OP39), 110–111

Operation 40 (OP40), 99–103
Operation 41 (OP41), 99–103
Operation 42 (OP42), 99–103
Operation 43 (OP43), 78–79, 81
Operation 44 (OP44), 78–79
Operation 45 (OP45), 58–60
Operation 46 (OP46), 81–85
Operation 47 (OP47), 89–91
Operation 48 (OP48), 50–53, 285
Operation 49 (OP49), 56–58
Operation 50 (OP50), 53
Operation 51 (OP51), 53–54
Operation 52 (OP52), 60–61
Operation 53 (OP53), 54–55
Operation 54 (OP54), 62–65
Operation 55 (CT-13), 122–123
Operation 56 (ST-1), 118–119
Operation 57 (CT-2), 123–125
Operation 58 (CT-6), 126–127, 345
Operation 59 (CT-5), 127
Operation 60 (CT-8), 127–129, 345
Operation 61 (CT-7), 129, 345
Operation 62 (OP62), 112–113
Operation 63 (ST-2), 119–120
Operation 64 (CT-12), 129, 131
Operation 65 (ST-3), 119–121
orangeware fragments, 51, 53, 267, 289
ornaments, 343
orogenic activity, 13
*Oxalis tuberosa*, 17

# P

Pachacamac-style ceramics, 363
Palacio del Inca, 32
paleoclimate, 20–21, 353–354
Pariacoto, 18
Pariamarca, 32
Pashash, 149, 150, 159, 176, 205, 361
pebble artifacts, 318–321
pelvic trowels, 340
pendants, figurine, 276–277
perforated ceramic whorls, 327–330
perforators, 337–338
*Phaseolus lunatus*, 17
Pierina mining zone, 215, 243, 246
Pikillacta, 31, 217, 257
pinkware
    fancy and imported ceramics, 275–276, 283
    figurines, 275–276
    Operation 12 (OP12), 77
    Operation 19 (OP19), 75
    Operation 35 (OP35), 107
    Operation 37 (OP37), 110
    Operation 48 (OP48), 51–52

Operation 64 (CT-12), 129
    spoons, 275
    Warmi phase ceramics, 289
Piruru, 23
plain burnished bottles, 251
plainware ceramics
    Chinchawas ceramic sequence, 38
    Chinchawasi 1 Ware D, 174–176
    Chinchawasi 2 Ware C, 187–205
    North Highlands, 243–245
    Operation 8 (OP8), 89
    Operation 11 (OP11), 70
    Operation 12 (OP12), 77
    Operation 15 (OP15), 86
    Operation 22 (OP22), 71
    Operation 27 (OP27), 112
    Operation 30 (OP30), 97
    Operation 57 (CT-2), 125
    Operation 62 (OP62), 113
Pleistocene, 13–14
Pliocene, 13–14
Pójoc, 243
polished stones, 83
polychrome kaolinite pottery, 257, 260–261
*Polylepis* sp., 15
Pomabamba, 32
post-Chakwas occupation, 246
potatoes, 17, 18, 292
pottery manufacture and decoration, 24–27, 30, 139–141
    *see also specific phases*
precipitation, 15–16
press-molded ceramics
    blackware, 253, 268–270
    chullpa tombs, 253
    fancy and imported ceramics, 253–254, 262–266
    non-Supe-style tumblers, 266–267
    North Central Coast-style redware, 267–268
    Operation 4 (OP4), 87
    Operation 23 (OP23), 95
    Operation 59 (CT-5), 127
    Operation 61 (CT-7), 129
    painted redware, 254
    slipped redware, 254
    sociocultural transformations, 363
    Supe-style tumblers, 262–266
    unslipped redware, 254
    Warmi phase ceramics, 288–289
projectile points
    Chinchawasi 1 phase, 305

Chinchawasi 2 phase,
    307–309
Warmi phase, 311
Punta Kallán, 293
purple iridescent-style ceramics,
    279–280, 285, 287

## Q

Qasawirka ceramic phase, 277
quartzites, 14, 300
    *see also* chipped stone artifacts
quartz/quartz crystals, 301
    *see also* chipped stone artifacts
Quebrada Aquilpo, 243
Quebrada Chihua Paccha, 19
Quebrada Chiliac, 19
Quebrada Honda, 31
Quebrada Pishan, 13
Quebrada Potrero Ruri, 13
Quebrada Tinco, 13
Quebrada Yupanca, 13
Quelccaya ice cores
    *see* ice core records
quenual, 15
Queyash Alto, 27, 149, 150, 361
Quillahuaca-style ceramics, 245
quinoa, 17, 18
Quispisisa obsidian source, 33,
    300, 357
Quitapampa A site, 158–159

## R

radiocarbon measurements
    Chakwas phase, 245–246
    Chinchawas ceramic sequence,
        37–38
    Chinchawasi 1 phase, 177
    Chinchawasi 2 phase,
        205–206
    chronology, 353
    chullpa tomb pottery, 255
    diagnostic assays, 48
    human premolar tooth,
        120–121
    human ulna fragment, 125
    Kayán phase ceramics, 150
    Operation 4 (OP4), 87
    Operation 9 (OP9), 76
    Operation 19 (OP19), 75
    Operation 20 (OP20), 92
    Operation 21 (OP21), 75
    Operation 26 (OP26), 47
    Operation 31 (OP31), 98–99
    Operation 36 (OP36), 108
    Operation 43 (OP43), 81
    Operation 49 (OP49), 57
    Operation 57 (CT-2), 125
    Operation 65 (ST-3), 120–121
    Recuay culture, 150
    textile fragment, 131
Wari provincial sites, 354
Warmi phase, 207, 217, 235
wood charcoal sample, 47,
    57, 75–76, 81, 87, 92,
    98–99, 108
rainfall, 15–16, 19–20
Ranrahirca, 215
Recuay culture
    ancestor veneration, 135
    architectural characteristics, 26
    artwork, 359
    Chinchawasi 1 Ware A,
        157–159
    Chinchawasi 1 Ware B, 161
    chronology, 353
    Early Intermediate Period,
        23–29, 359
    fancy ceramics, 250
    interregional interactions,
        357, 360–361
    Kayán phase ceramics,
        147–150, 282–283, 357
    Late Middle Horizon,
        362–364
    mortuary constructions, 117
    Operation 9 (OP9), 75–76
    Operation 35 (OP35), 107
    pottery sequence chronology,
        26–27
    settlement patterns, 25
    shell artifacts, 344–345
    sociocultural complexity,
        27–29
    sociocultural transformations,
        359–364
    warfare, 29
    Wari cultural influences,
        361–364
recycled ceramic sherds, 282
red-on-cream ceramics
    Chinchawasi 2 Ware A,
        177–178
    Moche-style ceramics, 276
    Operation 63 (ST-2),
        119–120
red-slipped ceramics, 145,
    163–165, 184–187
redware ceramics
    Chakwas phase ceramics,
        235–246
    Chinchawasi 1 Ware D, 166
    Chinchawasi 2 Ware C,
        187–205
    chullpa tombs, 254
    fancy ceramics, 254
    Middle Horizon, 244–245
    North Central Coast-style
        redware, 267–268
    Operation 61 (CT-7), 129
    Operation 64 (CT-12), 129
press-molded ceramics, 254
Warmi Ware A, 208–217
Warmi Ware B, 217–234
red, white, and black-style
    ceramics, 253
religious practices, 22–23,
    293–294, 358–359
research methodology
    community studies, 5–6, 365
    interregional interactions,
        6–8
    rural complexity, 8–10
research objectives, 1–3, 365
resist-painted ceramics, 261
rib tools, 340–341
Río Casma, 11, 13
Río Chacchan, 13
Río Pira, 13
river systems, 13
rodents, 101
Room Complex 1
    Operation 25 (OP25), 45–47
    Operation 26 (OP26), 47–48
Room Complex 2
    Operation 16 (OP16), 48–49
    Operation 17 (OP17), 49
Room Complex 3
    characteristics, 49–50
    Operation 48 (OP48), 50–53,
        285
    Operation 50 (OP50), 53
    Operation 51 (OP51), 53–54
    Operation 53 (OP53), 54–55
Room Complex 4
    characteristics, 55
    Operation 49 (OP49), 56–58
Room Complex 5
    characteristics, 58
    Operation 45 (OP45), 58–60
Room Complex 6, 60–61
room complexes
    characteristics, 45, 65–66
    Room Complex 1, 45–48
    Room Complex 2, 48–49
    Room Complex 3, 49–55
    Room Complex 4, 55–58
    Room Complex 5, 58–60
    Room Complex 6, 60–61
rural communities, 8–10

## S

San Diego, 261
San José de Moro, 294, 363–364
San Nicolás Molded ceramics,
    254, 267–268
Santa, 25, 215, 254, 267–268, 362
Santa Cruz area, 243
scapula scrapers, 341, 343
scrapers
    Chinchawasi 1 phase, 305

Chinchawasi 2 phase, 309
Kayán phase, 301
Warmi phase, 311
seasonal characteristics, 15–16
Sector 1 excavations
    archaeological fieldwork, 39–41
    Chinchawas ceramic sequence, 37–38
    enclosures, 41–45, 66–67
    excavations methodology, 39–41
    fancy ceramics, 255–282
    fieldwork methodology, 37–67
    room complexes, 45–61, 65–66
    Terrace 1, 69–85
    Torreón, 61–65, 67
Sector 2 excavations
    burial pits, 131
    chullpa tombs, 121–132, 253–255
    fancy ceramics, 249–251, 253–255
    fieldwork methodology, 115
    Operation 55 (CT-13), 122–123
    Operation 56 (ST-1), 118–119
    Operation 57 (CT-2), 123–125
    Operation 58 (CT-6), 126–127
    Operation 59 (CT-5), 127
    Operation 60 (CT-8), 127–129
    Operation 61 (CT-7), 129
    Operation 63 (ST-2), 119
    Operation 64 (CT-12), 129, 131
    Operation 65 (ST-3), 119–120
    research background, 115–118
    research summary, 121, 131–132
    subterranean tombs, 118–121, 249–251, 253
Shankaiyan, 157
shell artifacts
    characteristics, 344–345
    Middle Horizon, 133
    Operation 54 (OP54), 63
    Operation 55 (CT-13), 123
silex (chert), 14, 297, 300
    *see also* chipped stone artifacts
siliceous andesites, 300
    *see also* chipped stone artifacts
slate artifacts, 300–301
    *see also* chipped stone artifacts

slingstone objects, 318–321
small circular discs, 333
social organization, 358
sociocultural transformations, 359–364
sociopolitical complexity, 5, 358–359
soil characteristics
    Callejón de Huaylas, 16
    excavations methodology, 39–41
    Operation 4 (OP4), 87
    Operation 5 (OP5), 91
    Operation 6 (OP6), 91–92
    Operation 8 (OP8), 89
    Operation 9 (OP9), 73–76
    Operation 10 (OP10), 70–71
    Operation 11 (OP11), 70
    Operation 12 (OP12), 76–77
    Operation 13 (OP13), 85
    Operation 14 (OP14), 85–86
    Operation 15 (OP15), 86
    Operation 16 (OP16), 48–49
    Operation 17 (OP17), 49
    Operation 18 (OP18), 77–78
    Operation 20 (OP20), 92
    Operation 22 (OP22), 71–72
    Operation 23 (OP23), 95–96
    Operation 24 (OP24), 72–73
    Operation 25 (OP25), 45–47
    Operation 26 (OP26), 47–48
    Operation 27 (OP27), 111–112
    Operation 28 (OP28), 112
    Operation 29 (OP29), 96
    Operation 30 (OP30), 96–97
    Operation 31 (OP31), 97–99
    Operation 33 (OP33), 106
    Operation 34 (OP34), 106–107
    Operation 35 (OP35), 107–108
    Operation 36 (OP36), 108–109
    Operation 37 (OP37), 109–110
    Operation 38 (OP38), 99–103
    Operation 39 (OP39), 110–111
    Operation 40 (OP40), 99–103
    Operation 41 (OP41), 99–103
    Operation 42 (OP42), 99–103
    Operation 43 (OP43), 78–79, 81
    Operation 44 (OP44), 78–79
    Operation 45 (OP45), 59
    Operation 46 (OP46), 81–84
    Operation 47 (OP47), 89–91
    Operation 48 (OP48), 50–53
    Operation 49 (OP49), 57

    Operation 50 (OP50), 53
    Operation 51 (OP51), 53–54
    Operation 52 (OP52), 61
    Operation 53 (OP53), 54–55
    Operation 54 (OP54), 62–63
    Operation 62 (OP62), 112–113
*Solanum andigenum*, 17
spatulas, 335
spindle whorls and discs
    bone spindle whorls, 332
    ceramic spindle whorls, 327
    characteristics, 327
    economic trade, 352
    Operation 38 (OP38), 100
    Operation 40 (OP40), 100
    Operation 41 (OP41), 100
    Operation 42 (OP42), 100
    Operation 46 (OP46), 83
    Operation 48 (OP48), 52
    Operation 49 (OP49), 57
    Operation 52 (OP52), 61
    Operation 54 (OP54), 63
    Operation 57 (CT-2), 125
    perforated ceramic whorls, 327–330
    small circular discs, 333
    spindle whorl blanks, 330–332
    stone spindle whorls, 332–333
*Spondylus* sp., 7, 34, 269
spoons
    Chinchawasi 1 Ware D, 173
    Chinchawasi 2 Ware A, 180
    Chinchawasi 2 Ware B, 186
    Chinchawasi 2 Ware C, 191
    pinkware, 275
    Warmi Ware B, 226–227
stone artifacts
    Operation 46 (OP46), 83
    Operation 48 (OP48), 52
    stone spindle whorls, 332–333
stone sculpture
    ancestor veneration, 9, 135–137
    ceremonial practices, 3–4, 359
    Chinchawas, 9, 37
    defensive architecture, 360
    Enclosure 1, 41
    Enclosure 2, 43, 45
    Operation 57 (CT-2), 125
    prehistoric research, 22
    Recuay culture, 25, 27
    religious practices, 9
    Room Complex 3, 50, 53, 66
    surface locations, 40, 67, 116
    *see also* Torreón
stone spindle whorls, 332–333
subterranean tombs
    ancestor veneration, 135–137

bottles, 251
ceremonial practices, 359
characteristics, 118
Chinchawasi 1 Ware B, 161
cultural associations and functions, 133–134, 355
fancy ceramics, 249–251, 253
human skeletal remains, 134–135
metal artifacts, 346
Operation 56 (ST-1), 118–119
Operation 63 (ST-2), 119
Operation 65 (ST-3), 119–121
research summary, 121
Supe, 215
Supe-style tumblers
characteristics, 262–263
comparison studies, 265–266
Design A, 263
Design B, 263–265
Design C, 265

## T

taruca, 101, 103, 343
tectonic activity, 13, 19–20
Tello, Julio C., 22, 23–24
temples, 32
Terrace 1
larger exposures, 78–79
Operation 9 (OP9), 73–76
Operation 10 (OP10), 70–71
Operation 11 (OP11), 70
Operation 12 (OP12), 76–77
Operation 18 (OP18), 77–78
Operation 19 (OP19), 73–76
Operation 21 (OP21), 73–76
Operation 22 (OP22), 71–72
Operation 24 (OP24), 72–73
Operation 43 (OP43), 78–79, 81
Operation 44 (OP44), 78–79
Operation 46 (OP46), 81–84
research summary, 84–85
site characteristics, 69
Terrace 1 Center, 73–78
Terrace 1 East, 70
Terrace 1 West, 70–73
Terrace 2
characteristics, 86
Operation 13 (OP13), 85
Operation 14 (OP14), 85–86
Operation 15 (OP15), 86
Terrace 3
characteristics, 92–94
Operation 4 (OP4), 87
Operation 5 (OP5), 91–93
Operation 6 (OP6), 91–94
Operation 8 (OP8), 89
Operation 20 (OP20), 91–93
Operation 47 (OP47), 89–91

Terrace 3 East, 87–91
Terrace 3 West, 91–94
Terrace 4
characteristics, 94–95
larger exposures, 99–103
Operation 23 (OP23), 95–96
Operation 29 (OP29), 96
Operation 30 (OP30), 96–97
Operation 31 (OP31), 97–99
Operation 38 (OP38), 99–103
Operation 40 (OP40), 99–103
Operation 41 (OP41), 99–103
Operation 42 (OP42), 99–103
research summary, 103, 105
Terrace 5
characteristics, 106, 109
Operation 33 (OP33), 106
Operation 34 (OP34), 106–107
Operation 35 (OP35), 107–108
Operation 36 (OP36), 108–109
Terrace 6
characteristics, 109
Operation 37 (OP37), 109–110
Operation 39 (OP39), 110–111
Terrace 7, 111
Terrace 8
characteristics, 111
Operation 27 (OP27), 111–112
Operation 28 (OP28), 112
Terrace 9
characteristics, 112
Operation 62 (OP62), 112–113
terrace areas
characteristics, 69
fancy and imported ceramics, 282–283
research summary, 113–114
settlement organization, 355
Terrace 1, 69–85
Terrace 2, 85–86
Terrace 3, 87–94
Terrace 4, 94–105
Terrace 5, 106–109
Terrace 6, 109–111
Terrace 7, 111
Terrace 8, 111–112
Terrace 9, 112–113
Tertiary, 13
textiles
chullpa tombs, 131
domestic patterns, 356–357
Operation 64 (CT-12), 131
Recuay culture, 25

Tiahuanacoid, 117, 215
Tinco, 13, 16
*tinku*, 13
Tocroc, 32
Tomaval Period, 253, 254
tool production debris, 343
Tornapampa ceramics, 177, 205, 233
Torreón
characteristics, 67
fancy and imported ceramics, 283
functional role, 355
Operation 54 (OP54), 62–65
shell artifacts, 344–345
site location, 61–62
Transitional Period, 363–364
tumblers
non-Supe-style tumblers, 266–267
Supe-style tumblers, 262–266
Wari polychrome ceramics, 271

## U

ulluco, 17
usable meat, 101–102

## V

vegetation zones, 14–15
Viñaque style pottery, 31, 33, 284, 287, 363
Viracochapampa, 31
Virú, 25, 254, 267, 269
volcanism, 13

## W

Wamanga-style pottery, 272
Waman Wain, 243
wanka-pachilla walls
Enclosure 2, 42
Operation 23 (OP23), 95
Operation 34 (OP34), 106
Operation 37 (OP37), 109
Operation 39 (OP39), 110
Operation 45 (OP45), 59
Operation 47 (OP47), 90
Operation 56 (ST-1), 118–119
Operation 57 (CT-2), 123–124
Operation 58 (CT-6), 126–127
Recuay culture, 26
Terrace 9, 112–113
warfare, 29, 282, 360
Wari culture
architectural characteristics, 31–32
ceramics, 30, 33–34
Chinchawas ceramic sequence, 247

interregional interactions, 290–291, 357–358
sociocultural transformations, 362–363
Wari expansion
  economic patterns, 357–358
  Middle Horizon, 6–7, 29–34, 293–294, 361–364
  religious practices, 293
  significance, 29–32
Wari polychrome ceramics
  bowls, 272
  characteristics, 270
  comparison studies, 272–273, 275
  fancy and imported ceramics, 270–273, 275, 284, 287
  jars, 271–272
  Operation 23 (OP23), 95
  Operation 24 (OP24), 72
  Operation 30 (OP30), 96
  Operation 39 (OP39), 111
  Operation 46 (OP46), 84
  Operation 47 (OP47), 90
  Santa Valley, 215
  spatiotemporal distributions, 284
  tumblers, 271
Warmi phase ceramics
  ceremonial practices, 359
  characteristics, 207–208
  Chinchawas occupation, 356, 362
  chipped stone artifacts, 310–311
  chronology, 353
  chullpa tombs, 133, 253
  economic patterns, 357
  face-neck vessels, 277, 279
  fancy and imported ceramics, 287–289
  interregional interactions, 291–292
  non-Supe-style tumblers, 266–267
  Operation 4 (OP4), 87
  Operation 6 (OP6), 91–92
  Operation 8 (OP8), 89
  Operation 11 (OP11), 70
  Operation 15 (OP15), 86
  Operation 16 (OP16), 49
  Operation 20 (OP20), 92
  Operation 21 (OP21), 74–75
  Operation 22 (OP22), 71
  Operation 23 (OP23), 95
  Operation 24 (OP24), 72
  Operation 25 (OP25), 46
  Operation 26 (OP26), 46
  Operation 27 (OP27), 112
  Operation 28 (OP28), 112
  Operation 29 (OP29), 96
  Operation 34 (OP34), 107
  Operation 35 (OP35), 107
  Operation 36 (OP36), 108
  Operation 38 (OP38), 99–100
  Operation 39 (OP39), 111
  Operation 40 (OP40), 99–100
  Operation 41 (OP41), 99–100
  Operation 42 (OP42), 99–100
  Operation 43 (OP43), 79, 81
  Operation 46 (OP46), 82, 83–85
  Operation 47 (OP47), 90, 91
  Operation 48 (OP48), 51, 53
  Operation 49 (OP49), 57
  Operation 52 (OP52), 61
  Operation 57 (CT-2), 125
  Operation 61 (CT-7), 129
  Operation 62 (OP62), 113
  Operation 64 (CT-12), 129, 131
  radiocarbon dating measurements, 235
  shell artifacts, 345
  spatiotemporal distributions, 287–289
  stylistic features, 38
  Warmi Ware A, 208–217, 362
  Warmi Ware B, 217–234
Warmi Ware A
  characteristics, 208, 213–214
  Chinchawas occupation, 362
  painted decoration, 211–213
  paste characteristics, 209
  plastic decoration, 213
  surface treatment, 211
  vessel shapes, 209–210
Warmi Ware B
  characteristics, 217, 228–229, 231–233, 235
  painted decoration, 228
  paste characteristics, 218
  plastic decoration, 228–229
  surface treatment, 227–228
  vessel shapes, 218–225
water sources, 19–20, 356
Waullac, 33
weaving activities
  see textiles
wheat, 17
white-on-red ceramics, 25, 27, 161–163, 177, 184
  see also Huarás style pottery
white-tailed deer, 101, 103, 343
Wilkawaín area
  Chinchawasi 1 Ware C, 165

resist-painted ceramics, 261
Wari-influenced period, 27, 31, 33
Warmi Ware A, 214–215
window features, 84

# Y

Yaután, 18
Yayno, 32, 65, 362
Yungay, 33, 215